Essentials of
Marketing Research

DEL I. HAWKINS
DONALD S. TULL

Department of Marketing
University of Oregon

Essentials of
Marketing Research

MACMILLAN PUBLISHING COMPANY
NEW YORK

Maxwell Macmillan Canada
TORONTO

Maxwell Macmillan International
NEW YORK   OXFORD   SINGAPORE   SYDNEY

Editor: Denise Abbott
Production Supervisor: Dora Rizzuto
Production Manager: Lynn Pearlman
Text Designer: Robert Freese
Cover Designer: Robert Freese
Cover illustration: Viqui Maggio

This book was set in Palatino and Eras Type by Carlisle Communications, Ltd.
and was printed and bound by Rand McNally.
The cover was printed by Lehigh Press, Inc.

Macmillan Publishing Company is part
of the Maxwell Communication Group of Companies.

Macmillan Publishing Company
866 Third Avenue, New York, New York 10022

Maxwell Macmillan Canada, Inc.
1200 Eglinton Avenue East
Suite 200
Don Mills, Ontario M3C 3N1

Library of Congress Cataloging-in-Publication Data
Hawkins, Del I.
    Essentials of marketing research / Del I. Hawkins, Donald S. Tull.
        p.   cm.
    Portions of this book are taken from the author's Marketing
research, 6th ed., published in 1993.
    Includes indexes.
    ISBN 0-02-351831-6
    1. Marketing research.   2. Marketing research—Case studies.
I. Tull, Donald S.   II. Tull, Donald S.   Marketing research.
III. Title.
HF5415.2.H34   1993
658.8'3—dc20
                                                                                                        93-5979
                                                                                                            CIP

Printing: 1 2 3 4 5 6 7 8 Year: 4 5 6 7 8 9 0 1 2 3

Preface

This is an introductory text in marketing research. It is specifically designed for marketing research courses which do *not* have major responsibility for teaching advanced data analysis. It is appropriate for courses using a major project as a central part of the course as well as courses that rely on short cases, homework assignments, and/or mini-projects to reinforce the marketing research principles described in the text.

This text owes its philosophy and much of its content to its parent text: *Marketing Research: Measurement and Method,* 6th ed. (D. S. Tull and D. I. Hawkins, Macmillan Publishing Company, 1993). That text covers all aspects of the research process including advanced data analysis. This text focuses on the most essential or common research techniques and analytical methods. A student who masters the material in this text will be able to effectively evaluate more than 90 percent of all research conducted today.

Many current research texts state that they are designed for the *user* of marketing research rather than the *doer* of marketing research. We believe that this is increasingly a false dichotomy for three reasons. First, most large firms are rapidly reducing the size of their support staffs and expect line managers to be directly responsible for functions formerly performed by staff. Thus, future managers will be expected not only to deal very intelligently with internal research staff but also to contract directly with outside suppliers for needed research. Some companies such as 3–M even start high potential managers in the research department for the first three years of their careers.

Second, the majority of today's business graduates do not go to work for large firms. Instead, they work in much smaller organizations where research budgets are small and research staff nonexistent. These managers need to be able to design and conduct or contract appropriate small scale marketing research studies.

Finally, the "research user skills" required to decide if research is required and to evaluate research proposals and reports are the same skills required to design and conduct research. While conducting research may require a greater depth of knowledge and more competence at skill based tasks such as questionnaire construction than a general manager would need, the manager must have the same *basic* knowledge and skills if he or she is to effectively chose among competing research proposals or evaluate the accuracy of a research report. It is the purpose of this book to provide future researchers and managers with the basic understanding of the research process that both require.

As implied above, this text focuses exclusively on research designed to enhance marketing decisions. It attempts to acquaint students with the endless pressures for accurate data in the face of intense financial and time pressures. It deals explicitly with the trade offs between costs (time and financial) and data accuracy that practicing managers and researchers must make.

Like its parent, this text recognizes that business is global in scope. It integrates multinational research techniques into every chapter where they are appropriate. Thus, multinational issues in research design, survey methods, test marketing, sampling, questionnaire construction and so forth are covered in the relevant chapters.

A student finishing this text should have a good understanding of the nature of marketing research as it is practiced today. Not only does the text provide a detailed description of the widely used commercial research services, every chapter contains numerous research applications that illustrate how actual firms dealt with the issues covered in the chapters. In addition, section ending cases provide more detailed descriptions of actual firms dealing with real research problems.

It is never possible to provide adequate thanks to all those who assist with a project such as this. We owe particular thanks to those who served as reviewers for this text and/or its parent text:

David Andrus	*Kansas State University*
Ray DeCormier	*Central Connecticut State University*
Donald A. Fuller	*University of Central Florida*
Cathleen Jones	*Robert Morris College*
Peter F. Kaminski	*Northern Illinois University*
David R. Lamber	*San Francisco State University*
Nancy D. Marlow	*Eastern Illinois State University*
William Perttula	*San Francisco State University*
Judith D. Powell	*University of Richmond*
Jerry Scott	*South Eastern Oklahoma State University*
Han Srinivasan	*University of Connecticut*
Rita Wheat	*University of Southern California*

We are particularly grateful to the many practicing marketing researchers and managers who supplied examples, cases, and illustrations for this text and to our many users.

This book is much better than it would have been without all the help we received. Any shortcomings that remain are due to authors inability to incorporate all the valuable suggestions we received.

EUGENE, OREGON

Del I. Hawkins
Donald S. Tull

Supplementary Material for the Text

Data Disk and Software   The data from the quantitative cases, problems, and applications found in the text are available on computer disk to adopters. Computer software including "what-if" decision support and demonstration programs for computer-assisted questionnaire design and administration is also on this disk.

Instructor's Manual   This comprehensive resource contains teaching objectives, additional material for classroom presentation, quiz and demonstration questions and problems, answers to the end-of-chapter review and discussion questions, and transparencies.

Test Bank   This test bank contains over 2,500 multiple choice and true/false questions.

Microtest   A microcomputer testing system is available to adopters that provides the test bank on computer disk.

Brief Contents

I The Nature of Marketing Research   1

1 Marketing Research in Practice   2
2 Marketing Information and Decision Support Systems   22
3 The Research Process and Research Design   40

II The Sources of Research Data   77

4 Secondary Data   78
5 Standard Commercial Data Sources   106
6 Survey Research   130
7 Experimental Design   160
8 Experimental Environment   188

III Measurement Techniques in Marketing Research   225

9 Measurement in Marketing Research   226
10 Questionnaire Design   250
11 Measuring Attitudes and Emotions   280
12 Qualitative Research   304
13 Observation and Physiological Measures   324

IV Sampling and Data Analysis   359

14 The Sampling Process   360
15 Sample Size Determination   382
16 Data Reduction and Estimation   402
17 Hypothesis Tests of Differences   430
18 Measures of Association   462

V Marketing Research Reports and Ethical Issues   493

19 Preparing and Reading Research Reports   494
20 Ethical Issues in Marketing Research   518

Appendixes A–E   549

Indexes   I–1

Contents

I The Nature of Marketing Research   1

1   Marketing Research in Practice   2

The Function of Marketing Research   4
Information and Decision Making   7
International Marketing Research   13
The Marketing Research Department   13
The Research Industry   14
Marketing Research Careers   16
Questions/Problems/Projects   18

2   Marketing Information and Decision Support Systems   22

Marketing Information Systems (MIS)   24
Marketing Decision Support Systems (MDSS)   30
Expert Systems   36
Questions/Problems/Projects   37

3   The Research Process and Research Design   40

The Nature of Marketing Research Design   42
Types of Research Design   42
Steps in the Research Design Process   43
Potential Errors Affecting Research Designs   55
Multinational Research Design   59
Questions/Problems/Projects   60

Section I Cases

I–1   S.C. Johnson & Son, Inc.: Research Monday   63
I–2   Orange Juice Placement Study Proposal   68
I–3   Marketing Research at Sony Corporation   72
I–4   Marketing Research at Citicorp/Citibank   72
I–5   Marketing Research Careers at 3M   74
I–6   The FDA and "Fresh" Orange Juice   75

II The Sources of Research Data   77

4 Secondary Data   78

The Nature of Secondary Data   80
Internal Sources of Secondary Data   82
External Sources of Secondary Data   85
International Secondary Data   97
Questions/Problems/Projects   101
Appendix: External Sources of International Secondary Data   104

5 Standard Commercial Data Sources   106

Commercial Surveys   108
Audits   113
Panels   115
Applications of Commercial Surveys, Audits, and Panels   122
Standard International Commercial Data Sources   125
Questions/Problems/Projects   127

6 Survey Research   130

The Nature of Survey Research   132
Criteria for the Selection of a Survey Method   138
Nonresponse Error in Survey Research   143
Issues in Multinational Surveys   151
Questions/Problems/Projects   155

7 Experimental Design   160

The Nature of Experimentation   162
Types of Errors Affecting Experimental Results   163
Experimental Design   169
Conclusions Concerning Experimental Designs   181
Ex Post Facto Studies   181
Questions/Problems/Projects   184

8 Experimental Environment   188

Laboratory Experiments   191
Field Experiments   198
Test Marketing   198
Questions/Problems/Projects   211

Section II Cases

II–1 Iglo-Ola's "Circle of Housewives" Product Tests in Belgium   214
II–2 The Impact of R.J. Reynolds' "Old Joe the Camel" Advertising
          Campaign on Teenagers' Awareness of Camel Cigarettes   215
II–3 *Family Circle* Study of Print Advertising Effectiveness   216
II–4 Substantiation of Bufferin Advertising Claim   218
II–5 Northwest Marketers   219

II–6   Weyerhaeuser Survey Methodology   220
II–7   California Strawberry Advisory Board   223

III   *Measurement Techniques in Marketing Research*   *225*

9   *Measurement in Marketing Research*   226

The Concept of Measurement   228
Scales of Measurement   232
Components of Measurements   236
Measurement Accuracy   240
Questions/Problems/Projects   245

10   *Questionnaire Design*   250

The Nature of Questionnaire Design   252
Preliminary Decisions   253
Decisions About Question Content   255
Decisions About Question Phrasing   262
Decisions About the Response Format   266
Decisions About the Question Sequence   270
Physical Characteristics of the Questionnaire   270
Decisions About the Pretest   270
Multinational Questionnaire Design   272
Questions/Problems/Projects   275

11   *Measuring Attitudes and Emotions*   280

Rating Scales   283
Attitude Scales   294
Which Scale to Use?   298
Measuring Emotions   298
Questions/Problems/Projects   300

12   *Qualitative Research*   304

Depth Interviews   306
Projective Techniques   313
Questions/Problems/Projects   321

13   *Observation and Physiological Measures*   324

Observation   326
Physiological Measures   334
Questions/Problems/Projects   340

Section III Cases

III–1   Weyerhaeuser Lumber Purchase Criteria Questionnaire   343
III–2   The Impact of R.J. Reynolds' "Old Joe the Camel" Advertising
Campaign on Children's Awareness of Camel Cigarettes   346
III–3   Physicians' Attitudes Toward Hospital Services   348

III–4   Projective Research on Littering   352
III–5   Carlisle's Drugstores   354

IV   Sampling and Data Analysis   359

14   The Sampling Process   360

Census Versus Sample   362
The Sampling Process   363
Issues in Multinational Sampling   373
An Application of Sampling   375
Questions/Problems/Projects   378

15   Sample Size Determination   382

Methods of Determining Sample Size   384
The Sampling Distribution   386
Traditional Statistical Methods of Determining Sample Size   392
Sample Size, Incidence, and Nonresponse   395
Questions/Problems/Projects   398

16   Data Reduction and Estimation   402

An Example Involving New Product Research   405
Data Reduction   409
Statistical Estimation   420
Questions/Problems/Projects   424

17   Hypothesis Tests of Differences   430

The Nature of Hypothesis Tests   432
Univariate Hypothesis Tests Requiring Interval Data   433
Univariate Hypothesis Tests Using Ordinal Data   446
Univariate Hypothesis Tests Using Nominal Data   448
Multivariate Hypothesis Tests of Means   451
Questions/Problems   458

18   Measures of Association   462

Measuring Association   464
Measures of Association Between Two Variables   465
Multivariate Measures of Association   471
Questions/Problems   476

Section IV Cases

IV–1   Weyerhaeuser: Sample Design, Size, and Selection   479
IV–2   Cola Taste Test   482
IV–3   The Toni Company   486
IV–4   Carnations' Taste Test Comparison of Coffee-mate and Cream   488
IV–5   Kermit Steel Supply   489
IV–6   Labaume's Restaurant   491

V Marketing Research Reports and Ethical Issues   *493*

19 Preparing and Reading Research Reports   494

Preparing the Written Research Report   496
Preparing Oral Presentations   507
Reading Research Reports   510
Questions/Problems/Projects   512

20 Ethical Issues in Marketing Research   518

The Nature of Ethical Issues in Marketing Research   518
Questions/Problems/Projects   534

Section V Cases

V–1 Greenpeace Questionnaire   538
V–2 Methodology Section of a Telephone Provider Awareness
        Survey   538
V–3 Weyerhaeuser Report Format   541
V–4 Methodology Report for a Home Improvement Study   546
V–5 Hydra Products   546

Appendixes   *548*

Appendix A   Area Under the Normal Curve   548
Appendix B   Percentiles of the *t* Distribution (One- and Two-Tailed
                    Tests)   550
Appendix C   Percentiles of the *F*-Distribution for α Values of .01, .05,
                    and .10   552
Appendix D   Table of Values of Chi Square   556
Appendix E   Table of Random Numbers   558

Indexes   *559*

Name Index   I-1
Subject Index   I-7

The Nature of Marketing Research

Marketing research serves a single purpose—*that of providing information to assist marketing managers to make better decisions.*

Each year more than $6 billion is spent on marketing research worldwide (more than $2 billion in the United States). This money is spent on research projects that help *identify* marketing problems and opportunities, *select* the problems to solve and the opportunities to consider, and then obtain information to help *solve* the problems and take advantage of the opportunities that are selected. The first chapter discusses these functions of marketing research, along with the way in which it is organized, the nature of the research industry, and career opportunities in marketing research.

A marketing information system is designed to generate, store, and disseminate an orderly flow of pertinent information to marketing managers. Marketing decision support systems are databases with associated models and software that allow managers to interact directly with the database. They are designed to assist with specific types of marketing decisions. Chapter 2 covers both marketing information systems and marketing decision support systems.

The design of a research project is clearly critical to its success or failure. Chapter 3 concerns the steps involved in designing the project, how they are carried out, and estimating the value of the information the proposed design will provide.

CHAPTER 1

Marketing Research in Practice

LEARNING OBJECTIVES

Upon completing this chapter, you should be able to:

1. Explain the function of marketing research.

2. Describe the marketing decision-making process and indicate the role information generated by marketing research plays in that process.

3. Decide when research should be conducted internally and when it should be performed by external researchers.

4. Describe the U.S. and the international research industry.

5. Explain the nature and requirements of a career in marketing research.

Marketing Research at Amoco Oil Company

Abdul Azhari, manager of marketing research at Amoco Oil Company, describes the types of research performed by his organization as follows:

> Some of our research has become routine. For example, we determine market shares, using sample sizes of well over 400,000 a year, and we supplement these surveys for specific markets. Similarly, we track our own and competitors' customers' satisfaction: credit card account handling, service they receive on our driveway, repair and maintenance surveys, and motor club members. We also track the attitudes of our dealers and other distributors, as well as our own and our competitors' advertising and promotional campaigns, physical facilities, product quality, motor oil sales, pricing practices, and other activities.
>
> More fun are the unique problems such as working with research and development on improving our products and facilities; with pricing on uncovering principles that lead to policies; with corporate people on the impact of marketing activities on corporate image; with designers and architects on developing new company identities (e.g., facilities, equipment, packaging); with advertising people on testing new advertising and promotional approaches; with human resources and training departments on assessing present and developing new programs for salespeople, dealers, and others; with local operations on implementing new concepts; with the enterprise group on developing new products; and many others.
>
> Every week, if not every day, we have new challenges. In many instances, we do not recommend research because the problems are not intrinsically amenable to research or because the time and money costs are excessive. Instead, we draw on our marketing and research experiences and insights to provide consultation in the form of action recommendations and, perhaps more often, hand-holding.[1]

The Function of Marketing Research

The Amoco example illustrates the function of marketing research. The *function of marketing research is to provide information that will assist marketing managers in recognizing and reacting to marketing opportunities and problems.* In essence, marketing research exists to help marketing managers make better decisions. These decisions range from such global ones as "Is there a marketing opportunity or problem that I am not aware of?" to very specific decisions such as "Should we set the price at $1.79 or $1.69?" Research Application 1–1 illustrates the types of decisions Best Foods recently used marketing research to help resolve.

Marketing research:
a formalized means of obtaining information to be used in making marketing decisions.

An appropriate definition of **marketing research,** therefore, is that it is a formalized means of obtaining information to be used in making marketing decisions. The official American Marketing Association definition of marketing research reflects this theme, but in greater detail:

> Marketing Research is the function which links the consumer, customer, and public to the marketer through information—information used to identify and define marketing opportunities and problems; generate, refine, and evaluate marketing actions; monitor marketing performance; and improve understanding of marketing as a process.
>
> Marketing Research specifies the information required to address these issues; designs the method for collecting information; manages and implements the data collection process; analyzes the results; and communicates the findings and their implications.

These definitions are not theoretical abstractions; rather, they reflect the practice of marketing research. Consider the match between these definitions and the mission statements of the market research departments at Thomas J. Lipton, Marriott Corporation, and Coca-Cola.

> The mission of the Market Research Department is to gather, analyze, and interpret marketing and other relevant information needed for decision making at all levels of management. These activities are to be carried out in a cost-effective manner consistent with high professional standards.[2]

> Corporate Marketing Services' mission is to improve the quality of business decisions at Marriott through:
>
> 1. Building a knowledge base on customers, competitors, and markets for our major businesses, and transferring that knowledge between strategic business units and among key managers.
> 2. Conducting primary market research for strategic business units to ensure that projects meet their objectives, are cost effective, and avoid duplication of other work.
> 3. Providing quality control and oversight on all market research conducted for Marriott or its subsidiary companies.
> 4. Consulting with corporate and strategic business unit management on marketing strategy and tactics.[3]

> The Marketing Research Department will, by continuously extending our business insight into the changing nature of bottlers, consumers and

RESEARCH APPLICATION 1–1

Best Foods' Use of Marketing Research

Best Foods, a division of CPC International Inc., markets a variety of food products. They include Hellmann's and Best Foods Mayonnaise, Skippy Peanut Butter, Mazola Oil, Mueller's Pasta, and others.* The Marketing Research Department carries out and supervises studies for these established brands as well as for line extensions and new products.

In a recent year the Marketing Research Department undertook 139 research projects, categorized as follows:

- 64 for established products
- 36 related to line extensions
- 29 for new products
- 10 of a general nature

Examples of these studies are:

- A continuous tracking study to assess changes in awareness, usage, and attitudes for an established brand and key competitors.
- Focus groups and depth interviews among Hispanic consumers to explore ideas for a new advertising campaign.

- A price elasticity study using supermarket scanner data to assess the potential impact of alternative pricing actions on sales.
- Concept testing to determine appeal and the degree of fit with the parent brand for several line extension ideas.
- An idea-generation session to develop a list of possible brand names for a new product.
- Purchase of secondary data sources to assess potential acquisition candidates.
- Analysis of food usage diary data to identify emerging trends.

*Other brands marketed by Best Foods are Karo and Golden Griddle syrups, Mazola No Stick, Mazola margarine, Niagara laundry starches, Thomas' English Muffins, Arnold and Brownberry breads, Knorr soups and sauces, and Hellmann's and Best Foods Tartar Sauce and Sandwich Spread. All trademarks mentioned above are registered trademarks of CPC International Inc. or its affiliates.

SOURCE: Provided by John Carter and Aaron Strauss of Best Foods.

customers, proactively influence the sales and marketing decision-making process to achieve superior marketplace results. At the center of this mission is the commitment to provide growth challenges for all personnel in pursuit of the goal of becoming a premiere business information group.[4]

Each of these mission statements *explicitly* states that the primary function of marketing research is to improve management decision making. Think for a minute about the marketing manager's job. He or she must make *decisions* concerning which consumers to serve (market segmentation), and what product features, price levels, promotional strategies, and distribution channels to use.

Suppose you were in charge of programming at NBC. What decisions would you be required to make and how could marketing research assist you? NBC's vice president of marketing describes three major decision areas involving programming: (1) developing programs with audience appeal, (2) scheduling them in the appropriate time slots, and (3) promoting them

RESEARCH APPLICATION 1–2

Marketing Research Applications

• "It is our attention to basic research that has made Soft Care Apparel the largest manufacturer of infant apparel in the United States." Soft Care conducts a quarterly telephone survey that "gives us a snapshot of the marketplace, tracks trends, and offers us a picture of how attitudes change over time." Focus groups (moderated discussions involving 8–12 customers) are used to evaluate new product ideas. Test marketing (selling the product in a few cities) is used to determine demand for new products. Mall intercept interviews (questioning people in shopping malls) are also used to test new product ideas and new products. Research is also used to develop and test premiums and advertising appeals.[6]

• General Motors conducted a major research program to guide overall corporate strategy and particularly its communications strategy in the United Kingdom. It first conducted 14 focus groups with the general public and 6 with local audiences living near GM plants. It simultaneously conducted depth interviews with dealers, fleet operators, garage operators, insurance agents, pro- and anti-automobile pressure group members, government officials, members of the automobile press, the general editorial press and television, trade union leaders, and suppliers. Following this, 10 special surveys were developed, tested, and administered to approximately 4,000 respondents. The results produced major changes in GM's operations in the UK.[7]

• Spectra is Polaroid's most successful new product. "The market research effort was placed on a level of formal equality with every other link in the system." Positioning testing, targeting studies, and Polaroid's first use of name-generation research were used. Mall intercept interviews were conducted throughout Spectra's development. Consumers were given prototypes of the camera to use, then participated in extensive interviews concerning the camera and their attitudes toward it. These findings were used to revise the design of the camera.[8]

• US WEST was formed as one of seven regional telecommunications firms as a result of the AT&T divestiture. Shortly after divestiture, US WEST decided to reorganize around markets rather than products or functions. This resulted in a major research effort involving secondary research, depth interviews, focus groups, and thousands of questionnaires (mail, telephone, and personal) to organizations and households that had needs relating to the transmission of information (voice or data). The result was a revised understanding of the market, a complete restructuring of the organization, and the initiation of hundreds of follow-up studies focused on specific customer needs.

effectively. NBC uses research to help make all three types of decisions. For example, developing programs involves the following types of research:

• *Concept tests,* using phone surveys and focus groups, explore the reaction of the potential audience to the idea behind a proposed series. Hundreds of potential programs are screened each year.

- *Pilot tests* measure the reaction of the potential audience to a filmed episode of the proposed series. Selected cable subscribers are asked to watch a "special preview of a new series" on an unused cable channel. After viewing the pilot, they are asked a series of questions to determine their reaction to it.
- *Series research* is conducted after a series is launched. Viewers are interviewed by phone to determine those aspects of the program they like and dislike. This information is used by the writers and producers to improve the series.[5]

Research Application 1–2 provides several examples of how marketing research has improved marketing decisions.

Note that it is the output of the research process, *information,* that is useful to the manager. In today's highly competitive environment, the effective use of information is a critical managerial skill. For example, Taylor California Cellars was able to take $100 million of business away from entrenched competitors because the management group was more skilled at requesting and using information than its competitors.[9]

As information technology continues to improve, the ability to use information will become even more critical.[10] The effective use of information requires a thorough understanding of the types of information available and how this information is created. In this text, we are concerned with the general questions of *when, how,* and *how much* marketing research should be conducted. If you understand these issues, you will be a much better *consumer* of marketing research. That is, not only will you be able to evaluate the worth of a particular research project or proposal, but you will also know when and how to use the resultant information.

Information and Decision Making

The decision-making process in marketing is essentially the same as it is in any other area of human affairs. The management of NBC has to go through the same general steps in deciding to develop and introduce new programs as does Congress in voting on the defense budget or the Metropolitan Museum of Art in deciding to hold an exhibition of the paintings of Vincent van Gogh. In each case it is necessary for those involved in making the decision to (1) establish objectives, (2) measure performance/potential, (3) select the problem/opportunity to pursue, (4) develop alternatives, (5) choose the best alternative, and (6) implement the alternative. These steps, illustrated in Figure 1–1, can be summarized under the headings of problem/opportunity identification, problem/opportunity selection, and problem/opportunity resolution.

Problem/Opportunity Identification

Both opportunity and problem identification studies are common. For example, research for a major Canadian vacation package wholesaler, Suntours, revealed that despite two consecutive years of record sales and profits, its

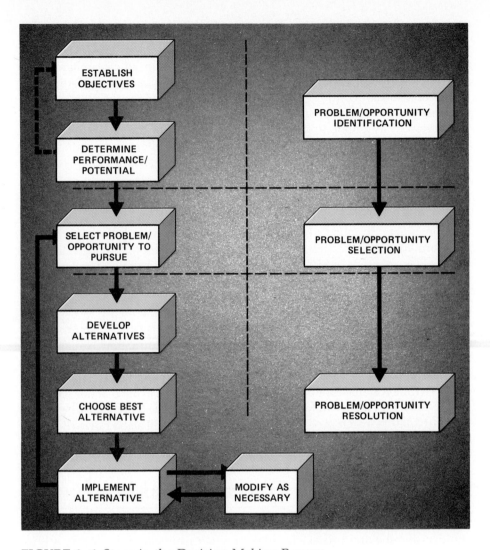

FIGURE 1–1 Steps in the Decision-Making Process

market share had declined by almost a third. Once the problem was recognized, Suntours was able to take steps to recapture its lost market share.[11]

Problems are identified when (1) objectives are established and (2) a measurement of performance indicates that the objectives are not being met. Opportunities occur when the potential to exceed objectives using a new approach is discovered. Marketing research can assist in setting objectives, measuring performance, and identifying opportunities and problems.

Think for a minute about setting or evaluating a market share or sales objective for a particular brand. What information would you like to have? Such data as number of customers, average purchase amount by customers, percentage of customers who are "heavy users," consumer purchase criteria, the nature of market segments, the number of competitors, marketing expenditures per competitor, relative product/service quality, and so forth would be useful. Marketing research can provide these types of data.

Marketing research can also be used to gather performance data such as sales by the firm and each competitor by customer type. For example, Procter & Gamble analyzes competitor sales by subscribing to a scanner-based sales reporting system (described in Chapter 5). Through this ongoing monitoring, it learned that a competitor's vacuum brick-packs of ground coffee were popular in the South. Recognizing an opportunity, P&G repackaged its Folgers brand into vacuum brick-packs for distribution in the South. This and related actions resulted in a 33 percent gain in market share.[12]

Opportunities, and problems, often arise quickly for firms. During the third week of January 1988, the National Institute of Health announced that regular use of aspirin might lower the incidence of some heart attacks. How much, and what type of action, should aspirin marketers and competing pain remedy marketers take? The answer depends, in part, on the impact the announcement has had on the public. On February 1, an R. H. Bruskin Associates syndicated marketing research report revealed that 90 percent of America's adults were aware of the announcement and one-third of these said they would be likely to take an aspirin every other day because of it.[13] Clearly, the research quickly revealed a major opportunity for aspirin marketers.

Nonprofit organizations and regulatory agencies also conduct problem-identification research. For example, the United Way of America

> . . . collects information covering the social, economic, political, technological, and philanthropic forces of change in the United States. The effort is aided by a volunteer committee of 45 individuals drawn from major U.S. corporations, consulting firms, universities, and labor and national associations, as well as 50+ "scanners" within the staff of United Way of America and local United Ways. More than 150 publications are monitored, content analysis is performed, and data are arranged for distribution to customers. These data are reported in several forms: a biennial publication entitled *What Lies Ahead*, United Way "Soundings" monthly newsletter, special focus publications like *Future World of Work*, and "Soundings" electronic database on our Human Care Network. In addition, these data are carried to United Way customers via slide and video presentations and are sold to the public to help offset the operational costs of data gathering. The data are used to identify the broad threats and opportunities posed for United Way of America and its customers as a result of changes in the marketplace.[14]

Problem-identification research often involves more than merely noting that sales, market share, or other relevant performance measures are not matching expectations. It often requires extensive research to determine exactly what the real problem is. This is discussed in depth in Chapter 3.

Problem/Opportunity Selection

Organizations often identify more problems and opportunities than they can work on at once. Research can often help prioritize identified problems and opportunities. Two dimensions determine the priorities—time and impact. The larger the impact and the less time until the problem occurs (or until the opportunity is lost), the higher is the priority.

Consider the following research program and its outcome:

> Two million dollars was spent on research for the Ronald Reagan presidential campaign. Sixteen national surveys, eighty-two statewide studies, and more

than fifty focus groups were conducted early in the campaign. During twenty days in October, an average of more than 2,400 persons were interviewed each night to provide information on voter awareness and attitudes.

This information went into a computerized simulation model known as the Political Information System (PINS). It was used to simulate the election to determine which were the major issues and what were the key coalitions of voters. Almost three hundred simulations were conducted.[15]

The PINS simulations, by allowing the major issues and key coalitions to be identified, permitted priorities to be set for both the content and the primary target audiences of Reagan campaign advertising and personal appearances.

Marketing research is commonly used to determine which new competitive activities—new products, advertising strategies, channels, and so forth—are most threatening. Those that pose serious threats in the near future are countered first.

Problem/Opportunity Resolution

Problem/opportunity resolution consists of two separate steps: (1) developing alternatives to meet objectives and (2) evaluating these alternatives in terms of the objectives.

Research Application 1–3 describes one of the earliest formal marketing research studies. In this case, information was provided through research that helped a potential customer evaluate an alternative (the alternative of advertising in the *Saturday Evening Post*).

More firms are spending more on marketing research of this nature than ever before.

- Lotus now spends about $1 million dollars a year on pricing studies for its software.[16]
- Taco Bell used marketing research to help redesign the exterior and interior of its outlets.[17]
- The *Seattle Post-Intelligencer* newspaper used extensive research before redesigning its editorial and feature content.[18]
- Miller Brewing Co. used research to change its familar tagline, "Tastes great, less filling" to "The feeling's right—Miller Lite" for advertisements targeting African-Americans.[19]
- L'eggs replaced its classic pantyhose package after consumer research showed a two-to-one preference for the new package.
- Riverside Methodist Hospital revamped its price structure for its Hotel-Care Program based on a competitor and customer analysis.
- Welch's recently began a major repositioning from being a "grape juice and jelly company" to a "fruit-products firm" based on marketing research.[20]
- Lipton Iced Tea in cans was positioned as "The softer soft drink" after extensive marketing research.[21]
- Cadillac based its recent, successful $25,000,000 campaign to reach younger (under 45), affluent customers on marketing research.[22]

We do not want to give the impression that marketing research projects either are, or should be, conducted to help with all marketing decisions. For example, California Cooler (and the entire "cooler" wine drink industry) was

RESEARCH APPLICATION 1–3

The Beginning of Marketing Research

The Curtis Publishing Company is the company generally acknowledged to have the first marketing research department in the United States, and a man named Charles Coolidge Parlin was its first head. In the early days of this century, a Curtis sales representative was attempting to sell the Campbell Soup Company space in the *Saturday Evening Post*. He was told that the *Post* was the wrong medium for prepared soup advertising—that it was a magazine read mainly by working people, whereas prepared soups were bought primarily by families with higher incomes. The wife in a working-class family prepared soup from scratch to save money, the argument went, while only the rich would pay 10¢ for a soup already prepared.

Parlin was asked to get data that would indicate whether or not the Campbell advertising department's view of the market for canned soups was correct. To do so, he drew a sample of garbage routes in Philadelphia and arranged to have the collected garbage from each dumped in a specified area of a National Guard Armory he had rented for that purpose. He then had the number of Campbell soup cans counted in each of the piles. He found that the piles from the garbage collection routes that served the wealthier parts of the city had few Campbell cans. Rather than buy canned soups, the wealthier families had their servants make it from scratch.

Most of the cans came from the blue-collar areas. Parlin theorized that it was probably more economical for the blue-collar wife to take the time saved in making soup and devote it to making clothes for herself and her family, an activity that really would save money.

When presented with these findings, Campbell soon became an advertiser in the *Post*.

SOURCE: "Garbage Dump Marks Long Ago Beginnings of Market Research," *Advertising Age*, April 30, 1970, 70.

---

launched with absolutely no marketing research.[23] Akio Morita, the famous leader of Sony, describes that company's view of marketing research:

> Our plan is to lead the public with new products rather than ask them what kind of products they want. The public does not know what is possible, but we do. So instead of doing a lot of market research, we refine our thinking on a product and its use and try to create a market for it by educating and communicating with the public.[24]

However, failure to conduct research greatly increases risks. TreeSweet Products spent $12 million to develop TreeSweet Lite, a line of six reduced-calorie juices. To beat competition, the product was launched nationally without test marketing. It failed completely and virtually forced the company into bankruptcy.[25] Patrick Mulcahy, chairman of Eveready Battery, explains his firm's logic in launching the "Jocko" commercials, which were tremendously successful in Australia, in the U.S. without research:

> It was one of those management things where you say, "We feel good about this, it's worked someplace else." So, without much real testing, we really stepped into it. And almost immediately, I was getting maybe ten negative letters a day on Jocko and how much he was hated.

> I directed Needham to do that campaign. They did not want to do it. And what we found was video vampirism with the poorly received campaign sucking the life out of the product in the marketplace.[26]

Despite this disaster caused by lack of research, Eveready also launched their next campaign without research. It was the immensely successful Energizer "Bunny" campaign. The issue of when research should be conducted is discussed in detail in Chapter 3.

The Marketing Decision

It is important to recognize that managers use information as they make decisions. The information may come from marketing research or it may come from intuition and experience. No matter the source, the *manager* needs to determine the information required and to decide how he or she will use it to reach a decision. If research is used, the researcher should work with the manager to ensure that the proper information is sought and interpreted correctly.

Suppose you as a manager needed to estimate the maximum market potential for a new video game. You might request the research department to estimate how many households own the appropriate hardware to play the game. And you might request them to measure consumers' reactions to a proposed price. Here is what happened when management at Atari did this:

> When research estimated the computer-hardware population in the U.S. at 19–20 million households, we used this as a base for calculating software sales—ignoring the fact that millions of units are stuck on the top shelves of closets (i.e., not used). And when focus groups of a handful of consumers said they would spend $40 for an E.T. video game, we produced more than 20 million, many of which can be found in a landfill in New Mexico.[27]

Both management and research failed in this situation. Management needed information on computers *being used*, not computers *owned*. Both the manager and the researcher should have recognized this. The researcher should have warned management that individuals who agree to participate in long discussions (focus groups) on video games are likely to be enthusiasts who will pay more for a game than the general population.

A danger of marketing research is that executives will substitute it for firsthand knowledge of their channels and customers. Marketing research should be a *complement to* rather than a *substitute for* managers' direct contacts with the marketplace. Unfortunately, some American managers rely too heavily on research data (perhaps supplemented by viewing a few focus group interviews) in making major decisions. Japanese managers (and technicians) are more likely to spend time face-to-face with wholesalers, retailers, and end-users.[28] Formal research can overcome the perceptual biases we all have when observing others, but experience with customers is helpful, if not necessary, to bring insight to the results of research studies. Case I–1 (page 63) describes how S. C. Johnson attempts to resolve this issue.

It is our hope that this text will enhance your appreciation of both the power and the pitfalls of market research. As one executive states:

> Research can be a very useful guide, but it has its limits. We need both the experienced management decision-maker and the best of what the research

community can offer, integrated in a productive way and with a healthy respect for the benefits and limitations of each.[29]

International Marketing Research

One of the most striking developments of the last two decades has been the globalization of business. There is little doubt that this trend will continue throughout the 1990s. Marketing research practices and techniques have yet to become truly global; however, rapid progress is being made in this area.[30] For example, the world's largest research firm, Nielsen, is headquartered in the U.S. but derives almost two-thirds of its revenue from outside the U.S. It is standardizing much of the data it routinely collects in 27 different countries. *

International marketing managers make the same basic types of decisions as do those who operate in only one country. Of course, they make these decisions in a more complicated environment. As with marketing decisions, the basic function of marketing research and the research process does not differ between domestic and multinational research. However, the process is complicated almost exponentially as more and more countries are involved in the same decision (and thus the same study).

In the appropriate chapters of the text, we will describe the complications involved in international research as they affect the research process.

The Marketing Research Department

The location of the marketing research function in the organization and the extent to which it is staffed vary from firm to firm. Some firms do most of their own research, whereas others depend heavily on their advertising agency, marketing research firms, and independent consultants. Some companies have only a single marketing research department that is responsible for all research projects, whereas others have decentralized the research responsibilities by business units, product lines, countries or other geographic units, or even customer types. Various combinations of these approaches are also utilized. There is no one optimum method of organization; the best organization for a particular company depends on its needs and the way it has organized the marketing and other functions of the firm.

It is not unusual for companies to have marketing research studies, or portions of studies such as the interviewing, conducted by outside firms. Many firms do research on a contract or fee basis, including all major advertising agencies, marketing research firms, and management consulting firms, as well as independent consultants, university bureaus of business and economic research, and some trade associations. The "make or buy" decision involves seven factors:[31]

1. *Economic factors:* Can an outside agency provide the information more economically? In the aspirin example described earlier, the cost of the consumer survey was shared by all the firms subscribing to the service.

Thus, using an outside agency was substantially more economical than conducting a special survey in-house.

2. *Expertise:* Is the necessary expertise available internally? Carnation did not have the expertise to conduct a laboratory test market for a prospective new product and so the company contracted with an outside agency to do it.

3. *Special equipment:* Does the study require special equipment not currently available in the firm? The acquisition of special rooms for focus group interviews, sophisticated devices for measuring physiological responses to commercials, and so forth are seldom justified for one-time studies.

4. *Political considerations:* Does the study involve deeply controversial issues within the organization? Studies designed to help resolve bitter internal disputes or that may reflect unfavorably on some segment of the organization should generally be conducted by an outside organization.

5. *Legal and/or promotional considerations:* Will the results of the study be used in a legal proceeding or as part of a promotional campaign? In either case, the presumption (not necessarily correct) that an outside agency is more objective suggests that one be used.

6. *Administrative facets:* Are current workloads and time pressures preventing the completion of needed research? If so, outside agencies can be used to handle temporary overloads.

7. *Confidentiality requirements:* Is it absolutely essential that the research be kept secret? As the need for confidentiality increases, the desirability of using an outside agency decreases.

It is not unusual for a research department to contract out parts of a study. In fact, most studies involving direct contact with consumers, such as surveys and taste tests, involve outside suppliers of research services. Thus, the pertinent question is often "What parts of this research project do we conduct ourselves and what parts do we contract out?" The seven factors we have just listed form the basis for answering this question, as well.

The Research Industry

Well over $2 billion was spent on commercial research in the United States in 1991. This figure does not include in-house work by governments, business firms, or advertising agencies. Thus, there is a large industry whose function is to supply research services to other organizations.

The firms that comprise this industry range in size from one person working part time to the Nielsen Co., which generated over $1 billion in worldwide research revenues in 1990.[32] The services offered range from conducting in-depth interviews or the analysis of questionnaire data to the installation and management of a complete marketing information system and decision support system. The most complete listing and description of the individual firms in the industry is the *Green Book.*[33] A brief overview of the industry follows.

Custom Research.   Firms that supply custom research will work with the client to develop and implement a complete research project. They help management specify the information needed and they collect the information. Some of these firms specialize in particular industries or types of problems; others are generalists.

Custom research firms are particularly useful for firms with small or nonexistent research departments. They are also frequently used by larger firms when their own research department is overloaded, when a new type of problem or environment is encountered, when a "fresh" approach is desired, when specialized equipment such as an eye-tracking machine is required, and so forth.

Field Services. Most interviewing is conducted by firms that specialize in this activity. This is particularly common in consumer interviews. The term *field* is generally used in the research industry to refer to that part of the research process in which data are actually collected from respondents. Asking respondents questions, whether in person, over the phone, or by mail, and recording their answers is referred to as **fieldwork.** Companies that specialize in interviewing are called *field organizations* or *field service organizations.*

Field organizations range from small offices with a few telephones to large multinational WATS-line interviewing services to extensive facilities for personal interviews in shopping malls (see Chapters 5 and 6 for detailed descriptions). Many field organizations specialize in *qualitative research.* Most such organizations offer *focus group* interviews, which involve 8 to 15 individuals and a moderator discussing a particular topic in depth. The interviews are generally videotaped (see Chapter 12).

Fieldwork: asking respondents questions and recording their answers.

Data Analysis. Firms that specialize in data analysis are sometimes referred to as *tab houses.* This term arose because such firms initially supplied simple tabulations (counts) and cross tabulations for surveys. Even though the spread of computers and related software has given many firms the ability to conduct their own statistical analyses, substantial demand still exists for outside analyses.

Syndicated Services. A number of research organizations, known as syndicated services, routinely collect information that they provide to firms subscribing to their services. Nielsen's television viewing panel is the most widely known service of this type. Reports on retail sales, radio listening, household purchasing patterns, food preparation and consumption, and other behaviors are available on a subscription basis from syndicated services (Chapter 5).

Branded Research Products. Many research firms have developed specialized techniques for the collection of information relevant to specific types of marketing problems. These techniques are given brand names and are marketed like branded products. Examples include:

NameLab: A specialized approach to developing brand names.
BehaviorScan: A test marketing service of Information Resources Inc.
BASES: Burke Marketing Services, Inc.'s program for incorporating consumer attitude measures into sales estimates throughout the new product development process.
PRIZM: A Claritas Corporation technique for identifying potential market segments based on life-style classifications of residential neighborhoods.

The International Research Industry

Most of the large research firms operating in the U.S. have operations throughout the world. In addition, the advanced economies have well-developed local research industries. The research industry in the European Community (EC) is similar to that in the U.S., although it is still focused more *within* than across countries. It is somewhat larger than the U.S. industry in terms of expenditures. Japan also has a research industry similar to that in the U.S., but it is much smaller. Most of the rest of the world has a very limited research infrastructure.[34]

Marketing Research Careers

Relatively few students in marketing research classes go on to careers in marketing research. However, marketing research has become a major staff function in many organizations. And, as the previous section indicates, there is a large marketing research industry consisting of a wide array of research suppliers. Thus, a variety of career paths are available in marketing research.

TABLE 1–1 Qualities Sought in Researchers

Qualities	Entry Level—%*	Junior Staff—%*	Senior Staff—%*
Strong writing skills	57	71	90
Strong analytic skills	50	67	90
Strong verbal skills	49	57	82
Professional appearance	19	28	59
Good grades	15	4	7
Strong quantitative (statistical) skills	13	19	41
Potential new business development skills	10	23	54
Graduate degree/some graduate training	6	11	16
Good schools	3	—	1
Managerial skills	†	†	49
Client-handling skills	†	†	83
National reputation	†	†	1
Expertise in a specific industry/industries	†	†	1
Expertise in a specific methodology/methodologies	†	†	4

*Indicating "very important" on four-point scale (very important, important, less important, not important at all).
†Not asked for this level.

SOURCE: Survey conducted by the Council of American Research Organizations of 74 (responding) large marketing research companies and reported in "Talking and Writing and Analysis," *Advertising Age,* October 26, 1981, S-28.

Marketing research organizations typically look for strong basic skills in analysis and communication, rather than expertise in a particular industry or methodology. As indicated by Table 1–1, strong writing, analytic, and verbal skills are the qualities that are most highly sought by research organizations.

RESEARCH APPLICATION 1–4

Jobs in Marketing Research

Burke Marketing Services. Inc., one of the nation's largest suppliers of custom designed marketing research has immediate needs for the following positions to meet our growing business needs

EXPERIENCED RESEARCH ANALYSTS
Responsibilities include consultation with clients, analysis of research data, and preparation of written reports

Qualified candidates must have an advanced degree in Marketing, the Social Sciences, or related discipline and 2-5 years' experience in marketing research analysis with a consumer goods company or research supplier. Strong statistical background required. Exceptional verbal and written communication skills are essential to successfully carry out this visible position.

EXPERIENCED PROJECT DIRECTORS
Responsibilities include coordinating research studies from field through final report, including regular client contact. Proven problem solving and organizational skills, excellent communication skills, two years of experience with a research supplier and college degree preferred

Burke
Marketing Services, Inc.

AMERICAN FLETCHER
NATIONAL BANK
AFNB
MARKETING RESEARCH

American Fletcher National Bank is currently seeking a Marketing Research Officer. Person is responsible for directing all research activities relative to the marketing process. Responsibilities including identifying needs, designing the projects, vendor selection and the interpretation and presentation of data. Candidate should have a BS degree minimum, 3 or more years of marketing research experience, possess good written, oral and interpersonal skills along with an analytical aptitude and innovative.

Equal Opportunity Employer M/F/H/V

MARKETING ANALYST

Aigner, a division of Avery International, is a recognized leader in the office products industry. Our rapid expansion makes this an excellent time to join our success team.

We currently seek an experienced Marketing Analyst to provide our marketing and sales departments with valuable information regarding market and product trends, sales forecasts, and new and existing product demands. Specific responsibilities include: designing methods of data gathering, examining statistical data, analyzing prices and distribution, working with government and research firms, analyzing our competitors, studying customer preferences and buying habits.

Qualified candidates will have a BS, MBA desirable; a degree in economics or marketing preferred. Related work experience is essential.

 Aigner
An Avery International Company

850 Algonquin Rd.. Schaumburg, IL 60195
equal opportunity employer m/f

MARKETING RESEARCH ANALYST

Armstrong, a leading manufacturer and marketer of a comprehensive line of interior furnishings including flooring, carpet, furniture, and ceiling systems for residential, commercial and institutional use, and industrial specialties for the automotive, textile, building and other markets, is seeking an individual with one to two years experience in marketing research projects from development through final presentation. Along with an MBA and good analytical skills, must be able to use a computer for statistical tasks.

Assignment involves close working relationship with marketing managers in a variety of business units and offers high visibility to an individual who is resourceful in producing actionable primary research through his or her own efforts as well as those of independent research firms.

Armstrong World Industries Inc.

An Equal Opportunity Employer M/F

 **Armstrong**

Research Application 1–4 contains several advertisements that indicate the nature of the researcher's job as well as the skills required to perform the job.

If interest and abilities qualify you, an entry level position in marketing research offers a number of advantages. It is interesting work that provides wide exposure to marketing problems at an early stage of one's career. It brings you in contact with the top management of the company for which the research is being conducted sooner and more often than almost any other position.

There are disadvantages, however. It is a *staff position*, and staff people always *recommend* rather than decide. And the line of promotion for top corporate positions typically does not pass through the marketing research director's office.

Summary

Marketing research is a formalized means of obtaining information to be used in making marketing decisions. The function of marketing research is to provide information that will assist marketing managers in recognizing and reacting to marketing opportunities and problems; that is, to help marketing managers make better decisions. Marketing decisions involve three steps: (1) problem/opportunity identification, (2) problem/opportunity selection, and (3) problem/opportunity resolution. Marketing research can provide useful information at each step.

Most firms of any size have a marketing research department. The location of the department in the firm depends on the organizational structure of the firm and the role assigned to the internal research department. Even firms with large internal research departments generally assign a substantial amount of research to outside research firms.

Firms specializing in marketing research in the U.S. had over $2 billion in revenues in 1991. The United States has a large, sophisticated research infrastructure. Europe's is similar. Japan is less developed than Europe or the U.S. in this area. The research infrastructure throughout most of the rest of the world is limited, but this is changing rapidly with economic development.

A career in marketing research can be very rewarding for anyone with a strong curiosity about human behavior, good business sense, and reasonable quantitative and analytical skills. However, sound written and oral communications skills are also essential to succeed.

Review Questions

1.1. What is the primary function of marketing research?

1.2. What is the definition of marketing research used in this text?

1.3. Describe the decision process.

1.4. How is research used in problem/opportunity identification?

1.5. How is research used in problem/opportunity selection?

1.6. How is research used in problem/opportunity resolution?

1.7. Is research always needed to assist with marketing decisions?

1.8. What considerations are involved in deciding whether to do a research project "in-house" versus having it done by an outside agency?

1.9. Is most research done "in-house"? Why?

1.10. What is meant by *custom research*?

1.11. What is meant by *field services*?

1.12. What is meant by *fieldwork*?

1.13. What is meant by *syndicated services*?

1.14. What is meant by *branded research projects*?

1.15. What are the three most important characteristics that marketing research organizations look for in entry-level job applicants?

1.16. How does international marketing research differ from domestic marketing research?

1.17. How does the international research industry differ from the research industry in the United States?

Discussion Questions/Problems

1.18. Should the marketing research department only provide information to help in decision making or should it also recommend courses of action? What are the advantages and disadvantages of each approach?

1.19. Can a parallel be drawn between an accounting system providing information on costs of products and a marketing information system providing information on demand for products? Explain.

1.20. Approximately 50 times as much is spent in the United States each year on informing and persuading consumers to buy (advertising) as on determining what they would like to buy and how it should be priced, distributed, and promoted (marketing research). Does this seem to be the (approximate) appropriate ratio for these two types of expenditures for a free-enterprise economy? Explain.

1.21. How can the following use marketing research?
    a. universities
    b. churches
    c. charities
    d. city governments
    e. libraries
    f. museums

1.22. Does the role of marketing research include a responsibility for providing information on ethical questions? Explain.

1.23. Should companies generally reduce, maintain at the same level, or increase their research expenditures during a recession? Explain.

1.24. The following statement appeared in an advertisement run by Xerox a few years ago:

    If you pick up a newspaper these days, it's easy to walk away with the impression that there's a worldwide shortage of everything.

There is an energy crisis and a food crisis and any number of other crises, all caused by vanishing resources.

But there is one that involves not a shortage, but an excess. A crisis where the resource isn't dwindling, but growing almost uncontrollably.

That resource is information.

Consider: Seventy-five percent of all the information available to mankind has been developed within the last two decades. Millions of pieces of information are created daily. And the total amount is doubling every ten years. . . .

With 72 billion new pieces of information arriving yearly, how do you cope with it all?

Is the information "explosion" a problem or an opportunity for marketing research? Explain.

1.25. As you seek employment after graduation, you will, in a sense, be a "product" that you are trying to "sell" to potential employers. What types of research should you be doing now to help design and position yourself as an "attractive" product?

1.26. Would you enjoy a career in marketing research? Why?

1.27. Describe the nature of a marketing executive's job at Best Foods based on Research Application 1–1.

1.28. Oil of Olay is a woman's skin-care product marketed throughout the world. What types of marketing decisions and marketing research are relevant for this brand?

Projects/Activities

1.29. Interview a manager in a nonprofit organization. What types of decisions does she or he make? How could (does) research help with those decisions?

1.30. Interview someone who has worked in marketing research for five years or more. Report on their perceptions of this type of career.

1.31. Interview someone in sales or marketing management. Determine their use of and attitudes toward marketing research.

1.32. Review publications such as the *Wall Street Journal, Advertising Age,* and *Business Week.* Find and report on five applications of marketing research.

1.33. Review the help wanted sections of the *Wall Street Journal, Advertising Age,* and/or *Marketing News.* Find 10 advertisements for marketing research analysts or other entry- or near-entry level research positions. List the attributes required and desired. What do you conclude?

Notes

1. A. G. Azhari, J. M. Kamen, "Marketing Research at Amoco Oil," *Marketing Research* (June 1989), 9.

2. D. W. von Arx, "The Many Faces of Market Research," *Journal of Consumer Marketing* (Spring 1986), 88.

3. F. E. Camacho, D. M. Knain, "Listening to Customers," *Marketing Research* (March 1989), 7.

4. J. L. Payne, "Marketing Insights in the 1990s," *Marketing Research* (December 1991), 3.

5. H. Stipps, N. Schiavone, "Research at a Commercial Television Network," *Marketing Research* (September 1990), 5.

6. E. E. Hinds, "Research Basic to Baby-Wear Business," *Marketing News*, February 13, 1987, 26.

7. E. Fountain, I. Parker, J. Samuels, "The Contributions of Research to General Motors' Corporate Communications Strategy in the UK," *Journal of the Market Research Society* (January 1986), 25–42.

8. K. T. Higgins, "Polaroid Stages Marketing Blitz," *Marketing News,* June 6, 1986, 4.

9. Based on C. E. Overholser, "Digging Beyond Research," *Marketing News*, April 26, 1985, 6; and C. E. Overholser, "Using Research to Create a $100 Million Brand," *ARF 31st Annual Conference* (New York: Advertising Research Foundation, 1985).

10. J. Raphael, I. R. Parket, "The Need for Market Research in Executive Decision Making," *The Journal of Business and Industrial Marketing* (Spring 1991), 15–21.

11. J. A. Schauer, "Use Research to Analyze Marketing Success," *Marketing News*, January 4, 1985, 53. Share had declined because market demand was shifting to areas not served by Suntours.

12. Z. Schiller, "Stalking the New Consumer," *Business Week*, August 28, 1989, 55.

13. "New Aspirin Claim," *Bruskin Report* 149 (March 1988), 1.

14. W. Wilkinson, "Getting and Using Information, The United Way," *Marketing Research* (September 1989), 6.

15. "Reagan's $2 Million Marketing Research Budget Paid Off," *Marketing News*, March 5, 1982, 12.

16. R. Brandt, "For Buyers of Business Programs, Money Is No Object," *Business Week*, August 10, 1987, 70.

17. T. Carsen, "Taco Bell Wants to Take a Bite Out of Burgers," *Business Week*, August 4, 1986, 63.

18. R. Edel, "Research Serves Editorial, Advertising Interests," *Advertising Age*, January 23, 1986, 24.

19. "Minority Shops Hinge Sell on Specialty," *Advertising Age*, July 1, 1991, 16.

20. J. S. Blyth, "Designers Becoming Enlightened About the Value of Research," *Marketing News*, March 30, 1991, 33.

21. L. G. Coleman, "Think Hard to Measure Soft Aspects of Behavior," *Marketing News*, May 27, 1991, 15.

22. R. Serafin, "Cadillac Winning Over Boomers," *Advertising Age*, December 2, 1991, 3.

23. "The Concoction That's Raising Spirits in the Wine Industry," *Business Week*, October 8, 1984, 182.

24. T. W. Malnight, *Sony Corporation: Globalization* (Cambridge, MA: Harvard Business School, Case #9-391-071, February 14, 1991), 2.

25. J. E. Davis, "A Juice Maker Squeezes Itself Dry," *Business Week*, August 10, 1987, 42.

26. J. Liesse, "How the Bunny Charged Eveready," *Advertising Age*, April 8, 1991, 20.

27. R. D. Arroyo, "Rapid Success Begat Atari Failure," *Marketing News*, May 10, 1985, 11.

28. See J. K. Johansson and I. Nonaka, "Market Research the Japanese Way," *Harvard Business Review* (May 1987), 16–22; M. Czinkota, M. Kotabe, "Product Development the Japanese Way," *The Journal of Business Strategy* (December 1990), 31–36; and C. L. Hodock, "The Decline and Fall of Marketing Research in Corporate America," *Marketing Research* (June 1991), 12–22.

29. J. E. Duffy, "TV, Researchers Must Blaze New Trails—Together," *Marketing News*, May 10, 1985, 8.

30. See M. van Hamersveld, "Marketing Research—Local, Multidomestic or International?" *Marketing and Research Today* (August 1989), 132–138; L. Caller, "Effective Management of International Research," *Marketing and Research Today* (June 1990), 109–114; N. Homma, J. Veltzhöffer, "The Internationalisation of Everyday-Life Research," *Marketing and Research Today* (November 1990), 197–207; and P. Bartram, "The Challenge for Research Internationally in the Decade of the 1990s," *Journal of Advertising Research* (January 1991), RC3–RC6.

31. For a different grouping see J. M. Sinkula, "Perceived Characteristics, Organizational Factors, and the Utilization of External Market Research Suppliers," *Journal of Business Research* (August 1990), 1–17.

32. J. Honomichl, "Top 50 U.S. Research Organizations," *Advertising Age*, May 27, 1991, H-4.

33. P. Ryan, *Green Book: International Directory of Marketing Research Houses and Services* (New York Chapter, American Marketing Association, annually).

34. J. Oostreen and J. Wouters, "The ESOMAR Annual Market Study," *Marketing and Research Today* (November 1991), 214–218.

2

Marketing Information and Decision Support Systems

LEARNING OBJECTIVES

Upon completing this chapter, you should be able to:

1. Differentiate a marketing information system from a marketing decision support system or an expert system.

2. Provide several examples of how different marketing managers could use a marketing information system.

3. Provide several examples of how different marketing managers could use a marketing decision support system.

4. Explain the value and potential applications of what-if and sensitivity analysis.

Motorola's Strategic Information System

Motorola Inc. has developed a computer-based strategic information system that "collects and distributes information on the general business environment, domestic and international events, companies, and related areas that are critical to market awareness and competitive success." Motorola personnel describe the development of the system as follows:

> Motorola believes that information as a competitive resource is becoming a major goal at many top companies. We began to organize and focus resources in this area in 1984. At that time, the company saw a need for more informed strategic planning. We began by looking for a software package that would support the information needs of the strategy office and the operational planning and marketing staffs.
>
> The demands of the users and the range of sources used to support the system required software with special capabilities. The system has to handle large volumes of text with a significant amount of flexibility. We have large quantities of random-sized abstracts. We need the ability to handle anything from a paragraph to a complete paper. When we do a search, we need the ability to look at the data from different analytical points of view. INQUIRE/Text software was selected for its ability to provide the needed flexibility.
>
> A wide variety of data sources, including newspapers, books, industry studies, government documents, on-line data services, marketing reports, consulting reports, technical analyses, and competitor reports are used in the system. However, we deal only with publicly available information. When we are searching for information, we always identify ourselves as representatives of Motorola. The key to building the system is knowing where the information exists and systematically collecting it.
>
> There is a distinction between simply collecting information and applying that knowledge strategically. Our department's primary objective is to develop actionable information. Information is analyzed and delivered to the individual in the company who can act on it.[1]

Marketing Information Systems (MIS)

Marketing information system: a system to generate, store, and disseminate information to marketing managers.

Marketing research was defined earlier as a formalized means of obtaining information to be used in making marketing decisions. A **marketing information system (MIS)** is a system designed to generate, store, and disseminate an orderly flow of pertinent information to marketing managers.[2] Thus, marketing research is concerned with the act of generating information, whereas the marketing information system is focused on managing the flow of information to marketing decision makers. Motorola's system is an example of a marketing information system that focuses on strategic issues.

The Nature of the Marketing Information System

The information provided by an MIS is used to assist in each of the three major tasks of marketing decision making; that is, the system helps identify, select, and resolve marketing problems or opportunities. For example, the J. C. Penney Co. has an MIS that provides data for all of these purposes.[3] A variety of sources of information are used to keep abreast of changes in consumer attitudes and purchasing behavior. The marketing research department monitors government and trade associations and subscribes to consumer spending forecasts from outside agencies (identification, selection). The company participates in a consumer purchase panel that provides detailed data on the purchases made by 7,000 U.S. households each month (identification, selection, resolution).

The marketing research department also conducts periodic surveys to track consumer awareness and attitudes on each major merchandise category (identification, selection, resolution). Each of the 1,700 Penney stores has electronic point-of-sale terminals (EPOS terminals) tied to a central computer that records the item number, size, style or model, and price of each unit sold. This information permits the early identification of changes in spending patterns, as well as the efficient management of inventories (identification, selection, resolution). In addition, tailored consumer research studies are conducted to help develop merchandising and marketing plans (resolution).

Figure 2–1 illustrates an MIS. The key task of an MIS is to provide needed information to the appropriate managers in a usable format and timely fashion. Obviously, this is a complicated task. Different managers require different types of information. Further, their information needs change, often in an unpredictable manner, over time. Flooding managers with more information than they need is generally counterproductive, as managers soon begin to ignore the relevant as well as the irrelevant information.

Thus, the most difficult task is to specify who receives what information, when, and in what format. This task requires considerable managerial effort. Once initiated, successful MISs continue to evolve and change over time.

Types of Information in an MIS

Three distinct types of information are generally supplied to marketing managers through the MIS—recurrent, monitoring, and requested.

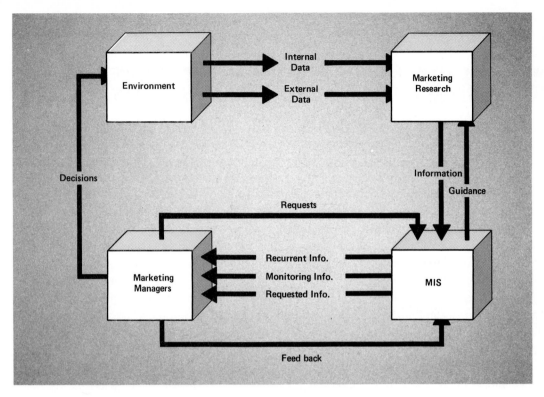

FIGURE 2–1 The Nature of a Marketing Information System

Recurrent Information

Recurrent information is information that is provided on a periodic basis. Market share by region, customer awareness of the firm's advertising, prices of the three leading competitors, customer satisfaction with the firm's products, and customer purchase intentions are examples of information that managers frequently receive on a weekly, monthly, quarterly, or annual basis.

Research Application 2–1 describes some of the recurrent reports used at Oscar Mayer. Recurrent information is particularly useful for indicating problems and opportunities. It can also be used to determine the effects of solutions to potential problems. For example, regular market share reports can be used to analyze the impact of price changes. The value of detailed, accessible recurrent data can be seen in this example:

> A large U.S. multinational active in Canada noticed a decline in its central division current month sales when in fact the commodity market in which it sold was known to be expanding rapidly. Through disaggregation down to the branch and customer group levels it was discovered that a number of the retail customers in specific branch trading areas were being offered extremely favorable prices by another U.S. producer attempting to gain a foothold in the central division. Because the market threat was quickly pinpointed by geographic trading area and customer group, the multinational was able to respond immediately by instituting price cuts that countered the market

Recurrent information: information provided by a marketing information system on a periodic basis.

RESEARCH APPLICATION 2–1

Recurrent Reports from Oscar Mayer's Marketing Systems and Analytics (MSA) Group

First, we have reduced the number of data measures available to users. Though it is possible to obtain thirty or forty measures from the providers of store scanner information, we maintain only about a dozen on our internal computer system. This approach enables us to conduct almost all the sales analyses that are relevant for our businesses, but prevents people from wasting their time examining the twenty to thirty other data measures that provide marginal additional insight.

Second, we issue topline reports each period on each business that probably go beyond the dictionary definition of *topline*. These batch reports are structured to provide trended information on category and segment sizes, plus market share, pricing, distribution, and retailer feature advertising support for both our brands and those of competitors. The intent is broad circulation of basic information that flags emerging business issues. We do not want the various marketing teams

to have to invent the best way to look at the data each period. We want to do it for them and provide the information in the most useful form.

Third, we have set up a system whereby our supplier of store-scanner data prepares sales analyses on each of our businesses and presents them to the marketing and sales planning organizations six times each year. Over a period of two days, our account team makes nine one-hour presentations. Like our toplines, these presentations are fairly structured to minimize the possibility of getting lost in detail and missing the big picture. The two-day marathon always ends with an executive presentation attended by our CEO and key senior executives. Tough business issues are discussed openly, and decisions often are made about how to respond to a marketplace event.

SOURCE: C. Etmekjian and J. Grede, "Marketing Research in a Team-Oriented Business: The Oscar Mayer Approach," *Marketing Research* (December 1990), 7–8.

---

penetration strategy of the potential invader. The report system in this instance told management which customers and trading areas were most vulnerable to competitors, thus allowing the firm to undertake specific price cuts without generally depressing margins throughout its national distribution system.[4]

Monitoring Information

Monitoring information: information derived from the regular scanning of selected sources.

Monitoring information is information derived from the regular scanning of certain sources. For example, a marketing manager may desire a summary of any articles on the competition or the industry. All relevant journals including trade association publications, government reports, and the general business press are examined as they are issued. Article summaries are prepared and distributed any time a relevant article appears.

Monitoring information comes primarily from external sources. Government reports, patents, articles, annual reports of competitors, and public activities of competitors are common sources that are monitored. Internal sales call reports and accounting records are also subject to monitoring. For example, sales call reports may be monitored for any mention of new product development activity by key competitors. If such activity is mentioned, the relevant marketing managers are notified.

Monitoring information is particularly useful for alerting firms to potential problems such as new competitors or new marketing activities by existing competitors. It can also help identify opportunities such as new product uses, new market segments, and improved product features.

Requested Information

Requested information is developed in response to a specific request by a marketing manager. Without such a request the information would not flow to the manager and might not exist in the system.

For example, a manager might request information on the size of a market not currently served by the firm along with an assessment of the intensity of competitive rivalry in the market and the level of customer satisfaction with the current brands in the market. Much of this information would not be available in the system and would have to be generated.

Another request might involve the response of one or more specific competitors to price changes initiated by other competitors. This information may well be in the system but may be difficult to access. Recall that the ability to access data from a variety of perspectives was a major concern of Motorola in our opening example. Here is an example of requested research at Oscar Mayer:

> . . . we use scanner-based models on a selective basis, when there are relevant business issues to be addressed. For example, about a year ago, we used a pricing and promotion model to estimate the price and trade promotion elasticities of twenty-two of our highest volume items. This information has enabled us to fine-tune our promotion programs and also to understand which items are likely to undergo the largest sales changes in response to price changes. Currently, we are trying to learn more about the impact of advertising and consumer promotion on sales and how this impact varies, if at all, geographically.[5]

Figure 2–2 provides examples of the types of information an MIS system might provide to various marketing managers.

> **Requested information:** information developed in response to a specific request by a marketing manager.

Specialized MISs

Thus far, we have discussed the MIS as though each firm had a single, integrated system designed to meet all the information needs of all the marketing managers. However, such systems are very rare. Instead, firms typically evolve smaller, specialized systems designed to meet the needs of a subset of managers such as sales managers or brand managers. Or systems are developed for specific types of information, such as data on competitors.

Specialized MISs frequently involve some duplication of effort and may not provide available information to all managers who could benefit from it.

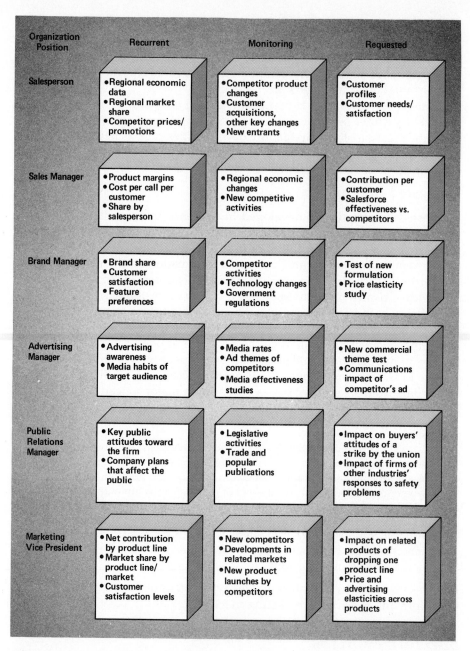

Organization Position	Recurrent	Monitoring	Requested
Salesperson	• Regional economic data • Regional market share • Competitor prices/promotions	• Competitor product changes • Customer acquisitions, other key changes • New entrants	• Customer profiles • Customer needs/satisfaction
Sales Manager	• Product margins • Cost per call per customer • Share by salesperson	• Regional economic changes • New competitive activities	• Contribution per customer • Salesforce effectiveness vs. competitors
Brand Manager	• Brand share • Customer satisfaction • Feature preferences	• Competitor activities • Technology changes • Government regulations	• Test of new formulation • Price elasticity study
Advertising Manager	• Advertising awareness • Media habits of target audience	• Media rates • Ad themes of competitors • Media effectiveness studies	• New commercial theme test • Communications impact of competitor's ad
Public Relations Manager	• Key public attitudes toward the firm • Company plans that affect the public	• Legislative activities • Trade and popular publications	• Impact on buyers' attitudes of a strike by the union • Impact of firms of other industries' responses to safety problems
Marketing Vice President	• Net contribution by product line • Market share by product line/market • Customer satisfaction levels	• New competitors • Developments in related markets • New product launches by competitors	• Impact on related products of dropping one product line • Price and advertising elasticities across products

FIGURE 2–2 Typical Information Requirements from an MIS

However, these systems have the tremendous advantage of being doable within the resources of most organizations. Furthermore, their benefits accrue to a few managers who are aware of the need for the data and who will therefore "champion" the system. Research Application 2–2 describes a specialized MIS focused on competitor activities.[6]

An MIS for Competitor Intelligence

Situation

This competitor MIS would work for virtually any product category. This system is particularly relevant for frequently purchased consumer goods such as soft drinks, detergents, and personal care items. The data are collected, analyzed, and summarized by a central staff. Periodic and "as-needed" reports are sent to the relevant managers.

In addition, the data summaries are stored on a computer system which all the managers can access from their offices.

Recurrent Information

Recurrent information in this system generally measures competitor actions and consumer responses to those actions after they have occurred.

Type, Frequency	Source	Recipient
Sales, market share trends by model and region, weekly	IRI InfoScan Nielsen ScanTrack	Brand and sales manager, regional sales managers
Customer satisfaction and perceptions, monthly	Special survey	Summary to all marketing personnel, details to brand, sales, and advertising managers
Advertising levels and themes, monthly	Advertising tracking service	Brand and advertising manager
Price levels, monthly	Nielsen audits	Brand and sales managers
Promotional activities (coupons, price reductions), monthly	Nielsen audits	Brand, advertising, and sales managers
Customer mix by model by region, monthly	IRI consumer panel	Brand manager
General strategies, strengths, and problems, annually	Arthur D. Little annual industry report	All marketing managers

Monitoring Information

Although the monitoring of information indicates prior competitor activities and consumer responses, its primary objective is to alert management to *future* actions by competitors.

Type	Source	Recipient
New product plans	Trade press, competitor's local newspaper, salesforce reports (including a "hot line")	Brand manager
New product tests	Salesforce reports, Nielsen audits, trade press	Brand manager
New research and development efforts	Trade press, annual and quarterly reports, want ad analysis	Brand manager
Production expansion, change	Local newspapers, building permits	Brand manager, production manager
New advertising themes	Trade press, salesforce reports, ad agency personnel	Brand manager, advertising, manager
New promotions	Salesforce reports, ad agency personnel	Brand manager, advertising, manager

Requested Information

These could involve a wide range of activities including quality testing of competitive products, cost analyses of competitor products or distribution systems, cash flow position of competitors, profiles of key competitor managers, and so forth. A sound system will build a base of this type of information over time and then update it periodically.

Marketing Decision Support Systems (MDSS)

Decision support system (DSS):
a computerized database containing one or more models and an interface that allows managers to interact directly with the models and the data.

Marketing decision support system (MDSS):
a DSS designed specifically for marketing decisions.

The term *decision support system* (DSS) is often used synonymously with *information system*, or, in a marketing context, with *marketing information system*. However, it is preferable to distinguish between the two concepts. MISs are centralized suppliers of information, as is shown in Figure 2–1. Although the managers can sometimes access information directly, it is generally supplied to them by staff personnel on a periodic, as-it-is-available, or requested basis as described in Research Application 2–2.

A **decision support system** is a computerized database containing one or more models and an interface that allows managers to interact directly with the models and the data. Stated more simply, a DSS allows managers to ask questions easily about the relationships among variables in the database or about the effect of changing one or more variables on other variables.

DSSs are decentralized and allow the managers to interact directly with the database. The systems are generally computerized and have one or more models (formulas) built in. These models are developed to assist with specific decisions faced by marketing personnel. Therefore, DSSs typically provide the results of analyses of decision situations rather than the more "factual" information generally supplied by an MIS.[7] Figure 2–3 illustrates a typical DSS. A **marketing decision support system (MDSS)** is one designed specifically for marketing decisions.

Consider a simple MDSS. An industrial salesperson handles a product that allows substantial customization. At a customer's site 1,500 miles from the home office, she is asked if she can match the price and delivery time of a competitor for a unique product configuration. A sound MDSS would allow the salesperson to plug a portable computer directly into a phone jack. The portable computer could then communicate with a mini- or mainframe computer in the home office. The salesperson types in the product configuration and desired delivery time. The database contains costs, inventory availability, assembly time needed, and margin requirements as well as a model to relate these variables. In a matter of minutes, the salesperson can respond with a price and delivery date. 3M Co. operates a system very similar to this.

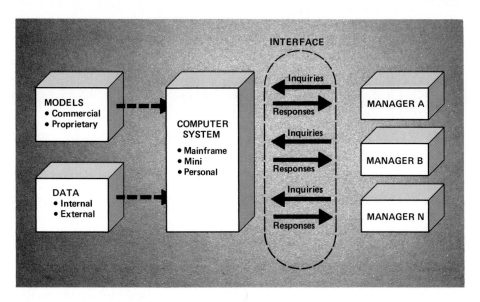

FIGURE 2–3 A Typical Decision Support System (DSS)

While the MDSS we have described is very valuable for the salesperson, it would have little value to the brand manager, strategic planner, advertising manager, or even the sales manager. Thus, rather than one MDSS, most firms have a series of MDSSs, some with shared components and some completely independent.

Components of an MDSS

As Figure 2–3 illustrates, MDSSs require five components: models, data, computers, an interface system, and managers.

Models

Models, as used in the context of an MDSS, are mathematical statements of the presumed relationship between two or more variables. A very simple model is

$$\text{Sales revenue} = \text{units sold} \times \text{average price per unit}$$

Although extremely simple, this model allows the manager to conduct *what-if* analysis or *scenarios*. **What-if analysis** involves determining *what* the impact on a decision outcome (sales revenue in our example) would be *if* one or more of the unknown or predicted variables (units sold and average price in our example) were different from its assumed value.

Suppose a manager believes that about 1,000 units of a new product will be sold at an average price of $100:

$$\text{Sales revenue} = 1,000 \times \$100$$
$$= \$100,000$$

Models: mathematical statements of the presumed relationship between two or more variables.

What-if analysis: determining what the impact on a decision outcome would be if one or more of the unknown or predicted variables were different from its assumed value.

However, the manager is uncertain about the exact number that will be sold and the average price level that will be obtained. Therefore, a series of what-if analyses are appropriate:

What if we sell only 900 units at $100 each?
What if we could sell 1,200 units at $90 each?
What if we could sell 800 units at $110 each?

Obviously, a model this simple requires no more than a pencil and paper to manipulate. Let's expand the model slightly to see how useful formal models can be.

Suppose management is considering introducing a new product. The firm uses a three-year planning horizon. Initial marketing research indicates that (1) the market demand is between 800,000 and 1,200,000 units a year, (2) the demand will grow between 10 and 14 percent a year, (3) the firm's market share will be between 20 and 30 percent, and (4) the average price will decline by $0.50 per year from the current $10.00 level.

If the manager has a reasonable understanding of the product's cost structure and the firm's marketing plans, a three-year projected income statement based on the initial marketing research estimates can be prepared. The first projection would be the "most likely" estimates produced by the researchers: perhaps 1,000,000 units current demand, a 12 percent growth rate, a 25 percent market share, and a $0.50 price decline each year.

An MDSS system for this situation might involve putting the projected income statements in formula form on a spreadsheet program such as *Lotus 1-2-3* or *Excel*. The manager can then conduct what-if analyses.

For example, the manager might ask, "What would our projected profits be if the initial market size were 900,000 units rather than 1,000,000?" Research Application 2–3 illustrates a very simple version of this type of analysis.

Sensitivity analysis: determining at what level or value, if any, each of the unknown or predicted variables has a meaningful impact on the decision to be made.

In addition to what-if analyses, models such as this allow managers to conduct sensitivity analyses. **Sensitivity analysis** is determining at what level or value, if any, each of the unknown variables has a meaningful impact on the decision to be made. Assume our manager needs to break even the first year and show a 20 percent return on sales for each of the next two years to justify launching the product. A simple sensitivity analysis could be done by conducting a what-if analysis with each unknown set at its highest and lowest likely value. If the decision would remain the same whether the variable was at its highest or lowest likely value, that variable could be ignored as far as the decision is concerned. If the decision would change, a critical variable has been identified. Additional research to specify its precise value may be justified.

A more thorough sensitivity analysis would involve varying the values of combinations of variables. Thus, it might be that the decision in our example would not change if the initial market size was 800,000 *given that all other unknowns were at their most likely values.* Likewise, the decision might not change if our market share was as low as 20 percent, *again given that all other unknowns are at their most likely levels.* However, if *both* initial market size *and* market share were low (800,000 and 20 percent), the decision might differ. Thus, a complete sensitivity analysis must cover all relevant combinations of unknown or assumed variables.

RESEARCH APPLICATION 2–3

"What-If" Analysis

Assumptions

	Most Likely	Most Favorable	Least Favorable
Market Size	1,000,000	1,200,000	800,000
Market Growth	12%	14%	10%
Market Share	25%	30%	20%
Price	$10.00 first year		
Price Decline/Year	$0.50	$0.20	$1.00
Cost of Goods Sold (COGS)	$5.00 first year		
Annual Decline in COGS	5%		
Marketing Expenses	$750,000 first year plus $0.50 per unit, $0.50 unit years 2–5		

Results

Most Likely	Year 1	Year 2	Year 3
Sales	$2,800,000	$2,979,200	$3,161,088
Cost of Goods	1,400,000	1,489,600	1,668,352
Gross Profits	1,400,000	1,489,600	1,492,736
Marketing Expense	890,000	156,800	175,616
Contribution	$ 510,000	$1,332,800	$1,317,120

Most Favorable			
Sales	$4,104,000	$4,584,989	$5,120,216
Cost of Goods	2,052,000	2,222,316	2,533,440
Gross Profits	2,052,000	2,362,637	2,586,776
Marketing Expense	955,200	233,928	266,678
Contribution	$1,096,800	$2,128,745	$2,320,098

Least Favorable			
Sales	$1,760,000	$1,742,400	$1,703,680
Cost of Goods	880,000	919,600	1,011,560
Gross Profits	880,000	822,800	692,120
Marketing Expense	838,000	96,000	106,480
Contribution	$ 42,000	$ 726,000	$ 585,640

Models are frequently developed for a specific decision such as the one just described. In addition, commercially available models for categories of problems can be used "as is" or modified slightly to fit the situation at hand.[8]

Data

MDSSs require varying amounts and types of data. In our first example of a price/delivery MDSS, only internal, "factual" data were involved. The new product launch MDSS that we just described required internal cost data as well as research data and assumptions about external factors such as market size, market share, and price level over time.

Suppose a brand manager for Procter & Gamble learns from the MIS that Colgate is test marketing a new competitive product in Denver and Buffalo. The manager would want answers to several questions, including, "How much share will my brand lose if Colgate goes national and I don't change my marketing mix?" Responding would require data on Procter & Gamble's brand's share trend nationally and in Denver and Buffalo, a measure of whether it or Colgate is unusually strong or weak in Denver or Buffalo, a reading of how its share is being affected in the two test cities, and estimates of how other competitors will respond if Colgate goes national.

As we will see in Chapters 4 and 5, such data are available from a variety of sources. However, for the data to prove useful, Procter & Gamble will have to have anticipated the need for it, arranged to acquire it, entered it into the system, and developed a model that will allow the data to be analyzed.

Computer System

Theoretically, the data in an MDSS could be analyzed using the relevant models and manual calculations. However, this is impractical for all but the very simplest systems. Increasingly, MDSSs are being developed for minicomputers and personal computers rather than mainframes. Given the fairly limited data storage requirements of most MDSSs and the rapidly increasing power and speed of personal computers, this trend toward personal computer systems will undoubtedly continue.

Interface

Interface:
software that
allows managers
to interact directly
with the data and
model(s) in an
MDSS.

More critical than the computer system is the **interface**—the software that allows the manager to interact with the data and the model. Most managers have limited computer programming skills and lack both the time and inclination to acquire them. Successful MDSSs are, therefore, exceedingly user friendly.

An MDSS has value only to the extent that *managers* will use it to test hypotheses and assumptions, change parameters, and clarify options. Thus, the interface must be more than "doable"; it must also be fun or at least easy.

A successful system was adopted by Kraft, Inc. Kraft has a five-member MDSS staff. They acquired a general system called ACCESS Marketing Analysis System from Dialogue, Inc.; to this, they added a series of sophisticated analysis functions addressing issues specific to Kraft. Today, over 200 managers in brand marketing, marketing services, sales, and advertising are active users of the

RESEARCH APPLICATION 2–4

Applications of Proprietary MDSSs

Hardee's MDSS is used by over 100 managers to estimate cannibalization of existing products by new menu additions, to maximize sales of its roast beef sandwich based on size changes, to evaluate price changes, to analyze the profit impact of various promotions, and to estimate the financial performance of proposed new restaurants.*

Zales uses its Store Placement Model (SPM) to evaluate potential outlet locations. The SPM's database contains data on each of Zales' current stores including financial and market area data. The market area data (demographics, traffic, and so forth) for a proposed site are entered into the model. Financial results from similar stores in markets similar to the proposed location are used to forecast the performance of the proposed outlet.†

Frito-Lay operates a large MDSS. It is capable of scenario analysis on a worldwide basis. A common application is to analyze the market share and

contribution margin implications of price and promotion changes within specific geographic areas.†

Northwestern Mutual Life Insurance has a decision support system designed to help it understand its current client base better. The new system allows analysis by client rather than by policy. Thus, it has allowed the firm to discover patterns of policy ownership. For example, it identified a group of "super clients" who had more coverage and loans than average. This knowledge allowed the development of special programs for this group as well as programs designed to attract similar customers.‡

*J. P. Stamen, "Decision Support Systems," *Journal of Business Strategy* (April 1990), 31.
†A. J. Greco and J. T. Hogue, "Developing Marketing Decision Support Systems in Consumer Goods Firms," *Journal of Consumer Marketing* (Winter 1990), 55–64.
‡L. A. Wallis, *Decision-Support Systems for Marketing* (New York: The Conference Board, 1989), 10.

system. With a staff of only 5 supporting over 200 users, it is clear that the managers are very comfortable interfacing with the system on their own.[9]

Managers

As stated earlier, managers are the most important aspect of an MDSS. If they fail to use the system or use it improperly, the system has no (or negative) value. Thus, not only must the interface system be user friendly, but managers also must understand how to do *what-if* and other relevant analyses. They must also understand and accept the models involved. Hence, managers should be actively involved in developing the models. In fact, active involvement in all aspects of the design of the system by all potential users is the key to a successful system.

MDSS Applications

A wide array of MDSSs are used by firms, ranging from Coca-Cola to General Electric to J. C. Penney to Esco (a specialty steel producer). Research Application 2–4 describes applications of several proprietary MDSSs.

Expert Systems

Expert system:
software that
attempts to
duplicate the
reasoning or logic
that a single
expert or group of
experts would use
to solve a class of
problems.

It is estimated that U.S. firms spent $4 billion on expert systems in 1990.[10] The distinction between a DSS and an expert system is one of degree. In general, an **expert system** attempts to duplicate the reasoning or logic that a single expert or group of experts would use to solve a class of problems such as making a competitive bid or setting an advertising budget. An expert system is more oriented toward providing an optimal or final answer than are most DSSs, which indicate probable outcomes of various potential decisions or states of nature.[11]

In addition to the requirements associated with developing a DSS, developing an expert system requires the following:

1. Marketing experts who can solve the problem demonstrably better than amateurs and who can clearly explain their thought processes to nonexperts.
2. A well-structured problem not significantly influenced by changes in the marketing environment.
3. A problem that occurs repetitively in the organization.
4. A problem that requires minimal common sense to solve.
5. A problem that experts can usually solve in two to three hours.[12]

As this list indicates, expert systems in marketing are currently limited to relatively straightforward, simple uses. Examples would include matching product features to customer use requirements, preparing competitive bids, selecting media schedules, and so forth. However, the range of applications is growing rapidly with gains in both computing power and knowledge about artificial intelligence. Expert systems will certainly play an increasingly important role in marketing decisions in the future. As an example, SCAN*EXPERT is a newly developed expert system that analyzes Nielsen's SCANTRACK scanner data to identify key competitors, find events in the data of interest to managers, and isolate possible causes of those events.[13]

Summary

A marketing information system (MIS) is a system designed to generate, store, and disseminate an orderly flow of pertinent information to marketing managers. MISs provide: (1) recurrent information—information provided periodically such as market share by region; (2) monitoring information—information derived from the regular scanning of certain sources and reported whenever it occurs, such as news of a new product launch by a competitor; and (3) requested information—information developed in response to a specific request such as a request for a test of consumer response to a proposed new product. These systems are widely used to identify, select, and help resolve marketing problems and opportunities.

A marketing decision support system (MDSS) is a computerized database containing one or more models and an interface that allows managers to interact directly with the models and the data. An MDSS allows managers to ask questions easily about the relationships among variables in the database or about the effect of changing one or more variables on the other variables. MDSSs are often used for what-if analyses—determining what the impact on a decision outcome such as sales revenue would be if one or more other variables, such as advertising or price, were changed. They are also used for sensitivity analysis—determining at what level or value, if any, each or any combination of the unknown or predicted variables would cause a change in the decision to be made.

An expert system is a computer model that attempts to duplicate the logic an expert or group of experts would use to solve a class of marketing problems such as making a competitive bid or developing a media schedule. Such systems are gaining in popularity and sophistication but are still limited to recurrent, structured problems for which experts can articulate a straightforward logic for solving.

MISs are focused primarily on providing managers with information. MDSSs allow managers to interact actively with data and models to test assumptions and ideas. Expert systems generally attempt to provide a single optimal answer to a specific type of problem or task.

Review Questions

2.1. What is a *marketing information system* (MIS)? How does it relate to marketing research?

2.2. What is *recurrent information?* Provide an example.

2.3. What is *monitoring information?* Provide an example.

2.4. What is *requested information?* Provide an example.

2.5. What is a *specialized MIS?*

2.6. Describe a *competitor intelligence MIS.*

2.7. What is a *decision support system?* How does it differ from a *marketing decision support system?*

2.8. How does an MDSS differ from an MIS?

2.9. What are the components of an MDSS? Describe each.

2.10. What is a *model?*

2.11. What is a *what-if analysis?*

2.12. What is a *sensitivity analysis?*

2.13. Describe Zales' SPM.

2.14. How does an expert system differ from an MDSS?

2.15. What is required for an expert system?

Discussion Questions/Problems

2.16. The developer of the Motorola DSS that we described at the beginning of the chapter stated: "There is a distinction between simply collecting information and applying that information strategically." What does this mean?

2.17. How would you determine what types of information an MIS should provide to different members of an organization?

2.18. How would you determine which types of MDSSs are required by different members of an organization?

2.19. Run a five-year what-if analysis using Research Application 2–3 as the base.[14] Use the most likely values and the following changes and report the annual contribution:
   a. market share = 22%
   b. market share = 23%
   c. market share = 28%
   d. market growth = 11%
   e. market growth = 14%
   f. market size = 850,000
   g. market size = 1,050,000
   h. price decline = $.70 per year
   i. price decline = $.30 per year
   j. a and d
   k. c and g

2.20. How do you insure that managers will make effective use of an MDSS?

2.21. How do you think the average marketing manager would react to the use of an expert system in his or her area?

Projects

2.22. Interview the managers of _____. Describe in detail a sound MIS for that organization.
   a. your student union
   b. the university bookstore
   c. a campus restaurant
   d. a local shopping center
   e. the university
   f. a local bank
   g. the United Way

2.23. Interview the managers of _____. Describe in detail a sound MDSS for that organization.
   a. your student union
   b. the university bookstore
   c. a campus restaurant
   d. a local shopping center
   e. the university
   f. a local bank
   g. the United Way

Notes

1. "Company Sees Benefits in Centralizing Its System of Competitor Intelligence," *Marketing News* (September 12, 1986), 4. See also J. P. Herring, "Building a Business Intelligence System," *Journal of Business Strategy* (May 1988), 4–9.

2. See L. Meredith, "Developing and Using a Data Base Marketing System," *Industrial Marketing Management* (4, 1989), 245–257; and L. F. Higgins, S. C. McIntyre, C. G. Raine, "Design of Global Marketing Information Systems," *Journal of Business and Industrial Marketing* (Fall 1991), 49–58.

3. Based on private correspondence and "Penney Sees 'Fairly Good' Retail Gains," *Advertising Age* (November 2, 1982), 20. See also H. G. M. Brinkhoff, "How Does Unilever Work with Its MIS?" *European Research* (April 1984), 88–95.

4. Meredith, "Developing and Using a Data Base Marketing Strategy," 252.

5. C. Etmekjian, J. Grede, "Marketing Research in a Team-Oriented Business," *Marketing Research* (December 1990), 10.

6. See K. Brockhoff, "Competitor Technology in German Companies," *Industrial Marketing Management* (2, 1991), 91–98; and L. Fuld, "A Recipe for Business Intelligence Success," *Journal of Business Strategy* (February 1991), 12–17.

7. M. D. Goslar, S. W. Brown, "Decision Support Systems," *Journal of Consumer Marketing* (Summer 1986), 43–50; J. T. Mentzer and R. Gomes, "Evaluating a Decision Support Forecasting System," *Industrial Marketing Management* (4, 1989), 313–323; A. J. Greco, J. T. Hogue, "Developing Marketing Decision Support Systems in Consumer Goods Firms," *Journal of Consumer Marketing* (Winter 1990), 55–64; and J. P. Stamen, "Decision Support Systems," *Journal of Business Strategy* (April 1990), 30–33.

8. See M. L. Laric, R. Stiff, *Lotus 1-2-3^R for Marketing and Sales* (Prentice-Hall Inc, 1984); G. L. Lilien, *Marketing Mix Analysis with Lotus 1-2-3^R* (The Scientific Press 1986); and G. L. Lilien, *Marketing Management: Analytic Exercises with Lotus 1-2-3^R* (The Scientific Press, 1988).

9. J. E. Ohlon, "Modified Computer System Helps Kraft Make Plans," *Marketing News* (May 23, 1986), 31.

10. T. H. Stevenson, D. A. Plath, C. M. Bush, "Using Expert Systems in Industrial Marketing," *Industrial Marketing Management* (3, 1990), 243–249.

11. See R. P. Morgan, J. R. Bond, "Methods of Artificial Intelligence," *Journal of the Market Research Society* (July 1989), 375–397; A. Rangaswamy, "Developing Marketing Expert Systems," *Journal of Marketing* (October 1989), 24–39; A. A. Mitchell, J. E. Russo, D. R. W. Hink, "Issues in the Development and Use of Expert Systems for Marketing Decisions," *International Journal of Research in Marketing* (April 1991), 41–50; and R. S. Sisodia, "Expert Systems for Services Marketing," *Journal of Services Marketing* (Summer 1991), 37–54.

12. Stevenson, Plath, Bush, "Using Expert Systems," 247.

13. J. Bayer, R. Harter, " 'Miner,' 'Manager,' and 'Researcher,' " *International Journal of Research in Marketing* (April 1991), 17–27.

14. A *Lotus 1-2-3* program is included in the software package available through Macmillan.

CHAPTER 3

Research Design

LEARNING OBJECTIVES

Upon completing this chapter, you should be able to:

1. Describe the marketing research process.

2. Explain the nature of marketing research design.

3. Differentiate exploratory research, descriptive research, and casual research.

4. List and describe the steps in the research design process.

5. Explain the importance of properly defining the research problem and the steps required to do so.

6. Construct a PERT chart for a research project and identify the critical path.

7. List and describe the elements of a research proposal.

8. List and describe the eight most serious potential errors confronting the researcher.

9. Describe the three general strategies the researcher can use to deal with potential research errors.

10. Explain why multinational research designs are much more difficult than single-country designs.

Marketing Research for a New Dairy Product in the United Kingdom

A British dairy was considering investing £100,000 for equipment to produce paneer and khoya. (Paneer is a cooking cheese used in the preparation of many Asian dishes. Khoya is a 70 percent solids dairy product that is the basis for a variety of Asian sweets.) The only khoya available in the United Kingdom was an artificial variety using powdered milk, and there was limited local production of paneer. Both products would be of interest to owners of Asian restaurants and sweet centers, to wholesale and retail food outlets that cater to Asian customers, and to food outlets that serve vegetarians and those interested in ethnic food specialties. The firm needed an estimate of the potential size of the market in order to make the investment decision. This represented a challenging task for several reasons. First, no data was available on sales of the products since they were largely unavailable. Second, authentic khoya is a new concept to many Asians in the United Kingdom since only an artificial version has been available. Third, the range of potential outlets was very wide (from small Asian restaurants to the specialty sections of large supermarkets). Finally, the dairy had limited funds for research.

The research firm was able to determine the number of potential outlets of each type for the two products through secondary data (previously published information). It was also able to get population estimates for the relevant Asian groups as well as insights into trends in the ethnic food market from secondary data. Next, 70 semi-structured interviews were conducted with Asian consumers, managers of Asian restaurants, sweet centers, and wholesale and retail food outlets, and managers of chain outlets and vegetarian/ethnic food specialty stores.

The interviews combined with the secondary data provided estimates of purchases by outlet type. This "high-side" estimate was subjectively deflated as extensive experience had convinced the researchers that buyers tend to overestimate the amount of a new product they will use. The resultant market size estimate was by no means exact, but the *go–no go* management decision did not require an exact estimate.[1]

In this chapter, we will provide an overview of the research design process. That is, we will describe the process the research firm working for the U.K. dairy went through to determine what information to collect and how to collect and analyze it. After we describe this process, we will describe the potential errors the researcher seeks to minimize through research design.

The Nature of Marketing Research Design

Marketing research process: identifying a management problem or opportunity; translating that into a research problem; and collecting, analyzing, and reporting the results.

The **marketing research process** involves identifying a management problem or opportunity; translating that problem/opportunity into a research problem; and collecting, analyzing, and reporting the information specified in the research problem.

A **management problem** deals with decisions managers must make. A research problem deals with providing information that will help management make better decisions. The management problem facing the dairy in our opening example was whether or not to invest £100,000 to produce two new products. The research problem was to discover the size of the potential market for the two products.

Management problem: determining the best course of action to take to maximize the organization's objectives.

Marketing research design is the specification of procedures for collecting and analyzing the data necessary to help identify or react to a problem or opportunity, such that the difference between the cost of obtaining various levels of accuracy and the expected value of the information associated with each level of accuracy is maximized.

Several aspects of this definition deserve emphasis. First, research design requires the *specification of procedures*. These procedures involve decisions on what information to generate, the data collection method, the measurement approach, the object to be measured, and the way in which the data are to be analyzed. Second, the data *are to be collected to help identify or react to a problem or opportunity*. All data collected should relate to decisions faced by management.

Marketing research design: the specification of procedures for collecting and analyzing data to help identify or react to a problem or opportunity.

A third implication of the preceding definition is that *information has value*. Information acquires value as it helps improve decisions. The fourth major implication is that *varying levels of accuracy of information can be generated in response to the same problem*. Information accuracy is affected by the occurrence of a number of potential errors. Finally, the goal of applied research design is not to generate the most accurate information possible. Rather, the objective is to *generate the most valuable information in relation to the cost of generating the information*.

Types of Research Designs

It is useful to consider three general categories of research based on the type of information required. These three categories are *exploratory*, *descriptive*, and *causal*.

Exploratory research is concerned with discovering the general nature of the problem and the variables that relate to it. Exploratory research is characterized by a high degree of flexibility, and it tends to rely on secondary data, convenience or judgment samples, small-scale surveys or simple experiments, case analyses, and subjective evaluation of the results.

Descriptive research is focused on the accurate description of the variables in the problem model. Consumer profile studies, market-potential studies, product-usage studies, attitude surveys, sales analyses, media research, and price surveys are examples of descriptive research. Any source of information can be used in a descriptive study, although most studies of this nature rely heavily on secondary data sources and survey research.

Causal research attempts to specify the nature of the functional relationship between two or more variables in the problem model. For example, studies on the effectiveness of advertising generally attempt to discover the extent to which advertising causes sales or attitude change. We can use three types of evidence to make inferences about causation: (1) *concomitant variation*, (2) *sequence of occurrence*, and (3) *absence of other potential causal factors.*

Concomitant variation, or invariant association, is a common basis for ascribing cause. Suppose we note that our advertising expenditures vary across a number of geographic areas and measure sales in each area. To the extent that high sales occur in areas with large advertising expenditures and low sales occur in areas with limited advertising expenditures, we may infer that advertising is a cause of sales. It must be stressed that we have only *inferred* this; we have not proven that increased advertising causes increased sales.

Sequence of occurrence can also provide evidence of causation. For one event to cause another, it must always precede it. An event that occurs after another event cannot be said to cause the first event. The importance of sequence can be demonstrated in our last example of advertising causing sales. Suppose that further investigation showed that the advertising allocation to the geographic regions had been based on the last period's sales such that the level of advertising was directly related to past sales. Suddenly, the nature of our causal relationship is reversed. Now, because of the sequence of events, we can infer that changes in sales levels cause changes in advertising levels.

A final type of evidence that we can use to infer causality is the *absence of other potential causal factors.* That is, if we could logically or through our research design eliminate all possible causative factors except the one we are interested in, we would have established that the variable we are concerned with was the causative factor. Unfortunately, it is never possible to control completely or to eliminate all possible causes for any particular event. Always we have the possibility that some factor of which we are not aware has influenced the results. However, if all reasonable alternatives are eliminated except one, we can have a high degree of confidence in the remaining variable.

Steps in the Research Design Process

Describing the research design process as a sequential series of distinct or separate steps is inherently misleading. The steps in the design process interact and often occur simultaneously. For example, the design of a measure-

Exploratory research: attempts to discover the general nature of the problem and the variables that relate to it.

Descriptive research: focuses on the accurate description of the variables in the problem model.

Causal research: attempts to specify the nature of the functional relationship between two or more variables in the problem model.

ment instrument is influenced by the type of analysis that will be conducted. However, the type of analysis is also influenced by the specific characteristics of the measurement instrument.

Because written communications must be presented sequentially, we present the research design process as a distinct series of steps. These steps, shown in Figure 3–1, represent the general order in which decisions are made in designing a research project. However, we must emphasize that the "early" decisions are made with simultaneous consideration of the "later"

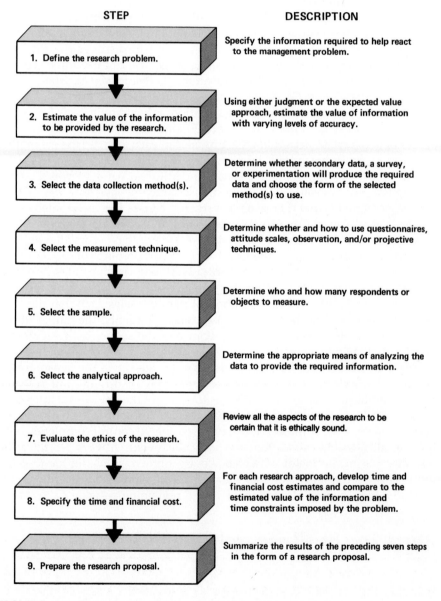

FIGURE 3–1 Steps in the Research Design Process

decisions. Furthermore, earlier decisions are constantly reconsidered in light of the later decisions.

Step 1: Define the Research Problem

Problem definition is the most critical part of the research process. **Research problem definition** involves specifying the information needed by management. Unless the problem is properly defined, the information produced by the research process is unlikely to have any value. Consider Research Application 3–1. Coca-Cola Company researchers utilized a very sound research design to collect information on taste preferences. Unfortunately for Coca-Cola, taste preferences are only part of what drives the soft drink purchase decision.

Research problem definition involves four interrelated steps: (1) management problem/opportunity clarification, (2) situation analyses, (3) model development, and (4) specification of information requirements.[2]

Research problem definition: specifying the information needed by management.

Management Problem/Opportunity Clarification

In a meeting with a marketing research consultant, the president of a chamber of commerce discussed a research project that would help merchants reduce the amount of shopping residents of their community do in two larger communities nearby. The management problem was apparently clear: how to reduce "outshopping" and so increase the amount of shopping done locally. Stated in this way, the task of the researcher was to help identify and evaluate various ways to increase the local merchants' share of the shopping done by residents.

However, additional probing revealed that the underlying problem was to convince a majority of the local retailers that there was a sufficient outflow of local trade to warrant joint action to reverse the flow. Only after the retailers were convinced of this would it be possible to utilize information on why local residents were shopping in surrounding communities. The more precise statement of the management problem implied a very different research problem from the initial statement. Now the researcher would become concerned with measuring the level of the retail trade outflow, in addition to the reasons for the outflow.

The basic goal of problem clarification is to ensure that the decision maker's initial description of the management decision is accurate and reflects the appropriate area of concern for research. If the wrong management problem is translated into a research problem, the probability of providing management with useful information is low.

Situation Analysis

The management problem can be understood only within the context of the decision situation. The situation analysis focuses on the variables that have produced the stated management problem or opportunity. The factors that have led to the problem/opportunity manifestations and the factors that have led to management's concern should be isolated. The situation analysis in-

RESEARCH APPLICATION 3–1

*Research Design for the Development of New Coke**

While doing research on the formula for what would become diet *Coke*, Coca-Cola USA chemists came up with a syrup that tasted "smoother" than regular *Coke*. Over the next three years the company conducted a series of taste tests comparing this and other formulations of *Coke* with the various cola brands on the market. During that time, the taste preferences of more than 190,000 persons were measured in the United States and selected foreign countries. The results of these taste tests ultimately convinced Coca-Cola USA management that "new" *Coke* should be introduced.

Although the overall design differed in some of the tests, the central design elements were as follows:

1. The tests were held in shopping malls.
2. Quota samples of 200 to 400 persons representing demographic groups of interest were selected.
3. All taste tests were conducted on a *double-blind* basis. That is, neither the person administering the test nor the person taking the test knew what actual brands and/or formulations were used in the tests in which they were involved.
4. The tests were conducted using two different designs, *double triangle discrimination* and *sequential monadic preference tests*. For the double triangle discrimination tests each sample member was asked to taste, in random order, two samples of *Coke* and one sample of *Pepsi-Cola*, and was then asked to tell the interviewer the one that was different from the other two. In a second triangle test, the sample member was asked to taste, in random order, two samples of *Pepsi* and one sample of *Coke*, and again was asked to

identify which sample was different from the other two.

After the second triangle discrimination test, the sequential monadic preference test was conducted. The procedure for this test was to give each sample member, in random order, samples of *Pepsi* and *Coke* and ask them to state a taste preference between the two.

Analysis of the results of the tests was performed on the total sample (including discriminators and nondiscriminators).

5. The taste preference tests were conducted on a paired comparison basis involving more than one formulation of *Coke*. For example, for the preference tests between regular *Coke* (now *Coca-Cola Classic*), regular *Pepsi*, and a new formulation of regular *Coke*, the sample member was asked to make the following comparisons:
   (i) regular *Coke*—regular *Pepsi*;
   (ii) new formulation of regular *Coke*—regular *Pepsi*;
   (iii) new formulation of regular *Coke*—regular *Coke*.

These pairs were administered in random order. The sample member was asked to rinse out her or his mouth with water and eat some unsalted crackers between tastes.

The results indicated a preference for the new formula *Coke* which was subsequently introduced. However, it now has less than a 2 percent market share while the original formula (now *Classic Coke*), *with the taste that consumers did not prefer*, has almost a 20 percent share.

*This description of the taste tests has been reviewed and approved by the corporate staff of the Coca-Cola Company.

volves giving careful attention to company records; appropriate secondary sources such as census data, industry sales figures, economic indicators, and so on; and interviews with knowledgeable individuals both internal and external to the firm. The persons interviewed will include the manager(s) involved and may include salespersons, other researchers, trade association officials, professionals, and consumers.

A situation analysis of the retail trade outflow problem revealed, among other things, that (1) the local population had grown 25 percent over the previous five years, (2) buying power per capita appeared to be growing at the national rate of 3 percent a year, and (3) local retail sales of nongrocery items had increased approximately 20 percent over the past five years. Thus, the local retailers' sales are clearly not keeping pace with the potential in the area.

Model Development

Once the researcher has a sound understanding of the decision situation, it is necessary to get as clear an understanding as possible of the *situation model* of the manager. A **situation model** is a description of the outcomes that are desired, the relevant variables, and the relationships of the variables to the outcomes. The researcher is therefore interested in having the manager answer the following questions:

Situation model: a description of the outcomes that are desired by a manager, the relevant variables, and the relationships of the variables to the outcomes.

1. What objective(s) is desired in solving the problem or taking advantage of the opportunity?
2. What variables determine whether the objective(s) will be met?
3. How do they relate to the objective(s)?

For example, the chamber president gave the following explanation about why local consumers shop in the larger communities nearby:

> It could be any of several things. Our prices are about the same as theirs but I'm not sure our local people recognize this. They advertise a lot more than we do and they have larger stores. Maybe it's just the excitement or fun of getting out-of-town. I think if more people recognized the impact on our local economy, they would spend more money in town. We really need to capture at least a third of the trade we are now losing.

Note that the president has suggested several causes for outshopping. He also has suggested a potential solution. In addition, he has stated his objective with respect to the problem. However, the researcher should not be satisfied to operate with only the manager's model of the problem. Instead, there should be an attempt to develop the best possible model of the decision at hand. Although there will usually be little latitude with respect to the objectives of the firm, the researcher should examine carefully the list of variables developed thus far that are believed to be the determining ones. Are all of these variables relevant? Are these the only relevant variables? How does each variable affect the outcome of the decision?

At least two sources of information may be helpful in this phase of research design. First, *secondary data* sources beyond those concerned directly with the situation analysis should be reviewed. These sources range from trade journal articles and special reports concerning the variable in a specific situation to more abstract theoretical treatments of the variable.

Case analyses: the in-depth analysis of a few selected situations, customers, or activities.

A second approach for getting information to help the researcher to develop a problem situation model involves using selected **case analyses.** Assume that a firm is concerned with the sales performance of its various branch offices. The case approach would involve an in-depth comparison of a "successful" branch and an "unsuccessful" branch. Those variables that differed the most between the two branches are considered relevant for additional study.

At the end of the model development stage, the researcher will have developed a list of variables relevant to the management problem *and* some known or tentative sets of relationships between the variables.

Specification of Information Requirements

Research cannot provide solutions. Solutions require executive judgment. Research provides information relevant to the decisions faced by the executive. *The output of the problem-definition process is a clear statement of the information required to assist the decision maker.* Thus, part of the information to be generated for the chamber president might include a price comparison of selected nongrocery items in the three towns and a measure of local residents' beliefs concerning the relative prices for the same items in the three towns.

A common temptation is to try to collect data on all possible variables. Unfortunately, this is generally impractical and always costly. The best approach for ensuring that any data collected are indeed relevant is to ask questions concerning the ultimate use of the data. Specifically, the researcher should list the research findings that seem possible and, in conjunction with the manager, trace the implications of each with respect to the decision. That is, the researcher must ask the question, "Given this finding, what would the firm do?"

The emphasis is on *what it will do,* or at least, *is likely to do, given certain findings.* In some companies such as Carnation it is the practice to have final research proposals signed by both the research director and the manager involved, and to include a statement to the effect that if X_1 results are obtained, Y_1 action will be taken; if X_2 is the finding, Y_2 action will be taken, and so on.

Step 2: Estimate the Value of the Information

As we have seen, information has value only to the extent that it improves decisions. The value of information increases as (1) the cost of a wrong decision increases, (2) our level of knowledge as to the correct decision decreases, and (3) the accuracy of the information the research will provide increases.

The principle involved in deciding whether to do more research is that *research should be conducted only when the value of the information to be obtained is expected to be greater than the cost of obtaining it.* The value of information from a research project is generally estimated intuitively by managers, though quantitative methods are available.[3]

Step 3: Select the Data Collection Approach

There are three basic data collection approaches in marketing research: (1) *secondary data,* (2) *survey data,* and (3) *experimental data.* **Secondary data** were collected for some purpose other than helping to solve the current problem, whereas **primary data** are collected expressly to help solve the problem at hand. Survey and experimental data are therefore secondary data if they were collected earlier for another study; they are primary data if they were collected for the present one. These data collection approaches and their major subareas are described in Table 3–1.

Secondary data are virtually always collected first because of their time and cost advantages. However, a researcher does not necessarily choose one of these approaches over the others. For example, in collecting data for a decision about introducing a new product, a researcher may (1) examine company records for information relating to past introductions of similar products (secondary data); (2) conduct a series of mall interviews to determine current consumer attitudes about the product category (survey data); and (3) conduct a controlled store test in which the impact of different package designs is measured (experimental data). Research Application 3–2 illustrates the series

Secondary data: data collected for some purpose other than helping solve the current problem.

Primary data: data collected specifically to help solve the problem at hand.

TABLE 3–1 Major Data Collection Methods

I. *Secondary Research*—utilization of data that were developed for some purpose other than to help solve the problem at hand.
  A. *Internal secondary data*—data generated within the organization itself, such as salesperson call reports, sales invoices, and accounting records.
  B. *External secondary data*—data generated by sources outside the organization, such as government reports, trade association data, and data collected by syndicated services.

II. *Survey Research*—systematic collection of information directly from respondents.
  A. *Telephone interviews*—collection of information from respondents by telephone.
  B. *Mail interviews*—collection of information from respondents by mail or similar techniques.
  C. *Personal interviews*—collection of information in a face-to-face situation.
    1. *Home interviews*—personal interviews in the respondent's home or office.
    2. *Intercept interviews*—personal interviews in a central location, generally a shopping mall.
  D. *Computer interviews*—respondents enter data directly into a computer in response to questions presented on the monitor.

III. *Experimental Research*—the researcher manipulates one or more variables in such a way that its effect on one or more other variables can be measured.
  A. *Laboratory experiments*—manipulation of the independent variable(s) in an artificial situation.
    1. *Basic designs* consider the impact of only one independent variable.
    2. *Statistical designs* consider the impact of more than one independent variable.
  B. *Field experiments*—manipulation of the independent variable(s) in a natural situation.

Typical Flow of Marketing Research at Kao

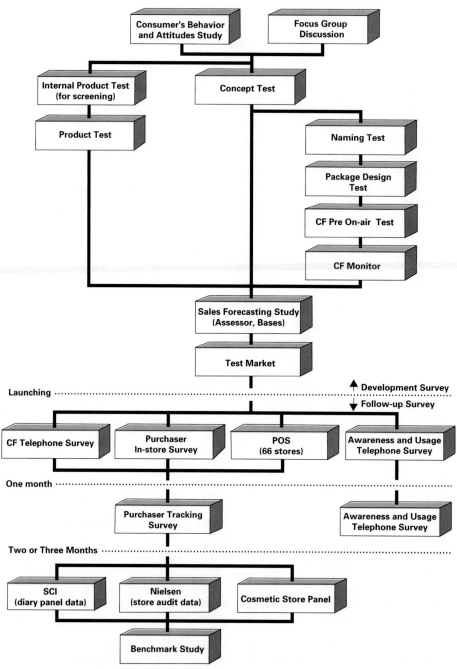

SOURCE: M. Kuga, "Kao's Marketing Strategy and Marketing Intelligence System," *Journal of Advertising Research* (April/May 1990), 24.

of research projects Kao, a leading Japanese consumer goods firm, uses in developing and launching a new product.

Step 4: Select the Measurement Technique

Four basic measurement techniques are used in marketing research: (1) *questionnaires*, (2) *attitude scales*, (3) *observation*, and (4) *depth interviews* and *projective techniques*. Each of these approaches is briefly described in Table 3–2. (Chapter 9 provides a discussion of the theory of measurement on which all four techniques are based. Chapters 10–13 discuss each technique.)

As with selecting the data collection method, selection of a measurement technique is influenced primarily by the nature of the information required and secondarily by the value of the information. This selection interacts with both the preceding and following steps in the design process. For example, it is difficult or impossible to use many projective techniques in telephone interviews. Similarly, it is impossible to use complex questionnaires or scales with young children. Selection of the appropriate measurement technique requires the simultaneous consideration of other characteristics of the research design.

Step 5: Select the Sample

Most marketing studies involve a *sample* or subgroup of the total population relevant to the problem, rather than a *census* of the entire group. The population is generally specified as a part of the problem definition process. As was

---

TABLE 3–2 Primary Measurement Techniques

I. *Questionnaire*—a formalized instrument for asking information directly from a respondent concerning behavior, demographic characteristics, level of knowledge, and/or attitudes, beliefs, and feelings.

II. *Attitude Scales*—a formalized instrument for eliciting self-reports of beliefs and feelings concerning an object(s).
   A. *Rating scales*—require the respondent to place the object being rated at some point along a numerically valued continuum or in one of a numerically ordered series of categories.
   B. *Composite scales*—require the respondent to express a degree of belief concerning various attributes of the object such that the attitude can be inferred from the pattern of responses.

III. *Observation*—the direct examination of behavior, the results of behavior, or physiological changes.

IV. *Projective Techniques and Depth Interviews*—designed to gather information that respondents are either unable or unwilling to provide in response to direct questioning.
   A. *Projective techniques*—allow respondents to project or express their own feelings as a characteristic of someone or something else.
   B. *Depth interviews*—allow individuals to express themselves without any fear of disapproval, dispute, or advice from the interviewer.

---

indicated in the previous section, the sampling process interacts with the other stages of the research design. For example, in most statistical techniques, probability sampling techniques are assumed. Therefore, the use of nonprobability samples restricts the types of analyses that can be performed. (The major considerations in sampling are described in Table 3–3 and discussed more fully in Chapters 14 and 15.)

Step 6: Select the Method(s) of Analysis

Data are useful only after analysis. Data analysis involves converting a series of recorded observations into descriptive statements and/or inferences about relationships. The types of analyses that can be conducted depend on the nature of the sampling process, the measurement instrument, and the data collection method.

It is imperative that the researcher select the analytic techniques *prior* to collecting the data. Once the analytic techniques are selected, the researcher should generate fictional responses (dummy data) to the measurement instrument. These dummy data are then analyzed by the analytic techniques selected to ensure that the results of this analysis will provide the information required by the problem at hand. Failure to carry out this step in advance can result in a completed research project that fails to provide some or all of the information required by the problem.[4] Further, it sometimes reveals that unneeded data are about to be collected.

Step 7: Evaluate the Ethics of the Research

It is essential that marketing researchers restrict their research activities to practices that are ethically sound. Ethically sound research considers the in-

---

TABLE 3–3 Primary Considerations in Sampling

    I. *Population*—determine who (or what objects) can provide the required information.

   II. *Sample Frame*—develop a list of population members.

  III. *Sampling Unit*—determine the basis for drawing the sample (individuals, households, city blocks, etc.).

  IV. *Sampling Method*—determine how the sample will be selected.
      A. *Probability*—members are selected by chance and there is a known chance of each unit being selected.
      B. *Nonprobability*—members are selected on the basis of convenience or judgment or by some means other than chance.

   V. *Sample Size*—determine how many population members are to be included in the sample.

  VI. *Sample Plan*—develop a method for selecting and contacting the sample members.

 VII. *Execution*—carry out the sampling plan.

terests of the general public, the respondents, the client, and the research profession as well as those of the researcher.

It is tempting to use simple ethical guidelines such as "Don't do anything you wouldn't want to explain on the six o'clock news"; however, the issues that arise in research are often too complex for such simple advice. For example, what are the ethics of rounding versus not rounding numbers in research reports? Chapter 20 thoroughly discusses this and many of the other ethical issues confronting the marketing researcher.

Step 8: Estimate Time and Financial Requirements

Once the research design(s) has been devised and checked for ethical soundness, the researcher must estimate the resource requirements. These requirements can be broken down into two broad categories: *time* and *financial*. Time refers to the time needed to complete the project. The financial requirement is the monetary representation of personnel time, computer time, and materials requirements. The time and finance requirements are not independent. As we shall see, on occasion, time and money are interchangeable.

The **program evaluation review technique (PERT)** coupled with the *critical path method* (CPM) offers a useful aid for estimating the resources needed for a project and clarifying the planning and control process. PERT involves dividing the total research project into its smallest component activities, determining the sequence in which these activities must be performed, attaching a time estimate for each activity, and presenting them in the form of a flow chart that allows a visual inspection of the overall process. The time estimates allow one to determine the **critical path** through the chart—that series of activities whose delay will hold up the completion of the project. Research Application 3–3 contains a simplified example.

Estimates of financial requirements must include the direct and indirect manpower costs, materials, transportation, overhead, and other costs. Commercial research organizations, particularly those that specialize in specific types of research, are often able to derive accurate rules of thumb. A common approach to estimating the cost of a survey is to use a variable cost of Y dollars per completed interview, plus a fixed cost of X dollars. Once the sample size is determined, the cost estimate can be quickly calculated.

Program evaluation review technique (PERT): divides the project into its component parts, determines the sequence, attaches a time estimate for each activity, and presents the process in the form of a flow chart.

Critical path: that sequence of activities in a PERT chart whose delay will delay the completion of the project.

Step 9: Prepare the Research Proposal

The research design process provides the researcher with a blueprint, or guide, for conducting and controlling the research project. This blueprint is written in the form of a *research proposal*. A written research proposal should precede any research project. The word *precede* here may be somewhat misleading. Obviously, a substantial amount of research effort is involved in the research planning process that must precede the research proposal. The research proposal helps ensure that the decision maker and the researcher are still in agreement on the basic management problem, the information required, and the research approach.

The basic elements of the research proposal are described in Table 3–4. The American Marketing Association provides a sample research contract for use between a firm and a research agency.[5]

PERT Chart for a Consumer Survey Comparison Shopping Research Project

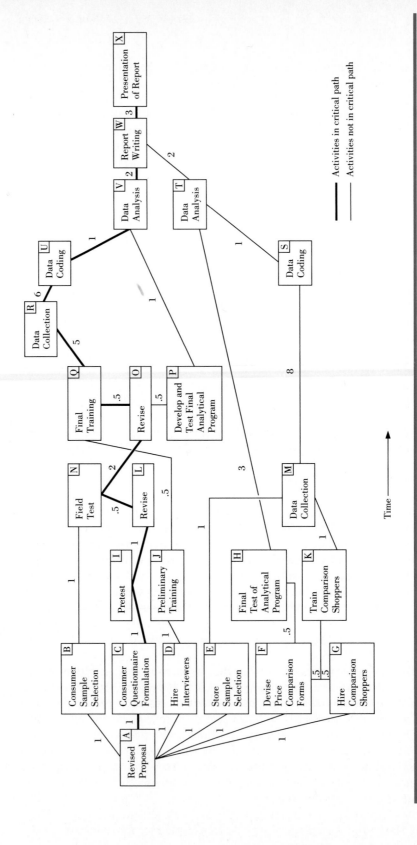

TABLE 3–4 Elements of the Research Proposal

1. *Executive Summary*—a brief statement of the major points from each of the other sections. The objective is to allow an executive to develop a basic understanding of the proposal *without* reading the entire proposal.
2. *Background*—a statement of the management problem and the factors that influence it.
3. *Objectives*—a description of the types of data the research project will generate and how these data are relevant to the management problem. A statement of the value of the information should generally be included in this section.
4. *Research Approach*—a nontechnical description of the data-collection method, measurement instrument, sample, and analytical techniques.
5. *Time and Cost Requirements*—an explanation of the time and costs required by the planned methodology accompanied by a PERT chart.
6. *Technical Appendixes*—any statistical or detailed information in which only a few of the potential readers may be interested.

As the definition given earlier in the chapter emphasizes, one of the primary goals of research design is to minimize the extent of the errors at any given budget level. It is therefore appropriate to consider the types of errors that can reduce the accuracy of research data.

Potential Errors Affecting Research Designs

Most readers of this text will have already completed one or more statistics courses. In these courses, you most likely covered sampling error and confidence intervals. In studying confidence intervals, you learned the meaning of such statements as "based on a random sample of households, we have a penetration percentage of 20 percent with a 99 percent confidence interval of plus or minus 2 percent." You might interpret this statement to mean, "I can be almost certain that our actual household penetration percentage is between 18 and 22 percent." However, if you interpreted the statement in this way, you would have made a common mistake. The mistake is confusing estimates of potential *sampling error* with estimates of *total error*. Unfortunately, sampling error is only one of eight types of potential errors that can influence research results. Research design must attempt to reduce this total error, *not* just one or two aspects of total error. Each type of potential error is described in the following sections.

Types of Errors
Surrogate Information Error

Surrogate information error is caused by a variation between the information required to solve the problem and the information sought by the researcher. The so-called price–quality relationship, where a consumer uses the price of

Surrogate information error: a variation between the information required to solve the problem and the information sought by the researcher.

a brand to represent its quality level, is a common example of a measure that is subject to surrogate information error (because price level does not always reflect quality level).

It has been argued that, in part, the taste test research done by Coca-Cola USA resulted in surrogate information. It is reported that "there was—as nearly as I can tell—no research to get at consumer attitudes about the pending change before the new formula introduction."[6] The company based its decision on taste preferences. The resultant consumer backlash was caused by surrogate information error, as consumers purchase *Coke* for reasons other than taste alone.

Measurement Error

Measurement error:
variation between the information sought by the researcher and the information produced by the measurement process.

Measurement error is caused by a difference between the information desired by the researcher and the information provided by the measurement process. In other words, not only is it possible to seek the wrong type of information (surrogate information error), but it is also possible to gather information that is different from what is being sought. This is one of the most common and serious errors. For example, respondents may exaggerate their income in order to impress an interviewer. The reported income will then reflect an unknown amount of measurement error. Measurement error is particularly difficult to control because it can arise from many different sources. (Techniques for dealing with measurement error are described in Chapters 9–13.)

Experimental Error

Experimental error:
variation between the actual impact of the independent variable(s) and the impact attributed to it.

Experiments are designed to measure the impact of one or more independent variables on a dependent variable. **Experimental error** occurs when the effect of the experimental situation itself is measured rather than the effect of the independent variable. For example, a retail chain may increase the price of selected items in four outlets and leave the price of the same items constant in four similar outlets, in an attempt to discover the best pricing strategy. However, unique weather patterns, traffic conditions, or competitors' activities may affect the sales at one set of stores and not the other. Thus, the experimental results will reflect the impact of variables other than price.

Like measurement error, experimental error can arise from a number of sources. (The various sources of experimental error and the methods by which they can be controlled are described in Chapters 7 and 8.)

Population Specification Error

Population specification error:
variation between the population required to provide the needed information and the population selected by the researcher.

Population specification error is caused by selecting an inappropriate universe or population from which to collect data. This is a potentially serious problem in both industrial and consumer research. A firm wishing to learn the criteria that are considered most important in the purchase of certain machine tools might conduct a survey among purchasing agents. Yet, in many firms, the purchasing agents do not determine or necessarily even know the criteria behind brand selections. These decisions may be made by the machine operators, by committee, or by higher-level executives. A study that focuses on the purchasing agent as the person who decides which brands to order may be subject to population specification error. (Population specification is described in more detail in Chapter 14.)

Frame Error

The *sampling frame* is the list of population members from which the sample units are selected. An ideal frame identifies each member of the population once and only once. **Frame error** is caused by using an inaccurate or incomplete sampling frame. For example, using the telephone directory as a sampling frame for the population of a community contains a potential for frame error. Those families who do not have listed numbers, both voluntarily and nonvoluntarily, are likely to differ from those with listed numbers in such respects as income, gender, and mobility. (Frame error is discussed in more detail in Chapters 6 and 14.)

Frame error: variation between the population as defined by the researcher and the list of population members used by the researchers.

Sampling Error

Sampling error is caused by the generation of a nonrepresentative sample by means of a probability sampling method. For example, a random sample of 100 university students *could* produce a sample composed of all females (or all seniors or all business majors). Such a sample would not be representative of the overall student body. Yet it could occur using probability sampling techniques. Sampling error is the focal point of concern in classical statistics. (It is discussed in more detail in Chapters 15–18.)

Sampling error: variation between a representative sample and the sample obtained by using a probability sampling method.

Selection Error

Selection error occurs when a nonrepresentative sample is obtained by nonprobability sampling methods. For example, one of the authors talked with an interviewer who was afraid of dogs. In surveys that allowed any freedom of choice, this interviewer avoided homes with dogs present. Obviously, such a practice may introduce error into the survey results. Selection error is a major problem in nonprobability samples. (It is discussed in more detail in Chapters 6, 7, and 14.)

Selection error: variation between a representative sample and the sample obtained by using a nonprobability sampling method.

Nonresponse Error

Nonresponse error is caused by (1) a failure to contact all members of a sample, and/or (2) the failure of some contacted members of the sample to respond to all or specific parts of the measurement instrument. Individuals who are difficult to contact or who are reluctant to cooperate will differ, on at least some characteristics, from those who are relatively easy to contact or who readily cooperate. If these differences include the variable of interest, nonresponse error has occurred. For example, people are more likely to respond to a survey on a topic that interests them. If a firm were to conduct a mail survey to estimate the incidence of athlete's foot among adults, nonresponse error would be of major concern. Why? Those most likely to be interested in athlete's foot, and thus most likely to respond to the survey, are

Nonresponse error: variation between the selected sample and the sample that actually participates in the study.

current or recent sufferers of the problem. If the firm were to use the percentage of those responding who report having athlete's foot as an estimate of the total population having athlete's foot, the company would probably greatly overestimate the extent of the problem. (Methods for dealing with nonresponse error are described in Chapter 6.)

Strategies for Handling Potential Research Errors

As stated earlier, the purpose of research design is, in part, to maximize the accuracy of the information that can be obtained for a given expense. Maximizing the accuracy of information requires minimizing errors in the information. There are three basic strategies for dealing with potential errors: (1) minimize individual errors through effective research design, (2) minimize total error through error trade-offs, and (3) measure or estimate the amount and/or impact of any residual error.

Strategy 1: Minimize Individual Error

The bulk of this book is devoted to describing techniques for reducing individual errors. Consider sampling error as an example. The probability and magnitude of sampling error can be reduced by increasing sample size; but increasing sample size also increases costs. However, it may be possible to reduce sampling error (and possibly sample size, as well) by moving from a simple random sample to a stratified sample (see Chapter 14).

The first stage of research design is generally devoted to selecting those research methods that will minimize each individual source of error, given budget (or value of information) constraints.

Strategy 2: Trade-off Individual Errors to Reduce Total Error

Assume that a researcher has initially selected a large sample for a mail survey. The sample is large enough to provide a low level of sampling error, but it has taken such a large proportion of the research budget that there are sufficient funds remaining for only one follow-up mailing. Past experience with surveys of this type indicates that, with one follow-up mailing, the total response rate will reach 40 percent; with four follow-ups, it will climb to 65 percent. Given the nature of the survey, the researcher thinks that the nonrespondents may differ significantly from the respondents.

One solution is to ask for an increase in the budget. However, such funds may not be available or the resultant data may not justify additional expenditures. A second solution is to "trade" sampling error for nonresponse error. Sample size could be reduced, which would increase the probable amount of sampling error. However, the funds thus freed could provide additional mailed follow-up questionnaires and telephone calls to the final group of nonrespondents. These efforts may reduce nonresponse error more than enough to offset the increase in sampling error. Thus, the result is a reduction in total error and an increase in total accuracy.

Strategy 3: Measure or Estimate Residual Error

It is seldom possible to eliminate all possible errors. Statisticians and others have recognized this with respect to sampling error. Virtually all studies dealing with random samples report confidence intervals and/or confidence levels. This is explicit recognition that sampling error may have occurred. Unfortunately, many researchers have tended to ignore the presence of other types of errors.

Measuring and/or estimating errors is preferred to ignoring them. Potential errors should never be completely ignored. It is possible and fairly common to estimate that the net effect of these errors is so small as to warrant no specific action. However, this is *not* the same as ignoring the potential errors. At a minimum, the researcher should *explicitly,* if subjectively, estimate the extent of each type of potential error. If individual errors or the combined effects of the errors are large, they should be reduced by means of the research design or their effects taken into account in the analysis of the data. Although a complete discussion of estimating and measuring individual and total error is beyond the scope of this text,[7] both approaches are described in detail with respect to nonresponse error in Chapter 6.

Multinational Research Design

Multinational research projects are designed in the same manner as single country projects. Unfortunately, each step in the design process is substantially more difficult when more than one country is involved. The reason for this increased difficulty is *the need for equivalent data across countries, not simply identical research techniques or designs.*

The same technique often cannot be used across countries (telephone interviews cannot be used in countries where the target population does not have phone service) or will produce differing results (purchasing agents may be decision makers in one country and not in another). Therefore, multinational research projects may require a series of coordinated research designs. The same is often true for research projects involving distinct population groups within a country such as children, the elderly, and various racial and ethnic subcultures.

We will consider the issues raised by multinational research in the appropriate chapters.

Summary

The marketing research process involves identifying a management problem or opportunity; translating that problem/opportunity into a research problem; and collecting, analyzing, and reporting the information specified in the research problem. A management problem deals with the decisions managers must make. A research problem deals with providing information that will help management make better decisions. Marketing research design is the specification of procedures for collecting and analyzing the data necessary to help identify or react to a problem or opportunity that minimize the cost of obtaining various levels of accuracy and maximize the expected value of the information associated with each level of accuracy.

There are three basic types of research designs. Exploratory research seeks to discover the general nature of the problem and the related variables. It is characterized by flexibility, secondary data, small convenience samples, simple experiments, case analyses, and so forth. Descriptive research focuses on the accurate description of the variables in the problem model. Secondary data and formal surveys are commonly used in this type of research. Causal research attempts to specify the functional relationship between two or more variables in the problem model. Evidence of causation is provided by concomitant variation, sequence of occurrence, and the absence of other potential causes. Experimentation is often used in this type research.

The research design process consists of nine interactive steps: (1) define the research problem, (2) estimate the value of the information to be provided by the research, (3) select the data collection method, (4) select the measurement instrument, (5) select the sample, (6) select the analytical approach, (7) evaluate the ethics of the research, (8) specify the time and financial cost, and (9) prepare the research proposal. Defining the research problem is a particularly important step since it determines what information will be collected. It involves clarifying the management problem, analyzing the problem situation, developing a model of the problem, and specifying the information required to help make the management decision. The time required for a study can be specified by means of a PERT chart.

Eight types of error can affect research results: (1) surrogate information error, (2) measurement error, (3) experimental error, (4) population specification error, (5) frame error, (6) sampling error, (7) selection error, and (8) nonresponse error. Researchers use three strategies to minimize total error: (1) minimize each individual error through sound research design, (2) trade off individual errors to reduce total error, and (3) measure or estimate residual error.

Multinational research projects are particularly difficult to design because of the need for equivalent data across countries, not simply identical research designs.

Review Questions

3.1. What are the steps in the *research process?*

3.2. What is the difference between the *management problem* and the *research problem?*

3.3. What is the definition of *research design?*

3.4. What are the steps involved in the *research design process?*

3.5. What are the three *basic data-collection approaches* in marketing research?

3.6. How do the three categories of *exploratory, descriptive,* and *causal* research differ from each other?

3.7. What are the *four basic measurement techniques* used in marketing research?

3.8. For what purposes are PERT charts used?

3.9. What is the *critical path* in a **PERT** chart?

3.10. What are the *potential errors* affecting research designs?

3.11. What are the *strategies for dealing with potential research errors*?

3.12. Why is design for multinational research projects more difficult than for single country projects?

Discussion Questions/Problems

3.13. Do you agree with the assertion "Research cannot provide solutions"? Explain.

3.14. It has been stated that "Marketing research need not be used only to predict future behavior; it can be used to predict present or past behavior as well." Is it ever useful to a company to predict present or past behavior? Explain.

3.15. Review the list of potential errors affecting research designs. Provide four examples of error trade-offs whereby the potential impact of one error might be increased to achieve a greater reduction in another error.

3.16. An underlying assumption of the Coca-Cola taste tests was that *taste preferences* lead to *purchase preferences*. Is this necessarily true? Explain.

3.17. As a newly hired researcher for Ford you have been asked to investigate the "household economic structure of Indonesia in 2010."
   a. How will you obtain a more precise statement of the management problem?
   b. Develop two distinct management problems that could have produced this request.
   c. To what extent do the two problems developed in (b) require different information?

3.18. Repeat 3.17 as a newly hired researcher for General Electric who has been asked to "estimate demand for clothes washers in the EC, Poland, Mexico, Taiwan, and Indonesia in 1999."

3.19. Most new products are not commercial successes despite the presence of a large research industry. Why is this the case?

3.20. How would you go about determining the market potential in Mexico and Brazil for a new soft drink for children fortified with vitamins and minerals?

3.21. In a research project for a chain of shoe stores, young children were asked about the importance of various features of children's shoes and shoe outlets. Which types of error do you think would be most critical for this study?

3.22. As a one-person research staff for a manufacturer of solar hot water heaters, you are asked to do a study to recommend in what market segments the marketing program of the firm should be concentrated.
   a. How would you obtain a more precise problem statement?
   b. Give a plausible statement of the management's problem and translate it into a statement of the research problem to be conducted to help solve it.

3.23. Find the path with the most *slack* (the amount of time required to complete the critical path minus the amount of time required to complete another path) in Research Application 3–3.

Projects/Activities

3.24. a. With two other members of your class, prepare a research design for Problem 3.22.
b. Prepare a PERT chart of your design with the same two other class members who helped develop the research design.

3.25. Conduct a taste test of *Coke, Classic Coke, Pepsi,* and *RC Cola* on five friends or acquaintances. Before telling them which soft drink they preferred, ask them which brand they would buy if they were going to stop by a store to buy a six-pack of soft drink. Compare their taste preference with their (stated) purchase preference. What do you conclude?

3.26. Interview a marketing manager and identify a marketing problem or opportunity with which the manager is concerned. Translate this into a research problem.

3.27. Prepare a research design for the research problem in 3.25 and prepare a proposal. What types of errors would be likely to affect the findings if the project were actually carried out?

Notes

1. D. Smith, "Small Is Beautiful, But Difficult," *Journal of the Market Research Society* (April 1990), 48–50.
2. See S. Jones, "Problem-Definition in Marketing Research," *Psychology & Marketing* (Summer 1985), 83–92; and R. G. Chapman, "Problem-Definition in Marketing Research Studies," *Journal of Consumer Marketing* (Spring 1989), 51–59.
3. For a somewhat different approach see J. W. Smith, "Beyond Anecdotes," *Marketing Research* (March 1991), 3–14. For coverage of the quantitative approach, see D. S. Tull, D. I. Hawkins, *Marketing Research* (Macmillan Publishing, 1993), 817–827.
4. A. R. Andreason, " 'Backward' Market Research," *Harvard Business Review* (May–June 1985), 176–182.
5. "AMA Attorneys Draft Sample Research Contract," *Marketing News* (September 11, 1989), 11–12.
6. J. Honomichl, "Missing Ingredient in 'New' Coke's Research," *Advertising Age* (July 22, 1985), 1, 58.
7. See D. S. Tull, G. S. Albaum, *Survey Research: A Decisional Approach* (Intext Educational Publishers, 1973), 67–77; and L. Bailey, "Toward a More Complete Analysis of the Total Mean Square Error of Census and Sample Survey Statistics," Bureau of the Census, undated.

SECTION I CASES

CASE I–1

S. C. Johnson & Son, Inc.:
Research Monday

Below are two internal memos that explain a concept called *Research Monday* that is gaining use within S. C. Johnson.

1. Exactly what is *Research Monday?*
2. What is the objective of *Research Monday?*
3. Evaluate *Research Monday* as a research technique and in terms of its value to S. C. Johnson.

From: G011628—VRNA   Date and time: 07/26/91 10:00:53
To: G994109—VRNA   Group * Argentina

From: T. R. Anderson
Subject: Research Monday

To: S. Chouhy Oria
Copy to: Alejandro Martinez de Hoz
          N. Di Bartolo

We are now in the process of consolidating the FY91/92 market research plans for the Americas region, and we look forward to receiving the Argentine plan when available.

"Research Monday" is the designation we have assigned to a methodology involving in-home visits by Johnson/Ad Agency personnel for the purpose of discussing a given subject with a target consumer. The subject could be insect control, floor care, or whatever. The interviews are made on a pre-arranged basis, and usually last about one hour. A team of five (5) interviewers, each doing eight (8) interviews per day, would conduct forty (40) interviews per day. In the evening, the team of interviewers would discuss what they saw, heard, and observed. The team would discuss "what is and importantly, what could be in terms of products, concepts, benefits/strategies/tactics/communications or whatever.

Originally we started to do in-home visits on the first day of the week. . . . For several consecutive weeks (until we ceased to learn anything new). Hence the designation "Research Monday."

In any event I thought you would find the following memo to be of interest. I hope that "Research Monday" becomes a part of your 91/92 plan.

Let me know if you have any questions or comments.

Regards,
Ted

*** Forwarding note from G011628—VRNA   07/23/91 14:48 ***
To: S013979—VRNA   Group * Australia

From: T. R. Anderson
Subject: Research Monday

To: Debbie Schubert (with copy to Ken Douglas)

Debbie: Research Monday is a conversation with the consumer. Research Monday does not involve a formal, written questionnaire. Rather Research Monday is a conversation with a purpose that involves a rather unstructured outline. A job search involves an interview . . . so does an application for a bank loan. New neighbors routinely interview each other, as do young people playing the dating game. We interview prospective mechanics, real estate agents, dentists, and medical doctors, especially if major surgery is involved. Men interview other men and women interview other women . . . in order to determine what type of space the other person occupies, to determine what type of person the other is, and whether he or she is worthy of pursuit/or how this particular person should be handled. The point is, we routinely conduct interviews in our daily lives. We set our objectives, we determine our info needs, we collect and process the data rather simultaneously, we adjust our outline and data collection technique to fit the current conditions, and we pursue our inquiry until we are satisfied that a decision can be prudently made on the existing information.

Taxi drivers are marvelous interviewers. A good taxi driver sets up a nonthreatening situation in terms of demeanor and driving. The passenger is relaxed and the driver starts asking a series of questions, and the passenger becomes engaged in a conversation that could lead to most anywhere, depending on the receptivity of passenger and the questioning skills of the taxi driver.

Marketing personnel are, or at least should be, good interviewers. Marketing personnel have strong interpersonal skills, inquirying/inquisitive minds, determination, good intuition, creative flair, seasoned (or soon-to-be-seasoned) judgment, appreciation of options and alternatives, etc. Marketing personnel must understand the consumer, her environment, her needs/problems and desires, her perceptions of existing products, the benefits delivered (or still desired, or alternatively, the problems created by an effective product with an offensive fragrance). Marketing personnel must also understand how the consumer perceives and reacts to possible new products (concepts).

The product manager tells R&D to formulate a product with XYZ characteristics based on his/her understanding of consumer needs/desires/aspirations, competitive conditions, production constraints, raw material availability and costs, and a whole series of other factors. The launch decision involves a series of questions involving the trade: alternative new product launches, pricing, ROI margins, deals and promotions, ad budgets, media plans, tracking studies, etc.

Note that the product manager communicates with R&D based on his/her understanding of the consumer. I would now like to assert that many product managers do not understand consumers, their environment, their needs/wants/problems, etc.

Product management attempts to understand the consumer by commissioning research. A project is discussed and initiated—one silver bullet to bring all parties up to speed on the consumer, and to help set the direction for R&D and the advertising agency. Everyone knows that the research community has been saying for years that we cannot/should not make decisions based on qualitative research. So since we are decision makers, we initiate a quantitative study. However, there is one key problem: we do not know enough about the subject matter to ask all of the right questions, so we ask just enough of the right questions to give a degree of credibility to this research. Yet we fail to ask certain questions, and thereby generate partial/limited information. We walk the cow's path and generate ordinary info, while truly creative insights and decisions are based on extraordinary insights. Good marketing requires the extraordinary. Unfortunately most research involves mechanical exercises that are put into motion with a minimum of thought by researchers who do not understand the marketing process and who are more concerned with driving the bus than with providing transportation.

Good research, like good whiskey, requires time. Good research also involves a lot of thought, effort, and commitment. War is too important to be left to the generals. Similarly, market research should not be delegated to the research community. Good research requires the active involvement of the marketing group. This involvement should not be at the analysis/interpretation stage. That's too late. The product management involvement must be up-front when decisions are made regarding the questions that are to be asked and the issues that are to be addressed. The GIGO principle will apply if we do not ask the right questions or address the right issues. The quantitative study can easily become an exercise in futility. Motion/activity can easily be confused with progress.

The basic tenet of Research Monday is that product managers must visit homes to see and to observe, and to talk with the consumer in a nonthreatening situation. Group interviews allow the respondent lots of room for deception. Respondents can live in fantasyland while in a group situation. Reality can be disguised by words. Another problem is with vocabulary and semantics. Words are defined differently by different people under different circumstances. Words like *bright/smooth/clean/even/porous* can mean different things to different people. One glance at a surface in a home will define the words the consumer uses to describe a given situation. It is difficult, if not impossible to define certain words/phases/terminologies in a group situation. As a result, we sometimes compound our problem when we think we understand but really do not.

Good research will help you to understand the consumer, your competition, your concepts, your opportunity. Inadequate research will distort your understanding and will lead to marketing errors.

Much if not all of our thinking is based on assumptions. Many times we are aware of the assumptions under which we are operating; many times we are not. That can lead to disaster, as we are eventually hit on the blind-side. Research Monday helps ensure that our assumptions are correct regarding the consumer, our competitors and our concepts. Research Monday forces us to understand the vocabulary of the consumer, and to adopt the consumer's frame of reference.

Unfortunately, we build false assumptions into much of our research. We employ an erroneous frame of reference and misuse words. We ask the wrong questions, and analyze the wrong data. Little wonder that the market research community is currently under attack and is searching for a more positive identity (that will only be achieved once we return to the basics of truly understanding the subjects being studied). The research community has gone off-track and has violated the kiss principle. We have confused ourselves and our clients with complicated test designs, elaborate methodologies and analysis patterns, and lots of industry vocabulary that sounds impressive at the outset but that has diminishing impact study after study. Many researchers are task-oriented as opposed to results-oriented. Unfortunately many marketing personnel delegate the research process to the researcher and do not intervene when necessary.

The product manager is a strategist. The product manager is also a tactician. Good information is a prerequisite for both roles. The research community can filter, alter, and contaminate good information by asking the wrong questions, by bringing the wrong assumptions to the party, and by misinterpreting the data. The PM is responsible for his/her own data bank, and what goes into that bank, when, and under what conditions. PMs should be wary of poor data in fine clothing.

Where should the marketing person begin to search for a good understanding of the consumer? My answer is "at the beginning, in the home of the consumer on a one-on-one basis." The marketing person should bring a list of questions and concerns to the interview and adjust his/her frame of reference and database as info is collected, digested, cross-referenced, dissected, challenged, labeled, and stored for easy reference and retrieval. New dimensions will be identified, and new weight will be assigned to old information. An altered perspective will be developed, and a new consumer vocabulary will emerge. Brand maps will appear in the mind of the interviewer and product/benefit opportunities will appear. Researchable issues will emerge during the Research Monday process that can be/must be pursued in subsequent qualitative or quantitative research. Research Monday is not the alpha and the omega. Research Monday is only the beginning of the overall research process required to understand the consumer, our opportunity, and how best to capitalize on that opportunity. In fact, the process of understanding the consumer and our opportunity is never-ending because the world in which we live is always changing.

So Research Monday is at the beginning of our never-ending journey to understand the consumer and our opportunity. Research Monday is our best departure point because it helps rid our minds of faulty assumptions, misleading vocabulary, and fuzzy visions of what toilets may look like in various homes. Once we have seen the reality of the situation it will never escape us and we will remain in touch with reality and the world in which we live.

After Research Monday we will know what our questions are and will know how to approach these questions in subsequent research. We will know what issues are important to us (and to consumers). We will easily establish the objectives of future research and we will know what we need to learn or to expand upon.

Importantly, we will be in a better position when analyzing and interpreting subsequent research because Research Monday will have broadened our horizons and will have made us more sensitive to certain pivotal issues.

Research Monday is a team exercise involving product management, marketing research personnel, R&D personnel, and ad agency personnel, as all these people are involved in the creation of the concept, the product, and the communications that eventually will be produced (label/copy/commercial). Each will serve as an interviewer and ask their own questions in their own way. Each will interpret their answers in their own way, and bring the strength/weaknesses of their particular discipline to the party. After the first day of forty interviews (five times eight—five interviewers doing eight interviews per day) you can talk about "what is and importantly, what could be." You will talk about a range of subjects . . . the consumer, competition, various strategies or tactics. You will have fed your creative systems with real-life info and insights and the creative juices will begin to flow regarding new-found opportunities.

Interviewing should take place in Sydney and elsewhere among a cross-section of possible target respondents. In time you will find it nonproductive to visit certain types of homes, or to talk with certain types of consumers. In time you will become more focused. In time you will be able to predict the results of the interview. In time you will be learning nothing new. That will be a good time to stop, and to then apply your learning to the enhancement of existing product or the introduction of new products.

So there it is, Debbie. A long answer to a short question regarding the availability of a suggested questionnaire.

Last week I sent you some material from Mexico that may help. Please also refer to the Research Monday proposal I previously sent to Tim Wilson.

Let me know if you have any additional questions. I promise a less laborious response to future inquiries.

All the best,
Ted

CASE I-2

Orange Juice Placement Study Proposal*

Dear Steve:

Subject: Research Proposal PAR #2897
           Chilled Orange Juice Replacement Study

This letter will confirm our several phone conversations of last week regarding the subject study. Our understanding of the project is as follows.

Background:	There are certain orange juices that are shelf stable that are offered for sale from the dairy cases of supermarkets. It is thought that if these products were removed from the dairy cases and their space reallocated to orange juices that need refrigeration, a sales improvement might be enjoyed.
Purpose:	To determine the results on sales when shelf stable orange juices are removed from the dairy cases and the resulting space reallocated among orange juices that require refrigeration. Evaluation would be made in terms of consumer sales using controlled store conditions.

*Used with permission of Product Acceptance & Research, Seaman & Associates, Inc.

Location:	Evansville, Indiana. A distribution study has been conducted and the nonrefrigerated product is in distribution, in dairy cases.
Number of Stores:	Either 12 or 16 stores would be required.
Tentative Stores:	Wesselman's Spalding's
Tentative Starting Date:	To be determined.
Length of Study:	Twelve (12) weeks divided into a four (4) week base period and an eight (8) week test period.
Audit Brands:	All brands and sizes of orange juices found in the dairy cases plus all orange juices packaged in glass found in the stores.
Product Handling:	PAR would not assume distribution of any item. Retail stores would be asked to stock extra product to prevent out-of-stocks. If the cooperating stores have dating problems as a result of this, PAR will buy the outdated product from the stores and destroy it. This will be done on an ex-budget basis.
Number of Facings:	The number of shelf facings has already been established. PAR will change facings only to meet test requirements.
Retail Pricing:	The retail pricing has been established and will remain constant throughout the study. Exceptions will have prior approval of the client.
Test Procedure:	The study is divided into a base period and a test period. The purpose of the base period is two-fold: (1) to establish sales "norms" for the items within the defined category, and (2) to establish data for panelization of the test stores. The purpose of the test period would be to measure the marketing variable panel against the control panel and each (in time) against the base period. On the initial store visit an audit would be taken followed by weekly audits throughout the study. In addition to the audit calls, weekly police calls will be made to each store. Using the data developed from the first two (2) weeks of the study, the stores would be divided into two (2) panels of either six (6) or eight (8) stores each, as follows:

	Number of Stores		
Panel	12-store study	16-store study	Test Period Marketing Variable
A	6	8	Normal store conditions
B	6	8	Shelf stable orange juice moved from refrigerated dairy cases to the regular dry grocery orange juice section

At the beginning of the fifth week of the study (end of a four (4) week base period), PAR would withdraw the shelf stable orange juice from the dairy cases of the test stores and reallocate that space among the remaining brands on some basis, yet to be determined.

Our research design is:

					Weeks							
	Base					Test						
1	2	3	4	5	6	7	8	9	10	11	12	13
A	A	A	A	A/SR	A	A	A	A	A	A	A	A/SR
P	P	P	P	P	P	P	P	P	P	P	P	P

A = audit of selected category; P = police/service of selected category; SR = shelf reallocation.

If more frequent than twice a week calls are necessary to properly control the study, the client will be immediately notified for a decision.

A 35mm picture would be taken in each store each week to show the test product in its in-store surroundings.

Reporting: Flash sales of the test product would be made available every week during the test period. This information would be made available within ten (10) days following the service call.

An interim report would be submitted within three (3) weeks following the close of each one (1) week audit period. These reports would include:

1. Unit sales by brand, by size, by store, and by panel.
2. Unit share by brand, by size, by store, and by panel.

3. Dollar sales by brand, by size, by store, and by panel.
4. Dollar share by brand, by size, by store, and by panel.
5. Number of shelf facings.
6. Retail price.
7. Competitive activity found on each scheduled store call.
8. Newspaper advertising report.

There would be a final report submitted to the client within four (4) weeks after the conclusion of the study.

Budget: To execute the study as outlined in this proposal using 12 stores would require a research budget of $_____ . In addition to the research budget, store cooperation payments (currently estimated at $_____) would be billed at actual cost. To execute the same project using 16 stores would require a budget of $_____ plus an estimated $_____ in store payments.†

All quotations are plus or minus the usual 10%.

These quotations will remain in effect for thirty (30) days. At the end of this period, they will be subject to review and possible revision by PAR.

Should PAR, as a result of a request of the client, or their agency, incur any special costs in connection with this project, and the project not be subsequently initiated, all such expenses will be billed to the client.

Steve, this covers our understanding. Your questions and comments are welcome. Thank you for the opportunity of submitting this proposal. We will look forward to working with you on this project.

Best regards,
E. Harvey Seaman

Discussion Questions

1. Evaluate the adequacy of this proposal as a research proposal.
2. Evaluate the proposed research design.

---

†Cost figures are omitted due to the competitive nature of bids such as this.

CASE I–3

Marketing Research at Sony Corporation

Sony Corporation has worldwide revenues of approximately $20 billion. It has sales throughout most of the world. Sony's business can be divided into four major areas. *Video hardware* includes televisions, monitors, home-use videotape recorders (VTRs), broadcast and professional-use VTRs, and HDTV equipment. These products are sold to both households and professionals. *Audio hardware* includes CD players, component stereos, radio-cassette tape recorders, headphone cassette players, car stereos, and other personal and professional audio equipment.

Sony's *audio software* products include CBS Records and related technologies. Its *video software* includes Columbia Pictures, products related to the manufacture and distribution of prerecorded videos and video disks, CATV systems, and so forth. Sony also manufactures and markets semiconductors, computer workstations and peripherals, telecommunications equipment, and audiovisual systems for airplanes.

Sony's business philosophy is "global localization"—manufacturing, marketing, and some research and development located in and managed from the major markets but positioned, coordinated, and controlled from Tokyo with a strong global view. In addition to Japan, Sony has established major organization structures (business units) in the United States (New York), Europe (Cologne), and Asia (Singapore). Sony's strategic vision for the 1990s is to become the global leader in the entertainment industry.

Discussion Questions

1. What role should research play in the daily operations of Sony?
2. What role should research play in the strategic decisions of Sony?
3. What types of research skills should Sony have "in-house" and what types should it buy?
4. How should a research division fit into a multiproduct, multinational firm such as Sony?
5. How would you establish a research budget for marketing research at Sony?

CASE I–4

Marketing Research at Citicorp/Citibank*

Citicorp is a global financial services holding company. It has several major brand names, including Citibank; Diners Club; Citicorp Mortgage, Inc.; and Quotron. The common element in each service is money: financial informa-

*SOURCE: Derived from S. Brock, S. Lipson, R. Levitt, "Trends in Marketing Research and Development at Citicorp/Citibank," *Marketing Research* (December 1989), 3–8.

tion, investments, transaction services, savings, and credit to individuals and organizations. Citibank operates more than 600 branches in nine states and the District of Columbia. Diners Club involves approximately 16 million cardholders. Citicorp Mortgage provides thousands of mortgages each year.

Citicorp believes in a strongly decentralized approach to business. It seeks to push profit responsibility down to a business that serves a homogeneous market.

Citicorp has a Development Division that concentrates on the development of long-term, capital intensive services. It maintains an experimental facility called The LAB. The LAB has simulated branch bank, home, and office environments. A standard method of evaluating consumer and/or staff interactive technology or software has been developed. The basic steps in this process are the following:

1. A sample from the relevant target group is asked to evaluate how a particular task is currently performed — "How do you determine if a recent check has cleared the bank? How easy is this?"
2. The respondents then react to a "white card" description (a written description) of the capability and process of a proposed new software or technology.
3. Next, the respondents use the new approach in The LAB. If the product involves bill paying via a PC, consumers would simulate paying actual bills on a PC in The LAB's den.
4. Finally, the respondents evaluate the experience of using the proposed approach. This includes both structured questions and a qualitative debriefing to collect reactions, attitudes, and feelings.
5. The respondents' evaluation of the new approach is compared to their view of how the task is currently performed, to their reaction to the white card description, and to how previous respondents reacted to earlier versions of the technology/software.

Discussion Questions

1. Evaluate Citicorp's method for evaluating new software/ technologies.
2. How does marketing research for services differ from research for products?
3. What role should research play in the daily operations of Citcorp/ Citibank?
4. What role should research play in the strategic decisions of Citicorp?
5. What types of research skills should Citicorp have in-house, and what types should it buy?
6. How should a research division fit into Citicorp?
7. How would you establish a research budget for marketing research at Citicorp?

CASE I–5
Marketing Research Careers at 3M*

3M has $13 billion in sales with almost half coming from outside the U.S. It has four operating sectors: (1) industrial and electronic, (2) information and imaging technologies, (3) life sciences, and (4) commercial and consumer. These four sectors contain 14 groups, which in turn have 60 operating divisions and departments with more than 50,000 products. The operating units are autonomous in most of their activities, including marketing. They have global strategic responsibilities for their product lines and tactical responsibilities for the U.S.

3M has a Corporate Marketing Research Department (see Figure 1). However, the operating units are not required to utilize it. In fact, some of the units have their own researchers and all the units can use outside research firms as well as or in addition to Corporate. This presents a challenge as each researcher at Corporate has an annual goal of a percentage of his/her time that must be sold to the operating units on approved projects.

The Corporate Marketing Research Department consists of about 30 people. About four new analysts are hired each year. These new hires are generally new MBAs. They are expected to spend approximately three years in marketing research and then move into marketing management in one of the operating companies.

During the analysts' first year, they spent about 60 percent of their time on research projects for the operating units. The balance of the time is spent in classes covering sampling, research design, questionnaire design, and so

*SOURCE: Derived from J. R. Kendall, "Corporate Marketing Research at 3M," *Marketing Research* (June 1991), 3–11.

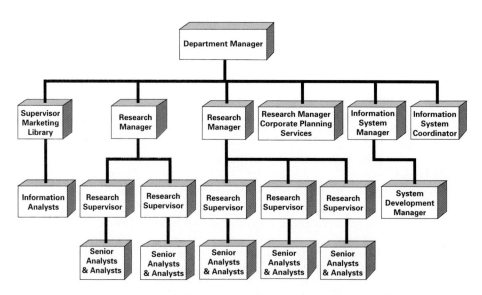

FIGURE 1 Organization of the Corporate Marketing Research Department

forth. Each analyst also takes sales training from a 3M divisional sales trainer (in part because the analysts must sell their services to the operating units).

After a successful year as an analyst, the person is promoted to senior analyst. The senior analyst is the workhorse of the project system. Senior analysts devote almost all their time to getting projects sold, performed, and reported. In general, analysts work primarily within a sector or group such as health care or imaging, though they will also be involved in projects outside their sector if they have skills that are required.

After about a year as senior analyst, the individual is promoted to research supervisor. The new supervisor is given one or two newly hired analysts to develop into researchers and future marketing managers. In addition to training, the supervisor is actively involved as a researcher in the more complex projects. The supervisor typically spends over half his or her time consulting with potential clients and selling the services of the Corporate Marketing Research Department.

At the end of a year as research supervisor, the researcher generally accepts an offer of a marketing position in one of the operating units.

Discussion Questions

1. What are the strengths and weaknesses of 3M's approach to developing marketing researchers?
2. What are the strengths and weaknesses of requiring the Corporate Marketing Research Department to be partially self funding by selling its services to the operating units?
3. How does industrial marketing research at a firm like 3M differ from consumer research at a firm like Procter & Gamble?
4. What role should research play in the daily operations of 3M?
5. What types of research skills should 3M have in-house and what types should it buy?
6. How would you establish a research budget for marketing research at 3M?

CASE 1–6

The FDA and "Fresh" Orange Juice

The FDA recently initiated a rule-making process concerning the use of the term *fresh* on food product labels. The rule-making is expected to take about a year. In the meantime the FDA is taking a tough stance on the use of the term by marketers.

An early case in this area involved Ragu Foods' brand *Ragu Fresh Italian* pasta sauce. The FDA ruled that the use of *fresh* is misleading since the product has been heat-processed. Ragu Foods offered to change the name to *Ragu Fresh Italian Brand* pasta sauce, but the FDA rejected it.

More recently, the FDA required Procter & Gamble to change the name of *Citrus Hill Fresh Choice* orange juice. The FDA's reasoning is that the use of the term *fresh* is "false or misleading on the label of orange juice made from concentrate." The FDA is also moving against Citrus World, a Florida growers' coop that markets *Fresh 'N Natural* orange juice because the use of the term *fresh* on a pasteurized product "would tend to confuse consumers."

Discussion Questions

1. What role should research play in the FDA's rule-making process?
2. How would you determine if consumers are misled by the labels described in this case?
3. Design a study that would help the FDA develop a rule to prevent consumer confusion while allowing marketers to make valid and meaningful claims.

The Sources of Research Data

The design of the research project specifies the data that are needed and how they are to be obtained. The first step in the data-collection process is to look for *secondary data.* The data still needed after that search is completed will have to be developed specifically for the research project, these are known as *primary data.*

The secondary data that are available are relatively quick and inexpensive to obtain. Chapter 4 is concerned with describing the various sources of the secondary data and how they can be obtained and used.

Some secondary data are generated by specialized firms and are sold to marketers. Nielsen's television ratings is the best-known example. Many of these services, broadly categorized as audits, commercial surveys, and panels, allow some degree of customization and thus fall between secondary and primary data. They are described in Chapter 5.

An important source of primary data is *survey research.* The various types of surveys (personal, mail, computer, and telephone) are described in Chapter 6.

Experiments are another important source of data. The nature of experimentation, the types of experimental designs, and the uses and limitations of experimentation are the subjects of Chapter 7.

Experiments are conducted in either a laboratory setting (most advertising copy pretests) or in a field setting (test marketing). Electronic and computer technologies have revolutionized both these environments, which are described in Chapter 8.

4

Secondary Data

LEARNING OBJECTIVES

Upon completing this chapter, you should be able to

1. Describe the difference between primary and secondary data.

2. Explain the advantages and problems associated with secondary data.

3. List and describe the primary sources of internal secondary data.

4. Specify a sound procedure for conducting a search of external secondary data.

5. List and describe the major sources of external secondary data.

6. Describe how marketing managers can use SIC codes and the Buying Power Index.

7. Explain the unique problems encountered when using international secondary data.

8. List and describe the major internal and external sources of international secondary data.

Buick's Use of Secondary Data to Develop Advertising Strategy for Its Roadmaster Station Wagon

In April 1991, Buick and its advertising agency, McCann-Erickson Worldwide, launched its new Roadmaster station wagon with a revolutionary new advertising approach. A major component of the advertising for Roadmaster is a print campaign with ads appearing in *Time, Newsweek, U.S. News & World Report, People, Sports Illustrated, Entertainment Weekly,* and *Money.* However, not all subscribers will see these ads. In fact, only 4,940 of the more than 40,000 ZIP codes in the United States will receive the ads. Subscribers in these ZIP codes will not only have a chance to see the ads, their magazines will come with a personally addressed card inviting them to send for more information on the Roadmaster.

The target households, which are located mainly in affluent suburbs in the Northeast and Midwest, represent less than 20 percent of U.S. households. However, these households buy over 50 percent of all large station wagons. Buick was able to select the appropriate ZIP codes by using McCann-Erickson's McMapping database. McMapping is based on data from several syndicated sources as well as the U.S. Census. It describes ZIP codes (and larger areas) in terms of standard demographics, values, primary motivations, life-styles, and media use. It works by matching the characteristics of the firm's target market with the characteristics of ZIP code residents.

McMapping does more than simply allow precise targeting of ads and efficient media buys. It also helps develop effective commercials. For example, a traditional system might describe the typical buyer of a specific pickup truck as a male between 25 and 54 with a household income of $30,000. The McMapping profile might add such information as he lives alone, owns a dog, likes sports which he often watches on cable with friends in a bar, and has a very macho self-image. Obviously, this added information would be invaluable in developing effective ad copy.[1]

In a few short years the increase in the number of commercially available databases and of computers on which to access them have brought about dramatic changes in the utilization of secondary data. In this chapter we describe this development and discuss the traditional sources of secondary data.

The Nature of Secondary Data

Primary data are data collected to help solve a problem or take advantage of an opportunity on which a decision is pending. Secondary data are data that were developed for some purpose other than helping to solve the problem at hand. Obviously, the U.S. Census was not conducted primarily to help target potential buyers of Buick station wagons. However, as the opening example illustrates, Census data and other data collected for other purposes can be used to target potential buyers or for other business applications.

Advantages of Secondary Data

Secondary data can be gathered *quickly* and *inexpensively*. It clearly would have been foolish for Buick to collect information directly on the population characteristics, values, and life-styles of every ZIP code in the United States. Such data are already available and can be obtained much faster and at a fraction of the cost of collecting them again.

Problems Encountered with Secondary Data

Secondary data tend to cost substantially less than primary data and can be collected in less time. Why, then, do we ever bother with primary data?

Before secondary data can be used as the only source of information to help solve a marketing problem, they must be *available, relevant, accurate,* and *sufficient.* If one or more of these criteria are not met, primary data may have to be used.

Availability

For some marketing problems, no secondary data are *available.* For example, suppose J.C. Penney's management was interested in obtaining consumer evaluations of the physical layout of the company's current catalog as a guide for developing next year's catalog. It is unlikely that such information is available from secondary sources. In this case, the company would have to conduct interviews of consumers to obtain the desired information.

Relevance

Relevance refers to the extent to which the data fit the information needs of the research problem. Even when data are available that cover the same general topic as the research problem requires, they may not fit the requirements of the particular problem.

Four general problems reduce the relevance of data that would otherwise be useful. First, there is often a *difference in the units of measurement.* For example, many retail decisions require detailed information on the characteristics of the population within the "trade area." However, available demographic statistics may be for counties, cities, census tracts, or ZIP code areas that do not match the trade area of the retail outlet.

A second factor that can reduce the relevance of secondary data is the necessity in some applications to use *surrogate data*. Surrogate data are a *substitute for more desirable data*. Had Buick had access only to data on new car purchases by ZIP code, it would have been much less relevant than data on purchases of new station wagons.

A third general problem that can reduce the relevance of secondary data is the *definition of classes*. Social class, age, income, firm size, and similar category-type breakdowns found in secondary data frequently do not coincide with the exact requirements of the research problem. For example, Gallup and other public opinion polls frequently collect data on alcohol consumption and attitudes toward alcohol as part of their periodic surveys. Bacardi Imports would like to use this readily available data. Unfortunately, Gallup and most other polls define adults as individuals 18 and over while Bacardi is interested in adults 21 and over. The different definitions of classes is one reason Gallup estimates that 56 percent of adults "ever consume" alcoholic beverages compared to the 70 percent indicated by Bacardi's surveys.[2]

The final major factor affecting relevancy is *time*. Generally, research problems require current data. Most secondary data, on the other hand, have been in existence for some time. For example, the *Census of Retail Trade* is conducted only every five years, and two years are required to process and publish the results. A researcher using this source could easily be using data that are over four years old. This is becoming less of a problem as more and more data are being placed directly into electronic databases. For example, *The Wall Street Journal* is available on-line before it is available in print.

Accuracy

Accuracy is the third major concern of the user of secondary data. For example, the 1990 Census is estimated to have undercounted the U.S. population by 5 million. The real problem is not so much obvious inaccuracy as it is *the difficulty of determining how inaccurate the data are likely to be*.

When using secondary data, the original source should be consulted if possible. This is important for two reasons. First, the original report is generally more complete than a second or third report. It often contains warnings, shortcomings, and methodological details not reported by the second or third source.

Second, using the original source allows the data to be examined in context and may provide a better basis for assessing the *competence* and *motivation* of the collector.

Examine Research Application 4–1 before reading further.

The table in Research Application 4–1 is in error, in that the total expenditure category should not be determined by multiplying the number of individuals in the category by the minimum expenditure in the next highest category. This procedure grossly overstates the total expenditures. The appropriate multiplier is the midpoint of each category. This table was taken from a report of a research project designed to persuade advertisers to purchase space in the newspaper that commissioned the project.

RESEARCH APPLICATION 4–1

Reported Annual Expenditures of a Sample of Consumers on Selected Products

Total Annual Expenditures	Sample (in %)	Estimated No.	Projected Expenditures
$199 or less	6.4	1,000	$ 200,000
$200 to $399	15.3	2,300	920,000
$400 to $599	13.2	2,000	1,200,000
$600 to $799	9.1	1,350	1,080,000
$800 to $999	8.7	1,325	1,325,000
$1,000 to $1,199	11.1	1,675	2,010,000
$1,200 to $1,399	4.9	750	1,050,000
$1,400 to $1,599	6.6	1,100	1,980,000
$1,600 to $1,799	5.9	950	1,710,000
$1,800 or more	19.0	2,900	5,800,000
Total	100.0	15,350	$17,275,000

Sufficiency

Secondary data may be *available, relevant,* and *accurate,* but still not *sufficient* to meet all the data requirements for the problem being researched. For example, a database that contained accurate, current demographic information on the purchases of various brands and types of automobiles could still be insufficient in terms of providing information to assist in developing new products or advertisements.

Internal Sources of Secondary Data

Internal sources can be classified into four broad categories: *accounting records, salesforce reports, miscellaneous records,* and *internal experts.*

Accounting Records

The basis for accounting records concerned with *sales* is the *sales invoice.* The usual sales invoice has a sizable amount of information on it, which generally includes *name of customer, location of customer, items ordered, quantities ordered, quantities shipped, dollar extensions, back orders, discounts allowed, date of shipment,* and *method of shipment.* In addition, the invoice often contains information on sales territory, sales representative, and warehouse of shipment.

This information, when supplemented by data on costs and industry and product classification, as well as from sales calls, provides the basis for a comprehensive analysis of sales by product, customer, industry, geographic area, sales territory, and sales representative, as well as the profitability of each sales category.

Unfortunately, most firms' accounting systems are designed primarily for tax reasons rather than for decision support. Currently, only a few organizations can readily retrieve the data required for the types of analyses just described. Competitive pressures, increasingly sophisticated managers, and enhanced computer systems are beginning to improve this situation.

Advertising expenditures, salesforce expenditures, and *data on inventories* are other types of data available from accounting records that are useful for research purposes. For example, a management trainee was asked to estimate the "best" price reduction for a store that frequently sold paint at a reduced price. An examination of the firm's advertising records allowed her to identify the timing of numerous sales at different discounts over the past several years. The firm's sales records allowed an estimate of the units sold during each sale. By combining these two data sources, the trainee was able to develop a useful estimate of the price elasticity of demand for the firm's paint. In addition, she was able to isolate one season of the year when the elasticity of demand was unusually high and one season when it was relatively low.

Salesforce Reports

Salesforce reports represent a rich and largely untapped *potential* source of marketing information.[3] The word *potential* is used because evidence indicates that valuable marketing information is generally *not* reported by sales personnel. An unfortunately typical example is reported in Research Application 4–2.

As Research Application 4–2 suggests, sales personnel often lack the motivation and/or the means to communicate key information to marketing managers. To obtain the valuable data available from most salesforces, several elements are necessary: (1) a clear, concise statement, repeated frequently, of the types of information desired; (2) a systematic, *simple* process for reporting the information; (3) financial and other rewards for reporting information; and (4) concrete examples of the actual use of the data.

Miscellaneous Reports

Miscellaneous reports represent the third internal data source. Previous marketing research studies, special audits, and reports purchased from outside for prior problems may be relevant to current problems. As a firm becomes more diversified, it is more likely to conduct studies that may be relevant to problems in other areas of the firm. For example, Procter & Gamble sells a variety of distinct products to identical or similar target markets. An analysis

RESEARCH APPLICATION 4–2

A Failure to Communicate

A manufacturer of specialized moldings had a serious sales decline in one of its major lines for almost a year. The marketing manager could not explain the decline and was considering either revising the firm's sales incentive plan to increase the rewards for selling this line or reducing the price of the line. At the annual industry trade show, the manager noticed that a major competitor had developed a clearly superior competitive product. Inquiry revealed that the launch of the competitive product coincided with the beginning of his line's sales decline. None of the 73 salespeople had reported the new product to management.

Why did these individuals fail to report such a significant piece of information? A variety of reasons emerged, as illustrated by the following statements:

"I figure management *knows* what's going on in the market. They don't need me to tell them."

"I used to tell them everything and they just ignored me. Not so much as a Thank You. So I figure the hell with it."

"I'm putting 60–70 hours a week trying to make a living *selling* this stuff. I don't have time to pass on every bit of gossip in the industry."

"I felt I should tell someone when I first saw it but Bob (the sales manager) is always on the road and I didn't know who to call at corporate."

"They knew about it. I told Bob's secretary right after it came out. We were talking about the new bonus plan and I said 'XYZ's new molding is going to give us fits.' She should have told Bob."

---

of the media habits conducted for one product could be very useful for a different product that appeals to the same target market. Again, this requires an efficient marketing information system to ensure that the relevant reports can be found by those who need them.

Research Application 4–3 describes how one consumer goods firm ensures that prior studies are consulted before primary data are collected.

Internal Experts

Internal expert: anyone employed by the firm who has special knowledge related to the question at hand.

One of the most overlooked sources of internal secondary data is internal experts. An **internal expert** *is anyone employed by the firm who has special knowledge related to the question at hand.* While this knowledge is stored in individuals' minds rather than on paper or computer disk, it can be as valid and valuable as more formal sources.

Reconsider Research Application 4–2. Had the marketing manager quickly asked the most obvious internal experts—members of the salesforce—to explain the sales decline, work on a competitive new product could have begun almost a year earlier. Companies have discovered that in addition to the salesforce, marketing research personnel, technical representatives, advertising agency personnel, product managers, and public relations personnel often have expert knowledge of relevance to marketing problems.

RESEARCH APPLICATION 4-3

An Effective Research Reports Library

The following statement by a senior research manager at a major consumer goods firm describes why his organization developed a research reports library and how they ensure its use.

On the average, each brand is assigned a new brand manager every two years. These brand managers are young, aspiring, talented MBA-types and they believe in the value of marketing research. They also know that their own upward mobility is pegged to the mark they leave on the brand. So, the first thing they require is marketing research: segmentation studies or attitude/usage surveys, typically followed by lots of qualitative studies in the copy concept or positioning/ad strategy areas. Hell, for most brands you don't need new segmentation or positioning studies every two years! Go to the file and find the last one done, learn from it before you decide a new study is required. The same is true for copy concept issues. If the concept is worth a damn, it has been researched before.

Reuse data, stretch it out to the max and reserve your budget for truly new, necessary primary studies. That's why we developed our "research library." Every thing we've ever done is in there, *including subsequent actions and results*. And it is organized for easy access. Now it is company policy that any research request has to include *proof* that the library has already been searched and found lacking— *before any new research can be conducted!*

External Sources of Secondary Data

Numerous sources external to the firm may have data relevant to the firm's requirements. Seven general categories of external secondary information are described in the sections that follow: (1) computerized databases, (2) associations, (3) government agencies, (4) syndicated services, (5) directories, (6) other published sources, and (7) external experts.

The best way to begin a search for external secondary data is to consult a general guide to secondary data sources. For example, suppose you are asked to develop background information on the motorcycle industry to assist your advertising agency prepare a proposal for Harley-Davidson's advertising account. Where would you begin? Research Application 4-4 shows the information sources that are referenced by one general guide, the *Encyclopedia of Business Information Sources*. This information would provide direction for beginning the search for secondary data. Table 4-1 lists several general and specific guides to secondary data.

Rather than conduct an external search "in house," it is often faster and more efficient to hire an *information broker*. These firms specialize in searching for external data using both computerized and manual techniques. Large

RESEARCH APPLICATION 4–4

Data Sources on the Motorcycle Industry from the Encyclopedia of Business Information Sources

Directories

Motorcycle Dealer News-Buyers Guide Issue. Harcourt Brace Jovanovich Publications, 1700 E. Dyer Rd., Suite 250, Santa Ana, CA 92705. (714) 250–8060. Annual. $25.00.

Motorcycle Product News Trade Directory. Joan Bratzman, editor. Freed-Crown Publishing Co., 6931 Van Nuys Boulevard, Suite 304, Van Nuys, CA 91405. (818) 977–0644. Annual. $12.00.

Encyclopedias and Dictionaries

Dictionary of Motorcycle Dictionary/Terminology. William H. Kosbab. Career Publishing, 910 N. Main St., Orange, CA 92613. (714) 771–5155. 1981. $8.95.

Periodicals and Newsletters

American Motorcyclist. American Motorcyclist Association, P.O. Box 141, 33 Collegeview R, Westerville, OH 43081. (614) 891–2425. Monthly. $7.50 per year.

Cycle. CBS Publications, 1515 Broadway, New York, NY 10036. (212) 725–3500. Monthly. $13.98 per year.

Cycle Guide. Cycle Guide Publications, Inc., 20916 Higgins Ct., Torrance, CA 90501. Monthly. $13.98 per year.

Cycle World. 1515 Broadway, 17th Fl., New York, NY 10036. (212) 719–6376. Monthly. $13.94 per year.

Dealernews. Edgell Communications, Inc., 1700 E. Dyer Rd., Suite 250, Santa Ana, CA 92705. (714) 250–8969. Monthly. $25.00 per year. Information for motorcycle and related power sports dealers and industry.

Motorcycle Product News. Crown Lee Pub. Co., Box 2338, Van Nuys, CA 91405. Monthly. $18.00 per year.

Motorcyclist. Peterson Publishing Co., 8490 Sunset Blvd., Los Angeles, CA 90069. (213) 854–2222. Monthly. $14.00 per year.

Price Sources

Motorcycle Appraisal Guide. N.A.D.A. Appraisal Guides, 8400 Westpark Dr., McLean, VA 22102. (703) 821–7000. Three times a year. $45.00 per year.

Trade Associations and Professional Societies

American Motorcyclist Association. P.O. Box 6114, Westerville, OH 43081. (614) 891–2425.

Motorcycle Industry Council. 3151 Airway Ave., Bldg. P-1, Costa Mesa, CA 92626. (714) 241–9251.

Other Sources

Chilton Book Company Automotive Editorial Department. Chilton Book Co., Chilton Way, Radnor, PA 19089. (800) 345–1214 or (215) 964–4000. Issues a variety of maintenance guides.

N.A.D.A. Motorcycle/Moped Appraisal Guide. National Automobile Dealers Association, P.O. Box 1407, Covina, CA 91722. Three issues per year. $35.00 per year. Used prices for 10 years and new prices.

SOURCE: P. Wasserman, et al., *Encyclopedia of Business Information Sources,* 7th ed. (Gale Research, Inc. 1988), 593.

TABLE 4–1 Guides to Secondary Data

American Statistics Index Microfiche (Washington, D.C.: Congressional Information Service, Annual, monthly updates): an index of statistical data available to the public from any agency of the federal government.

Directory of Directories, 6th ed. (Detroit: Gale Research, Annual): lists commercial and manufacturing directories, directories of individual industries, trades, and professions, rosters of professional and scientific societies, and others.

Directory of Online Databases (Santa Monica, Calif.: Cuadra Associates, Inc., Quarterly): describes more than 275 bibliographic and nonbibliographic databases.

Encyclopedia of Associations (Detroit: Gale Research, Annual): lists trade, business, and professional associations and describes their activities and publications.

Encyclopedia of Business Information Sources, 7th ed. (Detroit: Gale Research, 1988): a guide to the information available on various subjects, including basic statistical sources, associations, periodicals, directories, handbooks, and general literature.

Fuld, Leonard, M., *Competitor Intelligence* (New York: John Wiley & Sons, 1985): focus on sources relating to market and competitor characteristics.

Kruzas, Anthony T., Linda Varekamp Sullivan, eds., *Encyclopedia of Information Systems and Services*, 11th ed. (Detroit: Gale Research, 1991): describes over 3,000 organizations involved in data storage and retrieval including database producers and publishers, on-line vendors, information centers, research centers, banks, and database producers and publishers.

Nelson, Theodore A., *Measuring Markets: A Guide to the Use of Federal and State Statistical Data* (Washington, D.C.: Department of Commerce, 1979): a guide to both federal and state statistical data.

Social Sciences Citation Index (Philadelphia: Institute for Scientific Information, three times annually): indexes all articles in about 1,400 social science periodicals and selected articles in approximately 1,200 periodicals in other disciplines.

Wasserman, Paul, et al., *Statistics Sources*, 11th ed. (Detroit: Gale Research, 1989): a guide to federal, state, and private sources of statistics on a wide variety of subjects.

firms such as IBM and General Electric use information brokers to supplement their in-house expertise. Smaller firms use them in lieu of developing in-house expertise. FIND/SVP, one of the largest information search firms, has these characteristics:

- 11,000 company and subject files, 2,000 periodicals, access to 2,000 computer databases, and thousands of reference works.
- Access to the library networks in New York and Washington, D.C.
- 80 researchers, each a specialist in a subject area, who respond to telephone inquiries from client firms.
- 17 international centers with over 400 researchers to handle requests for international data that are not available in the U.S.

Computerized Databases

A **computerized database** is a collection of numeric data and/or textual information that is made available in computer-readable form for electronic distri-

Computerized database:
a collection of numeric data and/or textual information that is made available in computer-readable form for electronic distribution.

bution. More than 3,500 databases are available from over 550 on-line service enterprises (see Table 4–1). Databases are available that are useful in bibliographic search, site location, media planning, market planning, forecasting, and for many other purposes of interest to marketing researchers.

To use an on-line computerized database, the user links the receiving computer to the sending computer by telephone, using a coupler called a *modem*. The user dials a local telephone number, enters a special password to gain access to the sending computer, and then uses the interaction language of the system to retrieve and display the information of interest.

There is, of course, a charge for using a commercial database. Both the way charges are assessed and the amounts charged for using different databases vary substantially.

Bibliographic Databases

Bibliographic databases:
contain all or part of the text of articles and reports.

Bibliographic databases contain all or part of the text of articles and reports. A number of bibliographic databases are available for a wide variety of marketing research applications. *ABI* (Abstract Business Information)/*Inform* contains 150-word abstracts of articles published in approximately 1,300 business publications worldwide (the full text of articles from 100 of these publications are also available). Among the users of the service are sales representatives who are preparing proposals for potential customers. They use it to access available articles concerning the company so that a more customized presentation can be made.

Predicasts® PTS™ provides 11 on-line databases that are very useful to marketers:

- Predicasts Overview of Markets and Technology™ (PROMPT)—Over 500,000 150-word abstracts and full-text records added each year from trade and business publications worldwide. Provides competitor information and information on products, markets, and emerging technologies.
- Marketing and Advertising Reference Service® (MARS)—Multi-industry coverage of consumer products and services, including ad campaigns, budgets, slogans, marketing strategies, and market size and share.
- Aerospace/Defence Markets and Technology® (A/DM&T)—Worldwide coverage of aerospace and defense industries.
- Infomat International Business—International business information from hundreds of national trade journals, business publications, and newspapers. Focuses primarily on Europe.
- PTS Newsletter Database™—Multi-industry database covering over 450 business and industry newsletters focused on company activities, new technologies, industry trends, government policy, and international trade.
- F&S Index—Index to business information from worldwide business sources. Each one- or two-line entry contains a description of an article's content and a complete citation.
- Predicasts Forecasts®—Provides nearly 50,000 published forecasts for U.S. products, markets, industries, and the economy.
- Worldcasts®—Provides nearly 60,000 published forecasts for products and markets in countries other than the U.S.

- U.S. Time Series®—Provides over 26,000 time series on U.S. businesses, products, industries, and economic activities.
- New Product Announcements/*Plus*® (NPA/*Plus*)—Full-text company news releases, new product announcements, and newswires. Covers product introductions, new technologies, mergers and acquisitions, and license agreements.
- Annual Reports Abstracts (ARA)®—Provides texts of corporate annual reports.

Descriptions of several specialized bibliographic databases are given in Table 4–2.

Numeric Databases

Numeric databases contain numerical data such as sales, population, and so forth. A large number of Census-based numeric databases are useful for *market potential studies, segmentation studies,* and *site location evaluations.* These databases use the 1990 Census of Population and Housing (with proprietary and government updating) and provide data to the census tract and zip code levels. Included among the databases for the United States are those provided by the Bureau of the Census; Donnelly Marketing Information Services; CACI, Inc.; National Decision Systems; and the National Planning Data Corporation. Compusearch Market and Social Research, Ltd. produces a similar database for Canada.

Numeric databases: contain numerical data such as sales or population figures.

TABLE 4–2 Examples of Specialized Bibliographic Databases

The Information Bank Advertising & Marketing Intelligence Service

Advertising and marketing articles from over 60 trade and professional journals are summarized on topics such as new products, consumer trends, and sales promotions.

Bank Marketing Association: Financial Industry Information Service

Contains about 50,000 citations on the marketing of financial services by banks, credit companies, insurance firms, investment and real estate firms, thrift operations, and governmental agencies. Topics include advertising, pricing, sales, marketing, and new technologies.

FINDEX Reports and Studies

Indexes and describes industry and market research reports, studies, and surveys (more than 11,000 citations) from more than 500 research firms worldwide.

Frost & Sullivan Research Reports Abstracts

Contains citations and abstracts from approximately 1,500 market research reports providing analyses and forecasts of market size and share by product and company. Industries represented include chemicals, communications, consumer products, data processing, electronics, food, health, instrumentation, machinery, and transportation.

RESEARCH APPLICATION 4–5

The Washington Post's Use of the Claritas Database

Claritas Corporation has developed a database called PRISM, in which the U.S. population is broken into 40 life-style clusters. Claritas can estimate the percentage of households in every U.S. census tract block that fall into each life-style.* The *Washington Post* found that 87 percent of its subscribers fell into 14 of these clusters. The *Post* grouped these clusters into four similar groups and developed profiles of each based on data from PRISM as well as company data.

One group was labeled the Ozzie and Harriets. This group represented 10 percent of the market and the *Post* had a 40 percent penetration rate (over 75,000 members of this group did not subscribe to the *Post*). The group was described as predominantly middle-aged families. They are aspiring achievers with attention divided between career and family. They enjoy suburbia and have a limited identification with Washington. They are big consumers of home products and home-related entertainment. They are interested in community news/events, health and home information, and sports.

Separate direct mail campaigns were developed for nonsubscribers in each of the four groups. The campaign for the Ozzie and Harriet group positioned The *Post* as *the* family newspaper. These specific campaigns were tested against the general campaign traditionally used. The specific direct mail ads generated over twice as many new subscribers as did the general ads.

*For details, see D. I. Hawkins, R. J. Best, K. A. Coney, *Consumer Behavior* (Homewood, IL: Richard D. Irwin, 1992), 336–343.

SOURCE: Provided by Michael Custo, Circulation Marketing Manager, *The Washington Post*.

Another type of numeric database is that produced by *syndicated services*. Syndicated services collect data by conducting periodic surveys and sell them on a subscription basis. Included in these services are surveys of attitudes and life-styles (Monitor, Claritas), surveys of purchases by panels of households (Information Resources Inc.), information about movement of products at the retail level (Nielsen, Burgoyne, Information Resources Inc.), television viewing and radio listening (Nielsen, Arbitron), and magazine and newspaper readership (Simmons, Mediamark). We discuss these databases in the next chapter. Research Application 4–5 describes how *The Washington Post* used the Claritas database.

Database Systems

Finding the appropriate database, arranging to use it, and learning the access system is time-consuming. For firms needing to use a variety of databases, this time loss decreases the advantage of using a computerized database. A number of firms have responded by acquiring the right to distribute numerous databases through their computer system. Other firms then subscribe to this **database system** and can access any database contained on it using the same interaction language. Users are typically billed a subscription fee and a usage fee.

The largest of these systems is called DIALOG. It contains over 200 specific databases. NEXIS is another large system. Its bibliographic data contain entire articles rather than abstracts. It also has a large selection of newspaper databases. SDC/Orbit contains over 80 databases focused on scientific and technical data. It contains the most complete collection of patent information available.

Most of these database systems offer **Selective Dissemination of Information (SDI)** which allows a researcher to specify a company name or any specific subject and to receive all new information on that company or subject each time the database is updated.

Associations

Associations frequently publish or maintain detailed information on industry sales, operating characteristics, growth patterns, and the like. Furthermore, they may conduct special studies of factors relevant to their industry.

These materials may be published in the form of annual reports, as part of a regular trade journal, or as special reports. In some cases, they are available only on request from the association. Most libraries maintain reference works, such as the *Encyclopedia of Associations*, that list the various associations and provide a statement of the scope of their activities.

Suppose you were assigned the responsibility of researching the travel industry in the United States. The keyword index of the *Encyclopedia of Associations* lists 50 associations dealing with this area. One of these associations, the *Travel and Tourism Research Association*, provides the following services and publications:

- Sponsors Travel Research Student Contest and dissertation competition.
- Provides reference service to assist the travel industry in finding information sources and solving business problems.
- Maintains a library of 10,000 volumes.
- Publishes (1) *The Journal of Travel Research*, quarterly; (2) Member's Newsletter, 5/year; (3) *Directory of Members*, annual; (4) *Proceedings of the Annual Conference*; (5) *Travel Research Suppliers Directory*, semiannual.[4]

Clearly, one of your first steps would be to contact this association.

Government Agencies

Federal, state, and local government agencies produce a massive amount of data that are of relevance to marketers. In this section, the nature of the data produced by the federal government is described briefly. However, state and local government data should not be overlooked by the researcher.

Federal agencies produce five broad types of data of interest to marketers. There are data on (1) *population, housing, and income;* (2) *agricultural, industrial, and commercial product sales;* (3) *financial and other characteristics of firms;* (4) *employment;* and (5) *miscellaneous reports.*

Database system: a computer system on which subscribers can access numerous databases using the same interaction language.

Selective Dissemination of Information (SDI): automatically provides a subscriber all new information on selected topics or firms each time a database is updated.

Data on Population, Income, and Housing

Data of these types are of interest primarily for *estimating market potential* and for *segmenting markets* for consumer products. The principal federal sources for these data are the *Census of Population and Housing* (taken every 10 years) updated annually by the *Current Population Reports*.

A recent development by the Census Bureau called the *Tiger system* allows this and other data to be displayed on detailed maps of the appropriate geographic regions. The Tiger database does not contain any Census data. It is exclusively a digital description of geographic areas. It includes political and statistical boundaries, feature names and types, and, in metropolitan areas, address ranges. A large number of firms provide software that allows Census and other data (such as luxury car ownership) to be superimposed on the geographic maps. The potential applications in marketing include segmentation and media selection.[5]

Data on Industrial and Commercial Product Sales

Sales data for product categories can be used for such purposes as locating a plant, warehouse, retail store, or sales office, for setting sales quotas, or allocating advertising budgets by areas.

Sales statistics are available for each of the levels of distribution—manufacturers, agricultural producers, wholesalers, retailers for products, and suppliers for services. The principal sources of sales data for each of these levels are the censuses conducted for each. The *Census of Manufacturers, Census of Agriculture, Census of Wholesale Trade, Census of Retail Trade,* and *Census of Selected Services* are each conducted every five years (during years ending in 2 and 7). The *Current Industrial Reports, Agricultural Statistics, Current Wholesale Trade, Current Retail Trade,* and *Monthly Selected Services* series update these censuses at least annually.

Standard Industrial Classification (SIC): the classification system used by the U.S. government to classify and group business firms according to their primary activity.

Most government sales and industry statistics are based on the **Standard Industrial Classification (SIC)** Codes, used by the federal government to classify and group business firms. Reference to the SIC system definition is necessary for a full understanding of what products are included in the sales statistics. For example, SIC Code 521 is for "lumber and other building materials dealers." If one were considering using the sales for SIC Code 521 by area as a correlate of market potential for the do-it-yourself homeowner market, certain questions about the type of establishments and type of sales by those establishments must be answered. For example, what happens to the sales of those establishments selling both to contractors and to the do-it-yourselfers—are they included in SIC 521, excluded from SIC 521 and assigned to a wholesale trade code number, or are they somehow split, with part assigned to SIC 521 and part to a wholesale trade number? "Sales of hardware stores" is the definition given SIC Code 525. What happens to the hardware sales of SIC Code 521 establishments? Are structured steel dealer sales included in SIC 521 sales? What about cement dealers? floor covering dealers?

The answers to these and other questions can be found by looking up the definition of SIC group 521 and industry 5211 in the *Standard Industrial Classification Manual.*[6] These definitions are provided in Research Application 4–6. Given these definitions, what are the answers to the questions just raised?

RESEARCH APPLICATION 4–6

Description of SIC Major Group 52 and Industry 5211

Standard Industrial Classification Major Group 52 — Building Materials, Hardware, Garden Supply, and Mobile Home Dealers

The Major Group as a Whole

This major group includes retail establishments engaged primarily in selling lumber and other building materials; paint; glass and wallpaper; hardware; nursery stock; lawn and garden supplies; and mobile homes.

It includes lumber and other building materials dealers and paint, glass and wallpaper stores selling to the general public, even if sales to contractors account for a larger proportion of total sales. These establishments are known in the trade as retail.

Establishments primarily selling these products for use exclusively by businesses or to other wholesalers are classified in Wholesale Trade.

Establishments primarily selling plumbing, heating, and air conditioning equipment and electrical supplies are classified in Wholesale Trade.

Lumber and Other Building Materials Dealers

Group No.	Industry No.	
521	5211	*Lumber and Other Building Materials Dealers*

Establishments engaged in selling primarily lumber, or lumber and a general line of building materials, to the general public. While these establishments may sell to construction contractors, they are known as retail in the trade. The lumber they sell may include rough and dressed lumber, flooring, molding, doors, sashes, frames, and other millwork. The building materials may include roofing, siding, shingles, wallboard, paint, brick, tile, cement, sand, gravel, and other building materials and supplies. Hardware is often an important line of retail lumber and building materials dealers. Establishments which do not sell to the general public and those which are known in the trade as wholesale are classified in Wholesale Trade, Industry Group 503.

Brick and tile dealers—retail
Building materials dealers—retail
Buildings, prefabricated—retail
Cabinets, kitchen: to be installed—retail
Concrete and cinder block dealers—retail
Doors—retail
Fencing dealers—retail
Flooring, wood—retail
Garage doors—retail
Insulation material, building—retail

Lime and plaster dealers—retail
Lumber and building materials dealers—retail
Lumber and planing mill product dealers—retail
Millwork and lumber dealers—retail
Paneling—retail
Roofing material dealers—retail
Sand and gravel dealers—retail
Storm windows and sash, wood or metal—retail
Structural clay products—retail
Wallboard (composition) dealers—retail

Data on Financial and Other Characteristics of Firms

Data on financial characteristics, product line sales, joint ventures, staffing, and company history are valuable for market potential and segmentation studies, acquisition analyses, and competitor analyses. All publicly traded firms in the United States must provide detailed reports to the Securities and Exchange Commission (SEC). These SEC filings are available to the public.

10-K report:
an annual report containing data such as the income statement, balance sheet, sales by product line, debt structure, and so forth that all U.S. publicly traded firms must file.

The **10-K report** is the most widely used. It must be filed annually and contains such data as the income statement, balance sheet, sales by product line, debt structure, earnings per share, plants and property, subsidiaries, industry description, and so forth. This form is updated quarterly, though in less detail, by the 10-Q report.

Obtaining SEC data is simple. Disclosure, Inc. is the SEC's sole vendor for the private distribution of its data.[7] A call to Disclosure (800–638–8241) will produce any desired SEC material quickly and inexpensively.

Data on Employment

Employment data are used as an indicator of market potential for industrial products. They can be found in each of the economic censuses (Manufacturers, Wholesale, Trade, Retail Trade, Services, and Agriculture), in the *Annual Survey of Manufacturers,* and in *Employment and Earning Statistics, States and Areas* published by the U.S. Department of Labor.

Miscellaneous Reports

The federal government issues a staggering number of special reports each year covering a wide diversity of topics. Many of these are of interest to market researchers working on particular projects. Examples range from the *Construction Review,* a bimonthly report on residential and other construction published by the Department of Commerce, to *China: International Trade Annual Statistical Supplement,* published by the CIA.

The *National Technical Information Service* (NTIS) of the U.S. Department of Commerce provides many useful services to the marketing researcher. One of the most valuable services is its NTI Search. This is an on-line computer search of over 1 million unrestricted technical publications. It is updated every two weeks. For less than $50, an on-line search of the entire database can be made for an hour. (An average search requires considerably less time than that.) NTIS also has reports from more than 3,000 searches that have been made that can be purchased as documents through a catalog the service provides.

Syndicated Services

A wide array of data on both consumer and industrial markets is collected and sold by commercial organizations. This source of data is so important and complex that the next chapter is devoted to it.

Directories

Any sound marketing strategy requires an understanding of existing and potential competitors and customers. Suppose you were asked to prepare a report on the forest products industry to aid your organization in developing a sales and marketing approach to lumber manufacturers. How would you identify the potential customers and competitors by location and characteristics? A number of services and directories would prove useful.

A general industry directory such as *Thomas Register of American Manufacturers* (Thomas Publishing Company) is a good starting place. This 16-volume set lists manufacturers' products and services by product category. It provides the company name, address, telephone number, and an estimate of its asset size. It also contains an extensive trademark listing and samples of company catalogs.

Most industries have specific directories and buyers' guides published by a trade journal or the industry trade association. For the lumber industry, *Crow's Buyers and Sellers Guide to the Forest Products Industries* (C. C. Crow Publications) lists over 5,000 lumber products manufacturers indexed geographically, by product, and by firm name. In addition, *Forest Industries— Annual Equipment Catalog & Buyers' Guide Issue* lists numerous suppliers of equipment to the lumber industry by product.

Trade show directories (see Table 4–1) can also be very useful. A trade show directory allows one to identify the trade shows associated with an industry. The trade show organizer or sponsor can then be contacted and a list of exhibitors can usually be obtained, often with details about their products.

Other Published Sources

There is a virtually endless array of periodicals, books, dissertations, special reports, newspapers, and the like that contain information relevant to marketing decisions. Any attempt to list or describe the more important of these sources is beyond the scope of this book.

A starting point in a *manual* search for published sources on any particular topic is the subject heading in the local library's card catalog. This should be followed by consulting the relevant abstracts or literature guides, such as *Dissertation Abstracts, Psychological Abstracts, Sociological Abstracts, Business Periodicals Index,* the *Social Science Citation Index,* and the *Reader's Guide to Periodical Literature.*

One should consider starting with a *computerized* search rather than a manual one, however. The use of a computerized bibliographic service and the resulting printout of the references relating to the topic of interest may provide a more comprehensive search in the time available and, in many cases, is less costly. As an alternative, an information broker can be hired to conduct the search.

Research Application 4–7 provides an example of a widely used, published secondary source.

External Experts

External experts are individuals outside your organization whose job provides them with expertise on your industry or activity. State and government officials associated with the industry, trade association officials, editors and

External experts: individuals outside the organization whose job provides them with expertise on the problem at hand.

The Sales and Marketing Management Buying Power Index (BPI)

Each year *Sales and Marketing Management* magazine publishes a "Survey of Buying Power" issue that contains data for the United States on population, income, retail sales, and a "Buying Power Index" (BPI) down to the metropolitan area, county, and city levels. Similar data are also provided for Canada at the provincial and metropolitan area levels.

The Buying Power Index is a three-factor index. The factors and the factor weights are

$$\frac{f_{1,i}}{f_{1,t}} \times 100 = \text{percentage of the U.S. population in area } i, W_1 = .2,$$

$$\frac{f_{2,i}}{f_{2,t}} \times 100 = \text{percentage of U.S. retail sales in area } i, W_2 = .3, \text{ and}$$

$$\frac{f_{3,i}}{f_{3,t}} \times 100 = \text{percentage of effective buying income (disposable personal income) in area } i, W_3 = .5.$$

The calculation for the Davenport–Rock Island–Moline Metropolitan Statistical Area (MSA) is

Data on factors*	$\dfrac{f_{j,i}}{f_{j,t}}$	$\times$	100	$\times$	W_j	=	Weighted Factor Value
Population							
D-RI-M MSA = 367,500	.1471		$\times$		.2	=	.02942
United States = 249,830,048							
Retail Sales							
D-RI-M MSA = 2,473,393	.1437		$\times$		.3	=	.043110
United States = 1,721,219,903							
Effective Buying Income							
D-RI-M MSA = 4,995,095	.1519		$\times$		.5	=	.075950
United States = 3,288,410,138							
			Total—Buying Power Index Value			=	.14848

Recently, Orlando had a general BPI of .4316 while Phoenix's was .8796. Thus, all else equal, Phoenix has about twice the potential for sales of an average consumer product that Orlando has.

In addition to the general buying power index, three specific indexes are also provided: one each for economy-, moderate-, and premium-priced products. The BPI is widely used to set relative advertising budgets, to allocate salesforce efforts, to select areas for new product introductions or market tests, and to estimate market potential.

The BPI is concerned solely with the buying power of an area, *not* with product need. Therefore, the BPI should *not* be used to compare locations for products subject to strong geographic variations in demand unless the geographic influences are similar. Thus, comparisons for snow shovels between Houston and Denver would not make much sense, whereas they would be more reasonable for Denver and Salt Lake City.

*Given in the "1990 Survey of Buying Power," *Sales and Marketing Management*.

writers for trade and business publications, financial analysts focusing on the industry, government and university researchers, and distributors often have expert knowledge relevant to marketing problems. Referring to Research Application 4–2, a phone call to a few key retail department managers as soon as sales turned down would most likely have provided management with the required information.

Though not traditionally viewed as a source of secondary data, knowledgeable outsiders are frequently the fastest and most up-to-date sources available.

International Secondary Data

The Nature of International Secondary Data

Secondary data for international marketing decisions are subject to the same advantages and disadvantages as domestic secondary data. Unfortunately, many of the disadvantages are multiplied when the data involve more than one country. An additional problem is that most secondary data are available only in the host country's language. Thus, multicountry searches require utilizing specialist firms or maintaining a multilingual staff.

Data availability, recency, accessibility, and accuracy vary widely from country to country. Until recently, there were few commercial databases in Japan (because of the difficulty of using Japanese characters on computers—a problem that is now resolved). The Japanese government prepares many potentially useful reports, but even Japanese firms seldom use them because they are poorly organized and indexed.[8] Secondary data in many nondemocracies (as well as in democracies, on occasion) often reflect political interests more closely than reality. In general, the amount of secondary data available on a country varies directly with its level of economic development.

Even when recent, accurate data are readily accessible, it may not be possible to make multinational comparisons.[9] Data from several countries may not be comparable because the data were collected at different times, use different units of measurement, cover slightly different topics, or define the classes (such as age groups) differently. This has become a major problem in the European Community (EC) as firms begin to analyze the market as a whole rather than as a collection of individual countries. To resolve part of the problem, ESOMAR has proposed a standardized set of questions to gather demographic data in both government and private surveys. The English language version of these questions is shown in Research Application 4–8. The same group is also developing a pan-European economic status scale.[10] Similar work is underway in Brazil, India, and the Middle East.[11]

Internal Sources of International Secondary Data

The internal sources of data for international decisions are the same as for domestic decisions. As you might suspect, utilizing international internal data can be difficult. Different accounting systems, decentralized (often on a country basis) management and information systems, salesforces organized by country or region, and so forth, all combine to increase the difficulty of

RESEARCH APPLICATION 4–8

ESOMAR Working Party Recommended Demographic Questions

ESOMAR WORKING PARTY ON "HARMONISATION OF DEMOGRAPHICS"
RECOMMENDED QUESTIONNAIRE (1990)   ENGLISH

I

① - SEX: M ☐   F ☐

② - What is your age ?   ☐

③ - How many people live in your household, including yourself ?   ☐

④ - How many chidren under 15 are there ?   ☐

⑤ - Are you, in your household...
  • the person who contributes most to the household income ?
      YES ☐   NO ☐
  • the person mainly responsible for ordinary shopping and looking after the home ?
      YES ☐   NO ☐

⑥ - Are you... ?
  • married / living together
  • single
  • separated/divorced/widowed

⑦ - At what age did you finish full-time education ?   ☐
      Still studying (E10) ☐► q.13

⑧ - Any time after that, did you...
  • resume general education at a later stage in your life ?
      YES ☐► q.9   NO ☐
  • take any apprenticeship /professional training for your job ?
      YES ☐► q.9   NO ☐► q.10

⑨ - How many months did your ... (further education/prof. training) last in total ?   ☐

II

⑩ A - At present, are you...?
  • self-employed ☐►q11A
  • in a paid employment ☐►q11B
  • temporarily not working ☐►B
  • retired ☐►B
  • not working / responsible for ordinary shopping and looking after the home (E13) ☐►q13
  B - And formely, have you been...?

⑪ - What kind of work do you do ? (What position do you hold ?)
  A = SELF-EMPLOYED :
  • PROFESSIONAL (Doctor, Lawyer, Accountant, Architect)(E2) ☐►q12
  • OWNER OF SHOP/COMPANY
    How many employees do you have ? 0-5   (E6) ☐►q12
                     6 or +   (E7) ☐►q12
  • FARMER   (E12)   ☐►q12
  B = IN PAID EMPLOYMENT :
  • PROFESSIONAL   (E3) ☐► q12 (in actual profession)
  • GENERAL MANAGEMENT ☐ (Exec./Manag. Dir., Officer, Mgr)
  • MIDDLE MANAGEMENT ☐ (Dmt/Branch Head, Junior Mgr)
    - How many employees are you responsible for (heading) ?
                     GM   MM
      0-5 :   (E4) (E6) ☐►q12
      6 or + : (E1) (E5) ☐►q12
  • OTHER EMPLOYEE ☐► Do you work mainly in an office?
      YES (E8)☐►q12   NO☐
    - In your job, do you spend much of your time writing or working with figures ?
      YES (E11) ☐   NO (E14) ☐

III

⑫ - How many hours per week do you normally work ?   ☐

⑬ - Do you, or anyone else in your household, own ... ?
  • a colour TV set   Y☐ N☐
  • a video recorder   Y☐ N☐
  • a radio-clock   Y☐ N☐

  • a video camera/Camcorder Y☐ N☐
  • a PC/home computer   Y☐ N☐
  • an elec. deep fryer   Y☐ N☐

  • an electric drill   Y☐ N☐
  • a still camera   Y☐ N☐
  • at least 2 cars   Y☐ N☐

  • a second home or a vacation house/flat   Y☐ N☐

⑭ - Your main home : do you ... ?
      • rent it ☐
      • or own it ☐

⑮ - Which foreign languages do you understand well enough to read a newspaper or listen at radio news ?
      Danish ☐   Greek ☐
      Dutch ☐   Italian ☐
      English ☐   Portuguese ☐
      French ☐   Spanish ☐
      German ☐   Swedish ☐
                  Other ☐

  FULL ADDRESS
      ⬇⬇

⑯ • REGION

⑰ • SIZE OF TOWN

  USING THE LOCAL, USUAL CATEGORIES
  (AS DOCUMENTED IN AVAILABLE STATISTICS ON UNIVERSE)

SOURCE: Y. Marbeau, "Harmonization of Demographics," *Marketing and Research Today* (August 1990), 176.

acquiring and using internal data in a timely manner. Sophisticated global firms are beginning to deal with these problems by implementing global information systems and requiring some standardization across countries in terms of internal recordkeeping and reporting.

External Sources of International Secondary Data

The best way to begin an external search for international secondary data is to consult a general guide to this type of data, such as *The World Is Your Market*.[12] Contacting the U.S. Department of Commerce's International Trade Administration is also a wise early step.

An alternative to conducting such a search "in house" is to use a specialist firm such as FIND/SPV. As we saw previously, such firms have extensive resources for such searches.

Databases

As we described previously, both ABI/Inform and Predicasts have significant international content in their bibliographic databases. Predicasts coverage is particularly good and it is growing rapidly. In fact, half its information is on companies and industries from outside the U.S. Not only does its major bibliographic database, PROMPT, contain material from all over the world, but Predicasts maintains a number of international databases. Both Infomat International Business and Worldcasts (see page 88) are focused on companies, products, industries, economies, and so forth outside the U.S. Predicasts also has separate F&S Indexes (see page 88) for Europe and for the rest of the world excluding Europe and the U.S. A major advantage of these abstracts is that they are all in English. Copies of the entire articles are generally available in the original language.

Foreign Government Sources

All developed countries provide census-type data on their populations.[13] However, the frequency of data collection and the type and amount of data collected vary widely from country to country. Germany went 17 years between its last two censuses, and Holland has not conducted a census in 20 years. The U.S. collects income data in its census and marketers make extensive use of it. Most other nations, including Japan, Britain, France, Spain, and Italy, do not. (Australia, Mexico, Sweden, and Finland do.) While the Scandinavian countries, Japan, South Korea, Taiwan, and Thailand publish English-language versions of their main census reports, most countries report them only in their home language.[14] Contacting the country of interest's embassy in the U.S. or the U.S. Embassy in that country are the best ways to learn what is available.

U.S. Government

The U.S. government, as well as the various state governments, provide substantial data on foreign businesses, markets, and economies. The primary federal source of international secondary data is the International Trade Administration (ITA) in the Department of Commerce. The main services provided by ITA and other government agencies are described in the Appendix (page 104). *Inside Washington* is an excellent guide to the many sources of data and other assistance available from the federal government.[15]

International Political Organizations

Three major international political organizations provide significant amounts of data relevant to international marketing activities. The United Nations (UN) and its related organization, the United Nation's Educational, Scientific and Cultural Organization (UNESCO), provide hundreds of publications dealing with the population, economic, and social conditions of over 200 countries.

The World Bank lends funds, provides advice, and serves as a catalyst to stimulate investments in developing nations. To carry out its missions, it collects substantial amounts of useful data which can be purchased inexpensively.

The Organization of Economic Cooperation and Development (OECD) consists of 24 economically developed countries with the mission of promoting the members' economic and social welfare by coordinating national policies. As part of this mission, it publishes reports on a broad range of socioeconomic topics involving its members and the developing nations. (See the Appendix, page 104, for information on the publications of these organizations.)

Other Sources

There are numerous other sources of external international secondary data. A number of these are described in the Appendix to this chapter (page 104).

Summary

Primary data are data collected to help solve a problem or react to an opportunity on which a decision is pending. Secondary data are data that were developed for some purpose other than helping to solve the problem at hand.

Secondary data can be gathered quickly and inexpensively compared to primary data. However, to be used they must be available, relevant, accurate, and sufficient. Relevance is reduced by using (1) different units of measurement, (2) surrogate data, (3) different definitions of classes, and (4) different time periods.

Internal secondary data sources involve four broad categories: accounting records, salesforce reports, miscellaneous reports, and internal experts. External secondary data include computerized databases, associations, government agencies, syndicated services, directories, other published sources, and external experts. A sound beginning to a search of external data sources is to consult several general guides to secondary data. This step should be followed by contacting external experts and scanning several computerized databases if they are available. Another option is to use an information broker to conduct the search.

Marketers must understand SIC Codes—the federal government's method of classifying and grouping businesses—in order to use federal statistics on industries and sales. Another widely used source of data is *Sales and Marketing Management* magazine's annual Buying Power Index (BPI). The BPI provides an estimate of the general buying power as well as the buying power for economy-, moderate-, and premium-priced goods down to the metropolitan, county, and city levels.

Secondary data for international marketing decisions are subject to the same problems as domestic data, though they are multiplied as the number of countries involved increases. An additional problem is the frequent need to translate the data from its original language. The internal sources of international secondary data are the same as for domestic data. The external sources are similar, but different government agencies are involved and foreign governments and multinational political organizations are additional sources.

Review Questions

4.1. What are *secondary data*?

4.2. What are the major problems encountered with secondary data?

4.3. What are the major sources of *internal* secondary data?

4.4. What are the major sources of *external* secondary data?

4.5. What is an SIC code?

4.6. What are the *five broad types of data* published by the federal government that are of interest to marketers?

4.7. What is a *computerized* database?

4.8. Describe a specialized on-line database of use to marketing managers.

4.9. What are *two on-line bibliographic databases* that are broadly applicable to marketing research problems?

4.10. What does the Census Bureau's Tiger system make possible?

4.11. What is an *information broker*?

4.12. What is a *numeric database*?

4.13. What is a *database system*? What advantages does one offer?

4.14. What types of data are available from trade associations?

4.15. What is the *Buying Power Index*? What cautions should be observed in using the BPI?

4.16. What unique problems are encountered in using internal and external international secondary data?

4.17. Describe several databases that contain secondary data of use for international marketing decisions.

4.18. Describe the types of international secondary data available from the U.S. government.

4.19. What international political organizations provide useful international secondary data?

4.20. How can one find external experts on international marketing issues?

Discussion Questions/Problems

4.21. Describe a system that would enable a company to avoid the problems encountered in Research Application 4–2.

4.22. Most firms do not make effective use of internal secondary data. Why? How could this be altered?

4.23. Rank order the first five sources you would use from Research Application 4–4. Justify your answer.

4.24. Describe the steps you would go through to develop an estimate of the U.S. market size for cat food. Use only secondary data.

4.25. Describe the steps you would go through to develop a competitor profile on Apple Computer.

4.26. Describe the steps you would go through to develop a list of U.S. users of air compressors.

4.27. Repeat 4.24 for
   a. Latin America.
   b. Canada.
   c. the EC countries.
   d. Japan.

4.28. Repeat 4.25 for
   a. Siemens (a German firm).
   b. NEC (a Japanese firm).
   c. Kia Motor Company (a Korean firm).
   d. Autlan (a Mexican firm).

4.29. Repeat 4.26 for
   a. Latin America.
   b. Canada.
   c. The EC countries.
   d. Korea.

Projects/Activities

4.30. Give at least five *specific* potential sources of secondary data that you would consult to estimate the U.S. market potential for a new product (choose a product of interest to you).

4.31. Select a specialty retail store type—health foods and indoor plants are examples—that interests you. Assume that you are interested in opening such a store in the general area of the campus. Precisely what is your management problem? What is the research problem? What secondary sources are available that would provide data to help you decide whether to open such a store? Identify the specific individuals you would want to consult with to help in this decision. Gather and summarize the available secondary data that would bear on your decision of whether or not to open such a store.

4.32. Obtain data on wine sales in your state for the latest available year. Calculate the per-capita sales for your state and compare it to that for the country as a whole. Which is higher? What factors do you think explain the difference?

4.33. Select a company of interest to you and develop a competitive profile of that firm, indicating the source for each bit of data used.

4.34. Select a product category of interest and develop an estimate of market size, number of customers, number of competitors, geographic concentrations of customers and competitors, and a forecast of sales growth in the United States.

4.35. Using secondary data, describe the market for (i) dog food, (ii) wine, (iii) personal computers, or (iv) sheet metal in
   a. Japan.
   b. Spain.
   c. Brazil.
   d. Taiwan.

  e. Sweden.

  f. Indonesia.

4.36. Using secondary data, develop a detailed profile of

  a. Siemens.

  b. Samsung.

  c. Hitachi.

  d. Autlan.

4.37. What are the worldwide sales in units of

  a. personal computers?

  b. automobiles?

  c. watches?

  d. jet engines?

  e. industrial robots?

  f. soft drinks?

Notes

1. R. Serafin, C. Horton, "Buick Ads Target ZIP Codes," *Advertising Age* (April 1, 1991), 1; and P. Strnad, "McCann McMaps Ad Strategies," *Advertising Age* (April 22, 1991), 37.

2. P. H. Nelson, "Research and Information at Bacardi Imports," *Marketing Research* (March 1990), 8.

3. D. M. Lambert, H. Marmorstein, A. Sharma, "Industrial Sales People as a Source of Market Information," *Industrial Marketing Management* 2 (1990), 141–148.

4. *Encyclopedia of Associations*, Vol. 1 (Detroit: Gale Research, 1989), 353.

5. *Tiger* (Washington, D.C.: Bureau of the Census, November 1990).

6. *Standard Industrial Classification Manual* (Washington, D.C.: U.S. Government Printing Office, 1987).

7. Disclosure, Inc., 5161 River Road, Bethesda, MD 20816.

8. "How the Japanese Do It," *The Conference Board's Management Briefing* (1988), 2:6, 1.

9. R. Bartos, "International Demographic Data?" *Marketing and Research Today* (November 1989), 205–212.

10. Y. Marbeau, "Towards a Pan-European Economic Status Scale," *Marketing and Research Today* (August 1990), 180–184.

11. P. M. deAlmeida, H. Wickerhauser, "Finding a Better Socio-Economic Status Classification System for Brazil," *Marketing and Research Today* (November 1991), 240–250.

12. W. A. Delphos, *The World Is Your Market* (Washington, D.C.: Braddock Communications, 1990). A good overview of the process is I. MacFarlane, "Do-It-Yourself Marketing Research," *Management Review* (May 1991), 34–37.

13. See J. Treasure, "The Availability and Use of Public Statistics in the UK," *Journal of the Market Research Society* (October 1989), 581–589.

14. D. B. PiHenger, "Gathering Foreign Demographics Is No Easy Task," *Marketing News* (January 8, 1990), 23.

15. W. A. Delphos, *Inside Washington* (Venture Marketing Corporation, 1988).

Appendix: External Sources of International Secondary Data

U.S. Government Department of Commerce

International Trade Administration

(202) 377–3808. International trade specialists at ITA offices worldwide can individually tailor information packages on foreign business climates, import regulations, tariff and nontariff barriers, local and international competition, competitor firms and competitive forces, distribution practices, product standards, and so forth. ITA can provide market data (dollar value, quantity, unit value, market shares, etc.) on thousands of products in over 200 markets. Its staff can conduct in-country interviews to determine key marketing facts about products.

U.S. & Foreign Commercial Service

(202) 377–5777. The US&FCS works closely with the ITA. It provides background information on foreign companies, agency-finding services, market research, and similar services.

International Economic Policy

(202) 377–3022. The IEP provides information on trade potential in specific countries.

Trade Development

(202) 377–1461. The Trade Information and Analysis Office produces economic analyses, industry statistics, and trade, finance, and investment data and studies.

Center for International Research

(301) 763–2870. The CIR develops and maintains worldwide demographic and economic data. Much of this data can be accessed through its computerized International Data Base (IDB).

International Political Organizations

The United Nations

(212) 963–1234. The many special UN publications are listed in the annual *Catalogue of United Nations Publications*. In addition to its many specialized reports, three annual publications are valuable—*UN Statistical Yearbook, International Trade Statistics Yearbook,* and *Demographic Yearbook.* Each of these provides data on 220 countries. UNESCO's publications are distributed through UNIPUB (301) 459–7666. It also sells most UN publications.

The World Bank

(202) 473–2939. World Bank studies are listed in *The World Bank Index of Publications*. They can also be secured through NTIS (see page 94), which can be accessed through DIALOG and other search services. Its *World Bank Atlas* gives population, gross domestic product, and average growth rates for every country.

The Organization of Economic Cooperation and Development

(202) 785–6323. OECD's publications are listed in the *OECD Catalogue of Publications*. Particularly useful titles include *Economic Outlook/Historical Statistics* (semiannual), *Monthly Statistics on Foreign Trade* (monthly), *Foreign Trade by Commodity* (annual), and *OECD Economic Surveys*.

Private Databases

Predicasts

(800) 321–6388 or (216) 795–3000. As described in the text (pages 88, 89), F&S Europe, F&S International, Infomat International Business, and Worldcasts are international bibliographic and numeric databases. Its other databases also have significant international data.

Directories/Guides

Business On-Line: Management, Marketing and Administration. Describes over 200 on-line databases worldwide. Available from MacFarlane & Co., Inc., Atlanta, GA.

The European Directory of Marketing Information Sources. Available from Mac-Farlane & Co., Inc., Atlanta, GA.

Exporters' Encyclopaedia. Dun's Marketing Services, Parsippany, NJ.

International Directory of Business Information Agencies and Services. Gale Research Company, Detroit, MI.

The International Directory of Marketing Information Sources. This volume excludes Europe. Available from MacFarlane & Co., Inc., Atlanta, GA.

International Top Companies Series. Four volumes—Europe, Asia, United Kingdom, Latin America. Dun's Marketing Services, Parsippany, NJ.

Japan Trade Directory. Gale Research Company, Detroit, MI.

Principal International Businesses. Dun's Marketing Services, Parsippany, NJ.

Worldwide Government Directory. Cambridge Information Group, Bethesda, MD.

World Retail Directory and Source Book. Available from MacFarlane & Co., Inc., Atlanta, GA.

External Experts

District Export Councils

The Department of Commerce maintains numerous District Export Councils. These councils are composed of experienced exporters who volunteer their time to assist other firms as they begin international marketing.

CHAPTER 5

Standard Commercial Data Sources

Marketing Research to Determine Which Type of Coupon to Use to Attract New Customers

Brand managers at Procter & Gamble have substantial sales evidence that cents-off coupons produce significant sales increases. However, the coupons also lower margins and increase costs.

Coupons can be distributed in a variety of ways. Each method has a distinct cost and redemption rate. One approach to deciding whether to use coupons and how to distribute them is to calculate the gross contribution change during and immediately after the coupon period minus the cost of distributing the coupons. This is generally done by distributing coupons into selected regions and withholding them from a "matched" set of regions.

The brand manager can determine the coupon redemption rate through accounting records. However, accounting records would not reveal actual brand sales during the period. Why? Shipments into the channel of distribution precede retail sales by varying lengths of time. Therefore, to conduct this type of analysis, the brand manager at Procter & Gamble must obtain a measure of brand sales at retail.

Several sources are available. Nielsen Marketing Research provides weekly universal product code (UPC) scanner-based product-movement data from more than 3,000 stores. Information Resources, Inc., (IRI) provides a similar service called *InfoScan.*®

In this situation, the Procter & Gamble brand manager felt that *who* redeemed the coupons was more critical than the absolute number redeemed. The specific objective of couponing for this brand was to capture new users, not to encourage current users to stock up on the brand. How could these data be obtained?

Nielsen Household Services and IRI, among others, operate panels in which individual household purchases over time are recorded. By monitoring coupon redemption by specific households, the brand manager can determine the effect of various types of coupons on specific types of users. One such study revealed the following redemption patterns:[1]

| | Redemption Rate (%) | |
Customer Type	FSI Coupons	Target Direct Mail Coupons
New Users	13	48
Nonloyal Buyers	16	27
Loyal Buyers	71	25
Total	100	100

The data we have just described were not generated solely to solve Procter & Gamble's marketing problem. Therefore, they could be considered secondary data. However, these data are collected specifically to address this category of problem for firms like Procter & Gamble. Thus, they have much in common with primary data. Commercial surveys, audits, and panels occasionally generate primary data, sometimes secondary data, and, most often, data with characteristics of each. In this chapter we describe the characteristics of each of these three important data sources and then the major ways in which these data are used by marketing managers.

Commercial Surveys

Commercial surveys are conducted by research organizations and fall into three categories: periodic, panel, and shared.

Periodic Surveys

Periodic surveys: conducted at regular intervals using a new sample of respondents for each survey.

Periodic surveys are conducted at regular intervals, ranging from weekly to annually, using a new sample of respondents (individuals, households, or stores) for each survey, focusing on the same topic and allowing the analysis of trends over time, though changes in individual respondents cannot be traced. These surveys cover topics ranging from values to media usage and food preparation. Standard reports and special analyses are available to firms that subscribe to the service. Research Application 5–1 describes an annual periodic survey that Audits & Surveys has offered since 1964.

Panel Surveys

Panel surveys: a group of respondents who have agreed to be interviewed over time.

Panel surveys, sometimes called *interval panels,* are conducted among a group of respondents who have agreed to respond to a number of mail, telephone, or, occasionally, personal interviews over time. The interviews may cover virtually any topic and need not occur on a regular basis. In contrast, a *panel,* a *continuous panel,* or *panel data* refers to a group of individuals who agree to

RESEARCH APPLICATION 5–1

Audits & Surveys National Restaurant Market Index

- *Timing*—Annually in May.
- *Sample*—National probability sample of approximately 6,000 restaurants projectable to all commercial restaurants in the U.S.
- *Procedure*—Personal interviews with the chef, manager, or owner and an inspection of equipment and inventories.
- *Classification Data*—U.S. Census definitions as to type, service offered (counter, table, drive-in, etc.), and whether it is free standing or part of another establishment such as a hotel or retail store. Annual sales volume and the number of full- and part-time employees are also recorded.
- *Variables Measured*—The usage of specific categories of food and supplies (cleaning products, paper and plastic goods, dishes, and so forth), and the presence of specified equipment. Brand names of products actually found in the kitchen are recorded.
- *Reports*—Brands and sizes, equipment, product category usage, and so forth reported by total United States, type of restaurant, U.S. census, geographic region, and client sales regions.

report specified behaviors over time. This type of panel is discussed in the next section of this chapter.

In an interval panel, the research firm initially gathers detailed data on each respondent, including demographics and attitudinal and product-ownership items. Because the researchers need not collect this basic demographic data again, they can now obtain more relevant information from each respondent. These basic data also allow researchers to select very specific samples. For example, a researcher can select only those families within a panel that have one or more daughters between the ages of 12 and 16, or that own a dog, or that wear contact lens. This ability to select allows a tremendous savings over a random survey procedure if a study is to be made for a product for teenage girls, dog owners, or contact lens wearers, and so on.

Another advantage is the high response rate obtained by most interval panels. Return rates in the range of 70 to 90 percent are often obtained. However, the response rate when individuals are initially asked to join a panel may be quite low. Thus, panels do not eliminate nonresponse error. This issue is discussed in depth in the section on continuous panels.

In addition, the firm does not have to generate a sampling frame, a process that is both time-consuming and costly. Finally, since panel members are convinced of the legitimacy of the firm maintaining the panel, they may supply more detailed and accurate data to both neutral and sensitive questions.

Interval panels exist for the general U.S. and Canadian populations, for specific geographic regions within either country, and for specialized populations such as farmers. For example, the Doane Countrywide Farm Panel is

RESEARCH APPLICATION 5–2

Two Major Interval Panels

NFO

Size: Over 400,000 households (nearly 1 million people) with 40 continuously maintained subpanels of 5,000 households, each of which matches the demographics from the latest Census Bureau statistics.

Access: Mail-out/mail-back, mail-out/telephone collection, telephone, in-home videotape demonstrations, ability to recontact individual respondents, product placement for use testing.

Preidentified Characteristics: Geographic region; ADI (area of dominant influence); city size; stage of household life cycle; age; education; occupation (over 50 categories); employment status of household members; size and income of household; geodemographic and value segments (ACORN, ClusterPlus, PRIZM, VISION, and VALS); dwelling type and ownership; ownership of various products (11); travel patterns; dog or cat ownership; health information; and long-distance carrier.

CMP (Market Facts, Inc.)

Size: 340,000 households with nationally balanced subsamples available within geographic regions. An additional 35,000 households are available in Canada.

Access: Primarily mail-out/mail-back with phone interviewing also available. Products can be distributed for use testing and daily, or weekly diary reports from panel members can be obtained.

Preidentified Characteristics: Geographic region; ADI (area of dominant influence); city size; stage of household life cycle; age; education; occupation; employment status of household head; age of children; size and income of household; employment status of adult female household members; type and ownership of dwelling unit; and presence of dogs and/or cats.

---

composed of approximately 25,000 farmers and ranchers. NFO maintains a Hispanic Panel of over 16,000 households. Illinois Bell recently used this to test several versions of a Spanish-language television commercial. Three versions of the test ad and one control ad were placed on a videotape and, along with a questionnaire, were mailed to VCR-owning members of the Hispanic Panel. The results helped Illinois Bell develop its advertising strategy for the Hispanic market in its region.

Data are normally collected by mail, but telephone, personal, and even focus groups can be used. Clients can survey the entire panel, a stratified random sample of the larger panel, or a specific type, size, or location category. Research Application 5–2 describes two major consumer panels.

Shared Surveys

Shared surveys, sometimes referred to as *omnibus surveys,* are administered by a research firm and consist of questions supplied by multiple clients. Such surveys can involve mail, telephone, or personal interviews. The respondents may be drawn from either an interval panel or randomly from the larger

TABLE 5–1 Shared Surveys

Service	Method	Frequency	Sample
AIM (R. H. Bruskin Associates)	In-home personal	Bimonthly	2,000 homes, national probability, adults, half male
OmniTel (Bruskin/Goldring)	Telephone (CATI)	Weekly (Fri.–Sun.)	1,000 adults, half male, random digit dialing
TeleNation (Market Facts, Inc.)	Telephone (CATI)	Weekly (Fri.–Sun.)	1,000 adults, half male, random digit dialing
TeleNation Canada (Market Facts of Canada Limited)	Telephone (CATI)	Weekly (Thurs.–Sun.)	1,000 adults, half male, random digit dialing
Data Gage (Market Facts, Inc.)	Mail	Monthly	1,000 to 150,000 randomly selected from CMP's interval panel (see Research Application 5–2)
CMP National Omnibus (Market Facts of Canada, Limited)	Mail	Quarterly	3,000, 6,000, 10,000, or 14,000 randomly selected from CMP's Canadian mail panel (Research Application 5–2)
Multicard Survey (NFO)	Mail	Twice monthly	5,000 increments to 150,000 quota samples from NFO's interval panel (Research Application 5–2)
Insta-Vue (Home Testing Institute)	Mail	Monthly	5,000 increments to 150,000 quota samples from HTI's interval panel

population. Table 5–1 briefly describes several major shared surveys. Research Application 5–3 is a shared survey from Data Gage (Market Facts Inc).

Shared surveys offer the client several advantages. First, since the fixed cost of sample design and most of the variable surveying costs are shared by several clients, the cost per question is generally quite low. For example, a multiple-choice question asked of 1,000 respondents with the results cross-tabulated by four demographic variables costs only $750 in a shared telephone survey. The cost per question declines as the number of questions increases.

Since these data are collected frequently—weekly for telephone surveys—responses can be obtained *very* quickly. This feature is useful for measuring consumers' responses to competitive moves, adverse publicity, and environmental changes.

The frequent administration of the questionnaires also allows tracking of advertising awareness, product use, attitudes, and so forth. Note that such tracking or monitoring involves aggregate measures and does not measure *individual* changes over time since different respondents are involved in each wave.

Shared surveys conducted among interval panel members have the additional advantage of allowing the extensive demographic data associated with

Shared (omnibus) surveys: are administered by a research firm and consist of questions supplied by multiple clients.

RESEARCH APPLICATION 5–3

A Shared Survey from Data Gage (Market Facts Inc.)

(Please Read and Answer <u>these</u> questions)

1a. Are you currently married or are you planning to be married within the next 12 months?
Yes. . . . . ☐ 1
No. . . . . ☐ 2 (SKIP TO QU. 2)   (9)

1b. "X" one box below to indicate the date of your wedding.
Before <u>1990</u> . . . .☐ 1   (10)
Between January and June <u>1990</u>. . . . . .☐ 2
Between July and December <u>1990</u>. . . .☐ 3
Between January and June <u>1991</u>. . . . . .☐ 4
Between July and December <u>1991</u>. . . .☐ 5
During <u>1992</u>. . . . .☐ 6

2. What kind of video cassette recorder (VCR) do you own? (A video cassette recorder records and plays back TV shows, movies, etc.)
No VCR owned . . . .☐ 1   (11)
VHS . . . . ☐ 2
Beta . . . . ☐ 3

3. What kind of cameras are currently used by people in your household? ("X" ALL THAT APPLY)
35 mm camera . . . .☐ 1   (12)
110 cartridge camera. . . . .☐ 2
126 cartridge camera. . . . .☐ 3
Disc camera . . . .☐ 4
Instant print camera. . . . .☐ 5
Video camera/camcorder . . . .☐ 6
No cameras used. . . . .☐ X

4. Does any member of your household currently <u>smoke cigars</u> at least two times a week?
Yes. . . . . . ☐ 1   No. . . . . . ☐ 2   (13)

5. Which, if any, of the following <u>credit cards</u> are currently owned by any member of your household? ("X" ALL THAT APPLY)
Choice. . . . .☐ 1 (14)
Diner's Club . . . .☐ 2
Discover. . . . .☐ 3
NONE OF THESE . . . .☐ 4

6. Which, if any, of the following types of "specially flavored" block or sliced cheese—<u>not</u> spreads—(that is, cheeses that have been flavored with added bits and pieces of pepper, meats, onions, herbs/spices/seeds or have been smoked or are wine-flavored) have you or other members of your household purchased and eaten <u>in the past year</u>? ("X" ALL THAT APPLY)
<u>Block or Sliced. . .</u>   (15)
Pepper cheese (jalapeno, red, black pepper, etc.) . . . .☐ 1
Cheeses with bits of meat (pepperoni, bacon, ham, salami, etc.). . . . .☐ 2
Mexican or Cajun cheese . . . .☐ 3
Cheese with herbs/spices/seeds (onion, garlic, dill, chives, etc.) . . . .☐ 4
Smoked cheese (hickory smoked cheddar, etc.) . . . .☐ 5
Wine-flavored cheese . . . .☐ 6
NONE OF THESE. . . . .☐ X

7. "X" one box below to indicate how often you, or others in your household, <u>buy</u>. . .

RESEARCH APPLICATION 5–3 (continued)

	Once/Week or More Often	1–3 Times per Month	1–2 Times Every Three Mos.	Less than Every Three Mos.	Never
					(16)
Chocolate chip cookies..........	☐ 1	☐ 2	☐ 3	☐ 4	☐ 5
Sandwich cookies	☐ 1	☐ 2	☐ 3	☐ 4	☐ 5
Iced cookies	☐ 1	☐ 2	☐ 3	☐ 4	☐ 5
Other types of cookies	☐ 1	☐ 2	☐ 3	☐ 4	☐ 5
Frozen cakes....................	☐ 1	☐ 2	☐ 3	☐ 4	☐ 5
Frozen sweet rolls/coffee cake...	☐ 1	☐ 2	☐ 3	☐ 4	☐ 5
Potato/corn chips	☐ 1	☐ 2	☐ 3	☐ 4	☐ 5
Saltines........................	☐ 1	☐ 2	☐ 3	☐ 4	☐ 5
Snack crackers..................	☐ 1	☐ 2	☐ 3	☐ 4	☐ 5
					(24)

SOURCE: Reprinted with permission from Market Facts Inc.

each panel member to be used in an analysis of the responses. They also represent an economical way to develop a larger sample of individuals with unique characteristics such as allergies. These individuals can then be sent a custom survey on the topic of interest.

Research Application 5–4 contains part of an advertisement and rate sheet for the Omnitel shared telephone survey.

Audits

Audits involve the physical inspection of inventories, sales receipts, shelf facings, prices, and other aspects of the marketing mix to determine sales, market share, relative price, distribution, or other relevant information.

Store Audits

A **store audit** involves periodically visiting a set of stores and examining their inventories and purchases to determine the sales of specific brands.

The most widely used store audit service is the Nielsen Retail Index. It is based on audits every 30 or 60 days of a large national sample of food, drug, and mass merchandise stores. The index provides sales data on all the major packaged-goods product lines carried by these stores—foods, pharmaceuticals, drug sundries, tobacco, beverages, and the like (but not soft goods or durables). Nielsen contracts with the stores to allow their auditors to conduct the audits and pays for that right by providing them with their own data plus cash.

Store audit: periodically visiting a set of stores and examining their inventories and purchases to determine the sales of specific brands.

RESEARCH APPLICATION 5–4

Bruskin/Goldring's OmniTel

This weekly omnibus survey is conducted with freshly drawn samples of 1,000 adults, 18 years of age and older . . . half of the interviews are with men and half with women.

Each study is based on a comparably selected sample of homes utilizing our own random digit dialing computer-generated national probability sample. This RDD design thus takes into account unlisted as well as listed telephone households.

Our on-premise computer-assisted telephone interviewing (CATI) speeds up both the data collection and data processing of **OmniTel.** The Central Telephone Research Division (CTR) maintains continuous monitoring and supervision.

OmniTel has had many types of client studies, including point-in-time and multiwave awareness, attitude, and usage surveys; concept testing; im-
pact of ad campaigns; advertising claim substantiation; screening for qualified respondents for follow-up marketing and product placement studies; determination of incidence levels; media audience studies; and many others.

Regularly Scheduled:
- **OmniTel** is conducted weekly.
- Questionnaire deadline noon each Thursday.
- Top-line results on following Monday and complete tabs on Tuesday.

National Probability Sample:
- 1,000 telephone interviews each week; 52,000 per year.
- Male and female adults, 18 and over.
- Conducted on CATI on-premises.
- Random digit dialing sample based on latest updated telephone data.

OmniTel Price (Effective January 1992)

Number of Questions	Full Sample (1000)	Male/Female Sample (500)
1st–2nd(per)	$ 750	$ 550
3rd–4th(per)	$ 700	$ 500
5th or more	$ 550	$ 400
Open End	$1,300	$1,100

NOTE:
(1) Prices based on "yes–no" or "multiple choice" type questions.
(2) Special low prices available for participations based on low-incidence qualifications and multiple waves.
(3) Cost includes tabulation by sex, age, income, and area. Other variables available at a small additional cost.

SOURCE: Bruskin/Goldring documents.

The clients receive reports on the sales of their own brand and of competitors' brands, the resulting market shares, prices, shelf facings, in-store promotional activity, stockouts, retailer inventory and stock turn, and local advertising. These data are provided for the entire United States and by region, by size classes of stores, and by chains versus independents. The data are available to subscribers on-line by computer as well as in printed reports.

Product Audits

Product audits, such as Audits and Surveys' National Total Market Index, are similar to store audits but focus on products and attempt to cover all the types of retail outlets that handle a product category. Thus, a product audit for automotive wax would include grocery stores, mass merchandisers, and drugstores (in this way it is similar to the Nielsen store audits). In addition, it would include automotive supply houses, filling stations, hardware stores, and other potential outlets for automotive wax.

Product audits: store audits that cover all the types of outlets that sell a particular product.

Retail Distribution Audits

Retail distribution audits do not measure inventory or sales; instead, they are observational studies that measure how brands within specified product categories are displayed, priced, and so forth in retail outlets. Field agents enter stores unannounced. They observe and record the brands present, price, shelf facings, and other relevant data for selected product categories. NRTI (Erhardt-Babic) and BOS (Burgoyne, Inc.) are the major suppliers of this type of data. Research Application 5–5 provides additional information on the Burgoyne system.

Retail distribution audits: observational studies that measure how brands are displayed, priced, and so forth in retail outlets.

Panels

A panel is a group of individuals or organizations that have agreed to provide information to a researcher over a period of time. A *continuous panel,* the focus of this section, has agreed to report specified behaviors on a regular basis.

Retail Panels

A number of organizations provide **retail panels** by purchasing sales data from the checkout scanner tapes of a sample of supermarkets and other retailers that use electronic scanning systems and preparing and selling brand sales data. An estimated 99 percent of all packaged products in supermarkets carry the universal product code (UPC), often referred to as a bar code, and so are amenable to scanning. UPC codes are rapidly being expanded to soft goods and hardware; stores such as K mart, Wal-Mart, and Toys 'R' Us have or are installing scanners in all their outlets.

Closely related to UPC scanner methods are Electronic Point-of-Sale (EPOS) systems. EPOS systems are generally unique to a particular retail chain. They are common in catalog showrooms, home-improvement centers, hardware

Retail panels: groups of retail outlets that provide their scanner sales data to a firm which prepares and sells brand sales data.

RESEARCH APPLICATION 5–5

Burgoyne Observation Systems (BOS)

BOS can be applied within any defined set of retail outlet types or across outlet types for any given product category. Field work is normally completed in 72 to 96 hours, minimizing any time-related or competitor distortions. For the client's brand and its competitors, BOS measures on a one-time or ongoing basis:

- Distribution and Out-of-Stock
- Retail Price Levels and Feature Price Activity
- Shelf Space Allocation and Positioning
- In-Store Stocking Locations
- Display Activity
- Point-of-Purchase Material Presence
- Age-of-Stock/Type of Package/Damaged Product
- Depth-of-Line

BOS samples cover 200 major markets. Clients can share costs when using standard outlet samples. Standard sample panels correspond to other leading data sources so that sales results can be related to distribution intensity. Custom outlet samples can be created to cover any product category.

Common applications include the following:

- Evaluate salesforce/broker distribution efforts
- Track retail build for new/competitive products
- Guarantee sufficient penetration levels *prior to* advertising
- Gauge the quality of distribution at retail
- Determine channel strengths and weaknesses
- Investigate new items/categories/outlet types
- Integrate distribution data with sales/consumer information for an actionable MIS

Universal product code (UPC): a bar code attached to product packages by manufacturers that indicates the brand, size, and so forth.

stores, many specialty chains, and fast-food outlets. Research organizations arrange to buy **UPC** scanners or EPOS data from the retailers.

A. C. Nielsen's *ScanTrack,* and IRI's *InfoScan* are two of the larger scanning services. Scanning data are collected from a national sample of retail outlets. Each system has approximately 2,700 supermarkets, 500 drugstores, and 300 mass merchants in over 50 cities. Data on displays, advertising, couponing, and so forth are also collected. These data are analyzed to provide information on purchases by brand, size, price, flavor or formulation, and market share by user-specified definitions of time, area, and store classification. The data are collected weekly with reports available 30 days later.

Custom retail scanners and EPOS services are also offered by firms such as Burgoyne. These panels focus on unique markets or account types, geographic regions, and time periods. Such custom approaches greatly extend the range of applications for scanner panel data.

Scanning data have many applications in marketing research. Safeway Stores, for example, has a manager of scanner marketing research whose department conducts studies on such topics as price elasticities, placement of products in the stores, and the effects of in-store advertising. One such scanner test showed that the sales of candy bars increased 80 percent when they were put on front-end racks near the checkout counter. Another study indicated that foil-packaged sauce mixes sold better when they were placed near companion products—spaghetti sauce near the spaghetti, meat sauce in the refrigerated meat cases, and so on—rather than when they were displayed with other sauces.[2]

Scanner data compared to store audit data, have the advantages of (1) *greater frequency*—weekly instead of bimonthly collection, (2) *elimination of breakage and pilferage losses being counted as sales*, and (3) *more accurate price information*. They have certain problems, however, including (1) *not all supermarkets have scanners*, and (2) *the quality of the scanner data depends heavily on the checkout clerk*. Clerks sometimes do not lift heavy items (e.g., dog food and flour) for scanning, but ring them up instead. Rather than scan each individually packaged different flavor (of say, yogurt) in a multipackage purchase of the same product, the clerk often puts only one package through the scanner and rings in the number of packages. The purchase is then incorrectly recorded as consisting of only one flavor instead of the several different flavors actually purchased. Despite these problems, scanner data are widely used by consumer goods firms.[3]

Consumer Panels

Continuous consumer panels allow firms to monitor shifts in individual or specific household behaviors or attitudes over time. This allows the firm to determine how its own or competitors' marketing mix changes affect specific consumers or market segments. Consumer panel data are collected either electronically, by UPC scanners, or by diaries.[4]

Diary Panels

A **diary panel,** is a panel of individuals, households, or organizations who continuously record in a diary their purchases of selected products. It is used for those product categories for which purchase is frequent—primarily food, household, and personal-care products.

The largest suppliers of diary panel data are Nielsen Household Services and MRCA. Nielsen maintains two national panels of 6,500 families and a panel of 1,500 nonfamily households (primarily singles), plus a number of regional and other panels that are subsamples of the national ones. The client thus has the option of receiving purchase data from a sample of as many as 14,500 households.

Each panel household provides information on its purchases of products in each of approximately 50 product categories each month. For each product category, the respondent records the date of the purchase, the number and size(s) of the packages, the total cash paid, whether coupons were used or if there was a special price promotion, and the store at which the purchase was made. Special questions are asked for each product category; for example, for ready-to-eat breakfast cereals, *"Does the cereal have a special flavor or fruit or nuts added?—If yes, write in . . . ,"* and *"Is this cereal purchased specifically for one family member? If yes, write in age and sex."* The reporting forms for three products are shown in Research Application 5–6.

The panelists are classified by three geodemographic systems (PRIZM, ClusterPlus, VISION) and SRI's VALS II classification typology.[5] The data are available to subscribers on-line.

Diary panel:
a group of individuals, households, or organizations who record their purchases or other behaviors in a diary over time.

RESEARCH APPLICATION 5–6

Sample Reporting Form for a Consumer Diary Panel—Nielson, Inc.*

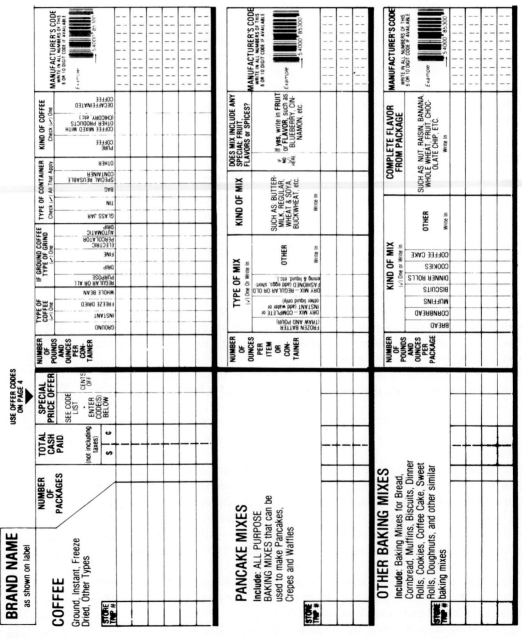

*Used by permission.

Nielsen provides the following information in its reports based on consumer panel data:

1. brand share (including brand and private label detail) by type of outlet
2. industry and brand volume (lbs., units, equivalent cases) by type of outlet
3. number of households buying (projected to U.S. total)
4. penetration (percentage of area households buying)
5. buying rate (units per buying occasion)
6. purchase frequency (number of purchases within a period)
7. percentage of volume bought with a cents-off deal
8. type of deal
9. dollars and dollar share
10. average price paid (by deal versus nondeal sales)

MRCA maintains a panel of 12,000 nationally and regionally representative households that report purchases weekly (as opposed to Nielsen's monthly diaries). MRCA provides information similar to that provided by Nielsen.

While the members of the Nielsen and MRCA panels report a wide range of purchase behaviors over a period of several years, other diary panels are established to collect relatively specific data over shorter intervals.

Electronic Panels

Electronic panels are composed of households whose television viewing behavior is recorded electronically. Nielsen Media Research is the main organization active in this area. Nielsen uses a national panel of homes equipped with people meters. A **people meter** is a device that (1) automatically records when a television is turned on and to which station, (2) has a remote control that allows each family member plus visitors (who also record their age and gender) to "log on" when they begin watching by punching an identifying button, and (3) sends these data by a telephone line for processing to a central computer that has the demographics of the panel in memory.[6] Thus, viewing by demographic segments can be determined. Although there is considerable controversy over the accuracy of people meters (the television networks feel they underestimate the number of viewers), they appear to be superior to the available alternatives.[7]

The Nielsen TV Index is now based on a national probability sample of 4,000 households (with a complete turnover every 2 years) equipped with people meters. This is supplemented four times a year by a large national sample of individuals who report their TV viewing for one week in a diary (these are known as *sweeps weeks*). Nielsen also plans to introduce an 800-Hispanic-household people meter panel in 1993. The Nielsen Station Index uses one-week diaries seven times a year to measure TV viewing in 200 local markets.

Arbitron Ratings is also very active in television (and radio) ratings. It has historically focused on providing detailed ratings for local markets. Its **ADI** (area of dominant influence) designations are used throughout the research and advertising industries. An ADI is a geographic area in which stations located within the geographic area receive the preponderance of total viewing

Electronic panels: group of households whose television viewing is recorded electronically.

People meter: a device that allows individuals to indicate when they are watching a television program.

ADI: the geographic area in which stations located within the area receive the preponderance of total viewing time.

hours. Arbitron is developing a 2,000-household people meter panel that will compete with Nielsen's national panel.

UPC Consumer Scanner Panels

UPC consumer scanner panels: composed of a group of households who record their purchases of UPC-coded items with an electronic scanner.

UPC consumer scanner panels are composed of households who record their purchases of UPC-coded items with an electronic scanner. Nielsen and IRI have scanner-based panels in selected cities. Two approaches are used in such panels—automatic in-store data collection at checkout using the store's scanner system and at-home data collection using a hand-held scanner (see Research Application 5–7.)

IRI is the largest supplier of consumer scanner panel data. Its panel consists of more than 60,000 households in 26 cities. Panel members are recruited to match national and local demographic profiles. Substantial demographic and other background data are collected on each participating household. Each panel member is then provided an ID number that is entered at the checkout counter as the purchases are scanned. The purchase data are automatically transmitted to IRI's central computer for analysis.

The second approach to using scanners for data collection is being used by Nielsen in its 40,000 member ScanTrack National Household Panel. ScanTrack panel members use hand-held scanners to record their packaged goods purchases from all outlets.

Compared to the automatic system used by IRI, the hand-held scanner system requires considerably more effort on the part of the respondent. Not only must the items be scanned at home, but store (once per trip), price (for the approximately 30 percent of total items not purchased at a cooperating store that provides prices directly to Nielsen), and deal data must be entered manually. Inaccurate recall or checking of price information, items consumed before they are brought home, and unscanned purchases due to time pressures may affect the accuracy of this approach. However, validation studies indicate that these are not major problems. The system has the *important* advantage of allowing purchases from all types of stores to be scanned rather than just those stores with scanners who have agreed to participate. Arbitron also uses wands in its UPC scanner panels.

As we will see in the next section, UPC consumer scanner panels are increasingly being combined with electronic panels to create *single-source data*.

Single-Source Data

Single-source data: continuous data derived from the same respondent or household, covering at least television viewing and product purchase information.

Single-source data are continuous data derived from the same respondent or household, covering at least television viewing and product purchase information. In general, the data are collected electronically and also contain in-store data such as price level, coupon use, and so forth. A complete system requires frequent in-store observation using an approach such as BOS (see Research Application 5–5) to measure stock-outs, displays, and so forth. The advantages of such a system are substantial, as it can produce virtually real-time measures of advertising effectiveness, the effects of repetition, product changes, and so forth.[8]

RESEARCH APPLICATION 5-7

Nielsen's UPC Household Panel Scanner Wand

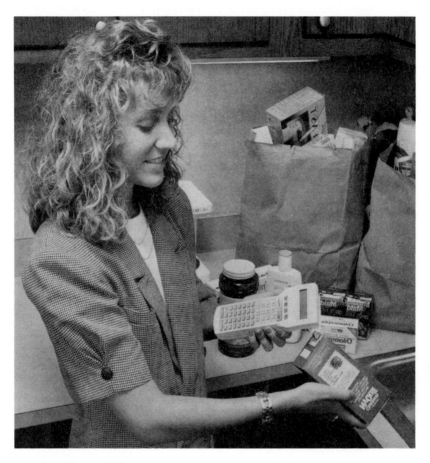

SOURCE: Courtesy of Nielsen Household Services.

A number of organizations have or are developing varying levels of single-source capability. IRI's BehaviorScan system is a subset of its scanner panel (discussed earlier) that has electronic monitoring of TV viewing. The Nielsen panel described earlier also has TV viewing monitored by meters in a 4,500-home subset of its at-home hand-held scanner panel. Panel members' newspaper and magazine readership are also recorded.

Applications of Commercial Surveys, Audits, and Panels

In the previous sections we described the characteristics of commercial surveys, audits, and panels. In this section we highlight the information available from such sources.

Retail Sales

Retail sales data are available from both audits and scanner-based retail panels. Scanner panels provide more current data at shorter time intervals than do audits. However, audits cover outlets not equipped with scanners.

Scanner data are useful to both retailers and manufacturers for measuring the aggregate impact of coupons, in-store promotions, point-of-purchase displays, price discounts, and so forth. Table 5–2 illustrates the use of this type of data to analyze price promotions. Measuring only the sales of the promoted brand would lead a manager to conclude that the fifth (least) most popular brand should be promoted. However, an analysis of category sales reveals that sales increases of minor brands on sale come as a result of the cannibalization of the more popular brands. In contrast, price reductions on the leading brands appear to increase overall category sales.

Data and analyses such as those shown in Table 5–2 are particularly useful for retailers. PromotionScan, a tracking service based on IRI's retail panel, is particularly useful to manufacturers. In one application, a snack-food manufacturer was running a national promotional campaign with no regional variation. PromotionScan analysis quickly revealed strong regional variations in response to the promotion. The manufacturer was then able to reduce spending in low-response areas. The results were stable overall revenues with a 20 percent reduction in promotion expenditures.[9]

TABLE 5–2 Sale Price Analysis Using Retail Scanner Data

	Percentage Increase in Margarine Brand (Category) Sales				
Price Discount (%)	Leading Brand	2nd Leading Brand	3rd Leading Brand	4th Leading Brand	5th Leading Brand
10	50 (5)	53 (5)	51 (2)	52 (1)	63 (1)
20	137 (16)	145 (14)	141 (6)	144 (6)	182 (1)
30	296 (38)	319 (35)	307 (16)	316 (16)	425 (5)

SOURCE: R. C. Blattberg, W. R. Bishop Jr., "Make Sense and Dollars from Scan Data," *The Nielsen Researcher* (Spring 1987), 19.

RESEARCH APPLICATION 5–8

Predicting New Product Sales Using Household Panel Data

The following graph shows Fruit Float's early share performance . . . by most measures an apparent success in the making in the $110,000,000 packaged pudding/whipped dessert market.

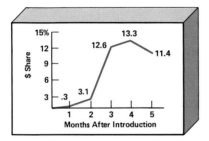

Period of Initial Trial	Share Contribution in Months After Introduction											
	1	2	3	4	5	6	7	8	9	10	11	12
1	.3	–	–	–	–	–	–	–	–	–	–	–
2		3.1	.7	.2	.2	.2	.2	.1	–	.1	–	.1
3			11.9	1.4	.5	–	–	.2	.1	.2	.1	–
4				11.7	1.7	.8	.2	.4	.2	.1	.1	.3
5					9.2	1.4	.8	.3	.1	.2	.1	.1
6						4.4	.8	.5	.2	.2	.1	.2
7							3.2	.8	.4	.4	.2	–
8								6.0	.9	.6	.4	.2
9									1.6	.3	.1	.1
10										5.5	.9	.5
11											3.4	.5
12												2.1
Total Share	.3	3.1	12.6	13.3	11.6	6.8	5.2	8.3	3.5	7.6	6.4	4.1
Trial Component	.3	3.1	11.9	11.7	9.2	4.4	3.2	6.0	1.6	5.5	3.4	2.1
Repeat Component	–	–	.7	1.6	2.4	2.4	2.0	2.3	1.9	2.1	2.0	2.0

COMPONENTS OF MARKET SHARE

But a detailed look at the composition of that early share indicated repeat purchases were slow to build; only strong continuing trial purchases supported sales . . . when trial purchases ceased, share declined dramatically.

This could easily be seen even at five months when total share was broken apart into the contribution from new buyers (trial component) versus repurchases by earlier triers (repeat component):

While the poor repeat purchase volume in this example was easily spotted even in the above simplistic manner, most products require more sophisticated analysis to predict long run share. To do this, NPD uses three different forecasting models.

SOURCE: *Sharpening Marketing Decisions with Diary Panels* (National Purchase Diary Panel, Inc., 1975), 13. Used with permission.

Household Purchases

Data on household consumption are available from both diary- and scanner-based household panels. Household consumption data allow the firm to monitor shifts in an individual's or market segment's purchasing patterns over time. This allows the firm to evaluate the effects of both its own and its competitors' marketing activities on specific market segments. For example, if a competitor introduces a larger package, the firm can tell what type (demographic and product usage characteristics) and how many people are switching to the new size.

Household panel data also serve as an important basis for forecasting the sales level or market share of a new product. A new product often attracts a number of purchasers simply because it is new. However, its ultimate success depends on how many of these initial purchasers become repeat purchasers. Research Application 5–8 illustrates this problem and describes one solution.

TABLE 5–3 Major Data Sources on Media Usage

Media	Organization	Methodology
Newspapers	Simmons Market Research	National personal interviews (annual)
	Birch/Scarborough	Top market telephone interviews (annual)
Magazines	Standard Rate and Data	Semiannual circulation data
	Birch/Scarborough	Top market telephone interviews (annual)
	Simmons Market Research	National personal interview (annual)
	Starch INRA Hooper	Recall of readership of specific ads based on personal interviews of 100 or more of each gender
Radio	Arbitron	Top market periodic one-week diaries
	Statistical Research	Repeat interviews (7 consecutive days) by phone with 12,000 respondents to measure network radio listening
Television	Nielsen TV Index	National people meter panel (can be combined with scanner panel data) and top market diaries
	Nielsen Station Index	One-week diaries 7 times a year in 200 local markets
	Simmons	National 2-week diary (annual)
	Arbitron	Top market (212) one-week diaries with television meters in 17 markets
		National panel using people meters is being developed
	IRI	Selected market television meters (can be combined with scanner panel data)
	Birch/Scarborough	Top market one-week diary (annual)
Billboards	Traffic Audit Bureau	Number of people passing specific locations
Yellow Pages	National Yellow Pages Monitor (NFO)	Two-week diaries in selected markets

Media Usage

Given the billions spent on advertising, it is not surprising that substantial effort is expended to measure media usage. Table 5–3 describes the major data sources available.

Attitudes/Knowledge/Behaviors

Commercial surveys, both periodic and panel-based, are the primary general sources of data on consumer attitudes, knowledge, and behavior. For example, a firm desiring to improve or alter its corporate image could engage in a variety of advertising and public relations programs in different regions of the country. Using one of the weekly shared-interview services, it could economically determine the relative impact on each approach over time.

MRCA provides a popular service for the food industry with its Menu Census. This service has the following characteristics:

- 2,000 households per year, containing over 5,500 members, based on rotating samples of 500 households per quarter
- Nationally representative samples—matched to U.S. Census figures for census regions, metro area size, household size, homemaker age, household income
- Diaries returned each day
- Each household reports the eatings of each household member for 14 consecutive days
- About 6 households start reporting each day of the year
- 77 diaries cover each day of the year
- All in-home and away-from-home food and beverage consumption is reported
- All ingredients and cooking agents used to prepare foods at home are included
- How dishes are prepared, including details on brand name, form as purchased, and packaging material
- Household demographics, household-member classifications, and attitudes, awareness, and interests of the homemaker are provided

Standard International Commercial Data Sources

The United States and Canada have the largest variety of standard commercial data sources. A similar though smaller array is available in most other developed countries.[10] For example, Nielsen operates people meter television viewing monitors in Australia, Finland, France, and Japan. (Video Research is the largest TV rating firm in Japan.) Nielsen also measures pan-European advertising using diaries kept by household who subscribe to European cable channels. AGB, a European firm, operates people meters in six other European countries.

INRA conducts a worldwide omnibus survey, INRABUS, 10 times a year in major international markets and four times in other markets. The field work is conducted simultaneously in all countries. In each survey, face-to-face interviews with 1,000 adults per country are conducted. Clients can choose the countries in which their questions are asked.

Nielsen operates a UPC household scanner panel in the United Kingdom that is similar to its U.S. operation. It tracks product sales through both store and household panels throughout the EC. The Henley Centre for Forecasting and Research International provides *Frontiers*, an annual in-depth examination and forecast of consumer attitudes and behaviors across Europe.

In Japan, Hakuhodo has developed a database containing over 100,000 recent Japanese print ads (with over 6,000 being added each month). This allows firms to monitor competitors' advertising strategies and to analyze the positions of the various brands in an industry. This development is consistent with the recent rapid increase in the use of formal marketing research, scanner data, commercial surveys, panel data, and related types of information by Japanese managers.[11]

The preceding examples barely scratch the surface of the data and services available in various countries. The international manager should utilize these sources in the same manner as their domestic counterparts.

Summary

Commercial surveys are conducted by research firms. Periodic surveys are conducted at regular intervals, focusing on the same topic but using a new sample of respondents for each survey. Panel surveys are conducted on the same respondents, generally at irregular intervals, covering a variety of topics. A continuous panel involves the same respondents providing information on the same topic over time. Shared surveys are administered by a research firm and consist of questions submitted by multiple clients.

A store audit involves periodically visiting a set of stores and examining their inventories and purchases to determine the sales of specific brands. Product audits are similar to store audits but focus on products and attempt to cover all the types of outlets for a product category. Retail distribution audits are observational studies that measure how brands within specified product categories are displayed, priced, and so forth in retail outlets.

A retail panel involves a research firm purchasing UPC scanner or EPOS data from a sample of retail outlets and preparing and selling brand sales data. A consumer diary panel is a sample of households who continuously record their purchases of selected products in a diary.

Electronic panels are composed of households whose television viewing behavior is recorded electronically, typically with people meters. A people meter is a device that (1) automatically records when a television is turned on and to which station, (2) has a remote control that allows each family member and visitors to "log on" when they begin watching, and (3) sends these data by telephone line to a central computer for processing.

UPC consumer scanner panels are composed of households who record their purchases of UPC-coded products with an electronic scanner. IRI's 60,000 panel members are given an ID number that is entered into participating stores' scanning systems when they make a purchase. These purchase data are automatically transferred to IRI's central computer for processing. Nielsen's 40,000 panel members scan their purchases at home using a hand-held scanner. The data from the scanner are then sent to Nielsen's computer over the telephone.

Single-source data are continuous data derived from the same respondents, covering at least television viewing and product purchases. Both IRI and Nielsen offer single-source panels in which television viewing is measured electronically, purchases are measured by scanners, and store-level variables are measured by observation.

Several standard commercial data sources measure the usage of each major type of media. There are also a variety of recurrent measures of attitudes, knowledge, values, and behaviors of both individuals and businesses.

While the U.S. and Canada have the largest variety of standard commercial data sources, a similar though smaller array is available in most developed economies.

Review Questions

5.1. What is a *commercial survey*? A *periodic survey*? A *panel survey*? A *shared survey*?

5.2. Describe the *National Restaurant Market Index*.

5.3. What is an *interval panel*? What are the advantages and problems of surveys based on interval panels?

5.4. How does the NFO interval panel differ from the CMP interval panel?

5.5. What are the advantages of a *shared survey*?

5.6. What is an *audit*?

5.7. How does a *store audit* differ from a *product audit*?

5.8. What is a *retail distribution audit*?

5.9. What is a *panel*? A *continuous panel*?

5.10. What are *retail panels*? What are their advantages?

5.11. What is a *UPC bar code*? An *EPOS*?

5.12. What is a *consumer diary panel*? What are its advantages?

5.13. What are *consumer scanner panels*? What are their advantages?

5.14. How does IRI's approach to consumer scanner panels differ from Nielsen's? What are the advantages of each?

5.15. What are *electronic panels*? What are their problems and benefits?

5.16. What is a *people meter*?

5.17. What is meant by *single-source* data?

5.18. Describe two single-source data systems.

5.19. What are the primary commercial data sources available for:
   a. retail sales
   b. household consumption
   c. consumer attitudes, knowledge, or behaviors

5.20. What are the primary commercial data sources available on consumers' use of
   a. newspapers
   b. magazines
   c. radio
   d. television
   e. billboards
   f. yellow pages

5.21. What types of standard commercial data sources are available outside the U.S.?

Discussion Questions/Problems

5.22. Do shared surveys generate primary or secondary data?

5.23. Describe how a brand manager could use Audits & Surveys National Restaurant Market Index (Research Application 5–1).

5.24. What type of nonresponse error is likely to affect interval panel surveys? What can be done about this?

5.25. Describe three marketing problems for which *each* of the following would be an appropriate technique (12 problems in total):
   a. a periodic commercial survey
   b. a one-time interval panel survey
   c. a one-time shared survey
   d. a series of shared surveys

5.26. Describe three marketing problems for which each of the following would be an appropriate technique (12 in total)
   a. retail store audit
   b. household diary panel
   c. household scanner panel
   d. single-source data

5.27. Do you think single-source data dominate the panel data field by 2000? Why or why not?

5.28. What problems do you see with people meters?

5.29. Describe three marketing problems for which INRABUS could provide useful information.

5.30. On Wednesday, the major news networks carried a story indicating that one of your firm's plants was causing significant pollution to a recreational waterway. While repairs to the plant have already begun, you need to assess the story's impact to decide if you need a communications campaign to counteract its effects. What data sources would you use?

Projects/Activities

5.31. Keep a record of your television viewing for two weeks. Have a friend do the same. How accurate is your record? How accurate do you think your friend's is? What could be done to improve the accuracy?

5.32. Keep a record of your radio listening for two weeks. Have a friend do the same. How accurate is your record? How accurate do you think your friend's is? What could be done to improve the accuracy?

5.33. Keep a record of the food and beverage you consume for two weeks. Have a friend do the same. How accurate is your record? How accurate do you think your friend's is? What could be done to improve the accuracy?

5.34. Keep a record of your personal grooming activities for two weeks. Have a friend do the same. How accurate is your record? How accurate do you think your friend's is? What could be done to improve the accuracy?

5.35. Interview one of the following people and ascertain the sources of media usage that he or she feels are most important.
   a. local radio station manager
   b. local television station manager
   c. local newspaper manager

5.36. Interview one of the following people and ascertain the sources of media usage that he or she feels are most important.
  a. media manager for a local ad agency
  b. advertising manager for a major department store
  c. marketing/advertising manager for a consumer goods manufacturer

Notes

1. *Insights into Consumer Behavior* (New York: The NPD Group, 1987), 8.
2. "Merchandise Ploys Effective? Scanners Know," *Marketing News* (January 4, 1985), 17. See also D. H. Schmalenese, "Exciting Breakthroughs in Sales Promotion Research," *Marketing Research* (September 1989), 34–42.
3. J. M. Sinlcula, "Some Factors Affecting the Adoption of Scanner-Based Research," *Journal of Advertising Research* (May 1991), 50–55.
4. For technical discussions see J. Hansen, "How Problematic Are Random Responses in Panel Studies," *European Research* (February 1988), 34–41; and A. M. Abernethy, "The Accuracy of Diary Measures of Car Radio Audiences," *Journal of Advertising* 3 (1989), 33–39.
5. A detailed description of geodemographic segmentation systems and the PRIZM system in particular is in D. I. Hawkins, R. J. Best, K. A. Coney, *Consumer Behavior* (Homewood, IL.: Irwin, 1992), 336–347. VALS II is described on pages 329–335.
6. A. S. C. Ehrenberg, J. Wakshlag, "Repeat-Viewing with People Meters," *Journal of Advertising Research* (February 1987), 9–13: "Nielsen People Meter Service Launched," *Nielsen Newscast* 3 (1987); L. R. Stoddard, Jr., "The History of People Meters," *Journal of Advertising Research*

(October 1987), 10–12; and P. Soong, "The Statistical Reliability of People Meter Ratings," *Journal of Advertising Research* (February 1988), 50–56.
7. L. G. Coleman, "People Meter Rerun," *Marketing News* (September 2, 1991), 1.
8. M. Prince, "Some Uses and Abuses of Single-Source Data for Promotional Decision Making," *Marketing Research* (December 1989), 18–22; G. D. Metzger, "Single Source: Yes and No," *Marketing Research* (December 1990), 27–33; and H. Assael, D. F. Poltrack, "Using Single-Source Data to Select TV Programs Based on Purchasing Behavior," *Journal of Advertising Research* (September 1991), 9–17.
9. J. Larkin, "Shifted Emphasis Cuts Costs," *InfoScan News* (November 1987), 7.
10. A. Wicks, "Advertising Research—An Eclectic View from the UK"; R. G. Stout, N. Dalvi, "Improving the Effectiveness of Multicountry Tracking"; and P. Freeman, "Continuous Surveys and Tracking in the UK"; all in *Journal of the Market Research Society* (October 1989), 526–565.
11. K. Kobayashi, P. Draper, "Reviews of Market Research in Japan"; and K. Fujitake, "The Transition and Future of Marketing Research"; both in *Journal of Advertising Research* (May 1990), 13–18, 58–67.

6

Survey Research

LEARNING OBJECTIVES

Upon completing this chapter, you should be able to:

1. Describe the four basic types of surveys.

2. Evaluate each of the four basic types of surveys on each of the seven primary criteria used to determine which type to use.

3. Describe the advantages and disadvantages of a mall intercept interview relative to an at-home personal interview.

4. Describe the advantages and disadvantages of a CATI relative to a standard telephone interview.

5. Explain random-digit dialing and why it is used.

6. Explain nonresponse error and indicate why it is a major concern in survey research.

7. Describe the best techniques for reducing nonresponse to surveys.

8. Discuss the three strategies for dealing with potential nonresponse error.

9. Discuss the unique issues encountered in multinational surveys.

Hallmark Cards Use of Computer Interviews

Hallmark Cards introduces hundreds of new cards each year, They must also delete cards with sentiments or expressions that are not current. By the late 1980s, research on new cards and card deletions involved almost 25,000 personal interviews per year. Hallmark's traditional paper-and-pencil survey methodology required up to 35 days to conduct and process a 200-interview survey. The increasing number of interviews and the need for rapid results to keep current in a rapidly changing world led Hallmark's research department to test and adopt computer interviews.

Traditionally, Hallmark would have respondents selected at a shopping mall come to a room that contained four or five six-foot tables. The tables were divided into 10 sections, each of which held five cards. Respondents would walk past the tables and evaluate each card on a six-point excellent-to-poor scale by writing the number of each card and its score on a form. They would then choose the eight cards they would be most likely to buy and record their numbers on the form. They would also indicate the age and relationship of the person who would receive the card. Finally, basic demographic and some attitude information would be solicited.

Each interview had to be edited to be sure that all card numbers had been entered correctly and that each card had been evaluated once and only once. Then the data were coded, key-punched, and verified.

Hallmark now uses Sawtooth Software's Ci2 computer interactive interviewing software. Greeting cards are grouped into 10 stacks of five each. Respondents are handed a stack and they read the card numbers and the scores they assign them to the interviewer, who enters this information into a PC. For each set of 10 stacks (50 cards), respondents hold up the eight cards they are most likely to buy. They also indicate the age and relationship of the recipient. The same demographic and attitude data are collected. The interview lasts only 18 minutes (having the respondents enter their responses directly into the PC without the assistance of an interviewer requires 28 minutes).

The Ci2 system eliminates the need for editing, coding, or verifying. The codes are built into the system. It will not accept invalid card numbers nor will it allow the same number to be entered twice. It also prevents the interviewer from moving on until all 50 cards in each set are evaluated.

After careful evaluation, Hallmark has concluded that computer interviewing is both faster and more accurate than their traditional approach. According to a Hallmark researcher: "Marketers need to make decisions based on today's preferences, and this technology brings them much closer to their goal."[1]

Survey research is concerned with the administration of questionnaires (interviewing). In this chapter, a number of issues associated with administering a questionnaire are examined. First, the various types of surveys are described. The criteria relevant for judging which type of survey to use in a particular situation are discussed in some detail. Next, an in-depth treatment of the problem of nonresponse error is provided. Finally, the problems and processes encountered in multinational surveys are discussed.

The Nature of Survey Research

Survey research:
the systematic
gathering of
information.

Survey research is the systematic gathering of information from respondents in an interview using a set of questions, generally in the form of a questionnaire. An **interview** is the administration of a questionnaire to an individual or group of individuals.

Types of Surveys

Interview:
the administration
of a questionnaire
to an individual
or group of
individuals.

Surveys are generally classified according to the method of communication used in the interviews: personal, telephone, mail, or computer. Figure 6–1 indicates the relative popularity of three of these techniques. (Personal interviews are broken into mall intercept and door-to-door categories.) Computer interviews are less common. Each of the four methods is described briefly in the following sections.

Personal Interviews

**Personal
interview:**
the administration
of the
questionnaire in a
face-to-face setting.

In a **personal interview,** the interviewer asks the questions of the respondent in a face-to-face situation. The interview may take place at the respondent's home or at a central location, such as a shopping mall or a research office.

**Mall intercept
interviews:**
selecting
respondents at a
shopping mall and
interviewing them
at the mall.

Mall intercept interviews involve stopping shoppers in a shopping mall at random, qualifying them if necessary, inviting them into the research firm's interviewing facilities that are located at the mall, and conducting the interview. Qualifying a respondent means ensuring that the respondent meets the sampling criteria. This could involve a quota sample when interviews are desired of a given number of people with certain demographic characteristics such as age and gender. Or it could involve ensuring that all the respondents use the product category being investigated.

As Figure 6–1 indicates, *mall intercept interviews* are the predominant type of personal interview. The popularity of this type of personal interview is the result of its cost advantage over door-to-door interviewing, the ability to demonstrate products or use equipment that is not easily transported, greater

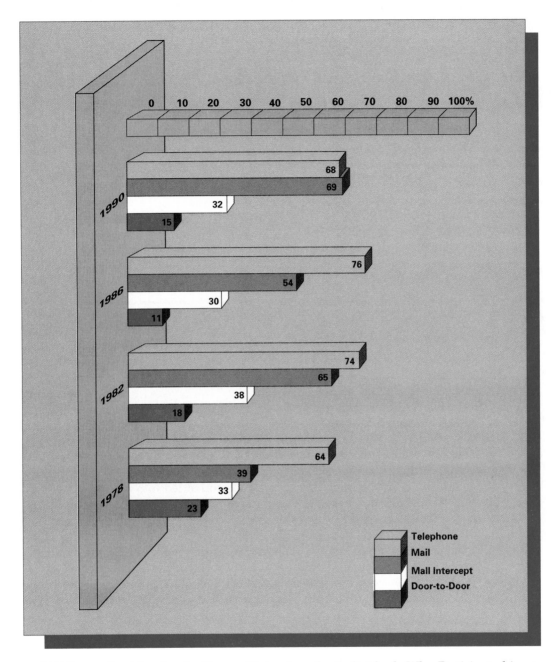

FIGURE 6–1 Participation by Type of Interview (by Individuals Who Participated in at Least One Survey in the Past Year)

SOURCE: "Participation Up," *Industry Image Survey* (Indianapolis, Walker Research, Inc. 1990), 2.

supervision of interviewers, and less elapsed time required. Research Application 6–1 describes the facilities available at a typical mall interview location.

Individuals who visit shopping malls are *not* representative of the entire population of the United States. However, most applied research studies do not require such a sample. For many consumer products, shopping mall

RESEARCH APPLICATION 6–1

Facilities Available at a Market Facts, Inc., Mall Interview Location

- Sound-conditioned interview rooms and booths
- Flexible areas for large displays
- Fully equipped kitchen with freezer storage
- Studio-quality monitoring system with three one-way mirrors, including kitchen observation
- Full-sound and closed-circuit TV monitors, cassette, reel-to-reel, and three-quarter-inch videotape recorders

- Focus group facilities
- Controlled track lighting
- Client conference room
- Twin vanity rooms
- INTERQUEST, an on-line CRT (computer) interviewing technique

---

customers constitute a major share of the market and therefore are an adequate sampling universe. In addition, careful control procedures can provide fairly representative samples (see Chapter 14).

Of course, intercept interviews are not limited to shopping malls. Increasingly, intercept interviews are conducted at locations relevant to the population of interest. For example, Burgoyne has conducted intercept interviews at specialty retail outlets such as pet stores, banks, fast food restaurants, truck stops, stadiums, movie theaters, golf courses, bowling alleys, and college campuses. Some research firms have vans converted into interview facilities which provide many of the features described in Research Application 6–1 in a "portable" format.

An emerging type of personal interviewing is the *in-store intercept*. In-store intercept interviews involve interviewing individuals inside retail outlets, generally immediately after they have purchased the product category in question. One version of this approach, the purchase intercept technique (PIT), is described in Research Application 6–2.

Telephone Interviews

Telephone interviews: presentation of the questionnaire by telephone.

Telephone interviews involve the presentation of the questionnaire by telephone. Low-priced WATS (Wide Area Telephone Service) lines have made nationwide telephone interviewing from a central location practical.

Computer-assisted telephone interviewing (CATI) requires the interviewer to read the questions from a computer screen and to enter the responses directly into the computer. A stand-alone CATI system involves programming a survey directly into one or more personal computers. The telephone interviewer then reads the questions from a television-type screen and records the answers directly on the terminal keyboard or directly on the screen with a light pen.

RESEARCH APPLICATION 6–2

The Purchase Intercept Technique

The purchase intercept technique (PIT) involves (1) observing shoppers purchasing the product category in a sample of stores, (2) recording relevant observational data such as brand(s) and size(s) purchased, and (3) interviewing the purchasers immediately to ascertain purchase motives, brands considered, and so forth.

This approach offers a number of advantages. First, the observational portion ensures accuracy in terms of brand and size purchased. This is a particularly important feature because consumers frequently are incorrect in reporting the last brand purchased. Second, the questions are presented while the decision is fresh in the respondent's mind. This not only improves recall but, since the questioning seems relevant, also results in high response rates. This in turn leads to a relatively low cost per completed interview. Third, there is no doubt that the actual purchaser is responding to the questions. Finally, the researcher can control, or at least measure, the actual purchase environment such as shelf facing and POP material.

This approach is particularly appropriate for items purchased infrequently and low-involvement products. In both cases, the closeness of the purchase and questioning enhances recall of the actual decision process used. It is also valuable when data are needed quickly on the impact of new marketing efforts by the firm or its competition. In addition, it can be used to generate a sample frame for subsequent detailed interviews.

The PIT approach has several weaknesses as well: (1) the sample is constrained to those who purchase during the time of the study, (2) the sample is limited to purchasers rather than users or deciders, (3) some stores will not allow in-store interviewing, (4) nonstore purchasers are excluded, and (5) it uses personal interviews and is subject to the problems associated with this form of data collection.

SOURCE: S. H. McIntyre, S.D.F.G. Bender, "The Purchase Intercept Technique (PIT) in Comparison to Telephone and Mail Surveys," *Journal of Retailing* (Winter 1986), 364–383; and G. Meyers, "Consumers Offer 'Fresh' Purchase Data When Questioned in the Store," *Marketing News* (January 2, 1987), 28–29.

CATI systems have a number of advantages. Often the exact set of questions a respondent is to receive depends on answers to earlier questions. For example, individuals who have a child under age three might receive one set of questions concerning food purchases whereas other individuals would receive a different set. The computer, in effect, allows the creation of an "individualized" questionnaire for each respondent based on answers to prior questions.

A second advantage is the ability of the computer to present different versions of the same question automatically. For example, when asking people questions that have several stated alternatives, it is desirable to rotate the order in which the alternatives are presented. This is easy with a CATI system.

Another advantage of CATI systems is the ease and speed with which a "bad" question can be changed or a new question added. CATI systems can also edit data as they are entered. That is, the computer can be programmed

Computer-assisted telephone interviewing (CATI): the interviewer reads the questions directly from a computer screen and enters the responses directly into the computer.

to highlight inconsistent answers across questions, to refuse answers outside a defined range, to ensure that constant sum question responses total properly, and so forth.

Finally, data can easily be analyzed and interim reports issued. Interim reports may allow one to stop a survey if the "answer" becomes clear before the scheduled number of interviews has been completed. Final reports can also be produced rapidly.

In addition to stand-alone CATI systems, network or linked systems are gaining widespread use. A network CATI system links up to 60 PCs to a main PC or larger computer. The system performs the same as the stand-alone CATI. In addition, it performs most aspects of survey administration. That is, the control unit handles random digit dialing or other sampling procedures, automatically schedules recalls for not-at-homes and busy signals, provides automatic quota controls as required, monitors call disposition by interviewer, performs interim data analysis, and so forth.

CATI systems are most appropriate for complex and/or large-sample surveys. The substantial amount of up-front programming required reduces their value for other applications. However, packaged systems such as Sawtooth Software's Ci2 CATI System™ handle most of the required programming and are reasonably priced ($7,500 for software to support a six-station network).[2]

Mail Interviews

Mail interviews:
are mailed to the respondent and the completed questionnaires are returned by mail.

Mail interviews are mailed to the respondent and the completed questionnaires are returned by mail to the researcher. As Figure 6–1 indicates, mail interviews are widely used.

Computer Interviews

Computer interview:
the computer presents the questions directly to the respondent on a screen and the respondent answers directly on the computer console.

In a **computer interview,** the computer presents the questions to the respondents on a screen and respondents answer via a console, or a computer-generated voice asks questions on the telephone and respondents answer by using the buttons on their touch-tone phones.[3] This system reduces interviewer bias and interaction problems. In addition, it provides the same flexibility and speed advantages associated with the CATI systems described earlier. However, it does require the respondent to be willing and able to interact directly with the computer. Open-ended questions are seldom practical as they would require a typed response.

Computer interviewing is gaining acceptance. Kentucky Fried Chicken recently converted their twice-a-month, 120-respondent Research Guidance Test (RGT) interviews from a personal format to a computer format using Sawtooth Software's Ci2 System™. The RGT surveys involve both attitude measures and taste tests. Preliminary studies found that 78–97 percent of the participants liked the computer interview experience "very much" (the variance was based on the type of hardware used). The firm has realized the following advantages since converting to computer interviews:

RESEARCH APPLICATION 6–3

Computer Interviewing of Automobile Consumers

The client needed detailed information involving complicated skip patterns as well as a large sample size of both recent and prospective new car buyers. It also had a limited budget. Computer interviews were conducted at the Chicago Auto Show.

Ten IBM PCs (640k, dual floppy, color monitor) were rented and placed in a booth at the show labeled with a banner "1989 Automobile Survey." As an incentive, each respondent was entered in a drawing for several prizes. Booth attendants were hired through a temporary employment agency. Two attendants were in the booth at all times. One served as a screener and only admitted respondents to the booth who (1) had purchased a new car in the past 12 months or planned to purchase one in the next 12 months, and (2) did not work in the automobile or advertising industries. The second attendant seated the respondent and provided the initial instructions. This attendant also changed the interview disks as required. A line of people was generally waiting to participate.

Almost 2,600 interviews were completed (1,000 purchasers and 1,600 prospects). Less than 1 percent terminated the interview before completion. Costs for the study were as follows:

PCs	$ 1,800
Booth	1,800
Attendants	4,200
Security	1,200
Disks	200
Prizes	850
Total	$10,050

SOURCE: L. Middleton, "Computer Interviewing—A Creative Approach," *Sawtooth News* (Winter 1990), 4.

- Questionnaire generation time has been cut from four hours to about one hour
- Paper requirements have been greatly reduced
- Average time per interview has been reduced by 50 percent
- Data analysis is completed the day after the interviews are completed
- The obtained data are more accurate[4]

Computer interviewing is most common in industrial and trade (distribution) applications. Trade shows are frequently used as locations for conducting interviews with engineers, purchasers, and other industrial respondents as well as with consumers. Research Application 6–3 describes how almost 2,600 computer interviews were completed in nine days for only $10,050 at the Chicago Auto Show.

One area in which computer interviewing is not gaining acceptance is in telephone applications. Refusal rates for computer interviews have been found to be twice those for identical traditional telephone interviews (53 percent vs. 26 percent). Other studies have obtained completion rates with computer interviews that were only one-tenth the rate for a similar traditional telephone interview (7.5 percent vs. 74 percent). However, one study found this approach to be superior for respondents under 50 years old.[5]

Criteria for the Selection of a Survey Method

A number of criteria are relevant for judging which type of survey to use in a particular situation. These criteria are (1) *complexity*, (2) *required amount of data*, (3) *desired accuracy*, (4) *sample control*, (5) *time requirements*, (6) *acceptable level of nonresponse*, and (7) *cost*.

Complexity of the Questionnaire

Although researchers generally attempt to minimize complexity, some subject areas still require relatively complex questionnaires. For example, the sequence or number of questions asked often depends on the answer to previous questions. Consider the following questions:

2a. Have you ever read a copy of the evening *Tribune?*
    __ YES
    __ NO (GO TO Q. 3a)

  b. Did you happen to read or look into a weekday copy—that is, a Monday to Friday copy, of the *Tribune* during the past seven days?
    __ YES, HAVE READ
    __ NO, HAVE NOT READ (GO TO Q. 3a)
    __ DON'T KNOW (GO TO Q. 3a)

  c. *Not counting today,* when was the last time you read or looked into a weekday copy of the *Tribune?*
(IF TODAY, ASK:) And when was the last time before today?
    __ YESTERDAY
    __ EARLIER THAN YESTERDAY
    __ DON'T KNOW

It would make very little sense to ask someone question 2b if the response to question 2a had been "No." A trained interviewer who has practiced administering a given questionnaire can handle such "skip" questions. Similarly, a computer will present such questions in the correct order, based on the respondent's earlier answers. However, a respondent seeing a questionnaire of this type for the first time can easily become confused or discouraged. Thus, computer, personal, and telephone interviews are better suited to collect this type of information than are mail interviews.

Other aspects of complexity also tend to favor the use of personal or computer interviews. Visual cues are necessary for many projective techniques, such as the picture response. Multiple-choice questions often require a visual presentation of the alternatives because the respondent cannot remember more than a few when they are presented orally. However, most attitude scales can be administered by phone.[6]

The telephone, and often mail, are inappropriate for studies that require the respondent to react to the actual product, advertising copy, package design, or other physical characteristics. Techniques that require relatively complex instructions are best administered by means of personal interviews. Similarly, if the response required by the technique is extensive, such as with many conjoint analysis studies, personal interviews are better, with computers second.

Amount of Data

Closely related to the issue of complexity is the amount of data to be generated by a given questionnaire. The amount of data actually involves two separate issues: (1) *How much time will it take to complete the entire questionnaire?* and (2) *How much effort is required by the respondent to complete the questionnaire?* For example, one open-ended question may take a respondent five minutes to answer, and a 25-item multiple-choice questionnaire may take the same length of time. Moreover, much more effort may go into writing down a five-minute essay than in checking off choices on 25 multiple-choice questions.

Personal interviews can, in general, be longer than other types. Social motives play an important role in personal interviews. It would be "impolite" to terminate an interview with someone in a face-to-face situation. However, the refusal rate has been found to double (from 21 to 41 percent) when either telephone or personal interviews last over five minutes.[7]

Telephone interviews are traditionally shorter than personal interviews. The ease of terminating a telephone conversation, coupled with the more suspicious nature of a telephone call, tends to limit the length of time a person will spend on a telephone.

Mail surveys are probably affected more by the type of questions than by the absolute length of the questionnaire. Open-ended questions require considerable effort on the part of the respondent, whereas an equally long multiple-choice response takes much less effort. The intuitive idea that short questionnaires will generate a higher response rate than longer questionnaires has *not* been supported by research on mail questionnaires but does hold for telephone and personal interviews.[8]

Accuracy of the Resultant Data

The accuracy of data obtained by surveys is affected by a number of factors, such as interviewer effects, sampling effects, and effects caused by questionnaire design. In this section, we are concerned with errors induced by the survey method itself, particularly responses to sensitive questions and interviewer effects.

Sensitive Questions

Personal interviews and, to a lesser extent, telephone interviews involve social interaction between the respondent and the interviewer. Therefore, there is concern that the respondent may not answer potentially embarrassing questions or questions with socially desirable responses accurately. Since mail and computer interviews reduce social interaction, it is often assumed that they will yield more accurate responses. However, research indicates that *well-constructed* and *well-administered* questionnaires *generally* yield similar results, regardless of the method of administration unless very sensitive topics such as illicit drug use are being investigated.[9]

Interviewer Effects

The ability of interviewers to alter questions, their appearance, their manner of speaking, the intentional and unintentional cues provided, and the way they probe can be a disadvantage. It means that, in effect, each respondent may receive a slightly different interview. Depending on the topic of the survey, the interviewer's social class, age, sex, race, authority, training, expectations, opinions, and voice *can* affect the results.[10]

The danger of interviewer effects is greatest in personal interviews. Telephone interviews are also subject to interviewer effects. Mail and computer surveys have minimal interviewer effects.

One final problem that arises with the use of telephone and personal interviews is *interviewer cheating*.[11] That is, for various reasons, interviewers may falsify all or parts of an interview. This is a severe enough problem that most commercial survey researchers engage in a process called *validation* or *verification*. For example, Sears requires that the local supervisor validate 10 percent of each interviewer's calls and that the central office validate an additional 15 percent. This is common throughout the industry.

Validation involves reinterviewing a sample of the population that completed the initial interview. In this reinterview, verification is sought that the interview took place and was conducted properly and completely.

Other Error Sources

Other types of inaccuracies can have a differential impact on the different methods of administration. The respondent cannot seek clarification of confusing questions or terms when mail surveys are used. In a personal interview the interviewer can, by observing the respondent closely, be sure that the respondent understands the question. Another potential problem with mail questionnaires is that respondents can read the entire questionnaire prior to answering the questions or they can change answers to earlier questions after seeing later questions. This may result in less spontaneous and less revealing answers. However, in general, all four methods of interviewing produce similar results.[12]

Sample Control

Each of the four interview techniques allows substantially different levels of control over *who* is interviewed. Personal interviews offer the most *potential* for control over the sample. An explicit list of individuals or households is *not* required. Although such lists are desirable, various forms of area sampling can help the researcher to overcome most of the problems caused by the absence of a complete sampling frame (see Chapter 14). In addition, the researcher can control who is interviewed within the sampling unit and how much assistance from other members of the unit is permitted.

Controlling *who* within the household is interviewed can be expensive. If the purpose of the research is to investigate *household* behavior, such as appliance ownership, any available adult will probably be satisfactory. However, if the purpose is to investigate *individual* behavior, interviewing the most readily available adult within the household often produces a biased sample.

Thus, the researcher must randomly select from among those living at each household. The simplest means of selection is to interview the adult who last had (or next will have) a birthday.[13] The odds of *a* household member being at home are substantially larger than the odds of a *specific* household member being available. This means that there will be more "not-at-homes," which increases interviewing costs substantially.

Personal and computer interviews conducted in central locations, such as shopping malls, lose much of the control possible with home interviews because the interview is limited to the individuals who visit the shopping mall.

Mail questionnaires require an explicit sampling frame composed of addresses, if not names and addresses. Such lists are generally unavailable for the general population.

Lists of specialized groups are more readily available. For example, a bank can easily compile a mailing list of its current checking account customers. Often, specific mailing lists can be purchased from firms that specialize in this area. One catalog contains approximately 20,000 lists, many of which can be subdivided on a state-by-state, regional, or ZIP sequence basis.[14] However, even with a good mailing list, the researcher maintains only limited control over *who* at the mailing address completes the questionnaire. Different family members frequently provide divergent answers to the same question. Although researchers can address the questionnaire to a specific household member, they cannot be sure who completes the questionnaire. Mailings to organizations have similar problems.

Telephone surveys are obviously limited to households with direct access to telephones. Although most businesses and U.S. households have a telephone, some groups, such as Hispanics, have a lower incidence of phone ownership.[15] However, the fact that telephone ownership is almost universal does not mean that lists of telephone numbers, such as telephone directories, are equally complete. Estimates of the percentage of phones not listed in a current telephone directory run as high as 60 percent for some areas, with a national average of approximately 31 percent.[16]

Unlisted phone numbers can be characterized as voluntarily unlisted and involuntarily unlisted. *Voluntarily unlisted* phone numbers are excluded at the owner's request. Voluntarily unlisted phone numbers are most common in urban areas and in the West. Research has shown significant differences between those with voluntarily unlisted numbers and those with listed numbers on such variables as ownership of luxury items and automobiles, housing characteristics, family composition, age, and other demographic and attitudinal variables.[17]

As the current telephone directory becomes older, the percentage of households with unlisted numbers increases because of new families moving into the area and others moving within the area. These *involuntarily unlisted* numbers generally consist of fewer than 10 percent of all phones.

Random Digit Dialing

To ensure more representative samples, researchers generally utilize some form of **random digit dialing** which requires that at least some of the digits of each sample phone number be generated randomly. The most popular technique, **plus-one** or **add-a-digit dialing,** simply requires the researcher to se-

Random digit dialing: requires that at least some of the digits of each sample phone number be generated randomly.

Plus-one (add-a-digit) dialing: involves randomly selecting a sample of phone numbers from a phone directory and adding *one* to each number selected.

lect a sample from an existing directory and add one to each number thus selected. Although the technique is more expensive than a sample selected directly from a directory,[18] and it has a higher refusal rate,[19] it produces a high contact rate and a fairly representative sample. A sophisticated version of this approach was found to reach 80 percent working numbers of which only 4 percent were business phones.[20]

Time Requirements

Telephone surveys generally require the least total time for completion. In addition, it is relatively easy to hire, train, control, and coordinate telephone interviewers. Therefore, the number of interviewers can often be expanded until any time constraint is satisfied.

The number of personal and computer interviewers can also be increased to reduce the total time required. However, problems with training, coordinating, and control tend to make this uneconomical after a certain point. Because "at-home" interviewers must travel between interviews, and often set up appointments, such interviews take substantially more time than telephone interviews. However, mall intercept interviews can be done fairly rapidly.

Mail surveys tend to take the longest time. Furthermore, there is relatively little the researcher can do to shorten this interval, except to reduce the number of follow-up attempts. It generally requires two weeks to receive most of the responses to a single mailing. A mail survey with only one follow-up mailing and no prenotification requires a minimum of three weeks for data collection.

Cost

The cost of the survey varies with the type of interview, the nature of the questionnaire, the response rate required, the geographic area covered, and the time at which the survey is made. However, personal interviews are generally much more expensive than the other approaches, particularly those conducted at the respondent's homes or offices. Intercept interviews are much more economical. Computer interviews involving the deliberate selection of respondents generally cost less than similar personal interviews. Computer interviews allowing self-selection cost much less.

Telephone interviews cost less than personal or computer interviews. They are usually more expensive than those conducted by mail. However, for short interviews, this relationship may not hold. Cost considerations for selecting a survey approach must include not only the costs of initial contacts but also the costs of any callbacks, remailings, or added telephone calls designed to increase the response rate.

Response Rate

The *response rate* refers to the percentage of the original sample that is interviewed. The potential impact of a low response rate is so critical for survey research that it is treated in depth in a later section of this chapter.

TABLE 6-1 Strengths of the Four Survey Methods

Criterion	Mail	Telephone	Personal*	Computer†
1. Ability to handle complex questionnaires	Poor	Good	Excellent	Good
2. Ability to collect large amounts of data	Fair	Good	Excellent	Good
3a. Accuracy on "sensitive" questions	Good	Good	Fair	Good
3b. Control of interviewer effects	Excellent	Fair	Poor	Excellent
4. Degree of sample control	Fair	Excellent‡	Fair	Fair
5. Time required	Poor	Excellent	Good	Good
6. Probable response rate	Fair	Fair	Fair	Fair
7. Cost	Good	Good	Fair	Fair

*Mall intercept interviews.
†Respondents deliberately selected at a mall or trade show.
‡Random-digit dialing.

Which Method to Use?

Obviously, no one method of survey data collection is best for all situations. The specific information requirements, the information that can be provided by each method, and time and monetary constraints determine which approach to use. The primary consideration is which technique is capable of generating *appropriate information* from the *appropriate sample* at the *lowest cost*. Table 6–1 provides a summary of the general strengths of the four techniques. It must be emphasized that the ratings shown in the table are of a general nature and do not hold true in all situations.

Thus far we have been considering the techniques as though they were mutually exclusive. However, two or more of the techniques often may be combined in a single survey. This approach, if properly performed, may allow the weakness of each technique to be offset by the strengths of the others. Research Application 6–4 provides an example of this approach.

Nonresponse Error in Survey Research

Questionnaires were mailed in March and April to 500 randomly selected subscribers of *Advertising Age;* 216 companies responded. The survey has a 6 percent margin of error.[21]

This quote, taken from a recent research report, is incorrect. The actual margin of error is unknown because the potential nonresponse error is ignored.

Table 6–2 indicates the characteristics of respondents reached on each of a series of calls. As can be seen, a no call-back policy would have produced different results from those actually obtained. Differences of those magnitudes could lead the researcher to erroneous conclusions. Likewise, respondents in a survey of small businesses had average monthly phone bills of

RESEARCH APPLICATION 6-4

Tri-Met's Multimethod Consumer Survey

Tri-Met (an urban bus company) used a combination of telephone and mail survey techniques in a ridership survey. Cost constraints ruled out at-home interviews. Mall intercept interviews were not practical because many bus riders did not visit shopping malls. "On-board" surveys were ruled out because of a desire to interview car drivers and "car poolers" as well as bus riders.

A standard mail survey was not feasible for two reasons. First, since only a very small percentage of the population rode the bus or car pooled to work, a huge random sample would be required. This would cost more than the study justified. Second, not enough time was available for a sound series of follow-ups to a mail survey.

A telephone survey seemed to be the only practical method. It could be used quickly and generate a quota sample (a fixed number of car drivers, car poolers, and bus riders). However, a very large amount of data was required from each respondent, and some of these data were too complex to generate by telephone.

Therefore, a three-phase survey methodology was developed. Using plus-one dialing, a quota sample based on method of commuting to work was contacted. In the initial phone interview, several questions concerning commuting behavior were asked, as were several nonsensitive demographic questions. The respondent was asked to provide his or her address, and a fairly lengthy and complex attitude questionnaire was *mailed* to each respondent.

The respondents were told that they should complete the questionnaire and keep it near the phone. In a few days they were recontacted by phone and asked to read their responses (generally attitude scale numbers) to the interviewer. They were then asked several additional questions, and the interview was completed.

This combination approach produced the required quota sample, a high response rate, and substantial amounts of complex information in a short time period at a reasonable cost.

TABLE 6-2 Response Variation by Call at Which Interviewed

| | Call at Which Interviewed | | | |
Behavior/Characteristic	First (N = 304)	Second (N = 114)	Third (N = 56)	Total Respondents (N = 474)
% Income > $25,000	31.5	48.0	64.8	39.5
% Male	36.8	41.2	57.1	40.3
% Democrat	40.8	34.1	19.6	36.7
% Voted for Democratic governor	53.8	43.0	57.1	51.7
% Feel President's economic policy is good	40.1	43.9	57.1	43.0
% Recalling a particular ad	24.1	27.2	37.5	26.4

SOURCE: Adapted from J. C. Ward, B. Russick, W. Rudelius, "A Test of Reducing Callbacks and Not-at-Home Bias in Personal Interviews by Weighting At-Home Respondents," *Journal of Marketing Research* (February 1985), 69.

$134, whereas the monthly bills of nonrespondents averaged only $95.[22] Again, a potentially misleading difference exists.

Nonresponse error is caused by a difference between those who respond to a survey and those who do not. Nonresponse can involve an entire questionnaire (refusal to answer any questions) or particular questions in the questionnaire (refusal to answer a subset of questions). It is one of the most significant problems faced by the survey researcher.

The **response rate** is the number of completed interviews with responding units divided by the number of eligible responding units in the sample.[23] In general, the lower the response rate to a survey, the higher the *probability* of nonresponse error. However, a low response rate does not automatically mean that there has been nonresponse error. Nonresponse error is a problem only when a difference between the respondents and the nonrespondents leads the researcher to an incorrect conclusion or decision.

Reducing Nonresponse in Telephone and Personal Surveys

Table 6–3 reveals the results of an analysis of almost 260,000 first-call attempts using the M/A/R/C Telno® System (a sophisticated random-digit dialing system). As can be seen, fewer than one call in 10 resulted in a completed interview with an adult (over 18). Approximately one-third of the calls produced "no answer" and a similar percentage were answered by someone under 18 with no one over 18 at home. Another 25 percent were either nonworking numbers or business firms. Only one call in 10 reached an adult of either sex, and 15 percent of those contacted refused to participate in the interview.

Table 6–4 indicates the refusal rates for various types of personal and telephone interviews, based on almost 1.7 million respondent contacts by 55 research firms. Refusals ranged from 19 percent to 56 percent with an overall rate of 38 percent.

Nonresponse error: is caused by a difference between those who respond to a survey and those who do not.

Response rate: the percent of those qualified to respond to a survey who do respond.

TABLE 6–3 Results of First Call Attempt
   (N = 259,088)

Outcome	Percent Occurring
No answer	34.7
No eligible person*	29.1
Nonworking number	20.3
Business	4.1
Busy	2.0
At home, eligible person	9.8
Refusal	1.4 (14.3)†
Completion	8.4 (85.7)†

*Any resident 18 years of age or older.
†Percent *given* that an eligible person is at home.

SOURCE: R. A. Kerin, R. A. Peterson, "Scheduling Telephone Interviews," *Journal of Advertising Research* (May 1983), 44.

TABLE 6–4 Refusal Rates for Telephone and Personal Interviews (Based on 1,687,000 Contacts)

Interviews	Refusal Rate (%)
Total	38
Telephone	32
Listed number	26
Random-digit dial	40
Personal	53
Mall	54
Other intercept	26
Door-to-door	36

SOURCE: Your Opinion Counts (Chicago: The Council of American Survey Research Organizations [CASRO]), 1988.

An analysis of 182 commercial telephone surveys of consumers involving a total sample of over 1 million reached the following conclusions:

- A large percentage of potential respondents/households was never contacted. The median noncontact rate was 40 percent.
- Of those individuals contacted, slightly more than one in four refused participation. The median refusal rate was 28 percent.
- Overall, response rates were low, with a median rate of 30 percent for surveys in the database.
- The low response rates were the result of controllable factors. In almost 40 percent of the surveys, only one attempt was made to contact a potential respondent, and research firms rarely made a concerted attempt to convert reluctant respondents.[24]

Clearly, nonresponse error is a potential problem for telephone, personal, and computer interviews.

Not-at-homes and refusals are the major factors that reduce response rates. The major focus in reducing nonresponse in telephone and personal interview situations has centered on contacting the potential respondent. This was based on the belief that the social motives that are present in a face-to-face or verbal interaction situation operate to minimize refusals. However, refusal rates are increasing for both personal and telephone interviews. Therefore, researchers must focus attention on gaining cooperation from, as well as making contact with, potential respondents.

Contacting Respondents

The percentage of not-at-homes in personal and telephone surveys can be reduced drastically with a series of *call-backs*. In general, the second round of calls produces only slightly fewer contacts than the first call.

The minimum number of calls in most consumer surveys should be three, and the contact rate can exceed 75 percent with seven calls.[25] Call-backs should generally be made at varying times of the day and on different days of the week. There is, as one might suspect, a definite relationship between both the day of the week and the time of day and the completion rate of telephone and personal interviews.[26]

Commercial survey research firms vary widely in the number of times they allow a phone to ring before dialing the next number. Some allow only three rings, whereas others go as high as 10. One study indicates that five rings may be optimal,[27] as shown below.

Number of Rings	Percent of At-Home Reached
3	88.0
4	96.7
5	99.2

Approximately one-third of American households with phones also have answering machines. While the widespread use of answering machines increases the cost of telephone surveys slightly due to the increased time required when a machine answers, they do not appear to have a negative impact on overall response rates.[28]

Motivating Respondents

Refusals are a problem in telephone and personal surveys. Most refusals occur immediately after the introductory remarks of the interviewer. After they begin, very few interviews are terminated prior to completion.

Explicitly mentioning the subject matter of the interview during the introduction lowers the refusal rate (34 percent versus 45 percent), although there are wide variations by *topic*, as shown in the following.[29]

Subject	Refusal Rate (%)
Household cleaners	57
Beauty aids	50
Foods	47
Retail	42
Personal care	30
Services	27
Media	26
Leisure time	19

Likewise, the *length of the interview* has a significant impact,[30] as can be seen from the following.

Length	Refusal Rate (%)
5 minutes or less	27
6–12 minutes	39
13 minutes or more	45

A number of techniques for improving response rates to personal and telephone surveys have been investigated. Following are some of the tentative findings:[31]

- *Gender* of the interviewer does not have an impact.
- *Prior notification* by letter (telephone) lowers the refusal rate for telephone (personal) interviews.
- *Monetary incentives* generally increase the response rate.
- *Foot-in-the-door* techniques—seeking cooperation on a short questionnaire and then asking the respondent to complete a longer questionnaire— generally produce a small gain in response rate. However, the gain often does not justify the added cost of this approach.
- *Refusal conversion or persuasion*—making additional pleas for cooperation after an initial refusal—causes a significant improvement in the response rate.
- The *time of day* influences refusals, with the evening being the best time to reach people at home and the time with the highest refusal rate.

Reducing Nonresponse in Mail Surveys

Attempts to increase the response rate to mail surveys focus on increasing the potential respondents' motivation to reply. Two complementary approaches are frequently used. The first is to increase the motivation as much as possible in the initial contacts with respondents. The second approach is to remind the respondents through repeated mailings or other contacts.[32]

The initial response rate to a mail survey is strongly influenced by the respondents' *interest* in the subject matter of the survey. For example, one study obtained a 54 percent response rate with an "interesting" questionnaire compared to 31 percent for a less interesting one.[33]

Interest level can be a serious source of nonresponse bias in the survey results. Consider a firm that is evaluating the potential for introducing a new tennis elbow remedy. A survey is conducted to determine the incidence and severity of the problem among the general population. Those individuals most interested in tennis elbow, and thus most likely to respond to the survey, are probably currently suffering from the problem or have recently suffered from it. Therefore, initial returns are likely to overstate the incidence of the problem. This could easily lead the firm to the wrong conclusion concerning the size of the market.

A number of techniques for motiving people to respond to mail surveys have been investigated. The major findings are listed here.[34]

- *Prenotification* by a card or letter is a cost-effective means of increasing the response rate.
- *Type of postage* has a modest impact of response rates. First-class, hand-stamped outgoing and return envelops have a higher response rate than other forms.
- The *length of the questionnaire* does not appear to affect the response rate, though this has not been thoroughly studied.

- *Prepaid monetary incentives* cause substantial increases in response rates in both commercial and general public populations. There is little difference in response rates to incentives under 50 cents, and sharply diminishing returns set in when the incentive is over $1.00.
- *Promised monetary incentives* and *promises of contributions to a charity* have very little effect on response rates.
- *Gift incentives* such as key rings have a small positive impact.
- *Promises of a copy of the results* do not increase responses even among industrial respondents.
- *Physical characteristics* of the questionnaire have very little impact on the response rate.
- *Promises of anonymity* increase responses to surveys on sensitive topics while *personalization* increases responses on nonsensitive surveys.
- The *identity of the survey sponsor* influences the response rate, with noncommercial sponsors obtaining a higher response rate.
- The *type of appeal* can influence the response rate. The best appeal depends on the audience and the other inducements being offered.
- *Return deadlines* do not increase response rates.
- The *foot-in-the-door* technique described earlier does not appear to produce significantly higher response rates than standard prenotification.

In addition to attempting to maximize the *initial* return of mail questionnaires, most mail surveys also utilize *follow-up contacts* to increase the overall response rate. Follow-up contacts generally consist of a postcard or letter requesting the respondent to complete and return the questionnaire, or the entire questionnaire may be resent.[35] Telephone and telegraph follow-ups are also used.[36] As the cumulative response rates in the following study indicate, follow-up contacts have a strong impact on the response rate (each mailing included the questionnaire, but only the first mailing included an incentive).[37]

	Incentive				
Mailing	0	$.25	$.50	$1.00	$2.00
First	54%	63%	63%	73%	78%
Second	72	75	78	88	88
Third	83	83	83	92	95
Fourth	88	86	87	93	96

Table 6–5 summarizes the effects of various approaches to reducing nonresponse to mail surveys. In any attempt to increase the total response rate to a survey, the researcher must try to balance the increased cost of each effort against the benefits of a more representative sample. The critical issue is how alike or different the respondents are from the nonrespondents on the variable(s) of concern. Methods of estimating the probable effect of nonresponse are described in the next section.

TABLE 6–5 Summary of Factors Affecting
Survey Response Rate

Factor	Effect
Limited Control	
Respondents' interest in topic	Strong
Questionnaire length	Weak
Identity of survey sponsor	Moderate
Full Control	
Follow-up contacts	Strong
Monetary incentives	Strong
Preliminary notification	Moderate
Type of return postage	Moderate
Nonmonetary gifts	Moderate
Promised monetary incentives	Weak
Physical characteristics	Weak
Degree of personalization	Weak
Anonymity and/or confidentiality	Weak
Type of appeal	Weak
Return deadlines	None
Foot-in-the-door	None

Strategies for Dealing with Nonresponse

Nonresponse sensitivity analysis: determining how different the nonrespondents would have to be from the respondents to alter the decision one would make with the currently available data.

After each successive wave of contacts with a particular group of potential respondents, the researcher should run a **nonresponse sensitivity analysis.**[38] That is, one should ascertain how different the nonrespondents would have to be from the respondents to alter one's decision based on the data supplied by the current respondents. If the most extreme foreseeable answers by the nonrespondents would not alter the decision, no further efforts are required. One recent study concluded that nonresponse error in mail surveys is extremely unlikely once the response rate reaches 50 to 60 percent.[39] Another study concluded that response rates of 65 to 75 percent virtually eliminate any chance of nonresponse error in telephone surveys.[40]

As an example, consider this decision rule: *If 20 percent or more of the population appear favorable, we will introduce the new product.* A mail survey is launched and provides a 50 percent return rate by the end of the second week. Of those responding, 44 percent favor the new product. If the remaining 50 percent of the potential respondents were unfavorable, the projected percentage of favorable attitudes would still be 22 percent. Since this is more than the amount needed for a "go" decision, any attempt to generate additional responses would be a waste of resources. However, if the nonrespondents *could* alter the decision, the researcher should use one (or more) of the following techniques.

Subjective Estimates

When it is no longer practical to increase the response rate, the researcher can estimate subjectively the nature and effect of the nonrespondents. That is, the researcher, based on experience and the nature of the survey, makes a subjective evaluation of the probable effects of the nonresponse error.

For example, the fact that those most interested in a product are most likely to return a mail questionnaire gives the researcher some confidence that nonrespondents are less interested in the topic than respondents. Similarly, the fact that young couples with no children are at home less than couples with small children provides the researcher with a basis for evaluating some aspects of not-at-homes in personal or telephone interviews.

Imputation Estimates

Imputation estimates involve imputing attributes to the nonrespondents based on the characteristics of the respondents.[41] These techniques can be used for missing respondents or for item nonresponse. For example, a respondent who does not report income may be assigned the average income of other respondents with similar occupations.

Trend Analysis

Trend analysis is similar to the imputation technique, except that the attributes of the nonrespondents are assumed to be similar to a projection of the trend shown between early and late respondents.

The data in Table 6–2 represent a fairly common finding when the results of several waves of a survey are compared. As can be seen, for five of the six questions, a trend exists such that responses to the third wave could be predicted based on the trend between responses from the first and second waves. When trends such as these appear, they can be used to estimate the characteristics or responses of the nonrespondents. However, trend analysis should be used only when there are logical reasons to believe the trend will extend to the nonrespondents.

Measurement Using Subsamples

Subsampling of nonrespondents, particularly when a mail survey was the original methodology, has been found effective in reducing nonresponse error. Concentrated attention on a subsample of nonrespondents, generally using telephone or personal interviews, can often yield a high response rate within that subsample. Using standard statistical procedures, the values obtained in the subsample can be projected to the entire group of nonrespondents and the overall survey results adjusted to take into account the nonrespondents. The primary drawback to this technique is the cost involved.

Issues in Multinational Surveys

The issues in multinational surveys mirror those in domestic surveys—which survey method is best and how do we minimize potential nonresponse error.[42] However, the issue is complicated because (1) the best method in one

TABLE 6–6 Relative Use (%) of Survey Methods Based on Expenditures
(and on the Number of Interviews)

Method	France	Nether-lands	Sweden	Switzer-land	West Germany	U.K.	U.S.
Mail	4 (19)	33	23	8	(22)	9 (17)	(40)
Telephone	15 (18)	18	44	21	(14)	16 (25)	(37)
Central location	52 (63)	37	15	5	(19)	10 (7)	(17)
Home/Work			8	44	(45)	54 (51)	(6)

SOURCE: J. Baim, "Response Rates: A Multinational Perspective," *Marketing and Research Today* (June 1991), 117.

country may be inappropriate in another and (2) different survey methods may produce differing results, making cross-country comparisons difficult.

Means of reducing and estimating nonresponse are the same across countries. Unfortunately, we have very little evidence on the effectiveness of the various techniques outside of the U.S. The available evidence suggests that techniques that are effective in the U.S. will also work elsewhere.

As Table 6–6 indicates, different conditions lead to sharply different usage rates for the various survey methods, even across the economically advanced countries.

Telephone Surveys

The ability to conduct telephone surveys in a given country depends on the sample having telephones and on their willingness to be interviewed on the phone. As Table 6–7 shows, the distribution of telephones differs widely across countries. The fact that a country has a low incidence of phones does not automatically mean that telephone surveys cannot be conducted. If the targeted sample is an upper-income group, a phone survey might be possible even in a country with relatively few phones.

Cultures differ in their willingness to grant interviews over the phone. In parts of Latin America, phones are used to speak with family members and close friends, and a telephone request for an interview would be considered inappropriate. In many Islamic cultures, such as Saudi Arabia, it is not appropriate for women to talk with strangers, particularly males. This problem is further complicated by the fact that telephone interviewing is viewed as an unacceptable job for Saudi Arabian women. In Japan, it is difficult to interview males and working females by phone because they tend to return from work late in the evening and are too tired for interviews. Futhermore, most Japanese would consider a telephone survey to be an invasion of privacy.[43]

Despite these difficulties, the use of telephone interviews appears to be growing in multicountry surveys, particularly in the EC.

Mail Surveys

Mail surveys require a high literacy rate among the sample, a well-developed postal system, and a list of addresses. Mail surveys are widely used in the EC countries, the United States, Canada, and Japan. They often are not a good

TABLE 6–7 Distribution of Telephones Across Countries

Country	Phones/ 1,000	Percent Homes	Country	Phones/ 1,000	Percent Homes
Argentina	100	—	Japan	535	—
Brazil	90	—	Mexico	90	—
Bulgaria	200	—	Netherlands	—	91
Canada	—	96	Poland	118	16
Czechoslovakia	226	—	Romania	130	—
Finland	—	93	South Korea	294	—
France	—	91	Spain	381 ′	59
East Germany	211	16	Sweden	—	99
West Germany	641	92	Taiwan	277	—
Greece	373	—	UK	—	85
Hungary	134	—	US	630	93
Ireland	235	49	USSR	115	—
Italy	—	75	Yugoslavia	122	—

SOURCE: A. J. Baim, "Response Rates: A Multinational Perspective," *Marketing and Research Today* (June 1991), 118; "Which Countries Lead the Good Life," *IMF Survey* 19 (9), 135.

method in other countries even if the literacy rate is high. For example, it is estimated that 30 percent of the domestic mail in Brazil is never delivered.[44] However, a multicountry industrial survey produced excellent results in the Caribbean.[45]

Personal Surveys

Personal interviews, both at-home and central-location, are popular in Europe, Japan, and developing countries (where they are often the only way the data can be collected).[46] Although shopping malls are not common outside the U.S. and Canada, intercept interviews can be conducted anywhere the target market gathers, such as shopping streets, markets, bazaars, sports events, and parks. However, at-home interviews are most common outside the U.S. Personal interviews in Islamic countries encounter the same problems described for phone interviews.

Computer Surveys

Computer interviews require a sample that is at least familiar with computer-type terminals. Thus, they are restricted to advanced economies and select segments of other countries. Multinational computer interviews are complicated by a variety of factors. In Japan, virtually all computers use the NEC operating system, which is incompatible with the DOS system most common in the U.S. Shipping computer disks across national boundaries can be difficult. For example, DOS cannot be sent internationally, so self-booting disks cannot be used; shipping diskettes to Brazil is prohibited; and so forth. However, international mailing firms such as TNT Express Worldwide have expertise in dealing with these issues.[47]

Multiple Survey Techniques in Multinational Surveys

As the preceding discussion indicates, it is sometimes desirable to use different survey methods in a multinational survey. When this is the case, it is desirable to test for method differences if the results are to be used for cross-country comparisons. For example, if a telephone survey is to be conducted in several countries and a personal interview in another, a small number of telephone surveys should be conducted in the personal interview country if possible. The results from these interviews can be compared to those from the personal interviews to test for method effects.

Summary

Survey research is the systematic collection of information from respondents in an interview using a set of questions, generally in the form of a questionnaire. An interview is the administration of a questionnaire to an individual or group of people. Surveys are classified according to their method of administration—personal, telephone, mail, and computer. The selection of a survey method involves consideration of seven criteria: (1) complexity of the required questions, (2) amount of data required, (3) required accuracy, (4) sample control needed, (5) time available, (6) acceptable level of nonresponse, and (7) value of the resultant information and funds available.

Most personal interviews are conducted as mall intercept interviews, though other locations are also used for intercept interviews. In an intercept interview, individuals are stopped at random, qualified, invited into a nearby interview facility, and interviewed. Compared to at-home interviews, they cost less, are faster, are easier to supervise, and allow the use of special equipment. However, the sample frame is limited to shoppers at the mall being used.

Computer-assisted telephone interviewing (CATI) requires the interviewer to read the questions from a computer screen and enter the responses directly into the computer. The computer can edit the responses as they are entered, handle skip patterns, rotate questions, and provide interim analyses quickly. However, CATIs do require up-front programming.

Unlisted phone numbers are as high as 60 percent in some cities. Thererore, the telephone directory is often not a good sample frame. To overcome this problem, random digit dialing is used. Random digit dialing requires the researcher to select at least one of the digits in each sample phone number randomly.

Nonresponse error is caused by a difference between those who respond to a survey and those who do not. Nonresponse error is a serious concern because most surveys have a low response rate, which increases the probability of nonresponse error occurring. Call-backs, monetary incentives, prior notification, and persuasion have been successful in increasing the response rate to personal and telephone surveys. Monetary incentives, follow-up contacts, prenotification, nonmonetary gifts, and first-class postage generally increase the response rate to mail surveys.

If the nonrespondents could alter the decision, the potential nonresponse error should be estimated by a subjective estimate, an imputation estimate, a trend analysis, or a measurement using a subsample.

The issues in multinational surveys mirror those in domestic surveys, but they are much more complex. The complexity occurs in part because (1) the best method in one country may be inappropriate in another, and (2) different survey methods may produce different results making cross-country comparisons difficult.

Review Questions

6.1. What is *survey research?*

6.2. What can be measured by surveys?

6.3. Define each of the following:
   a. *personal interview*
   b. *mail interview*
   c. *telephone interview*
   d. *computer interview*

6.4. What is a *mall intercept interview*? What are its advantages and disadvantages?

6.5. Describe the Purchase Intercept Technique (PIT).

6.6. Which interview approach is most common?

6.7. What is meant by each of the following, and which interview method(s) deal with each one most effectively?
   a. *complexity of the questionnaire*
   b. *required amount of data*
   c. *accuracy*
   d. *sample control*
   e. *time requirements*
   f. *level of nonresponse*
   g. *cost*

6.8. What is meant by *interviewer effects*? How does one control for them?

6.9. What is a *validation* or *verification procedure?*

6.10. What are the two types of unlisted numbers?

6.11. What is meant by *random-digit dialing*? *Plus-one dialing?*

6.12. What is a *CATI?*

6.13. What factors affect sample control for each of the interviewing techniques?

6.14. How many times should the phone ring in a telephone survey?

6.15. What is a typical response rate for phone interviews?

6.16. What is a typical refusal rate for phone interviews?

6.17. What is a typical refusal rate for mall intercept interviews?

6.18. What factors improve the response rate to phone interviews?

6.19. What factors improve the response rate to mall intercept interviews?

6.20. What factors affect the response rate to mail surveys?

6.21. What is a *sensitivity analysis?*

6.22. Describe each of the following as a means for dealing with nonresponse:
   a. *subjective estimate*
   b. *imputation estimate*
   c. *trend analysis*
   d. *subsample measurement*

6.23. What are the main issues in multinational surveys?

6.24. What variables must be considered in evaluating telephone surveys as a data collection method for a multinational survey?

6.25. What is required before mail surveys can be conducted in a country?

6.26. What concerns arise if more than one survey method is used in a multinational survey? What additional steps does this require?

Discussion Questions/Problems

6.27. How would you decide if a mall intercept interview approach is appropriate for a particular research project?

6.28. Why does a monetary gift enclosed with a questionnaire generally produce a higher response rate than the promise of a monetary gift if the questionnaire is returned?

6.29. An attitude survey conducted by mail by a city parks department obtained a 38 percent response. How are the nonrespondents likely to differ from the respondents with respect to (i) attitudes and (ii) voting behavior?

6.30. The following figures show the percentage of respondents having a favorable reaction to a new product on each successive wave of a telephone survey.

Wave	% Positive on This Wave	% of Total Sample Responding
1	64.3	32.2
2	58.1	25.8
3	51.9	13.1
4	44.9	6.0

A time deadline makes another wave of calls impossible. What should be the final estimate of the favorable percentage?

6.31. People tend to respond to surveys that deal with topics that interest them. How can this fact be used to increase the response rate from a mail survey of the general public on attitudes toward and usage of
   a. paper towels
   b. automobile tune-ups
   c. bicycles
   d. salt
   e. county government

6.32. Would you expect any nonresponse bias in the situations described in 6.31? Make a subjective estimate of the nature and extent of the bias if a 60 percent response rate were obtained in each situation.

6.33. What biases, if any, might be introduced by offering to give respondents $10.00 upon receipt of the questionnaire? The purpose of the payment is to ensure a high response rate. Will it work?

6.34. The manager of a shopping center recently conducted a computer survey to provide information on the types of stores that should be sought for the center's new wing, which was under construction. Self-administered computer terminals were placed near the entrances to the center. A large sign above each table said: "Help Us Plan the New Wing." The computers were left up for a two-week period. What type of errors are likely to be present in this study?

6.35. Describe and justify the survey methodology you would use in the following situations:
   a. A survey to measure teenagers' attitudes and behaviors toward a variety of soft drink brands in Mexico, Canada, the U.S., Japan, and Germany.
   b. A survey to measure the attitudes of women with children under the age of 16 living at home toward instant soups in Brazil, the U.S., Taiwan, France, Italy, and Great Britain.
   c. A survey to measure the attitudes of males aged 25–35 with incomes above the median for their country toward a new material for shoes in Japan, Mexico, Canada, the U.S., and the EC.

6.36. Westinghouse Credit Corp. sent a survey to 3,512 chief executive officers and chief financial officers by mail. Half received $1.00 with the survey and half did not. The response rate to the four-page questionnaire was 1.6 percent without the incentive and 17.5 percent with it. What would you do?

Projects/Activities

6.37. Conduct a series of telephone interviews in your area to develop a guide for when to conduct telephone interviews.

6.38. Conduct a series of telephone interviews designed to develop a guide for when to conduct telephone interviews with students on your campus.

6.39. Design and conduct a telephone survey among students on your campus. The purpose of the survey should be to determine attitudes and, if appropriate, behaviors toward _____ .
   a. regulating beer advertising on television
   b. men's ties
   c. coffee
   d. energy conservation
   e. charge card interest rates
   f. wine

6.40. Do 6.39 but using "hall" intercept interviews.

6.41. Do 6.39 and 6.40 for the same product. Discuss any differences in the results.

6.42. Do 6.39 using the general population and plus-one dialing.

6.43. Conduct a telephone survey of adults 18 and older in your area. Determine if they have been interviewed in the past 12 months, how many times, on what topics, by what means, and their attitude toward the interviews.

Notes

1. D. L. Pyle, "How to Interview Your Customers," *American Demographics* (December 1990), 44–45.

2. "Ci2 CATI Version 3.0 Released" *CATI News* (Ketchum, ID: Sawtooth Software, Spring 1991), 7.

3. See N. E. Synodinos, J. M. Brennan, "Computer Interactive Interviewing in Survey Research," *Psychology and Marketing* (Summer 1988), 117–137; N. E. Synodinos, J. M. Brennan, "Evaluating Microcomputer Interactive Software," *Journal of Business and Psychology* (Summer 1990), 483–493.

4. S. Cox, "Selecting Computer Interviewing Hardware at Kentucky Fried Chicken," *Sawtooth News* (Spring 1991), 3.

5. M. J. Havice, "Measuring Nonresponse and Refusals in an Electronic Survey," *Journalism Quarterly* (Autumn 1990); and M. J. Havice, M. J. Banks, "Live and Automated Telephone Surveys," *Journal of the Market Research Society* (April 1991), 91–101.

6. P. V. Miller, "Alternative Question Forms for Attitude Scale Questions on Telephone Interviews," *Public Opinion Quarterly* (Winter 1984), 766–778.

7. *Your Opinion Counts* (Chicago: The Council of American Survey Research Organizations [CASRO], 1986), 18.

8. See D. Jobber, "An Examination of the Effects of Questionnaire Factors on Response to an Industrial Mail Survey," *International Journal of Research in Marketing* (December 1989), 129–140; and *Your Opinion Counts* (Chicago: CASRO, 1988).

9. See W. S. Aquilino, L. A. LoSciuto, "Effects of Interview Mode on Self-Reported Drug Use," *Public Opinion Quarterly* (Fall 1990), 362–395.

10. R. M. Groves, L. J. Magilavy, "Measuring and Explaining Interviewer Effects in Centralized Telephone Surveys," *Public Opinion Quarterly* (Fall 1986), 251–266; L. G. Pol, T. G. Ponzurick, "Gender of Interviewer/Gender of Respondent Bias in Telephone Surveys," *Applied Marketing Research* (Spring 1989), 9–13; and S. E. Finkel, T. M. Guterbock, M. J. Borg, "Race-of-Interviewer Effects," *Public Opinion Quarterly* (Fall 1991), 313–330.

11. See P. L. Kiecker, J. E. Nelson, "Cheating Behavior by Telephone Interviews," in P. Bloom et al., eds. *Enhancing Development in Marketing* (Chicago: American Marketing Association, 1989), 182–188.

12. See J. P. Liefeld, "Response Effects in Computer-Administered Questioning," *Journal of Marketing Research* (November 1988), 405–409.

13. D. O'Rourke, J. Blair, "Improving Random Respondent Selection in Telephone Surveys," *Journal of Marketing Research* (November 1983), 428–432.

14. *Catalog of Mailing Lists* (New York: F. S. Hofheimer, Inc., issued periodically); and *SRDS Direct Mail List Rates and Data* (New York: Standard Rate and Data Service), issued twice annually.

15. N. F. Juárez, "Phone Surveys Most Efficient Way to Survey U.S. Hispanics," *Marketing News* (January 8, 1990), 28; and S. A. Hernandez, C. J. Kaufman, "Marketing Research in Hispanic Barrios," *Marketing Research* (March 1990), 11–27.

16. "Frame Quiz Results Are In," *The Frame* (Fairfield, CT: Survey Sampling Inc., Winter 1990), 3.

17. M. N. Segal, F. Hekmat, "Random Digit Dialing: A Comparison of Methods," *Journal of Advertising* (No. 4, 1985), 36–43; "Dialing Selection Techniques: Random Digit vs. Directory," *Research on Research* (Chicago: Market Facts, Inc., No. 10, undated); and L. Piekarski, "Unlisted Telephone Households Tied to Age," *The Frame* (Fairfield, CT: Survey Sampling, Inc, Summer 1989).

18. W. Lyons, R. F. Durant, "Interviewer Costs Associated with the Use of Random Digit Dialing in Large Area Samples," *Journal of Marketing* (Summer 1980), 65–69; and "Dialing Selection," loc. cit.

19. *Your Opinion Counts* (Chicago: The Council of American Survey Research Organizations [CASRO], 1986), 12.

20. R. A. Kerin, R. A. Peterson, "Scheduling Telephone Interviews," *Journal of Advertising Research* (May 1983), 41–47; and Segal and Hekmat, loc. cit.

21. S. Hume, "New Ideas, Old Barriers," *Advertising Age* (July 22, 1991), 6.

22. H. Assael, J. Keon, "Nonsampling vs. Sampling Errors in Survey Research," *Journal of Marketing* (Spring 1982), 114–123. See also L. Opatow, "Some Thoughts About How Interview Attempts Affect Survey Results," *Journal of Advertising Research* (March 1991), RC.6–RC.9.

23. F. Wiseman, M. Billington, "Comment on a Standard Definition of Response Rates," *Journal of Marketing Research* (August 1984), 336–338.

24. F. Wiseman, "Nonresponse in Consumer Surveys" in K. B. Monroe, *Advances in Consumer Research VII* (Provo: Association for Consumer Research, 1981), 267–269.

25. See L. Piekarski, "Answering Machine Households Not So Elusive," *The Frame* (Fairfield, CT: Survey Sampling Inc, Spring 1990).

26. M. F. Weeks, R. A. Kulka, S. A. Pierson, "Optimal Call Scheduling for a Telephone Survey," *Public Opinion Quarterly* (Winter 1987), 540–549; and W. Donsbach, H. B. Brasive, "Panel Surveys by Telephone," *Marketing and Research Today* (August 1991), 143–150.

27. R. J. Smead, J. Wilcox, "Ring Policy in Telephone Surveys," *Public Opinion Quarterly* (Spring 1980), 115.

28. Piekarski, "Answering Machine," op. cit.; and P. S. Tuckel, B. M. Feinberg, "The Answering Machine Poses Many Questions for Telephone Survey Researchers," *Public Opinion Quarterly* (Summer 1991), 200–217.

29. *Your Opinion Counts* (Chicago: CASRO, 1988).

30. Ibid.

31. For details and research references, see D. S. Tull, D. I. Hawkins, *Marketing Research* (Macmillan Publishing, 1993), 187.

32. For overviews, see J. Yu, H. Cooper, "A Quantitative Review of Research Design Effects on Response Rates," *Journal of Marketing Research* (February 1983), 36–44; D. Jobber, "Improving Response Rates in Industrial Mail Surveys," *Industrial Marketing Management* (3, 1986), 183–195; R. J. Fox, M. R. Crask, J. Kim, "Mail Survey Response Rate," *Public Opinion Quarterly* (Winter 1988), 467–491; and J. S. Conant, D. T. Smart, B. J. Walker, "Mail Survey Facilitation Techniques," *Journal of the Market Research Society* (October 1990), 569–580.

33. C. J. Dommeyer, "Does Response to an Offer of Mail Survey Results Interact with Questionnaire Interest?" *Journal of Marketing Research Society* (January 1985), 27–38. See also B. J. Kyzr-Sheeley, "Results of Walker's 1986 Survey," *The Marketing Researcher* 16, (3), 4; and S. W. McDaniel, C. S. Madden, P. Verille, "Do Topic Differences Affect Survey Non-Response?" *Journal of the Marketing Research Society* (January 1987), 55–66.

34. For details and references see Tull and Hawkins, op. cit., 189–191.

35. For an evaluation of various strategies and sequences, see R. A. Peterson, G. Albaum, R. A. Kerin, "A Note on Alternative Contact Strategies in Mail Surveys," *Journal of the Market Research Society* (July 1989), 409–418. See also H. Karimahahy and P.J. Brunn, "Postal Surveys of Small Manufacturers," *Industrial Marketing Management* 4 (1991), 319–326.

36. See T. G. Ponzurick, L. G. Pol, "An Integrated Method for Increasing Response to Mail Surveys," *Journal of Midwest Marketing* (Spring 1989), 188–192.

37. J. M. James, R. Bolstein, "The Effect of Monetary Incentives and Follow-up Mailings," *Public Opinion Quarterly* (Fall 1990), 346–361.

38. See also D. K. Pearl, D. Fairley, "Testing for the Potential of Nonresponse Bias in Sample Surveys?" *Public Opinion Quarterly* (Winter 1985), 553–560.

39. D. R. Berbie, "Reassessing the Value of High Response Rates to Mail Surveys," *Marketing Research* (September 1989), 52–63. See also L. Robinson, D. Lifton, "Reducing Market Research Costs," *Journal of the Market Research Society* (October 1991), 301–307.

40. D. R. Berbie, "Telephone Survey Response Rates," *Marketing Research* (March 1991), 35–44.

41. See T. Sharot, "Weighting Survey Results," *Journal of the Marketing Research Society* (July 1986), 269–284.

42. See N. K. Malhotra, "Administration of Questionnaires for Collecting Quantitative Data in International Marketing Research," *Journal of Global Marketing* 2 (1991), 63–92.

43. K. Kobagashi, P. Draper, "Reviews of Research in Japan," *Journal of Advertising Research* (May 1990), 13–18.

44. See G. Albaum, J. Strandskov, "Participation in a Mail Survey of International Marketers," *Journal of Global Marketing*, 4 (1989), 7–23; R. A. Jussaume, Jr., Y. Yamada, "A Comparison of the Viability of Mail Surveys in Japan and the United States," *Public Opinion Quarterly* (Summer 1990), 219–228; J. Baim, "Response Rates"; and E. Meier, "Response Trends in Britain," both in *Marketing and Research Today* (June 1991), 114–119 and 120–123.

45. A. Klose, "A Commercial Mail Survey in the Caribbean," *Journal of the Market Research Society* (October 1991), 343–346.

46. For excellent descriptions of personal interviews in LOCs, See D. R. Sopariwala, P. L. Roy, "Opinion Polling in India," *Journal of the Market Research Society* (April 1990), 173–186; and H. C. Steele, "Marketing Research in China," *Marketing and Research Today* (August 1990), 155–164.

47. "International Interviewing," *Sawtooth News* (Fall 1991), 4–6.

CHAPTER 7

Experimental Design

LEARNING OBJECTIVES

Upon completing this chapter, you should be able to

1. Explain the nature of experimentation.

2. Distinguish a dependent variable from an independent variable and a treatment group from a control group.

3. List and describe the potential errors that can affect experimental results.

4. List and describe the basic experimental designs and indicate the errors each controls.

5. List and describe the statistical experimental designs and the conditions for which each is appropriate.

6. Explain interaction and why it is important in marketing studies.

7. Describe how one decides which experimental design to use.

8. Explain what *ex post facto* studies are and why they are not experiments.

The American Heart Association's Experimental Test of Fund-Raising ''Teasers''

The American Heart Association uses direct mail as a major part of its fund-raising effort. A decision was made to develop and test alternative "teaser" lines for the outside of the fund solicitation envelopes. The six proposed envelopes are shown below.

The current method that involved a plain envelope was used as a control. A large mailing of each type of envelope was sent to randomly selected prospects (individuals who had not given before) and donors (individuals who had given before). Donations were measured for each envelope type, and the results for prospects and donors were analyzed separately. Which was the best envelope?

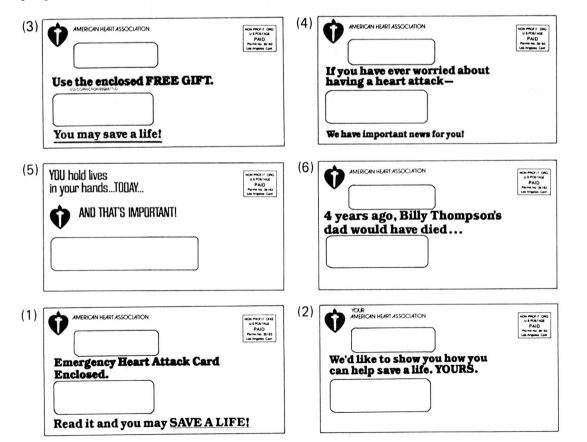

The Nature of Experimentation

Experimentation:
the manipulation of one or more variables in such a way that its effect on one or more other variables can be measured.

Independent variable:
the variable that is manipulated by the researcher in an experiment.

Dependent variable:
the variable that reflects the impact of the independent variable in an experiment.

Treatment group:
those subjects in an experiment who are exposed to a manipulation of the independent variable.

Control group:
those subjects in an experiment who are not exposed to a manipulation of the independent variable.

Randomization:
randomly assigning subjects to treatment and control groups in an experiment.

The American Heart Association study just described is an example of an *experiment.* Experimentation is a common part of our everyday lives. When we try on clothes, try a new route to school or work, or take a test drive in an automobile, we are engaged in experimentation.

Experimentation is also a common feature in the marketing activities of many firms: a grocer decides to use new point-of-purchase (P-O-P) material to see how it works; a manufacturer offers an additional bonus for sales of certain products; an advertising agency compares the cost of a computer-generated media schedule with the cost of a schedule generated manually.

Research Application 7–1 describes a marketing experiment. Would you feel confident making a decision on the use of P-O-P displays based on this experiment? Why? The purpose of this chapter is to enable you to evaluate marketing experiments from a decision-making perspective.

The characteristics of a controlled experiment are described first. Then the various types of errors that might affect an experiment are analyzed. The third section of the chapter is devoted to a description of the more common types of experimental designs that have been developed to control or reduce experimental errors. Finally, *ex post facto* studies that resemble experiments are described. The environments—laboratory and field—in which experiments are conducted are examined in the next chapter.

Experimentation involves the manipulation of one or more variables by the experimenter in such a way that its effect on one or more other variables can be measured. A variable being manipulated is called the **independent variable.** In Research Application 7–1, the P-O-P display is an independent variable. The envelope teaser line was the independent variable in the Heart Association study. A variable that reflects the impact of the independent variable is called a **dependent variable.** Its level depends at least partially on the level or magnitude of the independent variable(s). Unit sales is the dependent variable in the P-O-P experiment, as is donations in the Heart Association experiment.

That portion of the sample or population that is exposed to a manipulation of the independent variable is known as a **treatment group.** Thus, the stores receiving the static P-O-P display and the stores receiving the motion P-O-P display are the two treatment groups in Research Application 7–1. The six groups of prospects and the six groups of donors receiving an envelope with a "teaser" line are the treatment groups in the fund-raising study.

A group in which the independent variable is unchanged is called the **control group.** Those stores receiving no display constitute the control group in the Olympia beer example, while those individuals receiving the plain envelope served as the control group in the Heart Association experiment.

To be confident that any change (or lack of change) in the dependent variable is caused by the independent variable, the researcher must measure or control the effects of other variables. This control is generally achieved by one of two methods, randomization or matching. **Randomization** involves randomly assigning subjects to treatment and control groups. This technique

RESEARCH APPLICATION 7-1

Olympia Beer Point-of-Purchase Display Impact Experiment

The Point-of-Purchase Advertising Institute in cooperation with Olympia beer conducted a study to ascertain the impact of static and motion point-of-purchase displays on the sales of Olympia beer.* The displays were installed in 12 liquor stores and 12 supermarkets in two California cities with different demographics. Matching stores (stores in similar areas without displays) were used for control purposes. Sales were monitored for a four-week time period.

In the liquor stores, static displays increased sales by over 56 percent compared to the control

stores and motion displays produced a 107 percent sales increase. In the food stores, static displays improved sales by 18 percent over similar stores with no displays. Motion displays produced a 49 percent sales gain. Market share followed a similar pattern in both types of outlet.

*Fieldwork was conducted by Product Acceptance & Research, Inc., Evansville, Indiana.

SOURCE: *Two Studies on the Effectiveness of Static and Motion Displays for the Brewing Industry* (Point-of-Purchase Advertising Institute, Inc., undated), 1–2.

---

was used in the Heart Association study. **Matching** is the deliberate assignment of subjects to treatment and control groups to achieve balance on key dimensions. This was used in the P-O-P study. Both approaches attempt to ensure that the independent variable is the only variable that differs between the groups.

The purpose of the test involving Olympia beer was "to compare the difference in sales volume between no displays and a static display, and then to determine the impact of a static display versus a motion display." In other words, the experiment sought to establish the extent to which particular displays would *cause* a change in sales. Likewise, the Heart Association attempted to see if a teaser line on an envelope would *cause* an increase in donations. They found that envelope number two produced more donations than any other tested envelope.

Experimentation is oriented toward establishing and measuring causal relationships among the variables under consideration. Well-designed experiments are uniquely equipped to demonstrate causal relationships because they allow for or control other potential causal factors (extraneous variables). This is not possible with survey research or secondary data.

> **Matching:**
> deliberately
> assigning subjects
> to treatment and
> control groups in
> an experiment to
> achieve balance on
> key dimensions.

Types of Errors Affecting Experimental Results

Consider a retailer who has always charged $1.00 a unit for a particular product and has consistently sold 100 units per week. Curious about the effect of price level on sales, she increases the price to $1.20 a unit for a week and monitors sales. Sales drop to 50 units during the week. Price, in this example, is the independent variable and sales level is the dependent variable. Because sales changed, the retailer might be willing to conclude that price level does indeed affect sales level.

Before our retailer could reach such a conclusion, however, she would have to be sure that no other variable could have caused the change in sales. For example, if the area had had unusually bad weather, if the mass transit system had been closed because of a strike, or if a competitor had had a major sale, our retailer could not with any confidence attribute the cause of the sales decrease to the price increase. Thus, we must be concerned with potential errors that might affect the results of experiments.

The 10 types of errors that can confound experimental results are discussed in the following paragraphs.

Premeasurement Error

Assume that an interviewer knocks on your door and requests your cooperation for a marketing study. You agree and proceed to complete a questionnaire. The questions are concerned with a brand of soft drink that you have heard of but have not tried. Shortly afterward, you describe the interview to a friend and the next day you try one of the firm's soft drinks.

Two weeks later the interviewer returns and asks you to complete another questionnaire. This questionnaire is an alternative form of the one you completed earlier. You have continued to consume the firm's soft drinks and the second questionnaire reflects both increased consumption and a more favorable attitude toward the brand.

Premeasurement error: changes in the dependent variable that are solely the effect of the initial measurement.

What caused the shift in your behavior? Although the firm might have increased advertising, decreased price, altered the package design, or manipulated any of a number of other variables, the "cause" of your interest in and use of the product was the initial measurement. **Premeasurement error** occurs when the taking of a measurement has a direct effect on performance in a subsequent measurement.

Premeasurement is a major concern if the respondents realize they are being measured. However, if inanimate factors such as sales are being measured or if disguised measurement of human subjects is used, premeasurement no longer represents a potential error source and can be ignored.

Interaction Error

Interaction error: an increase or decrease in the effect of the independent variable because of a sensitizing effect of the premeasurement.

Interaction error occurs when a premeasure changes the respondents' sensitivity or responsiveness to the independent variable(s). This sensitizing effect is particularly important in studies involving attitudes, brand awareness, and opinions.

A group of individuals may be given a questionnaire containing several attitude scales concerned with a particular brand. These individuals are then likely to be particularly interested in, or sensitive to, advertisements and other activities involving this brand. Thus, an increase, decrease, or change in, say, advertising is more likely to be noticed and reacted to by these individuals than by a group who did not receive the initial questionnaire. This heightened sensitivity often increases the effect of whatever change was made in the marketing variable and is reflected in the postmeasurement.

It is important to note how interaction differs from direct premeasurement effects. In the example of direct premeasurement effects, the individual involved was never exposed to the independent variable. *All* of the change was caused by the initial measurement itself. In contrast, interaction does *not* require any *direct* effects from the initial measurement. It simply means that *the independent variable is more likely to be noticed and reacted to than it would be without the initial measurement*. Thus, premeasurement error occurs when the premeasurement, *by itself*, causes a change in the dependent variable. Interaction error occurs when the premeasurement *and the independent variable* have a unique, joint effect on the dependent variable. This distinction is important, as experimental designs that will control direct premeasurement effects do not necessarily control interaction effects.

Maturation

Maturation represents biological or psychological processes that systematically vary with the passage of time, independent of specific external events. Respondents may grow older, more tired, or thirstier between the pre- and postmeasurements.

For example, an experiment that begins at 1:00 P.M. and ends at 4:00 P.M. will begin with most of the respondents having just eaten and perhaps being somewhat sleepy from lunch. By the time the experiment ends, the respondents will, on the average, be hungrier, thirstier (unless fluids were provided), less sleepy, and more fatigued. Maturation can also be a severe problem in those experiments that persist over months or years, such as market tests and experiments dealing with the physiological response to such products as toothpaste, cosmetics, and medications.

Maturation: biological or psychological changes that are a function of the passage of time.

History

History is a somewhat confusing term. It does not refer to the occurrence of events prior to the experiment. Rather, **history error** refers to any variables or events, other than the one(s) manipulated by the experimenter, that occur between the pre- and postmeasures and affect the value of the dependent variable. A soft drink bottler may measure its level of sales in a region, launch a promotional campaign for four weeks, and monitor sales levels during and immediately after the campaign. However, such factors as unusually heavy advertising by a competitor or unseasonably warm or cold weather could each produce (or nullify) a change in sales. These extraneous variables are referred to as "history" and represent one of the major concerns in experimental design.

History error: changes in the independent variable caused by variables extraneous to the research design.

Instrumentation

Instrumentation error refers to changes in the measuring instrument itself over time. These changes are most likely to occur when the measurement involves humans, as either observers or interviewers. Thus, during a pre-

Instrumentation error: changes in the measuring instrument itself over time.

measurement, interviewers may be highly interested in the research and may take great care in explaining instructions and recording observations. By the time the postmeasurements are taken, the interviewers may have lost most or all of their interest and involvement, and their explanations may be less thorough and their recording less precise. Alternatively, interviewers or observers may become more skilled with practice and perform better during the postmeasure.

Selection

Selection error: caused by the treatment and control groups initially being unequal with respect to the dependent variable or in the propensity to respond to the independent variable.

In most experimental designs, at least two groups are formed. **Selection error** occurs when the groups formed for purposes of the experiment are initially unequal with respect to the dependent variable or in the propensity to respond to the independent variable.

Random assignment to groups, the *matching* of subjects assigned to each, or *blocking* (this technique is described later) can minimize this problem. However, random assignment to groups still leaves the potential for selection error. In this case it would be similar to sampling error. Any time subjects volunteer for particular groups, regardless of the basis for making the decision—that is, time of day, location, pay, or other reasons—selection error may occur. For example, an experiment that requires three hours to complete and requires three groups could run one group from 9 to 12 in the morning, one group from 2 to 5 in the afternoon, and the third group from 7 to 10 in the evening. The experimenter could then request volunteers for each of these time periods. However, it is likely that people able and willing to volunteer for a morning session differ in a number of respects from those who come at a different time.

Mortality

Mortality: the differential loss of respondents from the various groups in an experiment.

Mortality does not imply that some experiments reduce the population. Rather, **mortality** refers to the differential loss (refusal or inability to continue in the experiment) of respondents from the various groups. By a differential loss, we mean that some groups lose respondents that are different from those lost by other groups. If the experiment involves only one group, mortality error occurs when the respondents that remain in the study differ in responsiveness to the independent variable from those who withdraw.

Assume that a company has developed a new toothbrush that, although somewhat inconvenient to use, should reduce the incidence of cavities. A number of children, age 8 to 15, are selected and randomly assigned to two groups, one of which will receive the new toothbrushes. The respondents in each group are given dental checkups and told to brush their teeth in their normal manner for the following year. During the year's time, both groups will lose some members because of moving, loss of interest, and so forth. This may not involve any mortality error because, if the sample is large enough, it will affect both groups more or less equally.

However, the treatment group with the new "inconvenient" toothbrush will lose some members because of this inconvenience. Furthermore, those remaining in the treatment group are likely to be more concerned about their teeth than those who quit. Therefore, by the end of the year, the treatment group will have a higher percentage of respondents who are concerned about their teeth. These respondents are likely to brush more often, eat fewer sweets, and generally take better care of their teeth than the control group. This may be sufficient to cause a difference between the groups even if the new toothbrush itself has no effect.

Reactive Error

A **reactive error** occurs when the artificiality of the experimental situation or the behavior of the experimenter emphasizes, dampens, or alters any effects caused by the treatment variable. The reason for this is that human subjects do not respond passively to experimental situations. Rather, for some subjects at least, the experiment takes on aspects of a problem-solving experience in which the subject tries to discover the experimental hypothesis and then produce the anticipated behavior. Researchers generally use the term *demand characteristics* to refer to cues in the experimental environment that suggest the hypothesis. *Demand artifacts* is the term most often used to refer to the reactive error itself.[1]

A reactive error cannot be controlled for by the experimental design. Rather, it must be controlled for by the structure of the experimental situation. Since reactive arrangements are most critical in laboratory experiments, a detailed discussion of the problem they pose is provided in the next chapter.

Reactive error: effects on the dependent variable(s) caused by the artificiality of the experimental situation and/or the behavior of the experimenter.

Measurement Timing

We sometimes assume that the effect of any independent variable is both immediate and permanent. Thus, experiments occasionally manipulate an independent variable (price or advertising, for example), take an immediate measure of the dependent variable (sales), and then move on to the next problem. The danger in such an approach is that the immediate impact of the independent variable may be different from its long-range effect.

Measurement timing error occurs when pre- or postmeasurements are made at an inappropriate time to indicate the effect of the experimental treatment. Consider the following example. Weekly sales of a product are measured in two equivalent groups of stores. Average sales in each group equal 100 units per week per store. The product is placed in a P-O-P display in one group (treatment group) and is left in its usual shelf location in the second group (control group) of stores. Sales are measured for each group during the first week of the P-O-P display. Average sales for the treatment group are 120 units compared to 105 for the control group. The P-O-P display appears to have caused an average sales increase of 15 units per store.

If the researcher stops here, however, an incorrect conclusion concerning the magnitude of the effect of the display may be reached. Measurements made after the first week or so of a P-O-P display typically show a decline in sales, often below the initial level. Thus, a part of the impact is simply a result of consumers stocking up on the product. Table 7–1 illustrates the general nature of these findings.[2]

Measurement timing error: taking the pre- or postmeasures at a time when their levels are not representative or normal.

TABLE 7–1 Effect of Measurement Timing on Point-of-Purchase Experiments

	Measurement (1)	Introduction of P-O-P	Measurement			
			(2)	(3)	(4)	(5)
Point-of-purchase group	100	X	120	110	105	112
Control group	100		105	105	108	109

The researcher must be certain that both the pre- and postmeasurements are made over a sufficient time period to indicate the effect of the independent variable.

Surrogate Situation

Surrogate situation error occurs when the environment, the population(s) sampled, and/or the treatments administered are different from those that will be encountered in the actual situation. A radio advertising copy test in which recall is measured after listening while driving an automobile simulator is clearly a surrogate for having the radio on while driving and may lead to substantial predictive errors of the effectiveness of radio advertising directed toward drivers.

In market testing a potential change in price, the usual situation is that competitors are aware of the test and may decide either to do nothing or to "jam" the test by a promotional campaign or a price change of their own. In either case, if this is different from the action that the competitors would take in response to an actual price change, the results are a surrogate situation and consequently inaccurate. Bristol-Myers test marketed its Clairol brand hair conditioner, *Small Miracle*, in what turned out to be a surrogate situation. When *Small Miracle* was initially tested, it had few major competitors and performed well in tests. However, as *Small Miracle* went national, so did Gillette's *Silkience* and S. C. Johnson & Son's *Enhance*. Thus, the market situation encountered by *Small Miracle* was substantially different from its test situation and it was not successful.[3]

Experimental Errors and Experimental Design

The 10 types of experimental errors represent *potential* sources of error and do not necessarily affect all experiments. In general, experiments that use human respondents who are aware of some or all aspects of the experiment are most subject to these types of error.

All of the various types of error, except reactive error, measurement timing, and surrogate situation, can be controlled for by the experimental design. In general, the more controls that are built into the design, the more costly the experiment becomes. In addition, a design that is very efficient in controlling for some types of errors may be relatively inefficient with respect to others. Therefore, experiments should be designed to control for those errors that are *most probable* and are believed to be *most serious* in a given situation, not for all potential sources of error.

Experimental Design

Experimental design involves obtaining the proper information within an acceptable accuracy range for a cost that does not exceed the value of the information. As we saw in the previous section, a number of potential errors exist that can adversely affect the accuracy of the data from an experiment. Figure 7–1 illustrates how experimental design is affected by these factors.

Experimental designs can be categorized into two broad groups: **basic experimental designs** that consider the impact of only one independent variable at a time, and **statistical experimental designs** that allow the evaluation of the effect of more than one independent variable at a time.

Before specific designs can be described, it is necessary to introduce the symbols that are used in their descriptions:

> MB = *premeasurement:* a measurement made on the dependent variable before the introduction or manipulation of the independent variable
>
> MA = *postmeasurement:* a measurement made on the dependent variable after or during the introduction or manipulation of the independent variable
>
> X = *treatment:* the actual introduction or manipulation of the independent variable
>
> R = designation that the group is selected randomly

Any symbol that is to the *right* of another symbol indicates that the activity represented occurred *after* the one to its left. In the following discussion of experimental designs, we will show only one premeasurement and one postmeasurement. You should recognize that multiple pre- and postmeasurements are commonly used in practice.

Basic experimental designs: consider the effect of only one independent variable at a time.

Statistical experimental designs: allow the evaluation of more than one independent variable at a time.

Basic Experimental Designs

After-Only Design

The *after-only* design involves manipulating the independent variable and following this with a postmeasurement, or

$$X \quad MA$$

Ford Motor Co. spent $500,000 on an after-only experiment in Dallas and in San Diego. In this "experiment," women received engraved invitations to attend dealer showroom "parties" at which wine and cheese were served, the latest clothing fashions were displayed by models, and new Ford automobiles were shown in a "no pressure" situation. Subsequent purchases by those who attended the parties were one measure used to determine the "success" of the experiment.

The Ford example is typical of most new-product test markets. While after-only designs are often used, their results are difficult to interpret and are subject to numerous errors. Suppose 1 percent of the women attending a showroom "party" purchased a new Ford within six months after the party. What does this mean? Obviously, analyzing after-only experiments requires

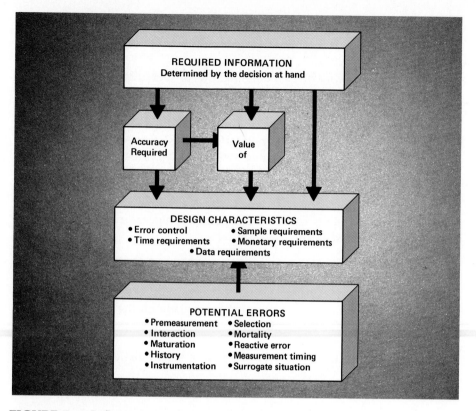

FIGURE 7-1 Influences on Experimental Design

substantial market knowledge and subjective judgment. In addition, after-only studies do not control for such serious potential error sources as history, maturation, selection, and mortality. For example, a history error might have occurred if Chevrolet dealers had run special sales to coincide with Ford's "experiment." Therefore, after-only designs should be used with care.

Before-After Design

The before-after design is like the after-only design, except that it also involves a premeasurement:

$$MB \quad X \quad MA$$

The result of interest is the *difference* between the pre- and postmeasurements *(MA − MB)*. This comparison gives this design a considerable advantage over the after-only design. If no errors exist, the difference between the two measures is caused by the independent variable.

Unfortunately, the before-after design is subject to a number of experimental errors. *History, maturation, premeasurement, instrumentation, mortality,* and *interaction* all *may* affect the results of this design. However, if our experimental units are stores and we are measuring sales, the only source of error that is likely to be important is history.

Assume this approach is used to estimate the effect of a price increase on market share. The price of the leading brand of piecrust mix is increased by $.15 per box within a supermarket chain. The prices of the other three brands remain the same. Market share is measured both before and after the price change; it is found to drop 13 percent.

Since history was not controlled for, attributing the market share decline to price involves judgment. The decline *may* have been caused by competitors' actions, quality-control problems, or other factors. The researcher may be willing to estimate subjectively the impact of any of these variables rather than go to the expense of adding a control group. However, the researcher must be alert to the possibility that extraneous variables caused the results, rather than the independent variable.

Because they lack a control group and thus cannot control history effects, both after-only and before-after designs are often referred to as *quasi-experimental designs*.

Before-After with Control Design

The *before-after with control* design involves the addition of a control group to the before-after design:

$$R \quad MB_1 \quad X \quad MA_1$$
$$R \quad MB_2 \quad \quad MA_2$$

The addition of the control group allows for the control of all potential sources of experimental error except *mortality* and *interaction*. For example, assume that a firm wishes to test the impact of a P-O-P display. Ten retail stores in the firm's trade area are selected at random for inclusion in the treatment group and 10 are selected for the control group. Sales are measured in each group of stores before and after the introduction of the new P-O-P display. The *change* in sales between the two groups is compared. That is, the measure of interest is

$$(MB_1 - MA_1) - (MB_2 - MA_2)$$

This comparison controls for any initial inequalities between the sales of the two groups. Similarly, direct premeasurement effects are controlled. Both groups receive the premeasurement, and any changes caused by this should influence both postmeasures equally. In this example, premeasurement effects are unlikely to influence sales (unless the sales personnel suspect that *their* performance is being monitored). *History, maturation,* and *instrumentation* should also affect both treatment and control groups equally.

The before-after with control group design is subject to *interaction* effects. Suppose a researcher is interested in the effect on attitudes of a single direct-mail advertisement. A group of respondents is selected and a premeasurement administered to all of them. Half of the respondents then receive the direct-mail advertisement (treatment group) and half receive nothing (control group). One week after the advertisement is delivered, both groups of respondents are remeasured.

Any *direct* effect, that is, learning or attitude change, caused by the premeasurement should affect both groups equally. However, if the premeasure serves to increase the respondent's interest or curiosity in the brand, the treatment and the control group may be affected differently. Those respondents in the treatment group will receive a direct-mail advertisement from the firm that they may read simply because of the interest generated by the premeasurement.

The effect of the premeasurement (increased interest) *interacts* with the independent variable (advertisement) to influence the postmeasurement (change of attitude). The control group may also experience increased interest because of the premeasure. However, because the control group will not be exposed to the advertising, the increased interest will dissipate without influencing the postmeasurement of attitudes. The overall result of this is that any conclusions about the effects of the advertising campaign may be generalized only to individuals who have taken the premeasurement.

In cases where interaction is unlikely and control for history and selection errors is important, the before-after with control group design is the best design in terms of cost and error control. An example of this design is shown in Research Application 7–2.

Simulated Before-After Design

The *simulated before-after design* was developed primarily to control for premeasurement and interaction errors in experiments dealing with attitudes and knowledge of human subjects. The design controls for these two errors by using separate groups for the pre- and postmeasurements:

$$R \quad MB$$
$$R \qquad X \quad MA$$

As in the before-after design, the measure of interest is the difference between *MA* and *MB.* Because different individuals receive the pre- and postmeasurements, there can be *no premeasurement* or *interaction effects.* However, the remaining problems associated with the standard before-after design, particularly *history,* remain.

This design is common in advertising research. A typical application involves giving a large sample of respondents a questionnaire to measure their attitude toward the product (premeasurement). An advertising campaign is then conducted (change in the independent variable). Finally, a *second* sample of respondents is given the same attitude questionnaire as the first group (postmeasurement). If the sampling is done properly and the two samples are large enough, they should be similar in terms of their initial attitude. Thus, any difference in the two scores can be attributed to the effects of the advertising campaign *and* any effects produced by history.

After-Only with Control

The premeasurements in the before-after with control group design introduce the possibility of uncontrolled *interaction* effects. In addition, premeasurements generally cost money and may increase the artificiality of the overall situation. They are necessary whenever there is a reasonable probability that the treatment and control groups are not initially equivalent on the depen-

RESEARCH APPLICATION 7-2

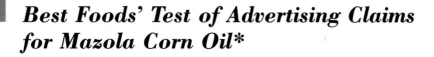

*Best Foods' Test of Advertising Claims for Mazola Corn Oil**

Best Foods, a division of CPC International Inc., used a before-after with control design to assess the desirability of three alternative advertising claims for its Mazola Corn Oil brand.†

The test employed a four-cell monadic design. Four independent groups of respondents were recruited in a mall intercept environment. Each respondent was exposed to a single advertising claim. The premeasurement in this test was a constant sum score—respondents were asked to divide their last 10 oil purchases among the various brands available.

The stimulus was in the form of a brief concept statement for the test cells. In the control cell, respondents were exposed to the brand's current advertising claim. (It was necessary to expose the control group to some stimulus rather than nothing; otherwise, it would be impossible to determine the extent to which seeing any Mazola concept in the test cell had a positive effect.)

The postmeasurement involved readministering the same constant sum measure used as a premeasurement, this time asking respondents to consider their *next* 10 purchases. A key evaluation measure was the average shift in respondents' point allocations to Mazola:

Average Pre–Post Shift for Mazola
(Number of Points Out of 10)

Control Cell	Adv. Claim A	Adv. Claim B	Adv. Claim C
+1.6	+1.6	+2.4	+1.9

In this case, Claim B significantly increased purchase interest over what was observed in the control cell. The claim was later incorporated into Mazola's advertising campaign.

*Provided by John Carter and Aaron Strauss of Best Foods.
†Mazola is a registered trademark of CPC International Inc.

---

dent variables. If it is likely that the groups are initially equal on the variable of interest, then there is no reason to go to the expense of a premeasurement. Instead, an *after-only with control* design can be used:

$$R \quad X_1 \quad MA_1$$
$$R \qquad\quad MA_2$$

This design explicitly controls for everything that the before-after with control design does except selection error. That is, even if random assignment is used, it is possible for the two groups to be initially unequal on the variable of interest. However, this design does eliminate the possibility of interaction. It is appropriate any time selection error is not likely to be a problem, such as when large random samples are used. It is uniquely appropriate when selection error is not a problem *and* interaction is.

After-only with control and before-after with control designs involving more than one level or version of the independent variable are sometimes called *completely randomized designs* (CRD). Such designs are subject to the

RESEARCH APPLICATION 7–3

In-Store Positioning Test for Equal

Equal, an artificial sweetener made by Nu-traSweet, is almost always consumed mixed with another product, primarily coffee or cereal. Equal is sold in small, lightweight packages that are generally stocked in the sugar section of the supermarket. Management felt that sales would increase if Equal were also stocked in the coffee and cereal sections. Safeway Scanner Marketing Research conducted an experiment to test management's idea.

Three matched groups of eight Safeway stores each in Houston were used. All 24 stores stocked Equal in its normal location during the 20-week test. Eight of the stores also placed Equal in a shelf extender in the coffee section and eight did the same in the cereal section. Sales were monitored daily using Safeway's scanner system. Sales were 15 percent higher in those stores with Equal in the coffee section as well as the sugar section. Sweetener sales were not significantly higher in those stores with Equal in the cereal section in addition to the sugar section.

SOURCE: L. Booth, "How to Get the Retailer's Attention," *Confectioner* (March/April 1990), 30–32.

same strengths and weaknesses as their simpler counterparts. Research Application 7–3 contains an example of such a design.

Solomon Four-Group Design

The *Solomon four-group design,* often called the *four-group six-study design,* consists of four groups, two treatment and two control, and six measurements, two premeasurements and four postmeasurements. An examination of the following diagram shows the overall design to consist of a before-after with control experiment and an after-only with control experiment run simultaneously:

$$
\begin{array}{llll}
R & MB_1 & X & MA_1 \\
R & MB_2 & & MA_2 \\
R & & X & MA_3 \\
R & & & MA_4
\end{array}
$$

The design explicitly controls for all sources of experimental error except *measurement timing, surrogate situation* and *reactive error,* which are not subject to control by designs. No single method of analysis makes use of all six measurements simultaneously. However, direct estimates of the effect of interaction and selection, as well as other experimental errors, can be made by various between-group analyses. The only time such an approach would be needed is when both selection error and interaction are likely to cause serious distortions of the data.

Conclusions Concerning Basic Designs

Table 7–2 summarizes the *potential* errors that may affect each design. A + indicates that the design controls for this type error; a − indicates that it is

TABLE 7–2 Experimental Designs and Potential Errors*

	History	Maturation	Premeasurement	Instrumentation	Selection	Mortality	Interaction Error	Reactive Error	Measurement Timing	Surrogate Situation
										Potential Error
1. *After-only*	−	−	+	+	−	−	+	0	0	0
2. *Before-after*	−	−	−	−	+	−	−	0	0	0
3. *Before-after with control*	+	+	+	+	+	−	−	0	0	0
4. *Simulated before-after*	−	−	+	−	−	+	+	0	0	0
5. *After-only with control*	+	+	+	+	−	−	+	0	0	0
6. *Solomon four-group*	+	+	+	+	+	+	+	0	0	0

*A + indicates that a method of controlling for the error is provided by the design; a − indicates no method of controlling is incorporated in the design; and an 0 indicates that the error is independent of the type of design.

vulnerable to it; and 0 indicates that the error is independent of the type of design. Remember that *potential errors* are not the same as *actual errors.*

Statistical Designs

Statistical designs permit the measurement of the effects of more than one independent variable. They also allow the researcher to control for specific extraneous variables that may confound the results. Finally, statistical designs permit an economical design when more than one measurement will be conducted on each respondent.

Statistical designs are actually a means of structuring a series of basic experiments to allow statistical control and analysis of extraneous variables. That is, statistical designs are simply several basic experiments run simultaneously. Therefore, statistical designs are subject to the same errors that can affect the particular basic design being used in a given experiment.

Randomized Blocks Design

Completely randomized designs are based on the assumptions that the experimental groups are initially similar on the dependent variable and that the members of these groups will react to the independent variable in a similar manner. These assumptions are frequently invalid.

Consider the following two experimental situations:

1. A field experiment to determine which of three price levels to use has a total of 27 stores available as experimental units. The sales volume of the stores ranges from $300,000 to $800,000 per month. Sales of the

product in question tend to vary closely with total store sales. In this situation, a CRD would not be appropriate since the probability of randomly selecting equivalent samples would be small.

2. A laboratory experiment is to be conducted to decide on an advertising theme for a new liqueur. The primary issue is whether to use a masculine theme, a feminine theme, or a gender-free theme. Six advertisements are prepared that represent different positions along a masculine–feminine appeal dimension. Management suspects that the reaction to the advertisement will be strongly influenced by the gender of the respondent. Again, a CRD would not be appropriate since the gender effects could not be easily determined.

Randomized block designs (RBD):
allow control of one major external variable in addition to one independent variable.

Randomized block designs (RBD) are appropriate for situations in which the researchers suspect that there is *one* major external variable, such as total sales or gender of the respondents, that might influence the results. Of course, one must be able to identify or measure this variable before one can utilize an RBD. In an RBD, the experimental units are *blocked*, that is, grouped or stratified, on the basis of the extraneous, or *blocking*, variable.

By ensuring that the various experimental and control groups are matched as closely as possible on the extraneous variable, we are assured that it affects all groups more or less equally. The principles and advantages of an RBD can be seen by reexamining the two research situations presented at the beginning of this section. In the first situation, the researcher was faced with the problem of selecting three groups from 27 stores with a wide range of sales. Total sales were believed to be an extraneous variable that could confound the experimental results. An RBD is appropriate since the stores can be grouped by sales level.

First, the stores are rank ordered in terms of sales. The total number of experimental units, 27, is divided by the number of experimental groups, 3, to determine how many blocks are needed, 9. The experimental units are then systematically assigned to the 9 blocks such that the top 3 ranked stores are assigned to the first block, the second 3 to the second block, and so forth. Finally, one unit from each block is *randomly assigned to each of the treatment groups*. Table 7–3 illustrates this process.

This process was recently used to compare the effectiveness of nutritional P-O-P signs, standard P-O-P signs, and no P-O-P signs for vegetables. The researchers used a procedure exactly like that shown in Table 7–3. The results of the study indicated that neither type of P-O-P sign affected vegetable sales.[4]

In the situation involving the masculine versus feminine advertisements, the concern is somewhat different. In this situation, it is possible to secure a large enough group of men and women to ensure adequate comparability of test and control groups. Rather than lack of comparability, the concern here is with isolating the effect of type of theme on the male and female subgroups as well as the total group. Again, an RBD represents an efficient approach.

Assume that a total sample of 800 males and 400 females is available. Individuals are assigned to blocks based on their gender, producing one block of 400 females and one block of 800 males. The individuals within each block are *randomly* assigned to treatment groups. The use of analysis of variance then allows the researcher to determine the impact of the commercial on the overall group as well as its effect on the male and female subgroups. The

TABLE 7-3 RBD to Increase Experimental Precision

Block No.	Store Rank	Treatment Groups		
		X_1	X_2	X_3
1	1,2,3	3	2	1
2	4,5,6	4	5	6
3	7,8,9	9	7	8
4	10,11,12	10	11	12
5	13,14,15	14	13	15
6	16,17,18	17	18	16
7	19,20,21	20	19	21
8	22,23,24	22	23	24
9	25,26,27	25	26	27

American Heart Association study described at the beginning of the chapter used a similar RBD; prospects and donors served as the two blocking groups. Likewise, the study described in Research Application 7–1 blocked on store type to allow the determination of any differential effects of P-O-P on the two types of outlets.

In general, RBDs are more useful than completely random designs because most marketing studies are affected by such extraneous variables as store type or size, region of the country, and gender, income, or social class of the respondent. The major shortcoming of RBDs is that they can control for only *one* extraneous variable. When there is a need to control for or block more than one variable, the researcher must use Latin square or factorial designs.

Latin Square Designs

Latin square designs allow the researcher to control statistically for two non-interacting extraneous variables in addition to the independent variable. This control is achieved by a blocking technique similar to that described in the previous section on randomized blocks designs.

This design requires that each extraneous or blocking variable be divided into an equal number of blocks or levels, such as drugstores, supermarkets, and discount stores. The independent variable must be divided into the same number of levels, such as high price, medium price, and low price. A Latin square design is shown in the form of a table with the rows representing the blocks on one extraneous variable and the columns representing the blocks on the other. The levels of the independent variable are then assigned to the cells in the table such that each level appears once, and only once, in each row and each column.

Latin square designs are described on the basis of the number of blocks on the extraneous variables. A design with three blocks is called a *3 × 3 Latin square*, four blocks is a *4 × 4 Latin square*, and so forth.

Suppose we wanted to test the impact on sales of three different price decreases for a personal care item. We suspect that the response may differ with the type of retail outlet—drugstore, supermarket, and discount store. In

Latin square designs: allow control of two noninteracting extraneous variables in addition to one independent variable.

addition, we feel that sales may vary over the time of the experiment. How should we proceed?

The first step in constructing a Latin square design is to construct a table with the blocks on the extraneous variables associated with the rows and columns. Since we have three levels of the independent variable (price) and three levels of one blocking or control variable (store type), we need three levels of the remaining blocking variable (time). Then, we can construct a table as follows:

		Store Type	
Time Period	Drug	Supermarket	Discount
1			
2			
3			

Next, we randomly assign the levels of the independent variable to the nine cells of the table, such that each of the three price levels is assigned once and only once to each row and each column.

This is, in fact, a simple procedure. The first step is to assign the three price levels randomly to each cell in row 1.

1	price 2	price 3	price 1

Next, price level 1 or 3 should be randomly assigned to row 2, column 1. Since price 2 is already in column 1, it is not eligible to appear there again.

1	price 2	price 3	price 1
2	price 1		

These four random assignments completely determine a 3 × 3 Latin square since the "once to each row and column" rule will automatically specify which treatment goes into each of the remaining cells:

		Store Type	
Time Period	Drug	Supermarket	Discount
1	price 2	price 3	price 1
2	price 1	price 2	price 3
3	price 3	price 1	price 2

This table represents the 3 × 3 Latin square design. From 5 to 20 stores of each type would generally be involved. In this case, during the first time period (say two weeks), five drugstores would price the product at price 2, five supermarket stores would be at price 3, and five discount stores would be price 1. The average sales in each cell would be recorded.

In the second time period the price levels would be shifted such that drugstores have price level 1, supermarkets have price level 2, and discount stores have price level 3. The same measurement procedure would be used. Price levels would be shifted among store types once again for the third time period.

This design has the sales effect of each price level recorded once in each time period and once in each store type. Analysis focuses on which price level produced the most sales (or profits) and whether or not there were differential effects across store types.

Latin square designs are widely used in marketing research. They are especially useful in retail studies where the need to control for store type or size and time period is particularly acute. The Latin square design also allows the minimization of sample size by allowing the same experimental units to react to all the different levels of the independent variable.

Latin square designs suffer from several limitations. First, the requirement of an equal number of rows, columns, and treatment levels can sometimes pose problems for specific research tasks. For example, if we want to test four versions of a product and control for time and store type, we must be able to isolate four store types. Furthermore, we must run the study for four time periods. If there are only three types of stores that carry this product, or if time is of critical importance, the Latin square must be altered. Another drawback to the Latin square design is that only two extraneous variables can be controlled for at once.

When several versions of a treatment variable, such as price, are applied to one control variable, such as a store, Latin square designs assume that there are no "carryover" effects from one condition to another. Thus, the design assumes that a low price in time period 1 will not affect the sales in time period 2 when a higher price is in effect. Clearly, such assumptions are not always valid, and several versions of the Latin square design have been created to deal with this type of problem.[5]

A final weakness of the Latin square design is the restriction that the control variables cannot interact with each other or with the independent variable. As demonstrated in the next section, interaction between variables is fairly common in marketing.

Factorial Design

Factorial designs are used to measure the effect of two or more independent variables at various levels. They are particularly useful when there is some reason to believe that interaction might occur. **Interaction** occurs when the simultaneous effect of two or more variables is different from the sum of their effects taken one at a time. For example, your favorite color might be gray and your favorite dessert might be ice cream. However, it does not follow that you would prefer gray ice cream.

Factorial designs: allow measurement of the effects of multiple independent variables and their interactions.

Interaction: the simultaneous effect of two or more variables is different from the sum of their effects taken one at a time.

RESEARCH APPLICATION 7–4

Measuring the Sales Response to Price Changes in Different Product Categories

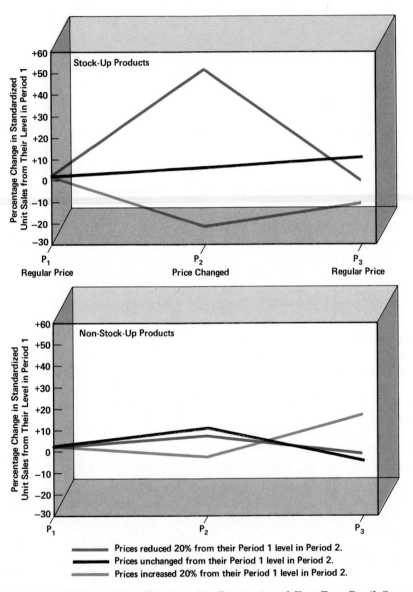

SOURCE: D. S. Lituack, R. J. Calantone, P. R. Warshaw, "An Examination of Short-Term Retail Grocery Price Effects," *Journal of Retailing* (Fall 1985), 20–21.

Interaction can involve any number of variables. Factorial designs coupled with analysis of variance statistical procedures are required to measure interaction.

A factorial design requires that all possible combinations of the independent variables be tested. Thus, if we are interested in three levels of sweetness, four levels of carbonation, and four colors for a proposed new soft drink, we would need to test $3 \times 4 \times 4 = 48$ versions of the product. If we also wanted to test three brand names, the number of versions to be tested would increase to 144!

A recent study investigated the sales impact of retail price changes on 72 supermarket items. A 3×2 factorial design was used with three levels of price (normal, 20 percent increase, 20 percent decrease) and two levels of product type (subject to stocking-up and not subject to stocking-up). Research Application 7–4 illustrates the results. As can be seen, very strong interaction occurs. Price changes have a major impact on stock-up items (decreases in price increase sales and vice versa) but have virtually no impact on non-stock-up items.

Conclusions Concerning Experimental Designs

The preceding sections have described a number of experimental designs. These designs range from the simple after-only design to factorial designs. No one design is *best*. The choice of the experimental design must balance cost constraints with accuracy requirements. Accuracy is related to the amount of error. However, we should not assume that the possibility of an experimental error means that the error *will* occur. It *is* possible that history will *not* bias the results in a before-after design, even though the design itself does not control for it. The researcher and the decision maker should apply judgment in deciding which errors represent sufficient potential danger to warrant additional outlays for control.

Figure 7–2 provides a very general guide for selecting an appropriate experimental design.

A research design that is similar to experimentation, but with the critical difference that the treatment and control group(s) are selected *after* the introduction of the potential causal variable, is the *ex post facto* design. Since it is often confused with a true experiment, its characteristics are described next.

Ex Post Facto Studies

Several department stores share details of their operations in order to improve their efficiency. A researcher selected one highly successful store and a relatively unsuccessful store. The study found "demographic differences and

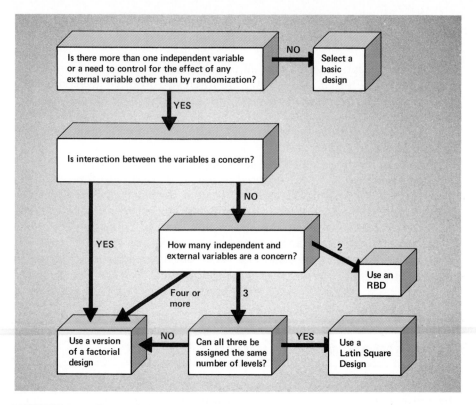

FIGURE 7–2 General Guide to Selecting an Experimental Design

differences in self-confidence, aggressiveness, and fashion leadership" between the two stores' buyers. The researcher concluded that "balance in the buyer team and the discretion given to buyers may be two of the keys to success."[6]

The study described is an example of *ex post facto* research. In **ex post facto studies** one starts with "the present situation as an effect of some previously acting causal factors and attempt to trace back over an interval of time to some assumed causal complex of factors.[7] Thus, this study began with the conditions "successful store" and "unsuccessful store" and examined one potential causative factor: characteristics of store buyers.

Ex post facto research is often treated as an experimental design. However, it does *not* meet the key characteristics of experimental designs: the researcher does *not* manipulate the independent variable nor control which subjects are exposed to the independent variable.

Ex post facto projects are common and useful in marketing research. For example, a Quebec law recently banned advertising to children on Quebec TV stations. This left American border stations as the only source of television ads for toys and children's cereals. As a result, English-speaking children, who watch substantial amounts of American TV, were exposed to substantially more toy and cereal ads than were French-speaking children, who tend

Ex post facto studies: start with the current situation and attempt to look backward in time for potential causes.

RESEARCH APPLICATION 7–5

National Cancer Institute of Canada: Study of Artificial Sweeteners and Cancer Using Ex Post Facto *Methodology*

A Canadian study linking bladder cancer in humans to saccharin consumption was very influential in the FOA's decision to request a ban on the sale of saccharin.

The study involved a specific "case-control" methodology that is fairly common in medical studies of this type.* All reported nonrecurrent cases of primary bladder cancer in British Columbia, Nova Scotia, and Newfoundland served as one set of respondents. All participants were interviewed within six months of the diagnosis.

For each of the 632 "cases" participating in the study, a control (another individual) was included that was matched on gender, age (within ± five years), and neighborhood. A questionnaire was developed that included questions on demographic variables, residential history, use of non-public water supplies, occupational history, consumption of beverages and meats containing preservatives, medical history, use of analgesics, and smoking. The questionnaires were administered in the respondents' homes by trained interviewers.

An analysis of the resulting data on saccharin use and the incidence of bladder cancer revealed a statistically significant ($P = .01$) relationship. The final paragraph of the report concluded:

> Our results suggest a causal relation between saccharin use and bladder cancer in males, especially when they are considered in conjunction with results in animals.

*For a complete description of the study, see G.R. Howe et al., "Artificial Sweeteners and Human Bladder Cancer," *The Lancet* (September 17, 1977), 578–581.

---

to watch local French-language stations. A study found that English-speaking children were able to recognize more toys available in the marketplace and had more children's cereals in their homes than did French-speaking children. This finding was further supported when the amount of American television watched was controlled for in each group. However, it could easily be that parents' attitudes, family life-style, or a host of other factors could influence both English-language TV viewing *and* toy knowledge and cereal consumption.[8]

Ex post facto studies will continue to enjoy widespread use because they provide *evidence* of causation in situations where experimentation is impractical or impossible. For example, Research Application 7–5 describes a controversial *ex post facto* study on the health effects of the consumption of artificial sweeteners.

Although frequently the only practical approach, *ex post facto* studies are not as desirable as experiments. They *cannot* be used to prove causation. Further, they are vulnerable to most of the errors described previously.

Summary

Experimentation involves the manipulation of one or more variables by the experimenter in such a way that its effect on one or more other variables can be measured. A variable being manipulated is called an independent variable. One that reflects the impact of the independent variable is called a dependent variable. The portion of the sample or population exposed to a manipulation of the independent variable is a treatment group. A group in which the independent variable is unchanged is the control group.

Experimental results can be affected by 10 types of errors: (1) premeasurement, (2) interaction, (3) maturation, (4) history, (5) instrumentation, (6) selection, (7) mortality, (8) reactive error, (9) measurement timing, and (10) surrogate situation.

There are six basic experimental designs: (1) after-only, (2) before-after, (3) before-after with control, (4) simulated before-after, (5) after-only with control, and (6) Solomon four-group. Each design controls for different combinations of errors, has different costs, and is appropriate for different situations.

There are three major types of statistical experimental designs: (1) randomized blocks, (2) Latin squares, and (3) factorial. They differ in terms of how many independent variables they can control for and in their ability to measure interaction. Interaction occurs when the simultaneous effect of two or more variables is different from the sum of their effects taken one at a time.

Ex post facto studies start with the present situation and look backward to determine the cause of the current situation. They are not experiments because the researcher does not manipulate the independent variable or control which subjects are exposed to it.

Review Questions

7.1. What does experimentation involve?

7.2. What do *ex post facto* studies involve?

7.3. Are *ex post facto* studies experiments? Why?

7.4. Describe and give an example of each of the following error types:

    a. premeasurement   f. selection
    b. interaction error   g. mortality
    c. maturation   h. reactive error
    d. history   i. measurement timing
    e. instrumentation   j. surrogate situation

7.5. How does *premeasurement error* differ from *interaction error*?

7.6. What is the difference between *demand characteristics* and *demand artifacts*?

7.7. Describe the following experimental designs using the appropriate symbols and indicate for which errors they control:

    a. after-only   d. before-after with control
    b. before-after   e. after-only with control
    c. simulated before-after   f. Solomon four-group

7.8. Is it always necessary to control for all types of experimental error? Why?

7.9. What is a *completely randomized design*?

7.10. What is the purpose of *randomization* and *matching* in experimental design?

7.11. What is *interaction*?

7.12. Describe each of the following designs:
   a. randomized block
   b. Latin square
   c. factorial

7.13. How do you decide which type of statistical design to use?

7.14. What is a *5 × 5 Latin square design*?

7.15. What is a *4 × 3 × 2 factorial design*?

7.16. What are the strengths and weaknesses of a *Latin square design*?

7.17. What are the strengths and weaknesses of a *factorial design*?

Discussion Questions/Problems

7.18. Why are simulated before-after designs sometimes used in field experiments on advertising effectiveness? What problems can arise in their use?

7.19. How will the increasing spread of UPC scanners affect marketing experiments?

7.20. Why is experimentation uniquely suited for determining causation?

7.21. Why is the Solomon four-group design seldom used in marketing studies?

7.22. Describe a specific situation for which you would recommend each of the following designs as being best (being sure to consider cost). Justify your answer.
   a. after-only
   b. before-after
   c. after-only with control
   d. before-after with control
   e. simulated before-after with control
   f. Solomon four-group
   g. randomized block
   h. Latin square
   i. factorial

7.23. Develop an alternative explanation for the results in Research Application 7–5. How would you test your explanation?

7.24. Design an experiment to determine which of two names for a new snack food is preferred by students on your campus.

7.25. Repeat 7.24, but introduce an explicit control for gender.

7.26. Repeat 7.24, but introduce explicit controls for gender and age (under 21, 21–25, and over 25).

7.27. Repeat 7.24, but with four names.

7.28. Repeat 7.25, but with four names.

7.29. Repeat 7.26, but with four names.

7.30. Repeat 7.26, but assume that you are concerned about the interaction between name and gender.

7.31. Develop a research design to provide information for each of the following questions:
   a. Will a 12-ounce version of a new product selling for $.99 produce more revenue for the firm than a 10-ounce version selling for $.89?
   b. Will decreasing the price by 10 percent increase unit sales by more than 20 percent?
   c. Will a blue, red, or yellow version of this be most preferred, and will preference vary by gender and age (under 30, 30–44, and 45 or older)?

7.32. What problems are encountered in experiments with human subjects that are not encountered in experiments with inanimate objects such as those a chemist might conduct?

Projects/Activities

7.33. Implement your design from problem _____ and write a managerial report on your results. What types of errors are most likely to have affected your results?
   a. 7.24   e. 7.28
   b. 7.25   f. 7.29
   c. 7.26   g. 7.30
   d. 7.27

7.34. Consult the latest issues of the *Journal of Marketing, Journal of Marketing Research,* or *Journal of Advertising Research.* Prepare and present to the class a description of an experiment reported in the journal. What errors may affect the results of the experiment?

7.35. Read the Goldberg article referenced in footnote 8. Prepare a report evaluating the strengths and weaknesses of the research design used.

Notes

1. T. A. Shimp, E. M. Hyatt, D. J. Snyder, "A Critical Appraisal of Demand Artifacts in Consumer Research," *Journal of Consumer Research* (December 1991), 273–283.

2. See D. S. Lituack, R. J. Calantone, P. R. Warshaw, "An Examination of Short-Term Retail Grocery Price Effects," *Journal of Retailing* (Fall 1985), 9–25; and S. Gupta, "Impact of Sales Promotions on When, What, and How Much to Buy," *Journal of Marketing Research* (November 1988), 342–355.

3. N. Giges, "No Miracle in Small Miracle: Story Behind Failure," *Advertising Age* (August 16, 1982), 76. See also L. Bogart, C. Lehman, "The Case of the 30-Second Commercial," *Journal of Advertising Research* (March 1983), 11–19.

4. D. D. Achabal, "The Effect of Nutrition P-O-P Signs," *Journal of Retailing* (Spring 1987), 9–24.

5. S. Banks, *Experimentation in Marketing* (New York: McGraw-Hill Book Co., 1965); G. T. McKinnon, J. P. Kelly, E. D. Robinson, "Sales Effects of Point-of-Purchase In-Store Signing," *Journal of Retailing* (Summer 1981), 49–63; and C. Paksog, J. B. Wilkinson, J. B. Mason, "Learning and Carryover Effects in Retail Experimentation," *Journal of the Market Research Society* (April 1985), 109–129.

6. C. R. Martin, Jr., "The Contribution of the Professional Buyer to a Store's Success or Failure," *Journal of Retailing* (Summer 1973), 69–70.

7. F. S. Chapin, *Experimental Designs in Sociological Research*, rev. ed. (New York: Harper & Row Publishers, 1955), 95.

8. M. E. Goldberg, "A Quasi-Experiment Assessing the Effectiveness of TV Advertising Directed to Children," *Journal of Marketing Research* (November 1990), 445–454.

8

Experimental Environment

LEARNING OBJECTIVES

Upon completing this chapter, you should be able to

1. Distinguish internal validity from external validity.

2. Explain the nature of reactive errors in laboratory experiments and discuss ways to minimize them.

3. List and describe the common applications of laboratory experiments.

4. Describe the common field experiments used for advertising copy tests.

5. Describe and evaluate standard test markets.

6. Describe and evaluate controlled-store test markets.

7. Describe and evaluate minimarket test markets.

8. Describe and evaluate electronic test markets.

9. Describe and evaluate simulated test markets.

10. Explain the unique problems encountered by multinational firms in test marketing.

The Advertising Research Foundation's Experiment to Determine the Effectiveness of Public Service Announcements

Recently, the Advertising Research Foundation attempted to determine the effectiveness of public service advertising (PSA) campaigns.[1] The research was sponsored by the Advertising Council. A PSA campaign by the American Cancer Society aimed at communicating the danger of colon cancer was selected for the test (see page 190). Colon cancer, the number two cancer killer, was felt to be a good topic for the test as it is a particularly sensitive issue, provoking both embarrassment and denial, especially among men. Some doctors are reluctant to bring up the subject, and many health insurers do not pay for preventive testing. If a PSA campaign would work for colon cancer, it should work with less sensitive issues as well. In addition, colon cancer was receiving little media attention, which would allow more confidence that the campaign itself is the cause of any observed changes in the respondents.

The PSA campaign ran and research was conducted within four Behavior-Scan test markets. An equal number of target households—which included the target audience of adults 40 to 69—were chosen in each market. Each market's split cable facilities were used to deliver the PSA to those households and to control the level of advertising received by each household.

Each market was then divided into two advertising cells: a cell exposed to an "average" level of advertising and a cell exposed to an "above average" level of advertising. This was done by means of cut-ins over donated time owned by Procter & Gamble Co., General Motors, and Gillette. Because 40 percent of the households had two-way meters on their TVs, it was also possible to measure actual exposure opportunities across both advertising levels; that is, the number of PSAs that ran while a household's TV set was actually on and tuned to the channel.

The campaign consisted of one 30-second PSA which ran from July 31, 1989, through July 23, 1990, with three waves of research being conducted:

- Benchmark wave in July 1989, prior to the campaign.
- Wave #1 in January 1990, six months into the campaign.
- Wave #2 in July 1990, 12 months into the campaign.

The sample size for each research wave was as follows:

· Benchmark wave: 757 households spread evenly across all four markets.
· Wave #1: 1,511 households.
· Wave #2: 1,500 households.

These sample sizes were chosen in order to be able to read small changes in behavior as statistically significant.

"Too Late"

(MUSIC UP AND UNDER THROUGHOUT) -...

...

...

...

...

...

WIFE: Ben, it says each year 60,000 men and women die of colon cancer. HUSBAND: Uh, huh.

WIFE: But it's 90% curable if treated early.

Maybe we should get a check-up.

HUSBAND: Honey, I have more important things to worry about right now.

(MUSIC)

(MUSIC UP AND OUT)

The experiment conducted by the Advertising Research Foundation was a *before-after* experiment as described in the previous chapter. As noted in that chapter, all experimental designs are influenced by a number of controllable and uncontrollable factors. One of the major influences this research project must contend with is the experimental environment.

Experimental environments can be classified according to the level of artificiality or realism they contain. Artificiality involves eliciting behavior from the respondents in a situation that is different from the normal situation in which that behavior would occur. Thus, a taste test in which respondents are brought to a firm's product development laboratory, given three different versions of a soft drink in glasses labeled *L*, *M*, and *P*, and asked of which version, if any, they would like to receive a free carton, contains a high degree of artificiality.

At the other extreme, the three versions could be introduced into a number of stores or geographic areas accompanied by regular P-O-P displays, advertising, and pricing. Such an experiment is characterized by a high degree of realism.

The first study described represents a **laboratory experiment,** whereas the second represents a *field experiment*. Laboratory experiments are characterized by a relatively high degree of artificiality. Field experiments have a relatively high level of realism. A given experiment may fall anywhere along this artificiality–realism continuum. Those nearer the artificiality end are termed "laboratory" experiments and those nearer the realism end are termed "field" experiments. The American Cancer Society study was a field experiment. Each general type of experiment has its particular strengths and weaknesses, as described in the following sections.

> **Laboratory experiments:** are conducted in a physical situation different from that in which the actual behavior of interest will occur.

Laboratory Experiments

Laboratory experiments involve isolating the research in a physical situation apart from the routine of ordinary living and by manipulating one or more independent variables under rigorously specified, operationalized, and controlled conditions."[2] This degree of control is seldom possible in field experiments.

This isolation provides a high level of **replicability** or **internal validity** in that the same experimental procedures will produce the same results if repeated with similar subjects. An advertisement that elicits a positive response from a subject group when viewed under strictly controlled laboratory conditions will elicit the same, or nearly the same, positive response when repeated with other groups of similar subjects in a similar laboratory setting.

However, the executive in charge of advertising is not concerned with the ability of the advertisement to elicit positive responses from other groups of respondents in a laboratory setting. The ultimate concern is the response of the market composed of individuals faced with real-world diversions, such as children who want to play, noise from the television, and projects that need completion; and retailers and/or wholesalers who make stock level and pro-

> **Internal validity (replicability):** indicates that observed changes in the dependent variable were indeed caused by changes in the independent variable.

RESEARCH APPLICATION 8–1

Green Giant's Laboratory Experiment for Oven Crock Baked Beans

Green Giant developed a highly flavored version of baked beans which it labeled Oven Crock baked beans. According to an executive involved in the development: "We did a series of *blind taste tests* and had a significant winner over bland pork and beans by a 3-to-1 or 4-to-1 margin."

Blind taste tests are laboratory experiments in which consumers evaluate various versions of a product without knowing the brand name. In general, the consumption environment is strictly controlled so that time of day, accompanying foods, or individually added flavors cannot distort the results of the test. Thus, taste tests are generally highly replicable (similar subjects will prefer the same version each time the study is repeated).

However, Oven Crock was a "disaster" in test market. Surveys later showed that people who ate heavily flavored baked beans preferred to add their own "special" flavorings to the bland variety and therefore would not buy preflavored beans.

The physical control over external variables that the laboratory test provided did not exist in the test market situation. Once individuals could "spice up" their own beans, the preflavored variety was no longer preferred.

External (predictive) validity: indicates that the observed changes in the dependent variable will occur in the environments in which the actual behavior of interest will occur.

motional decisions. **Predictive validity,** or **external validity** is the ability of the results in an experimental situation to predict the results in the actual situation of interest to the researcher.

Unfortunately, laboratory experiments are generally somewhat weak in generalizability. This weakness is a direct consequence of their primary strength. That is, the physical removal of most extraneous variables provides laboratory experiments with a high degree of replicability or internal validity at the same time that it limits their predictive validity. Research Application 8–1 provides an example of the problems this can cause.[3]

Laboratory experiments tend to cost substantially less in terms of resources and time than field experiments. Further, they enable a company to minimize the chance that competitors will learn of its new ideas. This has led many researchers to use laboratory experiments in the early stages of their research projects, when they are concerned with developing one or a limited number of advertisements or products. Then, if the costs and risks warrant it, these versions are subjected to further tests in field experiments. Appropriately designed laboratory experiments are also sometimes used as the final step before market introduction.[4]

Reactive Errors in Laboratory Experiments

A **reactive error** occurs when the experiment causes the respondent to react to the situation itself, rather than to the independent variable. Reactive errors have two aspects: the *experimental situation* and the *experimenter.*

Subjects do not remain passive in an experimental situation. They attempt to understand what is going on about them. In addition, they typically attempt to behave as "expected." If there are cues in the environment suggesting that a certain type of behavior is appropriate, many subjects will conform in order to be "good" subjects.

The main control for errors of this type is to use creative environments and/or to design separate control conditions for suspected reactive arrangements. Research Application 8–2 illustrates an attempt to develop a realistic experimental environment in which to pretest package designs. Theater tests (see page 197) are an attempt to develop a realistic laboratory environment in which to pretest television commercials.

The effect of the *experimenter* is very similar to the influence of the personal interviewer in survey research. For example, nonverbal behaviors by experimenters have been found to influence subjects' preferences in a cola taste test even though the subjects were not aware of the influence.[5]

Experimenter effects can be limited by some of the same techniques used to reduce interviewer bias. Thus, one should use highly trained experimenters, keep them uninformed about the research hypotheses, and minimize their contact with the respondents. Tape recordings, written instructions, and other impersonal means of communication with respondents should be used whenever feasible.

> **Reactive error:** effects on the dependent variable(s) caused by the artificiality of the experimental situation and/or the behavior of the experimenter.

Applications of Laboratory Experiments

Laboratory experiments are widely used in pretesting the impact of new or altered packages, advertisements, product concepts, and products. They are commonly used for evaluating pricing issues but are rarely used in assisting distribution decisions.

Package Tests.   Packages must attract attention, convey information, and reflect the image of the brand. Research Application 8–2 illustrated one approach to conducting package design experiments (various versions would be compared to each other or to the current package). Eye tracking and other physiological responses (see Chapter 13) are also used to test package designs.

Advertising Tests.   The **tachistoscope** is a slide projector with adjustable projection speeds and levels of illumination. Ads can be flashed on a screen with exposure times down to a small fraction of a second—$\frac{1}{32}$, $\frac{1}{64}$ of a second if desired—with varying levels of light. Ads are tested to determine at which speeds elements such as the product, brand, and headline are recognized.

Tachistoscopic tests are widely used for copy testing. The nature of the technique effectively limits its application to the evaluation of print, outdoor, P-O-P, packages, and individual frames of TV ads. The way in which Sears uses tachistoscopic tests for ad evaluation, and the perceived advantages of this technique over other tests for this purpose, are described in Research

> **Tachistoscope:** a slide projector with adjustable projection speeds and levels of illumination.

RESEARCH APPLICATION 8–2

The Pretesting Company's Laboratory Test Environment for Package Design Experiments

A. Exposure to Advertising Campaign (where appropriate)

Each qualified respondent will be given six rough or finished advertisements on six different product categories (one being the test brand) and questioned on each ad's target message communication. This pre-exposure to advertising is only used where strong advertising support will be provided in the "real world" when introducing the new product or line extension.

B. Brand Examination While "Shopping"

Each respondent will be seated in front of a five-and-one-half foot diagonal rear projection screen and told that he/she is to photographically go "shopping" through a supermarket and to choose three different brands (first, second, and third choice) for three different product categories from the photographic "shelves." The respondent will have the ability to use the close-up panel, which will photographically bring any product chosen on-shelf into a simulated one-foot distance view. The respondent will be able to photographically go back and forth on any shelf, examining any product for as long or short a period as he/she desires. The respondent will not be aware that a computer is keeping an accurate measure of which products are being photographically approached and for what duration.

C. Measurements While "Shopping"

Each respondent will be tested in terms of how quickly he/she can find the test package in a real-world setting, surrounded by competitive products on a life-size screen. The respondent will be told that he/she is about to see four shelf slides (one for each of the four product categories), one at a time. Each slide will show a product category in a natural shopping setting with full competitive surroundings. For each category, the slides may or may not actually contain the product to be found by the respondent. This is to prevent respondents from assuming that the test product is in view and quickly indicating the product has been "found."

As soon as the respondent believes he/she had identified the test product on-shelf, he/she is to touch the product with a special pointer which will remove the slide from view and will record his/her reaction time. The respondent will then be asked to identify the test package, both for package design and copy.

D. Competitive Imagery Measurement

Each respondent will be asked to rate the ideal product for the test category on a customized list of attributes in terms of the importance of each attribute.

SOURCE: *The Pretesting Company* (Englewood, NJ, undated). Used with permission.

RESEARCH APPLICATION 8–2 (continued)

Consumer presses button on joystick to freeze slide of store shelf showing life-sized laundry-detergent packaging.

Respondent uses joystick to zoom in on four competitive brands. Enlargement allows subject to read product prices on shelf facings.

RESEARCH APPLICATION 8–3

*Evaluation of Advertisements at Sears, Roebuck & Co. Using the Tachistoscope**

Uses of the Tachistoscope

1. *Screening a Number of Ads for Visual Impact*— 20 to 30 ads are sequentially presented to a viewer using a T-Scope to control duration of exposure, which is usually seven-tenths-of-a-second. A second series of 20 to 30 ads is shown one-by-one. About half of the shots were seen earlier; the other half are new. Respondents are told that some of the ads they will now see were seen before. As they view each ad, the respondents are asked a recognition question (How certain are you that you saw this ad before?), and a series of rating scales. Using two or more sample cells, recognition scores can be adjusted by subtracting false recognition percentages. In this way, ads with the strongest visual impact are identified.

2. *Communication Tests*—An ad is shown at 0.7 seconds, 3 seconds, and for as long as the viewer likes. Questions about what the ad says and shows follow each viewing. In this way, we can determine if an ad is quickly communicating what is intended. Results on two or more ads can be easily compared, and norms for product identification, and other measures, established.

3. *Design Assessment*—A sign or package is shown at 0.7 seconds, sometimes longer, via the T-Scope, and viewers are asked to describe what they saw. Next, they are told they will see an array of signs or packages, usually six to nine items in a three-column two-row or 3×3 grid. Using the T-Scope as a reaction timer, the respondents are told to release the button, blackening the screen when they see the item they saw earlier. When that happens, they are shown a grid, and asked to tell where they saw the item. If they answer correctly, and only then, their time is counted. We learn what they cue on through the T-Scope exposure and how visually impactful the cue is. The test is usually carried out in black and white with one sample, and in color with another. This is done so the contributions of both color and design can be measured.

Advantages of Using the Tachistoscope

1. Behavioral measures are more sensitive than attitudinal ones, more reliable, less subject to regional variations, and more stable with smaller samples.

2. Marketing managers are less likely to challenge such objective data, and they readily understand it.

3. The T-Scope itself is a more reliable, portable, flexible, and accurate device than others used in physiological measurements of advertising effects.

*Provided by and used through the courtesy of Sears, Roebuck & Co.

Application 8–3. Eye tracking (see Chapter 13) is also widely used in laboratory tests of advertisements.

Theater tests are another laboratory approach for testing television commercials. A test commercial is placed in a potential new television show that is shown to respondents in a movie theater. Pre- and postexposure attitudes and preferences are measured and the difference is taken as an indicator of the effectiveness of the commercial.

Theater tests are conducted on new television commercials by about one-half of all large television advertisers. These tests have the advantages of being inexpensive and providing a measure of the responses generated by the ad. Theater tests are conducted in a forced exposure setting, however, and so do not indicate how well the ad attracts attention.

A variety of other laboratory environments are available for pretesting different versions of print, radio, and television commercials. In general, these environments expose the commercials while the respondent is presumably focusing on the editorial or program content. Attitudes, affect, information recall, and/or purchase intentions are commonly used as the dependent variable(s). Before-after and after-only designs (with either an explicit control group or preestablished minimum "scores") are used. Focus groups and other in-depth questioning techniques are used to determine what the ad or package is communicating.

Pillsbury launched an advertising campaign for their new Crusty French Loaf using an Inspector Clouseau (the inspector portrayed by Peter Sellers in the Pink Panther movies) look-alike. Pretesting revealed that "the Clouseau character was so successful that he overshadowed the product . . . people tended to play back the character not the product." The commercial was revised to focus more on the product and the brand name. The revised version was successful in both the pretest situation and the market.[6]

Product Tests. Laboratory tests are widely used in the early stages of product development. Various versions of products that can be readily evaluated by consumers—such as foods, beverages, and most personal-care items—are routinely subjected to *blind* use tests (consumers rate performance without knowing the brand name) against each other and competitors. Procter & Gamble has a policy that no new product may be introduced unless it outperforms competitors in such a test.

While laboratory product tests such as taste tests offer a high degree of control over the consumption environment and produce data rapidly, they do not replicate the actual consumption environment. Research Application 8–1 and the Coca-Cola example described in Research Application 3–1 illustrate the problems this can cause.

Extended use tests, which are between a laboratory and field experiment, are frequently used as a follow-up to product taste tests or one-time use tests. In extended-use tests, consumers are given a supply of the product to use "normally" at home. While this method is still somewhat artificial (no purchase decision was made and there is pressure to use the product), it is substantially more realistic than a pure laboratory approach.

Theater tests: place a test commercial in a potential television show that is shown to respondents in a movie theater. The difference between pre- and postexposure attitudes and preferences serves as a measure of the commercial's effectiveness.

Extended-use tests: provide consumers with a supply of the test product to use at home.

Field Experiments

Field experiments:
are conducted in
an environment
similar to the one
in which the
actual behavior of
interest will occur.

Field experiments involve varying the independent variable in the market-place. Unfortunately, they are also characterized by a relative lack of control. This lack of control often extends to the independent variable as well as to extraneous variables.

For example, many field experiments require cooperation from wholesalers and/or retailers. However, this cooperation is often difficult to secure. Retailers who have a policy of price cutting may refuse to carry a product at the specified price, or they may be reluctant to assign prime shelf-facings to an untried product.

Control of extraneous variables is even more difficult. Such factors as bad weather, strikes in pertinent industries, and campaigns by competitors are beyond the control of the researcher. In fact, such events may occur without the researcher becoming aware of them. The problem is compounded even further by the fact that these extraneous variables may affect some regions where the experiment is being conducted and not others.

This lack of control reduces the *replicability* or *internal validity* of field experiments. However, their "real-world" setting tends to increase their *external validity*. The strengths and weaknesses of this approach can be seen in field experiments of advertising copy.

Advertising Copy Field Tests

**Day-after recall
(DAR):**
respondents are
asked to watch a
particular
television show
containing a test
commercial one
day and their
memory of the
commercial is
measured in a
telephone
interview the next
day.

Day-after recall (DAR) is the most widely used method to field test television ads. A leading supplier of DAR copy tests, ASI Market Research, conducts tests for television commercials using the research design described in Research Application 8–4.

ASI conducts a similar test for recall of magazine ads called Print Plus. In this methodology, the test ads are inserted into the current issue of magazines such as *Cosmopolitan, Sports Illustrated,* and *People*. Respondents are asked to help evaluate the magazine and are interviewed by phone the day after they are given the magazine. Persuasion is also measured by taking before and after measures of brand preference.

While a number of studies document the predictive validity of ASI's approach (somewhat similar methodologies are used by other researchers),[7] there is concern that recall measures are not appropriate for emotional or "feeling" ads.[8] In addition, recall measures do not directly measure the sales impact of advertising. For direct sales impact tests, electronic test markets are gaining popularity. The ARF example that opened this chapter and Research Application 8–5 illustrate this approach.

Test Marketing

Test marketing represents a particular type of field experiment that is often conducted in conjunction with the development of a new consumer product. **Test marketing** involves the duplication of all or part of the planned national

RESEARCH APPLICATION 8–4

ASI's Recall Plus ® Methodology

Sample. The purposive sample consists of 200 males and 200 females with 45 percent 18–34, 30 percent 35–49, and 25 percent 50–65. Samples with any other characteristics can be used at a higher cost. Respondents are randomly selected from cable subscribers in the cities in which ASI operates. Respondents are asked to "preview a new television program" that will be shown on an unused cable channel that evening. Records are kept so that respondents are used only once. Each test involves a minimum of two cities.

Treatment. The same unaired, 30-minute situation comedy is used in each test. It contains four noncompeting test commercials and one nontest "filler" commercial each time. The position of each commercial is rotated to avoid position bias. Re spondents are contacted by phone the day after viewing the program. Viewership is verified for both the program and the commercials. Questions about the program are asked first, followed by questions on the commercials. Four unaided product category cues are given to each respondent; if the respondent cannot correctly identify the advertised brand/company name, more specific brand/company name prompts are given. For each

commercial the respondent claims to remember, detailed prompts are administered to obtain levels of recall and communication.

Analysis. Norms, in the form of the percent recall of the ad and various levels of detail about the ad, have been established for a wide range of products, by length of commercial, and for males and females. Recall of the test commercial can be compared to these norms and/or to other versions of the commercial that are also tested.

Diagnostics. Optional diagnostic questions can be asked after the recall questions. These questions can be custom designed for the commercial being tested or they can be selected from a set of standard diagnostic questions (norms are available for these). These questions can be asked in a pure recall mode. However, the respondent is generally asked to turn the TV to an unused cable channel where the commercial is being shown continuously. The diagnostic questions are then asked immediately after viewing.

SOURCE: *ASI Recall Plus ® Methodology* (New York: ASI Market Research, undated).

---

marketing program for a product in one or more limited geographical areas (usually cities). Often, differing levels of marketing mix variables are used in the test markets to help management isolate the best combination for the national introduction.

Test markets are not limited to new products. As shown in Research Application 8–6, they can be used to evaluate any aspect of the marketing mix. Governmental and social agencies are also active users of test marketing. For example, the Department of Agriculture used Madison, WI, and Knoxville, TN, as test sites for a paid commercial campaign to steer schoolchildren and their parents toward healthy snacks.

Although many types of products, as well as other aspects of the marketing mix, are frequently examined in test markets, durable goods are seldom tested in this manner. The fact that only a very small percentage of the total

Test marketing: is the testing of all or part of a proposed national marketing program in a limited geographical area.

RESEARCH APPLICATION 8-5

Illinois Bell Telephone Company's Advertising Test

Illinois Bell Telephone Co. developed an advertising program to increase local telephone use (measured by the number of local calls made). However, before launching the campaign, they wanted to be confident that the program would indeed increase local calls. Therefore, they conducted a field experiment.

The Test Market Group maintains a split cable facility in Moline and East Moline, Illinois. This facility allows the company to send specific commercials into some households and withhold them from others.

Two matched samples of 600 households were used for the experiment. Local telephone use of each sample was monitored for 13 weeks to establish the before measure. Then the advertising campaign was presented to the treatment group at a level of 300 gross rating points (percentage of the audience reached × the number of times reached) per week for 38 weeks. The remaining sample, the control group, did not receive the advertising.

Over the 38-week period, the treatment group placed 7 percent more calls than the control group (statistically significant at the .01 level of confidence). Further, this difference was slowly increasing throughout the 38-week test period.

Based on this experiment, Illinois Bell could estimate the economic value of advertising at this level throughout the region. Based on demographic and usage data on the 600 households in the experimental group, it could also determine the characteristics of those most responsive to the ad campaign. However, since only one level of advertising was tested (300 gross rating points), Illinois Bell does not know if this is the optimal level of advertising.

market (perhaps as low as 3 percent) are potential purchasers of a durable good in a given year, coupled with the extremely high cost of tooling and production line changes, greatly limits the usefulness of such test markets. Research Application 8–7 provides a description of a modified test market used by Amana Refrigeration for a refrigerator.[9]

The two primary goals of most test market programs are the determination of market acceptance of the product and the testing of alternative marketing mixes. A major additional value comes from alerting management to unsuspected problems and opportunities associated with the new product. For example, Stamford Marketing found that many purchasers of a new snack food placed the packages into their shopping carts upside-down. Since the package was not designed for this, an unusual amount of compacting of the contents occurred and consumers were dissatisfied. A redesigned package allowed a successful introduction.

There are four basic types of market tests: *standard, controlled, electronic,* and *simulated.*

RESEARCH APPLICATION 8–6

Typical Test Market Experiments

1. Kentucky Fried Chicken conducted a test of a breakfast menu at 30 outlets in Singapore.
2. McCaw Cellular Communications and Telecommunications tested a moderately priced wireless telephone service in Medford, OR. The system is less expensive than cellular, with fewer features and less mobility.
3. Pepsi-Cola Co. tested All Sport, an isotonic drink, in Houston, Minneapolis, and Sacramento.
4. McDonald's Corp. tested McExtras, a refrigerated case containing such basic grocery items as milk, eggs, bread, and margarine for sale at the counter or drive-through in Bloomington, MN. It is also testing a double drive-through unit with no counter or seating in Raleigh, NC.
5. *TV Guide* tested a large-size version ($7\frac{1}{2} \times$ 10 inches) in Nashville, Pittsburgh, and Rochester.
6. Domino's Pizza Inc. tested a "universal" phone number (950-1430) in Lansing, MI, and Jacksonville, FL. A customer at any location dials this number, which is automatically transferred by computer to the Domino's outlet nearest them.
7. Quaker State Minit-Lube tested a new name, Q Lube, a redesigned format, and a new ad campaign at five centers in Reno, NV.
8. Procter & Gamble Co. tested Liquid Tide with Bleach in Indianapolis and a new toothbrush, Crest Complete, in Austin, Houston, and San Antonio.

Standard Market Tests

A **standard market test** is one in which a small sample of market areas— usually cities—is selected and the product is sold through regular distribution channels, using one or more combinations of product, price, and promotional levels. Standard market tests are also used for price, package, and advertising testing.

Standard market test: involves selling the product through regular distribution channels into one or more cities using one or more proposed marketing mixes.

Site Selection.   Selecting the market areas for a standard test marketing program is obviously an important decision. Random sampling is seldom used. Rather, purposive selections are made based on the following general criteria: (1) they must be large enough to produce meaningful data but not so large as to be prohibitive in cost (the combination should comprise at least 2 percent of the potential actual market to give projectable results); (2) they should have typical media availability and be self-contained from a media standpoint; (3) they should be demographically similar to the larger market area (region or entire United States); (4) the area should be a self-contained trading area, to avoid transhipments into and out of the area; (5) the areas should be representative with respect to competition; and (6) the combination of areas

RESEARCH APPLICATION 8–7

Amana Refrigeration's Modified Test Market of a Refrigerator

Amana Refrigeration, in conjunction with the Department of Energy, developed an energy-efficient refrigerator.

"With a product of this kind, final tooling can be in the order of $1,000,000 to $2,000,000," says Charles Mueller, manager of product planning at Amana. "We needed to have a good feeling about its acceptance." Amana manufactured prototypes of the unit, 25 of which were put into a field test market in stores in Norfolk, VA.

"Our goal was to find out both the consumer and distributor reaction. The refrigerator's price is higher than normal, so reaction to the higher cost vs. the models' payback—savings in electrical costs—was important. We also wanted to know what features were important to the consumer."

Consumers and dealers were not initially aware that the refrigerator they were buying was a pro-

totype of a new product. After one month, Amana advised the purchasers of this and offered them the use of the refrigerators for one full year if they would monitor the models' performance each month. Not only would the full purchase price be refunded at the end of the year, but the customer would be given $100 toward the purchase of another refrigerator.

From the in-store test, the company got feedback on the model's positioning to determine advertising emphasis, and also how it performed against the competition.

Working with the customers, Amana was able to make changes in the early design. For example, the thickness of the door was decreased to accommodate built-in installations.

Using the test market results, and with the refinements in place, Amana's Twin System refrigerator/freezer was rolled out nationally.

should allow testing under use conditions that are appropriate to the product (for example, both hard- and soft-water areas for a soap product, warm and cold climates for an all-weather tire). In addition, the firm needs to be aware of its "strength" in the test market area(s) relative to its strength nationally.

Site selection is uniquely difficult for multinational firms. Traditionally, such firms would conduct standard test markets in their domestic markets, launch the product, and, after it succeeded domestically, repeat the process sequentially in other countries. Today's interlinked global economy renders this approach impractical for most products, as global competitors will quickly launch competing products around the world. For example, Procter & Gamble's disposable diaper, Pampers, was beaten to the market in France, Italy, and the United Kingdom because it followed a country-by-country strategy. (It is going global with its new Pampers Phases almost simultaneously.)

Firms with a new multinational product can test the product simultaneously in several key markets (markets that are important to the product category). The product and/or the marketing mix may be standardized or altered for each major market. Another common option is to test, and often launch, a product in a lead market (a market whose consumers recognize a need for the product's benefits before consumers in other markets do). Procter & Gamble uses Germany as a lead market for environmentally friendly products such as Vidal Sassoon Airspray. Obviously, identifying lead markets is complex. Is Germany, France, the United States, or Japan the best lead market for cosmetics? Or is taste in cosmetics so culture-specific that lead markets do not exist?

Analysis.   Brand sales are monitored through store audits or, most commonly, UPC scanner data (see Chapter 5). Trial and repeat purchase rates, household penetration, substitution patterns, and user demographics are measured through existing or specially established household mail or scanner panels. Survey research can also be used for these purposes.

The length of time that a test market is conducted depends on the repurchase cycle for the product, the probability of a competitive response, the initial consumer response, and company philosophy. Evidence indicates that tests of new brands should run at least 10 months. Figure 8–1 illustrates the results of an analysis of 100 test markets that lasted at least 18 months. The final test market share was reached in 10 months 85 percent of the time and 95 percent of the time in 12 months.

Disadvantages of Standard Test Markets.   Standard test marketing is not without its disadvantages. All of the comments made earlier concerning after-only designs apply to most test market situations. In addition, standard market tests take a long time. Not only do most tests run for 12 to 18 months, but

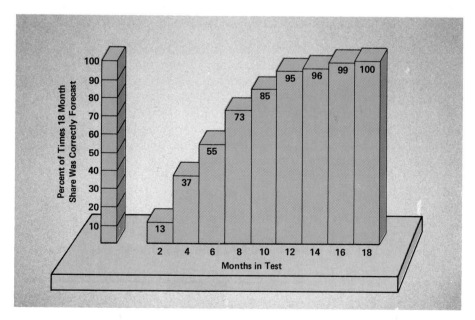

FIGURE 8–1 Time and Test Market Accuracy

SOURCE: "The True Test of Test Marketing Is Time," *Sale and Marketing Management* (March 14, 1983), 74.

the salesforce must also spend 2 to 3 months selling the product through the distribution channel before the consumer test can begin.

In most test markets only two or three versions of the overall marketing mix are tested. Thus, the fact that the test versions do not prove successful may not leave a clear-cut basis for eliminating other versions of the total product offering. Most organizations approach this problem by extensive consumer testing prior to test marketing. As a result of these preliminary tests, the researcher can often identify two to six versions of the total offering that appear most likely to succeed. These versions are then test marketed.

In addition to the normal types of problems associated with experimental designs, and particularly after-only designs, test marketing faces two unique problems. First, firms routinely take direct actions, such as lowering their prices, increasing their advertising, or even buying large quantities of the test product, to disrupt a competitor's test marketing program. This is commonly called *jamming*. Following are examples of such tactics:

- Vick Chemical distorted test results for a new Colgate cough preparation by distributing 25,000 Nyquil samples into Colgate's two test markets.[10]
- Ralston Purina often hands out thousands of coupons for free 5- or 10-pound bags of Purina Dog Chow in competitors' test areas.
- Competing toilet-paper producers disrupted American Can Co.'s test market of a premoistened toilet tissue by buying large quantities of the product.
- Chesebrough-Pond attempted to disrupt Procter & Gamble's test market of Wondra hand lotion in Milwaukee by offering huge discounts on its Vaseline Intensive Care lotion.[11]
- McDonald's "blew us away with promotion" when Wendy's tested a breakfast menu of biscuits and egg sandwiches.[12]

Another problem occurs when competitors successfully "read" a firm's test. This is particularly serious for multinational products. However, any market test is likely to alert competitors to the existence of the new product and its planned promotion. This allows competitors to begin to prepare their own versions of the product or to prepare other strategies. In addition, it is often possible for competitors to gain as much information from the test as the sponsoring firm because most test cities are included in various store auditing or scanning programs, to which many firms subscribe. An accurate reading of a competitor's test market may allow a firm to match or beat it to the national market. Examples of this include the following:

- Campbell Soup's Prego spaghetti sauce was beaten nationally by a similar product by Ragu.[13]
- General Foods' Maxim instant coffee was preceded by Nèstle's Taster's Choice.
- Hills Bros. High Yield coffee was introduced nationally after Procter & Gamble's Folger's Flakes.
- Hunt-Wesson's Prima Salsa tomato sauce was beaten nationally by Chesebrough-Pond's Ragu Extra Thick & Zesty.
- Carnation's Ground Round dog food was preceded by General Foods' Gaines Complete.[14]

RESEARCH APPLICATION 8–8

Surf's Test Market in Japan

Surf, a superconcentrated detergent made by Unilever, had a successful test market in Japan, gaining a 15 percent market share. However, it failed when it went national (less than a 3 percent share). Several problems caused the product failure. First, the test market ran from the spring through the summer and the national launch occurred in the fall. Apparently, the colder water temperatures encountered in the fall and winter reduced the detergent's ability to dissolve. This resulted in over 100 phoned-in complaints per week.

Surf was sold in premeasured packets somewhat like tea bags. Near the end of the test market, several firms introduced programmable, low-agitation washing machines which immediately became popular (1 million were sold by the end of the year). Surf was not designed to work in the new machine. Finally, the "fresh smell" positioning of Surf was not relevant to most Japanese, who hang their wash to dry outside in the fresh air.

SOURCE: D. Kilburn, "Unilever Struggles with Surf in Japan," *Advertising Age* (May 6, 1991), 22.

- Colgate-Palmolive's Fab 1 Shot beat Procter & Gamble's Tide brand version of a similar product to market.[15]

Concern over a competitor beating it to the national market apparently influenced Carnation to go national without market testing its Come'n Get It dry dog food. Other firms are also skipping tests. The chairman of National Presto explains his company's position:

> We can't afford to spend the time test-marketing anymore. They'll start copying us too soon. So we're flying by the seat of our pants. It's gutsy as hell but the rewards are worth the risk.[16]

Another disadvantage of standard test marketing is its cost. The cost of standard market tests often exceeds $1 million and sometimes runs as much as $10 million, with $3.5 million a typical figure. Tests of advertising campaigns cost over $1 million. Finally, as Research Application 8–8 indicates, standard test markets are not always accurate.

Advantages of Standard Test Markets. The primary reason for their continued use (over 40 percent of U.S. food and drug companies used a standard test market in 1989)[17] is the high cost of new-product failure coupled with the difficulty of projecting new-product success (or other marketing mix changes) without standard test markets. It is estimated that three out of four products that are introduced after standard test markets succeed. In contrast, four out of five products introduced without standard test marketing fail.[18]

One reason for the accuracy of standard test markets is the fact that trade (retailer and/or wholesaler) support is also tested. Products or brands that cannot achieve sufficient shelf facings are unlikely to succeed even if consumers find them superior to those of the competition. The average supermarket stocks 14,000 items. In 1988, there were 1,000 new products and line extensions introduced to supermarkets *per month*.[19] Obviously, supermarket managers cannot allocate shelf space to all new products. They allocate shelf space based on consumer demand, margin, handling costs, and fit with their overall product/ brand mix. A standard test market is the only method that measures salesforce and trade response on such key dimensions as the following:

- time to achieve target distribution levels
- actual versus planned distribution including stockouts
- actual pricing, shelf-space allocation, and so forth versus target
- "deal" levels and slotting allowances required to obtain distribution
- salesforce involvement and commitment

Controlled-Store and Minimarket Tests

Controlled-store test:
a market test in which a research firm places the product in a few outlets in several areas and handles all warehousing, stocking, and pricing activities.

Minimarket test:
a market test in which a research firm places the product in a high percentage of the relevant outlets in a modest-size city and performs all warehousing, stocking, and pricing activities.

To overcome some of the problems associated with standard market tests, controlled-store and minimarket tests are being used with increasing frequency (over 50 percent of U.S. food and drug companies used a controlled-store test in 1989).[20] In a standard market test, the product is distributed to the stores through the firm's regular distribution channels. In a **controlled-store test,** a market research firm places the product in a few outlets in several areas handling all warehousing, distribution, pricing, and stocking activities itself. In a **minimarket test,** a market research firm places the product in a high percentage of relevant outlets in a modest-size city (Ehrbart-Babic uses Portland, ME, Tuscon, Sacramento, and Spokane, among others) and performs all warehousing, distribution, pricing, and stocking activities.

In a controlled-store test, media advertising typically cannot be used because of the limited distribution of the product. The minimarket test overcomes this problem but increases the cost and visibility of the test.

Sales data are maintained by the research firm that is distributing the product. Existing or specially established household mail or UPC scanner panels can be used to provide trial- and repeat-purchase rates, household penetration, substitution patterns, and user demographics. Survey research can be used instead of panels or to supplement panel data.

These methods offer several important advantages over standard test markets. First, it is difficult for competitors to "read" the test results since the research company is the only source of sales data. Second, the tests are somewhat less visible to competitors, though most controlled stores and minimarkets are actively observed. Third, they are substantially faster since there is no need to move the product through a distribution channel. Finally, they are much less expensive than standard test markets.

Unfortunately, this approach suffers from four drawbacks. First, the limited number of stores and/or the small size of the communities involved makes projection of the results difficult. Second, these tests do *not* allow an estimate of the level of support the trade will give a product. If wholesalers do not push the product, or if retailers do not give it shelf space, it seldom succeeds. These tests provide no information on this critical component. Third, it is sometimes difficult to duplicate planned national advertising programs. Finally, the fact that the research firm ensures near-optimal positioning in each store, no stockouts, adequate shelf facings, correct use of P-O-P materials, and so forth produces a situation very different from that typically encountered during the national introduction.

Sophisticated firms are minimizing these drawbacks. A critical element is to specify distribution, shelf facings, and so forth at a level consistent with realistic expectations for the national introduction. Likewise, advertising expenditures in the minimarket are carefully constructed to match national levels. Projection from minimarket to national remains a problem, but use of historical data (relationships between past minimarket sales and subsequent national sales) and "what-if" analyses can provide some confidence.

In addition to testing new products, controlled-store tests are popular as a means of testing price and promotional variables such as displays, coupons, cents-off, and so forth. A before-after with control or after-only with control design is generally used. Matched panels of stores rather than random allocation is also the norm. These tests are fast, inexpensive ($20,000–$40,000), and realistic.

Electronic Test Markets

Electronic test markets (ETMs) operate like minimarket tests, except that the research firm (1) is able to collect ongoing scanner-based sales data from the major food and drug outlets in the area, and (2) has a UPC scanner-based household panel whose television viewing is monitored electronically. In other words, the research firm has "single-source" data capabilities (Chapter 5). In addition, the firm can send different commercials or different frequencies of commercials to various households in the panel.

Research Application 8–9 describes Information Resources Inc.'s (IRI) BehaviorScan® ETM. Although it is possible to use one of the BehaviorScan cities as a site for a standard test market, their rather small size generally precludes this (Eau Claire, WI, Midland, TX, Marion, IN, and Pittsfield, MA are typical cities). Instead, IRI handles the distribution as described in the research application.

ETMs are used to test new products and, even more commonly, advertising levels and themes. They allow relatively precise measurement of individual households' purchasing and television-viewing behavior. They also provide reasonable control over individual households' television commercial exposure as well as receipt of direct mail ads and coupons. Their disadvantages are the same as those associated with minimarket tests, with additional concerns about the representativeness of the electronic diary panel (because of the high refusal rate of those asked to join such panels) and the small size of the towns involved.

Simulated Test Markets

Simulated test markets (STMs) are very popular in both the United States and Europe (over 80 percent of U.S. food and drug companies reported using an STM in 1989).[21] STMs, often called laboratory tests, involve mathematical estimates of market share based on initial consumer reactions to the new product. A number of private companies such as Pillsbury have their own STM systems. In addition, a number of consulting firms offer STM services.

Electronic test markets (ETMs): a minimarket test with a research firm that (1) can collect ongoing scanner-based sales data from the major outlets in the area, (2) has a UPC scanner-based household panel whose television viewing is monitored electronically, and (3) can send different commercials or frequencies of commercials to various households in the panel.

Simulated test markets (STMs): produce estimates of market response to new products using mathematical models and measures of consumers' initial reactions to the new product.

RESEARCH APPLICATION 8–9

IRI's BehaviorScan® ETM

Currently available in eight markets

- Covers 95 percent of supermarket sales volume in all markets.
- Covers 85 percent of drugstore sales volume in four markets.

Receives direct feedback from UPC scanners
Maintains a panel of 3,000 households in each market

- Panel members have an ID number which is entered each time a purchase is made.
- IRI maintains complete demographics and product usage data on each panel member.
- IRI electronically monitors the television viewing of a subset of panel households.

Controlled distribution

- IRI controls in-store distribution, including shelf configuration, price, and P-O-P displays.
- IRI monitors competitive activity daily on a store-by-store basis.

- IRI monitors manufacturer and store coupon redemption by panel members.

Allows tests of various promotional activities

- Through proprietary technology, different television commercials can be sent to individual panel households (six markets). Groups can be formed based on past purchase behavior, demographics, or stores shopped.
- Direct mail, magazine, and newspaper inserts can be tested.

Feedback is rapid and cost-efficient

- Scanner-based reports are available four to six weeks sooner than traditional reports.
- Allows measures of trial and repeat, buying rate, loyalty, purchase cycles, brand shifting, buyer demographics, and response to market mix changes.
- Generally costs about half as much as a standard test market.

The major firms and their primary services are BASES Burke Institute, Inc. (BASES); M/A/R/C (MACRO Assessor); National Panel Data (ESP); Yankelovich, Clancy-Shulman (Litmus II).

STMs follow a similar basic procedure that is outlined in Figure 8–2 and that includes the following steps:

> **Step 1.** Potential respondents are contacted, generally in mall intercept interviews, and "qualified." Qualified means the respondents must fit the demographics and/or usage characteristics of the desired target market.
> **Step 2.** Qualified respondents are shown a description of the product concept, a finished or rough package, a finished or rough commercial, or a product prototype or finished product.
> **Step 3.** Respondents then express attitudes or purchase intentions toward the product. Those with positive attitudes or purchase intentions are given the product to try. The four firms listed previously also have simulated or real shopping environments

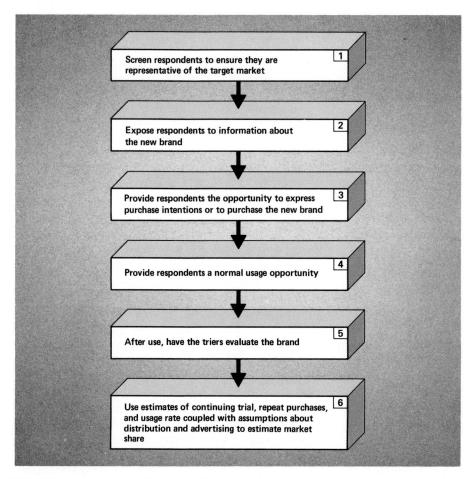

FIGURE 8–2 Steps in Simulated Test Markets

where respondents can buy the test product or competing products using real or "play" money. However, most STMs use purchase intent rather than simulated purchase data.

Step 4. The respondents take the item home and use it in a normal manner. The time allowed for usage depends on the "normal" consumption time for the product category.

Step 5. These respondents are then recontacted and asked to evaluate the product's performance. This evaluation generally includes repurchase intentions and likely usage rates. (Steps 4 and 5 are increasingly uncommon as more reliance is now placed on the purchase intentions data from Step 3.)

Step 6. The percentage of respondents who decide to try the new item is used to estimate the percentage of the target market population that would try the item *if* they were aware of the item and *if* it were available in the stores in which they shop. The firm's assumptions concerning advertising impact (target market awareness) and distribution are used with the "percent trying" figure to estimate actual market trial. The after-use evaluations (attitudes, statements of repurchase intentions, or actual repurchases) are used to estimate the percentage of the triers who will continue to use the product. The rate of usage is estimated from either respondent estimates or knowledge of the product category, or both. These three estimates are then combined to estimate volume and/or market share for the item.

It is clear from this description that STMs rely substantially on the behavior of respondents in an artificial situation. It seems intuitive that such behavior would differ from actual behavior in the marketplace. STMs do *not* assume that the behavior and attitudes displayed in the laboratory setting will be repeated exactly in the actual market. Instead, they rely on observed *relationships* between products' performances in the laboratory and their subsequent performances in actual market introductions.

An *extremely* simplified example will help make this process clear. Suppose 100 new products are run through the six-step procedure described and are then introduced in test markets or nationally. The researcher notices that in most cases, for every 10 people who try an item in the laboratory only 6 will try it in the actual market. Therefore, when product number 101 is tested and 40 percent of the laboratory respondents try it, the researcher would project that 24 percent (.60 times .40) of the target market would try it in an actual introduction. Although this example is *very* simplified, it reflects the general logic used in evaluating STM results.

STMs are fast, economical (generally costing under $100,000), confidential, easily controlled, and capable of substantial geographic spread. They do not measure trade response, competitors' reactions, or implementation difficulties. In addition, they depend critically on the mathematical model used in the STM *and* on management estimates of total market size, advertising reach, distribution penetration, and similar variables.

Johnson & Johnson used an STM creatively when a competitor introduced a new product that was positioned directly against its Reach toothbrush. Johnson & Johnson subjected the new product to an STM. The results indicated that the new product was not as much of a competitive threat as Johnson & Johnson had imagined. Therefore, the company was able to reduce its planned defensive campaign by $600,000.[22] Miles Labs used the same procedure to develop defensive strategy against Bristol-Myers' Dissolve.

Summary

Internal validity refers to the ability of an experiment to produce the same results if repeated with similar subjects. External validity refers to the ability of the results of an experiment to predict the results of a similar manipulation of the independent variable in the actual situation of interest to the researcher. Laboratory experiments tend to be high on internal validity but weak on external validity, whereas the opposite is often true for field experiments.

Laboratory experiments occur in an artificial setting. Reactive errors occur when respondents react to the setting rather than to the independent variable. Such errors are difficult to control. The use of realistic environments and special control conditions can help reduce or measure reactive error.

Laboratory experiments are commonly used to test packages, advertisements, product concepts, and products. Tachistoscope tests, eye tracking, and theater tests are commonly used laboratory experiments for testing various ad formats.

Field experiments involve manipulating the independent variable in the market. Day-after recall (DAR) and test markets are common field experiments for testing various advertisements.

Test marketing involves the duplication of the planned national marketing program in a limited geographic area. In a standard market test the product is sold through regular distribution channels into one or more cities or other geographic areas. Though expensive, time-consuming, and subject to competitor disruption or reading, standard market tests have very high predictive validity because they measure both trade and consumer response. Multinational firms have a difficult time selecting appropriate test sites that will provide the required information without alerting competition around the world of their intentions.

A minimarket test has a research firm handle all warehousing, distribution, pricing, shelving, and stocking of the product in most of the outlets in a relatively small community. A controlled-store test is similar except that it involves a few stores in a number of cities. These approaches are less expensive, faster, and less subject to competitor disruption or reading than standard market test. Unfortunately, they also have a lower predictive validity.

An electronic test market (ETM) is like a minimarket test except that the research firm (1) is able to collect ongoing scanner-based sales data from the major food and drug outlets in the area, and (2) has a scanner-based household panel whose television viewing is monitored electronically. ETMs are used primarily to test advertisements, though new products are also tested with this methodology. Simulated test markets (STMs) involve mathematical estimates of market share based on initial consumer response to the product in an artificial environment.

Review Questions

8.1. What is the difference between a *laboratory experiment* and a *field experiment?*

8.2. What are the strengths and weaknesses of laboratory experiments?

8.3. What is *predictive validity? external validity?*

8.4. What is *replicability? internal validity?*

8.5. What are *reactive errors?* Why is this important for laboratory experiments?

8.6. How does one control for reactive errors?

8.7. What is a *tachistoscope?* How are they used in copy testing?

8.8. Describe how ads and packages are copy tested in laboratory settings.

8.9. What is an *extended use test?*

8.10. What is a *blind use test?*

8.11. What are the strengths and weaknesses of *field experiments?*

8.12. What is *DAR?* What problems are associated with this approach?

8.13. What is a *standard test market?*

8.14. What are the strengths and weaknesses of a standard test market?

8.15. What criteria are used in selecting an area for a standard test market?

8.16. What issues arise in test marketing global products, and how do firms deal with them?

8.17. How does a *controlled-store test* differ from a *minimarket test*?

8.18. What are the advantages and disadvantages of *controlled-store* and *minimarket tests*?

8.19. What is an *electronic test market* (ETM)?

8.20. What are the strengths and weaknesses of ETMs?

8.21. Describe the BehaviorScan® system.

8.22. What is a *simulated test market* (STM)?

8.23. What steps are involved in most STMs?

8.24. What are the advantages and disadvantages of STMs?

8.25. How is the output from STMs used?

Discussion Questions/Problems

8.26. What are the broad research methodology implications of Research Application 8–1?

8.27. Evaluate the methodology used by the Advertising Research Foundation in the chapter's opening example.

8.28. What problems exist with theater tests of advertising copy?

8.29. Evaluate the experimental environment and procedure described in Research Application 8–2.

8.30. Evaluate the experimental environment and procedure described in Research Application 8–3.

8.31. Evaluate the experimental environment and procedure described in Research Application 8–4.

8.32. What are the ethical implications of the deception used by ASI in Research Application 8–4 and in its Print Plus® test?

8.33. If you felt you had to use a standard test market, what steps could you take to minimize disruption by competitors?

8.34. How would you select which cities in _____ should serve as sites for a standard test market?
   a. the EC
   b. the EC, Japan, and the U.S.
   c. North and South America

8.35. Design a laboratory experiment to test college students' reactions to _____ for a snack food.
   a. three flavor levels
   b. three packages
   c. three brand names
   d. three advertising themes
   e. three price levels
   f. three point-of-purchase displays
   g. three different levels of advertising
   h. *c* and *d*.

8.36. How would your design for 8.35 deal with reactive error? What other error sources would concern you?

8.37. To what extent do you think people who know their _____ behavior is being monitored change their behavior? In what ways?
   a. television viewing
   b. shopping

8.38. What factors would you consider in _____?
   a. deciding whether to conduct a test market
   b. deciding which type of test market to conduct

Projects/Activities

8.39. Interview three supermarket managers and determine their awareness of and attitudes toward test markets.

8.40. Design and conduct a field experiment on P-O-P display effectiveness with the cooperation of local retailers.

8.41. Interview 10 junior or senior business majors and 10 junior or senior liberal arts majors and determine their reactions to the deception described in Research Application 8–4. What do you conclude?

8.42. Develop three appeals for contributions to your favorite charity. Design and conduct an experiment to test their effectiveness.

Notes

1. *Establishing Accountability* (New York: Advertising Research Foundation, undated).

2. F. N. Kerlinger, *Foundations of Behavioral Research* (New York: Holt, Rinehart and Winston, Inc., 1973), 398.

3. L. Ingoassia, "A Matter of Taste," *Wall Street Journal* (February 26, 1980), 23.

4. R. Chatterjee, et al., "A Practical Bayesian Approach to Selection of Optimal Market Testing Strategies," *Journal of Marketing Research* (November 1988), 363–375.

5. C. E. Brown, et al., "The Effect of Experimenter Bias in a Cola Taste Test," *Psychology & Marketing* (Summer 1984), 21–26.

6. "Revised Pillsbury Spot in the Pink," *Advertising Age* (February 13, 1986), 15.

7. D. Walker, "Beyond Validation," paper presented at the Advertising Research Foundation's 7th Annual Copy Research Workshop, July 1990; and D. Walker, "Efficiency and Effectiveness," paper presented at the Advertising Research Foundation's 8th Annual Copy Research Conference, September 1991.

8. S. N. Singh, G. A. Churchill, Jr., "Response-Bias-Free Recognition Test to Measure Advertising Effects," *Journal of Advertising Research* (June 1987), 23–35.

9. G. Linda, "Those Test-Defying Goods," *Advertising Age* (February 22, 1982), M-36. Used with permission.

10. T. Angelus, "Experts' Choice: Top Test Markets," *Marketing/Communications* (May 1970), 29.

11. N. Howard, "Fighting It Out in the Test Market," *Dun's Review* (June 1979), 69.

12. R. Kreisman, "Wendy's Ready to Roll with Breakfast," *Advertising Age* (March 3, 1981), 3.

13. B. G. Yorovich, "Competition Jumps the Gun," *Advertising Age* (February 9, 1981), S-20.

14. J. Revett, L. Edwards, "Carnation Bites Back," *Advertising Age* (June 9, 1980), 78.

15. L. Freeman, "Colgate P&G," *Advertising Age* (August 31, 1987), 1.

16. L. Adler, "Test Marketing—Its Pitfalls," *Sales & Marketing Management* (March 15, 1982), 78.

17. M. E. Lieb, "The Test Market Balancing Act," *Food Business* (July 14, 1989), 36–39.

18. Adler, op. cit.

19. S. L. Hapoienu, "Product Glut Sparks Struggle for Shelf Space," *Marketing News* (January 16, 1989), 2.

20. Lieb, op. cit.

21. Ibid.

22. D. N. Scott, "Test Market Simulation Evaluates New Products," *Marketing News* (January 22, 1982), 10.

CASE II–1

Iglo-Ola's "Circle of Housewives" Product Tests in Belgium

Iglo-Ola uses a panel of housewives to test quick-frozen food products in Belgium. The firm has a panel of 1,400 housewives divided into 9 cells of 155 households each. Each panel is representative of the overall market. The quick-frozen foods to be tested are delivered by van to the panel members' homes along with the questionnaire and instructions. Each panel is used for a maximum of 10 tests per year. Participants are motivated by interest, the pleasure associated with being part of a group, and the small gifts provided at the end of each year.

The product tests are generally "blind." That is, no information other than preparation instructions is normally provided, since the objective is to test the intrinsic quality of the product. Occasionally additional positioning information is provided such as "this is a light health food."

Almost all of the tests are monadic. The logic is that this is the way frozen foods are consumed in everyday life. That is, consumers buy, or at least prepare, only one brand or version of a frozen food at a time. Furthermore, it is felt that having consumers compare two versions simultaneously would focus attention on attributes that might otherwise be irrelevant. It also tends to magnify the importance of minor differences (consumers feel compelled to differentiate between the two versions).

Monadic tests are simple to administer in unsupervised home tests such as these. They are also free of context effects (the taste of one version being influenced by the taste of the comparison brand) and so can be compared with the results of other monadic tests.

The questionnaire generally has five questions. Two open-ended questions ask for likes and dislikes about the product. Purchase intention is measured on a seven-point scale. Price receptiveness is measured by having respondents indicate the highest and lowest price they would expect to pay for the product. Finally, a question on eating habits relative to the product is asked.

When it is necessary to test multiple versions of the product, the monadic tests are structured in the appropriate experimental design. Following are the results (mean scores on the purchase intentions scale) of two such tests:

Breaded Fish

	Coating	
Shape	Raw	Precooked
Triangle	5.10	5.37
Square	5.22	5.53
Rectangle	5.25	5.54
Trapezoid	5.64	5.75

Ice Cream

	Fat Content	
Color	High	Low
White	4.80	4.45
Yellow	5.15	5.55

Discussion Questions

1. Evaluate this type of panel. What type of error would you be concerned with?
2. Evaluate their use of monadic tests. What weakness does this approach have?
3. Why do they use open-ended *likes* and *dislikes* questions? What advantages and disadvantages does their approach have?
4. How would you analyze the data for the breaded fish and the ice cream? Which, if any, versions should be introduced?

SOURCE: C. Forges, "A Circle of Housewives as Appraisers of Innovations and Product Improvements in Quick Frozen Foods," *Marketing and Research Today* (August 1991), 152–158.

CASE II–2

The Impact of R. J. Reynolds' "Old Joe the Camel" Advertising Campaign on Teenager's Awareness of Camel Cigarettes

High school students from Georgia, Massachusetts, Nebraska, New Mexico, and Washington were the teenage subjects. One school from each state was selected based on its administration's willingness to participate. A target of 60 students in each grade, 9 through 12, was set. Classes were selected to provide a sample of students at all levels of academic ability. The students were told that the study involved advertising and that their participation would be anonymous. The obtained sample size was 1,055.

Since adult brand preferences are available from national studies, the adult sample was limited to Massachusetts. All drivers renewing their licenses at the Registry of Motor Vehicles on the days of the study were asked to participate. Since licenses must be renewed in person, this provided a heterogeneous population. This produced a sample of 345.

Seven "Old Joe" ads that had appeared in popular magazines were used in the study. One was masked so that all clues as to the product and brand were hidden except the "Old Joe" character. A questionnaire was developed that measured tobacco use and attitudes as well as reactions to "Old Joe" and the other six "Old Joe" ads.

Subjects were first shown the masked ad and asked if they had seen the "Old Joe" character before and the product and brand he represents. They then were shown the other six ads one at a time and asked to indicate how the ad and the "Old Joe" character appealed to them. The key results are shown in the table.

Comparison of Student and Adult Responses to Camel's "Old Joe"
Cartoon Character Advertisements

	Massachusetts Students	Total Students*	Total Adults†
No. of subjects‡	224	1055	345
Have seen "Old Joe", %	99.6	97.7§	72.2§
Know product, %	100	97.5§	67.0§
Know brand, %	97.3	93.6§	57.7§
Think ads look cool, %	54.1	58.0§	39.9§
Ads are interesting, %	73.9	73.6§	55.1§
Like Joe as friend, %	31.1	35.0§	14.4§
Think Joe is cool, %	38.6	43.0§	25.7§
Smoke Camel, %¶	21.8	33.0§	8.7§

*Age range, 12 to 19 years.
†Age range, 21 to 87 years.
‡This is the total number of subjects in each category; due to incomplete questionnaires, respondents for some questions may be fewer.
§$P<.0001$.
¶Percentage of smokers who identify Camel as their favorite brand.

Discussion Questions

1. Evaluate the overall design of this study.
2. Evaluate the sampling technique used.
3. Evaluate the measurement technique used.
4. What conclusions would you draw from this study?
5. If you were to redesign this study, what changes would you make?

SOURCE: J. R. DiFranza, "RJR Nabisco's Cartoon Camel Promotes Camel Cigarettes to Children," *JAMA* (December 11, 1991), 3149–3153.

CASE II–3

Family Circle Study of Print Advertising Effectiveness

A recent study sponsored by *Family Circle* magazine tracked the purchases of approximately 100,000 households in 300 stores in three cities using scanner data. It reached the following conclusions:

- *Family Circle* readers spent 7 percent more per week ($71.09 vs. $66.38) than demographically similar nonreaders though both groups made 1.3 shopping trips per week.
- Sales to *Family Circle* reader households increased versus the nonreader households for 15 of the 22 advertised brands that were studied.
- For 21 of the 22 brands, cumulative sales to *Family Circle* households over the 28-week study period were higher than to the control group.

- As a result of print advertising, the market share increased for most of the brands as did product category sales.

The study used Citicorp's POS Information Services' scanner panel. Citicorp provides retailers with a customer retention program in exchange for data access. The supermarket chain then recruits customers into the program. The customers receive check cashing or debit card privileges and cash savings through rebates or electronic couponing. Each member household receives a coded ID card for each household shopper. The card must be presented when purchases are made at the supermarket in order to receive the discounts. The card is read by the scanner and the computer keeps a purchase history for each participating household.

The sample was limited to households that had been members of the panel since the beginning of 1990 and for whom purchases at the chain accounted for at least 70 percent of their estimated total grocery purchases.

Households that purchased the April 24 issue of *Family Circle* at the chain or that were members of the scanner panel and subscribed to *Family Circle* were identified. A matched sample (on age of household head, household income, and household size) of panel members who did not purchase this issue of *Family Circle* at the chain and who did not subscribe to it was created. The reader (purchaser) group had 8,700 members and the control group had over 90,000 members.

The sales of 22 brands advertised using one or more four-color pages in this issue of the magazine were measured for 28 weeks, broken down as follows:

- 12 weeks prior to the issue—base period
- 4 weeks immediately following the issue—observation period
- 12 weeks following the observation period—post period

The brands include beverages, dog biscuits, toilet paper, a cleaner, and food products.

Data from Simmons Market Research Bureau on the media consumption patterns of *Family Circle* readers indicate that they are near the national average in TV viewing but are very heavy magazine readers. Thus, the treatment group is likely to see substantially more magazine ads than is the control group.

Duncan Hines Frosting was one of the brands showing the largest impact. It had a major print media campaign run from April through June. It was advertised in *Family Circle* and seven other magazines. During the base period, the treatment group purchased 20 percent more Duncan Hines Frosting per household than the control group. During the observation period, this differential increased to 66 percent. It was 27 percent during the post period. Its market share was approximately equal in the two groups before the advertising. It was 2.5 points higher in the treatment group after the ads appeared.

Discussion Questions

1. What type of experiment is this (if it is indeed an experiment)? What types of experimental errors may be affecting the results?
2. Is this a good use of scanner panel data? Why?

3. What concerns do you have about this particular panel?
4. Evaluate the overall research design. What improvements would you suggest?
5. Do the conclusions appear justified by the research?

SOURCE: Derived from R. M. McPheters, *The Family Circle Study of Print Advertising Effectiveness* (New York: The New York Times Company, 1991).

CASE II–4

*Substantiation of Bufferin Advertising Claim**

The Bristol-Myers Company made an "establishment" claim (a claim asserted to have been established by a scientific test) in an advertisement that "*Bufferin's* laboratory test showed most of its pain reliever gets in the bloodstream 10 minutes sooner than plain aspirin." The Federal Trade Commission examined the proof offered by Bristol-Myers and was unconvinced that the claim was valid. The Commission issued a cease-and-desist order for the use of such a claim unless and until Bristol-Myers could substantiate, by conducting two well-controlled clinical experiments, that the claim was true.

The usual experimental design required by the Federal Trade Commission for over-the-counter pain relievers was called for in conducting the *Bufferin* tests. It is as follows:

1. Such proof must be in the form of two well-controlled clinical tests.
2. The tests must involve subjects who are experiencing the appropriate type of discomfort. In general, the appropriate type of pain is the pain for which the use of the drug is intended.
3. There should be a written protocol that describes the conduct of the study and its analysis.
4. Investigators who administer the test should be experienced, independent, and adequately trained.
5. Test subjects must be randomly assigned to the treatment groups within the study.
6. Where possible, tests comparing two analgesics should also compare those drugs against a placebo.
7. The test should be a double-blind test so that neither the test subject nor the person administering the test is able to tell which treatment is being administered.
8. After the clinical tests are completed, the results should be analyzed to determine their clinical and statistical significance. A 95 percent level of statistical significance is generally required.

*Bristol-Myers Company, Ted Bates & Co., Inc., and Young & Rubicam, Inc., *CCH Trade Regulation Reports*, Extra Edition, no. 604, July 19, 1983; and "Legal Developments in Marketing," *Journal of Marketing* (Spring 1984), 83, 84.

9. A determination should be made whether a statistically significant difference between two drugs is clinically significant. A difference is of no clinical significance if scientists regard the difference as being so small as to be of no importance.

Discussion Questions

1. Comment on design requirements 2 through 8.
2. How do the design requirements differ from the requirements a manager might have if the objective were to see which of two versions of a new pain reliever to introduce to the market?
3. What other design requirements might the Federal Trade Commission (reasonably) have required? Explain.

CASE II–5

Northwest Marketers

Bill Carlisle, a recent MBA graduate, was contemplating starting an export business. He had noted that there were a large number of small and medium-sized specialty food producers in the Pacific Northwest. These small firms took advantage of the region's high quality fruits, nuts, vegetables, spices, and fish to produce high-quality and/or unusual foods. These included smoked salmon, a variety of nuts smoked or otherwise flavored, jams and syrups based on berries and fruits, mustards, seasonings, and similar products. Most of these firms sold their products locally though several had direct mail sales as well. None of the firms had marketing programs though most could easily expand their production significantly if demand developed.

Bill had a few hundred dollars in the bank and a job that covered his living expenses. He was also convinced that there would be a significant market for these gourmet food products in Japan and perhaps in Taiwan and Europe as well. He hoped to buy the products from the local producers under his own label. He would then export them as premium-priced gift items.

Bill formed a firm, Northwest Marketers, and began to consider ways to make his dream a reality. Telephone contacts with a number of the local producers convinced him that he could obtain a significant supply of the various items. His next step before seeking the funding needed to launch the venture was to determine if there would actually be a demand for his products and what types of distribution might be possible. Unfortunately, he had no source of funds at this time other than his rather meager savings.

Discussion Questions

1. What is Bill's management problem? his research problem?
2. Specify precisely the information Bill requires.
3. How should Bill collect the needed data? Be detailed and precise.
4. What errors would you be concerned with in the data you have suggested he collect?

CASE II–6

Weyerhaeuser Survey Methodology

Weyerhaeuser's Building Products Group had been focusing considerable attention on the do-it-yourself (DIY) portion of the residential repair and remodel market for lumber. The repair and remodel market consumes 25 to 30 percent of the lumber used in the United States, with rapid growth projected for the next 10 years. DIYers purchase about half this total, with contractors buying the balance.

As this market has grown, the distribution channel has changed radically. Distribution of lumber materials to DIYers is now dominated by large "home center" and similar chains. Since most lumber products, particularly dimensional lumber (2×4's and similar items), are sold by grade rather than brand name, producers compete primarily on price and secondarily on delivery and service to the retailer. This allows large buyers to exert strong price pressures on producers. To counter these price pressures, provide greater value to customers, and take advantage of superior product quality, Weyerhaeuser was considering expanding its use of branding beyond the few specialty items currently branded.

For Weyerhaeuser to succeed in marketing premium quality products to DIYers, it was felt that both its general image and its product-specific image among this segment would have to improve. Image was conceptualized to include knowledge about the firm's offerings as well as beliefs about quality, value, trustworthiness, and so forth.

In addition, management was very interested in determining the relationship between a firm's image and the willingness of its customer to pay a premium for its products. Finally, management felt it needed more knowledge about the characteristics of DIYers, their homes, and their projects.

A series of nine focus groups (a 1.5–3 hour open discussion on a topic by 6–12 individuals led by a researcher) conducted among DIYers over the previous two years had provided some tentative insights into consumers' patterns:

- Most do not understand the lumber grading system and buy based on appearance.
- Price is important only for large jobs.
- Quality is important but most judge this based on appearance (they look for straightness, straight grain, few knots, sharp corners, dryness).
- Most desire helpful, skilled retailers but do not believe that many exist.
- Most believe you get what you pay for.
- Most are not satisfied with the quality of available lumber and do not believe that grade standards are enforced.
- They neither know nor care whose (which producer) wood they are buying. They do not look for brand names.
- Most are familiar with Weyerhaeuser and Georgia-Pacific but lack specific knowledge about either (though they remember Weyerhaeuser's reforestation ads).

Secondary data suggested that DIYers (1) are primarily married males, although females are increasingly active, (2) range in age from 25 to 44, (3) are both blue-collar and white-collar workers, (4) are homeowners, (5) earn middle-income salaries, and (6) are geographically dispersed.

As management was discussing options relating to the DIY market, the sponsorship of "This Old House" became available. "This Old House" is a very popular program on PBS (Public Broadcasting Service), providing advice and instruction on home repair and remodeling. While a firm sponsoring a PBS program is severely restricted in terms of the type of "commercials" it can show, it is possible to highlight the sponsor's name and products related to the DIY market. Owens-Corning had sponsored the show for several years.

Weyerhaeuser opted to sponsor the show with the objective of improving the company's image among viewers. Before its first season as sponsor, the company decided to develop a means of determining the effectiveness of the sponsorship. It also desired to determine (1) the impact the show had had on Owens-Corning's image, (2) the relationship between corporate image and price sensitivity, and (3) the characteristics of DIYers.

Weyerhaeuser management decided that the first priority was to determine the effects on the company image of sponsoring the television series "This Old House." Secondary issues would be (1) the relationship between company image and price sensitivity, (2) the characteristics of DIYers, their homes, and their projects, and (3) the effect that sponsoring "This Old House" had on Owens-Corning's image.

Since the first priority was to measure the impact of sponsoring "This Old House," this issue dominated the others. It was decided that an annual survey of Weyerhaeuser's image among viewers and nonviewers of the program would be the best way to measure the effect of sponsorship over time. This would allow an annual evaluation of the desirability of continued sponsorship.

Because the season sponsored by Weyerhaeuser was to begin in early October and the decision to measure its effectiveness was not made until late August, speed was very important. Weyerhaeuser wished to obtain a set of image measures before the shows began, in order to assess changes due to sponsorship.

Prior research indicated that DIYers spending over $200 per year on projects were the primary part of the market. Approximately 10 percent of all households were estimated to spend more than this per year. The questionnaire would not require the presentation of any visual aids or overly complex questions. The need for rapid response, limited questionnaire complexity, and the limited frequency of qualified respondents (which would require 10 or more household contacts for each qualified respondent even without nonrespondents) resulted in a telephone survey methodology.

Rather than use a national sample, Weyerhaeuser decided to conduct the surveys in Boston, Chicago, and Phoenix (see Case IV–1). Gilmore Research Group of Seattle conducted the surveys using random-digit dialing and three call-backs at varying times and days.

The questionnaire was developed and pretested in-house with the final revision and format prepared in conjunction with Gilmore. Part of Gilmore's agreement with Weyerhaeuser follows:

> Our costs are based on estimates that 10 percent of the population will qualify and that the interview is 10 to 11 minutes in length. We quoted a total fee of $XXXX* to complete 600 interviews, including the following services:

---

*Actual bid amount is omitted because of the competitive nature of such bids.

- Sample draw
- Questionnaire finalization and printing
- Data collection and quality control, including full-time supervision and monitoring, editing and clarification call backs, if necessary
- Long distance expense (calling will be done out of our WATS centers in Seattle and/or Omaha)
- Coding (listing of "others" and development of new code categories as needed)
- Data entry, together with 100 percent verification
- Data processing, resulting in one banner of cross-tab tables (up to 19 banner points). Additional banners run $250 each.
- Deliverables to include two copies of computer tables, a description of the sample disposition and incidence, and the actual questionnaires, if desired. If desired, data can also be provided on a diskette at no extra cost.

Our tentative schedule is:

- September 16—Draft questionnaire to you
- September 18 to 21—Into the field
- October 12 to 16—Out of the field
- October 21—Marginal dump of data, finalize processing specs
- October 29—Computer cross-tab tables run
- October 30—Printouts to you

Discussion Questions

1. What are the management problems confronting Weyerhaeuser? How would you clarify these problems?
2. What is the research problem facing Weyerhaeuser's researchers?
3. What data, if any, could audits and/or panels provide that would assist Weyerhaeuser? Describe precisely the data you would collect from each relevant service and specify how management would use such data in its decisions with respect to the DIY market. What concerns, if any, would you have about these data?
4. What useful data, if any, could a laboratory experiment provide Weyerhaeuser? Develop one or more laboratory experiments to provide these data, giving complete details on the research design. How would reactive errors affect your results? What other concerns would you have about these data? Describe precisely how management would use your results.
5. What useful data, if any, could a field experiment provide Weyerhaeuser? Develop one or more field experiments using (1) standard test markets, (2) minimarkets, (3) controlled-store tests, (4) electronic test markets, and (5) simulated test markets. What concerns would you have with the data from each? How would management use the data from each? What is best? Why?
6. Evaluate the survey methodology used and recommend appropriate improvements to this basic approach.
7. Assuming that either a few cities or a national sample could be used, what other survey approaches could be used? Develop, in detail, an alternative approach. Discuss the strengths and weaknesses of the alternative approach compared to the one used.

CASE II–7

California Strawberry Advisory Board

Television Advertising of Fresh Strawberries*

From mid-April to mid-May, a television advertising campaign for fresh California strawberries was conducted by the California Strawberry Advisory Board (CSAB) in a number of major metropolitan areas. The television campaign was part of an overall merchandising program designed to increase sales of fresh strawberries by stimulating retailers to increase or improve their marketing activities for strawberries. Several weeks in advance of the television campaign, the board's staff held meetings with many major food chains and wholesalers to inform them about the forthcoming television program.

Elrick and Lavidge, Inc., a marketing consulting firm, was retained to assess the effectiveness of the television campaign in meeting these goals. *Part* of the methodology used by Elrick and Lavidge is reported in the following paragraphs.

Study Procedure

The CSAB study consisted of two basic parts. One part was concerned with evaluating the effect of the television advertising and merchandising program on grocery chain store newspaper advertisements for fresh strawberries. The other part concerned the effect of the television advertising and merchandising program on store-level merchandising.

CSAB collected, measured, and tabulated all store sponsored newspaper advertisements for fresh strawberries appearing in the major newspapers of eight test and eight control markets. These measurements began two weeks before the television advertising campaign commenced, continued through the four weeks of the campaign, and continued two weeks after the campaign had ended. The eight metropolitan areas identified as test markets are those in which the television campaign was undertaken, and the eight markets identified as control markets are markets in which there was no television advertising for fresh strawberries. Comparisons have been made between the measurements of newspaper advertisements in the test cities with the measurements in the control cities in order to isolate the effects of the television advertising-merchandising program.

The tabulation of the newspaper advertisements has been analyzed by Elrick and Lavidge to determine whether the TV advertising program had any effect on the number of advertisements, the size of the advertisements, the use of illustrated advertisements, and advertised prices.

In order to determine the effect of the television advertising–merchandising program on store-level merchandising activity, a panel of 16 stores was selected in the test markets in which there was television advertising and another panel of 16 stores was selected in the control markets in which there was no television advertising.

*Used with permission of the California Strawberry Advisory Board and Elrick and Lavidge, Inc.

In both the test and control markets, suburban stores in middle-income areas were selected to represent the major chains in the markets. In each of the four geographical regions, one test city was matched with one control city. For each pair of cities, the sample of chains selected was restricted to chains that appeared to be a factor in only one of the markets. (The reason for this is that if a chain appeared in both markets in a pair, it would be conceivable that the chain would react to the television advertising campaign in such a way as to affect the entire region rather than just the test market.)

Observations and measurements were taken beginning two weeks before the television advertising, for the four weeks of the advertising campaign, and continuing two weeks after the television campaign.

The observations and measurements were made on Fridays, which were judged to be the most typical period for peak merchandising activity in the stores. These observations and measurements included an opinion rating by trained observers of the displays, the presence of point-of-purchase material, the physical size of the displays, and retail prices in the individual stores.

On either the seventh or eighth week of the observations (which was after the end of the television advertising campaign), brief interviews were conducted with the produce managers in the panel of stores to determine their awareness and opinions of the television advertising campaign. The major purpose of these interviews was to secure information that would aid in evaluating any changes, or lack of changes, that occurred in the in-store merchandising activity in the test markets as compared with the control markets.

Discussion Questions

1. Evaluate the experimental procedure used.
2. What specific changes, if any, would you recommend?

Measurement Techniques in Marketing Research

Measurement is central to the process of obtaining data. How, and how well, the measurements in a research project are made are critical in determining whether the project will be a success.

Because of their centrality and importance, *measurement concepts* are considered in the first chapter of this section. What measurement is, by what scales measurements can be made, and the components and accuracy of measurements are discussed in this chapter.

The next four chapters are concerned with measurements within a marketing research context. The considerations involved in sound *questionnaire design* are the concern of Chapter 10, while Chapter 11 describes the techniques used in *measuring attitudes and emotions. Depth interviews* and *projective techniques,* often termed *qualitative research,* are the subjects of Chapter 12. Chapter 13 covers the rapidly evolving areas of *observation* and *physiological measures.*

9

Measurement in Marketing Research

LEARNING OBJECTIVES

Upon completing this chapter, you should be able to:

1. Explain what is meant by *measurement* in marketing research.

2. Explain the difference between a conceptual definition and an operational definition.

3. List and describe the four types of measurement scales.

4. Cite and explain the various components of a measurement.

5. Explain the differences among measurement accuracy, reliability, and validity.

6. Cite and describe the major operational approaches to the estimation of reliability.

7. Cite and describe the major operational approaches to the estimation of validity.

The Traffic Audit Bureau's Attempt to Measure Exposure to Billboard Advertisements

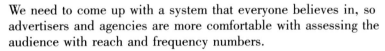

Exposure to outdoor advertisements such as billboards is based on vehicle counts multiplied by the average number of individuals per automobile (vehicle load factor). Vehicle counts are available from local or state governments or are conducted by local billboard firms according to standards used by the Traffic Audit Bureau (TAB). Since 1937, the TAB has used a vehicle load factor of 1.75. However, from 1960 to 1988 vehicle registrations grew four times as fast as the population. By 1990, over 60 percent of all households had two or more cars. As a result, many advertisers concluded that the TAB numbers were radically overstated and could not be relied on. This lack of faith led the president of the Institute of Outdoor Advertising to state:

> We need to come up with a system that everyone believes in, so advertisers and agencies are more comfortable with assessing the audience with reach and frequency numbers.

In response, TAB sponsored four studies of automobile occupancy rates. Two large-scale omnibus surveys (Simmons Market Research Bureau with 20,000 respondents and Mediamark Research, Inc. with 10,000) asked for the number of adults in the car on the respondent's last trip. The results were 1.35 and 1.36. Two observational studies by Market Research Services of America with 10,000 observations per study estimated average adult vehicle load at 1.36 and average total vehicle load at 1.46. Based on these studies, TAB began using 1.35 as its vehicle load factor.[1]

The TAB was using a method to measure exposure to billboards that had become inaccurate. Recognizing its lack of measurement accuracy, advertisers reached a point where they would not use it in deciding how to allocate advertising budgets.

Measurement is a familiar and common activity. College entrance examinations represent an attempt to measure an individual's potential to complete college successfully. An automobile speedometer measures how fast a car is going. Cooking recipes call for measures of the quantity of the various ingredients. Watches and calendars are used to measure the passage of time.

In this chapter, a discussion of the principles and problems involved in measurement as they apply to decision-oriented marketing research is presented. In the first section we attempt to clarify exactly what measurement is. This is followed by a discussion of the distinction between the characteristic being measured and the actual measurement operations.

As the list of common measurements at the beginning of this section indicates, there are several *types* of measurement. One approach to classifying the various types of scales used in measurement—*nominal, ordinal, interval,* and *ratio* scales—is described in the second section of this chapter. The third section discusses the various factors that can influence a specific measurement.

As we know from our own experience, measurements are often not correct: the gasoline gauge shows a quarter of a tank when we run out of gas, or the 10 o'clock news comes on at 9:45, according to our clock. The TAB example illustrates how serious inaccurate measurements can be in a marketing situation. Therefore, the fourth major section of this chapter is a discussion of measurement accuracy.

The Concept of Measurement

Measurement Defined

Measurement:
the assignment of numbers to characteristics of objects, persons, states, or events according to rules.

Measurement is the assignment of numbers to characteristics of objects, persons, states, or events, according to rules. What is measured is *not* the object, person, state, or event itself but some characteristic of it. When objects are counted, for example, we do not measure the object itself but only its characteristic of being present. We never measure *people,* only their *age, height, weight,* or some other characteristic. A study to determine whether a higher percentage of males or females purchases a given product measures the *male–female* and *purchaser–nonpurchaser* attributes of the persons sampled.

The term *number* in the definition of measurement does not always correspond to the usual meaning given this term by the nonresearcher. It does not necessarily mean numbers that can be added, subtracted, divided, or multiplied. Instead, numbers are used as symbols representing certain characteristics of the object. The nature of the meaning of the numbers—symbols—depends on the nature of the characteristics they represent and how they represent them. This issue is developed in some depth in the section on scales of measurement.

The most critical aspect of measurement is the creation of the rules that specify how the numbers are to be assigned to the characteristics to be measured. Once a measurement rule has been created and agreed on, the characteristics of events, persons, states, or objects are described in terms of it. Thus the statement: "Chrysler increased its market share by 2 percentage points during the past year," has a common meaning among those who know the measurement rule that is being applied. However, those who are not aware of the rule will not always be able to understand what has been measured.

This problem arises because the rules that specify *how* the numbers are assigned to the characteristics to be measured are *arbitrary.* Numbers are assigned on the basis of created or invented rules, not as a result of some divine revelation or undeniable natural law. Consider the previous statement concerning Chrysler's market share. Is market share based on units sold or dollar sales? on factory shipments or retail sales? on worldwide sales or U.S. sales? on U.S. sales of domestically produced autos or on imports as well? Each of these alternatives implies *a different measurement rule,* and unless one knows which rule is being applied, a figure is not completely understandable.

Measurement and Reality

If measurement is performed to a set of arbitrary rules, how do we evaluate measurements? Can we measure the *quality* of a measurement? The answer to the latter question is a qualified yes. Two aspects of the quality of a measurement can be evaluated.

First, *we can evaluate the extent to which the measurement rule has been followed.* For example, a researcher may decide on a measurement rule and issue instructions to "count the total number of people who walk past the P-O-P display and the number of people who 'examine' the item." An assistant who counts only those who physically handle the item as "examiners" is applying one interpretation of the rule. A second assistant who includes those who look at the item as "examiners" applies another interpretation of the rule. A third assistant who fails to count a number of examiners because of distractions makes errors in applying the rule. The count of "examiners" of either the first or second assistant is in error because of misunderstanding the rule. The court of the third assistant is in error because of misapplication of the rule.

Second, *we can evaluate how closely the rule corresponds to some aspect of "reality."* The extent of the correspondence required depends on the purpose of the research. Consider the example shown in Table 9–1. There is a perfect correspondence between the characteristic *relative size,* or *rank,* as measured and as it actually exists. If the researcher is interested only in rank order, perhaps to decide in which market to concentrate marketing efforts, the correspondence is satisfactory. This is true despite the errors in measuring the exact size of market potential that served as the basis for deriving the ranks.

TABLE 9–1 Measurement and Reality

| Area | Actual | | Measured | |
	Rank	Size	Rank	Size
A	1	24,800,000	1	29,600,000
B	2	16,500,000	2	25,300,000
C	3	15,200,000	3	14,900,000
D	4	12,100,000	4	6,300,000
E	5	1,700,000	5	4,900,000

RESEARCH APPLICATION 9–1

A Measurement Evaluation of the Consumer Price Index*

According to one economist: "The monthly consumer price index report should be like a cigarette package—Warning: Excess confidence in this index can be damaging to your investment health."

A recent study evaluated the consumer price index (CPI) on two criteria: How accurately does it pick up price changes, and to what extent does the CPI reflect consumer behavior in the marketplace?

The Bureau of Labor Statistics conducts a large-scale survey of consumers annually to determine what is being purchased and every four years to determine where items are being purchased. This information is used to guide the price checking of 350 field economists who spend three weeks of every month checking prices of items in the retail outlets where people report they shop. The prices obtained are then used to calculate the cost of an average "bundle of goods" that a typical consumer would use.

Shopping is very thorough. For example, limes were recently "3 for 99¢" in March and also in April at a shopped outlet. However, before they can conclude that there is no price change, the shoppers must weigh food items priced by the unit. In this case, the average lime weighed eight ounces in March and only five ounces in April. Thus, there had been a 60 percent price increase per ounce. Likewise, shoppers do not use the list price of automobiles but ask dealers to estimate the average discount given for the models being shopped.

Measuring other expenditures such as housing cost is more difficult. The CPI uses "equivalent rent" for the two-thirds of Americans who own their homes.

Despite some difficulties, the cost measures are relatively sound. However, the fact that the CPI is a fixed weight index (each item carries the same weight each month) does not correspond to the behavior of consumers who vary their purchases depending on relative price levels. For example, the CPI uses Macintosh apples every month. However, if they become relatively expensive, many consumers will shift to Golden Delicious apples or even to pears with little loss of quality of life. Likewise, the fact that average housing prices have increased sharply does not directly increase the cost of living for those who have owned their homes for some time.

*Derived from K. Madigan, "How Reliable Is the Consumer Price Index?," *Business Week* (April 29, 1991), 70.

If the researcher is concerned with preparing a sales forecast based on the size of market potential, however, the correspondence to reality is probably insufficient for all except area C. Thus, it is possible to have a "good" measurement when one level of measurement is considered and a "bad" measurement when another level is considered. The rule of measurement in this case was adequate to determine rank but inadequate to determine absolute level. It is important that "good" measurements occur on those characteristics that will influence the decision.

Research Application 9–1 provides an evaluation of the consumer price index using these two evaluative criteria.

Measurement and Concepts

A **concept** is an invented name for a property of an object, person, state, or event. The terms *construct* and *concept* are sometimes used interchangeably. We use concepts such as *sales, market share, attitude,* and *brand loyalty* to signify abstractions based on observations of numerous particular happenings. Concepts aid in thinking by subsuming a number of events under one heading. Thus, the concept *car* refers to the generalization of the characteristics that all cars have in common. The concept *car* is closely related to a physical reality.

Many concepts in marketing research do not have such easily observed physical referents. It is impossible to point to a physical example of an *attitude, product image,* or *social class.* Therefore, particular attention must be devoted to defining precisely what is meant by a given concept. Two approaches are necessary to define a concept adequately: (1) *conceptual definition* and (2) *operational definition.*

Concept: an invented name for a property of an object, person, state, or event.

Conceptual Definitions

A **conceptual definition** (sometimes called a *constitutive definition*) defines a concept in terms of other concepts. It states the central idea or essence of the concept. Very often it is the equivalent of a definition found in a dictionary. A good conceptual definition clearly delineates the major characteristics of the concept and allows one to distinguish the concept from similar but different concepts. Consider "brand loyalty" as a concept. How do you define it? Under your definition, is one loyal to a brand if one consistently buys it because it is the only brand of the product that is available at the stores at which one shops? Is this individual brand-loyal in the same sense as others who consistently select the same brand from among the many brands carried where they shop? An adequate conceptual definition of brand loyalty should distinguish it from similar concepts such as "repeat purchasing behavior."

Conceptual definition: defines a concept in terms of other concepts.

Operational Definitions

Once a conceptual definition has been established, an operational definition must be designed that will reflect accurately the major characteristics of the conceptual definition. An **operational definition** describes the activities the researcher must complete in order to assign a value to a concept. Concepts are abstractions; as such, they are not observable. Operational definitions translate the concept into one or more observable events. Thus, a conceptual definition should precede and guide the development of the operational definition.

Consider this conceptual definition of brand loyalty: "the preferential attitudinal and behavioral response toward one or more brands in a product category expressed over a period of time by a consumer (or buyer)." Brand loyalty defined in this way can be measured in a number of different ways. However, it is sufficiently precise to rule out many commonly used operational definitions of brand loyalty. For example, an operational definition involving a purchase sequence in which brand loyalty is defined as X consecutive purchases (usually three or four) of one brand is often used. This

Operational definition: describes the procedure to be used to assign a value to a concept.

operational definition is not adequate because it ignores the attitudinal component specified in the conceptual definition.

It is possible, and in fact common, to have several operational definitions for the same concept. This fact requires us to specify clearly the operational definitions we are using. Such terms as *profit, social class,* and *market share* should be accompanied by precise operational definitions when used in a research context. For example, a study of the market share of private-label grocery brands found that they had a 22.2 percent share based on unit sales but only a 15 percent share of dollar sales.[2] Likewise, Fisherman's Friend cough lozenges is number one in unit sales in drugstores with a 21 percent share but drops to fourth (12 percent) if dollar volume is the base.[3]

Scales of Measurement

In the preceding section, we saw that measurement consists of assigning numbers to characteristics of objects or events in such a way as to reflect some aspect of reality. The goal then is to assign numbers so that the properties of the numbers are the same as the properties of the objects or events we are measuring. This implies that we have different kinds of numbers. A moment's reflection will indicate that this is indeed the case. In a large university or class you may be identified by your university ID card number or your seat number. A number used in this manner is very different from the number that represents your score on the final exam. And score on the final examination is different in nature from your final rank in the class.

It is useful to distinguish four different types of numbers or scales of measurement: *nominal, ordinal, interval,* and *ratio.* The rules for assigning numbers constitute the essential criteria for defining each scale. As we move from nominal to ratio scales, we must meet increasingly restrictive rules. As the rules become more restrictive, the kinds of arithmetic operations for which the numbers can be used are increased. Examine Research Application 9–2 closely. Chances are you will not completely understand why three different results were obtained. The next few pages, which describe the four measurement scales, should resolve the mystery.

Nominal Measurements

Nominal scale: numbers used only to place objects or events into discrete categories.

Nominal scales are comprised of numbers used only to categorize objects or events. Perhaps the most common example is when we assign a female the number 1 and a male the number 0. Numbers used in this manner differ significantly from those used in more conventional ways. We could just as easily have assigned the 0 to the females and the 1 to the males, or we could have used the symbols A and B or the terms *male* and *female*. In fact, in the final research report, terms are generally substituted for numbers to describe nominal categories.

A nominally scaled number serves only as a label for a class or category. The objects in each class are viewed as equivalent with respect to the characteristic represented by the nominal number. In the example given, all those placed in category 0 would be regarded as equivalent in terms of "maleness"; those in

RESEARCH APPLICATION 9-2

Comparative Advertising, Measurement Scales, and Data Analysis

Suppose you see an advertisement that claims that *Vital* capsules are 50 percent more effective in easing tensions than the leading tranquilizer. As research director for the company that produces the leading tranquilizer, *Restease*, you immediately begin comparison tests. Using large sample sizes and a well-designed experiment, you have one group of individuals use *Vital* capsules and a second group use *Restease*. You then have each individual in each group rate the effectiveness of the brand they tried on a five-point scale as follows:

For easing tension, I found *Vital (Restease)* to be

____ a. Very effective
____ b. Effective
____ c. Neither effective nor ineffective
____ d. Ineffective
____ e. Very ineffective

For analysis, you decide to code the "very effective" response as $+2$; the "effective" response as $+1$; the "neither-nor" response as 0; the "ineffective" response as -1; and the "very ineffective" response as -2. This is a common way of coding data of this nature.

You calculate an average response for *Vital* and *Restease* and obtain scores of 1.2 and .8, respectively. Because the .4 difference is 50 percent more than the .8 level obtained by your brand, you conclude that the claims for *Vital* are valid. Shortly after reaching this conclusion, one of your assistants, who was also analyzing the data, enters your office with the good news that *Vital* was viewed as only 10.5 percent more effective than *Restease*. Immediately you examine his figures. He used the same data and made no computational mistakes. The only difference was that he assigned the "very ineffective" response at $+1$ and continued up to a $+5$ for the "very effective" response. This is also a widely used procedure.

Then, as you are puzzling over these results, another member of your department enters. She used the same approach as your assistant but assigned a $+5$ to "very ineffective" and a $+1$ to "very effective." Again, with no computational errors, she found *Vital* to be 18.2 percent more effective. What do you conclude?

SOURCE: Derived from B. Venkatesh, "Unthinking Data Interpretation Can Destroy Value of Research," *Marketing News* (January 27, 1978), 6, 9. Both brand names are completely fictitious.

---

category 1 would be equivalent in "femaleness." The number 1 *does not* imply a superior position to the number 0. The only rules involved are that *all members of a class* (every object that has a certain characteristic) *have the same number* and that *no two classes have the same number*.

An example of the use of nominal measurement is the case of a manager of a restaurant located in a shopping center who wants to determine whether noon customers select the establishment primarily because of its location or primarily because of its menu. The manager randomly selects and questions 100 customers and finds that 70 state that they eat there because of the location and 30 because of the menu. This represents a simple analysis using nominal data. The manager has formed a two-category scale, counted the number of cases in each category, and identified the modal category.

Any arithmetic operations performed on nominally scaled data can be carried out only on the *count* in each category. Numbers assigned to represent the categories (1 for male, 0 for female, for example) cannot meaningfully be added, subtracted, multiplied, or divided.

A *mean* or a *median* cannot be calculated for nominal data. A *mode* can be used, however. In the example given, location was the modal reason for choosing the restaurant. The *percentages* of items falling within each category also can be determined. A chi-square statistical test can be conducted to determine if differences between the numbers falling in the various categories is likely to be the result of chance or randomness.

Ordinal Measurements

Ordinal scale:
numbers used to place objects or events into rank-ordered categories.

Ordinal scales represent numbers, letters, or other symbols used to categorize and rank items. Items can be classified not only as to whether they share some characteristic with another item but also whether they have more or less of this characteristic than some other object. However, ordinally scaled numbers do not provide information on how much more or less of the characteristic various items possess. For an example, refer to the "actual" column of Table 9–1, in which five markets are ranked in terms of market potential and their actual sales are indicated.

The rank order (ordinal) scale in Table 9–1 accurately indicates that area A is the largest market, B the next largest, and so forth. Thus, it is a sound measure of the relative sizes of the five areas. Note that the difference in rank between markets A and B is 1, as it is between markets B and C. However, the difference in sales between markets A and B is approximately $8 million, whereas the difference between markets B and C is approximately $1 million. Thus, ordinal data indicate the relative position of two or more items on some characteristic but *not* the *magnitude* of the differences between the items.

A significant amount of marketing research relies on ordinal measures. The most common usage of ordinal scales is in obtaining preference measurements. For example, a consumer or a sample of experts may be asked to rank preferences for several brands, flavors, or package designs. The following task will produce ordinal data:

Read the list of brands of gasoline on the card I just gave you. Tell me which brand you think has the highest quality. Now tell me the one you think is next highest in quality.

(Continue until all brands are named or until the respondent says she does not know the remaining brands. Record DK if she does not know the brand.)

(1) _____   (3) _____   (5) _____

(2) _____   (4) _____

Suppose that Texaco is one of the brands of gasoline. Further suppose that the quality ratings it receives, compared with four other brands from a sample of 500 car owners, are as follows:

Quality Rating	Number of Respondents Giving Rating to Texaco
1	100
2	200
3	100
4	50
5	50

What kind of descriptive statistics can be used on these data?

A *mode* or a *median* may be used, but not a *mean*. The modal quality rating is "2," as it is for the median. A mean should not be calculated because the differences between ordinal scaled values are not necessarily the same. The *percentages* of the total appearing in each rank may be calculated and are meaningful. The branch of statistics that deals with ordinal (and nominal) measurements is called *nonparametric statistics*.

Interval Measurements

Interval scales represent numbers used to categorize and rank items such that numerically equal distances on the scale represent equal distances in the property being measured but the location of the zero point is not fixed. Both the zero point and the unit of measurement are arbitrary. The most familiar examples of interval scales are the temperature scales, both centigrade and Fahrenheit. The same natural phenomenon, the freezing point of water, is assigned a different value on each scale, 0 on centigrade and 32 on Fahrenheit. The 0 position, therefore, is arbitrary. The difference in the volume of mercury is the same between 20 and 30 degrees centigrade and 40 and 50 degrees centigrade. Thus, the measure of the underlying phenomenon is made in equal units. A value on either scale can be converted to the other by using the formula $F = 32 + 9/5C$.

The most frequent form of interval measurement in marketing is *index numbers*. An index number is calculated by setting one number, such as sales, for a particular year equal to 100. This is known as the *base period* or *base value*. Other numbers for subsequent years are then expressed as percentages of the base value. The Department of Labor provides a consumer price index with 1967 as the base year, whereas the Federal Reserve System uses 1977 as the base year for its industrial production index. Since any year or value, including a completely arbitrary value, can serve as the base value, index numbers have an arbitrary zero point and equal intervals between scale values.

Another common type of marketing research data generally treated as interval scale data is attitude measures. A Likert scale (described in Chapter 11), for example, requires the respondents to state their degree of agreement or disagreement with a statement by selecting a response from a list such as the following one:

1. Agree very strongly.
2. Agree fairly strongly.
3. Agree.

Interval scale: numbers used to categorize and rank objects or events such that numerically equal distances on the scale represent equal distances in the property but the location of the zero point is arbitrary.

4. Undecided.

5. Disagree.

6. Disagree fairly strongly.

7. Disagree very strongly.

It is doubtful that the interval between each of these items is exactly equal. However, most researchers treat the data from such scales as if they were equal interval in nature since the results of most standard statistical techniques are not affected greatly by small deviations from the interval requirement.[4] Where this is a concern, there are ways to transform most ordinal data used by marketers into workable interval data.[5]

Virtually the entire range of statistical analyses can be applied to interval scales. Such descriptive measures as the *mean, median, mode, range,* and *standard deviation* are applicable. *Bivariate correlation analyses, t-tests, analysis of variance tests,* and most multivariate techniques applied for purposes of drawing inferences can be used on intervally scaled data. However, as we saw in Research Application 9–1, ratios calculated on interval data are not meaningful. A ratio—twice as much, 50 percent more than, half as much—requires a ratio measurement scale.

Ratio Measurements

Ratio scale:
numbers used to categorize and rank objects or events such that numerically equal distances on the scale represent equal distances in the property and zero point is meaningful.

Ratio scales consist of numbers that categorize and rank items such that numerically equal distances on the scale represent equal distances in the property being measured *and* have a meaningful zero. In general, simple counting of any set of objects produces a ratio scale of the characteristic "existence." In this case, the number 0 has an absolute empirical meaning— none of the property being measured exists. Thus, such common measurements as *sales, costs, market potential, market share,* and *number of purchasers* are all made using ratio scales.

All descriptive measures and inferential techniques are applicable to ratio-scaled data. However, this produces only a minimal gain in analytic technique beyond those available for interval data. Table 9–2 provides a summary description of each of the four types of scales.

Components of Measurements

Supose an individual has completed a 10-item questionnaire designed to measure overall attitude toward the Honda Accord Coupe. The score (number) for this measurement was 68. We can assume any scaling system, nominal through ratio. The question that the researcher must ask is: *What factors or characteristics are reflected in this score?*

In an ideal situation, there would be only one component in the score and this component would be a direct reflection of the characteristic of interest— the individual's attitude toward the Accord. Unfortunately, such a state of affairs is seldom achieved.[6] The researcher must, therefore, be concerned about the extent to which any single measurement reflects the characteristic under consideration versus other characteristics.

Table 9–3 summarizes the components that may be reflected in any given measurement. As the table indicates, the characteristic of interest is only one of eight possible components of a measurement. The remaining components all constitute *measurement error* (sometimes referred to as *response error*). Each component of measurement error is described in the following paragraphs.

TABLE 9–2 Types of Measurement Scales

Scale	Basic Empirical Operations	Typical Usage	Typical Statistics*	
			Descriptive	Inferential
Nominal	Determination of equality	Classification: Male–female, purchaser–nonpurchaser	Percentages, mode	Chi-square, binomial test
Ordinal	Determination of greater or less	Rankings: Preference data, market position, attitude measures, many psychological measures	Median	Mann-Whitney U, Friedman two-way ANOVA, rank-order correlation
Interval	Determination of equality of intervals	Index numbers, attitude measures, level of knowledge about brands	Mean, range, standard deviation	Product–moment correlation, t-test, factor analysis, ANOVA
Ratio	Determination of equality of ratios	Sales, units produced, number of customers, costs		Coefficient of variation

*All statistics applicable to a given scale are also applicable to any higher scale in the table. For example, all the statistics applicable to an ordinal scale are also applicable to interval and ratio scales.

SOURCE: Adapted from S. S. Stevens, "On the Theory of Scales of Measurement," *Science* (June 7, 1946), 677–680.

TABLE 9–3 Components of Measurements

1. *True characteristic:* direct reflection of the characteristic of interest
2. *Additional stable characteristics of the respondent:* reflection of other permanent characteristics, such as social class or intelligence
3. *Short-term characteristics of the respondent:* reflection of temporary characteristics such as hunger, fatigue, or anger
4. *Situational characteristics:* reflection of the surroundings in which the measurement is taken
5. *Characteristics of the measurement process:* reflection of the interviewer, interviewing method, and the like
6. *Characteristics of the measuring instrument:* reflection of ambiguous or misleading questions
7. *Characteristics of the response process:* reflection of mistaken replies caused by checking the wrong response, and the like
8. *Characteristics of the analysis:* reflection of mistakes in coding, tabulating, and the like

Measurement Error's Impact on Hanes' Marketing Strategy

Hanes Corp. suffered substantial losses on its *L'erin* cosmetics line. Although its initial marketing strategy was weak in several areas, marketing research contributed to its problems. According to the division head of *L'erin,* the company "listened to the consumer too much." Hanes conducted a substantial number of interviews with target market consumers. In the interviews, the women described their ideal cosmetic in functional rather than in emotional terms. They stated a desire for cosmetics that could be worn all day without much upkeep.

Based on this research, *L'erin* was launched with a strong logical advertising theme. The slogan, delivered by a "plain-Jane" model in an ordinary setting, was: "Put your face on and forget it." The results were $30 million in losses over the first few years. The company shifted to a romantic theme with glamorous models and unusual settings.

Reflection of Additional Stable Characteristics

Perhaps the most troublesome measurement error occurs when the *measurement reflects a stable characteristic of the object or event in addition to the one of interest to the researcher.* Thus, the score of 68 in the example may reflect the respondent's tendency to be agreeable by making positive responses as well as the "true" attitude. Such "extraneous" variables as gender, education, and age have been found to be sources of bias in the measurement of attitudinal reactions to television commercials tested by the Leo Burnett Co.[7] Research Application 9–3 shows how Hanes developed an inappropriate advertising strategy for *L'erin* because it was misled by a tendency of the women it surveyed to describe comestic purchases in logical terms while (apparently) purchasing them on an emotional basis.[8]

Stable characteristics of the respondent are particularly troublesome when they differ across respondent groups of interest such as gender, subculture, or nationality groups. For example, evidence indicates that Hispanics are more likely than other groups to provide positive responses.[9] Likewise, the Japanese are generally reluctant to say *no* directly. This issue must be given careful consideration when conducting multinational or subcultural research studies.

Temporary Characteristics of the Respondent

An equally common source of error is the *influence of short-term characteristics of the object.* Such factors as fatigue, health, hunger, and emotional state may influence the measure of other characteristics. In the attitude measure example, some of the "68" could reflect the fact that the respondent was in a bad mood because of a cold. Fortunately, such temporary fluctuations are generally randomly distributed in their effect on the measurement and cancel each other out.

Situational Characteristics

Many measurements that involve human subjects reflect both the true characteristic under consideration and *the characteristics under which the measurement is taken.* For example, husbands and wives tend to report one level of influence in a purchase decision if their spouses are present and another level if their spouses are absent.

Characteristics of the Measurement Process

The measurement also can include *influences from the method of gathering the data.* Gender, age, ethnic background, and style of dress of the interviewer have been shown to influence an individual's response patterns on certain questions. In addition, various methods of interviewing—telephone, mail, personal interview, and the like—sometimes alter response patterns.

Characteristics of the Measuring Instrument

Aspects of *the measuring instrument itself can cause constant or random errors.* Unclear instructions, ambiguous questions, confusing terms, irrelevant questions, and omitted questions can all introduce errors. For example, the term *dinner* causes some people to think of the noon meal and others to think of the evening meal. Our 68 score may not be an accurate reflection of overall attitude toward the Accord if a key dimension such as safety was omitted from the questionnaire.

Characteristics of the Response Process

Response errors are another reason why responses may not reflect the "true" characteristic accurately. For example, our respondent may have inadvertently checked a positive response when the intention was to check a negative one. Part of the score of 68 would be caused by this mistake rather than the true attitude.

Characteristics of the Analysis

Finally, *mistakes can occur in interpreting, coding, tabulating, and analyzing an individual's or a group's response.* In our attitude example, the analyst might enter an 8 rather than a 3 for one of the questions. Again, the 68 would be composed of an error component in addition to the characteristic of interest.

The measurement errors described are subject to varying degrees of control by the researcher. The material in Chapters 10 through 13 provides explicit discussions of various approaches for controlling measurement error. The next section of this chapter describes the effect of the error components in terms of the accuracy of the measurement.

Measurement Accuracy

A measurement is a number designed to reflect some characteristic of an individual, object, or event. As such it is a specific observation or picture of this characteristic. Ideally, the observed measurement would be an exact representation of the true characteristic, or $M = C$ where M stands for the measurement and C stands for the true value of the characteristic being measured.

As we saw in the previous section, a number of errors tend to influence a measurement. Thus, the general situation is

$$M = C + E, \text{ where } E = \text{errors}$$

Systematic error (bias): occurs in a consistent manner each time something is measured.

Variable error: occurs randomly each time something is measured.

Reliability: the extent to which a measurement is free of variable errors.

Validity: the extent to which a measurement is free of systematic errors.

Measurement accuracy: the extent to which a measurement is free of both systematic and variable errors.

The smaller E is as a percentage of M, the more accurate is the measurement. Researchers should seek to achieve accuracy levels sufficient to solve the problem at hand while minimizing the cost of achieving the needed accuracy.

Although *validity, reliability,* and *accuracy* are often used interchangeably, each does have a specific meaning based on the type of measurement error that is present.[10] Measurement error impact can be either systematic or variable. A **systematic error,** also known as *bias,* is one that occurs in a consistent manner each time something is measured. In the Honda Accord example, a biased question would produce an error in the same direction each time it was asked. This would be a systematic error.

A **variable error** is one that occurs randomly each time something is measured. In the Accord example, a response that is less favorable than the true feeling because the respondent was in a bad mood (temporary characteristic) would *not* occur each time that individual's attitude is measured. In fact, an error in the opposite direction (overly favorable) would occur if the individual were in a very good mood. This represents a variable error.

Reliability is the extent to which a measurement is free of variable errors. This is reflected when repeated measures of the same stable characteristic in the same objects show limited variation.

A common conceptual definition for validity is the extent to which the measure accurately represents what one is trying to measure. In this conceptual definition, validity includes both *systematic* and *variable* error components. However, it is more useful to limit the meaning of the term *validity* to refer to the degree of consistent or systematic error in a measurement. Therefore, **validity** is the extent to which a measurement is free from systematic error.

Measurement accuracy is the extent to which a measurement is free from systematic and variable error. Accuracy is the ultimate concern of the researcher, since a lack of accuracy may lead to incorrect decisions. However, since systematic and variable errors are measured and controlled for in distinct ways, considering each separately under the concepts of reliability and validity is worthwhile. For example, the reliability of a score based on the sum of several similar items can be improved by increasing the number of items used to calculate the sum. The validity of the score is unaffected by this technique.[11]

Reliability

Table 9–4 summarizes the major operational approaches to the estimation of reliability. Each of these measures is discussed in some detail in the following paragraphs. No one approach is best; in fact, several different assessment approaches should generally be used. The selection of one or more means of assessing a measure's reliability depends on the errors likely to be present and the cost of each assessment method in the situation at hand.

Test–Retest Reliability

Test–retest reliability estimates are obtained by repeating the measurement using the same instrument under as nearly equivalent conditions as possible. The results of the two administrations are then compared and the degree of correspondence is determined. The greater the differences, the lower is the reliability.

A number of practical and computational difficulties are involved in measuring test–retest reliability.[12] First, *some items can be measured only once*. It would not be possible, for example, to remeasure an individual's initial reaction to a new advertising slogan. Second, in many situations, *the initial measurement may alter the characteristic being measured*. Thus, an attitude survey may focus the individual's attention on the topic and cause new or different attitudes to be formed about it. Third, *there may be some form of a carryover effect from the first measure*. The retaking of a measure may produce boredom, anger, or attempts to remember the answers given on the initial measurement. Finally, *factors extraneous to the measuring process may cause shifts in the characteristic being measured*. A favorable experience with a brand during the period between the test and the retest might cause a shift in individual ratings of that brand, for example.

Test–retest reliability: the ability of the measurement instrument to produce the same results when repeated under as equivalent conditions as possible.

Alternative-Form Reliability

Alternative-form reliability estimates are obtained by applying two equivalent forms of the measuring instrument to the same subjects. As in test–retest reliability, the results of the two instruments are compared on an item-by-item basis and the degree of similarity is determined. The basic logic is the same as in the test–retest approach. Two primary problems are associated with this approach. The first is the *extra time, expense, and trouble involved in obtaining two*

Alternative-form reliability: the ability of two equivalent forms of the instrument to produce the same results when given to the same subjects.

TABLE 9–4 Approaches to Assessing Reliability

1. *Test–retest reliability:* applying the same measure to the same objects a second time.
2. *Alternative-forms reliability:* measuring the same objects by two instruments that are designed to be as nearly alike as possible.
3. *Internal-comparison reliability:* comparing the responses among the various items on a multiple-item index designed to measure a homogeneous concept.
4. *Scorer reliability:* comparing the scores assigned the same item by two or more judges.

equivalent measures. The second, and more important, is *the problem of constructing two truly equivalent forms.* Thus, a low degree of response similarity may reflect either an unreliable instrument or nonequivalent forms. Despite these difficulties, researchers should use alternative measures of important concepts whenever possible to allow assessment of reliability (and validity) as well as to improve accuracy (by using the data from both measures).

Internal-Comparison Reliability

Internal-comparison reliability is estimated by the intercorrelation among the scores of the items on a multiple-item index. All items on the index must be designed to measure precisely the same thing.[13] For example, measures of store image generally involve assessing a number of specific dimensions of the store, such as price level, merchandise, service, and location. Because these are somewhat independent, an internal-comparison measure of reliability is not appropriate across dimensions. However, it can be used *within* each dimension if several items are used to measure each dimension.

Split-half reliability is the simplest type of internal comparison. It is obtained by comparing the results of half the items on a multi-item measure with the results from the remaining items. The usual approach to split-half reliability involves dividing the total number of items into two groups on a random basis and computing a measure of similarity (a correlation coefficient).

A better approach to internal comparison is known as *coefficient alpha.* This measurement, in effect, produces the mean of all possible split-half coefficients resulting from different splittings of the measurement instrument.[14]

Scorer Reliability

Marketing researchers frequently rely on judgment to classify a consumer's response. This occurs, for example, when projective techniques, focus groups, observation, or open-ended questions are used. In these situations, the judges, or scorers, may be unreliable, rather than the instrument or respondent. **Scorer reliability** is estimated by the correlations between the scores two or more judges assign a sample of items.[15]

Validity

Validity, like reliability, is concerned with error. However, it is *concerned with consistent or systematic error rather than variable error.* A valid measurement reflects only the characteristics of interest and random error. There are three basic types of validity: *content* validity, *construct* validity, and *criterion-related* validity (predictive and concurrent). These are defined in Table 9–5 and described in the following sections.[16]

Content Validity

Content validity estimates are systematic, but subjective, evaluations of the appropriateness of the measuring instrument for the task at hand. The term *face validity* has a similar meaning. However, face validity generally refers to

---

Internal-comparison reliability: the ability of two or more measurements of the same concept on the same instrument to produce the same results.

Scorer reliability: the ability of two or more judges to assign the same score to an item.

Content validity estimates: systematic, but subjective, estimates of the appropriateness of the measuring instrument.

TABLE 9–5 Basic Approaches to Validity Assessment

1. *Content validation* involves assessing the representativeness or the sampling adequacy of the items contained in the measuring instrument.
2. *Criterion-related validation* involves inferring an individual's score or standing on some measurement, called a *criterion*, from the measurement at hand.
   a. *Concurrent validation* involves assessing the extent to which the obtained score may be used to estimate an individual's present standing with respect to some other variable.
   b. *Predictive validation* involves assessing the extent to which the obtained score may be used to estimate an individual's future standing with respect to the criterion variable.
3. *Construct validation* involves understanding the meaning of the obtained measurements.

"nonexpert" judgments of individuals completing the instrument and/or executives who must approve its use. This does not mean that face validity is not important. Respondents may refuse to cooperate or may fail to treat seriously measurements that appear irrelevant to them. Managers may refuse to approve projects that utilize measurements lacking in face validity. Therefore, to the extent possible, researchers should strive for face validity.

The most common use of content validity is with multi-item measures. In this case, the researchers or some other individual or group of individuals assesses the representativeness, or sampling adequacy, of the included items in light of the purpose of the measuring instrument. Thus, an attitude scale designed to measure the overall attitude toward a shopping center would not be considered to have content validity if it omitted any major attributes such as location, layout, and so on. Content validation is the most common form of validation in applied marketing research.

Criterion-Related Validity

Criterion-related validity can take two forms, based on the time period involved: concurrent and predictive validity.

Concurrent validity is the extent to which one measure of a variable can be used to estimate an individual's current score on a different measure of the same, or a closely related, variable. For example, a researcher may be trying to relate social class to the use of savings and loan associations. In a pilot study, the researcher finds a useful relationship between attitudes toward savings and loan associations and social class, as defined by Warner's ISC scale. The researcher now wishes to test this relationship further in a national mail survey. Unfortunately, Warner's ISC is difficult to use in a mail survey. Therefore, the researcher develops brief verbal descriptions of each of Warner's six social classes. Respondents will be asked to indicate the social class that best describes their household. Before using this measure, the researcher should assess its concurrent validity with the standard ISC scale.

Predictive validity is the extent to which an individual's future level on some variable can be predicted by his or her performance on a current mea-

Concurrent validity: the ability of one measure of a variable to estimate an individual's current score on another measure of the same variable.

Predictive validity: the ability of one measure of a variable to estimate an individual's future score on the same or another measure of the same variable.

surement of the same or a different variable. Predictive validity is the primary concern of the applied marketing researcher. Some of the predictive validity questions that confront marketing researchers are (1) Will a measure of attitudes predict future purchases? (2) Will a measure of sales in a controlled store test predict future market share? (3) Will a measure of initial sales predict future sales? and (4) Will a measure of demographic characteristics of an area predict the success of a branch bank in the area?

Advertising researchers are trying to develop communications effects measures for use with storyboards that will accurately predict similar measures using "rough" commercials. Storyboards precede the development of commercials and cost substantially less than the $15,000 required to produce a rough commercial.[17] Thus, the economic benefits associated with a predictively valid measure of storyboard communications effects is substantial.

Construct Validity

Construct validity: involves understanding the factors that underlie the obtained measurement.

Construct validity involves understanding the factors that underlie the obtained measurement. It involves more than just knowing how well a given measure works; it also involves knowing *why* it works. Construct validity requires that the researcher have a sound theory of the nature of the concept being measured and how it relates to other concepts.

A number of approaches exist for assessing construct validity of which the most common is called the *multitrait–multimethod matrix* approach. These multiple measures (by methods as different from each other as possible) of multiple traits or concepts can be analyzed by the Campbell–Fiske procedure, confirmatory factor analysis, or the direct product model.[18]

Although a detailed description of these techniques is beyond the scope of this text, they generally involve ensuring that the measure correlates positively with other measures of the same construct (*convergent validity*), does not correlate with theoretically unrelated constructs (*discriminant validity*), correlates in the theoretically predicted way with measures of different but related constructs (*nomological validity,*) and correlates highly with itself (*reliability*).

Summary

Measurement is the assignment of numbers to characteristics of objects, persons, states, or events according to rules. An operational definition provides the rules the researcher must follow in order to assign a number to the concept under consideration. A conceptual definition defines a concept in terms of other concepts much like a dictionary definition.

Four commonly used types or scales of measurement are based on the restrictiveness of the measurement rules used. Nominal scales classify objects or events into categories. Ordinal scales classify objects and events into categories and rank order the categories. Interval scales classify objects or events into categories and rank order them such that equal distances on the scale represent equal distances in the property being measured but the location of the zero point is arbitrary. Ratio scales are the same as interval scales except that the zero point is fixed and meaningful.

Any given measurement can contain any combination of eight components: (1) the true characteristic being measured, (2) additional stable characteristics of the respondent, (3) short-term characteristics of the respondent, (4) situational influences, (5) characteristics of the measurement process, (6) characteristics of the measuring instrument, (7) characteristics of the response process, and (8) characteristics of the analysis.

Reliability is the extent to which a measurement is free of variable error. Validity is the extent to which a measurement is free of systematic error. Measurement accuracy is the extent to which a measurement is free of variable and systematic error.

Reliability is estimated by test–retest reliability, alternative-forms reliability, internal-comparison reliability, and scorer reliability. Validity is approached through content validation, criterion-based validation (concurrent and predictive validation), and construct validation.

Review Questions

9.1. What is meant by *measurement*?

9.2. How can we evaluate measurements?

9.3. What is a *concept*?

9.4. What is the difference between a *conceptual* definition and an *operational* definition?

9.5. What is a *nominal* scale? What statistical techniques can be used with a nominal scale?

9.6. What is an *ordinal* scale? What statistical techniques can be used with an ordinal scale?

9.7. What is an *interval* scale? What statistical techniques can be used with an interval scale?

9.8. What is a *ratio* scale? What statistical techniques can be used with a ratio scale?

9.9. What measurement components can exist in any specific measurement?

9.10. Describe the measurement component *temporary characteristics of the object*.

9.11. Describe the measurement component *additional stable characteristics of the object*.

9.12. Describe the measurement component *situational characteristics*.

9.13. Describe the measurement component *characteristics of the measurement process*.

9.14. Describe the measurement component *characteristics of the measuring instrument*.

9.15. Describe the measurement component *characteristics of the response process.*

9.16. Describe the measurement component *characteristics of the analysis.*

9.17. How are measurement accuracy, reliability, and validity related?

9.18. Describe each of the following:
   a. Test–retest reliability
   b. Alternative-forms reliability
   c. Internal-comparison reliability
   d. Split-half reliability
   e. Coefficient alpha
   f. Scorer reliability

9.19. What are the problems with test–retest reliability?

9.20. Describe each of the following:
   a. Content validity
   b. Face validity
   c. Criterion-related validity
   d. Concurrent validity
   e. Predictive validity
   f. Construct validity
   g. Convergent validity
   h. Discriminant validity
   i. Nomological validity

9.21. What is the *multitrait–multimethod* approach?

Discussion Questions/Problems

9.22. For each of the following measurements, indicate whether a nominal, ordinal, interval, or ratio scale was used. Briefly explain why you believe your answer is correct.
   a. A report indicating that Buick had fewer customer complaints per car sold than any other American car.
   b. A report indicating that men drink over three times as much beer per capita as women.
   c. A decision classifying pretzels as a snack food and thus subject to sales tax.
   d. A recommendation that yogurt be stored at 46°F or less.
   e. A study showing that Honda ranked third in terms of number of dealerships in California.

9.23. What kind of scale(s) is/are involved in the following situations? Is the analysis consistent with the scale(s) used?
   a. "Children under 10 receive aspirin as the most widely prescribed drug reducing the temperature of a fever. Most doctors prescribe aspirin when the temperature reaches 100°F or more. It reduces temperature at an average rate of 0.77°F per hour."

b. "A sample of 300 adults was asked to rank aspirin, Bufferin, Empirin, Excedrin, and Anacin in order of preference for treatment of headaches. The most preferred was given a ranking of '1,' and the least preferred a ranking of '5.' The median for aspirin was 1.72."

c. "Adults over 60 use twice as many grains of aspirin per year as adults between the ages of 20 and 30."

9.24. Give one conceptual and two or more operational definitions for each of the following concepts:

a. market share
b. light user
c. satisfied customer
d. department store

9.25. What measurement components do you think were or would be most important in the following situations?

a. Your score on your college entrance exam
b. A mall intercept survey during Christmas season to measure attitudes and behaviors related to gardening
c. An audit of your tapes and/or CDs to determine your taste in music
d. Your response to your instructor's question: "How do you like my class?"

9.26. In the Miss America Pageant, contestants are rated by each judge separately on a scale of 1 to 10 (10 highest) on talent, swimsuit appearance, evening gown appearance, and the results of an interview. These ratings are weighted one-third for talent, one-third for swimsuit appearance, one-sixth for evening gown appearance, and one-sixth for the interview. The weighted scores from each of these areas are first summed by judge and then for all judges. The contestant with the highest total score becomes the new Miss America.

Ignoring for a moment any concerns you might have about the appropriateness of such a contest, comment on the assumptions implicit in this procedure with respect to

a. the scales involved
b. interarea ratings by each judge
c. intraarea ratings across judges
d. the weights for the areas

9.27. As a manager, what indicators of measurement accuracy would you insist on in research reports?

9.28. Develop a series of index numbers using the following sales data:

a.	1983 =	730,000	g. 1989 = 1,340,000	
b.	1984 =	835,000	h. 1990 = 1,550,000	
c.	1985 =	955,000	i. 1991 = 1,760,000	
d.	1986 =	985,000	j. 1992 = 1,810,000	
e.	1987 =	1,130,000	k. 1993 = 1,550,000	
f.	1988 =	1,200,000	l. 1994 = 1,400,000	

Projects/Activities

9.29. Examine the marketing literature dealing with multiattribute attitude models. (Any recent consumer behavior text will describe the model and list additional references.) What type of validity has been stressed in this literature? What steps would you suggest to validate further these models?

9.30. Examine the marketing literature, and find and describe a marketing concept that has two or more distinct conceptual definitions.

9.31. Describe the assessment of reliability of the measurement instrument in a *recent* marketing study whose primary purpose did not relate to reliability assessment.

9.32. Describe the assessment of validity of the measurement instrument in a *recent* marketing study in which the primary purpose did not relate to validity assessment.

Notes

1. A. Fahey, "Outdoor Eyes Better Measurement," *Advertising Age* (June 5, 1989), 28; and *Addressing the Importance of the Vehicle Load Factor* (New York: Traffic Audit Bureau, undated).

2. J. Liesse, "Making a Name for Selves," *Advertising Age* (May 6, 1991), 36.

3. D. I. Hawkins, R. J. Best, K. A. Coney, *Consumer Behavior* (Homewood, IL: R. D. Irwin, 1992), 573.

4. M. R. Crask, R. J. Fox, "An Exploration of the Internal Properties of Three Commonly Used Research Scales," *Journal of the Market Research Society* (October 1987), 317–339.

5. G. R. Dowling, D. F. Midgley, "Using Rank Values as an Interval Scale," *Psychology and Marketing* (Spring 1991), 37–41.

6. J. A. Cote, M. R. Buckley, "Estimating Trait, Method, and Error Variance," *Journal of Marketing Research* (August 1987), 315–318.

7. M. J. R. Schlinger, "Respondent Characteristics That Affect Copy-Test Attitude Scales," *Journal of Advertising Research* (February/March 1982), 29–35.

8. B. Abrams, "Hanes Finds L'eggs Methods Don't Work with Cosmetics," *Wall Street Journal* (February 3, 1983), 33.

9. C. Goerne, "Go the Extra Mile to Catch Up with Hispanics," *Marketing News* (December 24, 1990), 13; and V. R. Wood, R. Howell, "A Note on Hispanic Values and Subcultural Research," *Journal of the Academy of Marketing Science* (Winter 1991), 61–68.

10. For a technical discussion of the relationship of these concepts, see F. N. Kerlinger, *Foundations of Behavioral Research* (New York: Holt, Rinehart and Winston, 1973).

11. G. A. Churchill, Jr., J. P. Peter, "Research Design Effects on the Reliability of Rating Scales," *Journal of Marketing Research* (November 1984), 360–375.

12. See A. Adams, "A Cautionary Note on the Reliability of Advertising Test–Retest Scores," *Journal of Advertising* 1 (1984), 41–45; and A. Adams, S. Mehrotra, S. Van Auken, "Reliability of Forced-Exposure Television Copytesting," *Journal of Advertising Research* (June/July 1983), 29–32.

13. See D. W.. Gerbing, J. C. Anderson, "An Updated Paradigm for Scale Development Incorporating Unidimensionality and Its Assessment," *Journal of Marketing Research* (May 1988), 186–192.

14. G. Vigderhous, "Coefficient of Reliability Alpha," *Journal of Marketing Research* (May 1974), 194; and R. G. Netemeyer, S. Durvasula, D. R. Lichtenstein, "A Cross-National Assessment of the Reliability and Validity of the CETSCALE," *Journal of Marketing Research* (August 1991), 320–327.

15. For more advanced methods see W. D. Perreault, Jr., L. E. Leigh, "Reliability of Nominal Data Based on Qualitative Judgments," *Journal of Marketing Research* (May 1989), 135–148.

16. This section is based on *Standards for Educational and Psychological Tests* (New York: American Psychological Association, 1974).

17. See R. L. Day, "Revisiting the Rough/Finished Issue in Advertisement Pretesting," *Marketing Research* (September 1990), 22–29.

18. R. P. Bagozzi, Y. Yi:"Multitrait-Multimethod Matrices in Consumer Research," *Journal of Consumer Research* (March 1991), 426–439.

ᴳ

Questionnaire Design

LEARNING OBJECTIVES

Upon completing this chapter, you should be able to

1. Describe the process one should go through to design a questionnaire.

2. Explain how to determine which questions should be included on a questionnaire.

3. Determine when and how to use aided and unaided questions.

4. Determine when and how to use open-ended, multiple-choice, and dichotomous questions.

5. Evaluate a questionnaire and determine any potential sources of measurement error.

6. Describe the issues involved in designing questionnaires for multinational studies.

7. Explain the difference between back-translation and parallel translation.

The Influence of Question Phrasing on Preferences for Burger King Versus McDonald's Hamburgers

Burger King ran a series of commercials in which it claimed that its method of cooking hamburgers was preferred 3 to 1 over McDonald's.[1] The question that was used to support this claim was

> *Do you prefer your hamburgers flame-broiled or fried?*

An independent researcher asked the "same" question a different way:

> *Do you prefer a hamburger that is grilled on a hot stainless-steel grill or cooked by passing the raw meat through an open gas flame?*

This version of the question resulted in 53 percent preferring McDonald's grilling process. When further description was added by noting that the gas-flame hamburgers are kept in a microwave oven before serving, the preference for grilled burgers was 85 percent. Thus, three technically correct descriptions of cooking methods produced preferences from 3 to 1 for Burger King to 5.5 to 1 for McDonald's.

Suppose we are curious about some aspect of another individual. Our curiosity could involve behavior, knowledge, personal characteristics, or attitudes. How would we satisfy this curiosity? For any one of a fairly wide range of topics, we would simply ask the individual to tell us the pertinent information. Questioning is a common, everyday approach to obtaining information. There are, however, some types of information for which questioning is appropriate and other types for which it is less appropriate. Furthermore, as the opening example illustrates, *how* we ask questions is critical.

The Nature of Questionnaire Design

Questionnaire:
a formalized set of questions for eliciting information.

A **questionnaire** is a formalized set of questions for eliciting information. Although the questionnaire generally is associated with survey research, it is also frequently the measurement instrument in experimental designs as well. When a questionnaire is administered by means of the telephone or by a personal interviewer, it often is termed an *interview schedule*, or simply *schedule*. However, the term *questionnaire* is used throughout this text to refer to a list of questions, regardless of the means of administration.

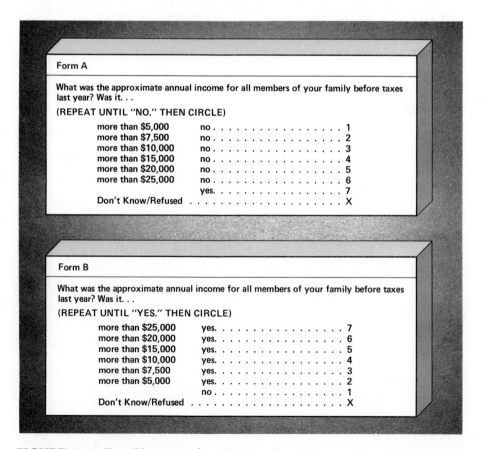

FIGURE 10–1 Two Versions of an Income Question

The most critical concern in questionnaire construction is *measurement error.* For example, consider Figure 10–1, which shows two very similar versions of the same basic question.[2] The median income reported in response to Form A was $12,711 compared to $17,184 for Form B! The Burger King–McDonald's questions described earlier produced equally dramatic differences.

As Figure 10–2 indicates, questionnaire construction involves seven major decision areas: (1) *preliminary considerations,* (2) *question content,* (3) *question wording,* (4) *response format,* (5) *question sequence,* (6) *physical characteristics of the questionnaire,* and (7) *pretest.*

The seven decision areas are interrelated. Not only do decisions made during the early stages influence the types of decisions that can be made later, but decisions made during the final stages may compel the reconsideration of earlier choices. For example, decisions on question sequence often influence the wording of the questions involved.

Software for personal computers is now available to assist in questionnaire design.[3] This software automatically formats various types of questions, provides instructions for answering, randomizes response orders, and checks for certain syntactical or logical errors.

Preliminary Decisions

Prior to constructing the actual questionnaire, the researcher must decide exactly *what information* is to be collected from *which respondents* by *what techniques.*

Required Information

We have already discussed the critical importance of clearly specifying exactly what information is needed (see Chapter 3). Obviously, data gained from a questionnaire are of limited value if they are on the wrong topic (surrogate information error) or if they are incomplete. The researcher must begin with a precise statement of what information is required to deal with the management problem at hand.

For example, Weyerhaeuser recently considered targeting the do-it-yourself home repair and remodel market and, among other things, wanted "to find out the characteristics of DIYers, their homes, and their projects." This objective led to the following information requirements:

a. respondents' gender, age, household size, stage in the household life cycle, social class, household income, ownership status, and tenure in current house
b. house age, size
c. last year's expenditures on DIY home improvement materials, last year's project descriptions, last year's lumber and building materials expenditures.

Which Respondents?

It is also essential to have a clear idea of exactly who the respondents are to be. Questions that are appropriate for a group of college graduates might not

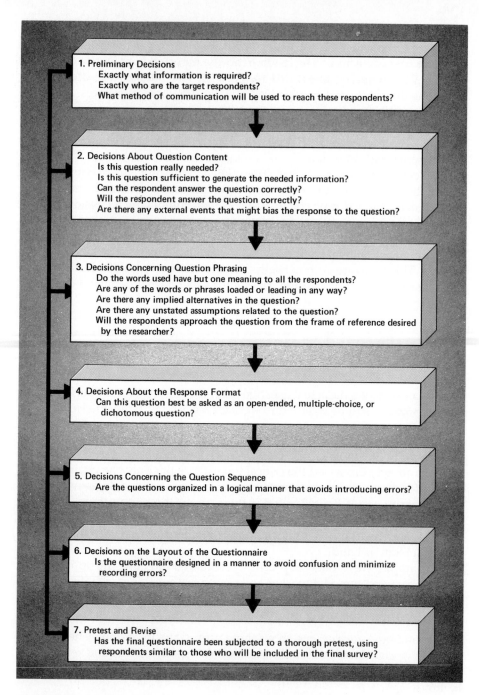

FIGURE 10–2 Questionnaire Construction Decisions

be appropriate for a group of high school graduates and would almost certainly be inappropriate for junior high or grade school children.

In general, the more diversified the potential respondents, the more difficult it is to construct a sound questionnaire that is appropriate for the entire group.

Interview Technique

Finally, one needs to decide on the method or technique of administering the questionnaire before designing it. The nature of the decision involving which method of administration to use was described in Chapter 6. However, it may be necessary to alter the method of administration if attempts at designing an effective questionnaire for the initial method of administration are unsuccessful.

Decisions About Question Content

Decisions concerning question content center on the general nature of the question and the information it is designed to produce, rather than on the form or specific working of the question. Five major issues, or problem areas, are involved with question content. For each question, the researcher must ascertain (1) *the need for the data*, (2) *the ability of the question to produce the data*, (3) *the ability of the respondent to answer accurately*, (4) *the willingness of the respondent to answer accurately*, and (5) *the potential for external events to bias the answer.*

The Need for the Data Asked for by the Question

The preliminary decisions will result in a list of informational items required to solve the problem. The next task is to generate one or more questions for each information item.

In general, every question on a questionnaire should contribute to the information on which the recommendation(s) to management is based.

Therefore, the first question a researcher should ask about each question is: "Exactly how am I going to use the data generated by this question?" If a satisfactory answer cannot be provided, the question should *not* be retained on the questionnaire.

The best way to approach this problem is to make up responses (contrived) to each question, analyze the results, and ensure that the results of the analysis provide sufficient information for the resolution of the management problem. Questions that provide data not needed to resolve the management problem should be deleted from the questionnaire unless they are deliberately created to disguise the purpose or sponsor of the study.

Ability of the Question to Produce the Data

Once we have assured ourselves that the question is *necessary,* we must make sure that it is *sufficient.* That is, will this one question generate the information we need or should we use two or more separate questions? For example, many questions ask individuals to express choices or preferences. If the researcher is also interested in how *strongly* or *intensely* the respondent holds these views, a separate question should be asked to ascertain this: *"How strongly do you feel about this—very strongly, somewhat strongly, or not at all strongly?"*

Double-barreled question:
two separate questions contained in a single question.

The **double-barreled question** is one in which two or more questions are asked as one. Consider the question, *"Do you prefer a small, economy car or a larger, sporty car?"* Would a response of "larger, sporty car" mean that the individual preferred larger cars, sporty cars, or larger, sporty cars? *"Do you consider the Triumph TR-7 to be a fast, powerful car?"* suffers from the same problem. Two or more separate questions are required in such cases.

We must also be sure that the question will elicit sufficient information that is directly relevant to the purpose underlying the question. Suppose we want to measure the occupation of respondents to ascertain if high-status occupation groups ride the bus as frequently as low-status groups. Is the question *"What do you do for a living?"* sufficient for our purposes? An attempt to characterize the status associated with the response "I'm a salesperson" will indicate the inadequacy of this question for its stated purpose.

Ability of the Respondent to Answer Accurately

Once we are sure that our question is necessary and sufficient, we must consider the respondent's ability to provide an accurate answer. Inability to answer a question arises from three major sources: (1) *having never been exposed to the answer*, (2) *having been exposed to the answer but forgetting*, and (3) *being unable to verbalize the answer*. The first two categories are concerned primarily with "factual" information, whereas the third is concerned more with attitudes and motives.

Uninformed Respondents

Respondents are frequently asked questions on topics about which they are uninformed. "Uninformed" in this sense means that they have never known the answer to the question. A common example is to ask an individual's opinion about a product, store, or brand that he or she has literally "never heard of."

In one study, over 95 percent of the respondents to a survey of lawyers and 97 percent of the respondents to a survey of the general public expressed an opinion on the performance of the National Bureau of Consumer Complaints. One might question the validity of the opinions, however, in view of the fact that no such organization exists! Even with a "Don't Know" option in the response set, over half of the lawyers and three-fourths of the general public still expressed an opinion on the performance of the nonexistent agency.[4]

Spurious awareness:
respondents falsely reporting awareness of brands, advertisements, logos, and so forth.

Respondents falsely reporting awareness or recognition of products, logos, advertisements or other specific stimuli in a survey is referred to as **spurious awareness** or *bogus recall*. A study of bogus recall of advertising slogans found a range of 12 to 52 percent, depending on the nature of the bogus slogan.[5]

One major research firm has established spurious awareness benchmarks for some product categories. Its studies indicate that around 8 percent of the population will report awareness of nonexistent health and beauty products. Thus, when awareness of an actual product is measured, the company reduces reported awareness by 8 percent.[6]

Current evidence indicates that spurious awareness (1) is associated with demographic characteristics and with an "agreeing" or "yea-saying" response style, and (2) may distort attempts to analyze the causes of awareness as well as measures of the level of awareness.[7]

Any time there is a possibility that the respondent may not have knowledge of the information requested, an attempt should be made to verify this fact. The question, *"What is the current assessed value of your home?"* implies that the respondent should know the answer. This, in turn, will encourage guessing. The following sequence of questions will provide a much more interpretable response:

Are you aware of the current assessed value of your home?
_____ Yes _____ No

What do you think the current assessed value of your home is? _____

How close to the actual assessed value do you think your estimate is?
_____ $100 _____ $1,000 _____ $5,000 _____ $10,000 _____ $15,000
_____ $25,000 _____ $50,000 _____ No idea

In addition, "Don't Know" options for multiple-choice questions and assurances that it is not necessary to answer every question reduce uninformed response, but only slightly.[8]

Forgetful Respondents

Another problem arises when respondents are forced to rely on memory for facts that they have been exposed to in the past. A simple test will indicate the delicate nature of memory. Answer the following questions from memory and then check the answers:

· How many pairs of shoes (of all types) do you own?
· What is the balance in your checking account?
· How much was your telephone bill last month?

Most of us do not know the answer to one or more of these rather simple questions. Three aspects of forgetting are of concern to the researcher: (1) **omission,** which occurs when an individual is unable to recall an event that actually took place; (2) **telescoping,** which occurs when an individual remembers an event as occurring more recently than it actually did; and (3) **creation,** which occurs when an individual "remembers" an event that did not occur.

Concern with all three types of forgetting increases with the length of the recall period. Recall periods as short as one week appear to create substantial telescoping effects.[9]

Telescoping and creation are minimized by using short recall periods. Research Application 10–1 illustrates a question format that appears to reduce telescoping in reporting past behaviors. Attempts to minimize omission generally involve various levels of *aided recall.*

Unaided Recall. **Unaided recall questions** do not provide any clues to potential answers, for example, *"What brands did you consider before purchasing your current bicycle?"* Such questions result in an understatement of *specific* events, such as brands in a choice set, shows watched, or small items purchased. In addition, more popular and known brands tend to be overstated in

Unaided recall questions: do not provide any clues to potential answers.

RESEARCH APPLICATION 10–1

Measuring Purchase Incidence Rates

Questionnaire Formats

I. One-step, direct question, three months
"Below are listed several products. Please 'X' each product you or anyone in your household *bought* in the PAST THREE MONTHS."

II. One-step, direct question, six months
"Below are listed several products. Please 'X' each product you or anyone in your household *bought* in the PAST SIX MONTHS."

III. Two-step, indirect question, multiple time periods
"Below are listed several products. Please 'X' each product you or anyone in your household *ever* bought. For each product ever bought, 'X' the box that best describes when the product was *purchased most recently*.
☐ Over 12 months ago
☐ 7–12 months ago
☐ 4–6 months ago
☐ within the past 3 months
(Note: The order of time periods was reversed on half the questionnaires.)

Results

Percent Reporting Purchase by Question Format

Product	I	III (3 mos)	II	III (6 mos)
White glue	46%	32%	54%	50%
Aspirin	68	57	73	72
Auto tires	32	24	39	39
Record album	41	32	48	41
N =	800	800	800	800

Conclusion

The two-step, indirect approach appears to reduce telescoping and provides more accurate responses, particularly for shorter time periods.

SOURCE: "Measuring Purchase Incidence Rates," *Research on Research* 5 (Chicago: Market Facts, Inc., undated).

---

response to questions asking for this kind of information. For example, a respondent may vaguely remember seeing an advertisement for soup and so report seeing an advertisement for *Campbell's Soup,* as this is the only brand name that comes to mind.

Aided recall questions: provide descriptions of some aspects of the original events.

Aided Recall.　Attempts to overcome problems with unaided recall focus on providing cues or aids to help the individual recall more accurately. **Aided recall questions** provide the respondents with descriptions of all or some aspects of the original events. The difference between an aided recall and an unaided recall question is similar to the difference between a multiple-choice and an essay examination question.

One measure of billboard advertising effectiveness is to ask respondents to *"name or describe any billboards that you have noticed while commuting to and from work in the past week."* This would be unaided recall. A second way of measuring the effectiveness of billboard advertisements is to present a list of product categories and ask the respondents to indicate whether they had noted billboards for each category and, if so, for which brands. A third approach is to present a list of brand names for each product category and ask the respondents which, if any, of these brands were advertised on billboards along their route to work. Finally, a picture of a billboard for each brand could be shown and the respondents asked to identify those that appeared along their route to work.

The level of "aid" increases at each stage in this example and, in general, so will the number of billboards identified. Unfortunately, the number identified may exceed the number along the route the individual takes to work; even worse, the correspondence between those identified and those actually on the individual's route may not be perfect. In part this is caused by the fact that aided recall techniques reduce omissions but increase telescoping and creation. Research Application 10–2 illustrates the effect that creation can have in aided recall studies.

Informing respondents in aided-recall situations in advance that some of the items they will be shown are bogus may reduce creation. That is, in the billboard situation respondents could be told that they will be shown a number of billboards, *several of which are definitely not in the area,* and then asked which ones they recall seeing on their commute to or from work.

Inarticulate Respondents

Questions such as *"Why did you buy that style of car?"* or *"Why did you decide to shop here?"* cannot always be answered by the respondent. If we think carefully, each of us can remember instances when we made purchases for which we did not really understand our motives.

We buy things from habit, for vanity, and other reasons of which we are not consciously aware. However, when we are asked *why* we buy a given product or brand we may respond with conventional reasons rather than the actual reasons. A method for overcoming a respondent's inability to verbalize answers to particular questions involves *projective techniques* (see Chapter 12).

Willingness of the Respondent to Answer Accurately

Assuming that the respondent *can* answer the question, we must still assess the likelihood that he or she *will* answer it. Why would a respondent refuse to answer one or more questions accurately? There are at least three possible reasons. The information request may be perceived by the respondents as (1) *personal in nature,* (2) *embarrassing,* or (3) *reflecting on prestige.*

Requests for Personal Information

Most people will provide answers to questions that they think are legitimate. By legitimate we mean that the questions are reasonable in light of the situation and the role of the person asking the question. However, many respondents who have willingly answered a lengthy series of questions on purchas-

RESEARCH APPLICATION 10–2

Time Inc.'s Test for Errors in Aided Recall Measures of Magazine Readership

Time Inc. sponsored a test to detect creation error in a popular method of measuring magazine readership. The method employed in the test is based on that used by a syndicated research service, Market Research Institute. Their standard method of determining readership and frequency of readership is as follows:

(1) Each respondent is given a deck of approximately 160 cards. Each card contains, in black and white, the logo of a magazine. The respondent is instructed to sort the cards into three piles: "definitely have read in the past six months," "definitely have not read in the past six months," and "not sure."

(2) For each magazine in the "definitely read" and "not sure" piles, the respondent is asked how many out of four issues he/she usually reads.

(3) Next, the readership question is asked separately by publishing interval (7 days for weeklies, 14 for bimonthly, etc.): "Did you happen to read any of these publications in the last *(publishing interval)* days? That is, any copy in the days since (specific date), not including today?" The respondent again sorts the cards into the same three categories based on behavior during the last publishing interval.

To test for creation error, logos for 22 fictitious or otherwise unavailable magazines were placed in with 140 regular magazines. The 22 nonexistent magazines had between 0.6 percent and 11.6 percent of the respondents reporting that they "definitely have read" one or more issues in the past six months. Of these respondents, over 20 percent reported that they usually read four out of four issues!

The readership during the publishing interval data also contained serious errors. Using standard projection techniques, the latest (nonexistent) issue of *Look* would have projected 6,690,000 readers. A nonexistent magazine, *Autocare*, would have projected almost 2,000,000 readers. Further, at least some aspects of the demographics of those who reported (inaccurately) reading the various magazines were consistent with the editorial content of the magazines (i.e., mostly males for *Autocare* and females for *Women's Weekly*). Thus, the errors do not appear to be random but reflect realistic errors of recall.

SOURCE: Adapted from C. Schitler, "Remembered, But Never Read," *Advertising Age* (October 26, 1981), S14–15.

---

ing and shopping patterns will refuse when suddenly asked without an explanation for their income, age, occupation, or other data. A brief explanation of why a particular piece of information is required will often suffice: *"To help us understand how people in different age and income groups view the shopping process, we need to know. . . ."*

Whenever it is practical and consistent with the information requirements, personal data should be requested in terms of broad categories rather than specific levels. In general, questions dealing with personal information should be placed near the end of the questionnaire.

Requests for Embarrassing Information

Answers to questions that ask for potentially embarrassing information are subject to distortion, especially when personal or telephone interviews are used. Questions on the consumption of alcoholic beverages, use of personal hygiene products, readership of certain magazines, and sexual or aggressive feelings aroused by particular advertisements are examples of topics on which questions are subject to refusals or distortions by the respondents.

Intuitively, anonymity would seem to enhance the likelihood of respondents answering, and answering accurately, sensitive questions. However, studies indicate that assurances of anonymity have little effect.[10]

Counterbiasing statements have been shown to improve responses to potentially embarrassing questions. **Counterbiasing statements** involve beginning a question with a statement that will make the potentially embarrassing responses seem common. For example, *"Recent studies have shown that a high percentage of males use their wives' cosmetics to hide blemishes. Have you used your wife's cosmetics in the past week?"*

Counterbiasing effects can also be obtained by carefully structuring the response options to multiple-choice questions. Consider the following response sets for this question: *"Think back over the past month. About how many bottles or cans of beer did you drink at home each week?"*

Counterbiasing statements: are statements placed in a question to make potentially embarrassing responses seem normal.

Version I	Version II
__ a. less than 6	__ a. less than 6
__ b. 6–11	__ b. 6–11
__ c. 12–17	__ c. 12–17
__ d. 18–23	__ d. 18–23
__ e. 24 or more	__ e. 24–29
	__ f. 30–35
	__ g. 36–41
	__ h. 42 or more

A test using similarly discrepant scales found that the extended-range version produced 47 percent more individuals reporting a consumption level of 24 or more.[11]

By expanding the range of response items at the potentially embarrassing end of the scale, it is easier for respondents to admit a high level of consumption because this level seems more normal. However, not all respondents will be so inclined. Furthermore, counterbiasing questions may cause some to admit to behavior they did not engage in because it may suddenly seem embarrassing *not* to have engaged in the behavior.

Another approach to overcoming nonresponse and measurement error caused by embarrassing questions is the **randomized response technique**.[12] It presents the respondent with two questions, one sensitive or potentially embarrassing, the other harmless or even meaningless. The respondent then flips a coin, looks at the last number on his or her Social Security card to see if it is odd or even, or in some other random manner selects which question

Randomized response technique: is a means of estimating the responses to a threatening question after respondents randomly answer either the threatening question or a neutral one.

to answer. Using appropriate mathematics, it is possible to calculate the aggregate response to the sensitive question.

Requests for "Prestige" or "Normative" Information

Prestige-oriented questions, such as those dealing with education obtained, income earned, or amount of time spent in reading newspapers, typically produce answers with an upward bias. For example, readership of high-prestige magazines is frequently overstated and readership of low-prestige magazines is often understated when self-report techniques are utilized.

Similarly, questions with a normative or socially accepted answer tend to have a consistent bias toward social norms. For example, the percentage of survey respondents who claim to have voted in the last election always exceeds the percentage of the population that actually voted.[13]

When possible, it is best to avoid questions with prestige and normative answers. When unavoidable, counterbiasing statements can sometimes be used to reduce measurement error. Careful wording and frequent pleas for candor, coupled with explanations of why candor is needed, can also reduce measurement error on these questions. Sometimes normative answers can be eliminated in the question itself: *"Other than nutrition, why do you serve . . .?"*

The Effect of External Events

A final issue involving question content is error caused by factors outside of the questionnaire itself. The time at which a question is asked is such a variable. A traffic planning commission was considering the need for bicycle paths. A questionnaire was designed and mailed to a sample of the population. One question asked for information on bicycle riding during the past week, which, in and of itself, was a reasonable question. However, the questionnaire was sent out after a week of particularly bad weather. Therefore, the bicycle-usage figures were most likely much less than would have been obtained had the weather been normal the preceding week.

For topics that are likely to be influenced by external events, particularly unpredictable external events such as weather, questions should generally be situation-free (e.g., "in a typical week" rather than "last week").

Decisions About Question Phrasing

Question phrasing is the translation of the desired question content into words and phrases that can be understood easily and clearly by the respondents. In general, questions should be as simple and straightforward as possible.

The primary concern with question phrasing is to ensure that the respondents and the researcher assign exactly the same meaning to the question. Five general issues are involved in question phrasing: (1) *Are the words, singularly and in total, understandable, to the respondents?* (2) *Are the words biased or "loaded" in any respect?* (3) *Are all the alternatives involved in the question clearly stated?* (4) *Are any assumptions implied by the question clearly stated?* and (5) *What frame of reference is the respondent being asked to assume?*

The Meaning of Words

Most of us would agree that questions designed for eight-year-olds should have a simpler vocabulary than questions designed for adult respondents. The researcher must take the vocabulary skills of the intended respondent group into account when designing a question. Such terms as *innovations*, *psychographics*, and *advertising medium* should be used only when dealing with specialized respondent groups.

Which of the following questions do you think will produce the highest level of reported new-product interest?

> *Would you be interested in buying any of these products?*
> *Which, if any, of these products would you be interested in buying?*

Fifty-three percent of a sample gave a positive response to the first question, whereas 64 percent did so for the second question.[14]

Even more critical problems can be introduced when the same term takes on different meanings to different groups of people. In the movie *Annie Hall* there is a scene with a split screen. On one side Alvie Singer talks to his psychiatrist; on the other side Annie Hall talks to hers. Alvie's therapist asks him, "How often do you sleep together?" and Alvie replies, "Hardly ever, maybe three times a week." Annie's therapist asks her, "Do you have sex often?" Annie replies, "Constantly, I'd say three times a week." That the same absolute frequency can be reported in very different ways is funny in a movie, but is a source of concern for researchers.[15]

The meaning of some terms is vague to most respondents. Alternative terms may be equally confusing. After substantial pretesting, a government health survey included a diagram indicating the location of the abdomen as attempts at verbal descriptions proved fruitless.[16]

It is important to remember that the objective is an understandable question, not a group of understandable words. Sometimes seeking the simplest terms results in a more complex question. Of the following two "identical" questions, which is easier to understand?

> *Should the state sales tax on prescription drugs be reduced from 5 percent to 1 percent?*
> *Should the state sales tax on those medicines that can only be bought under a doctor's order be lowered so that people would pay 1 cent tax instead of 5 cents tax for every dollar spent on such medicine?*[17]

Biased Words and Leading Questions

Biased, or **loaded**, **words and phrases** are emotionally colored and suggest an automatic feeling of approval or disapproval. **Leading questions** suggest what the answer should be.

Consider the following questions: *"Do you think the U.S. should allow public speeches against democracy?"* and *"Do you think the U.S. should forbid public speeches against democracy?"* Will they lead to the same conclusions? Slightly less than half (44 percent) of a sample said *no* (not allow) in response to the first question. However, only one-fourth (28 percent) of a similar sample said "yes" (forbid) to the second question.[18] Thus, it appears that the word *forbid* and/or the word *allow* induce bias.

Biased (loaded) words and phrases: trigger an emotional response and a feeling of approval or disapproval.

Leading questions: suggest what the answer should be.

Studies consistently find that about 60 percent of those responding favor increased spending/assistance for the *poor*. However, when the word *poor* is replaced with the term *welfare*, fewer than 25 percent support increased spending. Likewise, about half the population supports increased spending for *solving the problems of big cities*, but fewer than a fifth support increased spending for *assistance to big cities*.[19]

"*Do you think that General Motors is doing everything possible to reduce air pollution from the cars it manufactures?*" is a loaded question. General Motors is not doing "everything possible" in this area. This does not mean that it is not doing everything *reasonable*. Few firms or individuals ever do "all that is possible." The use of phrases such as *everything possible* (or its opposite, *anything*) tend to produce biased responses.

Implied Alternatives

Making an implied alternative explicit frequently, but not always, increases the percentage of people choosing the alternative. For example, the following question:

> *If there is a serious fuel shortage this winter, do you think there should be a law requiring people to lower the heat in their homes?*

produced 38.3 percent in favor of the law. Adding the phrase, "*or do you oppose such a law?*" reduced the percentage in favor of the law to 29.4. Adding the phrase, "*or do you think this should be left to individual families to decide?*" produced 25.9 percent in favor of the law.[20] Clearly, both the presence and nature of stated alternatives can influence responses.

Implied Assumptions

Questions are frequently asked in such a way that the answer depends on assumptions about factors outside the question itself. For example, the question "*Do you favor a ban on commercials in movie theaters?*" produced 44 percent in favor of the ban. Adding the assumption, "*even if it meant a $.50 increase in ticket prices?*" reduced the percent in favor of the ban to 22. Raising the assumed ticket price increase to $1.00 decreased the percent in favor of the ban to 11.[21]

Failure to state essential assumptions often produces (not always accidentally) inflated estimates of the public's demand for various products, social programs, or services.

Frame of Reference

The wording of the question often determines which frame of reference or viewpoint the respondent will assume. The frame of reference can be influenced by a variety of factors including preceding questions (see Decisions About the Question Sequence, page 270) and other brands or objects mentioned in the question. Research Application 10–3 illustrates the impact that different comparator groups had on perceptions of Chevrolet Nova's gas mileage.

RESEARCH APPLICATION 10–3

Frame of Reference Influences on Estimates of Chevrolet's Gas Mileage

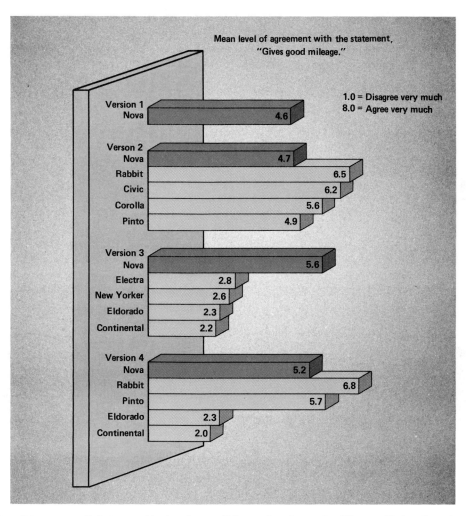

SOURCE: "Brand Perceptions: Relative vs. Absolute Ratings," *Research on Research* 6 (Chicago: Market Facts, Inc., undated).

Decisions About the Response Format

"Who do you think will win the Super Bowl this year?" "Who do you think will win the Super Bowl this year, the Cowboys, the Bears, or the Forty-Niners?" "Do you think the Cowboys will win the Super Bowl this year?" These three questions represent the three basic response formats that questions can assume. The first question is an example of an *open* or *open-ended* question. The respondent is free to choose any response deemed appropriate, within the limits implied by the question. The second question is an example of a *multiple-choice* response format. Here the respondent must select from among three or more prespecified responses. The final question represents a *dichotomous* question. Multiple-choice and dichotomous questions are often referred to as *closed* questions.

The decision as to which form of question to use must be based on the objective for the particular question. Each has its particular uses, advantages, and disadvantages. Most questionnaires contain all three types of questions.

Open-Ended Questions

Open-ended questions: allow respondents to answer in any manner they choose.

Open-ended questions leave the respondent free to offer any replies that seem appropriate in light of the question.

The degree of openness will vary from question to question. The question *"What do you think about cigarettes?"* allows almost total freedom to the respondent who may discuss cigarettes in general, particular brands, advertising slogans, health issues, ethics, and a host of other issues. The question *"What brand of cigarettes do you generally smoke?"* offers much less freedom.

Advantages of Open-Ended Questions.   Open-ended questions do not influence the respondent with a prestated set of response categories. Thus, opinions can be expressed that are quite divergent from what the researcher expected or what others had expressed. Related to this is the fact that open-ended questions elicit a wide variety of responses. These properties make open-ended questions particularly suitable for exploratory and problem-identification research.

Open-ended questions can provide the researcher with a basis for judging the actual values and views of the respondents that are often difficult to capture with more structured techniques. This "feel" for the quality of the information can be conveyed in the final report by the inclusion of quotes from representative responses. Finally, respondents generally like to have at least a few opportunities to express themselves openly.

Disadvantages of Open-Ended Questions.   Open-ended questions should be limited on self-administered questionnaires because most respondents will seldom write elaborate answers. Furthermore, these questions may measure *respondent articulateness*. Some respondents will answer clearly and in depth on almost any topic, whereas others, who may have equal knowledge, may be more reluctant to express themselves.[22]

A second source of error is *interviewer effects*. Interviewers vary in their ability to record the respondents' answers, in their intensity of probing, and in their objectivity.

An additional problem with open-ended questions is that except for very small surveys, the responses must eventually be coded or categorized. If the interviewers record the answers verbatim, or nearly so, the time and cost of coding becomes a sizable portion of the total cost of the research.

As an alternative to central coding, each interviewer can code or categorize the respondent's answer without showing the respondent the list of response alternatives. This technique is generally called *precoding.* The interviewer has, in effect, a multiple-choice question that is presented to the respondent as an open-ended question. The interviewer must then select the appropriate response category based on the respondent's verbal reply. Thus, the question *"Which brand of cigarettes did you last purchase?"* can be treated as open-ended by the respondent, but the interviewer may, instead of recording the response, have a list of the most popular brands and simply check which brand the respondent names, or an "other" category.

Multiple-Choice Questions

Do European, Japanese, or American cars represent the highest level of workmanship?
_____ European _____ Japanese _____ American

What was the brand name of the last soft drink you purchased?

_____ Pepsi	_____ Diet 7-Up
_____ Diet Pepsi	_____ Sprite
_____ Classic Coke	_____ Slice
_____ Coke	_____ Fresca
_____ Diet Coke	_____ Other
_____ 7-Up	

These questions represent versions of the **multiple-choice question.** The essential feature of a multiple-choice question is that it presents, either in the question proper or immediately following the question, the list of possible answers from which the respondent must choose.

Multiple-choice questions: restrict the answer to three or more prespecified choices.

Advantages of Multiple-Choice Questions.   Multiple-choice questions are generally easier for both the interviewer and the respondent. Indeed, they are almost essential for securing adequate cooperation in self-administered surveys. They also tend to reduce interviewer bias and bias caused by varying levels of respondent articulateness. In addition, tabulation and analysis are much simpler. Multiple-choice questions have an advantage over dichotomous questions whenever the answer naturally involves more than two choices or when some measure of gradation or degree is desired.

Disadvantages of Multiple-Choice Questions.   The development of a sound set of multiple-choice questions (or dichotomous questions) requires considerable effort. In addition, showing the respondents the list of potential answers can cause several types of distortion in the resulting data.

If all possible alternatives are not listed, no information can be gained on the omitted alternatives. Even if an "Other (Specify)" category is included, there is a strong tendency for respondents to choose from among those alternatives listed. Alternatives that the respondent had not thought about before may be selected over alternatives that would have been thought of independently.

Issues with Multiple-Choice Questions

Number of Alternatives.   A crucial issue in multiple-choice questions is how many alternatives to list. The standard answer to this question is that "each alternative should appear only once and all possible alternatives should be included." However, it is frequently impractical to include all possible alternatives. A list of all possible brands of cigarettes, for example, would have to include not only American brands but also all foreign brands that are available in local tobacco shops. A researcher is seldom interested in those brands or alternatives that only a few people will select. Therefore, the general approach is to list the more prevalent choices and an "Other" category, which is often accompanied by a "Please specify" and a short space to write in the answer. If the original list somehow excluded a major alternative, the "Other" category may uncover it.

Balanced or Unbalanced Alternatives.   Another important issue concerns the number of alternatives on each side of an issue. For example, consider the following two lists of alternatives for the same question:

Is Sears' advertising truthful or misleading?

____ *Extremely misleading*	____ *Neither misleading nor truthful*
____ *Very misleading*	____ *Truthful*
____ *Somewhat misleading*	

versus

Is Sears' advertising truthful or misleading?

____ *Extremely truthful*	____ *Neither truthful nor misleading*
____ *Very truthful*	____ *Misleading*
____ *Somewhat truthful*	

The results obtained form the two sets of response categories will differ significantly. Unless there is a specific reason (such as evidence that all respondents will respond on one side of the issue) to do otherwise, a balanced set of alternatives should be presented.

Position Bias.   Which of the two alternative response sets to the following question will produce the highest percent reporting that they eat out "much more often" than last year? Or will both sets produce similar results? The two versions of the questionnaire were administered by mail to over 750 respondents each.

Compared to a year ago, my household eats at a restaurant:

Version A	*Version B*
____ *Much more often*	____ *Much less often*
____ *Somewhat more often*	____ *Somewhat less often*
____ *About as often*	____ *About as often*
____ *Somewhat less often*	____ *Somewhat more often*
____ *Much less often*	____ *Much more often*

Version A produced twice as many "much more often" responses than version B (10 percent versus 5 percent). Similar results were obtained for questions on television viewing and the use of home repair professionals versus doing-it-yourself.[23]

It has been found that if three or four relatively long or complex alternatives are read to the respondents, there will be a bias in favor of the last alternative. However, if the alternatives are presented visually and all at the same time, the bias shifts to the alternative appearing at the top of the list.[24]

A list of numbers, such as amount of money spent, and estimates of facts, such as the number of outlets in a given chain store, is subject to a middle-position bias. That is, respondents tend to select those values that are near the middle of the range presented.

The labeling of alternatives can influence the respondent's choice. Table 10–1 contains a "favorableness" index of all the letters in the alphabet.

The **split-ballot technique**—using multiple versions of the questionnaire—minimizes these effects.

Dichotomous Questions

Dichotomous questions, which represent an extreme form of the multiple-choice question, allow only two responses, such as "yes–no," "agree–disagree," "male–female," and "did–did not." Often the two categories are supplemented by a neutral category such as "don't know," "no opinion," "both," or "neither."

The advantages of the dichotomous question are similar to those of the multiple-choice question. It is particularly well suited for determining certain points of fact, such as *"Did you purchase a new model car in the past year?"* and other clear-cut issues on which the respondents are likely to hold well-crystallized views. However, the researcher needs to be sure that the respondents think about the issue in dichotomous terms before using such questions.

Split-ballot technique: using multiple versions of the same basic question or questionnaire to overcome or detect problems such as position bias.

Dichotomous questions: restrict the answer to two prespecified choices.

TABLE 10–1 Favorableness Index for the Alphabet*

Letter	Index	Letter	Index	Letter	Index
A	116	J	61	S	82
B	92	K	49	T	68
C	73	L	71	U	14
D	53	M	78	V	20
E	64	N	44	W	38
F	12	O	50	X	8
G	56	P	44	Y	25
H	51	Q	8	Z	3
I	54	R	65		

*The higher the index, the more favorably the letter is viewed.

SOURCE: Adapted from G. J. Spagna, "Questionnaires: Which Approach Do You Use?" *Journal of Advertising Research* (February/March 1984), 70.

Decisions About the Question Sequence

Question sequence, the specific order in which the respondents receive the questions, is a potential source of error.[25] A number of general guidelines will reduce the probability of generating measurement error caused by the sequence of the questions.

The first questions should be simple, objective, and interesting. If the respondents cannot answer the first questions easily, or if they find them uninteresting, they may refuse to complete the remainder of the questionnaire.

In general, *the overall questionnaire should move from topic to topic in a logical manner, with all questions on one topic being completed before the respondent moves to the next.* Questions that are difficult to answer or that ask for controversial or sensitive information should be placed near the end of the questionnaire.

Initial questions should avoid providing a biased frame of reference or suggesting answers to following questions. Within groups of questions on a given topic, general questions should be asked first and more specific ones later. Consider the two following questions: *"How many miles per gallon does your present car get?"* and *"What things would you like to see improved in your car?"* If these questions are asked in the order presented, gas economy will be mentioned many more times in the second question than it would if the order were reversed.

Physical Characteristics of the Questionnaire

The physical characteristics of the questionnaire should be designed to make it easy to use.

The first and most important objective is to minimize the possibility of recording mistakes. Research Application 10–4 illustrates the effect that a confusing layout had on a questionnaire administered by Market Facts of Canada, Ltd.

The questionnaire must be designed so that the interviewer or respondent can easily move from one question to the next. This is particularly important when *skip* or *branching* instructions are involved. These instructions require the respondent to answer different following questions based on the answer to the current question.

Decisions About the Pretest

Burke Marketing Research designed a study to determine the extent and nature of consumer use of barbecue-style sauces at home.[26] One of the questions to be used on this questionnaire was:

In just the past 2 months, what types of barbecued foods have you eaten which were prepared at home?

RESEARCH APPLICATION 10–4

Impact of Questionnaire Layout on a Market Facts Survey

Form A of a question was used in a regular wave of Market Facts of Canada Ltd.'s Consumer Mail Panel. The households were known to have one or more of the products mentioned in the question.

Form A

Important: For Each Type, *If* You Have More Than One, Answer for the Newest
3a) What make or brand is it?

	Product X	Product Y	Product Z
Brand A	( )1	( )1	( )1
Brand B	( )2	( )2	( )2
Brand C	( )3	( )3	( )3
Brand D	( )4	( )4	( )4
Brand E	( )5	( )5	( )5
Brand F	( )6	( )6	( )6
Brand G	( )7	( )7	( )7
Other brand	_____	_____	_____

The year before, Brand G had 67, 39, and 55 percent ownership reported across the three products, and Brand F had had 5, 1, and 8 percent ownership. This year the results were 47, 27, and 35 percent, and 30, 18, and 27 percent, respectively. The client, Brand G, found changes of these magnitudes unbelievable. Telephone contacts with some reported Brand F owners indicated that they were, in reality, Brand G owners. Therefore, the question was revised into form B and readministered.

Form B

3. What make or brand is the newest one?

	Product X	Product Y	Product Z
Brand A	( )1	( )1	( )1
Brand B	( )2	( )2	( )2
Brand C	( )3	( )3	( )3
Brand D	( )4	( )4	( )4
Brand E	( )5	( )5	( )5
Brand F	( )6	( )6	( )6
Brand G	( )7	( )7	( )7
Other brand	( )8	( )8	( )8

The revised version produced Brand G ownership percentages of 71, 41, and 58, whereas Brand F percentages dropped to 3, 2, and 3! It appears that the respondents noticed that Brand G was the next-to-last response option (just above "other brand") and therefore looked for the next-to-last response box to check. However, in Form A the next-to-last response box was associated with Brand F because the *Other brand* option did not have a response category to mark. This error was eliminated by the Form B question.

SOURCE: Adapted from C. S. Mayer, C. Piper, "A Note on the Importance of Layout in Self-Administered Questionnaires," *Journal of Marketing Research* (August 1982), 390–391. The questions are reproduced with permission from the American Marketing Association.

However, during pretesting, it became clear that many respondents defined barbecued food as food cooked outside on a charcoal grill, *not* food cooked with barbecue sauce. This led to this question being revised to:

In just the past 2 months, what types of food have you eaten which were prepared at home using a barbecue sauce?

Only on rare occasions and for specific, explicit reasons should a questionnaire be administered without a *thorough* pretest.[27] A pretest requires five types of decisions. First, *what items should be pretested?* Obviously, one would want to be alert for problems with any aspect of the questionnaire such as layout, question sequence, branching instructions, word meaning, and question difficulty. However, in most questionnaires some question areas and sequences are of little concern because they have been presented in previous surveys and are very straightforward. Other areas are unique and more ambiguous and should receive the most attention.

Second, *how should the pretest be conducted?* At least part of the pretest should involve administering the questionnaire in the same manner planned for the final survey. This allows the researcher to discover which questions are likely to be skipped or refused in the actual administration, the likely range of responses, the use of "other" categories, and so forth.

Debriefing: interviewing pretest respondents after they complete the questionnaire to determine how they interpreted the questions and any difficulties they encountered.

In addition to a standard administration of the questionnaire, a **debriefing** and/or a *protocol* analysis should be conducted. In a *debriefing*, some of the pretest respondents are interviewed after they have completed the questionnaire. These respondents are asked to explain *why* they answered each question as they did, to state what each question meant to them, and to describe any problems or uncertainties they had in completing the questionnaire. A **protocol analysis** requires the respondent to "think aloud" while completing the questionnaire. The interviewer notes areas of confusion and terms with differing meanings among respondents.

Protocol analysis: having some pretest respondents "think aloud" while answering the questions.

Third, *who should conduct the pretest?* Telephone and personal pretest interviews should generally be conducted by several regular staff interviewers. Part of the purpose of the pretest is to discover problems for and with the interviewers. In addition, using regular interviewers allows a check on response rates and time per interview. This, in turn, allows a check on cost estimates.

In addition, the project director and/or the person charged with developing the questionnaire should conduct several interviews. Since it is the project director whose questions are being checked and who is responsible for the final report, he or she should be actively involved in testing and revising the questionnaire.

Fourth, *which respondents should be involved in the pretest?* The respondents should be as similar as possible to the target respondents.

Fifth, *how many respondents should be used?* There is no set answer to this question. A sufficient number of respondents should be used to satisfy the similarity-to-target-respondents consideration just described. Thus, the more varied the target respondents, the larger the pretest should be. Likewise, the more complex and unique the questionnaire, the larger the sample should be.

Multinational Questionnaire Design

As you might suspect, developing questionnaires for multinational surveys is particularly difficult. Variation in language, culturally defined behaviors, and the characteristics of the respondents all require the researcher's attention.[28]

These same concerns arise when research is conducted across subcultures within a single country, particularly if distinct languages are spoken by the subcultures.

Language

The most obvious task in multinational research is to secure equivalent versions of the questionnaire in the relevant languages. The fact that India has 16 distinct languages with over 1,600 dialects indicates the magnitude that the translation task can assume.

The simplest approach is to develop a questionnaire in the home country. This questionnaire is then translated into the second language by a bilingual who is a native speaker of the second language. The translated version of the questionnaire is then translated back into the original language by another bilingual who is a native speaker of the original language. This process is known as **back-translation.** This approach assigns priority to the home country language and strives for a loyal if not literal translation.

Back-translation often produces questionnaires with language structures inappropriate for some languages as well as "forced" equivalents for terms such as *mild* and *lonesome* when no such equivalence may exist.

Multinational research projects generally require data that have the same meaning, independent of the country from which they came (or that vary only in known ways). Thus, researchers should focus on securing equivalent answers (in terms of the meaning assigned those answers *by the respondents*) rather than on having identical questions.[29]

Parallel translation has this as its objective. Parallel translation involves a group of translators who, in total, represent all the languages involved with at least one native speaker. These translators are told the objective of the research project and of each question. Together with members of the research team, they work to simultaneously develop a set of questionnaires that will provide the required data in an equivalent form from each language group.

No matter what translation approach is used, thorough pretesting in each language group is necessary to minimize problems. Protocol analysis and debriefing are particularly useful in this situation.

Cultural Patterns

Unfortunately, we do not know as much as we need to concerning the influence of culture on the response to questionnaires. The Japanese are reluctant to say *no* directly. This may require different forms or interpretations of agree–disagree type questions. Cultures also appear to differ in terms of their tendency to exaggerate or understate, provide uninformed responses or refuse to answer some questions, and use extreme response categories.

Religion and other cultural variables influence behaviors in ways that, in turn, influence questionnaire responses. Ramadan in Muslim cultures, Lent in Catholic regions, and Christmas in Christian communities produce shopping and eating behaviors as well as attitudes that are not typical of the balance of the year. Researchers who ask about *last week's* or *last month's* activities must be aware of all such potentially distorting influences. Using competent local research associates is the most common way to avoid problems in this area.

Back-translation: translating a questionnaire from the domestic language into the foreign language and back into the domestic language to produce a close translation of the domestic questionnaire.

Parallel translation: simultaneously developing the questionnaire in multiple languages to provide answers with equivalent meanings across the language groups involved.

Respondent Characteristics

The characteristics of respondents to a survey often differ across countries. For example, a survey of bicycle riders in the United States would involve mainly younger individuals who ride primarily for recreation and exercise. In Holland, a much wider age group would be represented, and basic transport as well as recreation would be important. In developed countries, the market for a product may be quite literate while users of the same product in a developing country might have only limited literacy.

When the respondents are expected to differ sharply on important characteristics across countries, equivalent questionnaires may not be possible or desirable. Instead, the effort shifts to obtaining information appropriate to the problem at hand from each country. In this case, we may have a coordinated series of questionnaires rather than a multinational questionnaire.

Summary

A questionnaire is a formalized set of questions for eliciting information. Constructing a sound questionnaire involves seven decision areas: (1) preliminary considerations, (2) question content, (3) question wording, (4) response format, (5) question sequence, (6) physical characteristics of the questionnaire, and (7) pretest.

The information required is developed from the management problem. The problem statement should provide a list of the required information. For each piece of information required, the questionnaire should contain at least one question. After a questionnaire is designed, answers to the questions should be created and analyzed. The answers should provide sufficient information to deal with the decision at hand. Any question that provides data not needed to assist in the decision at hand should be dropped.

Respondents often remember events incorrectly. Omission occurs when an individual cannot recall an event that occurred. Telescoping occurs when an event is remembered as occurring more recently than it actually did. Creation occurs when an individual "remembers" an event that did not occur. Unaided recall asks respondents to remember events with minimum assistance. Aided recall provides varied levels of assistance. Compared to unaided recall, aided recall reduces omissions, but increases telescoping, creation, and bogus recall.

Requests for embarrassing information generally involve the use of counterbiasing statements or randomized response techniques. The key tasks in question phrasing are (1) to ensure that all respondents and the researcher assign the same meanings to the terms used and (2) to avoid leading or biasing the responses.

Open-ended questions provide the respondents with freedom to answer as they choose and can provide the researcher unexpected insights. However, they are harder for respondents to answer and require considerable effort to analyze. Multiple-choice and dichotomous questions are easier for the respondent to answer, allow less interviewer bias, and are easier to analyze. However, the alternatives must be developed with care and the split-ballot technique is often required when multiple-choice questions are used.

Questions should generally flow from the general to the specific. Personal or sensitive questions should be placed at the end of the questionnaire. Thorough pretest should be conducted on any new questionnaire.

Questionnaires being developed for multinational use must consider variations in language, culturally defined behaviors, and characteristics of the respondents. Back-translation strives for an accurate translation from the domestic language into a foreign language. Parallel translation strives to develop a questionnaire that will provide answers with equivalent meanings across the countries involved.

Review Questions

10.1. What is a *questionnaire?*

10.2. What is the most critical problem or concern in questionnaire design?

10.3. What are the steps in questionnaire design?

10.4. What preliminary decisions must be made before a questionnaire can be constructed?

10.5. What five major issues, or problem areas, are involved with question content?

10.6. What is the best way to ascertain the need for the information generated by a question?

10.7. Why would one put questions on a questionnaire that are not relevant to the management problem at hand?

10.8. What is a *double-barreled question?*

10.9. What factors can reduce the ability of a respondent to answer a question accurately?

10.10. What is an *uninformed respondent?*

10.11. Describe the three aspects of forgetting that concern researchers.

10.12. What counteracts the tendency to forget?

10.13. What are the advantages and disadvantages of *unaided recall?*

10.14. What are the advantages and disadvantages of *aided recall?*

10.15. What affects the willingness of respondents to answer accurately?

10.16. How can one secure "embarrassing" information from respondents?

10.17. What are *counterbiasing statements?*

10.18. Describe the *randomized response technique.*

10.19. How should one request normative or prestige information?

10.20. How can external events affect the response to questions?

10.21. What are the five general issues involved in question phrasing?

10.22. What is a *leading question?*

10.23. What is an *implied alternative?*

10.24. What is an *implied assumption?*

10.25. What is meant by *frame of reference?*

10.26. What are the advantages and disadvantages of *open-ended questions?*

10.27. What are the advantages and disadvantages of *multiple-choice questions?*

10.28. What are the advantages and disadvantages of *dichotomous questions?*

10.29. How many alternatives should be used in a *multiple-choice question?*

10.30. What is meant by *position bias* with respect to multiple-choice questions?

10.31. What are "branching" and "skip" instructions?

10.32. What are the five decisions involved in a pretest?

10.33. What are major influences on multinational questionnaire design? How do they operate?

10.34. What is the difference between *back-translation* and *parallel translation?*

Discussion Questions/Problems/Projects

10.35. Develop five *double-barreled* questions and corrected versions of each.

10.36. Develop two unaided recall questions of relevance to marketing. Develop three aided recall questions to replace each of the unaided questions. Have each aided question contain a different level of aid.

10.37. Develop a question for "drug use" using a counterbiasing statement.

10.38. Develop a question on consumption of alcohol for children aged 16 to 18 using a counterbiasing statement.

10.39. How would you select the response categories for a multiple-choice question on:
   a. weekly consumption of gum
   b. preferred television program
   c. hours spent studying per week
   d. favorite restaurant
   e. hours spent "goofing off" per week

10.40. Evaluate the following questions:
   a. We would like to know if anything you read or saw in *Travel and Travelers* during the past year or two interested you sufficiently to induce you to talk about it or to take any of the following actions: (You may check one or more)
      (1) discussed articles with others ____
      (2) visited a country or area ____
      (3) decided on or modified a travel plan ____
      (4) stayed at a hotel, motel, etc. ____
      (5) asked for more information on a product or service ____
      (6) bought or ordered a product ____
      (7) what else? ____
   b. Please indicate how much of an average issue of *High Walker* you usually read.
      (1) less than half ____
      (2) one-half to two-thirds ____
      (3) more than two-thirds ____
   c. Do you think federal control should be decreased or increased in the field of environment protection and antipollution?
      Should be decreased ____   Should be increased____

    d. Please check the following activities in which you participate as a private citizen interested in protection of the environment:
        ____ Read books and articles on the subject
        ____ Membership in business or professional groups on environment
        ____ Membership in conservationists, antipollution, ecology groups
        ____ Attend lectures and meetings on subject
        ____ Write letters to legislators, newspapers, or government officials
        ____ Make speeches, publish articles on subject
        ____ Other (specify) _____

    e. Have you bought powdered milk this week?   Yes ____   No____

    f. Where do you buy most of your meat?

    g. Where do you do most of your grocery shopping?

    h. How many times during the week do you usually eat breakfast?

    i. When you eat dinner out, do you usually eat at the same place?

    j. Are you currently planning any additions or expansions to your existing food services at this location?   Yes ____   No____

10.41. Develop a questionnaire to measure the reactions of families who acquired a camcorder for Christmas. Assume that the questionnaire will be administered on January 15 by mail to a nationwide sample (a mail panel has been used for initial screening so the sample frame is composed of qualified respondents).

10.42. Which version of the Burger King question described at the beginning of the chapter provides the most accurate information? Why?

10.43. Why do Form A and Form B in Figure 10–1 produce such dramatically different results?

10.44. How would you explain the results shown in Table 10–1?

Projects/Activities

10.45. Develop, pretest, and revise a telephone questionnaire that will allow you to estimate:
    a. the total amount of pizza consumed per week by full-time students on your campus
    b. the amount of money spent per day on pizza by the student body
    c. the top three types of pizza in terms of amount of money spent (1) by all students, (2) by undergraduates, (3) by graduates, (4) by women, (5) by men, and (6) by those with incomes above the median. Describe the major areas of concern you have with your revised questionnaire.

10.46. As 10.45 but for mail interviews.

10.47. As 10.45 but for personal interviews.

10.48. As 10.45 but for soft drinks (for part c estimate the top three brands).

10.49. As 10.46 but for soft drinks (for part c estimate the top three brands).

10.50. As 10.47 but for soft drinks (for part c estimate the top three brands).

10.51. Develop, pretest, and revise questionnaires to elicit information on the following topics from (1) first-graders, (2) high school sophomores, (3) college seniors.
   a. Food preferences and dislikes and the underlying reasons for these likes and dislikes
   b. Opinions about the seriousness of the pollution
   c. Opinions about TV and how many hours a week the respondent spends watching TV

10.52. Develop, pretest, and revise a telephone questionnaire to measure the music listening habits of students on your campus. What were your major concerns in developing this questionnaire?

Notes

1. "Have It Your Way with Research," *Advertising Age* (April 4, 1983), 16.

2. W. B. Locander, J. P. Burton, "The Effect of Question Form on Gathering Income Data by Telephone," *Journal of Marketing Research* (May 1976), 190.

3. P. E. Green, P. K. Kedia, R. S. Nikhil, *CAPPA* (Palo Alto, CA.: The Scientific Press, 1985).

4. See D. I. Hawkins, K. A. Coney, D. W. Jackson, Jr., "The Impact of Monetary Inducement on Uninformed Response Error," *Journal of the Academy of Marketing Science* (Summer 1988), 30–35.

5. M. Glassman, J. B. Ford, "An Empirical Investigation of Bogus Recall," *Journal of the Academy of Marketing Science* (Fall 1988), 38–41.

6. R. Goydon, "Phantom Products," *Forbes* (May 21, 1984), 292.

7. R. E. Goldsmith, "Personality and Uninformed Response Error," *Journal of Social Psychology* (February 1986), 37–45; R. E. Goldsmith, J. D. White, H. Walters, "Explanations for Spurious Response in Survey Research," *Business and Economic Review* (Summer 1988), 93–104; and R. E. Goldsmith, "Spurious Response Error in a New Product Survey," *Journal of Business Research* (December 1988), 271–281.

8. J. W. Cagley, K. C. Schneider, J. C. Johnson, "A Research Note on Techniques for Controlling Uninformed Responses," *Journal of the Market Research Society* (October 1988), 483–487; and R. E. Goldsmith, "Reducing Spurious Response in a Field Survey," *Journal of Social Psychology* (April 1989), 201–212.

9. W. A. Cook, "Telescoping and Memory's Other Tricks," *Journal of Advertising Research* (February 1987), 5–8. See also B. Walstra, "Validating the First-Time-Read-Yesterday Method," *Journal of Market Research Society* (April 1986), 157–173.

10. P. E. Downs, J. R. Kerr, "Recent Evidence on the Relationship Between Anonymity and Response Variables for Mail Surveys," *Journal of the Academy of Marketing Science* (Spring 1986), 72–82; J. H. Frey, "An Experiment with a Confidentiality Reminder in a Telephone Survey," *Public Opinion Quarterly* (Summer 1986), 267–269; and G. Albaum, "Do Source and Anonymity Affect Mail Survey Results," *Journal of the Academy of Marketing Science* (Fall 1987), 74–81.

11. A. D. Cox, R. L. Johnson, "Bias in Behavioral Self-Reports," in T. A. Shimp, ed., *1986 AMA Educator's Conference Proceedings* (Chicago: American Marketing Association, 1986), 387–392; and N. Schwartz, et al., "Response Scales," *Public Opinion Quarterly* (Fall 1985), 388–395.

12. D. E. Stem, Jr., R. K. Steinhorst, "Telephone Interview and Mail Questionnaire Applications of the Randomized Response Model," *Journal of the American Statistical Association* (September 1984), 555–564; and J. A Fox, P. E. Tracy, *Randomized Response* (Beverly Hills: Sage Publications, 1986).

13. S. Presser, "Can Changes in Context Reduce Vote Over-reporting in Surveys," *Public Opinion Quarterly* (Winter 1990), 586–593.

14. R. R. Batsell, Y. Wind, "Product Testing: Current Methods and Needed Developments," *Journal of the Market Research Society*, 2 (1980), 129.

15. N. C. Schaeffer, "Hardly Ever or Constantly?" *Public Opinion Quarterly* (Fall 1991), 395–423.

16. R. Jaroslovsky, "What's on Your Mind, America?" *Psychology Today* (July 1988), 57.

17. Taken from D. A. Dillman, *Mail and Telephone Surveys* (New York: John Wiley & Sons, 1978), 98.

18. H. Schuman, S. Presser, "Question Wording as an Independent Variable in Survey Analysis," *Sociological*

Methods and Research (November 1977), 155; and H. J. Hippler, N. Schwarz, "Not Forbidding Isn't Allowing," *Public Opinion Quarterly* (Spring 1986), 87–96.

19. K. A. Rasinski, "The Effect of Question Wording on Public Support for Government Spending," *Public Opinion Quarterly* (Fall 1989), 388–394.

20. H. Schuman, S. Presser, *Questions and Answers in Attitude Surveys* (Orlando: Academic Press, 1981), 191.

21. S. Hume, M. Magiera, "What Do Moviegoers Think of Ads?" *Advertising Age* (April 23, 1990), 4.

22. See J. G. Geer, "What Do Open-Ended Questions Measure?" *Public Opinion Quarterly* (Fall 1988), 365–371; and J. G. Geer, "Do Open-Ended Questions Measure 'Salient' Issues?" *Public Opinion Quarterly* (Fall 1991), 360–370.

23. "An Examination of Order Bias," *Research on Research* 1 (Chicago: Market Facts Inc. undated). See also S. A. Ayidiya, M. J. McClendon, "Response Effects in Mail Surveys," *Public Opinion Quarterly* (Summer 1990), 229–247.

24. See J. A. Krosnick, D. F. Alwin, "An Evaluation of a Cognitive Theory of Response-Order Effects in Survey Measurement," *Public Opinion Quarterly* (Summer 1987), 201–219.

25. S. Schröder, "Toward a Theory of How People Answer Questions," *European Research* (April 1985), 82–90; R. Tourangeau, et al., "Carryover Effects in Attitude Surveys," *Public Opinion Quarterly* (Winter 1989), 495–524; R. Tourangeau, K. A. Rasinski, N. Bradburn, "Measuring Happiness in Surveys," *Public Opinion Quarterly* (Summer 1991), 255–266; J. H. Barnes, Jr., M. J. Dotson, "The Effect of Mixed Grammar Chains on Response to Survey Questions," *Journal of Marketing Research* (November 1989), 468–472; and Ayidiya and McClendon, op. cit.

26. A. B. Blankenship, *Professional Telephone Surveys* (New York: McGraw Hill Book Company, 1977), 105.

27. S. D. Hunt, R. D. Sparkman, Jr., J. B. Wilcox, "The Pretest in Survey Research: Issues and Preliminary Findings," *Journal of Marketing Research* (May 1982), 269–273.

28. This section is based on S. P. Douglas, C. S. Craig, *International Marketing Research* (Englewood Cliffs, NJ: Prentice-Hall, 1983).

29. J. Williams, "Constant Questions or Constant Meanings?" *Marketing and Research Today* (August 1991), 169–177.

Measuring Attitudes and Emotions

LEARNING OBJECTIVES

Upon completing this chapter, you should be able to

1. Explain the difference between rating scales and attitude scales.

2. Distinguish comparative rating scales from noncomparative rating scales.

3. Discuss the issues involved in developing an itemized rating scale.

4. List and describe the various pairwise measures of preference and discrimination.

5. Explain how the constant-sum scale improves upon the rank-order scale.

6. Describe how response latency measures work.

7. Construct a Likert or semantic differential scale.

8. Describe several approaches to measuring emotions including BBDO's Emotion Measurement System.

The National Pork Producers Council's Use of Attitude Measures to Increase Sales of Pork

In the late 1980s, per capita sales of pork in the U.S. were declining as Americans became more concerned about health and diet. The National Pork Producers Council conducted research which found that consumers had negative *attitudes* toward pork that were unjustified by the product's characteristics. Following are some of the beliefs and attitudes uncovered in 1,200 interviews:

- White meat was preferred to red meat (42 percent to 28 percent).
- Females with college or technical education were most negative toward red meat.
- The preference for white meat was primarily because it was perceived to be leaner.
- Only 9 percent of the respondents thought of pork as a white meat.
- Taste was very important when selecting a cut of meat.
- Nutritional value, ease of preparation, versatility, and price have lesser importance.

Based on these findings, the Council developed and tested an advertising campaign to improve consumers' attitudes toward pork by repositioning it as a white meat and changing beliefs about its key attributes. One of the ads is on page 282. The amount of television advertising was varied by geographic area to allow an assessment of the impact of advertising intensity on attitudes.

After seven months of advertising, a telephone survey of 1,800 respondents was conducted to assess the program. The campaign was very successful in changing attitudes. Belief that pork is a white meat almost doubled. Its ratings on specific attributes such as versatility, amount of calories, ease of preparation, and level of cholesterol also improved dramatically. Based on these results, the campaign was continued and expanded.

Have you tried the other white meat?

If you think you have to serve fish or fowl to get the light, wholesome nutrition and easy convenience that today's life-styles demand, take a fresh look at pork — the *other* white meat.

Pork gives you the lighter meals and versatility you associate with white meat. Plus, it provides you and your family the great taste you want, and the nutrition and protein you need.

And of course the mouth-watering taste and savory flavor of pork blend deliciously with all kinds of sauces, spices, stuffings and side dishes.

Pork can easily be substituted for any other white meat in many recipes — in fact, in most meal preparation.

With a variety of new, leaner boneless cuts of pork to choose from, your menu plans have more flexibility than ever.

What's the best way to cook pork?

Often.

For a free recipe book containing light, easy, nutritious and creative ways to serve new meals with pork, just send a stamped self-addressed envelope to Pork Recipes, Box 10383-B, Des Moines, Iowa 50306.

The Other White Meat:

This message is brought to you by America's pork producers.

© 1987 National Pork Producers Council in cooperation with National Pork Board.

SOURCE: "The Other White Meat" campaign. © 1987 National Port Producers Council in cooperation with National Pork Board.

An **attitude** is an enduring organization of cognitive, affective, and behavioral components and processes with respect to some aspect of the individual's world. That is, attitude is generally conceived of as having three components: (1) a *cognitive* component—a person's beliefs or information about the object; (2) an *affective* component—a person's feelings of like or dislike concerning the object; and (3) a *behavioral* component—action tendencies or predispositions toward the object.

As the opening example indicates, a substantial proportion of all marketing effort is designed to influence the attitudes of consumers and intermediaries. Therefore, marketing managers frequently require information on attitudes and changes in attitudes induced by marketing activities.

Our treatment of attitude scales is divided into two major areas. The first of these is called *rating scales*. In this section, we discuss the construction of scales used to measure single dimensions or components of attitudes, such as the pleasantness of a taste. In the second section, we describe two of the more common *attitude scales*, which are combinations of rating scales designed to measure several or all aspects of an individual's attitude toward an object. Thus, although the division is somewhat arbitrary, we can say that attitude scales are composed of two or more rating scales.

In the final section of the chapter, we describe the difficulties and methods involved in measuring emotions.

> **Attitude:** an enduring organization of cognitive, affective, and behavioral components and processes with respect to some aspect of the world.

Rating Scales

The use of a **rating scale** requires the rater to place an attribute of the object being rated at some point along a numerically valued continuum or in one of a numerically ordered series of categories. Rating scales can focus on (1) overall attitude toward an object, such as *Pepsi Free;* (2) the degree to which an object contains a particular attribute, such as sweetness; (3) one's feelings toward an attribute, as in liking the taste; or (4) the importance attached to an attribute, such as the absence of caffeine.

Since individuals' evaluations of *specific* product attributes are influenced by the brand's reputation, measures of specific functional attributes, such as taste, are generally performed with the brand name removed. Such tests or comparisons are referred to as **blind tests.**

> **Rating scale:** requires the rater to place an attribute of the object at some point along a numerically valued continuum or in one of an ordered series of categories.

> **Blind tests:** involving rating an attribute of one or more brands without knowing the brand name.

Noncomparative Rating Scales

Noncomparative rating scales do not provide a standard to use in assigning the rating. If asked to rate a product, the respondent does so based on whatever standards seem appropriate. The researcher does not provide a comparison point such as an "average brand" or "your favorite brand." Noncomparative scales are often referred to as *monadic* scales since only one brand or product is evaluated. Such tests are common at the product-concept testing stage of the new product development process.

A standard monadic concept test involves a sample of 200 to 400 persons, with personal interviews conducted at a shopping center or in the respon-

Noncomparative rating scales: requires the rater to place an attribute of the object at some point along a numerically valued continuum or in one of an ordered series of categories without providing an explicit comparator or referent.

dents' homes. Each respondent is presented with the concept in written, pictorial, or finished print or television ad form for evaluation. The most popular evaluative question used involves intention to purchase. The 11-point Juster Scale shown below has been found to have good predictive validity.[1]

10	*Certain, practically certain (99 in 100)*
9	*Almost sure (9 in 10)*
8	*Very probably (8 in 10)*
7	*Probable (7 in 10)*
6	*Good possibility (6 in 10)*
5	*Fairly good possibility (5 in 10)*
4	*Fair possibility (4 in 10)*
3	*Some possibility (3 in 10)*
2	*Slight possibility (2 in 10)*
1	*Very slight possibility (1 in 10)*
0	*No chance, almost no chance (1 in 100)*

The order of appearance of the alternatives can be reversed on half of the questionnaires to avoid position bias.

The **top box score**—the percentage of respondents who mark the most favorable rating possible—is the one most often used for predictive purposes. If an 11-point scale is used, the percentage of respondents who mark one of the two most favorable ratings is usually used as the top box score.

Top box score: the percentage of respondents who choose the most favorable rating possible.

Given a history of top box scores on similar products that were subsequently introduced, norms can be established to separate the "winning" from the "losing" product concepts. If, for example, past experience indicates that a top box score of "30" (30 percent of the respondents marked the most favorable rating) is necessary for a new product of this type to be successful when introduced, this score can be established as the norm for deciding to continue or discontinue product development.[2]

Itemized Noncomparative Rating Scales

Itemized rating scale: requires the rater to select one of a limited number of ordered categories.

Itemized rating scales require the rater to select one of a limited number of categories that are ordered in terms of their scale positions. Research Application 11–1 illustrates three itemized rating scales that have been developed to measure satisfaction with a product or service.

Itemized rating scales are widely used in marketing research and are the basic building blocks for the more complex attitude scales.[3] Therefore, we examine the issues surrounding the use of itemized rating scales in some detail.

Nature and Degree of Verbal Description in Itemized Rating Scales. Scale categories can have verbal descriptions associated with them, as does the D-T Scale in Research Application 11–1, or they may be numerical, such as the Percentage Scale in the application. They may even be a completely unlabeled (except for the end points) series of categories, such as the Need S-D Scale in the application.

The presence and nature of verbal category descriptions have an effect on the responses. Techniques have been developed to assign values to category

RESEARCH APPLICATION 11–1

Alternative Itemized Rating Scales Designed to Measure Product/Service Satisfaction

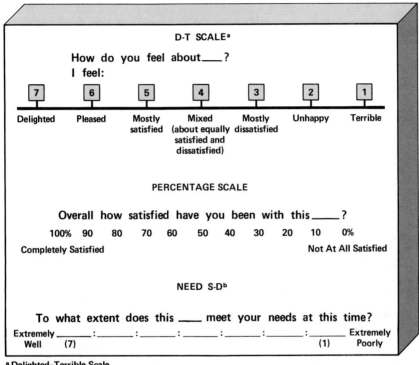

 D-T SCALE[a]

How do you feel about ____ ?
I feel:

| 7 | 6 | 5 | 4 | 3 | 2 | 1 |

| Delighted | Pleased | Mostly satisfied | Mixed (about equally satisfied and dissatisfied) | Mostly dissatisfied | Unhappy | Terrible |

PERCENTAGE SCALE

Overall how satisfied have you been with this ____ ?

100% 90 80 70 60 50 40 30 20 10 0%

Completely Satisfied   Not At All Satisfied

NEED S-D[b]

To what extent does this ____ meet your needs at this time?

Extremely ____ : ____ : ____ : ____ : ____ : ____ : ____ Extremely
Well   (7)   (1)   Poorly

[a] Delighted–Terrible Scale
[b] Need–Semantic Differential

SOURCE: R. A. Westbrook, "A Measuring Scale for Measuring Product/Service Satisfaction," *Journal of Marketing* (Fall 1980), 69. Used with permission from the American Marketing Association.

descriptors to ensure that balanced or equal interval scales are obtained, and several lists of category descriptors and their associated values are available.[4]

Instead of verbal descriptions, pictures have been used for special respondent groups. Research Application 11–2 illustrates a "smiling face" scale that was used successfully with children as young as five. A scale similar to this was used by Gillette in developing the marketing mix for PrestoMagiX (a toy).

The Number of Categories.   Any number of categories may be created, depending on the nature of the attitude being investigated. Rating scales should generally have between 5 and 10 response categories, though the measurement task may indicate a larger or smaller number. For example, 11-category 0–10 scales have been found to work well in telephone interviews.[5]

RESEARCH APPLICATION 11–2

Smiling Face Scale

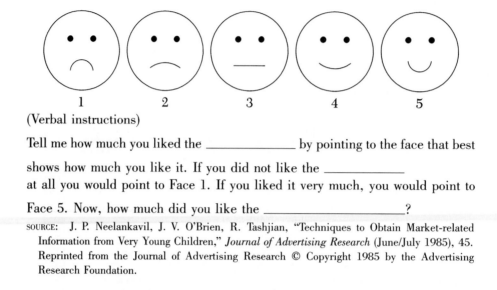

(Verbal instructions)

Tell me how much you liked the _____ by pointing to the face that best

shows how much you like it. If you did not like the _____

at all you would point to Face 1. If you liked it very much, you would point to

Face 5. Now, how much did you like the _____?

SOURCE: J. P. Neelankavil, J. V. O'Brien, R. Tashjian, "Techniques to Obtain Market-related Information from Very Young Children," *Journal of Advertising Research* (June/July 1985), 45. Reprinted from the Journal of Advertising Research © Copyright 1985 by the Advertising Research Foundation.

Balanced Versus Unbalanced Alternatives.   The researcher also must decide whether to use a *balanced* or *unbalanced* set of categories. A *balanced* scale provides an equal number of favorable and unfavorable categories. The decision to use a balanced scale should hinge on the type of information desired and the assumed distribution of attitudes in the population being studied. In a study of current consumers of a firm's brand, it may be reasonable to assume that most of the consumers have a favorable *overall* attitude toward the brand (this would *not* be a safe assumption if we were measuring attitudes toward specific attributes). In this case, an unbalanced scale with more favorable categories than unfavorable categories might provide more useful information.

Odd or Even Number of Categories.   The issue of an *odd* or *even* number of scale categories is a relevant issue when balanced scales (equal number of favorable and unfavorable categories) are being constructed. If an odd number of scale items is used, the middle item is generally designed as a neutral point.

Proponents of even-numbered categories prefer to avoid neutral points, arguing that attitudes cannot be neutral and that individuals should be forced to indicate some degree of favorableness or unfavorableness. However, in many issues, consumers may indeed be neutral and should be allowed to express that neutrality. Thus, the resolution of the odd/even question depends on whether at least some of the respondents may indeed be neutral on the topic being measured.

Forced Versus Nonforced Scales.   Another issue of importance with rating scales is the use of *forced* versus *nonforced scales.* A forced scale requires the respondent to indicate an attitude on the item. In this situation, respondents often mark the midpoint of a scale when in fact they have no attitude on the object or characteristic being rated. If a sufficient portion of the sample has no attitude on a topic, utilization of the midpoint in this manner will distort measures of central tendency and variance. On those occasions when the researcher expects a portion of the respondents to have no opinion, as opposed to merely being reluctant to reveal it, more accurate data may be obtained by providing a "no opinion" or "no knowledge" type of category.[6]

Conclusions on Itemized Rating Scales

Itemized rating scales are the most common means of measuring attitudes. There is no one "best" format for itemized rating scales. Instead, rating scales must be adjusted to the nature of the information required and the characteristics of the respondents. With this warning in mind, Table 11–1 summarizes our *general* recommendations on each of the key decision areas, while Figure 11–1 provides examples of a variety of types of itemized rating scales.

Comparative Rating Scales

In the graphic and itemized rating scales described previously, the rater evaluates the object without direct reference to a specified standard. This means that different respondents may be applying different standards or reference points. When asked to rate the overall quality of a particular brand, some respondents may compare it to their ideal brand, others to their current brand, and still others to their perception of the average brand. Therefore, when the researcher wants to ensure that all respondents are approaching the

TABLE 11–1 Summary of General Recommendations on Itemized
    Rating Scales

Issue	*General Recommendation*
1. Verbal category descriptions	Use precise descriptions for at least some categories.
2. Number of categories	Five when several scales are to be summed for one score, and up to nine when attributes are being compared across objects by interested, knowledgeable respondents.
3. Balanced or unbalanced	Balanced unless it is known that the respondents' attitudes are unbalanced, e.g., all favorable.
4. Odd or even categories	Odd if respondents could feel neutral, even if this is unlikely.
5. Forced or nonforced choice	Nonforced unless it is likely that all respondents will have knowledge on the issue.

1. Balanced, forced-choice, odd-interval scale focusing on an attitude toward a specific attribute.

   How do you like the taste of Classic Coke?

Like it very much	Like it	Neither like it nor dislike it	Dislike it	Strongly dislike it
_____	_____	_____	_____	_____

2. Balanced, forced-choice, even-interval scale focusing on an overall attitude.

   Overall, how would you rate Ultra Bright toothpaste?

Extremely good	Very good	Somewhat good	Somewhat bad	Very bad	Extremely bad
_____	_____	_____	_____	_____	_____

3. Unbalanced, forced-choice, odd-interval scale focusing on an overall attitude.

   What is your reaction to this advertisement?

Enthusiastic	Very favorable	Favorable	Neutral	Unfavorable
_____	_____	_____	_____	_____

4. Balanced, nonforced, odd-interval scale focusing on a specific attribute.

   How would you rate the friendliness of the sales personnel at Sears' downtown store?

Very friendly	Moderately friendly	Slightly friendly	Neither friendly nor un- friendly	Slighty unfriendly	Moderately unfriendly	Very un- friendly	Don't know
_____	_____	_____	_____	_____	_____	_____	_____

* When used in a written format, the scales may appear either horizontally, as shown in this table, or vertically. In general, the particular layout can be based on how the scale will best fit on the questionnaire.

FIGURE 11–1 Examples of Itemized Rating Scales*

Comparative rating scale: requires the rater to evaluate an attribute of the object relative to an explicit comparator or referent.

rating task from the same known reference point, some version of a comparative rating scale should be used. It is for this reason that comparative scales are generally required to substantiate comparative advertising claims.[7] However, the brand(s) or other standards used for comparison have a major impact on the evaluation given the brand of interest.[8]

A **comparative rating scale** provides the respondent with an explicit standard against which the object of interest is to be compared as shown below:

How do you like the taste of "new" Coke compared to Classic Coke?

Like it much more	Like it more	Like it about the same	Like it less	Like it much less	Don't know
_____	_____	_____	_____	_____	_____

The issues and recommendations discussed under noncomparative scales also apply to comparative scales.

Pairwise Measures of Preference and Discrimination

Suppose a firm wants to reduce the cost of its beverage product by lowering its sugar content. However, it does not want consumers to notice any taste difference. Therefore, it must determine how much of a reduction it can obtain without affecting the noticeable taste of the product. Problems such as this one require measures of consumers' ability to discriminate between brands or product versions.

Another common problem confronting marketers is to decide which of two similar product versions to introduce. A related problem is whether consumers prefer a new product to a leading competitor's product (or vice versa). Problems such as these require measures both of consumers' ability to discriminate between similar products and of their preference for one of the products.[9]

Paired Comparisons. The **paired comparison technique** involves presenting the respondent with two objects at a time and requiring the selection of one of the two according to some criterion. Thus, the respondent must make a series of judgments of the nature: A tastes better than B; overall, B is better than A; or A is more important than B.

Each respondent must compare all possible pairs of objects. If the researcher is interested in 5 brands ($n = 5$), there will be 10 comparisons [$n(n - 1)/2$]. If there are 10 brands, the number of required comparisons increases to 45. Furthermore, there must be a comparison for each attribute of interest. If we are interested in 10 brands and 5 attributes, our respondents will each be required to make 225 comparisons. Thus, paired comparisons are generally limited to a few brands and attributes.

Double-Paired Comparison. Paired comparison tests force the respondent to choose one item over the other. However, in many cases a significant portion of the respondents cannot distinguish one version from the other. Even when provided a "no preference" option, many of these "nondiscriminators" will express a preference. Obviously, this confounds the measure of preference.

A *double-paired comparison* test attempts to measure both discrimination and preference simultaneously. Respondents are provided four objects to compare consisting of two identical samples of Product A and two identical samples of Product B. The respondents are *not* told that there are only two products involved. Instead, they are required to rank order all four "brands." Those who can discriminate should rank both samples of the preferred product version over the two samples from the less preferred version. Those who do not, cannot clearly discriminate between the two products.

This approach places considerable demands on the respondents and is therefore limited to a relatively few brands or product versions.

Consistent Preference Discrimination Test. Another approach to measuring discrimination and preference simultaneously is known as *consistent preference discrimination testing*. This technique requires the subject to repeat the paired

Paired comparison techniques: present the respondent with two objects at a time and require the selection of one according to some specified criterion.

comparison task several (generally 4 to 8) times. Consider a 7-Up versus Sprite blind (unlabeled) taste test. If a person cannot discriminate between the two, a series of 8 paired comparisons will generally result in each brand "winning" approximately half the time. A person who can discriminate between the brands should consistently prefer one over the other.

Triangle Discrimination and Triangle Preference Tests.   The *triangle discrimination test* and the *triangle preference test* are conducted in the same manner as the paired-comparison test except that the respondent has two samples of one product and one of the other. In the triangle discrimination test, the respondent simply identifies the version that differs from the other two. No measure of preference is taken. Those who can differentiate then respond to additional preference and attitude questions.

The triangle preference test, sometimes referred to as *preference ranking,* asks the respondent to rank order the three brands. Those who can discriminate should rank the odd brand either first or third. Thus, both discrimination and preference is measured.

Double Triangle Discrimination and Double Triangle Preference Tests.   These tests are identical to the versions described, except that a second triangle test is performed in which the minority version in the first trial is the majority version in the second.

Response latency: the time delay between the presentation of a question or rating task and the beginning of the response.

Response Latency.   **Response latency,** the time delay before a respondent answers a question, indicates the respondent's certainty or confidence in the answer. It has been found to be a useful indicator of "guessing" responses to factual questions. However, the most common use of response latency is with paired comparisons. When used in conjunction with a paired-comparison preference test, the faster the choice is made, the stronger is the preference for the chosen brand.[10]

Response latency preference measures are particularly useful in telephone surveys since (1) they are unobtrusive, (2) automated equipment can make the measurements, and (3) more complex scales such as rank order and constant sum are difficult to administer by telephone. These advantages led duPont's marketing research department to use response latency in a major corporate image telephone survey.

Response latency times and brand selections can be converted into a scale known as the affective value distance (**AVD**) scale.[11] This indicates the degree to which one brand or product version is preferred over another. Research Application 11–3 illustrates the output of this approach. Respondents saw a television program with several commercials. Some saw a Coke commercial that was known to be successful, others saw a Heinz catsup commercial that was known to be unsuccessful, and a final group saw neither commercial. After viewing the program, the respondents performed a paired-comparison preference task with response latencies measured for five brands of cola and five brands of catsup. As Research Application 11–3 indicates, this technique clearly reflected the effects of the two commercials.

RESEARCH APPLICATION 11–3

Response Latency Measures of Advertising Impact

AVD Scale Scores*

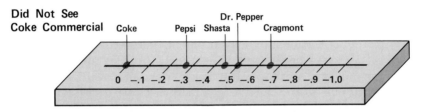

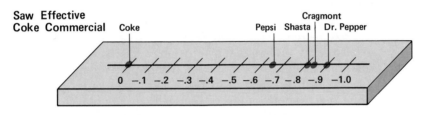

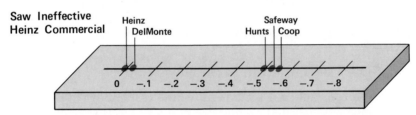

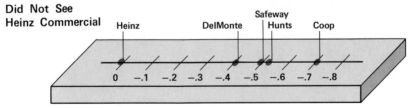

*The most preferred is set at zero, lesser preferred items have negative scores.

*The most preferred is set at zero, lesser preferred items have negative scores.

SOURCE: J. MacLachlan, J. G. Myers, "Using Response Latency to Identify Commercials That Motivate," *Journal of Advertising Research* (October/November 1983), 54. Reprinted from the Journal of Advertising Research © Copyright 1983, by the Advertising Research Foundation.

Rank-Order Rating Scale

Rank-order scale: requires the respondent to rank a set of objects or events according to a specified criterion.

The **rank-order scale** requires the respondent to rank a set of objects according to some criterion. Thus, a respondent may be asked to rank 5 brands of a snack food based on overall preference, flavor, saltiness, or package design. This approach, like the paired-comparison approach, is purely comparative in nature. An individual may rank 10 brands in descending order of preference and still "dislike" the brand rated as 1 because the ranking is based solely on the individual's reactions to the *set of objects presented for evaluation.* For example, a brand might be ranked number 5 compared with brands **A, B, C,** and **D** and yet be ranked first when compared to brands **E, F, G,** and **H.** Therefore, it is essential that the researcher include all the relevant competing brands, product versions, or advertisements in the comparison set.

The rank-order method is widely used to measure preference for both brands and attributes. It forces respondents to discriminate among the relevant objects and does so in a manner closer to the actual shopping environment than does the paired-comparison technique. It is also substantially less time-consuming than paired comparisons. Ranking 10 items is considerably faster and easier for most people than making the 45 judgments required to generate paired-comparison data for 10 brands. The instructions for ranking are also easily understood by most individuals, a fact that makes it useful for self-administered questionnaires where more complex instructions may reduce the response rate or increase measurement error.

The major shortcoming of the technique is that it produces only ordinal data. As discussed in Chapter 9, the number of statistical analyses permissible with ordinal data is limited. For example, we cannot calculate a *mean* from rank-order data; a *median* must be used instead.

The Constant-Sum Scale

Constant-sum scale: requires the respondent to divide a number, generally 10 or 100, among two or more objects such that the division reflects the relative standing of the objects on a specified dimension.

The **constant-sum scale** requires the respondent to divide a constant sum, generally 10 or 100, among two or more objects or attributes in order to reflect the relative standing of the objects or attributes on a specified dimension such as importance or preference. The constant-sum technique can be used for two objects at a time (paired comparison) or more than two objects at a time (quadric comparison).

Most common applications in marketing involve quadric comparisons. In these situations, the respondent is asked to divide the 100 points among *all* the brands or attributes under consideration. The resulting values can be averaged across individuals to produce an *approximate* interval scale value for the brands or attributes being considered.

The value of the constant-sum approach can be seen in the following example. Suppose a sample of respondents from a target market is requested to rank order several automobile characteristics with 1 being more important. Assume the individual ranks are similar and produce the following median ranks for each attribute:

Price	1	Safety	4
Economy	2	Comfort	5
Dependability	3	Style	6

A constant-sum measure of the importance of the same attributes could be obtained from the following procedure:

Divide 100 points among the characteristics listed so that the division will reflect how important each characteristic is to you in your selection of a new automobile.

Economy
Style
Comfort
Safety
Price
Dependability ____
   Total   *100*

All three of the following groups' average responses to the constant-sum scale would be consistent with the rank-order results just described:

	Group A	Group B	Group C
Price	35	20	65
Economy	30	18	9
Dependability	20	17	8
Safety	10	16	7
Comfort	3	15	6
Style	2	14	5
	100	100	100

However, with rank-order data, the researcher has no way of knowing if price is of overwhelming importance (Group C); part of a general, strong concern for overall cost (Group A); or not much more important than other attributes (Group B). Constant-sum data provide such evidence.

Simulated-Purchase Chip Testing

Simulated-purchase chip testing is used by Coca-Cola Company and other firms in international markets where respondents are not comfortable with more sophisticated methods.[12] However, it can be used anytime that budget, software, or expertise restricts access to more advanced methods.

Simulated-purchase chip testing (chip testing) is basically a before–after experiment with the constant sum as the measurement of the dependent variable. Respondents are given 10 chips to allocate among a set of brands, such as soft drinks, in a manner that will reflect their next 10 purchases. All the chips may be allocated to one brand or they may be spread out as much as the respondent desires. After the first allocation, the respondent repeats the tasks among a second set of brands in which the change of interest to the researcher (a new brand, a new package, an added feature, etc.) has been added. This allows an assessment of the purchase response to the change and an estimate of which brands or product versions will lose share to the change.

Simulated-purchase chip testing:
a before–after experiment with the constant sum used to measure the independent variable, which is generally preference or purchase intentions.

Results of a test replacing the standard bottle cap on the liter bottle of Coca-Cola with a screw cap are as follows:

Product	Simulated Market Shares (%)		
	Control	Test	Difference
Coca-Cola Screw Cap	—	42.6	42.6
Coca-Cola Crown Cap	33.9	—	−33.9
Coca-Cola	33.9	42.6	8.8
Other corporate	19.1	17.3	−1.9
Total corporate	53.0	59.9	6.9
PepsiCo	14.2	10.5	−3.7
All other	32.8	29.6	−3.2

Coca-Cola has conducted numerous tests of this approach and concludes that it is very useful for most applications *except* price level tests and when many scenarios need to be tested. It is easy and realistic for respondents, most decision makers are comfortable with it, it is inexpensive and takes little time to conduct, and it requires little expertise to conduct or analyze.

Attitude Scales

Attitude scale: a carefully constructed set of rating scales designed to measure one or more aspects of an individual's attitude toward an object or event.

Attitude scales are carefully constructed sets of rating scales designed to measure one or more aspects of an individual's attitude toward some object. The individual's responses to the various scales may be summed to provide a single attitude score for the individual. Or, more commonly, the responses to each scale item or subgroup of scale items may be examined independently of the other scale items.

Two unique forms of the itemized rating scale are commonly used to construct attitude scales in applied marketing research studies. These are known as *Likert scales* and *semantic differential scales*. These scale types and their use in attitude scales are discussed in some detail in the following sections. Since these are versions of the itemized rating scale, we must keep in mind the various issues and problems associated with itemized rating scales.

The Semantic Differential Scale

The **semantic differential scale** requires the respondent to rate the attitude object on a number of itemized, seven-point rating scales bounded at each end by one of two bipolar adjectives or phrases. For example:

Semantic differential scale: requires the respondent to rate the object or event on a number of itemized, seven-point rating scales bounded at each end by one of two bipolar adjectives or phrases.

Camaro Z28

Fast	____	____	X	____	____	____	____	*Slow*
Plain	____	____	____	____	____	X		*Stylish*
Large	____	____	____	X	____	____	____	*Small*
Inexpensive	____	____	____	____	X	____	____	*Expensive*

The instructions indicate that the respondent is to mark the blank that best indicates how accurately one or the other term describes or fits the attitude object. The end positions indicate "extremely," the next pair indicate "very," the middlemost pair indicate "somewhat," and the middle position indicates "neither–nor." Thus, the respondent in the example described the Camaro Z28 as somewhat fast, extremely stylish, somewhat expensive, and neither large nor small.

Any number of scale positions can be used with the semantic differential, with six or seven being most common. It is generally recommended that the more favorable adjective or phrase be randomly assigned to the left or right side of the scale.[13]

The widespread use of the semantic differential has promoted a number of attempts to improve the format in which it is presented to respondents. The most common alteration is to have the respondent rate two or more brands or stores on the *same scales* (as shown below). This approach is referred to as the *upgraded semantic differential* or the *graphic positioning scale*.[14] It takes less space than the standard semantic differential and appears to give similar results.

Camaro Z28 (Z)   *Plymouth Laser (L)*
Ford Escort GT (F)   *Ideal sports car (I)*

Fast	____	FZ	I	L	____	____	____	*Slow*
Plain	____	____	____	Z	____	LF	I	*Stylish*
Large	____	____	Z	____	IL	F	____	*Small*
Inexpensive	____	____	____	F	L	IZ	____	*Expensive*

A recently tested enhancement of this scale, known as the *numerical comparative scale*, is shown in the following example. The instructions are similar to those for the semantic differential, except that the respondent records the category number for each concept being measured beside each scale. An initial test indicates that, in a mail survey, it provides a response rate comparable to the graphic positioning scale but with an increased questionnaire completion rate and higher data quality.[15]

			Camaro Z28	Ford Escort GT	Plymouth Laser	Ideal Sports Car
Fast 1 2 3 4 5 6 7	*Slow*		2	3	4	2
Plain 1 2 3 4 5 6 7	*Stylish*		6	7	5	7
Large 1 2 3 4 5 6 7	*Small*		4	6	5	5
Inexpensive 1 2 3 4 5 6 7	*Expensive*		4	4	5	6

Coca-Cola Company has found that the simple "yes–no" version of the semantic differential works as well as or better than the standard version with large sample sizes (more than 250).[16]

If you think a phrase describes a brand, circle the number for that brand. If you think a phrase does not describe a brand, do not circle that brand's number. If you think a phrase does not describe any of the brands listed, circle zero to the right indicating "none."

	Coca-Cola	*Pepsi-Cola*	*Fanta*	*Sinalco*	*Miranda*	*Lift*	*Sprite*	*Schweppes*	*Appollnaris*	*None*
Modern	1	2	3	4	5	6	7	8	9	0
Sweet	1	2	3	4	5	6	7	8	9	0
Lively	1	2	3	4	5	6	7	8	9	0

Semantic differential data can be analyzed in a number of ways. The versatility is increased by the widely accepted assumption that the resultant data are interval in nature. Two general approaches to analysis are of interest to us—aggregate analysis and profile analysis. The first step in either approach is to assign each interval a value of 1 through 7. For aggregate analysis, it is essential (and helpful for profile analysis) that the larger numbers are consistently assigned to the blanks nearer the more favorable terms.

Aggregate analysis requires that the scores across all adjective pairs be summed for *each individual*. Each individual is thus assigned a summated

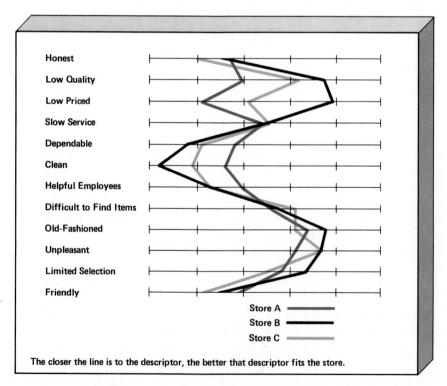

FIGURE 11–2 Profile Analysis Using Semantic Differential Data

score. The individual or group of individuals can then be compared to other individuals on the basis of their total scores, or two or more objects (products, brands, or stores) can be compared for the same group of individuals. Aggregate analysis is most useful for predicting preference or brand share. However, disaggregate, or profile analysis, appears to provide more useful data for marketing decision making.

Profile analysis involves computing the mean, or median, value assigned to each adjective pair for an object by a specified group. This profile can then be compared with the profile of another object, an "ideal" version of the object, or another group. Figure 11–2 provides an example of a profile comparison of two department stores.

Profile analysis is used to isolate strong and weak attributes of products, brands, stores, and so forth. Marketing strategies are then devised to offset weak attributes and/or to capitalize on strong ones. For example, General Motors has used profile analysis of a 35-item semantic differential to develop advertising strategies. Container Corporation of America has used profile analysis to evaluate direct mail approaches. General Electric has used the semantic differential to isolate attributes of persuasive appliance advertisements.

Likert Scales

Likert scales, sometimes referred to as *summated scales*, require a respondent to indicate a degree of agreement or disagreement with each of a series of statements related to the attitude object such as the following:

1. *Macy's is one of the most attractive stores in town.*

____ Strongly ____ Agree ____ Neither agree ____ Disagree ____ Strongly
   agree   nor disagree   disagree

2. *The service at Macy's is not satisfactory.*

____ Strongly ____ Agree ____ Neither agree ____ Disagree ____ Strongly
   agree   nor disagree   disagree

3. *The service at a retail store is very important to me.*

____ Strongly ____ Agree ____ Neither agree ____ Disagree ____ Strongly
   agree   nor disagree   disagree

To analyze responses to a Likert scale, each response category is assigned a numerical value. These examples could be assigned values, such as strongly agree = 1 through strongly disagree = 5, or the scoring could be reversed, or a −2 through +2 system could be used.

Like the semantic differential and Stapel scales, Likert scales can be analyzed on an item-by-item basis (profile analysis), or they can be summed to form a single score for each individual. If a summated approach is used, the scoring system for *each* item must be such that a high (or low) score *consistently* reflects a favorable response. Thus, for statement 1, *strongly agree* might be assigned a 5 and *strongly disagree* a 1. If so, the reverse would be required for statement 2.

The Likert scale offers a number of advantages. First, it is relatively easy to construct and administer. The instructions that must accompany the scale are easily understood, which makes the technique useful for mail surveys of the general population as well as in personal interviews with children. It can also

Likert scales: require a respondent to indicate a degree of agreement or disagreement with each of a series of statements about the object or event.

be used in telephone surveys. It does, however, take longer to complete than Stapel or semantic differential scales. Care should be taken when using Likert scales in cross-cultural research, as there may be cultural variations in willingness to express disagreement.

Which Scale to Use?

The preceding pages describe a number of techniques, all of which purport to measure some aspect of attitudes. In addition to these techniques, numerous less well-known techniques and various versions and alterations of the popular scales are available.

When various scaling techniques have been compared, the results generally have been equivalent across the techniques.[17] Therefore, the selection of a scaling technique depends on the information requirements of the problem, the characteristics of the respondents, the proposed means of administration, and the cost of each technique. In general, multiple measures should be used. That is, no matter what type of scale is used, whenever it is practical, several scale items should be used to measure each object, attribute, belief, or preference under consideration. Summing these several items will provide a more accurate measurement than a single measurement.

Measuring Emotions

Emotions:
strong, relatively
uncontrolled
feelings that affect
behavior.

Marketers have always been interested in the affective, like–dislike, component of attitudes. In recent years this interest has expanded into an interest in emotions themselves.[18] **Emotions** are strong, relatively uncontrolled feelings that affect our behavior. Emotions are generally triggered by *environmental events*, are accompanied by *physiological changes*, often cause *cognitive thoughts*, have *associated behaviors*, and, most important, involve *subjective feelings*. Marketers need to measure emotions, particularly the subjective feelings aspect, as emotional arousal or reduction is often an important product benefit and advertisements that arouse appropriate emotions are often more effective than those that do not.

Projective techniques (Chapter 12) and physiological measures (Chapter 13) can be used to measure emotional responses to ads, products, or product use. Semantic differentials, and Likert scales are commonly used to measure emotions. The phrases are selected from lists developed for this purpose[19] as in the following:

While driving the Ford Escort, I felt

	Not at all						Very
Excited	1	2	3	4	5	6	7
Mad	1	2	3	4	5	6	7
Playful	1	2	3	4	5	6	7
Fearful	1	2	3	4	5	6	7
Desirous	1	2	3	4	5	6	7

RESEARCH APPLICATION 11–4

Pictures Used in BBDO's Emotional Measurement System

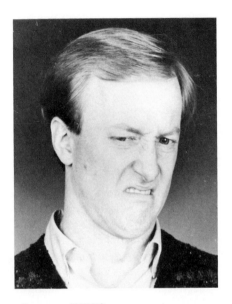 

SOURCE: Courtesy of BBDO.

BBDO, a major ad agency, has a list of 26 emotions they believe can be triggered by advertising. To measure the emotions triggered by an ad, they developed the **Emotional Measurement System.** Starting with 1,800 pictures of six actors portraying various emotions, the firm used extensive research to narrow the list to 53 that reflect the 26 emotions of interest. Research Application 11–4 shows the types of pictures used.

To test a commercial, respondents quickly sort through the 53 pictures and set aside all that reflect how they *felt* while watching the commercial. The percentage of respondents selecting particular pictures provides a profile of the emotional response to the commercial.

The system has been used for such companies as Gillette, Pepsi-Cola, Polaroid, and Wrigley. The Gillette commercial—"The Best a Man Can Get"—arouses feelings of "pride" and "confidence" among men and "happiness" and "joyfulness" among women.[20]

Emotional Measurement System:
a series of pictures of faces showing emotions that respondents use to indicate the feelings triggered while viewing an ad.

Summary

Rating scales are single-scale items used to measure one dimension of a component of an attitude such as pleasantness of taste. Attitude scales are basically combinations of rating scales designed to measure several or all aspects of an individual's attitude toward an object.

A noncomparative rating scale, often called a monadic scale, does not provide an explicit standard against which the object of interest is to be compared. A comparative rating scale does. Itemized rating scales require the rater to place the object in one of a limited number of categories that are ordered in terms of the attitude dimension in question. Itemized scales are most widely used and require attention to (1) the verbal descriptions of the categories, (2) the number of categories, (3) balanced or unbalanced categories, (4) an odd or even number of categories, and (5) forced or nonforced answers.

There are a number of pairwise techniques for measuring individuals' ability to distinguish various product versions and/or their relative preferences for a set of items, including paired comparisons, double paired comparisons, consistent preference tests, triangle discrimination and preference tests, and double triangle discrimination and preference tests. Response latency, the length of time it takes to respond to a preference question such as a paired comparison, indicates the strength of the preference.

The rank-order scale requires the respondent to rank a set of objects according to some criterion. The constant sum adds the requirement that 100 points be allocated among the objects to reflect their relative standing on the criterion.

The semantic differential requires the respondent to rate the attitude object on a number of itemized, seven-point rating scales bounded at each end by one of two bipolar adjectives. The Likert scale requires the respondent to indicate a level of agreement or disagreement with a series of statements about the attitude object.

Emotions can be measured using projective techniques or physiological measures. Semantic differential scales and Likert scales are often used to measure emotions. BBDO has developed a set of pictures of faces that indicate various emotions. Respondents select those pictures that reflect how they felt while watching a commercial.

Review Questions

11.1. What is a *rating scale*?

11.2. What is an *attitude scale*?

11.3. What is a *noncomparative rating scale*?

11.4. What is a "top box" score?

11.5. What is a *monadic scale*?

11.6. What is a *blind test*?

11.7. What is an *itemized rating scale*?

11.8. What are the major issues or decisions involved in constructing an itemized rating scale?

11.9. Does the presence and nature of verbal description affect the response to itemized rating scales?

11.10. How many categories should be used in itemized rating scales?

11.11. What factors affect the appropriate number of categories to use with itemized rating scales?

11.12. What is meant by *balanced* versus *unbalanced alternatives*?

11.13. Should an *odd* or *even* number of response categories be used? Why?

11.14. Should *forced* or *nonforced* scales be used? Why?

11.15. What is a *comparative rating scale*?

11.16. What is a *paired comparison*?

11.17. What is a *double paired comparison*?

11.18. What is *consistent preference discrimination testing*?

11.19. How does a *triangle discrimination test* differ from a *triangle preference test*?

11.20. What is a *double triangle discrimination test*?

11.21. What is *response latency*? How does it relate to paired comparison preference tests?

11.22. What is the *rank-order rating scale*? What are its advantages and disadvantages?

11.23. What problems can arise when the analysis of rank-order data focuses only on the number one rank (top box)?

11.24. What is the *constant-sum scale*? What are its advantages and disadvantages?

11.25. What is a *simulated purchase chip test*? What are its advantages and disadvantages?

11.26. How do you construct an *attitude scale*?

11.27. Describe the *semantic differential scale*.

11.28. Describe the *graphic positioning scale (upgraded semantic differential scale)*.

11.29. Describe the *numerical comparative scale*.

11.30. What is meant by *profile analysis*?

11.31. Describe the *Likert scale*.

11.32. What are the advantages of the Likert scale?

11.33. What criteria influence which scale should be used?

11.34. What are the various approaches to measuring emotions?

11.35. Describe BBDO's Emotional Measurement System.

Discussion Questions

11.36. "A product could receive the highest median rank on a rank-order scale of all brands available in the market and still have virtually no sales." Explain how this could occur. Could a paired comparison technique overcome the problem?

11.37. Develop an attitude scale to measure the following groups' attitude toward (1) reading, (2) the environment, or (3) alcoholic beverages.
   a. Children age 10–12
   b. Children age 14–17
   c. Young adults age 18–22
   d. Parents
   e. Grade-school teachers

11.38. Develop_____to measure college students' attitudes toward three restaurants. Measure their overall liking; their beliefs about relevant attributes and the importance they attach to each of these attributes. Assume a personal interview format.
a. noncomparative graphic rating scales
b. noncomparative itemized rating scales
c. comparative graphic rating scales
d. comparative itemized rating scales
e. paired comparisons
f. rank-order scales
g. constant-sum scales

11.39. Develop a set of items (adjectives, phrases, and the like) for use in a semantic differential scale to study the attitude college students have toward
a. their hometown
b. Classic Coke
c. General Motors
d. alcohol consumption by college students

11.40. Develop a scale to measure the emotional response to
a. a television advertisement
b. a popular song
c. a sports car
d. an environmental problem

Projects/Activities

11.41. Use the (a) semantic differential, and (b) Likert scale to measure a sample of 10 students' attitudes toward (1) basketball, (2) accounting as a career, (3) Big Mac, (4) Harley Davidson and Honda motorcycles, (5) Japan. Use a separate sample for each technique.

11.42. Conduct a double triangle discrimination test on the following products using a sample of 20 students. Follow each by a paired comparison preference test using a constant-sum (100 points) expression of preference. Analyze the constant-sum preference of those who correctly discriminate 0, 1, and 2 times separately.
a. 7-Up versus Sprite
b. Classic Coke versus Coke
c. Diet Coke versus Diet Pepsi

11.43. For 3 different samples of 20 students each, use (a) paired comparison, (b) rank-order scale, and (c) constant-sum scale to measure preferences for 6 popular TV shows. What do you conclude?

11.44. Implement_____(a) 11.38, (b) 11.39, (c) 11.40, (d) 11.41.

Notes

1. P. Gendall, D. Esslemont, D. Day, "A Comparison of Two Versions of the Juster Scale Using Self-Completion Questionnaires," *Journal of the Market Research Society* (July 1991), 257–263.

2. See L. F. Jamieson, F. M. Bass, "Adjusting Stated Intention Measures to Predict Trial Purchase of New Products," *Journal of Marketing Research* (August 1989), 336–345; and R. Gillett, "The Top-Box Paradox," *Marketing Research* (September 1991), 37–39.

3. L. W. Friedman, H. H. Friedman, "Comparison of Itemized vs. Graphic Rating Scales," *Journal of the Market Research Society* (July 1986), 285–290.

4. C. B. Schertzer, J. B. Kernan, "More on the Robustness of Response Scales," *Journal of the Market Research Society* (October 1985), 261–282; and M. R. Crask, R. J. Fox, "An Exploration of the Internal Properties of Three Commonly Used Marketing Research Scales," *Journal of the Market Research Society* (July 1987), 317–339.

5. B. Loken, et al., "The Use of 0–10 Scales in Telephone Surveys," *Journal of the Market Research Society* (July 1987), 353–362.

6. See O. D. Duncan, M. Stenbeck, "No Opinion or Not Sure," *Public Opinion Quarterly* (Winter 1988), 513–525.

7. B. Buchanan, "Can You Pass the Comparative Ad Challenge?" *Harvard Business Review* (July/August 1985), 108; and B. Buchanan, R. H. Smithies, "Taste Claims and Their Substantiation," *Journal of Advertising Research* (July 1991), 19–35.

8. See "Brand Perceptions: Relative v. Absolute Ratings," *Research on Research* 6 (Chicago: Market Facts Inc., undated). The primary findings are reproduced in Research Application 10–3, pp. 265.

9. For an excellent discussion of these issues see R. M. Johnson, "Simultaneous Measurement of Discrimination and Preference," *Research on Research* 33 (Chicago: Market Facts, Inc., undated); B. Buchanan, M. Givon, A. Goldman, "Measurement of Discrimination Ability in Taste Tests," *Journal of Marketing Research* (May 1987), 154–163; B. S. Buchanan, D. G. Morrison, "Taste Tests," *Psychology and Marketing* (Spring 1984), 69–91; and B. S. Buchanan, D. G. Morrison, "Measuring Simple Preferences," *Marketing Science* (Spring 1985), 93–109.

10. J. MacLachlan, J. Czepiel, and P. LaBarbera, "Implementation of Response Latency," *Journal of Marketing Research*

(November 1979), 573–577; T. T. Tyebjee, "Response Latency: A New Measure for Scaling Brand Preference," *Journal of Marketing Research* (February 1979), 96–101; and D. A. Aaker, et al., "On Using Response Latency to Measure Preference," *Journal of Marketing Research* (May 1980), 237–244.

11. J. MacLachlan, J. G. Myers, "Using Response Latency to Identify Commercials that Motivate," *Journal of Advertising Research* (October/November 1983), 51–57. See also W. J. Burroughs, R. A. Feinberg, "Using Response Latency to Assess Spokesperson Effectiveness," *Journal of Consumer Research* (September 1987), 295–299.

12. This section is based on N. C. Mohn, "Simulated Purchase Chip Testing," *Marketing and Research Today* (November 1989), 240–244; and N. C. Mohn, "Simulated-Purchase Chip Testing vs. Tradeoff Analysis," *Marketing Research* (March 1990), 49–54.

13. H. H. Friedman, L. W. Friedman, B. Gluck, "The Effects of Scale-Checking Styles on Responses to a Semantic Differential Scale," *Journal of the Market Research Society* (October 1988), 477–481.

14. D. E. Stem, S. Noazin, "Effects of Number of Objects and Scale Positions on Graphic Position Scale Reliability," in R. F. Lusch, *1985 AMA Educators' Proceedings* (Chicago: American Marketing Association, 1985), 370–372.

15. L. L. Golden, G. Albaum, M. Zimmer, "The Numerical Comparative Scale," *Journal of Retailing* (Winter 1987), 393–410.

16. N. C. Mohn, "Comparing the Statistical Quality of Two Methods for Collecting Brand Image Data," *Marketing and Research Today* (August 1989), 167–171.

17. See N. R. Barnard, A. S. C. Ehrenberg, "Robust Measures of Consumer Brand Beliefs," *Journal of Marketing Research* (November 1990), 477–484.

18. This section is based on D. I. Hawkins, R. J. Best, K. A. Coney, *Consumer Behavior* (Homewood, IL: Irwin, 1992), 312–318.

19. R. Batra, M. B. Holbrook, "Developing a Typology of Affective Responses to Advertising," *Psychology & Marketing* (Spring 1990), 22.

20. G. Levin, "Emotion Guides BBDO's Ad Tests," *Advertising Age* (January 29, 1990), 12.

CHAPTER 12

Qualitative Research

LEARNING OBJECTIVES

Upon completing this chapter, you should be able to:

1. Explain why qualitative research is used.

2. Describe individual depth interviews including their advantages and disadvantages.

3. Describe focus group interviews including their advantages and disadvantages.

4. Describe minigroup interviews including their advantages and disadvantages.

5. List and describe the major types of projective techniques.

6. Explain the reasoning underlying projective techniques and discuss their problems and potential.

Curlee Clothing's Use of Focus Group Research

The marketing department of Curlee Clothing undertook a major marketing research effort to help management evaluate current advertising and product strategy. As part of this effort, it brought together various groups of six or seven young men with similar demographic characteristics, such as college students, blue-collar workers, or sales representatives. These groups were placed in comfortable surroundings, provided refreshments, and asked to discuss clothing in terms of why and how they purchased it, their likes and dislikes, and so forth. Each session was taped and analyzed.

Management anticipated that the discussions would focus on styles, prices, quality, and perhaps advertising. However, what emerged from each session was a critical discussion of the retail sales personnel. Most of the individuals, once relaxed, expressed a feeling of insecurity in purchasing men's fashion-oriented clothing. This insecurity was coupled with a distrust of both the intentions and competence of the retail salesperson. As a result of these findings, Curlee embarked on a major effort at training the retail sales personnel through specially prepared films and training sessions.

The most common method of obtaining information about the behavior, attitudes, and other characteristics of people is to ask them. In Chapters 10 and 11 we were concerned with the preparation of structured, direct questionnaires for that purpose.

It is not always possible, or desirable, to use direct questioning to obtain information. People may be either *unwilling* or *unable* to answer questions because they consider them to be an invasion of their privacy, to adversely affect their self-perception or prestige, to be embarrassing, to concern motivations they do not fully understand or cannot verbalize, or for other reasons. Therefore, additional approaches to obtaining such information may be necessary.

Depth interviews and *projective techniques* are frequently used by marketing researchers when direct questioning is impractical, more costly, or less accurate. These techniques, generally referred to as *qualitative research*, are described in this chapter.[1] Over the past decade, qualitative research has grown rapidly in popularity worldwide, particularly in the United States and Europe.[2]

Depth Interviews

Depth interviews can involve one respondent and one interviewer or they may involve a small group (8 to 12 respondents) and an interviewer. The latter are called *focus group interviews*, and the former are termed *individual depth interviews* or *one-on-ones*. Groups of four or five are often referred to as *mini-group interviews*.

Of the three "types" of depth interviews—*individual*, *minigroup*, and *focus group*—the focus group is by far the most popular. However, both individual and minigroup interviews are widely used as well.

Individual Depth Interviews

Individual depth interviews (one-on-one): involve one respondent and an interviewer who does not follow a prespecified set of questions that must be asked in a predetermined order but probes and questions as necessary to develop the required data.

Individual depth interviews typically last 30 to 45 minutes, involve one interviewer and one respondent, but do not follow a set of prespecified questions that must be asked according to the order imposed by a questionnaire. Instead, there is freedom to create questions, to probe those responses that appear relevant, and generally to try to develop the best set of data in any way practical. However, the interviewer must follow one rule: one must not consciously try to affect the content of the answers given by the respondent. The respondent must feel free to reply to the various questions, probes, and other, more subtle, ways of encouraging responses in the manner deemed most appropriate.

In addition to the relatively direct pursuit of detailed information as described, Durgee recommends three questioning techniques for use in individual depth interviews.[3] *Laddering* involves having respondents identify attributes that distinguish brands by asking questions such as "In what way is Pepsi different from Classic Coke and Dr. Pepper?" Each distinguishing attribute is then probed to determine why it is important or meaningful. These reasons are then probed to determine why they are important, and so forth. The purpose is to uncover the "network of meanings" associated with the product, brand, or concept.

Hidden-issue questioning focuses on individual respondents' feelings about sensitive issues such as wanting to have an affair or having a desire for power. Analysis focuses on common themes across respondents. These themes can then be used to guide advertising development. *Symbolic questioning* requires respondents to describe the opposites of the product/activity of interest or a specific attribute of the product/activity. For example, a segment might describe the opposite of beer as skim milk—thin, flat, watery, nonalcoholic, staid, healthy, but almost medicinal. This suggests that beer is perceived as lively, full, rich, fun, but not entirely good for you, which further suggests guilt about consuming it. Another segment might consider the opposite of beer to be fine wine—sophisticated, glamorous, upscale, expensive, subtle, and consumed primarily with excellent food. This suggests that they view beer as unsophisticated, common, inexpensive, straightforward, and inappropriate with good food. Obviously, these two segments would require dramatically different marketing approaches.

Individual depth interviews have been found to generate more and higher-quality ideas on a per respondent basis than either focus or minigroups. They are particularly appropriate when

1. detailed probing of an individual's behavior, attitudes, or needs is required;
2. the subject matter under discussion is likely to be of a highly confidential nature (e.g., personal investments);
3. the subject matter is of an emotionally charged or embarrassing nature;
4. certain strong, socially acceptable norms exist (e.g., baby feeding) and the need to conform in a group discussion may influence responses;
5. where highly detailed (step-by-step) understanding of complicated behavior or decision-making patterns (e.g., planning the family holiday) are required; or
6. the interviews are with professional people or on the subject of the interviewee's job.

For example, one-on-one interviews were conducted for Merrill Lynch with individuals who make large financial investments.[4] This research revealed that the "Bullish on America" advertising theme that stressed patriotism did not appeal to this group. The heavy investor wanted an investment firm that would help him or her achieve larger financial gains. Merrill Lynch changed its advertising content and used a new theme—"A breed apart." It is quite possible that in a group setting these respondents would not have revealed the importance of financial gain relative to patriotism.

One-on-ones are very common in industrial research. Research Application 12–1 describes a particularly complicated industrial study that used this approach.

At least one consulting firm is successfully conducting depth interviews by telephone. Using skilled interviewers, the firm has respondents tell stories about both typical and atypical times they have used a certain product. The interviewer probes for additional details concerning the story. (How did you

Individual Depth Interviews in a High Technology Environment

U.S. WEST, one of the seven regional telephone operating companies formed after the break-up of AT&T, launched a major research project to help it understand the evolving communications needs of its customers. One customer group of interest was composed of the large, sophisticated business and government users. These organizations viewed voice and data communications as either a key competitive tool or a central cost center.

The initial phase of the research project involved specification of a population of such firms based on billings, growth, industry characteristics, and the judgment of industry experts. Next, a judgment sample of firms was selected to represent the relevant range of industries, firm size, communications applications, and in-house communications expertise.

The third phase involved extensive semistructured telephone interviews with the selected firms to identify the key participants in the evaluation of the firm's communications needs. Titles such as telecommunications manager, data communications manager, and information systems manager were most common, but a wide array of other job titles such as controller also appeared.

The one-to-two hour interviews took place at the respondent's location, either in his or her office or in a conference room. The respondent was frequently assisted by one to four assistants such as engineers and computer scientists.

The interview involved a long semistructured questionnaire that served as a guideline, but the interviewer was not bound to follow it. The interview team consisted of a highly trained interviewer (graduate degree, extensive interviewing experience, experience with the telecommunications industry), an engineer or other technical person from U.S. WEST, and a member of the U.S. WEST research project team.

Each member of the interviewing team took notes during the interview and wrote out a long summary of his or her impressions and conclusions following the interview. The summary followed the format of the semistructured questionnaire to provide comparability across interviews. The interviews were also tape recorded so that additional notes and quotes could be taken. Finally, most respondents agreed to respond to telephone inquiries to clear up any uncertainty as the interviews were being analyzed.

---

feel? How were you dressed? What else was happening?) A series of such interviews revealed that chicken and cooking chicken has strong, warm associations with home and family:

> I have such happy memories of the big family picnics on Labor Day. There was such excitement and anticipation. I remember my mother frying chicken all day in the kitchen, just enormous platters full. Everyone brought fried chicken, but she always made extra because hers was the best; the crustiest, the crispiest. She fried chicken from morning to night and would be just worn out, but it was worth it. The picnics were at my uncle's out in the country near Nashville. She put out picnic tables under the elm trees and everyone just ate and ate: potato salad, chicken, green beans, fried corn, cole

slaw, baked beans, pecan pie. I want to convey those good memories to my son, and I always feel that way when I make my mother's fried chicken for him.[5]

Such associations provide useful information for product positioning and advertising decisions.

A vice-president of Elrick and Lavidge, a major consulting firm, describes the advantages and disadvantages of individual depth interviews as follows:

> Compared with group interviews, individual in-depth interviews can provide more detail, point out personal preferences and idiosyncrasies, and describe subtleties, nuances, and shades of difference that are masked in the group setting. Such results cannot, however, be accomplished within the time and cost parameters generally associated with focus group studies. Interviewing 35 individuals in a series of four groups takes approximately one-fourth the time required to conduct one-on-ones with that same number on an individual basis.[6]

Another factor that must be considered when conducting individual in-depth studies is interviewer burnout. No matter how experienced or intrepid the interviewer/discussion leader, it is not often possible to complete more than four or five hour-long interviews in one day without sacrificing quality.

It also should be kept in mind that whatever is said must be analyzed;[7] stimulus overload can also take place once the interviews are completed and the conversations are compiled.

Focus Group Interviews

A **focus group interview** is a depth interview with one interviewer and 6 to 12 respondents. The typical focus group interview in the United States involves 8 to 12 individuals and lasts about 2 hours. Normally, each group is designed to reflect the characteristics of a particular market segment. Research Application 12–2 illustrates the importance of including groups from each major market segment. The respondents are selected according to the relevant sampling plan and meet at a central location that generally has facilities for taping and/or filming the interviews. In Europe, focus groups tend to consist of 6 to 8 respondents, vary in length from 1.5 to 4 hours, and are often conducted in the home of the recruiter.[8] Otherwise, the interviews are similar.

The discussion itself is "led" by a moderator. The moderator attempts to progress through three stages during the interview: (1) establish rapport with the group, structure the rules of group interaction, and set objectives; (2) provoke intense discussion in the relevant areas; and (3) summarize the group's responses to determine the extent of agreement.[9]

LKP International, a large advertising agency, uses what it terms *modular research* in designing advertisements. Modular research involves presenting every element that might appear in a particular advertisement to a focus group for a discussion of its appropriateness. For example, before LKP launched its Prego spaghetti sauce campaign, it used focus groups to identify the details of the setting—from room to pot to people—that would be most effective. Among other things, LKP learned that steel gourmet kitchens and

Focus group interviews: involve 6 to 12 respondents and an interviewer who does not follow a prespecified set of questions that must be asked in a predetermined order but probes and questions as necessary to develop the required data.

RESEARCH APPLICATION 12–2

Focus Group Discussions on Bread Consumption

Four focus groups were held on bread consumption. The groups consisted of individuals who made most of the bread purchases for their households. The groups were organized by type of bread consumed. The following differing reactions of two groups indicate the importance of having separate focus groups from each major market segment.

Group 1 (Wheat-bread consumers, primarily middle-class)

Speaker	Comment	Group Reactions
Moderator:	Let's take just a minute and let me ask you one final question. Is there any advice that you would give a bakery about bread?	Several folding napkins, picking up coffee cups. It is the end of the session.
Gayle (responding quickly):	Tell us more about what you put in and why.	All except Billie stop their preparations.
Joan (emphatically):	Yeah!	General nodding agreement but no one speaks.
Moderator:	More educational materials?	
Gayle:	Even if it was just posted in the bakery so you could just look. It wouldn't have to be on the package.	General nodding agreement from group.
Lori:	Give us a primer to tell us what all those long complicated words mean.	
Joan:	A lot of times, it will say "no preservatives" and then you read a lot of these words that you don't understand. The layman doesn't know. Those are not common words in my vocabulary.	Light laughter accompanied by nods of agreement.
Susan:	I think it would be nice to have just a little pamphlet that you could read. That they could tack it up there.	Billie looks at doors, others remain attentive.
Gayle:	I'd like to know that it is a real necessity that they add all those nonartificial preservatives. I understand that a smaller bakery like that (referring to a small local bakery discussed earlier) is selling things on a bigger turnover rate and not baking in such large quantities. I suppose that is why they don't have to add any preservatives at all.	Joan nods and starts to speak but Patty speaks first.
Patty:	A variety of sizes would be good. Maybe make this a smaller loaf too because when I am by myself I have to put half of it in the freezer.	The discussion shifts to package size, then to price. The session lasts about 5 more minutes.

Group 2 (White-bread consumers, primarily working-class)

Speaker	Comment	Group Reactions
		It is at the end of the session. Moderator has made several probes for "advice" for bakeries. Additional information has *not* been mentioned. The group is not particularly restless but is rather passive.
Moderator:	What about more information? Are any of you interested in bakeries doing more to educate you in terms of what all these things on the labels mean?	Several shrugs, no one speaks.
Moderator:	Would that be of interest to anybody?	Moderator looks around the room at the participants who appear to be thinking about the question.
Doug:	Don't they put their address on it for people who are interested in wanting to know more?	After a pause.
Moderator:	So you wouldn't be interested?	Sylvia and Ann nod, others seem uninterested.
Doug:	It just seems like that most people who are interested in knowing more usually write.	A brief pause.
Moderator:	So no one here thinks that would be a good idea?	Most of the group nods.
Doris:	Would it be possible to find out why they don't identify McKenzie Farm bread as being made by Williams? It just says on the label: baked for McKenzie Farm bakery.	Group interest perks up somewhat.
Moderator:	That is a concern to you?	General discussion of private labels follows. Session ends after 10 more minutes.

formal dining rooms were inappropriate for the preparation and consumption of spaghetti.[10]

Focus groups played a major role in the development of Fisher-Price's line of preschool playwear. Group members were mothers with children less than six years of age. The topics discussed were children's clothing and dressing children. The discussions revealed deep dissatisfaction with many of the functional aspects of children's clothing, particularly zippers, buckles, buttons, and other features that made it difficult for children to dress themselves. As one researcher summarized: "Oshkosh overalls are beautifully designed but kids being toilet trained need to be Houdini to get out of them." The new Fisher-Price line has Velcro fasteners, padded knees and elbows, extra-long shirttails, and cuffs that can be lowered as kids grow.[11]

Focus groups are also useful in industrial research. Weyerhaeuser has used such groups to analyze the purchasing process and problems encountered by building contractors. U.S. WEST used them in an analysis of demand for a new property maintenance service for "technologically sophisticated" buildings. This research revealed dramatic differences in the problems and needs confronting managers of public buildings (such as cities and universities) and managers of private buildings (such as IBM).

Advantages of Focus Groups

The interaction process induced by the group situation produces a number of *potential* advantages. Each individual is able to expand and refine their opinions in the interactions with the other members. This process provides more detailed and accurate information than could be derived from each separately.

A group interview situation is generally more exciting and offers more *stimulation* to the participants than a standard depth interview. This heightened interest and excitement make more meaningful comments likely. In addition, the *security* of being in a crowd encourages some members to speak out when they otherwise would not. Because any questions raised by the moderator are to the group as a whole rather than to individuals, the answers contain a degree of *spontaneity* not produced by other techniques. Furthermore, individuals are not under any pressure to "make up" answers to questions.

Focus groups can be used successfully with children over five.[12] They are also very useful with adults in developing countries where literacy rates are low and survey research is difficult.[13]

A final, major advantage of focus groups is that executives often observe the interview (from behind mirrors) or watch films of the interviews. For many executives, this is their only "direct" contact with customers (dealers, suppliers, or whomever the research focuses on). This helps provide a "feel" for the market that is beyond the scope of the more quantitative approaches. Unfortunately, this dramatic impact causes some executives to place too much reliance on focus group results.

Disadvantages of Focus Group Interviews

Given these benefits, it is not surprising that focus group interviews are widely used. However, a number of disadvantages are associated with focus groups. Since focus group interviews last 1.5 to 3 hours and take place at a central location, securing cooperation from a random sample is difficult. Those who attend group interviews and actively participate in them are likely to be different in many respects from those who do not. Participants may "play games" in the group setting, go along with the group rather than express their own opinions, or otherwise provide inaccurate or incomplete information. One vocal person with a strong opinion on the topic being discussed may alter the expressed views of the group substantially. The presence of a one-way mirror and/or an observer(s) has been found to distort participants' responses.[14]

The moderator can introduce serious biases in the interview by shifting topics too rapidly, verbally or nonverbally encouraging certain answers, failing to cover specific areas, and so forth. Focus groups are expensive on a per-respondent basis. Securing a sample, paying the participants, using a central location, and paying trained interviewers and analysts generally cost over $2,000 per group.

The combined effects of potential nonresponse errors, small sample sizes caused by high costs, abnormal behavior by participants, and the potential for interviewer effects makes generalization from a few focus groups to the larger population a risky undertaking. Unfortunately, many researchers and managers do make such generalizations. This tendency to generalize without adequate concern for the potential errors is a serious problem.

Focus groups, although widely used, remain controversial. Chrysler Corporation conducts over 13,000 interviews a year, "many" of which are focus group interviews. In contrast, a research manager of Ford discounts focus groups, claiming that they "generate random, top-of-the-head remarks instead of substantive suggestions and ideas."[15]

Minigroups

Minigroups are focus groups with 4 or 5 respondents rather than the 8 to 12 used in most focus groups. They are used when the issue being investigated requires more extensive probing than is possible in a larger group.

Minigroups do not allow the collection of as confidential or highly sensitive data as might be possible in an individual depth interview. However, they do allow the researcher to obtain substantial depth of response on the topics that are covered. Further, the intimacy of the small group often allows discussion of quite sensitive issues. For example, Predictor, a home pregnancy test marketer, used minigroups, each composed of five women closely matched in terms of age and life cycle, to develop advertising for its product. The minigroups proved as effective as earlier one-on-ones and were more cost-effective.[16]

The advantages and disadvantages of minigroups are similar to those of standard focus groups, but on a smaller scale.

Minigroups: involve 4 or 5 respondents and an interviewer who does not follow a prespecified set of questions that must be asked in a predetermined order but probes and questions as necessary to develop the required data.

Projective Techniques

Projective techniques require individuals to respond to vague or incomplete stimuli. This approach is based on the theory that the description of vague objects requires interpretation, and this interpretation can be based only on the individual's own background, attitudes, and values. The more vague or ambiguous the object to be described, the more one must reveal of oneself to complete the description.

The following general categories of projective techniques are described: *association, completion, construction,* and *expression*. All of these techniques have been adopted from clinical psychology. Marketing researchers have tended to use these techniques out of context and to expect more from them than they were designed to deliver. However, when properly used, projective techniques can provide extremely useful data.[17]

Projective techniques: require individuals to respond to vague, incomplete, or unstructured stimuli.

Association Techniques

Association techniques require the subject to respond to the presentation of a stimulus with the first thing or things that come to mind. The *word association* technique requires the respondent to give the first word or thought that comes to mind after the researcher presents a word or phrase. In *free word association*, only the first word or thought is required. In *successive word association*, the respondent is asked to give a series of words or thoughts that occur after hearing a given word. The respondent is generally read a number of relatively neutral terms to establish the technique. Then the words of interest to the researcher are presented, each separated by several neutral terms. The order of presentation of the key words is randomized to prevent any position or order bias from affecting the results.

The most common approach to analyzing the resulting data is to analyze the frequency with which a particular word or category of word (favorable, unfavorable, neutral) is given in response to the word of interest to the researcher.

Word association techniques are used in testing potential brand names and occasionally for measuring attitudes about particular products, product attributes, brands, packages, or advertisements.

Compton Advertising uses a version of this approach that it refers to as a *benefit chain*. A product, brand, or product description is shown to the respondent, who names all the benefits that possession or use of that product might provide. Then, for each benefit mentioned, the respondent is asked to name two other benefits and for each of these benefits, two more benefits. This continues until the respondent is unable to name additional benefits.

For example, a respondent might mention "fewer colds" as a benefit of taking a daily vitamin. When asked the benefit of fewer colds, one respondent might identify "more efficient at work" and "more energy." Another might name "more skiing" and "fewer problems dating."

A similar approach is to use the terms generated in either a free or successive word association task as the stimulus words in a second round of associations. For example, the term *soap* generates relatively few associations. Among these are *clean* and *fresh*. Clean and fresh, however, generate additional responses such as *free, relaxed, unhindered, nature, country,* and *sensual.*[18] The value of information of this type for product positioning and advertising is apparent.

Completion Techniques

Completion techniques require the respondent to complete an incomplete stimulus. Two types of completion techniques are of interest to marketing researchers—*sentence completion* and *story completion*.

Sentence completion, as the name implies, requires the respondent to complete a sentence. To some extent, it merely rephrases an open-ended question. For example, "What kind of people prefer filter cigarettes?" and "People who prefer filter cigarettes are _____" represent two approaches to the same information. However, in direct questioning, respondents are giving *their* answers. In most sentence-completion tests, the respondents are asked to complete the sentence with *a* phrase. Generally they are told to use the first thought that comes to mind or "anything that makes sense." Because the individual is not required directly to associate himself or herself with the answer, conscious and subconscious defenses are more likely to be relaxed and allow a more revealing answer. A study of smokers obtained the following results using direct questioning and sentence completion:

> The majority gave responses [to direct questions] such as, "Pleasure is more important than health," "Moderation is OK," "I like to smoke." One gets the impression that smokers are not dissatisfied with their lot. However, in a portion of the study involving sentence-completion tests, smokers responded to the question, "People who never smoke are _____," with comments such as "better off," "happier," "smarter," "wiser, more informed."
>
> To the question, "Teenagers who smoke are _____," smokers responded with, "foolish," "crazy," "uninformed," "stupid," "showing off," "immature," "wrong."[19]

Clearly, the impression one gets from the sentence completion test is that smokers are anxious, uncomfortable, dissonant, and dissatisfied with their habit. This is quite different from the results obtained with the direct question. This finding was further supported in other phases of the study, indicating that it is probably the more valid of the findings.

Story completion is an expanded version of sentence completion. As the name suggests, part of a story is told and the respondent is asked to complete it. In a study on the role of husbands and wives in the purchase of furniture, for example, the respondents could be presented a story that included a visit to a furniture store and a disagreement as to which brand to purchase. The respondents would be asked to complete the story. Because respondents do not know how the people in the story will react, they must create the end of the story based on their own experiences and attitudes.

Consider a manufacturer who introduces a major appliance innovation that generates a great deal of consumer interest but few sales. A story could be created about a couple who were interested in the product but did not purchase it. The respondents would then be asked to complete the story, beginning as the couple were driving home after looking at the product, with one saying to the other: "That widget was nice, but. . . ." This would serve to direct the remainder of the story along the lines of interest to the researcher.

Construction Techniques

Construction techniques require the respondent to produce or construct something, generally a story, dialogue, or description. They are similar to completion techniques, except that less initial structure is provided.

Cartoon techniques present cartoon-type drawings of one or more people in a particular situation. One or more of the individuals are shown with a sentence in bubble form above their heads and one of the others is shown with a blank bubble that the respondent is to "fill in."

Instead of having the bubble show replies or comments, it can be drawn to indicate the unspoken thoughts of one or more of the characters. This device allows the respondent to avoid any restraints that might be felt against having even a cartoon character *speak*, as opposed to *think*, certain thoughts. Research Application 12–3 illustrates both approaches. Other opening phrases could

Construction techniques: require the respondent to construct something, generally a story, dialogue, or description.

RESEARCH APPLICATION 12–3

A Cartoon Technique to Measure Attitudes Toward Macintosh Computers

include such statements as: "My boyfriend bought a new Honda," "The Joneses are building a new swimming pool," "We are thinking about carpeting the living room," and the like. The reply and "unspoken" thoughts of the other person would be supplied by the respondent.

The basic idea in this technique is the same as in other projective techniques. The individual is allowed to project any "subconscious" or socially unacceptable general feelings onto the cartoon character. The analysis is the same as it is for word association and sentence completion.

Third-person techniques allow the respondent to project attitudes onto some vague third person. This third person is generally "an average woman," "your neighbors," "the guys where you work," "most doctors," or the like. Thus, instead of asking the respondent why he or she did something or what he or she thinks about something, the researcher asks what friends, neighbors, or the average person thinks about the issue.

The following quote illustrates the theory and use of this technique:

> Realizing that consumers might not want to admit spending on luxuries when many believe they should be scrimping, BBDO (Batton, Barton, Durstine & Osborne, a large advertising agency) first asked what they thought others were splurging on. The agency believes these figures are more indicative of what respondents were spending themselves than what they said about their own behavior.
>
> For example, 30 percent said they thought others were buying major appliances while only 17 percent said they themselves were. For movies, 29 percent said others were splurging while only 13 percent admitted they themselves were.[20]

A useful version of this technique is to provide a description of a set of an individual's possessions, purchases, or activities and ask the respondents to describe the individual's personality, interests, or other characteristics of interest. The respondent's feelings toward the items on the list will be reflected in the description of the owner. Mason Haire provides a now classic example of the use of this technique. When instant coffee was first introduced, many housewives refused to use the product. When questioned why, the standard response was "It doesn't taste good." Haire, who had taste tests indicating that this was not the case, prepared two brief shopping lists. The lists were identical except that one contained "Nescafé instant coffee" and the other "Maxwell House coffee (drip grind)." One group of 100 women was given one list and a second group received the second list. Each woman was asked to "write a brief description of the personality and character" of the woman who would purchase the set of items on the list.

The differences in the descriptions provided by the two lists (which differed only in the type of coffee) were both striking and revealing. The hypothetical woman whose shopping list contained drip grind coffee was described as being more or less average. In contrast, the woman with instant coffee on her shopping list was characterized as being lazier, more of a spendthrift, and not as good a cook. These responses were more revealing about the women's attitudes toward instant coffee than the "I don't like the taste" response generated by direct questions.[21]

Picture response, another useful construction technique, involves using pictures to elicit stories. These pictures are usually relatively vague, so that the respondent must use his or her imagination to describe what is occurring.

Fantasy scenarios require the respondents to make up a fantasy about the product or brand.[22] For example, they might be asked to imagine that they are at a reunion of various brands of beer. They might be asked to "describe each beer in terms of its 'occupation,' physical characteristics (athletic, pretty, tall, intelligent, etc.), recent adventures, family status, future plans and concerns, and its behavior during the reunion."

Personification asks the respondents to create a personality for the products or brands. One approach is to "name the best spokesperson for _____." Another is to "tell us what animal _____ would be if it were an animal." Or respondents could be asked to "describe the personality would have if it were a person."[23]

RESEARCH APPLICATION 12–4

Perceived Cake-Mix Customers

SOURCE: Illustration by McCann-Erickson Worldwide, Inc. Used with permission.

McCann-Erickson, a major advertising agency, has asked consumers to write obituaries for various companies. They also have interviewees draw likely buyers of competing brands. In one study, consumers consistently portrayed Pillsbury customers as "grandmotherly" types and Duncan Hines purchasers as svelte, contemporary women (see Research Application 12–4).[24]

Expressive Techniques

Role playing: requires the respondent to assume the behavior of another person or even an object such as a brand in a particular situation.

Role playing is the only expressive technique used to any extent by marketing researchers. In **role playing,** the consumer is asked to *assume the role or behavior of an object or another person,* such as a sales representative for a particular department store. The role-playing customer can then be asked to try to sell a given product to a number of different "consumers" who raise varying objections. The means by which the role player attempts to overcome these objections can reveal a great deal about his or her attitudes. Another version of the technique involves studying the role player's approach to shoppers from various social class backgrounds. This could reveal the role player's attitudes on what type of people "should" shop at the store in question. Research Application 12–5 describes an example of role playing.

Problems and Promise of Projective Techniques

As projective techniques generally require personal interviews with highly trained interviewers and interpreters to evaluate the responses, they tend to be very expensive. This, in turn, has led to small sample sizes, which increase

RESEARCH APPLICATION 12–5

Psychological Motivations, Inc., Use of Role Playing in a Focus Group Context

Problem

Schenley has a premium brand of Canadian Whiskey called O.F.C. whose sales were considerably below par. Past marketing efforts for O.F.C. were generally unsuccessful or short-lived. The client gave us the open-ended assignment: "See what you can recommend."

Approach and Results

We conducted a series of focus group sessions among people who consumed at least three drinks of Canadian whiskey per week. During the sessions we asked a volunteer to role play a bottle of O.F.C. Canadian Whiskey. After the initial laughter and disclaimers ("I'm a person and not a bottle of booze") the volunteer settled into the task. We handed him a bottle of O.F.C. to help him along.

Starting from the very general, we asked the gentleman what his name was. "Pastor Bushman," he replied. Our moderator reminded him that he was role playing. "Excuse me," he said, "My name is O.F.C." From there the discussion proceeded.

Eventually, we asked our bottle of O.F.C. to tell us what his fears were. He confided that he was afraid no one liked him; that no one could really get to know him, since he did not have a name.

The role play continued and, after awhile, we asked our bottle of O.F.C. to tell us what he would like to have most. He quickly responded, "A *real* name."

We then observed that this participant was closely examining the O.F.C. bottle in his hand. We asked, "What are you thinking about?" He explained, "I see this product is both distilled and bottled in Valley Rand, Canada. That's the French Canadian area of Quebec. Why not call the product 'French Canadian?' You know, like 'Canadian Club?' " Our moderator probed further: "And what do we do with the 'O'?" "Use it; call it '*Old* French Canadian!' "

We played this back to several other groups and observed that it immediately caught on. The client and its agency likewise recognized the potential.

Today, O.F.C. is being test marketed as Old French Canadian. The results, thus far, are encouraging.

SOURCE: Supplied by Dr. H. Clarke Noyes, Psychological Motivations Incorporated, Dobbs Ferry, New York. Used with permission.

---

the probability of substantial sampling error. Furthermore, the reliance on small samples often has been accompanied by nonprobability selection procedures. Thus, selection error is also likely to be present. These potential errors are not an integral aspect of the technique. They have become associated with projective techniques because of the costs and the predispositions of some of the practitioners, not because of the techniques themselves. These problems can be minimized with proper sampling.

Nonresponse is more serious. Some of the projective techniques require the respondents to engage in behavior that may well seem strange to them. This is particularly true for techniques such as role playing. It is therefore reasonable to assume that those who agree to participate differ in a number of ways from those who refuse to participate. This is a strong argument for testing the

RESEARCH APPLICATION 12–6

Using Unfinished Scenarios (Story Completion) in a Focus Group to Develop New Product Concepts

Kane, Bortree & Associates find unfinished scenarios to be a particularly effective technique. A description of an open-ended situation is read aloud to focus group respondents, who complete the story in their own words in writing. Individual answers are then discussed as a group, and specific issues are probed by the moderator.

In an effort to learn about consumers' changing drinking patterns for Seagram's, we used the following unfinished scenario:

> There are so few choices if you want something light, said Liz. I get tired of Perrier but don't want a heavy drink. I wish . . .

Respondents' answers led us to believe that there was a growing desire for a light drink with more taste. Women in particular were bored with the limited selection available, especially white wine and Perrier. Other scenarios were used to explore other pertinent issues, such as the following to explore image:

> Sarah hadn't seen Jane for a long time. She seemed very sophisticated and self-assured these days. At the bar she ordered. . . .

Completions of this scenario by female groups had Jane most often ordering a glass of wine. Women felt that this selection reflected her higher level of knowledge and sophistication.

Based on our learning through these and other scenarios, we developed the concept for a wine-based beverage with a twist of citrus to liven it up. The result: Taylor California Cellar's Chablis with a Twist.

SOURCE: Kane, Bortree & Associates, Inc., New York, New York.

findings generated by projective techniques with other techniques that may permit a more representative sample to be taken.

Measurement error is also a serious issue with respect to projective techniques. The possibility of interpreter bias is obvious. The responses to all except the word association techniques are open-ended. The opportunity for error in attempting to decide what a fairly vague and contradictory story or phrase means is great.

The typical approach to analyzing the responses of all the techniques is to look for common, underlying themes. Each stimulus type (Ford, Plymouth) or respondent group (blue-collar, white-collar) is scored based on the percentage of the respondents who mention the key theme. This can be developed into a relatively efficient and reliable scoring system.

Projective techniques are a valuable and useful marketing research tool. For example, Research Application 12–6 illustrates how Kane, Bortree & Associates, Inc., used unfinished scenarios (story completion) to develop a successful new product concept. As the examples presented indicate, they can help to uncover information not available through direct questioning or observation. They are particularly useful in the exploratory stages of research. They can generate hypotheses for further testing and provide attribute lists and terms for more structured techniques, such as the semantic differential. The results of projective techniques can also be used directly for decision making. However, the techniques are complex and should not be used naïvely.

Summary

Depth interviews and projective techniques, often termed qualitative research, are used when consumers are unable or unwilling to respond to direct, structured questionnaires or the researcher does not have sufficient knowledge to construct such questionnaires. They are widely used in the United States and Europe.

Individual depth interviews typically last 30 to 45 minutes, involve one interviewer and one respondent, and do not follow a prespecified set of questions. Instead, the interviewer probes, creates questions, and generally tries to create the best data possible in light of the issue at hand.

Focus group interviews are based on the same principle but they involve multiple respondents (8 to 12 in the United States) simultaneously. They are generally conducted at a central location such as the research firm's office or a special facility in a shopping mall. They cost less per respondent than individual depth interviews, they offer more stimulation and spontaneity, and the interaction of the participants may generate unique insights. However, they are subject to moderator bias, high nonresponse errors, and domination by one or two individuals. Minigroup interviews are focus group interviews with four or five respondents.

Projective techniques are based on the theory that the description of vague or incomplete stimuli requires interpretation and this interpretation can be based only on the respondent's own background, values, and attitudes. Used properly, projective techniques provide insights into attitudes and values that other approaches cannot reveal. However, they are subject to nonresponse and measurement error and must be used with caution. The four general types of projective techniques are (1) association, (2) completion, (3) construction, and (4) expression.

Review Questions

12.1. Describe each of the following types of *depth interviews,* including appropriate uses and advantages and disadvantages:
  a. one-on-one
  b. minigroup
  c. focus group

12.2. What is *laddering?*

12.3. What is *hidden-issue questioning?*

12.4. What is *symbolic questioning?*

12.5. What are the stages of a focus group interview?

12.6. Describe and give examples of each of the following types of projective techniques:
  a. association
  b. completion
  c. construction
  d. expression

12.7. How does *free word association* differ from *successive word association?*

12.8. How does a *cartoon* technique differ from a *picture-response* technique?

12.9. How do *third-person* techniques differ from *sentence-completion* techniques? How are these different from *fantasy scenarios?*

12.10. What is *role playing?*

Discussion Questions/Problems

12.11. Develop a projective technique to determine students' attitudes toward
   a. cheating on exams
   b. exercise
   c. drinking and driving
   d. United Way contributions
   e. Porsche automobile
   f. Japan

12.12. Under what conditions would individual depth interviews be more appropriate than projective techniques? less appropriate? Under what conditions should both be used?

12.13. Evaluate the procedure used in Research Application 12–1.

12.14. What conclusions does Research Application 12–2 suggest?

12.15. Evaluate the procedure described in Research Application 12–5.

12.16. What techniques would you use to help develop a campaign to reduce "unsafe sex" by college students? Why would you choose these methods?

12.17. Would your answer to 12.16 change if the target audience were (a) young blue-collar workers or (b) professions such as doctors, lawyers, and managers? Why?

12.18. Would minigroups or individual depth interviews provide better data on college students' attitudes toward _____? Why?
   a. cheating on exams
   b. Japan
   c. United Way contributions
   d. drinking and driving

12.19. What ethical issues are involved in using projective techniques? How would you resolve these issues?

Projects/Activities

12.20. Select an item from the list below. Administer each of the following techniques to five fellow students (different students for each technique) to develop an idea of their feelings toward the selected item: (a) successive word association, (b) sentence or story completion, (c) cartoon, and (d) third person. Report your results and conclusions.
   a. imported beer
   b. pork

  c. *60 Minutes*
  d. ecologists
  e. Catholic church
  f. accountants

12.21. Complete 12.11 using a sample of 10 students. Report your results and conclusions.

12.22. Complete 12.16 using a sample of 10 students. Report your results and conclusions.

12.23. Complete 12.18 using a sample of 10 students. Report your results and conclusions.

Notes

1. For a discussion of the issues surrounding qualitative research see D. T. Seymour, *Marketing Research: Qualitative Methods for the Marketing Professional* (Probus Publishing Co., 1988); J. Colwell, "Qualitative Market Research," *Journal of the Market Research Society* (January 1990), 13–36; W. Sykes, "Validity and Reliability in Qualitative Market Research," *Journal of the Market Research Society* (July 1990), 289–328; C. Gabriel, "The Validity of Qualitative Market Research," *Journal of the Market Research Society* (October 1990), 507–520; and W. Sykes, "Taking Stock"; M. Warren, "Another Day, Another Debrief"; L. F. Collins, "Everything Is True"; and S. Wells, "Wet Towels"; all in *Journal of the Market Research Society* (January 1991).

2. P. Cooper, "Comparison Between the UK and US," *Journal of the Market Research Society* (October 1989), 509–520.

3. J. T. Durgee, "Depth-Interview Techniques for Creative Advertising," *Journal of Advertising Research* (December 1985), 29–37.

4. J. T. Plummer, "Emotions Important for Successful Advertising," *Marketing News* (April 12, 1985), 18.

5. J. Langer, "Story Time Is Alternate Research Technique," *Marketing News* (September 13, 1985), 19.

6. M. S. Payne, "Individual In-Depth Interviews Can Provide More Details than Groups," *Marketing Today* (Elrick and Lavidge, 1982).

7. See S. Griggs, "Analyzing Qualitative Data," *Journal of Market Research Society* (January 1987), 15–34; C. J. Fedder, "Listening to Qualitative Research," *Journal of Advertising Research* (December 1985), 57–59; and R. M. Bolton, T. M. Bronkhorst, "Quantitative Analyses of Depth Interviews," *Psychology and Marketing* (Winter 1991), 275–298.

8. Cooper, op. cit.

9. See also J. Durgee, "New Product Ideas from Focus Groups," *Journal of Consumer Marketing* (Fall 1987), 57–65; and "Special Issue on Focus Groups," *Marketing News* (May 27, 1991).

10. "How an Agency Lifted Its Admakers' Creativity," *Business Week* (November 30, 1981), 114.

11. R. Alsop, "Fisher-Price Banks on Name," *Wall Street Journal* (August 2, 1984), 23.

12. W. J. McDonald, "Approaches to Group Research with Children," *Journal of the Academy of Marketing Science* (Fall 1982), 490–499.

13. M. Goodyear, "Qualitative Research in Developing Countries," *Journal of the Market Research Society* (April 1982), 86–96.

14. D. Checkman, "Focus Group Research as Theater," *Marketing Research* (December 1989), 33–40; and S. Robson, J. Wardle, "Who's Watching Whom?" *Journal of the Market Research Society* (July 1988), 333–359.

15. "Panelists Provide a Glimpse of Automotive Marketing Research," *Marketing News* (September 30, 1983), 3.

16. H. Mulholland, "Advertising Home Pregnancy Tests," *European Research* (November 1987), 242–247.

17. P. Sampson, "Qualitative Research and Motivation Research," in R. M. Worcester, J. Downham, eds., *Consumer Market Research Handbook* (New York: North Holland, 1986), 29–55; E. Day, "Share of Heart," *Journal of Consumer Marketing* (Winter 1989), 5–12; and J. F. Durgee, "Qualitative Methods," *Journal of Consumer Marketing* (Winter 1990), 15–21.

18. Langer, op. cit., 24. See also L. L. Golden, M. I. Alpert, J. F. Betak, "Psychological Meaning," *Psychology and Marketing* (Spring 1989), 33–50; and M. D. Reilly, "Free Elicitation of Descriptive Adjectives for Tourism Image Assessment," *Journal of Travel Research* (Spring 1990), 21–26.

19. H. H. Kassarjian, "Projective Methods," in R. Ferber, *Handbook of Marketing Research* (New York: McGraw-Hill Book Company, 1974), 3·85–3·100.

20. N. Giges, "Inflation Doesn't Deflate Luxury Spending," *Advertising Age* (January 23, 1980), 1.

21. M. Haire, "Projective Techniques in Marketing Research," *Journal of Marketing* (April 1950), 649–656; see also C. Anderson, "The Validity of Haire's Shopping List Projective Technique," *Journal of Marketing Research* (November 1978), 644–649.

22. Day, op. cit.

23. Ibid.

24. A. Miller, D. Tsiantar, "Psyching Out Consumers," *Newsweek* (February 27, 1989), 46–47.

13

Observation and Physiological Measures

LEARNING OBJECTIVES

Upon completing this chapter, you should be able to:

1. Explain when observational techniques should be used.

2. Describe the five basic dimensions along which observational approaches can vary.

3. Explain marketing ethnography.

4. Describe brain-wave analysis.

5. Indicate how brain-wave analysis uses hemispheral lateralization.

6. Describe eye tracking and list a number of applications for this methodology.

Clairol's Use of Observation in the Development of Small Miracle Hair Conditioner

The Park Avenue offices of the Clairol Products division of Bristol-Myers house something called the Consumer Research Forum, a test salon at which Clairol tries out all kinds of hair-care items on women volunteers.

Staffers watch the women through a one-way mirror as they shampoo, condition, or color their hair with Bristol-Myers' and competing products. The volunteers, who realize they are testing products, are given a free hair styling for their help.

In return, the company gets some idea of how consumers react to products and learns whether they understand and correctly follow label directions. It sometimes also obtains "verbatims," or favorable comments from the volunteers that can be used in advertising.

An observational study in this facility of women using the hair conditioner *Small Miracle* prior to its introduction predicted failure. The observers noticed that it caused fine, thin hair to stick together. Standard research, including an in-home use test by more than 1,000 women, did not uncover this weakness. Despite the warning from the observational study, *Small Miracle* was introduced and became a commercial failure.[1]

This example indicates the potential value of observation of consumers' behaviors. Monitoring individual's physiological changes, a specialized type of observation, offers equally valuable insights. Both of these approaches are described in this chapter.

Observation

Observation:
a data collection technique in which the situation of interest is watched according to prespecified rules based on a stated objective.

A British ice cream manufacturer was concerned that sales of some of its products in neighborhood shops were not achieving the levels that had been expected from children's enthusiasm for these products as measured through interviews. A direct-observation study in a sample of shops revealed why. The ice cream was kept in top-loading refrigerators with sides that were so high that many of the children could not see in to pick out the products they wanted. Nor did the young children ask for the product by name. A picture display was devised for the side of the cabinet to enable the children to recognize each product and to indicate their choice by pointing to it. Sales increased substantially.[2]

The purpose of this section is to describe **observation** and the conditions under which it should be used.

Conditions for Use

Before observation can be used in applied marketing research, three minimum conditions must be met. First, the *data must be accessible* to observation. Motivations, attitudes, and other "internal" conditions cannot be readily observed. However, it is possible to make inferences about attitudes and motivations from behavior that can be observed. For example, facial expressions have been used as an indicator of babies' preferences for various food flavorings.

A second condition is that the *behavior be repetitive, frequent, or otherwise predictable*. Although it is possible to observe infrequent, unpredictable occurrences, the amount of time that would have to be spent waiting would be excessive for most purposes.

Finally, an *event must cover a reasonably short time span*. To observe the entire decision-making process that a couple might go through as it considers purchasing a new home could easily take months, if not years. The time and monetary costs associated with this are beyond the value of most applied studies. Thus, we are usually restricted to observing activities that can be completed in a relatively short time span or to observing phases, such as store visits, of activities with a longer time span.

Reasons for Preferring Observational Data

The fact that a given type of data *can* be gathered by observational techniques does not imply that it *should* be gathered by such techniques. There are two conditions under which observational techniques are preferred over alternative methods. In some cases, *observation is the only technique that can be used to collect accurate information*. Two of the most obvious examples are food or toy

RESEARCH APPLICATION 13–1

Requirements for an Observational Study of Child-Resistant Packaging

(1) Use 200 children between the ages of 42 and 51 months inclusive, evenly distributed by age and sex, to test the ability of the special packaging to resist opening by children. The even age distribution shall be determined by having 20 children (plus or minus 10 percent) whose nearest age is 42 months, 20 whose nearest age is 43 months, 20 at 44 months, etc., up to and including 20 at 51 months of age. There should be no more than a 10 percent preponderance of either sex in each age group. The children selected should be healthy and normal and should have no obvious physical or mental handicap.

(2) The children shall be divided into groups of two each. The testing shall be done in a location that is familiar to the children; for example, their customary nursery school or regular kindergarten. No child shall test more than two special packages, and each package shall be of a different type. For each test, the paired children shall receive the same special packaging simultaneously. When more than one special packaging is being tested, they shall be presented to the paired children in random order, and this order shall be recorded. The special packaging, each test unit of which, if appropriate, has previously been opened and properly resecured by the tester, shall be given to each of the two children with a request for them to open it. Each child shall be allowed up to 5 minutes to open the special packaging. For those children unable to open the special packaging after the first 5 minutes, a single visual demonstration, without verbal explanation, shall be given by the demonstrator. A second 5 minutes shall then be allowed for opening the special packaging. If a child fails to use his teeth to open the special packaging during the first 5 minutes, the demonstrator shall instruct him, before the start of the second 5-minute period, that he is permitted to use his teeth if he wishes.

SOURCE: Consumer Product Safety Commission, "1700.20 Testing Procedure for Special Packaging," *Title 16-Commercial Practices*, updated, 580–581.

preferences among children who cannot yet talk and pet food preferences. Research Application 13–1 describes the federally mandated observational study required for child-resistant packaging.

At times people are not aware of, cannot remember, or will not admit to certain behaviors. For example, many retailers monitor their competitors' prices and advertising efforts. In this way, they can remain informed despite the fact that the competitors would not voluntarily supply them with this information.

A study of the influence of various family members in purchase decisions found that children were rarely described as influential in verbal reports. However, observational studies found that most of the children had a substantial level of influence.[3]

Observational studies of garbage have found that individuals tend to underreport consumption of "negative" product such as beer.[4] Thus, observational studies can sometimes provide more accurate data than other methods.

In fact, the Advertising Research Foundation used observational data as the baseline for evaluating various self-report measures of ad readership.[5]

The second reason for preferring observational data is that in some situations the *relationship between the accuracy of the data and the cost of the data is more favorable for observation than for other techniques.* For example, traffic counts, both of in-store and external traffic, can often be made by means of observational techniques more accurately and for less expense than some other technique such as a survey.

Observing the general public or competitors without their knowledge and consent raises serious ethical questions (see Chapter 20). In the authors' opinion, observation of *public* behaviors for which individuals would expect to be subject to at least casual observation is acceptable if it does not harm those observed in any way and if anonymity is protected. However, others feel strongly that individuals should not be systematically observed in any environment without their prior consent.[6]

Types of Observational Approaches

Observational approaches can vary along five basic dimensions: (1) *natural or contrived situation,* (2) *open or disguised observation,* (3) *structured or unstructured observation,* (4) *direct or indirect observation,* and (5) *human or mechanical observers.* These five dimensions are not dichotomous; they represent continuums. That is, a situation is more or less natural, and more or less open, rather than being natural *or* contrived, open *or* disguised.

Natural Versus Contrived Situation

The researcher who sits near the entrance to a restaurant and notes how many couples, groups of couples, or families of various sizes enter during specified time periods is operating in a natural situation. Nothing has been done to encourage or restrain people from entering. It is likely that those entering the restaurant view the situation as being natural in every way.

Unfortunately, many behaviors that a researcher might like to observe occur so seldom or under such specialized conditions that it is impractical for the researcher to attempt to observe them in the natural state. Research Application 13–2 provides an example of a contrived situation, in which the "applicant" was a trained observer with no intention of opening an account at the bank. This is a widely used research technique in the retailing area that is known as *service shopping* or *mystery shopper* programs.

In mystery shopper programs, the respondent is unlikely to notice the contrived nature of the study. At other times, the research objective requires a contrived situation that is completely obvious. For example, a researcher might need to control precisely the length of time a message designed for a billboard is shown to a respondent. A common approach requires the respondent to look into a rather large machine (a tachistoscope) while the "billboard" is shown. This is a contrived situation that would be noticeable to the respondent. Research Application 13–3 describes an obviously contrived situation.

RESEARCH APPLICATION 13–2

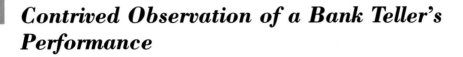

Contrived Observation of a Bank Teller's Performance

Bank: Competitor B
Location: Cranston   *Time:*   10:20 A.M.
Clerk: Mrs. L.   *Account:*   Savings

I entered the bank and approached a teller, Miss I., and asked who I would see to find out about a savings account. She said I should see Mrs. L., indicating her. Mrs. L. had a customer at her desk, so the teller suggested I have a seat and wait. She said, "There's a pamphlet on savings accounts on the rack over there you might like to look over while you're waiting." I thanked her, took a pamphlet, and sat down. After about two minutes Mrs. L. was free and I told her I was interested in a savings account. She took out a pamphlet and said, "I see you have one of these; maybe it would be best if we go through it together." She then went over each type of savings plan offered, adding comments on each that were not in the brochure. She told me I could save by

mail or come in to the office and gave me their hours. She also mentioned that if I had a checking account I could have money saved automatically. I said I did not have a checking account, so she went over them fully, giving me literature. At the end she said, "We're a full service bank—we have loans, safe deposit boxes, even a credit card!" I had already told her I wouldn't be opening anything "until payday." She said, "Right over where you got that first brochure, we have literature on all our services; why don't you take one of each and look them over, and come back and see me on payday?"

Mrs. L. was extremely knowledgeable, well organized, and very pleasant.

SOURCE: *Specialized Marketing Services for the Banking Industry.* A special report by Bank Marketing Group, a division of Sheldon Spencer Associates, Inc., Warwick, Rhode Island. Used with permission.

Open Versus Disguised Observation

The example presented in Research Application 13–2 was basically a disguised approach. Had the teller known she was under observation, she would probably have altered her behavior in some manner. One-way mirrors, observers dressed as stock clerks, and hidden cameras are a few of many ways used to prevent respondents from becoming aware that they are being observed.

It is not always possible or desirable to prevent the respondent from being aware of the observer. Our opening example described an open observation system used by Bristol-Myers.

The known presence of an observer offers the same potential for error as the presence of an interviewer in survey research. The magnitude of observer effects is probably closely related to how obvious the observer is to the subject. Therefore, it seems wise always to minimize the presence of the observer to the extent possible. Notice that this was done in our opening example, even though the women knew that they were being observed. Likewise, the respondents in Research Application 13–3 were not aware that their commercial viewing was being recorded.

RESEARCH APPLICATION 13–3

Observation of Television Commercial Viewing

The Pretesting Company maintains a "Simulated Network" facility in 64 shopping-mall locations as well as portable versions. The firm inserts test commercials (usually two versions for each test) into videotapes of actual network TV programs. Subjects are recruited to match the client's target market and are told they are to evaluate TV programs.

The participants watch a standard television set for 25–30 minutes. Each respondent has a remote-control changer and can switch channels, and thus avoid commercials, at will. The test commercials are shown twice, at 12-minute intervals. A computer ensures that each respondent is exposed to each test commercial and records if the commercial is viewed or not. A variety of before and after measures of attitude, purchase intention, and brand and commercial liking are made.

While the technique is used primarily for proprietary commercial testing, a number of general findings have begun to emerge. For example, "forced exposure" testing of commercials in focus group settings often produces high scores for fact based, hard data commercials. However, these same commercials are frequently "zapped" in the more realistic "Simulated Network."

SOURCE: The Pretesting Company Inc., Englewood, NJ. Used with permission

Structured Versus Unstructured Observation

In structured observation, the observer knows in advance precisely which aspects of the situation are to be observed or recorded. All other behaviors are to be "ignored." Research Application 13–4 provides an example of part of a form for use in a structured observation.

Highly structured observations typically require a considerable amount of inference on the part of the observer. For example, in Research Application 13–4 the observer is required to note whether the teller is well groomed. This is a judgment task that is influenced by personal tastes. However, well-trained observers can achieve a high degree of agreement as to the category in which a given individual should be placed.

Completely unstructured observation places no restriction on what the observer should note. Thus, an observer for a department store might be told to mingle with the shoppers and notice whatever seems relevant. Completely unstructured observation is often useful in exploratory research.

Direct Versus Indirect Observation

We can generally observe current behavior directly. That is, if we are interested in purchasing behavior, we can observe people actually making purchases. Most of the examples described so far have focused on direct observation. However, to observe other types of behavior, such as past behavior, we must turn to some record of the behavior or indirect observation. That is, we must observe the effects or results of the behavior rather than the behavior itself.

RESEARCH APPLICATION 13-4

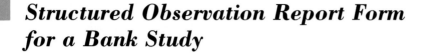

Structured Observation Report Form for a Bank Study

Bank _____   Date _____

Location _____   Time _____

Teller _____   Transaction _____

Appearance
Well groomed   Yes _____ No _____

Behavior
Chewing gum or eating _____
Smoking _____
Personal conversations:
   with customer _____
   with other employees _____
   on telephone _____
Other poor behavior _____

Window
Nameplate visible   Yes _____ No _____
Loose cash or checks   Yes _____ No _____
Cluttered work area   Yes _____ No _____
Personal belongings visible   Yes _____ No _____

Transactions (General)
Waited on immediately   Yes _____ No _____
  If no, waited (_____) minutes
   presence acknowledged   Yes _____ No _____
   teller was:
     helping customer _____
     talking with employee:
       business _____
       personal _____
     working:
       at station _____
       at back counter _____
       at drive-in window _____
     other _____

SOURCE: Specialized Marketing Services for the Banking Industry. A special report by Bank Marketing Group, a division of Sheldon Spencer Associates, Inc., Warwick, Rhode Island. Used with permission.

One type of indirect observation involves *physical traces.* Physical traces are physical evidence of past behavior, such as empty packages. Analysis of garbage from various areas of a community has been used to infer consumption of a variety of products.

Another use of physical traces is known as the *pantry audit.* In a pantry audit, respondents' homes are examined (with the owners' permission) for the presence and quantity of prespecified items. The basic assumption of this approach is that possession is related to purchase and/or usage. Unfortunately, this is often a tenuous assumption. For example, one of the authors has had a bottle of Ouzo (a Greek liqueur) in his pantry for several years, and it is likely to remain there for several more. To infer that this product is liked or consumed because of its presence would be incorrect.

Human Versus Mechanical Observations

Most of the examples and discussions thus far have emphasized human observers. However, it is sometimes both possible and desirable to replace the human observer with some form of mechanical observer. This may be done for accuracy, cost, or functional reasons.

Traffic counts of automobiles can generally be performed more accurately and for less expense by machine than by human observers. Even these machines are subject to some error. One of the authors remembers being in a group, as a teenager, that took great delight in finding traffic counters and driving back and forth across them. Research Application 13–5 illustrates the use of a videocamera to increase the accuracy of observations of children's reactions to a television commercial.

An electric utility group found that fuel-use projections based in part on survey research reports of where people set their home-heating thermostats were not sufficiently accurate. A research firm focused unobtrusive video cameras on the thermostats in 150 homes. The findings were quite revealing:

> People might say they kept the things at 68 degrees, but it turned out that they fiddled with them all day. Older relatives and kids—especially teenagers—tended to turn them up, and so did cleaning ladies. Even visitors did it. In a lot of homes, it was guerrilla warfare over the thermostat between the person who paid the bill and everyone else.[7]

Time-lapse photography is proving very useful in analyzing in-store traffic flows and the effect of point-of-purchase displays. In addition, measures of physiological reactions to advertisements, package designs, and the like rely on mechanical observers that can "observe" or measure changes which are beyond the capabilities of human observers. These physiological measures have become so important in marketing research that the next major section of this chapter is devoted to them.

Conclusions on Observational Studies

Relatively structured observational studies have become increasingly popular. Toyota recently sent observers to Cadillac, Mercedes, and BMW showrooms to watch customers inspect cars. They also noted how they dressed, what questions they asked, whether they appeared timid or confident, and so

An Observational Study of Children's Responses to Three Competing Television Commercials

Three commercials based on three different cartoon characters were to be tested. Each child was exposed to only one of the new characters. The children were 6 to 11 years old. The sample was 150 per commercial.

The purpose of the test was camouflaged. Children came in to watch a show. Viewing was done in groups of six at a time. They saw a 10-minute cartoon with two commercial breaks. The test commercial played in the middle position of both breaks. It was shown twice because we have found that children's reactions to a commercial often shift on second exposure. It was inserted in naturalistic clutter because that is the context in which commercials are viewed at home.

The layout of the room was standardized. Chair placement, set size, and set placement matched the previous copytests we have done on children's commercials. A low-level distractor (a random sequence of slides playing on an adjacent screen) was provided to give the children something else to look at if their interest faded. Commercials have to compete with simultaneous distractions in the real world, so we provide simultaneous distractions in our test.

While the children sat and watched the shows, a videocamera recorded their faces. Subsequent analysis of the videotapes let us calculate the percent of children actually looking at the commercials every two seconds during their first and second exposure.

After the viewing session, the children were given one-on-one interviews. A picture-based brand choice item showed them six different snacks and had them mark all the ones they wanted. It turned out that viewers of Commercial A were most likely to choose the test brand. Open-ended questions got children to reconstruct what they remembered from the commercial, and explored what they thought it said about the product. Later questions got children to rate the commercial, the various characters, and some key attributes of the product. The latter ratings all asked for binary judgments: Is it sweet? Yes/no/not sure, etc. Children do not generally perceive qualities in a dimensional fashion. A product either has a property or it does not. By concentrating on yes/no's, we find that interviewing goes much faster and more pleasurably with young children, and we feel secure that it more accurately reflects the thinking they actually do in the real world, where children are anything but slow, deliberative, and measured.

In this study, the most actionable findings came from the attention data. Comparing the executions, we were able to establish that the commercial featuring Character A significantly outpulled the others. A check of the norms showed that it did very well indeed—and it did so by holding on to older children, who often lose interest in animated characters. By examining the attention on a moment-to-moment basis, we were able to confirm that the character was strong. There was a tendency for interest to peak every time the character was actively involved in the plot—even on second exposure.

There were two spots where attention fell. One was where the screen portrayed one thing while the sound-track talked about something else—a problem that frequently afflicts animatics and would be straightened out in a finished production. The other drop-off came when the scene cut abruptly to a new setting with a new secondary character. Viewers appeared to have gotten disoriented, and some of them just turned away. This problem required some rewriting to solve.

SOURCE: L. Rust, C. Hyatt, "Qualitative and Quantitative Approaches to Child Research," in R. H. Holman, M. R. Solomon, eds., *Advances in Consumer Research, XVIII* (Provo, UT: Association for Consumer Research, 1991), 21–22.

RESEARCH APPLICATION 13-6

Do-House Research in Japan

Do-House is a Japanese research firm that specializes in consumer goods studies. The firm has 660 *Do-sans*, housewives who serve as interviewers and analysts. A typical consumer product study is conducted by five or six *Do-sans*. Each *Do-san* will host a party inviting five or six housewives. The party will involve the product under study. For example, they may prepare a meal using a food product that is being evaluated. The *Do-sans* pay close attention to their guest's comments and behaviors concerning the product in question. After the party, all the *Do-sans* who hosted a party for a given product meet and analyze the relevant behaviors and comments. The results of their analysis and their recommendations are sent to the sponsoring firm.

SOURCE: K. Katori, "Recent Developments and Future Trends in Marketing Research in Japan Using New Electronic Media," *Journal of Advertising Research* (April/May 1990), 56.

---

forth. Saatchi & Saatchi, a major advertising agency, reports that it uses observational studies for every one of its major clients.[8]

In addition to the types of studies we have described, a combination observation/depth interview study is gaining increasing acceptance. **Marketing ethnography** involves openly observing consumers engaged in an activity and questioning them about that activity after having established rapport with them. Once rapport is established, respondents will hopefully act naturally in front of the observer and explain their actions truthfully. The following example illustrates this approach.

Marketing ethnography: involves openly observing consumers engaged in an activity and questioning about that activity after having established rapport with them.

> Researchers for Breyers Ice Cream spent time with six families at their homes. They photographed people lounging in their favorite chairs and eating ice cream. They looked in freezers, inspected bowls and utensils, and watched as people added various toppings to the ice cream. One woman described how she likes to dim the lights and turn on the stereo before having a bowl of ice cream. The result: "We learned about people's emotional response to ice cream and found that it is a very sensual, inner-directed experience. Hopefully, this will guide the agency in developing more effective advertisings."[9]

Research Application 13-6 describes a Japanese version of this approach.

Physiological Measures

Physiological measures are direct observations of physical responses to a stimulus such as an advertisement. These responses may be controllable, as are eye movements, or uncontrollable, as the galvanic skin response. Physiological measures are used for the same reasons that other observations are used: to obtain more accurate or more economical data. Since physiological measures generally cost more than verbal reports, they are used when it is felt that respondents cannot or will not provide accurate verbal responses.[10]

Brain-Wave Analysis

The human brain emits a number of electrical "signals" that can be monitored. Some of the signals reflect the level of interest the respondent has in whatever stimulus he or she is confronted with.[11] Thus, **brain wave analysis** may indicate a respondent's interest in a commercial, package, or product. By carefully controlling which aspects of the commercial or package are shown, the researcher can measure interest in the components of the stimulus.

Both the left and the right hemispheres of the brain produce brain waves. The level of brain waves being emitted by each side indicates how actively involved that side of the brain is with the stimulus at hand. This is useful to the marketing researcher because of **hemispheral lateralization**—the fact that the left hemisphere of the brain deals with verbal, sequential, and rational activities while the right side of the brain specializes in pictorial, time free, and emotional responses. Much of the activity of the right brain is not "available" to the individual for verbal reporting.

Brain-wave analysis offers the potential of evaluating the interest generated by a commercial or package and the nature—emotional or rational—of that interest. A consulting firm in this area, Neuro-Communication Research Laboratories, breaks commercials down into five-second "epochs." The degree of right and left hemisphere activity is recorded for each epoch. Research Application 13–7 shows the brain-wave patterns elicited by an award-winning commercial. The first 20 seconds (epochs 1–4) presented a problem. The left (analytical) hemisphere was actively seeking solutions during this portion of the commercial. The solution to the problem (a brand) was presented in epoch 5. This produced a strong right-hemisphere or emotional response. The final epoch presented brand information that elicited a high level of left-brain, or rational, processing.

One weakness of brain-wave research is the artificial environment in which the measurements take place. These studies are generally conducted in a research laboratory and involve a forced exposure to the advertisement or package while the respondent is literally wired to a machine. An individual may respond differently in the hectic environment of the supermarket than he or she would in a quiet research facility. Of course, any technique short of test marketing suffers from this problem to some degree.

Eye Tracking

Eye tracking is the use of computer/video technology to record movements of the eye in relation to a stimulus, such as a package or commercial.[12] This allows the determination of the order and amount of time an individual spends looking at the various parts of an advertisement or package, or which of two competing stimuli receives the most attention.

The procedure involves the respondent sitting in a chair and reading magazines, observing television commercials or slides of print advertisements, billboards, packages, shelf facings, point-of-purchase displays, and the like. For all except television commercials and billboard tests, the respondents

Physiological measures: are direct observations of physical responses to a stimulus.

Brain wave analysis: monitoring electrical impulses emitted by the brain to ascertain the level and nature of a respondent's interest in a stimulus.

Hemispheral laterization: the left hemisphere of the brain focuses on verbal, sequential, rational activities and the right hemisphere specializes in pictorial, time free, and emotional responses.

Eye tracking: uses computer and video technology to record the focal point of one's eyes relative to a stimulus object over time.

RESEARCH APPLICATION 13–7

Brain-Wave Activity and Television Commercial Evaluation

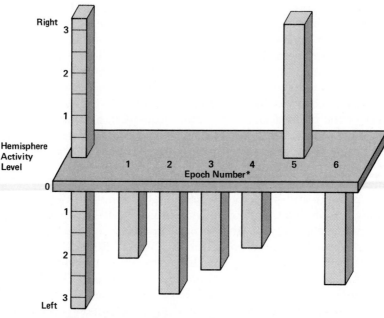

*5-second segments of the commercial.

SOURCE: S. Weinstein, "Advances in Brain Wave Analysis Allow Researchers to Test Effectiveness of Ads," *Marketing News* (September 17, 1982), 22.

control how long they view each scene. An eye-tracking device sends an undetectable beam of filtered light which is reflected off the respondent's eyes. This reflected beam represents the visual focal point and can be super-imposed on whatever is being viewed. These data are stored in computer memory that allows a complete analysis of the viewing sequence. Portable, inconspicuous equipment is now available, as shown in Research Application 13–8. In Germany, respondents wear a large pair of "goggles" which allows them to sit or stand in a natural manner.

Knowing the time spent on viewing an advertisement or package, the sequence in which it was examined, and which elements were examined has obvious value. For example, Samantha Eggar appeared in a conservative dress in a television commercial for RCA Colortrack. Eye tracking indicated that viewers focused substantial attention on the product. Seventy-two hours later, brand-name recall was 36 percent. In contrast, a similar commercial used Linda Day George dressed in a "revealing" gown. Eye tracking showed

RESEARCH APPLICATION 13-8

The Pretesting Company's People Reader Eye Camera

Used with permission from The Pretesting Company Inc., Englewood, NJ.

that most attention was focused on Ms. George, and subsequent brand name recall was only 9 percent. Similar results were obtained when Catherine Deneuve appeared in a low-cut dress to advertise Lincoln-Mercury.[13]

Research Application 13–9 describes how one firm uses eye tracking to evaluate package designs (Research Application 8–2 described another firm's use of a similar methodology for the same problem). Notice that eye tracking is used in combination with verbal interviews. Eye tracking measures *what* is attended to; it does not measure *why*. Thus, a package could attract attention and still be inappropriate for the product.

Eye tracking has become widely accepted among consumer packaged-good marketers. It is used to evaluate all aspects of advertisements and packages as well as related variables such as ad location within a magazine and on a page. As technological advances continue, eye tracking may become a standard pretest for marketing communications.

RESEARCH APPLICATION 13–9

The Use of Eye Tracking to Evaluate Shelf Impact of Package Designs

Perception Research Services, Inc. (PRS) is a research agency that specializes in the use of physiological measures. A description of its research design using eye cameras to evaluate package changes follows.

1. Test Materials

To simulate a competitive environment for the viewer, PRS uses an actual store for photographing test packages. Packages are photographed in an actual display alongside major competition. Packages are rotated on the shelf so positioning will not bias results. 35-mm slides are used for testing purposes.

2. Sample

PRS recommends that all interviewing be conducted with target market respondents as defined by the advertiser and agency. Interviewing is generally conducted with one hundred (100) participants per package.

3. Research Procedure

Screening. PRS interviewers approach respondents at central location facilities (shopping malls). Screening questions are administered, though care is taken to disguise the nature of the test.

Shelf Impact. The participant is seated at the PRS eye-tracking recorder. He or she views a screen onto which 35-mm slides of the test material will be projected. These slides include a series of in-store displays which simulate a walk through a store. The participant is instructed that she will see a series of displays that she might normally encounter during a shopping trip to a specific outlet, i.e., supermarket, drugstore, liquor store, etc. She controls the viewing time, and is told to take as much or as little time with each scene as desired. Eye movements are recorded for the test scene.

Eye tracking determines precisely what a respondent looks at in a display and in what order she notes the individual packages. More specifically, PRS can report how quickly each brand draws attention, the number of times a consumer looks at a particular package, and the total time she spends with the facings on the shelf.

PRS can evaluate packaging for different brands with the same individual, thus conserving time and cost in maintaining a consistent audience sample from one brand or package to the next.

After the respondent has been exposed to the store walk-through, recall questioning is administered. This provides insight into the ability of the packaging to register brand name.

Package Readability. Respondents are presented close-up pictures of packages including the test design for a time period voluntarily controlled by the participant. Eye movements are tracked to determine the extent to which each element on the package (brand name, product type, illustration, ingredient content, etc.) is noted, the speed of noting, sequence of viewing (i.e., element seen first, second, etc.), incidence of copy readership, and time spent with each element. Importantly, eye tracking documents those elements quickly bypassed or totally overlooked.

Recall questions are administered to determine the saliency of package components.

Verbal Interview. Participants are now shown the actual package or a slide, if prototypes are not available. A comprehensive interview is administered, generally covering the following areas:

Aesthetic Appeal: Does the consumer like the package? Is it pleasant to look at?

RESEARCH APPLICATION 13-9 (continued)

Brand Image Connotations: The kinds of images generated for the product are important.

Functional Characteristics: Most packages do more than identify and promote the product. In use, they protect the product from contamination or damage and provide a convenient means of storing and dispensing.

Likes and Dislikes: Open-ended questioning offers the consumer an opportunity to convey spontaneous reactions to the package and product.

Purchase Interest: Responses to this line of questioning demonstrate degrees of commitment or resistance to product trial.

Product Usage and Demographics: Questioning during the verbal interview typically concludes with specified product usage and demographic information.

SOURCE: E. Young, *Multidimensional Communications Research* (Perception Research Services, Inc., undated), 3. Used with permission.

Other Physiological Measures

A number of other physiological measures are occasionally used by marketing researchers.

The **psychogalvanometer** measures emotional reactions to various stimuli by measuring changes in the rate of perspiration. Because this reaction is beyond the control of the subject, there is no chance for the respondent to deliberately distort the response. Through the use of this device, researchers can determine whether subjects have an emotional reaction to various slogans, brand names, or advertisements. Unfortunately, the machine provides only limited information about the nature of the response and it is seldom used in marketing research.

Walt Wesley Associates, a consulting firm, used psychogalvanometer measurements to determine why one advertisement for V-8 juice was successful, whereas a similar advertisement was not. By testing the response to various elements of the advertisements, the firm found that "the ad with the high emotional punch, the ad which sold cases and cases of V-8, showed only the product display. The weak ads added a drawing of a housewife holding the horn of plenty. The resultant split attention between the woman and the product display killed the appetite appeal of the illustration and the ad died in the market."[14]

> **Psychogalvanometer:** measures emotional responses to a stimulus by measuring changes in the rate of perspiration.

Summary

Observational techniques are used when they are the only means of obtaining the required data or they provide a better relationship between cost and accuracy than do other techniques. In general, observational techniques require that the behavior of interest (1) be accessible to observation, (2) be repetitive, frequent, or predictable, and (3) cover a reasonably short time frame. Observational studies can vary along five basic dimensions: (1) natural/contrived, (2) open/disguised, (3) structured/ unstructured, (4) direct/indirect, and (5) human/mechanical.

Marketing ethnography involves openly observing consumers engaged in an activity and questioning them about that activity after establishing rapport with them.

Physiological measures are direct measures of physical responses to a stimulus. Brain-wave analysis involves monitoring electrical impulses emitted by the brain to ascertain the level and nature of a respondent's interest in a stimulus. It is based in part on hemispheral lateralization—the fact that the left hemisphere of the brain deals with verbal, sequential, and rational activities while the right specializes in pictorial, time free, and emotional responses.

Eye tracking is the use of computer and video technology to record movements of the eye in relation to a stimulus. This allows determination of which aspects of packages, ads, store shelves, and so forth attract the most attention.

The psychogalvanometer measures emotional reactions to various stimuli by measuring changes in the rate of perspiration. It has seen only limited use in marketing research.

Review Questions

13.1. What conditions must be met before *observation* can be used in applied marketing research?

13.2. Under what conditions are observational techniques preferred over other methods?

13.3. Describe each of the following dimensions of an observational study:
   a. natural/contrived situation
   b. open/disguised observation
   c. structured/unstructured observation
   d. direct/indirect observation
   e. human/mechanical observers

13.4. What is *marketing ethnography?*

13.5. Describe *brain-wave analysis* and how it can be of use to marketing managers.

13.6. Describe *eye tracking* and how it can be of use to marketing managers.

13.7. Describe the information provided by the *psychogalvanometer.* Of what value is it to marketing researchers?

Discussion Questions/Problems

13.8. A national retail chain has 900 outlets. The stores are located in all types of neighborhoods and are open from 10:00 A.M. until 9:00 P.M., 6 days per week. Management would like to test reactions to a new point-of-purchase display. The display is large, brightly colored, and has several moving parts. Design an observational study of the display, including details on each of the five dimensions involved in an observational study and other research technique(s), if any, that would be more suitable for this problem.

13.9. Design an observation approach for evaluating the relative effectiveness of the service at two competing banks.

13.10. Will physiological measures become common in marketing research by 2005? Justify your response.

13.11. What advantages would be associated with combining brain-wave analysis and eye tracking?

13.12. If you were manager of _____, what observational studies, if any, would you want to have conducted on a regular basis? on a sporadic basis?
   a. Texaco
   b. Safeway
   c. Apple Computers
   d. Ford Taurus
   e. Domino's Pizza
   f. DuPont solvents

13.13. For what kinds of products is an analysis of garbage likely to be useful? What kinds of errors would you expect to arise in garbage analysis that are not present in self-reports? What kinds of errors would you expect to arise in self-reports that are not present in garbage analysis?

13.14. Compare Research Applications 13–9 and 8–2. Which approach is best? Why?

13.15. Evaluate the procedure in Research Application 13–1.

13.16. Evaluate the procedure in Research Application 13–3.

13.17. Evaluate the form in Research Application 13–4.

13.18. If you were manager of _____, how would you use eye tracking?
   a. Texaco
   b. Safeway
   c. Apple Computers
   d. GTE Phones
   e. Kentucky Fried Chicken
   f. United Way

13.19. What ethical issues are involved in observation studies? What is your position on these issues?

13.20. What problems do you see associated with "marketing ethnography"?

Projects/Activities

13.21. Observe shoppers purchasing _____. What hypotheses or insights have you gained from this observation?
   a. bread
   b. compact disks
   c. bicycles
   d. hamburgers
   e. cereals
   f. wine

13.22. Implement 13.11 and report the results.

13.23. Form a group of three. Develop a form similar to the one in Research Application 13–4 for a store type of interest. Enter the store and observe the same behaviors. Complete the form without discussing it with your colleagues. Explain any differences in your group's responses.

Notes

1. N. Giges, "No Miracle in Small Miracle: Story Behind Clairol Failure," *Advertising Age* (August 16, 1982), 76.

2. J. Richer, "Observation, Ethology and Marketing Research," *European Research* (January 1981), 22.

3. C. K. Atkins, "Observation of Parent–Child Interaction in Supermarket Decision-Making," *Journal of Marketing* (October 1978), 41–45.

4. R. Alsop, "People Watchers Seek Clues to Consumers' True Behavior," *Wall Street Journal* (September 4, 1986), B1.

5. R. L. Lysaker, "The Search for the Gold," speech given at the 37th Annual Advertising Research Foundation Conference (New York: Advertising Research Foundation, 1991).

6. See A. Finn, "Consumer Acceptance of Unobtrusive Observation in a Shopping Center," in P. Bloom, et al., eds., *Enhancing Development in Marketing* (Chicago: American Marketing Association, 1989), 176–181.

7. F. C. Klein, "Researcher Probes Consumers Using Anthropological Skills," *Wall Street Journal* (July 7, 1983), 23.

8. K. Foltz, "People-Watching Latest Trend," *The Register-Guard* (December 18, 1989), 6A.

9. Alsop, op. cit. See also A. Miller, "You Are What You Buy," *Newsweek* (June 4, 1990), 59–60.

10. J. T. Cacioppo, R. E. Petty, "Physiological Responses and Advertising Effects," *Psychology and Marketing* (Summer 1985), 115–126.

11. An excellent literature review is M. L. Rothschild, et al., "Hemispherically Lateralized EEG as a Response to Television Commercials," *Journal of Consumer Research* (September 1988), 185–198. See also J. Meyers-Levy, "Priming Effects on Product Judgments: A Hemispheric Interpretation," *Journal of Consumer Research* (June 1989), 76–86.

12. B. von Keitz, "Eye Movement Research," *European Research* (November 1988), 217–224.

13. *What the Eye Does Not See, the Mind Does Not Remember* (Telecom Research, Inc., undated).

14. "Psychogalvanometer Testing 'Most Predictive'" *Marketing News* (June 16, 1981), 11.

SECTION III

CASE III–1

Weyerhaeuser Lumber Purchase Criteria Questionnaire

Weyerhaeuser wanted to expand its sales in the do-it-yourself market. As a pilot study, a consulting firm prepared a questionnaire to administer in a parking lot intercept study. The purpose was to determine the extent to which consumers understood and relied on lumber grades in buying 2×4s. In addition, it sought to determine the other attributes that influence purchases of 2×4s. The questionnaire is shown here.

Evaluate the questionnaire and make any needed improvements.

Do-It-Yourself Home Improvement Questionnaire

Have you repaired, remodeled, or added on to your home within the last 5 years?

     YES ____ NO ____

Are you considering repairing, remodeling, or adding on to your home within the next 5 years?

     YES ____ NO ____

Who did or will do each of these tasks on your largest home improvement project? (Leave item blank if work was not needed)

	Contractor	*Homeowner*	*Other*
Design	____	____	____
Bought materials	____	____	____
Concrete work	____	____	____
Framing (Floor, wall, or roof)	____	____	____
Roofing	____	____	____
Siding	____	____	____
Electrical	____	____	____
Plumbing	____	____	____
Sheetrock/drywall	____	____	____
Paneling	____	____	____
Painting	____	____	____
Other _____	____	____	____
_____	____	____	____

	Yes	No	No Opinion
Have you ever used 2×4s in any construction work?	___	___	___
Do you think the grade stamped on a 2×4 is meaningful?	___	___	___
Does a better grade always mean a higher quality 2×4?	___	___	___
Is the best grade one you can depend on for the best 2×4?	___	___	___

From your experience, how would you rate these grades of 2×4? (Place a mark on each line)

	Bad	OK	Good	No Opinion
Stud				___
No. 1				___
Standard & Better				___
Economy				___
No. 2				___

When you choose a 2×4, how much does grade influence your choice?

Not At All	Somewhat	Extremely	Depends on Use	No Opinion
			___	___

Would you use these grades in your home?

	Yes	No	Depends on Price	Depends on Quality	No Opinion
Stud	___	___	___	___	___
No. 1	___	___	___	___	___
Standard & Better	___	___	___	___	___
Economy	___	___	___	___	___
No. 2	___	___	___	___	___

How *consistent* would you say lumber grading standards are? (If you choose a certain grade, do you always get boards that are similar?)

Not At All	Somewhat	Extremely	No Opinion
			___

How *meaningful* would you say lumber grading standards are? (Can you choose a certain grade to get a certain kind of board?)

Not At All	Somewhat	Extremely	No Opinion
			___

Do you think there could be a better grade than the best grade available now?

Yes ___   No ___   Maybe ___   No Opinion ___

If so, would the new best grade be more reliable?   Yes ____   No ____

Would the new best grade be a higher quality?   Yes ____   No ____
How much does each of these characteristics affect the quality of a 2×4?

	Not At All			Somewhat			Extremely	No Opinion
Straightness of board								
Closeness of grain								
Bark on the edges								
Moisture content								
Checks (tiny cracks)								
Dirt or stain								
Knots								
Weight								
Rough ends								
Straightness of grain								
White or black mildew								
Twist								
Heaviness or density								
Rounded corners								
Exact length								

When you choose a 2×4, how much does each characteristic influence your choice?

	Not At All			Somewhat			Extremely
Straightness of board							
Closeness of grain							
Bark on the edges							
Moisture content							
Checks (tiny cracks)							
Dirt or stain							
Knots							
Weight							
Rough ends							
Straightness of grain							
White or black mildew							
Twist							
Heaviness or density							
Rounded corners							
Exact length							

What do you think is the *market* value of your home today?

____ Less than $40,000   ____ $80,000 to $100,000
____ $40,000 to $60,000   ____ $100,000 to $120,000
____ $60,000 to $80,000   ____ More than $120,000

What is your approximate household income?

____ Less than $10,000   ____ $20,000 to $30,000
____ $10,000 to $15,000   ____ $30,000 to $40,000
____ $15,000 to $20,000   ____ More than $40,000

What is your age:

_____ Less than 25

_____ 26 to 35

_____ 36 to 45

_____ 46 to 55

_____ Over 55

Do you have a spouse, or spousal equivalent?   YES _____   NO _____

THANK YOU FOR PARTICIPATING

CASE III–2

The Impact of R. J. Reynolds' "Old Joe the Camel" Advertising Campaign on Childrens' Awareness of Camel Cigarettes

Two hundred twenty-nine children aged three to six were recruited from 10 preschools in Augusta and Atlanta. The preschools were selected judgmentally to produce a balanced sample in terms of socioeconomic variables. The sample had these characteristics: age—3 (35 percent), 4 (29 percent), 5 (26 percent), 6 (10 percent); gender—male (54 percent), female (46 percent); race—black (27 percent), white (73 percent); parents' education—less than 12 years (29 percent), 12–16 years (54 percent), over 16 years (17 percent); and parent(s) smokes (34 percent).

Each child was tested separately in a quiet part of the classroom. The child was told that he or she would play a game matching cards (which had pictures of company logos on them) with pictures of products. The 12 products (see table) pictured on the game board were then named and a sample matching was done. The child was then given a test logo to match. After the card was placed on the board, the child was told, "That's good." No other instructions were given. Following each match, the card was removed from the board and the child was given the next card. Each child matched 22 logos.

The "Old Joe" logo was a picture of the head and shoulders of the "Old Joe" cartoon-type character used in the Camel advertising campaign.

Logos Tested,* Correct Product Response, and Recognition Rates for 229 Subjects Aged 3 to 6 Years

Product Category	Logo	Correct Product Response	Recognition Rate (%)
Children's brands	Disney Channel	Mickey Mouse	91.7
	"McDonald's"	Hamburger	81.7
	"Burger King"	Hamburger	79.9
	"Domino's Pizza"	Pizza	78.2

Product Category	Logo	Correct Product Response	Recognition Rate (%)
	"Coca Cola"	Glass of cola	76.0
	"Pepsi"	Glass of cola	68.6
	"Nike"	Athletic shoe	56.8
	"Walt Disney"	Mickey Mouse	48.9
	"Kellogg's"	Bowl of cereal	38.0
	"Cheerios"	Bowl of cereal	25.3
Cigarette brands	"Old Joe"	Cigarette	51.1
	"Marlboro" and red roof	Cigarette	32.8
	Marlboro man	Cigarette	27.9
	Camel and pyramids	Cigarette	27.1
	"Camel"	Cigarette	18.0
Adult brands	"Chevrolet"	Automobile	54.1
	"Ford"	Automobile	52.8
	Apple	Computer	29.3
	"CBS"	Television	23.1
	"NBC"	Television	21.0
	"Kodak"	Camera	17.9
	"IBM"	Computer	16.2
Surgeon General's warning		Cigarette	10.0

*Quotation marks on the logo indicate that the brand name is part of the test item.

The results are provided in the table. Of the various sociodemographic variables, only age affected recognition of the picture of "Old Joe" as a cigarette logo (from 30 percent of the three-year-olds to 91 percent of the six-year-olds). Thus, although cigarettes are not advertised on television, "Old Joe" is as widely recognized by six-year-olds as is Mickey Mouse.

Discussion Questions

1. Evaluate the overall design of this study.
2. Evaluate the sampling technique used.
3. Evaluate the measurement technique used.
4. What conclusions would you draw from this study?
5. If you were to redesign this study, what changes would you make?

SOURCE: P. M. Fischer, et al. "Brand Logo Recognition by Children Aged 3 to 6 Years," *JAMA* (December 11, 1991), 3145–3148.

CASE III–3

Physicians' Attitudes Toward Hospital Services

As competition in the medical field has increased, hospitals have begun to adopt modern marketing practices. The management of XYZ Hospital, a large metropolitan hospital, was concerned with keeping a high occupancy rate in the face of an oversupply of hospital beds in the area. The management team was well aware that success required the active support of area physicians. Therefore, it undertook a survey of all practicing physicians in its primary service area. The purpose of the survey was to discover ways to increase the physicians' satisfaction with, and thereby support of, XYZ Hospital. The questionnaire that was used is represented here.

Evaluate the questionnaire, making improvements where appropriate.

Physician Satisfaction Survey

Dear Doctor:

The Administration of XYZ Hospital is concerned about your satisfaction with how services are provided—both to you and your patients. Please tell us what you really think. Your individual answers will never be seen by the XYZ Administration—only combined responses will be reviewed.

I. Nursing Staff

A. Please evaluate each of the following components of physician satisfaction using a rating scale where "5" means "Very Satisfied" and "1" means "Not At All Satisfied." You may circle any number from "5" to "1". If you don't know the answer to a question, please circle the "DK" (Don't Know). Please begin by thinking about your level of satisfaction with the NURSING STAFF . . .

	XYZ Ratings	
	Very Satisfied	Not at All Satisfied
1. CARING ATTITUDE toward patients	5 · 4 · 3 · 2 · 1 · DK	
2. COURTESY to patients	5 · 4 · 3 · 2 · 1 · DK	
3. RESPONSIVENESS to patient preferences and needs	5 · 4 · 3 · 2 · 1 · DK	
4. TECHNICAL SKILLS of nursing staff	5 · 4 · 3 · 2 · 1 · DK	
5. Reaction to "PRIMARY CARE NURSING"	5 · 4 · 3 · 2 · 1 · DK	
6. OVERALL SATISFACTION with nursing care	5 · 4 · 3 · 2 · 1 · DK	

B. What is the single most important thing related to PATIENT CARE that XYZ Hospital could do to improve your satisfaction with the hospital?

————————————————————————————————— (11) ——

————————————————————————————————— (12) ——

C. Is there a specific nursing unit at XYZ which does an ESPECIALLY GOOD job of providing high quality patient care?

Yes   1   Please identify the unit number: __

No   2

Don't know   3

D. Is there a specific nursing unit at XYZ which NEEDS SPECIAL ATTENTION TO IMPROVE its ability to provide high quality patient care?

Yes   1   Please identify the unit number: __

No   2

Don't know   3

E. How useful do you find XYZ NURSING CLINICIANS to your practice at the hospital? (Please circle one number below.)

Very Useful   5 · 4 · 3 · 2 · 1   Not At All Useful

II. Operations/Clinical Areas

	XYZ Ratings	
	Very Satisfied	Not at All Satisfied

A. Key Clinical Areas:
  1. Inpatient Admitting:

a. Scheduling	5 · 4 · 3 · 2 · 1 · DK	
b. Room Assignments	5 · 4 · 3 · 2 · 1 · DK	
c. Staff Performance	5 · 4 · 3 · 2 · 1 · DK	

  2. Surgery/Operating Room:

a. Scheduling	5 · 4 · 3 · 2 · 1 · DK
b. Anesthesia Services	5 · 4 · 3 · 2 · 1 · DK
c. Staff Performance	5 · 4 · 3 · 2 · 1 · DK

  3. Same Day Surgery:

a. Scheduling	5 · 4 · 3 · 2 · 1 · DK
b. Overall Patient Care	5 · 4 · 3 · 2 · 1 · DK

  4. Emergency Room:

a. Physicians' Attitudes and Cooperation	5 · 4 · 3 · 2 · 1 · DK
b. Quality of Services Provided	5 · 4 · 3 · 2 · 1 · DK
c. Nursing and Ancillary Care	5 · 4 · 3 · 2 · 1 · DK

  5. Radiology Department:

a. Physicians' Attitudes and Cooperation	5 · 4 · 3 · 2 · 1 · DK
b. Quality of Services Provided	5 · 4 · 3 · 2 · 1 · DK
c. Technologists' Support	5 · 4 · 3 · 2 · 1 · DK

  6. Laboratory/Pathology:

a. Physicians' Attitudes and Cooperation	5 · 4 · 3 · 2 · 1 · DK
b. Quality of Services Provided	5 · 4 · 3 · 2 · 1 · DK

	XYZ Ratings	
	Very Satisfied	Not at All Satisfied

B. Other Clinical Areas and Departments: (Overall)

1. Respiratory Care	5 · 4 · 3 · 2 · 1 · DK	
2. Pharmacy	5 · 4 · 3 · 2 · 1 · DK	
3. Physical Medicine	5 · 4 · 3 · 2 · 1 · DK	
4. CareUnit (Substance Abuse)	5 · 4 · 3 · 2 · 1 · DK	
5. Radiation Therapy	5 · 4 · 3 · 2 · 1 · DK	
6. Inpatient Rehabilitation	5 · 4 · 3 · 2 · 1 · DK	
7. Social Services	5 · 4 · 3 · 2 · 1 · DK	
8. Home Care	5 · 4 · 3 · 2 · 1 · DK	
9. Medical Records	5 · 4 · 3 · 2 · 1 · DK	
10. Pediatrics (3100)	5 · 4 · 3 · 2 · 1 · DK	
11. Maternity	5 · 4 · 3 · 2 · 1 · DK	
12. Dietetics	5 · 4 · 3 · 2 · 1 · DK	
13. Family Practice Residency	5 · 4 · 3 · 2 · 1 · DK	

C. Please state additional comments regarding any clinical areas or departments:

_____ (53) _____

_____ (54) _____

III. Administration/Medical Staff Relations

This portion of the questionnaire deals with relations between XYZ Hospital and the Medical Staff. Please indicate your views by circling the answer which best represents your opinion.

A. Generally speaking, I feel that Hospital Administration is genuinely interested in and receptive to the needs of the Medical Staff.
STRONGLY AGREE 5 · 4 · 3 · 2 · 1 STRONGLY DISAGREE

B. Generally speaking, I feel the President of XYZ Hospital is responsive to the needs of the Medical Staff.
STRONGLY AGREE 5 · 4 · 3 · 2 · 1 STRONGLY DISAGREE

C. Generally speaking, I feel the Nursing Management is genuinely interested in and receptive to the needs of the Medical Staff.
STRONGLY AGREE 5 · 4 · 3 · 2 · 1 STRONGLY DISAGREE

D. There is sufficient communication and contact between the Administration and the Medical Staff.
STRONGLY AGREE 5 · 4 · 3 · 2 · 1 STRONGLY DISAGREE

E. The Medical Staff Director plays an important role in facilitating Administration/Medical Staff relations.
STRONGLY AGREE 5 · 4 · 3 · 2 · 1 STRONGLY DISAGREE

F. What needs to be done to improve Administration/Medical Staff relations?

_____ (60) _____

_____ (61) _____

IV. Overall Comparison: XYZ vs. ABC

Recognizing that a large number of physicians who practice at XYZ also admit patients to ABC, we would like you to rate your satisfaction level for each of the two hospitals on the following points. (If you are not familiar with ABC, please complete the XYZ ratings only.)

	XYZ Ratings		ABC Ratings	
	Very Satisfied	Not At All Satisfied	Very Satisfied	Not At All Satisfied
A. Overall Nursing Care	5 · 4 · 3 · 2 · 1 · DK		5 · 4 · 3 · 2 · 1 · DK	
B. Projecting a Caring Attitude	5 · 4 · 3 · 2 · 1 · DK		5 · 4 · 3 · 2 · 1 · DK	
C. Overall Facilities/ Technology	5 · 4 · 3 · 2 · 1 · DK		5 · 4 · 3 · 2 · 1 · DK	
D. Administration (Daily Operations)	5 · 4 · 3 · 2 · 1 · DK		5 · 4 · 3 · 2 · 1 · DK	
E. Administration Leadership (Addressing the Future)	5 · 4 · 3 · 2 · 1 · DK		5 · 4 · 3 · 2 · 1 · DK	

V. Private Practice of Physicians

A. Thinking of your current practice level, would you describe your capacity as

100% capacity	1
90% capacity	2
80% capacity	3
70% capacity	4
60% capacity or less	5

B. Do you expect that your practice level will increase, decrease, or remain about the same in the next 12 months?

Increase	1
Decrease	2
Remain about the same	3

C. Approximately what percentage of your patients do you refer to area hospitals? (Total should equal 100%)

XYZ: _____ %   ABC: _____ %   QRS: _____ %   Other: _____ %

D. Do you anticipate the need for the addition of a partner in the next 2 to 3 years?

Yes	1	Would you welcome assistance from
No	2	XYZ in recruiting a partner at
Don't know	3	the appropriate time?

Yes	1
No	2
Don't know	3

E. Is it appropriate for hospitals to work with physicians to further develop their practices (i.e., assistance with office automation, purchasing, promotional efforts)?

Yes   1   No   2   Don't know   3

F. Do you feel there is value in promoting the medical staff and the hospital to the public?

Yes   1   No   2   Don't know   3

VI. Miscellaneous Issues

A. What is the single greatest **WEAKNESS** of XYZ Hospital?

_____ (11) _____

_____ (12) _____

B. What is the single greatest **STRENGTH** of XYZ Hospital?

_____ (13) _____

_____ (14) _____

C. What is the single most important thing XYZ could do to improve your satisfaction with the hospital?

_____ (15) _____

_____ (16) _____

D. Aside from quality of care, what is the single most important thing the XYZ Administration should not lose sight of as they manage the business of the hospital?

_____ (17) _____

_____ (18) _____

E. Do you feel that XYZ should move toward a smoke-free hospital environment for each of the following groups of people?

	Yes	No	Dont't Know
Hospital employees	1	2	3
Patients of the hospital	1	2	3
Guests of the patients	1	2	3
Doctors	1	2	3

CASE III–4

Projective Research on Littering

The Highway Department of a large state has become increasingly concerned about the annual costs of cleaning litter from the state's roadways. Littering is prohibited by law and carries a maximum fine of $500. However, it is difficult for law enforcement officers to apprehend litterers, and the state and local police tend to believe that littering is a minor offense compared to the many other violations they must attempt to control.

The Highway Department has sponsored a number of publicity and advertising campaigns aimed at reducing littering. Two basic themes have been utilized—pride in the state and the cost to taxpayers for removing litter.

Neither theme appears to have had a substantial impact on the amount of litter being deposited on the state's highways. The state legislature is considering a number of potential programs to deal with the problem. These programs range from instituting special police "litter patrols," whose primary duty is to apprehend litterers, to starting a major educational campaign on littering in the state's schools.

Stu Billington, director of the state's Highway Department, recently testified before a subcommittee investigating litter. In his testimony he stated that: "The reason our programs don't work is that we have absolutely no idea why people litter. If we don't know why they do it, how can we persuade them to stop?" The Senate subcommittee decided that Billington was correct in his assessment, and four months later he received authorization to spend $60,000 to isolate the underlying reasons why people litter.

Billington asked Motivation Research, Inc.,* to submit a proposal on this problem. Parts of the proposal are presented in the paragraphs that follow.

> Littering, although all too widely practiced, is not socially acceptable to the general society. Most individuals will not openly admit to littering even on anonymous questionnaires. Littering on the surface appears to be a simple act. One removes something from one's car in a simple, convenient, and direct manner. However, we do not believe that littering is, in reality, such a simple process. Otherwise, it would not persist in the face of so much stated opposition.
>
> We do not pretend to know the underlying dynamics of littering at this time. However, we can venture several guesses. Littering may be viewed subconsciously as an act of rebellion. Children rebel against parental commands, including the command to clean up. Governmental agencies issue orders ("do not litter") much like parents. Therefore, littering may be an act of rebellion against authority. Other facts may be involved. The private automobile is cherished for the amount of freedom it provides the individual. Littering while in an automobile may represent an extension of this freedom. In this case, it is freedom from the rules of neatness that generally apply in the home.
>
> Other potential motives could be suggested. However, it is the purpose of this study to discover the underlying motives. Therefore, we will begin with an open mind rather than a prespecified set of hypotheses.
>
> The research will involve two approaches. First, group depth interviews (10 respondents per group) will be conducted, with one group selected from each of the relevant populations described earlier. These interviews will last approximately 2.5 hours. Because littering is not a socially acceptable activity, one member of each group will actually be a member of our organization. This member will admit to littering early in the discussion, which will make it easier for others to confess. In addition, the "plant" will admit to or agree with antisocial motives for littering. Again, this will make it easier for others to admit to the same feelings.
>
> The second approach to the problem will involve separate samples of 50 from each of the relevant population groups. These groups will complete several projective techniques. First, each group will complete a successive word association test involving 10 words. Litter, highway, and cleanliness will be the key words. The remaining seven terms will be relatively neutral.
>
> The second projective technique is a version of the picture technique. Half of each sample will see a vague drawing of a car traveling down a highway. The car will have two adults in the front seat and two children in the back

seat. The other half of each sample will see the same picture, except that several pieces of litter will be shown coming from the car. The respondents will be asked to tell a story about the people in the car, including where they are going, where they have been, what they are like, what they are thinking, and so forth. The stories will be analyzed to reveal differences between those who saw the car with litter and those who saw the car without litter.

The final projective technique will utilize the cartoon approach. Two characters (line drawings) will be shown in conversation. One will be saying: "I threw some junk out of the window of my car on the Interstate the other day and got a $20 ticket." The respondents will be asked to provide *both* the verbal reply and the unspoken thoughts of the second character.

The depth interviews and the three techniques described will provide us a clearer understanding of the underlying dynamics of the behavior that results in littering.

*This is a fictitious name.

Discussion Questions

1. Should Billington authorize the study?
2. Will the "plants" in the group depth interviews introduce any potential error?
3. Is it ethical to use "plants" in an interview situation of this type?
4. Are both depth interviews *and* projective techniques required? What information will each give that the other will not?
5. What other specific projective techniques could be used?
6. Are all three projective techniques required? Explain.

CASE III–5

Carlisle's Drugstores

Carlisle's is a local drug chain (five outlets) that provides high service levels, stamps, and quality merchandise at average prices. The weak economy and the emergence of severe price competition from several new, large chain stores had drastically reduced Carlisle's profits. Before developing a strategic response to the changed competitive scene, Sandra Carlisle, the owner of the chain, requested a study to determine (1) what criteria various market segments desire in a drugstore, and (2) how Carlisle's compared to its competitors on these criteria.

A local consulting firm proposed a telephone survey. The sample would be chosen by randomly selecting names from the phone book and adding 1 to the phone number associated with the selected name. The interview would involve any adult that answered the phone and was willing to be interviewed. Each selected number would be called three times (unless it was answered or out of service) before being replaced. The first call to each number had to be between 6 and 9 P.M. One of the two remaining calls had to be between 8 A.M. and 5 P.M. Calls were to be made until 500 interviews were completed.

The basic questionnaire is shown here. There were actually five versions of the questionnaire. Each version was the same except for question 16. Each version contained a different competitor's name in the blanks shown in question 16. Thus, there were 100 completed interviews measuring the image of each of five major competitors.

Questionnaire

Hello, my name is _____ and I'm conducting a survey for a local retail establishment. I'd like to ask you a few questions that will take only a few minutes.

1. What stores in the Eugene/Springfield area do you think of when I say "drugstores"?
   Record a 1 by the store mentioned first, a 2 by the one named second, and a 3 by the one mentioned third. Probe with "any others?" Until three are named.
   ___ Bi-Mart   ___ K mart
   ___ Family Drug   ___ Payless
   ___ Fred Meyer   ___ Shopko
   ___ Gerlachs   ___ Thrifty
   ___ Gold Cross   ___ Tiffany's
   ___ Hiron's   ___ _____

2. Which drugstore do you shop at most frequently?
   ___ Bi-Mart   ___ K mart
   ___ Family Drug   ___ Payless
   ___ Fred Meyer   ___ Shopko
   ___ Gerlachs   ___ Thrifty
   ___ Gold Cross   ___ Tiffany's
   ___ Hiron's   ___ _____

3. What other drugstores have you shopped at in the past two months?
   Place an X by all that are mentioned.
   ___ Bi-Mart   ___ K mart
   ___ Family Drug   ___ Payless
   ___ Fred Meyer   ___ Shopko
   ___ Gerlachs   ___ Thrifty
   ___ Gold Cross   ___ Tiffany's
   ___ Hiron's   ___ _____

4. Think back to a recent trip to a drugstore. PAUSE. What types of items did you purchase?
   Check all that apply. If in doubt, write down the name(s) of the item(s) below the checklist. Probe with "anything else?"
   ___ Beer/wine   ___ Prescription drugs
   ___ Cards/stationery   ___ Reading materials
   ___ Cosmetics   ___ School supplies
   ___ Film   ___ Small appliances
   ___ Gifts_____   ___ Sporting goods
   ___ Hardware   ___ Stereo/radio/TV
   ___ Household supplies   ___ Tennis shoes/clothing
   ___ Nonprescription drugs   ___ Toys
   ___ Pets/pet supplies   ___ Other_____
   ___ Plants

5. Did anyone go with you on this particular trip? Who?

____ No   ____ Relatives
____ Children   ____ Spouse
____ Friends   ____ Other _____

6. Do you generally do most of your shopping during the week or on weekends?

____ During the week
____ Weekends

7. Do you have most of your prescriptions filled at one pharmacy?

____No *Ask Question 8*
____Yes *Ask 7a and 7b*

7a. What is the most important reason you use this pharmacy?

____ Always have   ____ Friendly/nice atmosphere/know me
____ Fast service   ____ Purchase other things there
____ Convenient location   ____ Stamps
____ Recordkeeping services ____ Price
                            ____ Other _____

7b. Is this pharmacy located in the same drugstore where you usually shop for nonprescription merchandise?

____ Yes
____ No

8. If you were a new resident in town and wanted to select *one* pharmacy or drugstore, where would you make most of your purchases of *prescription drugs?* _____

What characteristic or feature would you consider *most* important in choosing the store?

What characteristic or feature would you consider *second* most important in choosing the store?

Mark the most important as 1, second most important as 2.

____ Price ____ Selection of merchandise
____ Convenient location   ____ Stamps
____ Service   ____ Friendly/nice atmosphere
____ Quality of merchandise ____ Fast service
____ Reputation   ____ Other _____

9. If you were new to the area and wanted to select one outlet, where you would purchase most of your *nonprescription* drugstore items?

What characteristics or feature would you consider *most* important in choosing the store?

What characteristic or feature would you consider *second* most important in choosing the store?

Mark the most important as 1, second most important as 2.

____ Price   ____ Selection of merchandise
____ Convenient location   ____ Stamps
____ Service   ____ Friendly/nice atmosphere
____ Quality of merchandise ____ Fast service
____ Reputation   ____ Other

10. Do you save green stamps if a store provides them?

____ Yes *Ask Question 11*
____ No *Omit Question 11*

11. Do you prefer stores that give green stamps?
    ___ Yes *Omit Question 12*
    ___ No
12. Do you avoid stores that give green stamps?
    ___ Yes
    ___ No
13. Do you check newspaper ads before purchasing drugstore items?
    ___ Yes
    ___ No *Omit Questions 14 and 15*
14. What day of the week do you check newspaper ads for drugstore items?
    Check all that apply.
    ___ Sunday   ___ Thursday
    ___ Monday   ___ Friday
    ___ Tuesday   ___ Saturday
    ___ Wednesday
15. What newspapers do you consult for ads?
    ___ Register-Guard
    ___ Valley News
    ___ Oregonian
    ___ Other _____
16. I will now read you a series of statements. Please indicate your level of agreement or disagreement after each sentence by saying "strongly agree," "agree," "disagree," or "strongly disagree."

    For example, if I were to say, "It rains a lot in Eugene," you might respond "strongly agree" or perhaps "agree."

    Is that clear? Okay. There are no right or wrong answers. We are interested only in your initial reactions.

    Record the responses as
    1 = *Strongly Agree*
    2 = *Agree*
    3 = *Disagree*
    4 = *Strongly Disagree*
    5 = *Don't Know/No Opinion*

                                                         Response
    a. Friendly store clerks are very important to me.   ___
    b. A drugstore's appearance and layout are very important to me.   ___
    c. When possible I shop a locally owned store.   ___
    d. When having a prescription filled, it is important for me to deal directly with the pharmacist rather than with a pharmacist's helper.   ___
    e. A Carlisle's Drugstore is conveniently located for me.   ___
    f. Carlisle's Drugstores are expensive.   ___
    g. Carlisle's Drugstores have well-trained personnel in their cosmetics departments.   ___
    h. _____ have high-quality pharmacies.   ___
    i. _____ are *un*pleasant stores to shop in.   ___
    j. _____ have helpful personnel.   ___

Response

k. Carlisle's Drugstores carry a wide range of merchandise. ____
l. Carlisle's Drugstores have high-quality pharmacies. ____
m. Carlisle's Drugstores are *un*pleasant stores to shop in. ____
n. Carlisle's Drugstores have helpful personnel. ____
o. A _____ is conveniently located for me. ____
p. _____ are expensive. ____
q. _____ have well-trained personnel in their cosmetics departments. ____
r. _____ carry a wide range of merchandise. ____
s. Drugstores are locally owned. ____

Now, so that we may compare the attitudes and opinions of different groups of people, we would like to ask you a couple of individual questions.

17. What is your occupation?_____

_____

18. What is your husband/wife's occupation?_____

_____

Provide enough details to enable the coder to place the family into a Blue-Collar, White-Collar, or Managerial-Professional category. Probe with "what does that job involve?"

19. How many children, if any, do you have living at home?_____
    Ask 19a only if there are children living at home.
19a. What is the age of the youngest?
    ____under 6
    ____over 6
20. *About how old are you?*____
21. What is your zip code?_____
    If they don't know or refuse to answer 21, ask 21a.
21a. What area of town do you live in?_____

_____

22. ____ Male ____ Female
    Record question 22 without asking, if possible.

Discussion Questions

1. What other approaches could have been taken to provide the required information? What changes, if any, would you make in the research design?
2. Evaluate the survey methodology used. Suggest improvements where appropriate.
3. Evaluate the questionnaire suggesting improvements where necessary.

Sampling and Data Analysis

Sampling and data analysis each play an important role in the research project. Without a sound sampling plan and a suitable sample size, the data will be collected from neither the proper respondents nor the appropriate number of them. And inadequate or inappropriate data analysis can negate the efforts going into an otherwise soundly designed and competently conducted project.

The first two chapters of this section are concerned with sampling. Chapter 14 deals with devising the *sampling plan,* and then putting it into effect. Determining the appropriate *size of the sample* is the subject of Chapter 15.

The next three chapters are devoted to data analysis. *Data reduction,* the process of getting the data ready for analysis, and *statistical estimation* are the subjects of Chapter 16. *Hypothesis tests of differences* are considered in Chapter 17, while *measures of association* between variables are covered in Chapter 18.

14

The Sampling Process

LEARNING OBJECTIVES

Upon completing this chapter, you should be able to:

1. Explain why a sample rather than a census is commonly used in marketing research studies.

2. List the steps in the sampling process.

3. Evaluate the adequacy of the definition of a population for a research study.

4. Describe a desirable sampling frame.

5. Explain the difference between a probability and a nonprobability sample.

6. List and describe the common nonprobability sampling methods.

7. Explain the advantages of stratified sampling and unequal unit probability sampling.

8. Describe the major issues and problems encountered in sampling for multinational studies.

Frontier Stoves' Sampling Plan for a Focus Group Study

The president of Frontier Stoves, a wood stove manufacturer, asked the person in charge of marketing research for the company to conduct focus group interviews of blue-collar, white-collar, and managerial/professional owners of wood stoves to determine what they see as the principal benefits and problems arising from the use of wood stoves.

The primary benefits from focus group research are indications of attitudes and beliefs, and perhaps the suggestion of new courses of action, rather than provision of statistically reliable, projectable responses. One of the requirements for a successful focus group interview is to have reasonably outgoing, verbal persons who will respond to questions and participate in group discussions. For this reason, sample members for focus groups, however they are selected initially, usually require prequalification.

At the time the samples for the focus groups were taken, the city in which Frontier was located had an ordinance requiring permits to operate a wood stove. A list of permit holders was obtained and households were called randomly until the 48 sample households necessary to provide participants for six focus groups (one adult member from each household, eight persons per focus group, two focus groups each from the blue-collar, white-collar, and managerial/professional social classes) were selected. Selection involved verification that the wood stove was still owned, open-ended questions on the benefits of it were asked to assess how verbal the respondents were. If they qualified on these counts and were willing to participate, demographic data were obtained to determine to which focus group they should be assigned.

If all possible information needed to solve a problem could be collected, there would be no need to sample. We can rarely do this, however, because of limitations on the amount we can afford to spend, on the available time, or for other reasons. We, therefore, must take samples.

This chapter begins with a discussion of the reasons for sampling. The steps in the sampling process are then discussed, including a description of the various types of samples that may be taken, and the principal factors involved in their selection. Next, we consider the special issues associated with multinational sampling. Finally, the sample plan used in a major research project is described.

Census Versus Sample

Sample:
a subset of the population of interest that is selected for study.

Census:
studying all the members of the population of interest.

A **sample** is a subset of the population of interest that is selected for study. A **census** is the selection of all the members of the population of interest. Censuses are occasionally taken in marketing studies, but *cost, time, accuracy,* and *the destructive nature of the measurement* generally mandate the use of a sample.

Cost is an obvious constraint on the determination of whether a census should be taken. If information is desired on grocery purchase and use behavior (frequencies and amounts of purchase of each product category, average amount kept at home, and the like) and the population of interest is all households in the U.S., the cost will preclude a census being taken. The budget for the 1990 Decennial Census of Population was more than $2.5 billion. As an approximation of the cost of a census of households to obtain the information on groceries, it is apparent that this cost would far exceed any conceivable value of such information for a marketer of this type of product.

Even if a census of households to obtain information on grocery purchase and use behavior were practical from a cost standpoint, it might not be so when the time required to conduct the census is considered. Data collection for the 1990 Census in the U.S. was begun in March 1990 (planning began in 1984), and yet the detailed characteristics of the population were not published until 1993. Most of the kinds of decisions made by business firms need to be made in less time than that.

A census contains no sampling error. However, it may contain any of the other types of errors discussed in Chapter 3. For example, the 1990 census undercounted the U.S. population by an estimated 5.3 million people! It is often desirable to take a sample rather than a census and use the funds thus freed for more call-backs, more skilled interviewers, and so forth to produce a lower total error. This is the concept of error trade-off, discussed in Chapters 3 and 6.

Measurements are sometimes destructive in nature. When they are, it is apparent that taking a census would usually defeat the purpose of the measurement. If one were producing firecrackers, electrical fuses, or grass seed, performing a functional use test on all products for quality-control purposes would not be considered from an economic standpoint. A sample is the only practical choice. On the other hand, if bicycles or electrical appliances are to be tested, a 100 percent sample (census) may be entirely reasonable.

The Sampling Process

The sampling process consists of seven sequential steps. These steps are listed and a brief summary description is given in Table 14–1. A more detailed treatment of each step is given in the sections that follow.

Step 1. Define the Population

The **population** for a survey of purchasing agents might be defined as "all purchasing agents in companies and government agencies that have bought any of our products in the last three years." To be complete, a population must be defined in terms of *elements, sampling units, extent,* and *time.* In relation to these constituent parts, the population of purchasing agents is

(element)	purchasing agents in
(sampling unit)	companies and governmental agencies that have
(extent)	bought any of our products
(time)	in the last three years.

Defining a population incorrectly may render the results of the study meaningless or even misleading for the decision at hand. For example, the population for a study of the eating habits of single persons was defined as

(element)	All persons 18 years of age or older who live by themselves and are shopping in
(sampling unit)	supermarkets
(extent)	in Los Angeles, California
(time)	during the week of January 18–24.

Population: the entire group of persons, events, or objects of interest to the researcher.

TABLE 14–1 Steps in the Sampling Process

Step	Description
1. Define the population	The population is defined in terms of (a) element, (b) units, (c) extent, and (d) time.
2. Specify sampling frame	The means of representing the elements of the population—for example, telephone book, map, or city directory—are described.
3. Specify sampling unit	The unit for sampling—for example, city block, company, or household—is selected. The sampling unit may contain one or several population elements.
4. Specify sampling method	The method by which the sampling units are to be selected is described.
5. Determine sample size	The number of elements of the population to be sampled is chosen.
6. Specify sampling plan	The operational procedures for selection of the sampling units are selected.
7. Select the sample	The office and fieldwork necessary for the selection of the sample are carried out.

One of the findings of the research was that "singles do not eat meals away from home as frequently as previously thought."[1] This result could hardly have come as a surprise given that the singles interviewed were all shopping in supermarkets. If the interviews had been conducted in restaurants, the finding would almost certainly have been that "singles eat meals away from home *more* frequently than previously thought." What the finding would have been on this issue if a probability sample of all singles had been taken is not known.

Research Application 14–1 illustrates how misspecifying a population almost led Johnson & Johnson into making an incorrect advertising decision.

Step 2. Specify the Sampling Frame

Sampling frame:
a list or other means of representing the sampling units for a study.

If a probability sample is to be taken, a **sampling frame** is required. A sampling frame is a means of representing the sampling units. A sampling frame may be a telephone book, a city directory, an employee roster, a listing of all students attending a university, or a list of all possible phone numbers.

A perfect sampling frame is one in which *every element of the population is represented once but only once*. The listing of stock prices in the *Wall Street Journal* provides a perfect frame for sampling listed stocks on the New York Stock Exchange. Examples of perfect frames are rare, however, when one is interested in sampling from any appreciable segment of a human population.

A tempting frame for sampling human populations is the telephone book. Although 93 percent of the households in the U.S. have telephones,[2] the distribution of telephone ownership is not even across all groups. Low-income, rural, and inner-city homes constitute the primary source of homes without telephones. In addition, many homes with telephones do not have their numbers listed in the telephone directory. For the U.S. as a whole, it is estimated that 31 percent of all households have unlisted telephone numbers, with rates above 60 percent in some metropolitan areas.[3]

People with unlisted telephone numbers tend to live in metropolitan areas, be younger, and have a somewhat lower income, and are more likely to be single than those with listed numbers. Nonwhites are about three times as likely to have an unlisted number as are whites (see Chapter 6). In contrast, middle-income and affluent households with children are likely to have multiple phone numbers, a factor that enhances their likelihood of inclusion in a telephone book–based sample.

These omissions and dual listings may lead to *frame errors* in a study in which the telephone book is used as a sampling frame. This is true of city directories, maps, census tract information, or any other listing or representation of a population that is incomplete or out of date. Unfortunately, some frame error is probably unavoidable in most surveys of human populations. Research Application 14–2 describes Survey Sampling, Inc.'s procedure for developing a sampling frame for random-digit dialing samples (see Chapter 6, page 141).

Step 3. Specify Sampling Unit

The **sampling unit** is the basic unit containing the elements of the population to be sampled. It may be the element itself or a unit in which the element is contained. For example, if one wanted a sample of males over 13 years of age, it might be possible to sample them directly. In this case, the sampling unit

The Effect of Population Specification on Day-After-Recall Measures of Advertising Effectiveness

Day-after-recall (DAR) is one of the most popular methods for copy testing television commercials. The method involves running the commercial on the air and telephoning a random sample of individuals the next day to determine their recall of the copy of the commercial. A recall score is computed as the percentage of those watching television when the commercial was aired who can recall some aspect of the commercial. Substantial evidence suggests that recall is not strongly affected by product usage. The following results were obtained from an analysis of 611 DAR studies.

Recall Scores

Total	Product Users	Product Nonusers
24	26	21

Based on evidence of this nature and the high cost of sampling only users, the population for most DAR studies is defined as all adults (or males or females) at homes with telephones who were at a television set when the commercial was aired. This approach was used by Johnson & Johnson to test two commercials for a skin-conditioning product. The results were:

	Recall Score
Commercial A	14
Commercial B	15
Norm	23

The norm represents the average recall score for commercials this length (30 seconds).

Based on these results, neither commercial would be used. However, the commercials were also tested in a theater test (people are brought to a theater to view programs that contain the com-

mercials). The theater test used a sample composed primarily of product category users. Using a somewhat different measure of copy effectiveness, the following results were obtained:

	Effectiveness Score
Commercial A	20
Commercial B	12
Norm	8

Using this sample and measurement technique, both commercials could be used, but A is clearly superior.

Given these conflicting results, Johnson & Johnson retested commercial A on a DAR basis with a sample selected from a universe defined as "purchasers of any brand in the product category in the past year." A third DAR test was conducted on a sample selected from a universe defined as "users of any brand in the produce category in the past month." The results were:

	Recall Score
Total audience	14
Past year purchasers	47
Past month users	59
Norm	23

Clearly, measured recall for some types of commercials depends on the specification of the population. Since the Johnson & Johnson campaign was designed to influence current product users, relying on the normal population specification for DAR tests would have caused the company to make the wrong decision.

SOURCE: Derived from C. L. Hodock, "Copy Testing and Strategic Positioning," *Journal of Advertising Research* (February 1980), 33–38.

RESEARCH APPLICATION 14–2

Survey Sampling, Inc.'s Sample Frame for Random-Digit Dialed Surveys

By starting out with an extensive cleaning and validation process, we can ensure that all phone numbers in our database are assigned to the correct area code and fall within an appropriate set of ZIP codes. Once this cleaning has been done, we determine working blocks.

A block is defined as the first two digits of a phone number within an exchange. The phone number 226-7558 falls within block 75 of exchange 226. A working block is a block which contains at least three listed residential telephone numbers. Nonworking blocks—those with zero, one, or two listed numbers—are eliminated from consideration in our database, as many of these turn out to be data entry errors.

Currently, there are estimated to be 87 million households in the United States. About 93 percent of these households have telephones, projecting to a national telephone household base of 80.9 million. AT&T currently reports 36,827 exchanges nationally, projecting to 368.27 million possible telephone numbers.

Only 31,530 of these exchanges contain valid residential listings, projecting to 315.5 million possible phone numbers. If all the blocks within these exchanges were considered eligible for random-digit samples, the incidence would be 25.6 percent (not very efficient).

To improve this incidence, our first step is to eliminate from the universe of potential numbers those blocks with fewer than three listed telephone numbers. Currently, this represents approximately 1.76 million blocks.

That means that almost 56 percent of all blocks in active exchanges are inactive. By limiting the universe to working blocks only, 139 million potential numbers, the incidence of reaching a working residential number is raised to 58 percent. This incidence is further improved to 62 percent after eliminating the 9.2 million business phone numbers listed in our Yellow Page database.

There are, on average, 43 listed numbers per active block. The median, however, is between 53 and 54 numbers per block. While the ratio of listed to unlisted phones may vary greatly from one exchange to another, there is no evidence that telephone companies assign unlisted numbers differently than they assign listed numbers.

Therefore, by weighing each working block in an exchange in proportion to its share of the listed phones in that exchange, the overall incidence of working residential phones can be raised by as much as 10 points.

Used with permission from Survey Sampling, Inc.

Sampling unit:
the initial contact point that contains the elements to be sampled.

would be identical with the element. However, it might be easier to select households as the sampling unit and interview all males over 13 years of age in each household. Here the sampling unit and the population element are not the same.

The sampling unit selected often depends on the sampling frame. If a relatively complete and accurate listing of elements is available—a register of purchasing agents, for example—one may well want to sample them directly. If no such register is available, one may need to sample companies as the basic sampling unit.

Step 4. Selection of Sampling Method

The sampling method is the way the sample units are to be selected. Five basic choices must be made in deciding on a sampling method:

> *probability versus nonprobability,*
> *single unit versus cluster of units,*
> *unstratified versus stratified,*
> *equal unit probability versus unequal unit probability,* and
> *single stage versus multistage.*

Probability Versus Nonprobability Sampling

We have listed the most crucial decision first: the choice of a probability versus a nonprobability selection procedure. A **probability sample** is one in which the sampling units are selected by chance and for which there is a known chance of each unit being selected. A **nonprobability sample** is one in which chance selection procedures are not used.

Probability Samples.   Suppose there are 50 students in your class and you wish to select 10 randomly. You could assign each a number from 1 to 50. Next you could go to the table of random numbers in Appendix E, randomly select a column, say column 5, and move down that column until you have found 10 numbers between 1 and 50. The students associated with those numbers would be your sample.

This would result in a particular kind of random sample being taken. It is known as a **simple random sample** (often abbreviated as *srs*) and, in addition to being a *probability* sample, it would have the characteristics of consisting of *single units*, each of which was drawn from an *unstratified* population with an *equal probability of each unit's being selected* by a *single-stage* procedure. It is a frequently used sampling technique.

It should be emphasized that a probability sample does not ensure a *representative* sample. If an *srs* of 100 students were taken from the students on your campus, for example, it is possible that the sample selected would consist of 100 sophomore men. This sample obviously is not representative of the total student body demographically, and probably not in most other respects.

Nonprobability Samples.   Several kinds of nonprobability samples are in common use. They include *convenience, judgment, quota,* and *purposive* samples.

Convenience Samples.   A **convenience sample** is one in which the only criterion for selecting the sampling units is the convenience of the sampler. An example of convenience sampling is the testing by food product manufacturers of potential new products by adding them to the menu of the company cafeteria. A potential new cake mix, for example, can be tested by adding it to the dessert section and noting how well it sells relative to the other kinds of cake offered.

Convenience samples are often used in exploratory situations when there is a need to get only an approximation of the actual value quickly and inexpensively. Commonly used convenience samples are associates, friends, family members, and "passers by." However, such samples contain unknown levels and types of errors and should generally be avoided.

Probability sample:
the sampling units are selected by chance and there is a known chance of each unit being selected.

Nonprobability sample:
the sampling units are selected by other than chance procedures.

Simple random sample (srs):
a probability sample consisting of single units selected from an unstratified population by a single-stage procedure with each unit having an equal probability of being selected.

Convenience sample:
one selected for the convenience of the researcher.

Judgment sample:
one selected to be
representative of
the population of
interest based on
the researcher's
judgment.

Judgment Samples.   A **judgment sample** is one in which there is an attempt to draw a representative sample of the population using judgmental selection procedures. An example is a sample of addresses taken by a municipal agency to which questionnaires on bicycle-riding habits were sent. A judgment sample was taken after researchers looked at traffic maps of the city, considered the tax assessment on houses and apartment buildings (per unit), and kept the location of schools and parks in mind.

Judgment samples are common in industrial marketing research. In this environment, very small samples of lead users, key accounts, or technologically sophisticated firms or individuals are regularly used to test new product/service concepts, pricing programs, and so forth.

Quota sample:
one selected
purposively so
that its most
important
demographic
characteristics
match those of the
population of
interest.

Quota Samples.   A **quota sample** is one selected purposively in such a way that the demographic characteristics of interest are represented in the sample in the same proportion as they are in the population.[4] If one were selecting a quota sample of persons for a use test of pizza-flavored catsup, for example, one might want to control by ethnic background, age, income, and geographic location. That is, the sample taken would have the same proportion of people in each income bracket, ethnic group, age group, and geographic area as the population. However, in a quota sample, the interviewers have at least some discretion in how they select respondents to fill each cell.

The controls used in quota samples of human populations (1) *must be available and should be recent,* (2) *should be easy for the interviewer to classify by,* (3) *should be closely related to the variables being measured in the study,* and (4) *should be kept to a reasonable number so as not to produce too many cells.* Each possible set of controls produces a separate *cell* in a quota sample. If the selection of respondents is controlled by five income brackets, three ethnic backgrounds, four age brackets, and six areas, for example, there would be $5 \times 3 \times 4 \times 6 = 360$ different cells in the sample. The interviewers would have trouble filling the quota assigned to many of these cells, and the costs of taking the sample would rise as a result.

The number of cells is not the only concern in designing a low-cost quota sample; the rate of occurrence, or percentage, of persons eligible to fill each cell—the *incidence* for each cell—can also increase costs. For example, suppose that in a study of cold cereals a quota sample is being used for which one of the cells calls for "female heads of households aged 25–44." Of women between the ages of 18 and 54—women who might reasonably be approached to see if they qualify—approximately 14 percent are heads of households between the ages of 25 and 44. This means that on the average about 7 women would have to be approached to obtain one respondent on this dimension. If a second control—has eaten cold cereal for breakfast in the past week—is added and 20 percent of the women aged 25 to 44 meet this criterion, our incidence drops to less than 3 percent ($.14 \times .20 = .028$). Now we must contact 35 women to find one who is qualified for this cell!

Quota samples are usually "validated" after they are taken. The process of validation involves a comparison of the sample and the population with respect to characteristics *not* used as control variables. In a quota sample taken to form a consumer panel for which income, education, and age were used as control variables, for example, a comparison of the panel and the population might be made with respect to such characteristics as average number of children, the occupation of the chief wage earner, and home ownership. If the panel differed significantly from the population with respect to any of these characteristics, it would be an indication of potential bias in the selection procedures.

Purposive Samples.   A **purposive sample** is one that is purposefully chosen to be nonrepresentative, to achieve some specific objective(s). The most common approach is to follow the procedure just described for a quota sample but to overrepresent some cells. In practice, purposive samples are often referred to (incorrectly) as quota samples.

Purposive samples frequently "overrepresent" heavy users, frequent viewers, potential users, and small population groups. Obviously, results from such samples cannot be generalized to the larger population without appropriate weighting. Even then, the cautions required for quota samples still apply.

Purposive sample: one selected purposively to have overrepresentation from some parts of the population of interest.

The Choice Between Probability and Nonprobability Samples.   The choice between probability and nonprobability samples is based on the *cost versus value* principle. We want to take whichever kind of sample yields the greatest margin of value over cost.

No one would question this principle; the problems come in applying it. The real question at issue is, "How can I estimate with a reasonable degree of confidence whether a probability sample will give more or give less value for its cost than a nonprobability sample?"

Generally speaking, the need for *projectable totals, low allowable errors, high population heterogeneity, small nonsampling errors, and high expected costs of errors* favors the use of probability sampling. A tight error tolerance means that the elimination of selection bias and the ability to calculate sampling error become more important considerations in the selection of the sampling plan; and so favor a probability sample. Small nonsampling errors likewise favor probability samples: the sampling error becomes relatively more important the smaller the other errors are. The more diversified and heterogeneous the population is, the greater is the need to ensure representativeness through a probability sampling procedure.

Single-Unit Versus Cluster Sampling

In a **single-unit sample** each sampling unit is selected separately; in a **cluster sample** the units are selected in groups. If the unit is a household, for example, single-unit sampling would require that each household be selected separately. One form of cluster sampling is to change the sampling unit to city blocks and to take every household on each block selected.

The choice between single-unit and cluster sampling is, again, an economic tug-of-war between cost and value. Cluster sampling usually costs less (and often substantially less) per sampling unit than does single-unit sampling. For samples of the same size, the sampling error for a cluster sample is usually greater than that of a single-unit sample because of less within-cluster variability than for the population as a whole.

Single-unit sample: each unit is selected separately.

Cluster sample: the sample units are selected in groups.

Consider a sample of 100 households to be selected for personal interviews. If selected on a single-unit basis, they will most likely be scattered around the city. This will increase the chance of getting a representative cross-section of the various ethnic groups, social classes, and so on. In contrast, a cluster sample in which 10 blocks are selected and 10 households interviewed on each block is likely to miss more of the social groups since members of social groups tend to live near each other. The costs of personal interviews per unit in a cluster sample will be low, however, because of the close proximity of the units in each cluster. Low error tolerance, high population heterogeneity, and high expected costs of errors all favor single-unit sampling.

Unstratified Versus Stratified Sampling

A *stratum* in a population is a segment of that population that has one or more common characteristics. It might be an age stratum (age 35–49), an income stratum (all families with incomes over $50,000 per year), or a gender stratum.

Stratified sampling: treating each stratum or segment of the population as a separate population for sampling purposes.

Stratified sampling involves treating each stratum as a separate subpopulation for sampling purposes. If the head-of-household age strata "18–34," "35–49," "50 and over" are of interest in a study on household furnishings, each of these age groups could be treated separately for sampling purposes. That is, the total population could be divided into age groups and a separate sample drawn from each group.

The reasons for stratifying a population for sampling purposes are that (1) it may be administratively convenient (if one wanted to take a sample of customers of a bank, for example, it would probably be more convenient to take separate subsamples from each of the lists of checking account customers, saving account customers, mortgagees, etc. than to merge all of the lists to take an unstratified sample); (2) one may want estimates of the means, proportions, or other parameters of strata in the population (if one were sampling users of a product, one might well want to know the mean consumption for each of the segments that comprise the market, for example); and (3) the required sample size for a well-designed stratified sample will usually be smaller than for a well-designed unstratified sample.

The saving in the size of the sample, although still obtaining the same level of sampling error as a nonstratified sample, may not be intuitively obvious but is easily explained. In the household furnishings study referred to previously, the age group 18–34 is that of family formation and initial acquisition of most furnishings; age 35–44 is the time when original purchases are replaced and more marginal items acquired; and age 50 and over is generally a time of limited purchasing of any kind of furnishings. To the extent that these generalizations hold, the households that fall within each of these strata should be more like each other than they are like those in any other stratum.

The greater the degree to which this within-stratum similarity holds, the smaller is the sample size required in each stratum to provide information about that stratum. Consider the extreme case in which all units in each stratum are *identical*. If this were true, a sample of *one* would be all that was required from each stratum to give complete information on the subpopulation of interest. Thus, the more homogeneous each stratum is with respect to the variable of interest, the smaller is the sample required.

The primary reason that stratified samples are not used more widely is the difficulty of obtaining adequate sample frames. A stratified sample requires that members of each stratum be selected *randomly* from that stratum. Thus, a separate sampling frame is required for each stratum. In the household furnishing example, separate sample frames for individuals in each of the age groups are not available.

Equal Unit Probability Versus Unequal Unit Probability Sampling

Another method of good sampling that is not intuitively obvious is having *unequal* probabilities of selection. The example of the household furnishing study just described affords an example.

Suppose we are interested in the average amount spent on household furnishings by families in each of the age strata. It seems reasonable to assume that the variation in expenditures of the 18–34 and the 35–49 age group households are likely to be higher than those for the 50-and-over group. If this is the case, it is more efficient statistically to take a smaller sample of the 50-and-overs and allocate part of its proportionate share to the two groups with the higher variation in purchase amounts.

Stated differently, it is only when we have no reason to believe that the variation (variance) is different among the strata that we would take a proportional sample, to give each sampling unit an equal chance of representation.

Single-Stage Versus Multistage Sampling

The number of stages involved in the sampling method is partially a function of the kind of sampling frame available. If a perfect frame were always available complete with all the associated information one might want for purposes of stratifying, far fewer multistage samples would be taken than now. In practice, it is not uncommon to have a first-stage area sample of, say, census tracts, followed by a second-stage sample of blocks, and completed with a systematic sample of households within each block. These stages would not be necessary if a complete listing of households were available. Research Application 14–3 illustrates A. C. Nielsen's use of a multistage procedure to select households for its National PeopleMeter panel.[5]

Step 5. Determination of the Sample Size

The determination of the proper sample size has traditionally been taught by one method in statistics classes and often practiced by an entirely different approach in the field. The reason for this is that traditional sampling theory generally ignores the concept of the cost versus the value of the information to be provided by various sized samples. Practitioners have been forced to deal with the realities of sampling economics regardless of whether theory recognizes them.

The problem of determining sample size is dealt with in the next chapter.

RESEARCH APPLICATION 14-3

A. C. Nielsen's Multistage Sampling Procedure to Select Its PeopleMeter Panel

The first stage involves the selection of counties using a stratified random sample based on population. Next, within the selected counties there is a random selection of blocks or enumeration districts. These blocks then go through a process called *prelisting*. A trained field representative visits the selected blocks and creates a list of all of the individual housing units. This list is then returned to the home office where it is checked for internal consistency and external agreement with other data. Finally, individual household units are randomly selected from each block.

This approach is also used by Simmons Market Research Bureau to select the sample for its annual magazine audience survey. The U.S. Census Bureau uses it in many of its household surveys and the federal government requires it in many of the surveys it sponsors.

Step 6. Specify the Sampling Plan

The *sampling plan* involves specification of how each of the decisions made thus far is to be implemented. It may have been decided that the household will be the element and the block the sampling unit. How is a household defined operationally? How is the interviewer to be instructed to take a systematic sample of households on the block? What should the interviewer do when a housing unit selected is vacant? What is the call-back procedure for households at which no one is at home? What age respondent speaking for the household is acceptable?

Research Application 14-4 provides an example of part of a sampling plan for a systematic sample. The special situations shown in the application represent problems that an interviewer might encounter in "starting with the first occupied dwelling unit to the left of the preliminary address, attempt to interview every third occupied dwelling unit in the block until four completed interviews are obtained in homes with listed phone numbers."

Step 7. Select the Sample

The final step in the sampling process is the actual selection of the sample elements. This requires a substantial amount of office and fieldwork, particularly if personal interviews are involved. Many of the difficulties encountered in this stage were described in the chapter on surveys, generally because it is the interviewer who completes this stage of the process.

RESEARCH APPLICATION 14-4

*Special Situations Encountered in Systematic Sampling by Circling a Block**

In the instructions that follow, reference is made to follow your route around a "block." In cities this will be a city block. In rural areas, a "block" is a segment of land surrounded by roads.

1. If you come to a dead end along your route, proceed down the opposite side of the street, road, or alley, traveling in the other direction. Continue making right turns, where possible, calling at every third occupied dwelling.

2. If you go all the way around a block and return to the starting address without completing four interviews in listed telephone homes, attempt an interview at the starting address. (This should seldom be necessary.)

3. If you work an entire block and do not complete the required interviews, proceed to the dwelling on the opposite side of the street (or rural route) that is *nearest* the starting address. Treat it as the next address on your Area Location Sheet and interview that house only if the address appears next

to an "X" on your sheet. If it does not, continue your interviewing to the left of that address. Always follow the right turn rule.

4. If there are no dwellings on the street or road opposite the starting address for an area, circle the block opposite the starting address, following the right turn rule. (This means that you will circle the block following a clockwise direction.) Attempt interviews at every third dwelling along this route.

5. If, after circling the adjacent block opposite the starting address, you do not complete the necessary interviews, take the next block found, *following a clockwise direction*.

6. If the third block does not yield the dwellings necessary to complete your assignment, proceed to as many blocks as necessary to find the required dwellings; these blocks follow a clockwise path around the primary block.

*Reprinted from an actual interviewer guide by permission of Belden Associates, Dallas, Texas. The complete guide was over 30 pages long and contained maps and other aids for the interviewer.

Issues in Multinational Sampling

As in most other aspects of research, sampling is more difficult in multinational research than it is in single-country research. This is particularly true when the research objectives focus on between-country comparisons or on the development of standard data across countries. Multinational research poses difficult problems for each step in the sampling process.[6]

Step 1. Define the Population

Properly defining the population is often difficult in multinational surveys. Suppose you were interested in demand for a relatively expensive breakfast food for children. What is the appropriate population? In the U.S., children and their mothers would be the primary decision makers, although fathers are increasingly involved. In England, the opinions of children would probably be less critical. In Argentina and Brazil, the maid may play the critical role in middle- and upper-income households.

Similar difficulties arise in industrial studies. In the U.S., substantial purchasing authority may be allocated to the purchasing department for a given product while in Japan a group of line managers may make the decision.

The researcher's task is to determine the type of information required and then to define the population for *each* country in a manner most likely to produce the required information. This often means that different types of people will be interviewed in different countries. It also means that the researcher must have or acquire substantial knowledge about the purchasing process for the product in question in each country.

Step 2. Specify the Sampling Frame

There are relatively few global sampling frames except for lists of large or highly specialized industrial or service firms. At the regional level, such as the EC, directories of industrial and service firms tend to be more comprehensive. However, for most multinational surveys, country-specific sampling frames must be used. Unfortunately, such frames often vary considerably across countries in both their availability and content.

The absence of reasonable sample frames for many populations in many parts of the world requires the researcher to depend more on judgment, quota, or purposive samples than would otherwise be the case. Again, the researcher must strive for *equivalent respondents* across countries, not *identical sample frames*. Thus, the Yellow Pages or state licensing bureaus may provide a workable sample frame for barbershops in a set of American cities, while local interviewers may have to compile a frame by interviewing taxi drivers and barber supply wholesalers in a set of Mexican cities.

Step 3. Specify the Sampling Unit

Since different countries often have different sampling frames available, it may be necessary to use different sampling units across countries. For example, in a country that licenses automobile mechanics, a complete sampling frame composed of individual mechanics may be available from the government. Given such a list, using individual mechanics as the sampling unit would be natural. In a country that does not license mechanics, a list of garages could be developed from Yellow Pages ads or other sources. Here the initial sampling unit is garages, followed by a selection of mechanics from the selected garages.

Step 4. Selection of the Sampling Method

As you might guess from the preceding discussion, it is often impossible, or at least unwise, to use the same sampling method across countries. For example, in Japan secondary data may allow a stratified probability sample of various types of industrial firms to be drawn. In Indonesia, such data may not be available and a quota sample may be the best available alternative. Again, the objective is to obtain comparable data. This means that significant effort should be devoted to detecting any potential biases in nonrandom samples.

Step 5. Determine the Sample Size

Sample size determination is discussed in the next chapter. However, in multinational studies a key decision affecting sample size is *how many countries must be included?* Will a survey covering France and Germany allow you to draw conclusions about the EC for your product? If your study includes France and Holland, does it also need to include Belgium? Answering these questions requires substantial insight into the countries involved, as well as balancing the cost of an error relative to the cost of collecting the additional data.

Step 6. Specify the Sampling Plan

Again, the sampling plan may need to be adjusted to meet the unique environment of each country. While the same sampling plan will probably work in both Holland and Germany, it may require alteration for Japan and almost certainly will for Indonesia.

Step 7. Select the Sample

The multinational issues associated with this step are described in Chapter 6.

An Application of Sampling

Elrick and Lavidge, a research agency, has interviewing facilities located in 19 shopping malls throughout the United States. A client wanted a mall-intercept quota sample of 250 adult women (18 years of age or older) *selected to obtain information about preferences concerning alternative formulations of a proposed new food product.*

One of the most frequently used methods of collecting data is to interview a sample of respondents in a shopping center. It is (relatively) inexpensive and provides the opportunity for new products, packages, and advertisements to be displayed and tested, capabilities that are not present in telephone interviews.

Unless the sampling plan is devised carefully, however, the results of mall-intercept sampling are subject to potentially large selection biases. These biases result from variations in the demographic composition of shoppers from that of the population as a whole by shopping center, by day and time of day, and by location in the shopping center, as well as the biases that potentially arise from how individual shoppers are selected. Elrick and Lavidge uses the following generally accepted methods to reduce the biases that could result from each of these causes:

1. Selection of the shopping center. The client decided that one of the Elrick and Lavidge mall facilities in Chicago would be acceptable from a bias standpoint and would keep the costs of the study down.

2. Allowance for unrepresentative demographic composition of shoppers. Data indicate that persons aged 25 to 54, women, and unemployed persons make more than a proportional number of visits to shopping centers. There is wide variation among persons in each of these groups with respect to the number of visits to a shopping mall in any given time period. Those people who visit shopping malls most often have a higher than proportional probability of being selected in any given sample. This unrepresentative demographic composition can be allowed for by taking a quota sample. The allowance for the number of visits can be made by obtaining information from the respondent on frequency of visits and either (i) weighting responses appropriately or (ii) subsampling respondents on the basis of frequency.[7] It may also be necessary to adjust for the varying lengths of time that different individuals spend at the mall.[8]

3. Allowance for location within the center. Buses typically stop at only one or two of several entrances. Those shoppers who arrive by bus are likely to have different demographic characteristics (be less affluent, for example) than those who drive to the center. The simplest adjustment procedure is to station an interviewer or interviewers at every entrance and instruct them to select every kth customer who enters. If this is not feasible, entrances can be sampled with equal probability and every kth customer is interviewed at the selected entrances.

4. Allowance for variation in demographic composition of shoppers by day and time of day. The characteristics of shoppers vary by season, by day of the week, by time of day, by whether there are sales, and by weather.

   How can allowance be made for these variations? The season in which the study is to be taken presumably will have been decided upon and so can be ignored as a source of bias insofar as the sample design is concerned. Day of the week and time of day variations can be allowed for by taking a probability sample. If a shopping center is open from 10:00 A.M. to 9:00 P.M. 7 days a week, there are 77 one-hour periods or 154 half-hour periods to be sampled. The length of the time period chosen should depend on the length of the interview and other administrative considerations. The time periods should be selected with a probability proportionate to the number of customers visiting then (necessitating information from a prior count) and the probability of each customer being selected within the time period should be inverse to that probability.

   Adjustments for sales and weather effects typically have to be made in terms of the quantity visiting rather than for differences in composition. Sampling rates are adjusted downward to allow for a larger number of shoppers because of a sale, for example, or adjusted upward to allow for a lower number resulting from a snowstorm.

5. Instructions for selecting respondents. If every *k*th person is to be selected, a continuing count has to be taken during the sample time period. Unambiguous rules have to be established to ensure that the count is accurate if potential biases are to be avoided.

    A line, or lines, at intersections of corridors, need to be specified as the point(s) to be crossed before a person becomes eligible for selection. Rules for how to select persons from ties (persons crossing the line simultaneously as, for example, two or more persons shopping together) need to be specified. ("Select the person who is farthest north who meets the characteristics of the cell in the quota to be added to next," is an example of such a rule.)

A final point needs to be made about sampling in practice as opposed to sampling in theory: *judgment has to be exercised at every step of the sampling procedure.* As the sampling situations just described illustrate, at each of the steps in devising and carrying out the sampling plan many alternatives are available from which to choose. Someone had to make the choices and, although objective criteria were available for some of these choices, the final decisions depended at least in part on the judgment of the person(s) who made the decisions. The sample taken can be no better than the quality of the judgments made.

Summary

Sampling involves the selection of a subset of the population of interest. A census is the selection of all of the population of interest. Samples are generally used in marketing studies because of cost, time, accuracy, and/or the destructive nature of the measurement reasons.

    The sampling process consists of seven steps: (1) define the population in terms of element, unit, extent, and time, (2) specify the sampling frame, (3) specify the sampling unit, (4) specify the sampling method, (5) determine the sample size, (6) specify the sampling plan, and (7) select the sample.

    The sampling frame is a list of sampling units of the population. A good sampling frame lists every member of the population once and only once.

    In a probability sample, the sampling units are selected by chance and each unit has a known chance of being selected. A nonprobability sample is not based on chance selection procedures. Common nonprobability sampling methods include convenience samples, judgment samples, quota samples, and purposive samples.

    Stratified sampling involves segmenting the population into groups before the sample is taken and then taking separate samples from each group. To the extent the members of each group are similar to each other and different from members of the other groups on the variable of interest, the same total sample size will produce more accurate results. Likewise, taking an unequal unit probability sample (a disproportionately large sample from those groups whose members are most diverse on the variable of interest) also increases accuracy with the same total sample size.

Sampling for multinational studies is particularly challenging. It is frequently necessary to have a unique population definition for each country or culture in the study. The quality and nature of sample frames typically varies across countries. It is often necessary to use different sampling units and even methods across countries. Yet all these decisions must be made in such a way as to produce compatible data.

Review Questions

14.1. What are the reasons a *sample* is usually preferable to a *census?*

14.2. What are the steps in the *sampling process?*

14.3. What are the necessary parts of the definition of a *population?*

14.4. What is a *sampling frame?*

14.5. What are the five basic choices that can be made among sampling methods?

14.6. What is a *probability* sample?

14.7. What is a
   a. *convenience* sample?
   b. *quota* sample?
   c. *judgment* sample?
   d. *purposive* sample?

14.8. What are the major factors to consider in *choosing between a probability and a nonprobability sample?*

14.9. What is a *stratum* in the population?

14.10. What is a *cluster* of sampling units?

14.11. What is the *incidence* for a cell in a sample?

14.12. How does multinational research affect each step in the sampling process?

Discussion Questions/Problems

14.13. Evaluate the procedure described in Research Application 14–3.

14.14. Describe three decisional situations in which a census might be preferable to a sample. Explain why this would be the case in each instance.

14.15. Would you expect that a carefully designed and well executed plan for a sample of households would yield a better, or worse, sample of adults of the general population than on an equally well-designed and executed mall-intercept sampling plan? Why?

14.16. Trade shows and industry conferences are common locations for intercept interviews in industrial research. What sampling issues does this fact pose?

14.17. Assume that the sample size for each of the following paired choices of sampling methods is the same. Given that, state which you think would be

      i. less costly

     ii. have the lower sampling variance:

        a. quota vs. stratified

        b. simple random vs. systematic

        c. convenience vs. purposive

        d. cluster vs. simple random

    Explain your reasoning in each case.

14.18. How would you define the population from which to select a sample for a survey for the design of

    a. a new line of living room furniture

    b. a lathe for use in small machine shops

    c. a super computer for large organizations

    d. an antidrug campaign aimed at high school students

14.19. Would your definition in question 14.18 change if the survey were multinational, involving the U.S., Canada, France, Japan, Mexico, and Indonesia? If so, how?

14.20. Suppose a quota sample was desired for each of the surveys described in questions 14.18 and 14.19. How would you go about deciding which controls to use for each survey?

14.21. Suppose that each of the surveys described in questions 14.18 and 14.19 are to involve personal interviews.

    a. What sampling frame(s) would you use for each survey?

    b. How would you go about selecting the sample for each survey?

14.22. Suppose you were asked to design a probability sample to obtain the names and addresses of 500 individuals in your state for a taste test of a new soft drink. Describe how you would proceed through the first six steps in Table 14–1.

14.23. A local sporting goods retailer has asked you to select a sample of 50 "opinion leaders." These leaders will be paid $20 each to evaluate the store's layout and merchandise selection. The store carries equipment for a wide range of sports activities. How would you proceed?

14.24. A quota sample is being developed for use in forming a 5,000-member national consumer panel of gardeners. What quota variables and levels of variables should be used, and how many persons should be included in each cell?

14.25. For each situation below, critique the method used and suggest alternatives you consider better where appropriate:

    a. To study attitudes toward a bank, interviewers were stationed in the parking lots of the bank's branches and questioned all those willing to answer.

    b. In studying the results of a screening method for credit card applications for a department store, folders of applicants were selected at a fixed interval beginning at the front of each file drawer. The folders were filed alphabetically by the name of the applicant and each file drawer contained the folders associated with one letter of the alphabet (i.e., all the "A's" were in the first drawer, the "B's" in the second, and so forth).

   c. To develop information on the *purchasers* of its new video game, *Space Cowboys*, the manufacturer made the activation of the product warranty conditional on the receipt of the warranty card, which also contained a short questionnaire.

14.26. Suppose that mall-intercept interviews are to be made in a regional U.S. shopping mall of male sport car owners between the ages of 25 and 44 who live in households with annual incomes of $25,000 or more. Further suppose that 3.1 percent of all U.S. males aged 25 to 44 own sport cars, and 48.1 percent of all U.S. males aged 25 to 44 live in households with incomes of $25,000 per year or more. Assuming independence between sport car ownership and income, what percentage of males between the ages 25 to 44 approached in the mall would you expect to be found to be qualified to be interviewed?

Projects/Activities

14.27. Determine the cell sizes for an 800-person quota sample of students on your campus, given the following quota variables (a) gender, (b) classification (freshman, sophomore, junior, senior, graduate), (c) full time or part time, (d) domestic or foreign, and (e) marital status.

14.28. Develop a sample of 25 classes from which you will select one member each to provide a representative sample of your university.

14.29. A firm wishes to estimate the number of portable computers being used by _____
   a. business firms
   b. nonprofit organizations
   c. service organizations
   d. retailers
   in your state. Using material available from your university library, develop a sampling plan that uses a stratified random sample. Justify your selection of strata.

Notes

1. "Single People Are Traditional Grocery Shoppers: Survey," *Marketing News* (July 10, 1981), 6. The *extent* and *time* of the population definition given are illustrative rather than actual.
2. L. Smith, "How the Average American Gets By," *Fortune* (October 21, 1991), 55.
3. "Frame Quiz Results Are In," *The Frame* (Fairfield, CN: Survey Sampling, Inc., Winter, 1990), 3.
4. See C. Marsh, E. Scarbrough, "Testing Nine Hypotheses About Quota Sampling," *Journal of the Market Research Society* (October 1990), 485–505. See also P. Cornish, "Geodemographic Sampling in Readership Surveys," *Journal of*

the Market Research Society (January 1989), 45–51; M. R. Frankel, "Current Research Practices"; and J. Rothman, D. Mitchell, "Statisticians Can Be Creative Too," both in *Journal of the Market Research Society* (October 1989), 447–455 and 456–466.
5. Frankel, op. cit., 448–449.
6. See D. J. Casley, D. A. Lury, *Data Collection in Developing Countries* (Oxford: Clarendon Press, 1987); H. C. Steele, "Marketing Research in China," *Marketing and Research Today* (August 1990), 155–164, and J. Foreman, M. Collins, "The Viability of Random Digit Dialling in the UK," *Journal of the Market Research Society* (July 1991), 219–227.

7. The weighting assigned will be equal to the inverse of the frequency of visits. Those who had not visited any other time during the period (except the present visit) have a weighting of 1, those who had visited one other time a weighting of $\frac{1}{2}$, those visiting two other times a weighting of $\frac{1}{3}$, and so forth. The subsampling procedure is similar. The sampling rate would be 100 percent of those initially selected who had not visited any other time during the period, 50 percent of those who had visited one other time, and so forth. For a critical discussion of this issue, see T. D. Dupont, "Do Frequent Mall Shoppers Distort Mall-Intercept Survey Results?" *Journal of Advertising Research* (August 1987), 45–51.

8. C. Nowell, L. R. Stanley, "Length-Biased Sampling in Mall-Intercept Surveys," *Journal of Marketing Research* (November 1991), 475–479.

CHAPTER 15

Sample Size Determination

LEARNING OBJECTIVES

Upon completing this chapter, you should be able to:

1. List and evaluate the various approaches to determining sample size.

2. Explain the nature of a sampling distribution of the mean or proportion.

3. Explain the logic underlying statistical estimation of the mean and proportion.

4. Describe the process of statistical estimation of the mean and proportion.

5. Calculate the sample size required to estimate the mean given a problem for which a simple random sample is appropriate.

6. Calculate the sample size required to estimate the proportion given a problem for which a simple random sample is appropriate.

7. Describe the impact of the incidence of the characteristics of interest in a survey and the anticipated response rate to the survey on the required initial sample size.

Public Interest Opinion Research's Approach to Sample Size Determination

Public Interest Opinion Research (PIOR) explained its rationale for using a sample size of 800 in its national surveys with the following logic. "As shown in the following table, a sample size of 800 nationwide produces a likely margin of sampling error falling in the 3 to 4 percent range. This is the normal margin of sampling error found in all national opinion surveys. As the table indicates, doubling the sample size to 1,600 persons, which would mean a 75 percent cost increase to the client, would reduce the sample error by only one point (to the 2−3 percent range)."[1]

Sample Size	Allowance (%) for Sampling Error (95% Confidence)
200	5−8
400	4−6
600	3−5
800	3−4
1,000	2−4
1,500	2−3

A number of things about PIOR's explanation are interesting. First, they are clearly using some formula to calculate an appropriate sample size. Second, they are confident that a sample of only 800 will provide sound information on the entire adult population of the U.S. Third, the margin of sampling error does *not* decrease in direct relation to increases in sample size (doubling sample size does not half the margin of sampling error). Finally, PIOR does not seek to completely minimize or eliminate possible sampling error. Instead, *they explicitly consider the cost of reducing sampling error and select a sample size based on cost and accuracy trade-offs.* The purpose of this chapter is to help you understand both the logic and mathematics of sample size determination.

An inescapable part of taking a sample is determining what size it should be. At least six different methods of determining sample size are used in marketing research. These are (1) *unaided judgment*, (2) *all you can afford*, (3) *the average for samples for similar studies*, (4) *required size per cell*, (5) *use of a traditional statistical model*, and (6) *use of a Bayesian statistical model*.

We briefly describe each of these methods and then turn to a more detailed discussion of the use of traditional statistical models for determining the size of probability samples. This discussion is introduced by a description (and simulation) of a sampling distribution.

Methods of Determining Sample Size

Unaided Judgment

It is not unusual to hear a client for a research project say, "I want a sample of 50 (or 100 or 200) persons for this study." When the client is asked why he or she thinks this is the appropriate sample size, not an uncommon response is "For this problem that is about the size we need."

This arbitrary approach to arriving at sample size gives no explicit consideration to either the likely *precision* of the sample results or the *cost* of obtaining them, characteristics in which any client should have an interest. It is an approach to be avoided.

All-You-Can-Afford

In this method, a budget for the project is set by some (generally unspecified) process and, after the estimated fixed costs of designing the project, preparing a questionnaire (if required), analyzing the data, and preparing the report are deducted, the remainder of the budget is allocated to sampling. Dividing this remaining amount by the estimated cost per sampling unit gives the sample size.

This method concentrates on the cost of the information to the exclusion of concern about its value. Although cost always has to be considered in any systematic approach to sample size determination, one also needs to give consideration to how much the information to be provided by the sample will be worth.

Average Size for Samples for Similar Studies

The sample sizes reported in several hundred studies are shown in Table 15–1.[2] Depending on the number of subgroup analyses to be run, national studies of individuals or households had samples ranging in size from 1,000 to 2,500 or more, and regional studies had samples of 200 to 1,000 or more. National samples of institutions (companies, for example) ranged in size from 200 to 1,000 or more, and regional or special studies from 50 to 500 or more. The sample sizes for institutional studies tended to be smaller because of the use of stratified sampling and because the sample frequently comprised a large fraction of the total population.

These typical sample sizes can be used as an initial aid in deciding what size sample to take, but not as a substitute for formal judgment.

Required Size Per Cell

This method of determining sample size can be used on *simple random, stratified random, purposive,* and *quota* samples. For example, in a study of attitudes about fast food establishments in a local marketing area it was decided that information was desired for two occupational groups (blue-collar and white-collar/managerial-professional) and for each of four age groups (12–17, 18–24, 35–44, and 45 and over). This resulted in $2 \times 4 = 8$ sample cells. A sample size of 30 was needed per cell for the types of statistical analyses that were to be conducted. The overall sample size was therefore $8 \times 30 = 240$.

Use of a Bayesian Statistical Model

The Bayesian model involves finding the difference between the expected value of the information to be provided by the sample and the cost of taking the sample for each potential sample size. This difference is known as the *expected net gain from sampling* (ENGS). The sample size with the largest *positive* ENGS is chosen.[3]

The Bayesian model is not as widely used as the traditional statistical models for determining sample size, even though it incorporates the cost of sam-

TABLE 15–1 Typical Sample Sizes for Studies of Human and Institutional Populations

Number of Subgroup Analyses	People or Households		Institutions	
	National	*Regional or Special*	*National*	*Regional or Special*
None or few	1,000–1,500	200–500	200–500	50–200
Average	1,500–2,500	500–1,000	500–1,000	200–1,000
Many	2,500 +	1,000 +	1,000 +	1,000 +

pling and the traditional models do not. The reasons for the relatively infrequent use of the Bayesian model are related to the greater complexity and perceived difficulty of making the estimates required for the Bayesian model as compared to the traditional models.

Use of a Traditional Statistical Model

If you have taken one or more courses in inferential statistics, you will already have been introduced to the traditional statistical formulas for determining the size of probability samples. Although the formula varies depending on the type of sample to be taken, it always incorporates three common variables: (1) an estimate of the *variance in the population* from which the sample is to be drawn, (2) the *error from sampling* that the researcher will allow, and (3) the desired *level of confidence* that the actual sampling error will be within the allowable limits.

The balance of this chapter discusses more extensively the traditional statistical formulas for determining sample size. These formulas are all based on a *sampling distribution*, which is considered first.

The Sampling Distribution

Sampling theory rests on the concept of a *sampling distribution*. Having a basic understanding of what a sampling distribution is and how it is used removes much of the mystery from sampling theory.

To help understand the concept of a sampling distribution, we illustrate a *sampling distribution of the mean* by drawing samples from a population of 1,250 sales invoices from a local retailer's Easter sale catalog. We use simple random samples of size $n = 50$ from this population for the illustration.

Sampling distribution of the mean: the relative frequency distribution of the means of all possible samples of size n taken from a population of size N.

A **sampling distribution of the mean** is the relative frequency distribution of the means of all possible samples of size n taken from a population of size N.[4] The definition specifies that *all* possible samples of size n from population size N should be taken, and the mean of *each* sample be calculated and plotted in a relative frequency distribution. With a sample of size 50 from a population of size 1,250, this would require approximately 2×10^{91} samples. Because such an undertaking is possible in theory but not in practice, we have to settle for a more modest number of samples in our illustration.

Illustration of Sampling Distribution of the Mean

Five hundred simple random samples of size 50 were taken from 1,250 invoices whose values ranged from $1 to $100, and the mean was calculated for *each* sample. These sample means were sorted into intervals based on their values. The resulting frequency distribution is shown in Table 15–2.

The relative frequencies in column 2 of Table 15–2 were calculated by dividing the absolute number in each interval (the figure in column 1) by the total number of samples taken, 500. Thus, a relative frequency for a class

TABLE 15–2 Frequencies and Relative Frequencies of 500 Sample Means

	Column 1	Column 2
	Frequency of Sample Means	Relative Frequency of Sample Means
$38.00–39.99	1	1/500 = .002
40.00–41.99	2	2/500 = .004
42.00–43.99	17	17/500 = .034
44.00–45.99	39	39/500 = .078
46.00–47.99	52	52/500 = .104
48.00–49.99	85	85/500 = .170
50.00–51.99	110	110/500 = .220
52.00–53.99	77	77/500 = .154
54.00–55.99	64	64/500 = .128
56.00–57.99	37	37/500 = .074
58.00–59.99	10	10/500 = .020
60.00–61.99	4	4/500 = .008
62.00–63.99	2	2/500 = .004
Total	500	1.000

(interval) is nothing more than the percentage of times means with values falling within the class limits occurred.

A relative frequency, then, is a measure of a *probability*. If one were asked to predict the probability of a random sample of size 50 taken from this population having a mean between $50.00 and $51.99, the best estimate is .22, based on the table. That is, we would expect about 2 out of every 10 simple random samples of size 50 drawn from this population to have a mean within this range.

The relative frequencies in Table 15–2 are shown in a histogram in Figure 15–1. A normal curve is shown in the same figure. It may be seen that the relative frequency distribution is very close to being normally distributed. Had *all* possible samples been drawn rather than only 500, it *would* have been normally distributed. The normal curve in Figure 15–1 is the *sampling distribution of the mean* for the sampling problem with which we are working. A sampling distribution of the mean for *simple random* samples that are large (30 or more) has

1. *a normal distribution*
2. *a mean equal to the population mean (M)*
3. *a standard deviation, called the standard error of the mean ($\sigma_{\bar{x}}$), that is equal to the population standard deviation (σ) divided by the square root of the sample size ($\sqrt{n}$):*

$$\sigma_{\bar{x}} = \frac{\sigma}{\sqrt{n}} \qquad (15\text{-}1)$$

It is important to note that the **standard error of the mean** is simply the standard deviation of the sampling distribution of the mean. The only reason

Standard error of the mean: the standard deviation of the sampling distribution of the mean.

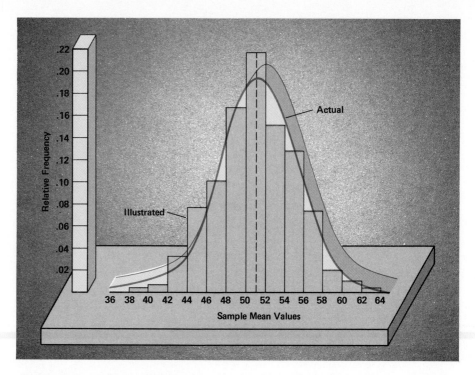

FIGURE 15–1 Illustrated and Actual Sampling Distribution of the Mean
for Sales Invoice Problem ($n = 50$)

that a standard error of the mean is called that instead of a standard deviation is to indicate that it applies to a *distribution of sample means* and not to a single sample or a population.

A *basic characteristic of a sampling distribution is that the area under it between any two points can be calculated as long as each point is defined by the number of standard errors it is away from the mean.* The number of standard errors a point is away from the mean is referred to as the **Z value** for that point. For example, the areas under one side of the curve between the mean and points that have Z values of 1.0, 2.0, and 3.0, respectively, are as follows:

Z value: the number of standard errors a point is from the mean of a sampling distribution.

Z Value (number of standard errors)	Area Under the Curve from the Mean to the Point Defined by the Z Value
1.0	0.3413
2.0	0.4772
3.0	0.4986

(A complete table of areas under the normal curve is given in Appendix A.)

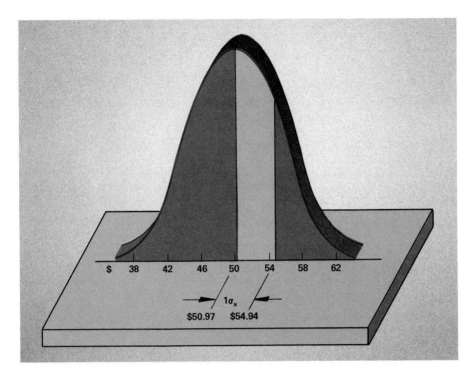

FIGURE 15–2 Determination of Probability of Getting a Sample Mean with a Value of $50.97 to $54.94

Thus, the area between the population mean (M) and a sample mean ($\bar{x}$) that is one standard error to the right of the mean ($Z = +1.0$) is 0.3413. This area is shown as the shaded area in Figure 15–2.

The dollar value for one standard error in the sales invoice problem is $3.97. It is calculated from the values for the standard deviation ($\sigma = \$28.06$) and the sample size ($n = 50$) as follows:

$$\sigma_{\bar{x}} = \frac{\sigma}{\sqrt{n}} = \frac{\$28.06}{\sqrt{50}} = \$3.97.$$

Thus, the dollar values shown in Figure 15–2 for the mean and one standard deviation to the right of it in the sales invoice problem are as follows:

$$M = \$50.97, \text{ and}$$
$$M + 1.0\sigma_{\bar{x}} = \$50.97 + \$3.97 = \$54.94.$$

The area between two points under a sampling distribution is a *probability*. For our example, if we took all possible samples of size 50 from the population, the relative frequency of occurrence of those with means falling from $50.97 to $54.94 would be .3413. That is, slightly more than one-third of them would fall between $50.97 and $54.94.

The fact that the *relative frequency* of occurrence of *all possible* samples of size 50 with a mean of plus (or minus) 1 standard error from the population mean is .3413 means that the *probability* of *one* sample with a mean falling within this range is .3413 (or 34.13 percent). That is, if we know the population mean and the standard error, we know that the probability of any given sample mean being within one standard error ($Z = 1.0$) on one side of the population mean is .3413. We can determine the comparable probability for any Z value (number of standard errors) from the table of areas under the normal curve.

Statistical Estimation and the Sampling Distribution of the Mean

In statistical estimation problems involving the mean, we want to estimate a *population mean* that *we do not know* from a sample mean that *we do know*. Two kinds of estimates of a population mean may be made, *point* and *interval*.

A *point estimate* of the mean is an estimate involving only a single value. If a random sample is taken, the sample mean is the best estimate that can be made from the sample data. If we have taken a random sample of 50 invoices from the population of 1,250 sales invoices and want to estimate the population mean, we simply use the sample mean as the best guess, or estimate, of the value of the population mean.

A visual examination of the sampling distribution of the mean in Figure 15–2 shows that the mean of an *srs* of size 50 is likely to be quite close to the actual population mean. Most of the sample means are clustered near the center of the sampling distribution; that is, near the true mean. But the mean of a particular *srs* of size 50 could be any one of the sample means in the distribution, and some are a substantial distance from the true mean. The distance between the sample value and the true value of the mean is the *sampling error*.

Increasing sample size will reduce the potential sampling error, because as sample size increases the sampling distribution becomes clustered more closely around the true population value. Or, stated differently, *the standard error of the mean becomes smaller as the sample size increases*. This can be seen easily by examining formula (15–1).

The fact that point estimates based on sample means are seldom *exactly* correct makes the *interval estimate* quite useful. An **interval estimate** is an estimate concerning an interval, or range of values with the probability that the interval will enclose the true value of the mean also given. This probability is called a **confidence coefficient** and the interval is called a **confidence interval.**

An interval estimate of the mean is arrived at by the following procedure. A sample is taken and the sample mean is calculated. We know that this sample mean falls somewhere within the sampling distribution, but not at what location. We do know, however, that there is a probability of .3413 (34.13 percent) that it lies within 1 standard error above and a probability of .3413 (34.13 percent) that it lies within 1 standard error below the actual population mean. We may, therefore, make an interval estimate that *allows us to be 68.26 percent confident* (34.13 + 34.13 percent) *that the population mean (M) lies within the interval formed by the sample mean ($\bar{x}$) plus 1 standard error ($\sigma_{\bar{x}}$) and the sample mean minus 1 standard error.*

In symbols this confidence interval may be shown as

$$\bar{x} - 1.0\sigma_{\bar{x}} \leq M \leq \bar{x} + 1.0\sigma_{\bar{x}}$$

Interval estimate: an estimate that a population value will fall within a specified range of values and a probability that the estimate is correct.

Confidence coefficient: the probability that the confidence interval encloses the population value.

Confidence interval: the range of values within which a population value is estimated to be.

The 68.26 percent is the *confidence coefficient* of the estimate.

We may extend the interval to be more confident that the true value of the population mean is enclosed by the estimating process. We might enlarge the interval to plus or minus 2 standard errors. Reference to Appendix A indicates that the appropriate confidence coefficient is 95.44 percent. Although we are more confident of our interval estimate now, it is a larger interval and, therefore, may not be as useful.

The question may be asked, "This seems all right if you know the value of the standard deviation of the population. But what do you do when you don't know that either?" One answer is that you may estimate it from the sample.[5] If we let $\hat{\sigma}$ stand for an *estimate* of the standard deviation of the population and s represent the sample standard deviation, an estimate is given by

$$\hat{\sigma} = s, \text{ where } s = \sqrt{\frac{\sum\limits_{i=1}^{n} (x_i - \bar{x})^2}{n - 1}} \tag{15-2}$$

The Sampling Distribution of the Proportion

Researchers are often interested in proportions (percentages) as well as in means. For example, marketers are concerned about the percentage of magazine readers who remember a specific advertisement, the percentage of a group that prefers brand A over brand B, and so on. Therefore, marketing researchers are often dealing with proportions and, of necessity, with the sampling distribution of the proportion.

The **sampling distribution of the proportion** is the relative frequency distribution of the proportion (p) of all possible samples of size n taken from a population of size N.[6] The same basic reasoning used to determine the sampling distribution of the mean applies to the sampling distribution of the proportion. A sampling distribution of a proportion for a simple random sample has a

1. *normal distribution*
2. *a mean equal to the population proportion (P)*
3. *a standard error (σ_p) equal to*

$$\sigma_p = \sqrt{\frac{P(1 - P)}{n}} \tag{15-3}$$

The estimated standard error of the proportion (given a large sample size that is a small proportion of the population) is

$$\hat{\sigma}_p = \sqrt{\frac{p(1 - p)}{n - 1}} \tag{15-4}$$

where p represents the sample proportion.

Having briefly reviewed the critical concept of the sampling distribution, we now turn our attention to how this concept can be used in determining sample size.

Sampling distribution of the proportion: the relative frequency distribution of the proportion of all possible samples of size n taken from a population of size N.

Traditional Statistical Methods of Determining Sample Size

Calculation of Sample Size in Estimation Problems Involving Means

Suppose an estimate of the mean dollar amount per invoice is required for a decision concerning the continuation of the direct mail campaign that generated the invoices. A simple random sample is to be taken from the 1,250 invoices described earlier to make the estimate. What information is needed before a calculation of the sample size can be made?

Three kinds of specifications have to be made before the sample size necessary to estimate the population mean can be determined:

1. *Specification of the error (e) that can be allowed*—how close must the estimate be (how accurate do we need to be)?
2. *Specification of the confidence coefficient*—what level of confidence is required that the actual sampling error does not exceed that specified (how sure do we want to be that we have achieved our desired accuracy)?
3. *Estimate of the population standard deviation (σ)*—what is the standard deviation of the population (how "spread out" or diverse is the population)?

The first two of these specifications are matters of judgment involving the *use* of the data. The questions of "How much error in the estimate is acceptable?" and "How confident do you want to be that the error really isn't any greater than that?" need to be raised.

Suppose that, after discussing these questions, it is decided that the allowable error is ±$8.00 and that a confidence level of 90 percent is desired.

The third specification, the estimate of the standard deviation of the population, is the responsibility of the analyst. Estimates of the standard deviation sometimes are available from previous studies. Most government agencies that collect data report means and deviations. Standard deviations are either available directly or can be calculated for such demographic and other variables as personal income, corporate income, age, education, labor rates, and housing values. Research Application 15–1 provides estimates of variances (σ^2) associated with rating scales commonly used in marketing research.

If other sources are not available for estimating the standard deviation, one can sometimes design the sampling plan so that a small sample is taken for that purpose. The sample standard deviation is calculated and used to estimate the population standard deviation and the final sample size is determined.

Assume that, based on past studies, we estimate the standard deviation of the population of invoice values to be $28.90. With the allowable error already set at $8.00 and the confidence coefficient at 90 percent, all the specifications needed to calculate sample size are complete.

RESEARCH APPLICATION 15–1

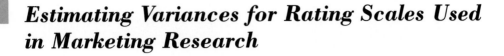

Estimating Variances for Rating Scales Used in Marketing Research

Rating scales are "doubly-bounded": on a 5-point scale, for instance, responses cannot be less than 1 or greater than 5. This constraint leads to a relationship between the mean and the variance. For example, if a sample mean is 4.6 on a 5-point scale, then there must be a large proportion of responses of "5" and it follows that the variance must be relatively small. On the other hand, if the mean is near 3.0, the variance can be potentially much greater. The nature of the relationship between the mean and the variance depends on the number of scale points and on the "shape" of the distribution of responses (e.g., approximately normal or symmetrically "clustered" around some central scale value, or skewed, or uniformly spread among the scale values). By considering the types of distribution shapes typically encountered in practice, it is possible to estimate variances for use in calculating sample size requirements for a given number of scale points.

Typical variances for various numbers of scale points are shown below.

Number of Scale Points	Typical Variances
3	.67
4	1.0
5	1.8
6	2.5
7	3.5
8	4.0
9	5.0
10	6.0

SOURCE: "Sample Size Tables for Significance Tests," *Research on Research* 45 (Chicago: Market Facts Inc., undated), 3.

The three specifications are related in the following way:

$$\frac{\text{number of standard errors}}{\text{implied by confidence coefficient}} = \frac{\text{allowable error}}{\text{standard error}}$$

or in symbols,

$$Z = \frac{e}{\dfrac{\sigma}{\sqrt{n}}} \qquad\qquad (15\text{-}5)$$

The only unknown variable is the sample size.

This equation is the direct result of the logic of the sampling distribution. We know that the sample mean ($\bar{x}$) lies somewhere on the sampling distribution, which has as its mean the population mean (M). In order to be 90 percent confident that the population mean will be included, we must construct an interval that includes the population mean in all cases except those in which the sample mean happens to fall in the last 5 percent of the area at the two ends of the distribution. This interval is shown in Figure 15–3.

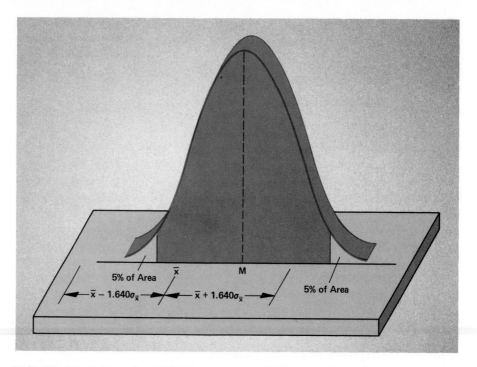

FIGURE 15–3 Sampling Distribution and 90 Percent Confidence
Interval—Estimate of Mean

A simpler formula for the size of simple random samples can be derived
from equation (15–5).[7] It is

$$n = \frac{Z^2\sigma^2}{e^2} \tag{15-6}$$

$$n = \frac{(1.64)^2(28.90)^2}{(8.00)^2}$$

$$n = 35$$

The Z value of 1.64 is determined from Appendix A as the number of standard errors that includes 45 percent of one side of the sampling distribution.

Specifications Required for Estimation Problems Involving Proportions

Suppose an estimate of the proportion of invoices that have dollar amounts of
$20.00 or less is to be made. A simple random sample is to be taken from the
population of 1,250 invoices described earlier. What additional information is
needed before one can determine the sample size to take?

The specifications that must be made to determine the sample size for an
estimation problem involving a proportion are very similar to those for the
mean:

1. *Specification of error (e) that can be allowed*—how close must the estimate be?
2. *Specification of confidence coefficient*—what level of confidence is required that the actual sampling error does not exceed that specified?
3. *Estimate of population proportion ($\hat{P}$) using prior information*—what is the approximate or estimated population proportion?

The reasoning for these specifications and the methods of obtaining them are the same as that for the mean. They, along with the sample size, collectively determine the sampling distribution for the problem. Because sample size is the only remaining unknown, it can be calculated.

As was the case with the sample mean, the three specifications are related as follows:

$$\frac{\text{number of standard errors implied}}{\text{by confidence coefficient}} = \frac{\text{allowable error}}{\text{standard error}}$$

The formula for the estimated standard error of the proportion is

$$\hat{\sigma}_P = \sqrt{\frac{\hat{P}(1.0 - \hat{P})}{n}} \tag{15-7}$$

The relation among specifications may be shown symbolically as

$$Z = \frac{e}{\sqrt{\dfrac{\hat{P}(1.0 - \hat{P})}{n}}} \tag{15-8}$$

Because the logic for this relationship is the same as it is for problems involving estimation of means, we do not repeat it here. The calculation of sample size can also be made in the same way.[8]

The formula for determining n directly is

$$n = \frac{Z^2[\hat{P}(1.0 - \hat{P})]}{(e)^2} \tag{15-9}$$

The sample size required for estimating the proportion of invoices with dollar amounts of $20.00 or less where the specification of *error that can be allowed (e)* is .08 (8 percentage points), *the confidence level* is 95.4 percent (thus, $Z = 2.0$) and the estimate of the *population proportion* is $P = .20$ (20.0 percent) is

$$n = \frac{2^2[.20(1.0 - .20)]}{(.08)^2}$$
$$= 100$$

Sample Size, Incidence, and Nonresponse

Our discussion of sample size determination thus far has ignored incidence and nonresponse.[9] **Incidence** is the percentage of individuals who have the traits necessary to be included in a survey, such as product category user,

Incidence:
the percentage of individuals in the sample frame who have the characteristics to be included in the study.

male, viewed program, or a host of other variables. *Nonresponse*, as described in Chapter 6, refers to the percentage of respondents who refuse to participate in a survey or who cannot be contacted.

The formulas we have described are based on a population of qualified respondents with a 100 percent response rate. Suppose you need to conduct a mail survey of owners of aquariums. Using the formulas described previously, you calculate a required sample size of 200. However, previous research indicates that only 8 percent of all households have aquariums. Further, the mail panel company you are using estimates a 75 percent response rate to your questionnaire. How many questionnaires do you mail out?

A simple approach is to use the formula:

$$\text{Initial sample size} = \text{required response} \div (\text{incidence} \times \text{response rate})$$
$$= 200 \div (.08 \times .75)$$
$$= 3{,}333$$

This will yield 200 or more qualified respondents only about half the time. A formula for determining the required initial sample size to achieve an obtained sample size with a specified level of confidence is available.[10] Using that formula in this case indicates that an initial sample size of 3,631 is required to produce 200 completed interviews 90 percent of the time.

Several Sample Sizes Must Be Calculated for Most Survey Research Studies—Largest Is Ruling

In most survey research projects there are questions on the questionnaire that, when the answers are analyzed, involve proportions *(Do you own a microwave oven? At which of the following supermarkets have you shopped in the past two weeks?)* and other questions that involve means *(On the average, how many times a week would you say you use your microwave oven? At how many different supermarkets would you say you shop during an average month?)* The answers to these questions are almost always analyzed to provide estimates of population values. They are also often used to test hypotheses.

Thus, the usual situation is that more than one sample size has to be calculated. When this occurs, the *largest* sample size should be taken. Reflecting for a moment will reveal that this is the only way the specifications concerning allowable error and confidence level can be met for the estimate or hypothesis test that requires the largest sample.

Summary

Sample size can be determined by a variety of methods including (1) unaided judgment, (2) all-you-can-afford, (3) average size for similar studies, (4) required size per cell, (5) use of a Bayesian statistical model, and (6) use of a traditional statistical model. The Bayesian approach has much to recommend it, but nonstatistical approaches, particularly the all-you-can-afford and the required size per cell, and the traditional statistical model are more widely used.

The traditional statistical model is based on the concept of a sampling distribution. A sampling distribution of the mean is the relative frequency distribution of the means of all possible samples of a given size taken from a particular population. A sampling distribution of the mean based on a large (greater than 30) simple random sample has (1) a normal distribution, (2) a mean equal to the population mean, and (3) a standard deviation, called the standard error of the mean, that is equal to the population standard deviation divided by the square root of the sample size.

Since the sampling distribution of the mean is a normally distributed relative frequency distribution, the area under it between any two points can be calculated as long as each point is defined by the number of standard errors it is away from the mean. The number of standard errors (standard deviations of the sampling distribution) a point is from the mean is known as its Z value. An area between the mean and a point 1 standard area away (a Z value of 1) is .3413. This means that 34 percent of all possible means of random samples of this size from this population will have a value between the mean and this point. Likewise, the probability of any one mean falling within this range is .34.

These characteristics allow us to make an interval estimate, which is an estimate the probability (called the confidence coefficient) that the true mean falls with a specified interval (called the confidence interval). It is calculated by adding and subtracting a specified number of standard errors to the obtained sample mean. The interval thus formed is the confidence interval and the area enclosed on either side of the mean by the number of standard errors chosen is the confidence coefficient.

The standard error of the proportion is the relative frequency distribution of the proportion of all possible samples of a given size taken from a particular population. It has characteristics similar to those of the sampling distribution of the mean and is used in similar ways.

Given our knowledge of the characteristics of the sampling distribution of the mean, we can calculate the required sample size by making the following specifications: (1) the error that we will allow—how close we need to be to the true answer, (2) the confidence coefficient—how sure we need to be that we are as close to the answer as we need to be, and (3) as estimate of the population standard deviation—how diverse or spread out the population is. The same specifications are required to determine the sample size required for a problem involving proportions, except that an estimate of the population proportion is required rather than the population standard deviation.

Incidence is the percentage of persons in the sample frame who have the traits to be included in a survey. Nonresponse is the percentage of respondents who refuse to participate in a survey or who cannot be reached. The initial sample size for surveys that require respondents with specific characteristics and/or that have some level of nonresponse must be increased accordingly.

Review Questions

15.1. What are *six* different methods of *determining sample size?*

15.2. What is a *sampling distribution of the mean?*

15.3. What is the difference between a *population standard deviation* and a *standard error of the mean?*

15.4. What is the formula for the *standard error of the mean* for a simple random sample?

15.5. What is a *point estimate* of the mean? an *interval estimate* of the mean?

15.6. What is a *confidence coefficient?*

15.7. What is a *confidence interval?*

15.8. What is a *sampling distribution of the proportion?*

15.9. What is the formula for the *standard error of the proportion* for a simple random sample?

15.10. What specifications must be made to determine the sample size required to estimate the population mean using a *simple random sample?*

15.11. What specifications must be made to determine the sample size required to estimate the population proportion using a *simple random sample?*

15.12. What is the formula for the sample size for an estimate of the population mean using a simple random sample?

15.13. What is the formula for the sample size for an estimate of the population proportion using a simple random sample?

15.14. How do incidence and response rate affect the initial sample size requirements?

Discussion Questions/Problems

15.15. Suppose that there is a population of 40 users of an industrial raw material. The mean of the sampling distribution of the mean for a simple random sample of size $n = 8$ of the amount of the material used last year is 1,000 lbs. The mean of the amount of the same material used last year by the 20 companies is 1,150 lbs. What conclusion(s) can you draw concerning the difference in the two means? Explain.

15.16. A congressional committee investigating television ratings in the U.S. stated its belief that the samples of households on which ratings are based are far too small for a country with more than 80 million households. The sample used by the research agencies that provided the ratings is typically in the range of 1,000 to 1,500 households. Would Congress have less cause for concern about the sample size if the number of households were 8 million instead of 80 million? Why or why not?

15.17. The American Testing Institute provides both static and dynamic tests of automobile characteristics and performance. Such tests are used for comparison advertising and advertising documentation purposes. Static tests are measures of relatively uniform characteristics such as head room or leg room. Dynamic tests involve performance characteristics such as acceleration, braking, handling, and so forth. According to the firm's president, a valid dynamic test requires a minimum sample size of five cars of each model tested. What assumptions about the performance characteristics of cars does this statement imply?

15.18. A simple random sample is to be taken from a population of 50,000 sales invoices to estimate the mean amount per invoice. Suppose that the population mean is actually $6,000 and the standard deviation of the population is $1,500. The allowable error is set at $200 and the confidence coefficient at 95 percent.
   a. What size sample is required? (You may ignore the finite population correction factor.)
   b. Suppose the sample means turns out to be 6,286. What is the interval estimate?

15.19. Evaluate the following quote from a recent report.
   "Questionnaires were mailed in March and April to 500 randomly selected subscribers of *Advertising Age*; 216 companies responded. The survey has a 6 percent margin of error."[11]

15.20. Evaluate the following quote from a recent report.
   "The poll was conducted Wednesday with 512 adults nationwide, all of whom had been interviewed before in the September survey. The poll has a margin of error of plus or minus 5 percentage points."[12]

15.21. A mail survey is to be conductd to estimate pet food expenditures among households that have one or more pets. A completed sample size of 300 is desired. The sample frame is a list of household addresses. It is estimated that half of all households have a pet. The response rate to this survey is estimated to be 40 percent among pet owners and 20 percent from households that do not own a pet. How large should the initial sample be?

Projects/Activities

15.22. Form a project group with three other members of your class. Design a sampling plan and a questionnaire and conduct a poll among the students on your campus to determine the percentage that plan to go directly into graduate school after graduation from their undergraduate program. Design the sample so that the allowable error is $e = P - p = \pm .02$ with a confidence level of 90 percent.

15.23. Form a project team with three other members of your class. Design a sampling plan and conduct a poll among students at your university to determine the mean number of soft drinks consumed in the past week. Justify all aspects of your sampling plan.

Notes

1. *National Opinion Survey: Sampling and Interview Procedure* (Alexandria, VA: Public Interest Opinion Research, undated).

2. S. Sudman, *Applied Sampling* (New York: Academic Press, 1976), 87.

3. For a discussion and illustration of the use of the Bayesian statistical model in determining sample size, see Sudman, op. cit. 88–104.

4. This definition assumes that the sampling is from a population of finite rather than infinite size. This is usually

the situation in marketing and, if the sampling is from an infinite population, presents no conceptual problem.

5. For more advanced treatments, see R. E. Shiffler, A. J. Adams, "A Correction for Biasing Effects of Pilot Sample Size on Sample Size Determine," *Journal of Marketing Research* (August 1987), 319–321; R. Gillett, "Confidence Interval Construction By Stein's Method," and A. J. Adams, R. E. Shiffler, "Commentary on Biasing Effects of Pilot Samples," both in *Journal of Marketing Research* (May 1989), 237–240, 241–243.

6. This definition also assumes that the sampling is from a population of finite size.

7. These formulas assume an infinite rather than a finite population. If the population is finite and sample size calculated by equation (15–6) is 5 percent or more of the population, it is larger than necessary. In such cases, the formula that should be used for calculating sample size is

$$n = \frac{\hat{\sigma}^2}{\dfrac{e^2}{Z^2} + \dfrac{\hat{\sigma}^2}{N}}$$

8. These formulas assume an infinite rather than a finite population. If the population is finite and sample size calculated by equation (15–9) is 5 percent or more of the population, it is larger than necessary. In such cases, the formula that should be used for calculating the sample size is

$$n = \frac{\hat{P}(1 - \hat{P})}{\dfrac{(e)^2}{Z^2} + \dfrac{\hat{P}(1 - \hat{P})}{N}}$$

9. This section is based on "Estimating Sample Sizes for Mailouts," *Research on Research* 32 (Chicago: Market Facts, Inc., updated).

10.

$$IS = \frac{2X + Z(ZQ + \sqrt{(ZQ)^2 + 4XQ})}{2P}$$

where IS = initial sample;

X = required sample (number of people with characteristic of interest) minus .5;

= 200 − .5 = 199.5;

P = the incidence (proportion) for the characteristic times the estimated response rate = .08 × .75 = .06;

$Q = 1 − P = 1 − .06 = .94$;

C = the desired probability or confidence that the initial sample will produce the desired sample, say .90 for this case; and

Z = the value that exceeds 100(C)% of the standard normal distribution = 1.282 (from Appendix A).

11. S. Hume, "New Ideas, Old Barriers," *Advertising Age* (July 22, 1991), 6.

12. E. Kolbert, "Many Harassed But Few Report," *The Register Guard* (October 15, 1991), A1.

CHAPTER 16

Data Reduction and Estimation

LEARNING OBJECTIVES

Upon completing this chapter, you should be able to:

1. Describe the steps necessary to create a basic data array.

2. Explain the importance of sound field controls.

3. Describe the tasks involved in editing survey data.

4. Discuss the issues involved in coding.

5. Explain why it is often desirable to generate new variables before data analysis.

6. Explain the differences between a one-way frequency distribution and a cross tabulation.

7. Examine a cross tabulation or banner table for evidence of causation.

8. Describe the common measures of central tendency and dispersion.

9. Calculate point and interval estimates of the mean and proportion based on simple random samples.

Analyzing Taste Reactions to a New Potato Chip

The following numbers represent the reactions of 200 individuals to a new vinegar-and-salt flavored potato chip. The taste of the chips was rated on a 10-point scale with 1 representing terrible and 10 representing fantastic. What is the overall response to the taste of the chips? Do people like the taste, dislike it, or are they neutral toward it? Do males and females differ in their responses to the taste of the chip?

Males					Females				
1	3	2	9	1	10	6	3	10	5
9	3	2	4	1	7	10	1	2	9
5	2	1	10	1	2	3	9	4	2
9	10	2	5	8	3	2	9	10	1
2	3	10	1	2	6	2	10	8	2
10	8	1	1	1	2	4	2	3	5
2	1	2	3	10	1	1	6	9	10
1	1	8	9	2	9	10	1	1	1
5	2	1	10	1	2	3	9	4	2
9	3	2	1	3	1	1	4	2	9
1	3	2	9	1	2	1	1	10	2
9	10	6	3	10	5	3	4	2	1
3	9	4	2	7	6	1	3	3	2
9	10	2	5	8	3	2	9	10	1
10	8	1	1	1	2	4	2	3	5
2	1	2	3	10	1	1	6	9	10
1	1	8	9	2	9	1	10	1	1
9	3	2	1	3	1	1	4	2	9
2	3	10	1	2	6	2	1	2	2
6	1	3	3	2	9	5	1	1	3

Few of us can answer these simple questions just by looking at the numbers presented in the table. If we calculated a simple average for the entire sample (4.25), and for males (4.27) and females (4.23) separately, we easily see that overall the group was not enthusiastic about the taste and that males and females had a similar reaction to it. In fact, the means

403

are very close to the midpoint of the scale, and we might be tempted to conclude that the respondents are neutral about the chip's taste. However, if we presented the data in the form of a graph of a frequency distribution, as shown in the following figure, we quickly see that, though most individuals strongly dislike the chip's taste, a sizable minority of both genders like it. In fact, it appears that a market segment for the new chip does indeed exist.

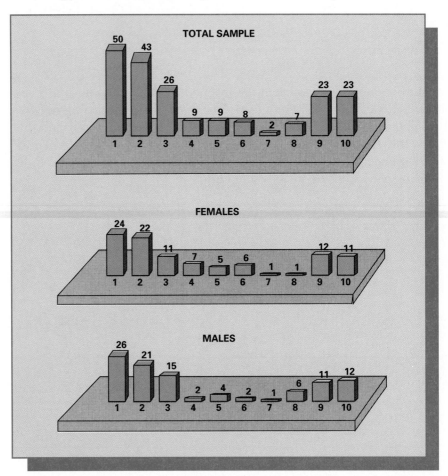

Data analysis: converting a series of observations into descriptive statements about variables and/or inferences about relationships among variables.

As the opening example illustrates, data become useful only after they are analyzed. **Data analysis** involves converting a series of observations (data) into descriptive statements about variables and/or inferences about relationships among variables. Put more simply, *data analysis provides answers to questions we might want to ask of a set of data.* Some examples are as follows:

> *How many pairs of jeans does the average teenager buy per year?*
> *Do boys or girls buy more jeans?*
> *Is there a relationship between social class and brands of jeans bought?*
> *Do social class, sex, age, and geographic region combine in some way to influence jean buying?*

Data reduction: the process of getting the data ready for analysis and the calculation of summarizing statistics.

In this chapter, we deal with **data reduction,** which is the process of getting the data ready for analysis and the calculation of summarizing or descriptive statistics. Estimation techniques are also discussed in this chapter. Estimation techniques involve inferring the value of some group (called a *population*) from a subset of that group (a *sample*). Since virtually all marketing studies involve samples, estimation techniques are very important.

An Example Involving New Product Research

In this section, we present a very simplified example of a set of observations. A regional soft drink firm is evaluating the potential introduction of a non-alcoholic carbonated apple cider. One market segment of interest is the college student market. As a means of examining the nature and extent of potential student demand for the product, the firm commissioned a small "pilot" experiment using students from a state university in the area (26,000 students). The experiment and the data collected in conjunction with it were designed to determine a number of things:

1. The percentage of males, females, and all students who consume a carbonated beverage at least one day a week.
2. The amount of carbonated beverages consumed per week by males, females, and all students.
3. The importance of price in general to students.
4. The importance to students of image or status for items used in public.
5. The taste reaction of male and female students to the new product.
6. The relative preference by male and female students for this product compared to four potential competitors.
7. The likelihood of purchasing the product by males, females, and all students.
8. Which of two brand names is better for the product.
9. The differences in reactions between males and females to the product and the brand names.

It was decided that the study would involve a sample of 100 students. To provide a sampling frame, a list of all students registered at the university was generated. Approximately 60 percent of the students were male. A random sample of 100 students produced 60 male and 40 female respondents.

The selected students completed a questionnaire dealing with their demographics, attitudes toward a variety of beverages, and beverage-consumption patterns. Then they tasted the new beverage.

Half of each group (30 males and 20 females) tasted the beverage with the label *Bravo* while the other half tasted the identical beverage labeled *Delight*. The students then rated the taste of the product, ranked its overall appeal compared to four competitors, stated their likelihood of purchasing the product, and finally chose either a six-pack of the version they had tasted or $3 as a payment for their participation in the study.

Table 16–1 contains some of the questions used in the study and Table 16–2 contains the responses to these questions.

TABLE 16–1 Selected Questions and Measurements from the Student Beverage Preference Study

1. Gender: _____(1) Male _____ (2) Female
2. Age:_____
3. How many bottles, cans, and/or glasses of carbonated beverages do you drink in a typical week?_____
4. How many days in a typical week do you drink at least one carbonated beverage?_____
5. How important is price to you when you purchase beverages?
   (1) Extremely Important ___ (2) Very Important ___ (3) Somewhat Important ___
   (4) Neither Important Nor Unimportant ___ (5) Somewhat Unimportant ___
   (6) Very Unimportant ___ (7) Extremely Unimportant___
6. How important is the quality image of a brand to you when you purchase beverages?
   (1) Extremely Important ___ (2) Very Important ___ (3) Somewhat Important ___
   (4) Neither Important Nor Unimportant ___ (5) Somewhat Unimportant ___
   (6) Very Unimportant ___ (7) Extremely Unimportant___
7. Having tasted Bravo (Delight), indicate how much you like its taste by assigning 0 to 100 points, where 0 indicates extreme dislike, 50 indicates indifference (neither like nor dislike), and 100 indicates extreme liking. (Use any value between 0 and 100)_____
8. Please rank the following five brands in order of your overall preference. Let a "1" represent your most preferred brand and a "5" your least preferred brand. No ties, please. (*Note: the order of the brands shown was rotated across the questionnaires.*)
   Rank
   _____ a. Perrier (or similar brands)
   _____ b. Coke (or similar brands)
   _____ c. 7-Up (or similar brands)
   _____ d. Hi-C (or other fruit drinks)
   _____ e. Bravo (Delight)
9. Please indicate the likelihood or probability that you would purchase six or more bottles of Bravo (Delight) per month if it were available for $3.00 per six-pack. Indicate by allocating 100 points such that 0 indicates that there is no possibility that you would purchase the product, 50 indicates that you are equally likely to purchase or not purchase the product, and 100 indicates certainty that you would purchase the product. (Use *any* number between 0 and 100) _____
10. As an expression of our appreciation for your assistance, you may have either $3.00 or a six-pack of Bravo (Delight). Which would you prefer? _____ (1) $3.00 _____ (2) Bravo (Delight)
    Completed by Editor
    　Respondent #_____
    　Treatment: _____ (1) Bravo _____ (2) Delight

TABLE 16–2 Responses to Selected Questions and Measurements from a Beverage Preference Test

Respondent #	Treatment #	Gender	Age	Bottles Consumed per Week	Days Consumed per Week	Price Importance	Image Importance	Taste Reaction	Rank This Brand	Rank Brand A	Rank Brand B	Rank Brand C	Rank Brand D	Purchase Probability	Choice
1	1	1	21	1	1	2	6	45	4	2	5	1	3	30	1
2	1	1	21	0	0	7	4	90	1	2	5	4	3	100	2
3	1	1	23	3	1	4	6	50	4	3	5	2	1	15	1
4	1	1	20	12	4	2	2	65	4	2	3	1	5	30	2
5	1	1	25	0	0	6	5	62	2	3	5	1	4	80	1
6	1	1	19	24	5	1	1	60	3	1	2	5	4	0	1
7	1	1	19	0	0	1	5	56	2	5	4	1	3	50	2
8	1	1	45	36	5	5	1	72	1	2	5	4	3	75	1
9	1	1	22	18	4	3	4	62	3	4	5	2	1	50	1
10	1	1	38	6	4	7	6	35	5	1	2	4	3	0	1
11	1	1	18	12	4	2	1	60	2	1	3	5	4	20	1
12	1	1	19	0	0	7	1	60	1	2	4	3	5	50	1
13	1	1	27	24	5	7	1	64	2	3	5	1	4	80	1
14	1	1	21	10	3	1	6	70	2	1	5	3	4	90	2
15	1	1	20	18	4	7	4	54	3	4	5	1	2	0	1
16	1	1	23	12	3	2	7	40	3	2	4	1	5	50	2
17	1	1	19	24	5	7	3	58	3	1	2	4	5	20	1
18	1	1	20	0	0	4	4	66	2	1	3	5	4	100	2
19	1	1	21	0	0	1	7	70	1	2	4	3	5	90	2
20	1	1	19	12	4	6	1	58	2	3	4	5	1	50	1
21	1	1	21	18	4	2	7	62	3	1	2	5	4	50	2
22	1	1	19	2	1	6	5	35	5	3	4	2	1	0	1
23	1	1	23	0	0	4	6	56	3	4	5	1	2	50	1
24	1	1	19	12	4	4	4	70	2	3	5	1	4	30	2
25	1	1	41	24	5	7	1	58	2	1	5	4	3	80	1
26	1	1	20	12	3	7	4	45	4	2	5	3	1	100	2
27	1	1	26	36	5	1	6	90	1	2	4	5	3	75	1
28	1	1	21	0	0	7	4	60	2	5	3	4	1	20	1
29	1	1	19	0	0	2	1	65	2	1	5	3	4	90	2
30	1	1	20	13	6	2	6	70	2	1	5	4	3	70	2
31	1	2	22	1	1	6	1	60	5	3	2	4	1	60	1
32	1	2	18	0	0	7	4	70	2	1	3	4	5	70	1
33	1	2	24	0	0	4	5	59	3	1	5	4	2	20	1
34	1	2	20	12	5	2	7	67	1	2	4	3	5	100	2
35	1	2	19	8	4	7	2	30	5	3	4	1	2	0	1
36	1	2	20	0	0	6	3	62	3	2	4	1	5	50	1
37	1	2	24	2	1	1	7	65	2	3	5	1	4	0	1
38	1	2	19	12	4	4	4	72	3	2	5	4	1	20	1
39	1	2	22	0	0	1	3	85	1	2	3	5	4	90	2
40	1	2	20	18	6	5	3	66	4	1	5	2	3	0	1
41	1	2	31	6	1	2	5	58	2	1	4	3	5	90	2
42	1	2	21	0	0	7	2	64	2	3	4	1	5	75	1
43	1	2	18	0	0	2	6	65	3	1	4	2	5	0	1
44	1	2	29	12	7	6	2	69	1	2	5	4	3	100	1
45	1	2	32	0	0	1	7	85	2	1	5	3	4	100	2
46	1	2	24	6	2	2	7	70	1	2	5	3	4	50	2
47	1	2	20	0	0	6	6	61	3	2	1	4	5	20	1
48	1	2	28	6	3	5	5	63	3	1	5	2	4	0	1
49	1	2	19	0	0	7	6	65	2	3	1	4	5	90	1
50	1	2	24	2	2	2	5	40	3	1	4	5	2	30	1

TABLE 16–2 *(continued)*

Respondent #	Treatment #	Gender	Age	Bottles Consumed per Week	Days Consumed per Week	Price Importance	Image Importance	Taste Reaction	Rank This Brand	Rank Brand A	Rank Brand B	Rank Brand C	Rank Brand D	Purchase Probability	Choice
51	2	1	21	12	2	4	3	35	5	4	3	1	2	0	1
52	2	1	20	6	3	7	2	38	4	1	5	3	2	10	1
53	2	1	22	42	6	3	3	46	4	1	3	2	5	0	1
54	2	1	18	0	0	6	2	52	2	1	5	4	3	50	1
55	2	1	19	1	1	2	5	45	2	4	3	5	1	60	2
56	2	1	23	10	4	2	6	41	3	1	5	2	4	75	2
57	2	1	24	0	0	7	1	25	5	3	2	1	4	0	1
58	2	1	19	18	2	4	7	36	2	1	4	5	3	100	2
59	2	1	21	0	0	7	3	44	4	2	5	1	3	0	1
60	2	1	22	0	0	1	4	80	1	2	3	4	5	100	2
61	2	1	20	2	2	5	4	42	2	1	4	3	5	50	1
62	2	1	26	0	0	2	7	39	3	2	1	5	4	0	1
63	2	1	21	10	4	7	3	40	3	1	5	4	2	0	1
64	2	1	23	12	3	4	1	38	4	2	5	1	3	10	1
65	2	1	18	18	3	1	6	28	5	4	2	3	1	0	1
66	2	1	22	0	0	6	3	40	5	1	3	4	2	0	1
67	2	1	20	12	4	2	6	42	2	3	4	1	5	50	2
68	2	1	20	6	2	2	7	34	4	3	5	2	1	0	1
69	2	1	19	12	4	6	2	25	5	1	4	2	3	0	1
70	2	1	21	0	0	7	2	35	4	2	5	1	3	10	1
71	2	1	20	6	2	3	3	34	4	1	5	2	3	50	1
72	2	1	18	2	1	2	6	39	4	2	5	1	3	75	2
73	2	1	23	40	5	7	1	42	2	1	4	3	5	0	1
74	2	1	25	0	0	1	4	25	5	1	3	4	2	10	1
75	2	1	20	12	4	7	3	46	2	3	5	4	1	0	1
76	2	1	19	0	0	5	2	40	4	3	2	1	5	0	1
77	2	1	22	10	4	7	7	75	1	4	5	3	2	0	1
78	2	1	21	18	3	2	6	36	5	2	3	1	4	100	2
79	2	1	18	14	4	7	1	80	1	3	2	4	5	80	2
80	2	1	21	0	0	4	3	38	3	1	4	2	5	50	2
81	2	2	23	72	7	1	6	85	2	1	3	5	4	100	2
82	2	2	28	12	4	4	2	95	1	3	5	2	4	90	2
83	2	2	19	6	4	5	4	90	3	2	5	1	4	0	1
84	2	2	38	1	1	3	5	80	2	5	3	4	1	90	1
85	2	2	21	6	2	6	7	77	1	2	3	4	5	50	1
86	2	2	18	0	0	4	3	81	3	1	5	2	4	50	2
87	2	2	52	0	0	1	2	79	2	1	4	3	5	75	2
88	2	2	21	6	1	3	2	87	1	3	4	2	5	90	2
89	2	2	20	0	0	7	1	50	5	2	4	1	3	0	1
90	2	2	35	18	3	1	7	87	2	1	3	5	4	50	2
91	2	2	19	0	0	4	4	90	1	4	5	2	3	100	2
92	2	2	23	0	0	7	2	85	1	3	2	5	4	90	1
93	2	2	20	6	2	6	2	60	3	1	4	2	5	50	2
94	2	2	19	0	0	7	7	30	5	2	3	1	4	0	1
95	2	2	22	0	0	1	4	80	2	1	5	4	3	100	2
96	2	2	20	1	1	7	1	78	3	2	4	5	1	50	1
97	2	2	18	0	0	4	4	92	1	3	4	2	5	90	2
98	2	2	21	0	0	1	6	86	1	2	5	3	4	75	2
99	2	2	20	0	0	6	4	96	1	2	3	4	5	100	1
100	2	2	20	10	5	3	4	40	3	2	4	5	1	80	2

Data Reduction

The steps involved in the reduction of data are (1) *field controls,* (2) *editing,* (3) *coding,* (4) *transcribing,* (5) *generating new variables,* and (6) *calculating summarizing statistics.* The first five of these steps concern developing a basic data array that is as complete and error-free as possible. The last step involves calculations made from the array.

A **basic data array** is a table composed of the value of each variable for each sample element. Table 16–2 is the basic array for the beverage study described in the previous section. It consists of the values for 15 variables for 100 subjects, or a total of 1,500 measurements. This is a small data array compared to those encountered in most marketing studies.

> **Basic data array:** a table composed of the value of each variable for each sample element.

Field Controls

Field controls are procedures designed to minimize errors during the actual collection of data. These controls involve ensuring that the sampling, data collection, and measurement tasks are carried out as specified.

Sound field controls require both monitoring and validation procedures. **Monitoring** is the observation of fieldwork by supervisors or project directors as it occurs. Monitoring is common in central location telephone interviewing. In such situations a supervisor will "listen in" on several interviews by each interviewer.

Validation involves checking the accuracy of fieldwork after it has been conducted. Survey research validation involves a supervisor or a separate interviewer recontacting a sample of respondents (generally 10–20 percent) from each interviewer's list of completed interviews. The purpose is to ensure that the interview took place and that the respondent was asked all the questions on the questionnaire.

> **Field controls:** procedures designed to minimize errors during the actual collection of data.
>
> **Monitoring:** observation of fieldwork by supervisors as it occurs.
>
> **Validation:** checking the accuracy of fieldwork after it has been conducted.

Effective field controls and editing require several variables in addition to the variables required by the research problem. Every sample unit should be assigned a number and the result of the contact attempt(s) recorded. Contact attempts can result in completed interviews, refusals, or noncontacts. The time of each contact attempt should also be recorded. This allows a validation of noncontact and refusal responses. Although noncontacts and refusals are not entered as part of the basic data array, it is important to have a record of them for estimating the potential for nonresponse bias.

Every sample unit in a study involving more than one interviewer or observer should also have the *interviewer code* attached to its record. This allows an analysis of interviewer variations that can indicate potential problems such as interviewer bias.

Each completed interview should also be assigned a *respondent number.* The first three columns in Table 16–2 are the respondent numbers from the beverage experiment.

Editing

The responsibility of the editor is to ensure that the data requested are *present, readable,* and *accurate.* Unless the questionnaire and analysis are very simple, or the responses are being entered directly into the computer in CATI systems, an editor should examine every completed questionnaire before it is transcribed onto disks. In addition, after the data are entered into the computer, computer editing should be conducted.

Missing Data

Item nonresponse: failure of a respondent to answer some questions in an otherwise complete interview.

It is very common for a questionnaire to be returned with one or more specific questions unanswered. This is known as **item nonresponse.** The editor must decide what to do about such missing data. Often it is possible and desirable to use the data "as are." That is, the unanswered questions are assigned a missing data code and entered into the computer along with the other observations.

On occasion, the editor can have respondents recontacted to collect key bits of missing information. Alternatively, **plug values,** values developed in advance to use for missing data, can be used. For example, an editor could have a list of the average salaries associated with a wide array of occupations. One of these values could be used for respondents who reported their occupations but not their incomes. Such values can also be developed from the database itself.

Plug values: values used to substitute for missing data due to item nonresponse.

Questions such as number 8 in Table 16–1 often produce only partial answers. Respondents often refuse to rank brands or products with which they are not familiar. If a respondent ranked only four of the five brands in question 8, the editor would have to decide if the unranked brand should be assigned a "5" indicating "least liked" or a missing data code or perhaps another value indicating that the brand was unfamiliar to the respondent.

Some questionnaires contain more missing data than others. The editor must decide how much and what types of missing data constitute sufficient grounds for "tossing" or deleting the entire questionnaire.

Ambiguous Answers

Many questionnaires contain one or more responses whose meaning is not clear. This occurs even in questionnaires composed entirely of "closed" questions. Question 3 in Table 16–1 requests the respondent to provide a numerical answer. However, answers similar to the following will also appear a significant number of times:

> "I almost never drink carbonated drinks, but when I do I usually have several."
> "10–15 Cokes and several fruit drinks."
> "12 if you count mixed drinks."
> "6–summer, 0–winter."

The editor must assign values to responses such as these. Question 8 in Table 16–1 requests a rank order of five brands without ties. Some respondents will assign tied ranks anyway. Again the editor must determine how to break ties (generally randomly or systematically in a manner designed to minimize bias).

Suppose a respondent answered "0" to question 3 in Table 16–1 and "3" to Question 4. Both answers cannot be correct. Again, the editor must decide whether to "guess" which answer is correct based on other responses in the questionnaire, to discard the entire questionnaire, to treat both answers as missing data, to recontact the respondent, or to take other relevant action.

Accuracy/Quality

As editors review a series of questionnaires, they should note suspect responses. Respondents sometimes rush through questionnaires carelessly. This tends to produce a number of inconsistent responses such as a high-income category and a low-paying job category, or unawareness of a brand that is also reported as frequently used. Questionnaires containing such inconsistencies should be examined carefully and deleted from the database if it appears that the respondents completed them haphazardly.

Editors should also be alert for inconsistencies between the responses obtained by different interviewers. Such inconsistencies may be expected if the interviewers are contacting different respondent groups, such as in distinct geographic areas. However, they may also reflect interviewer bias, question interpretation, interviewer quality, or even interviewer cheating. Thus, the cause of inconsistencies between interviewers should be determined as rapidly as possible. For this reason, interviews should be turned in and edited daily, if practical.

Computer Editing.   Computer editing can be used instead of, or preferably in addition to, manual editing. The computer can be instructed to examine each set of coded responses for values that lie outside the permissible range, or for conflicting responses to similar questions. The respondent number associated with the problem measurement is printed out as an indication of the nature of the problem (e.g., for respondent 044 an "8" is coded for question 5 and it has only seven response categories). The editor or supervisor can then check the original questionnaire and take the appropriate action.

The computer can supply prespecified "plugs" for missing data or it can calculate values for missing data based on the responses in the overall data array. It can also be used to run checks for variations in responses between interviewers. Computer editing is relatively inexpensive and should generally be used in addition to manual editing.

Coding

Coding involves establishing categories and assigning data to them.

Establishing Categories

Categories for the answers to multiple-choice or dichotomous questions are established at the time the question is formulated. (See Chapter 10.) Open-ended questions may also have response categories established at the time they are formulated. However, it is common to create some or all of the response categories to open-ended questions after at least some of the questionnaires have been returned.

Coding: establishing categories and assigning data to them.

Since almost all marketing studies are analyzed by computer, each category must be assigned a numerical value. Thus, in Table 16–2, Male was assigned the value "1" and Female the value "2." It is important that a category be available for every response, which often requires the use of a "catchall" category such as "Other." Likewise, it is important to have a specified category for nonresponses or missing data.

Assigning Data to Categories

After categories have been established and questionnaires or other measuring instruments have been completed by at least some respondents, the observations must be assigned to categories.

Many questionnaires, particularly those administered by telephone or personal interview, are *precoded*. That is, appropriate category values and column numbers are listed on the questionnaire. Had question 3 in Table 16–1 been precoded according to the input format shown, it would have taken the following form:

> **3.** *How many bottles, cans, and/or glasses of beer do you consume in a typical week?*
> _____ 8–9

The 8–9 to the right of the question indicates that the response should be entered into the eighth and ninth columns. By reserving only two spaces for the response, the researcher is assuming that 99 is the largest response which will be obtained. Should someone report an amount larger than this, it will have to be coded as a 99, or the entire coding system would have to be restructured.

Postcoding involves the same procedure as precoding except that it is done after the questionnaires are received. The advantage of postcoding is that the range of responses to the open-end questions are known before category values are assigned and columns reserved.

Coding open-ended responses is difficult and requires sound instructions to ensure consistency between coders. Because of the complexity involved, a *codebook*, which provides explicit instructions for coding each variable and indicates the columns to be used for each response, should be developed. Research Application 16–1 illustrates codebook instructions as well as the difficulty that one may encounter in following these instructions.

It is not uncommon to have questionnaires coded independently by two persons to reduce errors.

Transcription of Data

Transcription of data is the process of physically transferring data from the measuring instruments onto magnetic tape or disk, or directly into the computer.

Available analytical programs have varying data entry requirements. As shown in Table 16–2, the basic data array is a matrix, where rows typically represent respondents (or cases) and columns represent values of variables. The variable values may be entered into the computer with each value separated by a comma, a blank space, or nothing.

Coding an Open-Ended Question

A consumer survey conducted by the Institute for Social Research* contained these questions:

C19 *Do you (or your family) do any of your own repair work on cars?*

_____ Yes _____ No (go to Section D)

(If yes)

C20 *What kind of work have you done on your cars in the last year?*

_____

_____

The Codebook for question C20 gave the following codes and examples for each:

Code	Example of Answer for Code
5	*Yes, complex repairs that usually take a skilled mechanic (rebuilt engine or transmission).*
4	*Yes, extensive repairs taking much skill (rings, valves, bearings), install factory rebuilt engine, kingpins, ball joints, transmission work, motor work, or "I do anything that needs doing."*
3	*Yes, some skill required (brakes, wheel bearings, exhaust system, starter).*
2	*Yes, some skill (tune-up, points, plugs, adjust carburetor, fuel pump).*
1	*Yes, little or no skill, mostly maintenance (oil change, greasing, tire switching, touch-up painting).*
0	*Inappropriate, family does not have car, does no repair work.*
9	*Answer not given whether repairs were done or what kind of repairs.*
7	*Yes, but not in the last year.*

How should the following replies be coded? (All indicated yes to C19.)

(a) My car has been running fine the past year, but I completely overhauled the motor in the washing machine."

(b) "I put in a new tape deck."

(c) "My husband and I made and installed new rugs for the floor."

(d) "I've changed the oil in my car a few times. I also helped my cousin overhaul his car's engine."

(e) "I always give it a tune-up every year."

(f) "I changed a flat last spring."

(g) "I took the carburetor off, but I had a mechanic overhaul it before I put it back in."

(h) "I do all the repairs, but it hasn't needed anything recently."

*J. B. Lansing, J. N. Morgan, *Economic Survey Methods* (Institute for Social Research, 1971), 247. Copyright © 1971 by the University of Michigan; reprinted by permission of the publisher, the Survey Research Center of the Institute for Social Research.

Generating New Variables

It is often necessary to create new variables as a part of the analysis procedure.

First, *new variables are often generated from combinations of other variables in the data.* For example, data on a person's age, marital status, and presence and age of children may be combined to generate a new variable called "stage in the family life cycle." Or measures of household consumption of a product such as bread or milk may be combined with measures of household size to produce *per person* consumption measures.

Second, *it may be desirable to collect intervally scaled data as such and later assign them to classes.* Family income is often collected in dollars, for example, and later classified by a convenient number of income brackets or deciles. The coder can classify by brackets but would have to examine the entire income array to code by decile. A new variable generated by the computer, *income decile,* is the usual way this is done.

Third, *new variables may be added from secondary data.* It may be desirable to add such information as the median level of income and education in the county of residence of the respondent to be used in the analysis.

Fourth, *transforming the data into another functional form* may be desirable. An example is transforming intervally scaled data into logarithmic form for use in certain kinds of analyses.

Tabulation of Frequency Distributions and Calculations of Summarizing Statistics for Each Variable

Unless the research project is a very small one, it will be tabulated and the data analyzed by computer. A large number of computer programs with differing capabilities are available for these purposes. Since the same program is typically used for tabulation and analysis of the data, it is important for the analyst to choose a program that is suited to the overall needs of the project.

Tabulation of Frequency Distributions

The tabulation process starts with the preparation of the *basic data array* described earlier. The next steps in the tabulation process are the preparation of *one-way* and *n-way* frequency distributions.

One-way frequency distribution: the number and/or percent of responses given to each response category of a single question or variable.

One-Way Frequency Distributions.   Examine the responses to the image importance question shown in Table 16–2. Is it easy for you to understand what these responses mean? The odds are that it is not. Imagine how much more difficult it would be to develop a "feel" for the data if there were 1,000 respondents instead of 100! Now examine Table 16–3, which represents a **one-way frequency distribution** of the same data from the SPSS program. The frequency distribution provides a much more concise portrayal of the data.

The *frequency* is simply the number of respondents who provided that particular value (14 respondents gave image an importance rating of 2). The

TABLE 16–3 One-Way Frequency Distribution and Summary Statistics

Frequency Distribution for Variable Image Importance

Value	Label	Frequency	Percent	Valid Percent	Cumulative Percent
1	Extremely Imp.	15	15.0	15.0	15.0
2	Very Imp.	14	14.0	14.0	29.0
3	Somewhat Imp.	13	13.0	13.0	42.0
4	Neither Imp. Nor Unimp.	18	18.0	18.0	60.0
5	Somewhat Unimp.	9	9.0	09.0	69.0
6	Very Unimp.	17	17.0	17.0	86.0
7	Extremely Unimp.	14	14.0	14.0	100.0
	Total	100	100.0	100.0	

Summary Statistics

Mean:	3.990	Mode:	4.000	Median:	4.000
Maximum:	7.000	Range:	6.000	Minimum:	1.000
Std. dev:	2.028	Variance:	4.111		
Valid cases:	100	Missing cases:	0		

percent or *relative frequency* is the percentage of all respondents who provide a particular value (14 percent of the respondents—14/100—gave image an importance rating of 2). The valid percent is the same as the percent except that any nonrespondents have been removed from the analysis.

The *cumulative* percent is the percentage of all respondents who provide a response equal to or less than a particular value (42 percent of the respondents—42/100—gave image an importance rating of 3 or less).

When categorical data are being analyzed, all of the categories are normally used in the construction of a frequency distribution. However, if there are a large number of categories, or if interval or ratio data are involved, it is useful to group the responses into a smaller set of categories. For example, the 100 respondents in Table 16–2 provided 46 different values in response to the taste-reaction question. A frequency distribution with 46 responses for 100 respondents would do little to clarify the nature of the response.

In such situations, the researcher may use a smaller number of categories determined either *a priori* or by the distribution of the data. For example, in the taste-reaction case, we might specify 10 categories of equal range of response starting at 1–10 and continuing through 91–100. Or the computer could construct 10 categories with an equal number of responses in each (deciles).

A one-way frequency distribution is a frequency distribution for a single variable. It is also called a *simple tabulation* and is to be distinguished from a *two-way* or *n-way* frequency distribution (two variables, *n* variables). These *n*-way frequency distributions, one form of which is known as *cross tabulations*, and another form as *banners*, are described next.[1]

Cross tabulation:
a table showing
the distribution of
responses to two
or more questions
or variables
considered
simultaneously.

Cross Tabulations.   **Cross tabulation** involves constructing a table so that one can see how respondents with various values on one variable responded to one or more other variables.

Suppose we are interested in examining the relationship between the choice of money or product and the brand name of the beverage sample tasted by the respondent. First, we would place the two categories for choice on the horizontal axis and the two brand names on the vertical axis, to form four cells of a table. Then we would count and record the number of respondents falling in each cell.

Table 16–4 shows the cross tabulation for all 100 respondents as produced by the SPSS program. A visual examination of this table indicates that (1) most respondents chose option 1 — money, and (2) the brand name may have affected this choice.

SPSS, like most other programs that produce cross tabulations, calculates and prints percentages for each cell of the table. Three different bases are used for the percentages in each cell — the percentage that the frequency in that cell is of the frequency for the row in which it appears; the percentage that the frequency in that cell is of the frequency of the column in which it appears; and the percentage that the frequency in that cell is of the total number of cases.

In drawing interpretations with respect to potential causal relationships, one should use the row- or the column-based percentage *that is calculated across the levels (or categories) of the dependent variable.* In using Table 16–4, for example, we would be interested in determining whether tasting the beverage labeled *Bravo* or tasting the one labeled *Delight* (the *independent* variable) had any apparent effect on whether money or product was chosen (the *de-*

TABLE 16–4 Cross Tabulation of All Respondents

	Count Row % Column % Total %	REWARD		
		$3.00 Cash 1.00	Six Pack of Soda 2.00	Row Total
TREATNUM				
Bravo	1.00	33 66.0 53.2 33.0	17 34.0 44.7 17.0	50 50.0
Delight	2.00	29 58.0 46.8 29.0	21 42.0 55.3 21.0	50 50.0
Column Total		62 62.0	38 38.0	100 100.0

Number of Missing Observations: 0

pendent variable). Applying the rule just stated, we would want to use the *row* percentages in Table 16–4 since they are calculated across the two categories of the dependent variable. We find that for *Bravo* the percentage that chose "money" (66 percent) was higher than the percentage for *Delight* that chose "money" (58 percent). Thus, it appears that the brand label of the sample tested *may* have had a causal relationship with the "money" versus "product" choice made.

It is perhaps unnecessary to warn that even if an apparent association is found between levels of the independent and dependent variables it may be the result only of chance, or of some third variable that affects both the other two.

Banners.   **Banners** are a way of displaying several cross tabulations in one table. In a banner, the values for a variable of interest (preferably a dependent variable) are arrayed down the first column on the left and the values of potentially associated variables are arrayed in columns to the right in the table.

Banners: a means of showing several cross tabulations in one table.

An example of a banner from the beverage study is given in Table 16–5. The values of the variable of interest, the number of points assigned for taste on a 0–100 scale, are arrayed in five categories in the first column. The cross tabulated values for variables that could be associated with taste—beverage name, gender and age of the taster, bottles of soft drinks consumed per week, and reported purchase probabilities of *Bravo* and *Delight*—are arrayed in columns to the right. (As we shall see shortly, some of these variables should *not* have been included in this banner. Before reading the next three paragraphs, can you tell which ones—and why?)

Banners are widely used, especially in reports prepared by research agencies. Banners allow a large amount of data to be presented concisely. Percentages for each cell based on the column total are usually supplied. When the variable of interest is the dependent variable, these percentages are calculated across it, the proper direction for use in drawing inferences for potential causal relationships.

For example, in Table 16–5 the number of points assigned for taste may depend on the name of the beverage tasted, and the gender, age, and number of bottles consumed per week by the taster. Therefore, taste is the dependent variable and the cell percentages ought to be calculated across it. A glance at Table 16–5 will indicate that this is the way they were in fact calculated.

However, the reported purchase probabilities for *Bravo* and *Delight* will very likely depend on taste, rather than the reverse. For the cross tabulations of points assigned for taste with these variables, therefore, taste is the *independent* variable. Since the purchase probabilities for *Bravo* and *Delight* are dependent variables in these cross tabulations, the cell percentages for the purchase probabilities ought to be calculated across them, rather than across the taste variable, as in Table 16–5.

Summarizing Statistics

There are two major kinds of summarizing statistics. *Measures of central tendency* provide measures of the midpoint of the distribution. *Measures of dispersion* indicate the amount of variation in the data comprising the distribution.

TABLE 16–5 Example of Banner Format for Question 7: Having Tasted Bravo (Delight), Indicate How Much You Like Its Taste

Taste Reaction	Total Sample	Brand		Gender		Age		
		Bravo	Delight	Females	Males	18–24	25–34	35 or Over
	100	50	50	40	60	84	10	6
	(100%)	(100%)	(100%)	(100%)	(100%)	(100%)	(100%)	(100%)
0–20	0	0	0	0	0	0	0	0
	(0.0)	(0.0)	(0.0)	(0.0)	(0.0)	(0.0)	(0.0)	(0.0)
21–40	25	5	20	4	21	22	2	1
	(25.0)	(10.0)	(40.0)	(10.0)	(35.0)	(26.2)	(20.0)	(16.7)
41–60	27	16	11	5	22	25	1	1
	(27.0)	(32.0)	(22.0)	(12.5)	(36.7)	(29.8)	(10.0)	(16.7)
61–80	33	25	8	18	15	26	4	3
	(31.0)	(50.0)	(16.0)	(45.0)	(25.0)	(31.0)	(40.0)	(50.0)
81–100	15	4	11	13	2	11	3	1
	(15.0)	(8.0)	(22.0)	(32.5)	(3.3)	(13.1)	(30.0)	(16.7)

Measures of Central Tendency. The three primary measures of central tendency are the *mean*, the *median*, and the *mode*.

Mean:
the sum of the values for the variable under consideration divided by the number of cases involved.

The **mean** should be computed only from intervally or ratio-scaled data. It is obtained by adding all the observations and dividing the sum by the number of observations. When the exact value of each observation is known, this is a simple process. Often, however, means must be calculated from absolute frequency distributions. In these cases, the midpoint of each category is multiplied by the number of observations in that category, the resultant category values are summed, and the total is divided by the total number of observations, or:

$$\bar{x} = \frac{\sum_{i=1}^{h} f_i x_i}{n} \tag{16-1}$$

where f_i = the frequency of the ith class
x_i = the midpoint of that class
h = the number of classes
n = the total number of observations

Median:
the value for a variable below which 50 percent of the observations lie.

The **median**, which requires only ordinal data, is obtained by finding the value below which 50 percent of the observations lie. If cumulative frequencies were calculated for the data array, it would be the value for which the cumulative frequency was 50 percent.

Mode:
the value for a variable that appears most frequently.

The **mode**, requiring only nominal data, is found by determining the value that appears most frequently. In a relative frequency distribution, the mode is the class that has the highest frequency. Data can have more than one mode if two or more values tie for most frequent appearance.

The three measures will *not* be the same for distributions of values that are not symmetrical and, when different, they are useful for different purposes.

TABLE 16-5 *(continued)*

Bottles Consumed Per Week				Purchase Probability—Bravo				Purchase Probability—Delight			
0	1–10	11–20	>20	0–25	26–50	51–75	76–100	0–25	26–50	51–75	76–100
38	28	25	9	16	13	6	15	21	10	5	14
(100%)	(100%)	(100%)	(100%)	(100%)	(100%)	(100%)	(100%)	(100%)	(100%)	(100%)	(100%)
0	0	0	0	0	0	0	0	0	0	0	0
(0.0)	(0.0)	(0.0)	(0.0)	(0.0)	(0.0)	(0.0)	(0.0)	(0.0)	(0.0)	(0.0)	(0.0)
8	10	7	0	3	2	0	0	14	2	1	3
(21.1)	(35.7)	(28.0)	(0.0)	(18.8)	(15.4)	(0.0)	(0.0)	(66.7)	(20.0)	(20.0)	(21.4)
8	8	6	5	7	5	1	3	5	4	2	0
(21.1)	(28.6)	(24.0)	(55.6)	(43.8)	(38.5)	(16.7)	(20.0)	(23.8)	(40.0)	(40.0)	(0.0)
13	8	10	2	6	6	4	9	1	2	1	4
(34.2)	(28.6)	(40.0)	(22.2)	(37.5)	(46.2)	(66.7)	(60.0)	(4.8)	(20.0)	(20.0)	(28.6)
9	2	2	2	0	0	1	3	1	2	1	7
(23.7)	(7.1)	(8.0)	(22.2)	(0.0)	(0.0)	(16.7)	(20.0)	(4.8)	(20.0)	(20.0)	(50.0)

For obtaining an *estimate of a population total,* the sample *mean* times the number of population units provides the best estimate. If one wants an *estimate of the most representative amount,* the *mode* should be used. If we want an average that is *unaffected by extremes,* the *median* is the best estimator.

In our example, using the mean to reflect average consumption by females who consumed carbonated beverages would be misleading. Weekly consumption reported by those who consume such products was

1, 12, 8, 2, 12, 18, 6, 12, 6, 6, 2, 72, 12, 6, 1, 6, 6, 18, 6, 1, 10

The arithmetic mean is 10.6, which exceeds the consumption of all but 7 of the respondents. In contrast, the median is 6 (as is the mode). The arithmetic mean is severely distorted by the single respondent who reported very heavy usage (ignoring this respondent changes the arithmetic mean from 10.6 to 7.5).

Measures of Dispersion.   The *standard deviation, variance,* and *range* are common measures of how "spread out" the data are. The smaller these three values are, the more compact are the data.

The formula for the standard deviation of a sample calculated from an array of the sample data is[2]

$$s = \sqrt{\frac{\sum_{i=1}^{n}(x_i - \bar{x})^2}{n - 1}} \qquad (16\text{-}2)$$

s = sample standard deviation
x_i = the value of the ith observation
x = the sample mean, and
n = the sample size

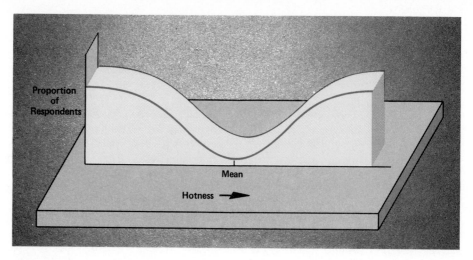

FIGURE 16–1 Preferences for Degree of Hotness in a Sauce

The *variance*, the square of the standard deviation, is found by the same formula with the square-root sign removed. The *range* is equal to the maximum minus the minimum value in the data array.

Calculating the mean of a data set without determining its distribution can sometimes lead to mistaken interpretations. Data developed from a study concerning a new sauce product illustrates this point. The *mean* preference for "hotness" of the sauce turned out to be about halfway between very mild and very hot. If the distribution of the responses on the hotness scale had not been reported, a sauce with a medium degree of hotness would have been introduced. The distribution of the responses indicated that preferences were really as shown in Figure 16–1, however; bimodal with roughly one-half of the respondents preferring a mild sauce and the other half a hot sauce. The company therefore introduced two sauces, one mild and one hot, rather than only one with a medium degree of hotness.[3] The message is clear: *always examine the distribution of the data in addition to measures of central tendency.*

Statistical Estimation

Statistical estimation: estimating a population value we do not know from a sample value we do know.

Statistical estimation involves the estimation of a population value we do not know from a sample value we do know. Estimates of the mean amount of a product bought per person per time period, the market share of a brand, or the proportion of outlets that carry the brand are common estimates used in making marketing decisions.

As was pointed out in Chapter 15, there are two kinds of estimation procedures, *point estimation* and *interval estimation*. A brief review and illustration of each of these procedures is useful here. Estimation is based on the sampling distribution; therefore, it would be wise to review the treatment of that concept in the previous chapter. If you do not have a sound understanding of the concept of a sampling distribution, you will not fully understand either estimation or hypothesis testing procedures.

Point Estimation

A **point estimate** is a single number, or point, that is used to estimate a population value of interest. A point estimate may be made for any population value, but the estimates most commonly made are for the *mean* and the *proportion* of the population.

Point estimate: a single number used to estimate a population value.

Point Estimates of Population Means

The management group in our example was interested in estimating the average taste rating that all students on the campus would give the product if they were to taste it with the *Bravo* label. The average of the 50 students (30 male and 20 female) in the sample is 61.7. This unadjusted average is the best single estimate of the population mean when either a simple random sample or a proportional stratified sample is used. A nonproportional stratified sample, which is quite common in marketing research, requires an adjustment.[4]

Point Estimates of Population Proportions

Management also wanted to estimate the proportion of students that consume a carbonated beverage at least once per week. The overall sample proportion is .62 (the number of students reporting this level of consumption divided by the total number of students). Again, this is the best estimate for a simple random sample or a proportional stratified sample, but a nonproportional stratified sample would require an adjustment.[5]

Interval Estimation

An **interval estimate** consists of two points between which the population value is estimated to lie with some stated level of confidence. Rather than report to management that the estimated proportion of consumers is .62, as shown previously, it is possible and preferable to report: "There is a 90 percent probability that the proportion of the population that consumes a carbonated beverage at least once a week is between .54 and .70." In this section, we describe how to construct such intervals.

Interval estimate: an estimate that a population value falls within a specified range of values and a probability that the estimate is correct.

Interval Estimate of the Mean: $n = 30$ or Larger

How is an interval estimate of the mean made? Recall from the discussion in Chapter 15 that an interval estimate with a specified level of confidence is obtained from an interval formed by the two points,

$$\bar{x} - Z\sigma_{\bar{x}} = \text{lower point, and}$$
$$\bar{x} + Z\sigma_{\bar{x}} = \text{upper point}$$

where Z represents the number of standard errors for the desired confidence level and $\sigma_{\bar{x}}$ is the size of the standard error. A confidence level of 68 percent is obtained when $Z = 1.0$, 90 percent when $Z = 1.64$, and 95 percent when $Z = 1.96$ (see Appendix A). Each Z value gives the indicated level of confidence because that percentage of the samples that could be taken (of that size from that population) would have means falling between the lower and upper ends of the interval formed using that Z value.

Remember that $\sigma_{\bar{x}}$ the standard error of the mean, is the standard deviation of the distribution of all possible sample means of a simple random sample of a given size from a given population. It can be calculated by dividing the *population* standard deviation by the square root of the sample size [see equation (15–1)]. If the population standard deviation is not known, $\sigma_{\bar{x}}$ can be estimated by using the sample standard deviation. When $\sigma_{\bar{x}}$ is estimated from sample data, it is written as $\hat{\sigma}_{\bar{x}}$ Thus,

$$\hat{\sigma}_{\bar{x}} = \frac{\hat{\sigma}}{\sqrt{n}} \tag{16-3}$$

where

$$\hat{\sigma} = s = \text{sample standard deviation.}$$

Suppose we want to estimate the average weekly consumption of carbonated beverages per student with 68 percent and 95 percent confidence intervals. How would we proceed?

1. The sample mean is calculated as $\bar{x} = 5.575$.
2. The sample standard deviation is determined using equation (16–2). This gives us a value of 11.97.
3. This value is divided by the square root of the sample size to provide the estimated standard error of the mean:

$$\sqrt{40} = 6.32$$
$$\hat{\sigma}_{\bar{x}} = 11.97/6.32 = 1.89$$

4. The appropriate number of standard errors are placed around the estimated mean to create the desired confidence interval:

68% confidence interval	95% confidence interval
$\bar{x} \pm 1.0\ \hat{\sigma}_{\bar{x}} = 5.575 \pm 1.0(1.89)$	$\bar{x} \pm 1.96\ \hat{\sigma}_{\bar{x}} = 5.575 \pm 1.96(1.89)$
$= 3.685 - 7.465$	$= 1.875 - 9.275$

Notice that the 95 percent confidence interval is substantially larger than the 68 percent confidence interval. It makes intuitive sense that one would be more confident that the correct value would fall within a wider interval.

Equation (16–3) is designed for a simple random sample. An estimate based on a stratified sample follows exactly the same procedure *except* that a different formula for calculating the estimated standard error of the mean would be required.[6]

Interval Estimate of the Mean: n Less than 30

For an interval estimate in which the sample size is less than 30 and for which the sample standard deviation, s, is used to estimate the population standard deviation, $\hat{\sigma}$, the sampling distribution is no longer normal. Because the distribution of the Z statistic is normal, it is not applicable in small sample situations. The Student t distribution is used instead of the normal distribution when the sample size is less than 30. The t statistic is calculated and used in the same way as the Z statistic, except that the values for areas of the sampling distribution are looked up in a different table (see Appendix B).

The t distribution changes as the sample size changes. Therefore, when using Appendix B, we must find a t value based on the number of *degrees of freedom (df)* in our sample. The df in this situation is equal to $n - 1$. Thus, the t value for a 90 percent confidence interval with a sample size of 20 (19 degrees of freedom) is 1.729. This value used exactly the same as the Z value for a 90 percent confidence interval as described in the preceding section.

Interval Estimate of a Proportion

Interval estimation for proportions is carried out by a procedure similar to that for means. The estimated standard error of the proportion, $\hat{\sigma}_p$, must be determined; then the interval is formed around the sample proportion such that

$$p - Z\hat{\sigma}_p = \text{lower point, and}$$
$$p + Z\hat{\sigma}_p = \text{upper point}$$

where Z = the number of standard errors for the desired confidence level.

When the sample is an srs and the population proportion is known, the formula for the standard error of the proportion is

$$\sigma_p = \sqrt{\frac{P(1 - P)}{n - 1}} \tag{16-4}$$

If the population proportion is not known, it can be estimated from the sample proportion p and the estimated standard error, $\hat{\sigma}_p$, found from the formula

$$\hat{\sigma}_p = \sqrt{\frac{p(1 - p)}{n - 1}} \tag{16-5}$$

If the sample is a stratified random sample, the estimated standard error is the weighted average of the estimated stratum standard errors.[7]

Management wanted to estimate with a 90 percent confidence interval the proportion of males and the proportion of females that drink a carbonated beverage at least once a week. The procedure for males is

1. Calculate the sample proportion: $p = .68$
2. Calculate the estimated standard error:

$$\hat{\sigma}_p = \sqrt{\frac{.68(.32)}{60 - 1}}$$
$$= .06$$

3. The appropriate number of standard errors are placed around the sample proportion to create the desired confidence interval:

$$p \pm 1.64\hat{\sigma}_p = .68 \pm 1.64(.06)$$
$$= .58 \text{ to } .78$$

To ensure that you understand this process, verify that the 90 percent confidence interval for the proportion of females who consume at least one carbonated beverage per week is .39 to .66.

Summary

Data reduction is the process of getting the data ready for analysis and calculating summarizing statistics. It involves six steps: (1) field controls, (2) editing, (3) coding, (4) transcribing, (5) generating new variables, and (6) calculating summarizing statistics. The first five steps produce a basic data array—a table containing the value of each variable for each sample unit.

Field controls are procedures designed to minimize errors during the actual collection of data. Field controls include monitoring data collection while it is in progress and validating that it was done properly after the fact.

Editing involves dealing with missing data and ambiguous answers as well as evaluating the accuracy and quality of completed surveys. Both human and computer editing are common. Coding requires the researcher to establish categories for question responses and to assign responses to those categories.

New variables are often generated before data analysis (1) from combinations of existing variables, (2) by recoding existing data into different categories, (3) by adding data from sources outside the survey, and (4) by mathematically transforming existing data.

A one-way frequency distribution simply displays the number and percentage of the respondents that fall into the various response categories of interest. A cross tabulation or n-way frequency distribution shows the number and percentage of respondents that fall into two or more response categories simultaneously. Banners are a way of displaying several cross tabulations at once. In drawing inferences about possible casual relationships, one should use the percentages based on either the row or the column that is associated with the dependent variable.

The mean, median, and mode are commonly used measures of central tendency, while the standard deviation, variance, and range are measures of dispersion.

Statistical estimation involves estimating a population value we do not know from a sample value we do know. A point estimate of a population mean or proportion from a simple random sample is the sample mean or proportion. An interval estimate consists of two points between which the population value is estimated to lie with some stated level of confidence. These estimates are based on the sampling distibution.

Review Questions

16.1. What are the steps involved in *data reduction?*

16.2. What is the purpose of *field controls?*

16.3. What do sound field controls require?

16.4. Describe *monitoring and validation* as field controls.

16.5. What variables in addition to the variables required by the research problem are often necessary for field controls and editing?

16.6. Why is an *interviewer code* useful?

16.7. What is the purpose of *editing?*

16.8. In what ways can one deal with *missing data?*

16.9. How can editors assess the accuracy/quality of questionnaire data?

16.10. What is *computer editing?*

16.11. Why should questionnaires be turned in and edited promptly?

16.12. What is meant by *coding?*

16.13. What is *precoding? postcoding?*

16.14. What is a *codebook?*

16.15. What is meant by *transcription of data?*

16.16. Why are new variables generated?

16.17. What is a *one-way frequency distribution?*

16.18. How does the *absolute frequency* differ from the *relative frequency* in a one-way frequency distribution?

16.19. What are *cross tabulations?*

16.20. What is the appropriate direction in which to calculate percentages in the cells of a two-way cross tabulation if one is interested in investigating the possibility of a causal relationship between the independent and the dependent variable?

16.21. What is a *banner?*

16.22. When would you use a _____to describe the central tendency of a distribution:
   a. mean
   b. median
   c. mode

16.23. Describe each of the following:
   a. standard deviation
   b. variance
   c. range

16.24. How would you calculate a point estimate for a population mean from a simple random sample? a population proportion?

16.25. Would your answer to 16.24 change if a nonproportional stratified sample were used?

16.26. What is an *interval estimate?*

16.27. What is a *Z value?*

16.28. What is a *t value?*

16.29. When is a *t* table used?

Discussion Questions/Problems

16.30. A recording company is about to hire a new A & R (artist and repertoire) director. Four candidates are being considered, all presently employed by other recording companies. The company has the data given below for each person. Which one should be hired, if only past sales performance is to be considered?

A & R Person	Sales of Last 25 Records (in units)				
	Mean	Median	Mode	Variance	Range
A	160,317	40,249	30–40,000	226,315	1,005–1,616,503
B	158,608	52,512	40–50,000	158,733	8,693– 744,604
C	154,772	61,712	50–60,000	110,410	18,614– 505,842
D	150,219	74,847	70–80,000	80,693	24,830– 476,966

16.31. Precode the following questions and develop the codebook. Assume that this is the order in which the questions will appear on the questionnaire and that the first three columns of the code sheet are to be used for the respondent code.

a. _____Male _____ Female
b. Marital status: _____
c. What is your age? _____
d. How many nonfiction books have you read in the past 2 months? _____
   (If none, skip to J.)
e. What is your favorite type of nonfiction book? _____
f. Why did you select the last nonfiction book that you read?
   _____

16.32. Code the responses in Research Application 16–1.

16.33. An analyst for the Farmer's Group of insurance companies took a stratified random sample of 1,500 smokers and 1,500 nonsmokers from among the company's policyholders. He found that the number of automobile accidents during the preceding year was 56 for nonsmokers and 97 for smokers. Thirty-eight percent of the company's policyholders were smokers.
a. What is the point estimate of the automobile accident rate (proportion of policyholders who had automobile accidents during the year)?
b. What is the interval estimate of the accident rate, using a 90 percent confidence interval?

16.34. Refer to Tables 16–1 and 16–2 to perform the following tasks.
a. Prepare a one-way frequency distribution and summary statistics for
   i. age: entire sample
   ii. age: males and females separately
   iii. bottles consumed per week: entire sample
   iv. bottles consumed per week: males and females separately
   v. price importance: entire sample
   vi. price importance: males and females separately
   vii. rank brand C: entire sample
   viii. rank brand C: males and females separately
   ix. choice: entire sample
   x. choice: males and females separately

b. Prepare a two-way cross tabulation using
    i. gender and image importance
    ii. price importance and image importance
    iii. choice and rank this brand
    iv. taste reaction and treatment

c. Prepare a point estimate and a 90 percent confidence interval for
    i. the average age of the students
    ii. the average age of males and females separately
    iii. the average taste reaction of all students
    iv. the average taste reaction of males and females separately
    v. image importance (assume interval data) for all students
    vi. image importance (assume interval data): males and females separately

16.35. Perform the tasks specified in 16.34(c) but with a 68 percent confidence level.

16.36. Repeat 16.34(c) ii, iv, and vi using only those students who received treatment 2 *(Delight)*.

16.37. Prepare a point estimate and a 90 percent confidence interval for
a. the proportion of students tasting *Bravo* who choose *Bravo* rather than money.
b. the proportion of students tasting *Delight* who choose *Delight* rather than money.
c. Repeat (a) for males and females separately.
d. Repeat (b) for males and females separately.
e. the percentage who assigned price importance a "7."

16.38. Repeat 16.37 using a 68 percent confidence interval.

16.39. "The mean is generally meaningless in marketing research." Comment on this remark (ignoring the quality of the pun).

Projects/Activities

16.40. Pick three frequently purchased products and survey students on your campus concerning their purchase levels. Estimate total expenditures on these products by students registered on your campus during the nine-month school year. Prepare separate estimates for (a) male/female, (b) graduate/undergraduate, and (c) overall.

16.41. Repeat 16.40 for _____ .
a. hours studying per week
b. hours exercising per week
c. hours watching TV per week
d. percentage riding bicycles to school at least once a week
e. percentage owning a car
f. percentage who smoke

Notes

1. R. Maguire and T. C. Wilson, "Banners or Cross-Tabs? Before Deciding, Weigh Data-Format Pros, Cons," *Marketing News* (May 13, 1983), 10.
2. The formula for the sample standard deviation calculated from data in a frequency distribution is

$$s = \sqrt{\frac{\sum\limits_{i=1}^{h} f_i(x_i - \bar{x})^2}{n-1}}$$

where f_i = the frequency of the ith class, x_i = the midpoint of the ith class, h = the number of classes, and all of the other symbols are the same as the formula for arrayed data.
3. Reported in Elrick and Lavidge Inc., "How to Mislead Product Planners, or Marketing Research Mistakes to Avoid," *Marketing Today* 2 (1984).
4. The correction simply involves computing the weighted average of the sample means of the groups where the weights equal each group's percentage of the total population, or

$$\bar{x} = \sum_{i=1}^{n} W_i \bar{x}_i$$

5. The corrected sample proportion can be found by the following formula, using the same weights derived to correct the sample mean:

$$p = \sum_{i=1}^{n} W_i p_i$$

6. The formula is

$$\hat{\sigma}_{\bar{x}_{st}} = \sqrt{\sum_{h=1}^{k} W_h^2 \frac{S_h^2}{n_h}}$$

where h = each stratum sampled
W_h = the percentage of the population in stratum h
S_h = the sample standard deviation from stratum h
n_h = the sample size taken from stratum h

7.

$$\hat{\sigma}_{p_{st}} = \sqrt{\sum_{h=1}^{k} W_h^2 \frac{p_h(1 - p_h)}{n_h - 1}}$$

17

Hypothesis Tests of Differences

LEARNING OBJECTIVES

Upon completing this chapter, you should be able to:

1. Describe the process involved in testing a hypothesis about differences between two or more groups.

2. Explain the difference between a univariate hypothesis test and a multivariate hypothesis test.

3. Determine the appropriate univariate statistical technique to use to test a hypothesis based on the nature of the data available.

4. Conduct univariate hypothesis tests using the most common statistical techniques.

5. Explain the importance of calculating the probability that a given result is due to chance rather than just accepting or rejecting the null hypothesis.

6. Select the appropriate ANOVA technique based on the experimental design used and the assumptions made about the presence of interaction.

7. Explain the meaning of an ANOVA output table.

Market Facts' Test of Two Measures of Product Attribute Importance

Market Facts is a large research firm. It is often called upon to measure consumers' ratings of the importance of various product characteristics as part of a survey research project. It has found measuring importance on standard 5-, 7-, or 10-point scales where "1" is "not at all important" and the highest scale point is "extremely important" to be unsatisfactory for some applications. A major weakness is that many consumers report that most or all characteristics are more than moderately important. This makes it difficult to identify either key attributes or distinct consumer groups.

In an attempt to overcome this problem, Market Facts compared a "concern scale" (*When thinking of purchasing oil how concerned are you with . . .*) with a standard importance scale (*How important is it that the oil you buy . . .*). The hope was that the concern scale would reflect fewer high responses (a lower mean) and more variance across respondents. The means are shown below.

Which, if any, of the differences in means are likely to represent genuinely lower means rather than differences due to sampling variation? (All except the last four differences are significant at the .05 level. That is, they are very unlikely to have occurred only because of sampling variation.)[1]

Characteristic	Concern Mean	Importance Mean
Taste of oil	5.88	6.15
Oil's value for money	5.75	6.16
Consistent quality of oil	5.57	6.09
Oil smoking when heated	5.39	5.65
Messiness of using oil	4.82	5.56
Frying uses of oil	4.78	5.46
Baking uses of oil	4.68	5.55
Color of oil	3.90	4.24
Nutritional content of oil	5.17	5.74
Oil liked by entire family	5.08	5.65
Oil for everyday use	5.08	5.97
Oil is natural	5.32	5.40
Cost of oil	5.24	5.32
Cholesterol level of oil	5.92	6.00
Artificial ingredients in oil	5.07	5.28

As indicated at the beginning of Chapter 16, statistical techniques are simply ways of asking questions of a set of data. In this chapter, we examine statistical approaches to a particular type of question:

Is the difference between one or more sample values and one or more other values likely to be the result of random characteristics of the sample or of some other factor?

Answering this type of question generally involves some form of a hypothesis test.

The Nature of Hypothesis Tests

Hypothesis test: determine if observed differences between one or more sample values and one or more other values are due to random variations.

Null hypothesis: any observed differences are no more than one would expect by chance.

Alternate hypothesis: the observed differences reflect real differences between the populations the samples represent.

Type I error: concluding that the null hypothesis should be rejected when, in fact, it is true.

Hypothesis tests attempt to ascertain if observed differences between one or more sample values and one or more other values are due to random variations. Two hypotheses are involved in each hypothesis test. The **null hypothesis,** designated by H_0, is generally that the sample values do not differ by more than one would expect due to chance. In decisional research, it is generally stated such that, if accepted, no change or new action will be undertaken. The **alternate hypothesis,** designated by H_1, is that differences observed in the sample values represent real differences in the populations the samples represent. In a decisional context, if the alternate hypothesis is accepted, it generally leads to changes or new actions being initiated.

Statistical tests of hypotheses are designed to allow us to *reject* or *not reject* the null hypothesis with some stated level of confidence. We cannot prove that the null is true because we never have complete information when we are using samples. However, we can provide evidence that it is not true. If we can reject the null, then we are able to accept the alternate hypothesis. Thus, if we reject the null hypothesis that two sample means are equal (there is no difference in taste preference between our current formulation and the new formulation), we can accept the alternate hypothesis that there is a difference.

The hypothesis test just described is known as a two-tailed or nondirectional test because the null hypothesis left both sides open for the alternate. That is, a more favorable or a less favorable taste rating would allow the null to be rejected. When we want to take an action only if the difference is in a particular direction, we need to structure a one-tailed or directional test (consumers rate the taste of our current formulation as high as or higher than the new formulation). Rejecting this null leads to accepting the alternative that consumers rate the taste of the new formulation higher than our current formulation. This, in turn, would lead to plans to use the new formulation (all other things being equal).

Two types of errors can be made in hypothesis tests. A **type I error** occurs when the null hypothesis is true but it is concluded that it should be rejected. **Alpha (α)** is the designation for the probability of making a type I error. This is also the significance level of the test. One minus alpha is known as the confidence level of the test (the probability of not rejecting a correct null).

TABLE 17–1 Possible Outcomes of a Hypotheses Test

Research Conclusion	True Situation	
	H_0 = True	H_1 = False
Do not reject H_0	Correct decision	Error: Type II
	Confidence level	
	Probability = $1 - \alpha$	Probability = β
	Error: Type I	Correct decision
Reject H_0	Significance level	Power of test
	Probability = α	Probability = $1 - \beta$

Alpha is specified in advance and is traditionally set at .01, .05, or .10, though the only logic for these levels is tradition. In fact, as we will see in the next section, naively using these levels can result in serious errors in decisional research.

A **type II error** occurs when the null hypothesis is false but the decision is made to not reject it. **Beta (β)** is the probability of a type II error. Beta is generally calculated after the fact, but it can be specified in advance and the sample size adjusted accordingly. One minus beta is known as the power of the test (the probability of correctly rejecting a false null). Table 17–1 illustrates these relationships.

Selecting an appropriate statistical technique for hypothesis testing requires the answers to five questions:

1. Are the effects of more than one variable being examined?
2. Are the data *ratio, interval, ordinal,* or *nominal?*
3. How many groups are to be compared?
4. Are the samples from the group(s) to be compared independent? (Does the selection of a sample element from one population limit the sample elements that can be selected from the second population?)
5. How large are the samples that were taken?

A **multivariate hypothesis test** is required to examine the effects of more than one variable. Such tests are common and are described in the last section of this chapter. First, we describe **univariate hypothesis tests,** which focus on the effects of only one variable.

Table 17–2 indicates some of the appropriate techniques for testing hypotheses based on the answers to the last four questions. We briefly describe the more widely used of these techniques.[2] Where appropriate, we illustrate their computation and application using the example from Chapter 16.

Alpha (α): the probability of making a type I error (the significance level of a hypothesis test).

Type II error: concluding that the null hypothesis should not be rejected when, in fact, it is false.

Beta (β): the probability of making a type II error.

Multivariate hypothesis test: examines the effects of more than one variable.

Univariate hypothesis test: examines the effects of only one variable.

Univariate Hypothesis Tests Requiring Interval Data

As indicated in Chapter 9, techniques that are appropriate for lower levels of measurement, such as nominal and ordinal scales, can be applied to higher

TABLE 17-2 Univariate Statistical Techniques

Level of Data	No. of Samples	Independent Samples?	Sample Size	Appropriate Statistical Techniques
Interval	1	N.A.*	≥ 30	Z test
Interval	1	N.A.	<30	t test
Interval	2	Yes	≥ 30	Z test
Interval	2	Yes	<30	t test
Interval	2	No	a†	t_r test
Interval	2†	Yes	a	One-way ANOVA
Interval	2†	No	a	t_r tests of all pairs
Ordinal	1	N.A.	a	Kolmogorov–Smirnov one-sample test
Ordinal	2	Yes	a	Mann–Whitney U, median test, Kolmogorov–Smirnov two-sample test
Ordinal	2	No	a	Sign test, Wilcoxon matched-pairs
Ordinal	2†	Yes	a	Kruskal–Wallis one-way ANOVA
Ordinal	2†	No	a	Friedman two-way ANOVA
Nominal	1	N.A.	a	Binomial test, X^2 one-sample test
Nominal	2	Yes	a	Fisher test, X^2 two-sample test
Nominal	2	No	a	McNemar test
Nominal	2†	Yes	a	X^2 k-sample test
Nominal	2†	No	a	Cochran Q test

*N.A. = Not Applicable.
†a = Sample size is not a determinant of the appropriate technique.

levels such as ratio and interval. The reverse is not true. Since there are no commonly used techniques that require ratio data, we begin our discussion with techniques requiring interval data.

Test of a Sample Mean, One Sample: $n \geq 30$

The management of the firm in our example (pages 405–408) believed that the average consumption of carbonated beverages per female student per week was more than four bottles. If the consumption were found to be this high, the firm would test a product positioning strategy designed specifically for females. However, the firm wants to be "very" sure that actual average consumption is over four bottles per week before developing and testing this strategy. The average consumption found in the sample was 5.575 bottles per week. Can management be "very" sure that overall consumption by females is over 4 bottles per week?

Three specifications are necessary in hypothesis tests of a single mean against a null hypothesis:

1. *the hypothesis to be tested;*
2. *the level of sampling error (alpha, or α) permitted in the test; and*
3. *the standard error of the mean for the sample size taken.*

The hypothesis was developed by management. As analysts, we need to restate the hypothesis in its null form; that is, that the average consumption

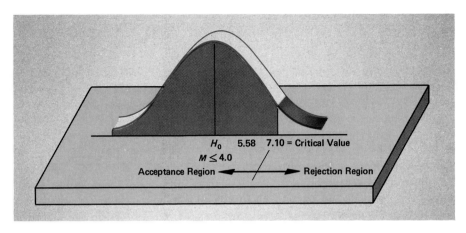

FIGURE 17–1 Test of Hypothesis H_0: $M \leq 4.00$

was no more than four bottles, glasses, or cans per week. This is written formally as

$$H_0: M \leq 4 \text{ bottles, glasses, or cans per female per week}$$

The desire to be "very" sure that the mean female consumption is indeed above four bottles we will interpret to mean a chance of being wrong as a result of a sampling error of no more than .05 (an α of .05). All that remains is to calculate $\hat{\sigma}_{\bar{x}}$, by the use of equation (16–3). The steps to be performed are

1. *Determine the sample standard deviation using equation (16–2):*

$$s = \sqrt{\frac{\sum_{i=1}^{n}(x_i - \bar{x})^2}{n - 1}} = 11.97$$

2. *Divide this deviation by the square root of the sample size:*

$$\hat{\sigma}_{\bar{x}} = \frac{11.97}{\sqrt{40}} = 1.89$$

The value of the mean specified in the null hypothesis, the α value, and $\hat{\sigma}_{\bar{x}}$ are combined to create a *rejection region* for H_0. This is done by assuming that the mean specified in the null is the mean of the sampling distribution (a normal distribution). The rejection region is any value outside the *critical value* created by moving the number of standard errors from the mean required by the alpha level chosen. The required number of standard errors (Z values) required by various alpha levels can be determined from Appendix A (Area Under the Normal Curve). Any sample value (mean) lower than the critical value in this case indicates that H_0 should be accepted.

This test is illustrated for our problem in Figure 17–1. The distance to the critical value from the mean of the sampling distribution as specified by the null hypothesis ($M \leq 4.00$) is

$$Z_\alpha \hat{\sigma}_{\bar{x}} = 1.64 \ (1.89) = 3.10$$

The critical value is then

$$M + Z_\alpha \hat{\sigma}_{\bar{x}} = 4.00 + 3.10 = 7.10$$

The critical value is greater than the sample value of 5.58 and so *the null hypothesis is accepted*. That is, management cannot be "very" sure that females consume an average of more than four bottles per week.

A natural question for a manager to ask, given these results is: "O.K. I can't be *very sure* that these results are due to sampling error. What is the exact probability that they are indeed caused by sampling variation?"

This probability is determined by finding the shaded area of the sampling distribution shown in Figure 17–2. To find this area, the Z value for the distance of the sample mean from the hypothesized mean is calculated and the area of the sampling distribution excluded by this value is determined from Appendix A. Or

$$Z = \frac{|M - \bar{x}|}{\hat{\sigma}_{\bar{x}}} \tag{17-1}$$

$$Z = \frac{|4.00 - 5.58|}{1.89} = .84$$

The probability corresponding to this Z value is .20. Stated another way, our test has shown that (1) given the sample size used and (2) given the variance in consumption in our sample, we would obtain a sample consumption value of 5.58 or larger 20 percent of the time *if the actual population mean were 4.0*. In a decisional context, a substantially different interpretation may be given to the conclusion, "there is a 20 percent chance we would obtain these results if the null hypothesis is correct" than to the conclusion, "the null hypothesis is accepted." For this reason, the exact probability should always be reported in decisional research projects.

Our discussion has centered on *one-tailed* tests, that is, our hypothesis specified the direction of the anticipated difference (*more than* four glasses per

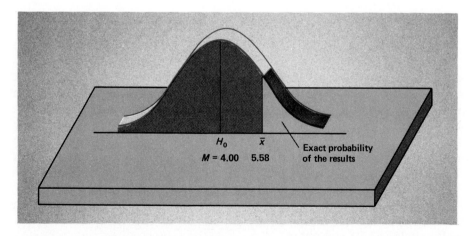

FIGURE 17–2 Probability That H_0 Is True

week). Occasionally, we need to test for differences in either direction (more or less than four glasses per week). This would be a *two-tailed test* because values in either tail of the normal distribution could lead to the rejection of the null. The basic procedures are identical except that two critical values are required, that is,

$$\text{higher critical value} = M + Z_\alpha \hat{\sigma}_{\bar{x}}$$
$$\text{lower critical value} = M - Z_\alpha \hat{\sigma}_{\bar{x}}$$

(17-2)

The Z values would also reflect the fact that both ends of the distribution are involved. That is, an α level of .05 would require a Z value that would cut off 2.5 percent of the area under the normal curve at each end ($Z = 1.96$).

Test of a Proportion, One Sample

The hypothesis test of a proportion follows the same logic and procedure as a test of a mean. The only difference is that the estimated standard error of the proportion, $\hat{\sigma}_p$, is used instead of the estimated standard error of the mean ($\hat{\sigma}_{\bar{x}}$).

Management believed that more than 50 percent of college males would consume six or more glasses of carbonated beverages per week. If so, the firm would develop an extensive strategy aimed at males. Again, management wants to be "very" sure that the actual percentage is at least this high before developing the program. An examination of Table 16–2 reveals that 58 percent (35/60) of the males reported a consumption rate of six glasses or more per week. The following procedure is employed.

1. *Specify the null hypothesis:*
   $H_0: P \le .50$
2. *Specify the level of sampling error allowed:*
   α = "very" sure, use .05; thus $Z = 1.64$
3. *Calculate the estimated standard error using the p specified in the null hypothesis:*

$$\hat{\sigma}_p = \sqrt{\frac{P(1 - P)}{n - 1}} = \sqrt{\frac{.50(1 - .50)}{60 - 1}} = .065$$

4. *Calculate the critical value:*
   critical value = .50 + (1.64).065 = .61
5. *Since the observed value, .58, is less than the critical value, the null hypothesis cannot be rejected.* That is, we cannot, with a .05 confidence level, conclude that the null hypothesis is false.
6. *However, as stated earlier, in decisional research we should also report the exact probability. This involves calculating the Z value for the distance the sample proportion is from the null hypothesis proportion and looking up in Appendix A the area of the sampling distribution excluded by this value. This calculation is*

$$Z = \frac{|P - p|}{\hat{\sigma}_p} = \frac{.08}{.065} = 1.23$$

(17-3)

A Z value of 1.23 cuts off about 11 percent of one tail of the distribution. Thus, given our sample size, we would obtain by chance a sample proportion of .58 or larger *if the actual population proportion were* .50 about 11 percent of the time.

A two-tailed test of a proportion is conducted in the same manner as a two-tailed test of a mean.

Test of a Mean, One Sample: $n < 30$

The Z test used in the initial section on a hypothesis test of the mean is based on the sampling distribution of the mean being normally distributed. For samples less than 30, this is not the case. Instead, the sampling distribution of the mean follows one of the Student t distributions. There is a unique Student t distribution for every sample size. As the sample size increases, the t distribution increasingly resembles the normal distribution.

The appropriate t distribution to use is determined by the *degrees of freedom*, or *df*. For a hypothesis test of a single mean, the degrees of freedom are one less than the sample size ($n - 1$). A table of t distributions is provided in Appendix B.

Hypothesis tests of a mean with a sample of less than 30 are conducted in exactly the same manner as those involving larger samples, except that a t value and the t distribution are used instead of a Z value and the normal distribution.

We illustrate this procedure by testing management's feeling that females who taste *Delight* will assign it an average taste rating greater than 70. From Table 16–2 we calculate the sample mean of the 20 females who tasted *Delight* as 77.40 and the sample standard deviation as 18.19. The following steps are required:

1. *Specify the null hypothesis:*

$$H_0: M \leq 70.00$$

2. *Specify the level of sampling error allowed:*

$$\text{let } \alpha = .05, \text{ thus } t \text{ for 19 } df = 1.73$$

3. *Calculate the estimated standard error:*

$$\hat{\sigma}_{\bar{x}} = \frac{s}{\sqrt{n}} = \frac{18.19}{\sqrt{20}} = 4.07$$

4. *Calculate the critical value:*

$$\text{critical value} = 70 + 1.73(4.07) = 77.04$$

5. *Since the sample value (77.40) is larger than the critical value (77.04), we can reject the null hypothesis that the average taste rating is 70.00 or less.*
6. *The exact probability given our sample results is calculated:*

$$t = \frac{|M - \bar{x}|}{\hat{\sigma}_{\bar{x}}} = \frac{7.4}{4.07} = 1.82$$

The area of the t distribution with 19 degrees of freedom excluded by $t = 1.82$ about .04.

Test of Differences in Two Means, Independent Samples: $n \geq 30$

Marketers are frequently interested in learning of differences between groups created by exposure to marketing variables, such as the taste reactions of those tasting *Bravo* compared to those tasting *Delight*. Likewise, different responses to the same variable by groups with different characteristics are frequently of interest. The management group in our example was interested in differences between males and females in the consumption of carbonated beverages; it believed that males consumed more than females. Testing this "hypothesis" involves the use of the same logic and procedures used to test hypotheses about a single mean as described in the previous section. The only real difference in these procedures is that the *standard error of the difference between two means* is used rather than the standard error of the mean. Testing this hypothesis involves the following:

1. *The null hypothesis to be tested:* the null would be that mean consumption by males, M_m, is the same as or less than mean consumption by females, M_f. Thus H_0: $M_m - M_f \leq 0$. From Table 16–2, we calculate the sample difference as $9.87 - 5.58 = 4.29$.
2. *The level of sampling error permitted:* judgmentally set at $\alpha = .10$ ($Z = 1.28$)
3. *The estimated standard error of the differences between two means:* calculate using

$$\hat{\sigma}_{\bar{x}_{m-f}} = \sqrt{\frac{\hat{\sigma}_m^2}{n_m} + \frac{\hat{\sigma}_f^2}{n_f}} \qquad (17\text{-}4)$$

where $\hat{\sigma}_m$ = estimated standard deviation of population m (males).
This is calculated as before using equation (16–2)
$\hat{\sigma}_f$ = estimated standard deviation of population f (females) calculated as for males
n_m = sample size for sample m
n_f = sample size for sample f

$$\hat{\sigma}_{\bar{x}_{m-f}} = \sqrt{\frac{(10.80)^2}{60} + \frac{(11.97)^2}{40}} = 2.35$$

4. *The critical value is determined as*

$$\text{Critical value} = (M_m - M_f) + Z_\alpha \hat{\sigma}_{\bar{x}_{m-f}} \qquad (17\text{-}5)$$
$$= 0 + 1.28(2.35) = 3.01$$

5. *Since the sample difference, 4.29, is larger than the critical value (3.01), we can reject the null hypothesis that male consumption is equal to or less than female consumption.*

6. *The exact probability given our results can be calculated as*

$$Z = \frac{|(\bar{x}_m - \bar{x}_f) - (M_m - M_f)|}{\hat{\sigma}_{x_{m-f}}} \tag{17-6}$$

$$= \frac{4.29 - 0}{2.35} = 1.83$$

This value cuts off approximately $3\frac{1}{3}$ percent of the distribution (see Appendix A). Therefore, the exact probability of obtaining a sample difference of 4.29 or larger, given our sample sizes and the variances in our samples, if the male and female populations actually consume the same amount, is .033.

A nondirectional or two-tailed test can be conducted for a difference in two means using the same procedure that is appropriate for one mean.

Test of Differences Between Two Means, Independent Samples: $n < 30$

If the size of one or both samples is below 30, a different method of calculating the standard error of the difference between two means must be used, and the appropriate t distribution must be used instead of the Z distribution. The appropriate t distribution is based on the degrees of freedom which is, $n_1 + n_2 - 2$. The formula for t is

$$t = \frac{(\bar{x}_1 - \bar{x}_2) - (M_1 - M_2)}{\sqrt{\frac{(n_1 - 1)s_1^2 + (n_2 - 1)s_2^2}{n_1 + n_2 - 2}\left(\frac{1}{n_1} + \frac{1}{n_2}\right)}} \tag{17-7}$$

The denominator of (17–7) is the appropriate formula for the standard error of the difference between two means when the sample size is less than 30.

Other than these changes, the same six steps described in the previous section are followed. To test your understanding of this type of test, verify that the exact probability given the sample results and a null hypothesis of no difference in taste reaction between females tasting the *Bravo* brand and females tasting the *Delight* brand is .006. The mean and standard deviation for the females tasting *Bravo* are 63.80 and 12.13, and for the females tasting Delight they are 77.40 and 18.19. This is a two-tailed test, and once *df* exceeds 30, the Z distribution can be used as an approximation for the *t* distribution (if the *t* distribution is used, the probability is .009).

Test of Differences Between Two Proportions, Independent Samples

Managers, and therefore researchers, are often interested in the difference between the proportion of two groups that engage in a certain activity or have a certain characteristic. In our example, management believed that the percentage of females who report a zero level of carbonated beverage consumption would be larger than the percentage of males. Testing this hypothesis involves the use of the same logic and procedure used to test a difference between two means.

The only difference is that the *standard error of the difference between two proportions* is used instead of the standard error of the difference between two means. The specifications required and the procedure for using them are as follows:

1. *The null hypothesis to be tested:* the null would be that the proportion of females, P_f, reporting no consumption is equal to or less than the proportion of males, P_m. Thus, $H_0: P_f - P_m \leq 0$. From Table 16–2, we calculate the sample proportions and the difference as $.50 - .317 = .183$
2. *The level of sampling error permitted:* judgmentally set at $\alpha = .10$ ($Z = 1.28$)
3. *The estimated standard error of the differences between two proportions:* calculate using

$$\hat{\sigma}_{P_{f-m}} = \sqrt{\bar{p}(1 - \bar{p}) \left[\frac{1}{n_f} + \frac{1}{n_m} \right]} \qquad (17\text{-}8)$$

where $\bar{p} = \dfrac{n_f p_f + n_m p_m}{n_f + n_m}$

p_f = proportion in sample f (females) who are nonconsumers

p_m = proportion in sample m (males) who are nonconsumers

n_f = size of sample f

n_m = size of sample m

Therefore,

$$\bar{p} = \frac{40(.475) + 60(.317)}{40 + 60} = .39,$$

and

$$\hat{\sigma}_{P_{f-m}} = \sqrt{.38(.62) \left[\frac{1}{40} + \frac{1}{60} \right]} = .10$$

4. The null hypothesis is $H_0: P_f - P_m \leq 0$. *The critical value is* then

$$(P_f - P_m) + Z_\alpha \hat{\sigma}_{P_{f-m}} \qquad (17\text{-}9)$$

$$0 + 1.28(.10) = .128$$

5. *Since the sample difference,* .183, *is larger than the critical value, we reject the null hypothesis and conclude that more females report no consumption than males.*
6. *The exact probability given our results can be determined as*

$$Z = \frac{|(p_f - p_m) - (P_f - P_m)|}{\hat{\sigma}_{P_{f-m}}} \qquad (17\text{-}10)$$

$$= \frac{.183 - 0}{.10} = 1.83$$

This value cuts off approximately 3 percent of the distribution.

There are no separate large and small sample versions of hypothesis tests involving proportions. As long as the population proportion is midrange, say .3 to .7, small samples (10 or more) can be used in the tests described.

Tests of Differences Among Two or More Means, Independent Samples

Analysis of variance (ANOVA) is a set of techniques that can be used to test differences in means caused by two, three, or more levels of one variable, multiple variables, and even multiple variables that interact with each other. We describe multivariate versions of ANOVA in the last section of this chapter. Univariate ANOVA is often referred to as *one-way* ANOVA.

One-way ANOVA is commonly used in the analysis of experimental results. It is a method of determining the probability that the observed differences of the mean responses of experimental groups receiving different levels of a single independent variable are the result of sampling variation.

This procedure can help answer such questions as: "Is there a significant difference in sales per salesperson between our straight salary, straight commission, and combination salary/commission plans?"; "Does the color of our package—red, blue, green, or yellow—affect sales?"; and "Which, if any, of these five advertisements will produce the greatest attitude change?"

The bases of one-way ANOVA—both intuitive and mathematical—are explained in the following steps. We use a hypothetical example involving our new carbonated beverage. Suppose management is considering three different types of bottles: A—a tall, slender, clear bottle; B—a tall, slender, shaded bottle; and C—a short, shaded bottle. Since the costs of the bottles are not equal, management will use the least expensive version (C) unless there is a sales advantage associated with the other designs.

Three random samples of 25 stores each are selected and one version of the bottle is placed in each sample of stores. The same point-of-purchase display is used in all three stores. The sales results are shown in Table 17–3. Does the type of bottle affect sales?

1. Intuitive Logic.   In an experiment, the greater the effect of the treatment, the greater is the variation between group (treatment) means.

TABLE 17–3 Unit Sales Response to Varying Bottle Types

A		B		C	
125	142	143	125	146	137
149	160	116	171	91	160
189	145	170	162	148	123
107	131	201	148	130	168
136	162	141	185	138	139
153	155	168	98	145	141
156	165	126	137	169	138
196	188	138	149	168	196
151	153	140	139	140	97
139	162	146	140	114	138
148	142	87	132	124	183
154	134	150	141	96	135
133	$\bar{x}=151$	147	$\bar{x}=144$	136	$\bar{x}=140$

Mathematical Measurement. The variation among group means is measured by the *mean squares* between groups *(MST)* calculation. *MST* is calculated as

$$MST = \frac{\text{sum of squares among groups}}{\text{degrees of freedom}} = \frac{(SST)}{df}$$

$$= \frac{\begin{array}{c}\text{sum of squared deviations of group sample}\\ \text{means } (\bar{x}_j) \text{ from overall sample mean } (\bar{x}_t),\\ \text{weighted by sample size } (n_j)\end{array}}{\text{number of groups } (G) - 1} \qquad (17\text{-}11)$$

$$MST = \frac{\sum\limits_{j=1}^{G} n_j(\bar{x}_j - \bar{x}_t)^2}{G - 1}$$

Example: The overall sample mean is calculated from Table 17–2 as

$$\bar{x}_t = \frac{25(151) + 25(144) + 25(140)}{75}$$

$$\bar{x}_t = 145$$

Then,

$$MST = \frac{25(151 - 145)^2 + 25(144 - 145)^2 + 25(140 - 145)^2}{3 - 1}$$

$$= 775$$

Notice that the greater the differences among the sample means (evidence of strong treatment effects), the larger *MST* will be.

2. Intuitive Logic. Although the variation among group sample means will change as a result of treatment effects (as just discussed), the variation *within* the group samples should not. The addition (or subtraction) of a fixed amount to each of a series of numbers does not change the variation of the numbers. Thus, the variance of the series [1, 3] (not from the carbonated beverage bottle example) is

$$\hat{\sigma}^2 = \frac{(1 - 2)^2 + (3 - 2)^2}{2} = 1.0,$$

which is the same as the variance of the series [1 + 4, 3 + 4], or

$$\hat{\sigma}^2 = \frac{(5 - 6)^2 + (7 - 6)^2}{2} = 1.0$$

Therefore, a variable such as the bottle type could be presented in a different form to each of three sample groups. It could affect the *means* of each group, but it should not affect the *variance* of each group.

Illustration. The means for the sample groups are different, as shown in Table 17–3. Because the three groups of stores were randomly selected, one would expect that the variances of the three samples would have been the same (within sampling error) before the test was conducted. There is no reason to believe that they are different (again, beyond sampling error differences) for the period of the test. Therefore, we need an estimate of the variance within the samples.

Mathematical Measurement.　The variation within the sample groups is measured as the *mean sum of squares within groups*. Generally referred to as *mean square error (MSE)*, it represents the natural and random variation in the data. It is calculated as

$$MSE = \frac{\text{sum of squares within groups}}{\text{degrees of freedom}} = \frac{SSE}{df}$$

$$= \frac{\begin{array}{c}\text{sum of the squared deviations of each} \\ \text{observation in the group sample } (x_{ij}) \text{ from} \\ \text{the mean of the observations for that group} \\ \text{sample } (x_j), \text{ summed for all group samples}\end{array}}{\begin{array}{c}\text{sum of the sample sizes for all groups} \\ \text{minus the number of groups } (G)\end{array}} \quad (17\text{-}12)$$

$$MSE = \frac{\displaystyle\sum_{j=1}^{G}\sum_{i=1}^{n}(x_{ij} - \bar{x}_j)^2}{\displaystyle\sum_{j=1}^{k} n_j - G}$$

The sum of the squared deviations for group A is obtained by taking each observation in the group A sample (125, 149, ... 134, as shown in Table 17–2), subtracting the group A mean from each ($x = 151$, also shown in Table 17–2) squaring the resulting difference for each observation, and summing the results, or

$$(125 - 151)^2 + (149 - 151)^2 + \ldots + (134 - 151)^2 = 9{,}620$$

The same procedure is followed to obtain the sum of the squared deviations for group B (14,464) and for group C (15,490). The result of this procedure is

$$= \frac{(9{,}620) + (14{,}464) + (15{,}490)}{(25 + 25 + 25 - 3)} = 549.64$$

3. Intuitive Logic.　Although the variation between sample means will increase as the effect of the treatment increases, variation within each of the samples should not change with treatment effects. The ratio of measurements of

$$\frac{\text{variation } between \text{ sample means}}{\text{variation } within \text{ samples}}$$

should, therefore, reflect the effect of the treatment, if any. The higher the ratio, the more probable it is that the treatment(s) actually had an effect.

Illustration.　If we compute a ratio of measurements of the *between* variation to the *within* variation, we should be able to make an inference about the probability that the observed difference between the group sample means was the result of packaging and not of sampling variation.

Mathematical Measurement.   A sampling distribution known as the F distribution allows us to determine the probability that an observed value of F, where

$$F = \frac{MST}{MSE} \qquad (17\text{-}13)$$

(with specified degrees of freedom in both the numerator and denominator) could have occurred by chance rather than as the result of the treatment effect.

The F distribution is a sampling distribution just like the Z and t distributions described earlier. Like the t distribution, the F distribution is really a set of distributions whose shape changes slightly depending upon the number and size of the samples involved. Therefore, using the F distribution requires that we calculate the degrees of freedom for the numerator and the denominator.

The numerator is MST and the degrees of freedom for it are the number of groups minus one ($G - 1$). The denominator is MSE and the degrees of freedom for it are the total number of units in all the samples minus the number of samples

(G) or $\sum_{j=1}^{G} n_j - G = 25 + 25 + 25 - 3 = 72$ for the problem at hand.

We can calculate F as

$$F = \frac{775}{549.64} = 1.41$$

Our null hypothesis is that there are no treatment effects, or

$$H_0: M_1 = M_2 = M_3.$$

Using an alpha of .10, we find that the critical value for F with 2 and 72 degrees of freedom in Appendix C is approximately 2.38. Since 1.41 is less than the critical value, we cannot reject the null hypothesis of no differences between the groups. (Consulting a more detailed set of F distribution tables reveals that the exact probability is approximately .25.) Since management was concerned about the differential cost of the bottles, it might decide to use the least expensive version.

Table 17–4 shows a common way of displaying the results of an ANOVA. Most computer programs display results in this manner. The usefulness of this display will be more apparent later in this chapter when we consider ANOVA with more than one variable.

TABLE 17–4 ANOVA Output

Source	DF	Sum of Squares	Mean Squared	F Ratio	F Prob.
Total	74	41124.00			
Between	2	1550.00	775.00	1.410	.2508
Within	72	39574.00	549.64		

Thus far, we have not described the formal assumptions involved in the ANOVA model. They are as follows:

1. *Treatments are assigned at random to test units.*
2. *Measurements are at least intervally scaled and are taken from a population that is normally distributed.*
3. *The variances in the test and control groups are equal.*
4. *The effects of treatments on response are additive.*

One of the assumptions of the ANOVA is that treatments are assigned at random to test units. This is often overlooked in practice by using pseudo-treatments such as occupation, stage of life cycle, or urban or rural residency, and analyzing to see what effect these factors have on the mean amounts of a particular product purchased. This use of nonrandomly assigned pseudotreatments greatly increases the possibility that other variables associated with them will affect responses, and these effects will be attributed to the pseudotreatment.

Univariate Hypothesis Tests Using Ordinal Data

Test of Differences in Rank Orders of Two Independent Samples

Does the rank assigned *Bravo* by females differ from the rank females assigned to *Delight*? As indicated in Table 17–2, the question can be answered by several techniques. However, the Mann–Whitney U test is generally the best approach. It is basically the ordinal data substitute for the t and Z tests for differences between sample means described earlier. In fact, there are even large and small sample versions of this test. We illustrate the large-sample version that can be used if one sample is larger than 20 or if both samples are larger than 10.[3]

1. *The null hypothesis implied by our question at the beginning of this section is that the two distributions are equal.*
2. *The raw scores (rank assigned Bravo or Delight by each individual respondent) from the two groups are treated as one set and are placed in order of increasing size. Each raw score is then assigned to a rank. Ties are assigned the average rank of the group of raw scores they are in. In Table 17–5 the ranks are*

Raw Score	Number with Same Raw Score	Range of Ranks	Combined Average Rank
1	12	1–12	6.5
2	11	13–23	18.0
3	12	24–35	29.5
4	1	35–36	36.0
5	4	37–40	38.5

TABLE 17–5 Combined Rank Calculation for the Mann–Whitney U Test

Raw Scores		Combined Ranks	
Bravo	Delight	Bravo	Delight
5	2	38.5	18.0
2	1	18.0	6.5
3	3	29.5	29.5
1	2	6.5	18.0
5	1	38.5	6.5
3	3	29.5	29.5
2	2	18.0	18.0
3	1	29.5	6.5
1	5	6.5	38.5
4	2	36.0	18.0
2	1	18.0	6.5
2	1	18.0	6.5
3	3	29.5	29.5
1	5	6.5	38.5
2	2	18.0	18.0
1	3	6.5	29.5
3	1	29.5	6.5
3	1	29.5	6.5
2	1	18.0	6.5
3	3	29.5	29.5
		$R_1 = 453.5$	$R_2 = 366.5$

3. *The ranks for each treatment group are then summed.*
4. *A statistic called U is computed as*

$$U = n_1 n_2 + \frac{n_1(n_1 + 1)}{2} - R_1 \qquad (17\text{-}14)$$

or

$$U = n_1 n_2 + \frac{n_2(n_2 + 1)}{2} - R_2 \qquad (17\text{-}15)$$

where n_1, n_2 = sample size in groups 1 and 2, respectively
$\quad R_1, R_2$ = sum of the ranks assigned to groups 1 and 2, respectively

Thus,

$$U = (20)(20) + \frac{20(21)}{2} - 366.5$$

$$U = 243.5$$

5. *For small samples, the critical value for U with a specified alpha is ascertained with special tables.[4] For large-sample cases such as this one, a Z value is calculated and the standard Z table or normal distribution is used. The value for Z is calculated as[5]*

$$Z = \frac{U - \dfrac{n_1 n_2}{2}}{\sqrt{\dfrac{(n_1)(n_2)(n_1 + n_2 + 1)}{12}}}$$

$$= \frac{243.5 - \dfrac{(20)(20)}{2}}{\sqrt{\dfrac{(20)(20)(20 + 20 + 1)}{12}}} = 1.17 \qquad (17\text{-}16)$$

Appendix A reveals that the probability of obtaining these results if the null hypothesis of no difference in the rankings assigned the two brands is correct is approximately .24. Therefore, the null hypothesis cannot be rejected.

Univariate Hypothesis Tests Using Nominal Data

Test of Distributions by Categories of a Single Sample

Often a researcher needs to determine if the number of subjects, objects, or responses that fall into some set of categories differs from chance (or some other hypothesized distribution). This could involve the partitioning of users into gender, geographic, or social-status categories. Conversely, it could involve the distribution of a particular sample, such as males, into heavy user, light user, or nonuser categories.

Suppose the advertising manager for our beverage wants to test three direct mail formats, each of which offers a $.75 discount coupon for a purchase of a six-pack of *Delight* at the campus bookstore. Five hundred of each version are mailed to students selected at random. The coupons were redeemed as follows:

Version A	135
Version B	130
Version C	155
Total	420

Is there a significant difference?

The chi-square (χ^2) one-sample test is an appropriate way to answer this question. The χ^2 test requires the following steps:

1. *Determine the number that would be in each category if the null hypothesis were correct (E_i).* In our example, the null hypothesis would be that there is no difference in the response to each version. Therefore, we would expect an equal number of the total responses to fall into each category, or $E = 420/3 = 140$ per category. Check for small expected frequencies which can distort X^2 results. No more than 20 percent of the categories

should have expected frequencies less than 5, and none should have an expected frequency less than 1.

2. Calculate X^2 as follows

$$\chi^2 = \sum_{i=1}^{k} \frac{(O_i - E_i)^2}{E_i} \qquad (17\text{-}17)$$

where O_i = observed number in ith category
$\quad E_i$ = expected number in ith category
$\quad k$ = number of categories

For our example

$$\chi^2 = \frac{(135 - 140)^2}{140} + \frac{(130 - 140)^2}{140} + \frac{(155 - 140)^2}{140}$$
$$= 2.5$$

3. *The probability associated with this value is determined from Appendix D with k − 1 degrees of freedom.* The probability is slightly less than .30.

Test of Distributions by Categories of Two Independent Samples

We often need to determine if two sample groups differ in the way they are distributed into a number of discrete categories. This involves questions such as: "Are males and females equally divided into heavy, medium, and light user categories?" and "Are purchasers and nonpurchasers equally divided into blue-collar, white-collar, and managerial–professional occupation categories?" An appropriate test for such questions is the chi-square (χ^2) test for two independent samples.

We illustrate this technique using the data from Table 16–2 and the following question: "Is there a difference between males and females in terms of their reported frequency of carbonated beverage consumption?" Our null hypothesis is that there is no difference. For convenience, we collapse the eight response categories into three: 0, 1–3, and 4–7 days per week. The steps are as follows:

1. *Place the observed (sample) frequencies into a* k × r *table (called a contingency table) using the* k *columns for the sample groups and the* r *rows for the conditions or treatments. Calculate the sum for all the rows and columns. Record those totals at the margins of the table (they are called marginal totals). Also calculate the total for the entire table* (N). *For our example:*

Frequency	Male	Female	Totals
0	19	19	38
1–3	17	12	29
4–7	24	9	33
Totals	60	40	100

2. *Determine the expected frequency for each cell in the contingency table by finding the product of the two marginal totals common to that cell and dividing that value by N. Thus:*

	Male	Female
0	$\dfrac{60 \times 38}{100} = 22.8$	$\dfrac{40 \times 38}{100} = 15.2$
1–3	$\dfrac{60 \times 29}{100} = 17.4$	$\dfrac{40 \times 29}{100} = 11.6$
4–7	$\dfrac{60 \times 33}{100} = 19.8$	$\dfrac{40 \times 33}{100} = 13.20$

The χ^2 value will be distorted if more than 20 percent of the cells have an expected frequency of less than 5, or if any cell has an expected frequency of 0. It should not be used in these conditions. In this case all cells exceed 5 so we may continue.

3. *Calculate the value of χ^2 using*

$$\chi^2 = \sum_{i=1}^{r}\sum_{j=1}^{k} \frac{(O_{ij} - E_{ij})^2}{E_{ij}} \tag{17-18}$$

where O_{ij} = observed number in the ith row of the jth column
E_{ij} = expected number in the ith row of the jth column

For our example

$$\chi^2 = \frac{(19 - 22.8)^2}{22.8} + \frac{(19 - 15.2)^2}{15.2} + \frac{(17 - 17.4)^2}{17.4} + \frac{(12 - 11.6)^2}{11.6}$$

$$+ \frac{(24 - 19.8)^2}{19.8} + \frac{(9 - 13.2)^2}{13.2}$$

$$\chi^2 = 3.83$$

4. *The probability associated with our results can be determined from Appendix D with (r − 1) (k − 1) = 2 degrees of freedom.* The chance of obtaining these results if the null hypothesis of no difference is correct is approximately .16. We therefore cannot reject the null.

Test of Distributions by Categories of Two or More Independent Samples

Do white-collar, blue-collar, and managerial–professional groups differ in terms of being heavy, medium, light, and nonusers of this product? Do purchasing agents, operators, and supervisors differ in terms of having favorable, neutral, or unfavorable attitudes toward our brand? Such questions, which involve categorical (nominal) data and two or more independent samples, can be answered by using the chi-square (χ^2) test for k independent samples. The procedure and formula for three or more samples are the same as for two samples. Therefore, we do not repeat them here.

Multivariate Hypothesis Tests of Means

In this section, we examine techniques for testing hypotheses about differences between groups when more than one variable may be causing these differences. This will enable us to answer questions such as the following: *"Do differing price levels, package sizes, and point-of-purchase displays combine to have a unique influence on sales? Which has the strongest effect? Are their effects when used simultaneously different from the sum of their individual effects?"* When we examine the effects of two or more variables on a dependent variable, we must make one of two assumptions. We can assume that the effects of the independent variables are independent of each other and that no interactions (joint effects) occur. Or we can assume that the effect of the independent variables taken together is different from the sum of their effects one at a time. This latter situation is known as *interaction*. You may recall from Chapter 7 that different experimental designs may be required if interaction is likely to occur. Different analytical techniques are also required when interaction may be present.

Recall also from Chapter 7 that randomized blocks designs (RBD) and Latin square designs are used when more than one variable may affect the results and no interaction is expected. The basic ANOVA approach is the same for both designs. However, since the Latin square design involves an additional variable, some additional calculations are required. We illustrate both approaches.

ANOVA for Randomized Blocks Designs (RBD)

Assume that the experimental design described in the main example in Chapter 16 was a simple RBD with gender as the blocking variable and brand name as the treatment variable. This means we are assuming that gender and treatment do not interact. We would, in effect, be saying, "I think gender will affect response to this product and I want to see if brand name will. I'm sure that gender won't affect the response to the brand name. Therefore, I will control for gender's effects on response to the product by blocking on it."

Let us accept this logic for a moment and test the null hypothesis that the brand name has no effect on the stated purchase probability. The results from Table 16–2 are summarized in Table 17–6 with two treatments and two blocks. Treatments generally form the columns (c) and blocks form the rows (r).

How do we proceed? Recall that ANOVA utilizes an F ratio that has a measure of the variance associated with a treatment (MST) as the numerator

TABLE 17–6 Mean Purchase Probability by Gender and Brand Name*

	Bravo (c = 1)	Delight (c = 2)	$\bar{X}$
Male (r = 1)	51.50	29.33	40.42
Female (r = 2)	48.25	66.50	57.38
$\bar{X}_j$	50.20	44.20	47.20

*Derived from Table 16–2.

and a measure of random, natural, or unexplained variances (MSE) as the denominator. Extending the one-way ANOVA to the RBD requires computing a mean sum of squares for blocks as well as for treatments. In addition, the calculation of the mean sum of squares error is altered to reflect the effect of the blocks. The required formulas are as follows:

$$\text{Mean square treatment } (MST) = \frac{\text{Sum of squares treatments } (SST)}{df}$$

$$= \frac{\sum\limits_{j=1}^{c} n_j(\bar{X}_j - \bar{X}_T)^2}{c - 1} \tag{17-19}$$

$$\text{Mean square blocking } (MSB) = \frac{\text{Sum of squares blocking } (SSB)}{df}$$

$$= \frac{\sum\limits_{i=1}^{r} n_i(\bar{X}_i - X_T)^2}{r - 1} \tag{17-20}$$

$$\text{Total mean square } (TMS) = \frac{\text{Total sum of squares } (TSS)}{df}$$

$$= \frac{\sum\limits_{i=1}^{r}\sum\limits_{j=1}^{c}\sum\limits_{k=1}^{n_{ij}} (X_{ijk} - \bar{X}_T)^2}{n_T - 1} \tag{17-21}$$

$$\text{Mean square error } (MSE) = \frac{\text{Sum of squares error } (SSE)}{df}$$

$$= \frac{\sum\limits_{i=1}^{r}\sum\limits_{j=1}^{c}\sum\limits_{k=1}^{n_{ij}} (X_{ijk} - \bar{X}_i - \bar{X}_j + \bar{X}_T)^2}{n_T - r - c + 1} \tag{17-22}$$

$$= \frac{TSS - SSB - SST}{n_T - r - c + 1}$$

where n_j = sample size of treatment group j

n_i = sample size of block group i

$\overline{X}_j$ = mean of treatment j

$\overline{X}_i$ = mean of block i

$\overline{X}_T$ = total or grand mean

n_{ij} = number of respondents (observations) receiving treatment i and blocking variable j

X_{ijk} = the kth observation in treatment i *and* block j

n_T = total number of observations

These values are then used for calculating F ratios with the formulas

$$F_{Treatment} = \frac{MST}{MSE}, \quad F_{Blocks} = \frac{MSB}{MSE}$$

The ANOVA table takes the form shown in Table 17–7. The results are shown in Table 17–8. The data in the table indicate that the blocking variable, gender, is associated with a differential purchase probability. However, the observed differences between the treatment groups could have easily occurred by chance. Remember that we assumed there was no interaction between our treatment and blocking variables. In the section on ANOVA with interaction (pages 456–457), we reexamine these same data. We reach strikingly different conclusions, which indicates the importance of specifying properly both the experimental design and the ANOVA version.

ANOVA for Latin Square Designs

Latin square designs are an efficient way of blocking or controlling two variables that might affect our experimental results. Like the RBD, Latin square designs assume no interaction occurs among the variables.

The calculations are similar to those described for the RBD. However, it is necessary to calculate the effects of the second blocking variable. Table 17–9

TABLE 17–7 ANOVA Output Format for RBD

Source of Variation	Degrees of Freedom	Sum of Squares	Mean Square	F	P
Between blocks	$r - 1$	SSB	$\dfrac{SSB}{r - 1}$	$\dfrac{MSB}{MSE}$	F Table
Between treatments	$c - 1$	SST	$\dfrac{SST}{c - 1}$	$\dfrac{MST}{MSE}$	F Table
Error	$n_T - r - c + 1$	SSE	$\dfrac{SSE}{n_T - r - c + 1}$		
Total	$n_T - 1$	TSS	$\dfrac{TSS}{n_T - 1}$		

TABLE 17–8 ANOVA Output for Purchase Probability in an RBD

Source of Variation	Degrees of Freedom	Sum of Squares	Mean Square	F	P
Gender	1	6902.04	6,902.04	5.11	.026
Name	1	900.00	900.00	.67	.416
Error	97	131,013.96	1,350.66		
Total	99	138,816.00			

TABLE 17–9 Latin Square Experiment Design and Results

	Design				Results (Sales)			
	Store Type					Store Type		
Store Location	Gr	Di	De	Store Location	Gr	Di	De	$\overline{X}$
U	C	A	B	U	51	59	67	59
S	A	B	C	S	32	66	49	49
R	B	C	A	R	37	52	37	42
				$\overline{X}$	40	59	51	50

where U = urban   Gr = grocery   A = point-of-purchase display A
       S = suburban   Di = discount   B = point-of-purchase display B
       R = rural   De = department   C = point-of-purchase display C

illustrates a Latin square design in which the effects of three versions of a point-of-purchase display were tested. The Latin square design was used to control for store type (grocery, discount, and department) and store location (urban, suburban, and rural). The required formulas are

$$\text{Total means square } (TMS) = \frac{\text{Total sum of squares } (TSS)}{df}$$

$$= \frac{\displaystyle\sum_{i=1}^{r} \sum_{j=1}^{c} (X_{ij} - \overline{X}_T)^2}{rc - 1} \tag{17-23}$$

$$\text{Mean square row block } (MSR) = \frac{\text{Sum of squares row block } (SSR)}{df}$$

$$= \frac{r \displaystyle\sum_{i=1}^{r} (\overline{X}_i - \overline{X}_T)^2}{r - 1} \tag{17-24}$$

Mean square column block $(MSC) = \dfrac{\text{Sum of squares column block } (SSC)}{df}$

$$= \dfrac{c \displaystyle\sum_{j=1}^{c} (\overline{X}_j - \overline{X}_T)^2}{c - 1} \qquad (17\text{-}25)$$

Mean square treatment $(MST) = \dfrac{\text{Sum of squares treatment } (SST)}{df}$

$$= \dfrac{t \displaystyle\sum_{k=1}^{t} (\overline{X}_k - \overline{X}_T)^2}{t - 1} \qquad (17\text{-}26)$$

Mean square error $(MSE) = \dfrac{\text{Sum of squares error}}{df}$

$$= \dfrac{TTS - SSR - SSC - SST}{(r - 1)(c - 2)}$$

F for column block $= \dfrac{MSC}{MSE}$

F for row block $= \dfrac{MSR}{MSE}$

F for treatment $= \dfrac{MST}{MSE}$

where $c = r = t =$ number of columns, rows, and treatments respectively
$\overline{X}_T =$ grand mean (mean of all cells),
$\overline{X}_j =$ mean of column j,
$\overline{X}_i =$ means row i, and
$\overline{X}_k =$ mean of cells having treatment k.

The ANOVA table for this problem is Table 17–10. As the table indicates, store location, store type, and type of point-of-purchase display all appear to affect sales.

TABLE 17–10 ANOVA Output for a Latin Square Design

Source of Variation	Degrees of Freedom	Sum of Squares	Mean Square	F	P
Location	2	438	219	31.29	.031
Type	2	546	273	39.00	.025
Point-of-purchase	2	296	148	21.14	.045
Error	2	14	7		
Total	8	1294			

ANOVA with Interaction: Factorial Designs

In Chapter 7, we indicated that factorial experimental designs are required when interaction is suspected. Let us now consider our example as a factorial design with brand name and gender as treatment variables. As pointed out earlier (page 453), it could also be treated as an RBD. Let's reanalyze the data used to illustrate the RBD design (Table 17–6). However, this time we will take advantage of the factorial nature of our design and test for interaction. The appropriate formulas are as follows:

Mean square 1st treatment or block (MST_1) —use equation (17–19)
Mean square 2nd treatment or block (MST_2)—use equation (17–20)
Total mean square (TMS)   —use equation (17–21)

$$\text{Mean square interaction } (MSI) = \frac{\text{Sum of squares interaction } (SSI)}{df}$$

$$= \frac{\sum_{i=1}^{r} \sum_{j=1}^{c} n_{ij}(\overline{X}_{ij} - \overline{X}_i - \overline{X}_j + \overline{X}_T)^2}{(r-1)(c-1)} \qquad (17\text{-}27)$$

$$\text{Mean square error} = \frac{\text{Sum of squares error } (SSE)}{df}$$

$$= \frac{\sum_{i=1}^{r} \sum_{j=1}^{c} \sum_{k=1}^{n_{ij}} (X_{ijk} - \overline{X}_{ij})^2}{n_T - rc} \qquad (17\text{-}28)$$

$$= \frac{TSS - SST_1 - SST_2 - SSE}{n_T - rc}$$

$$F \text{ treatment } 1 = \frac{MST_1}{MSE}$$

$$F \text{ treatment } 2 = \frac{MST_2}{MSE}$$

$$F \text{ interaction} = \frac{MSI}{MSE}$$

where n_{ij} = observations per cell.

These results are summarized in Table 17–11, which indicates that brand name has an effect when considered in conjunction with gender. Reexamine Table 17–6. Males and females have a similar response to Bravo; however, males appear to dislike *Delight* whereas females like it. Thus, brand name interacts with gender to influence purchase probability. Compare these conclusions with the conclusions reached from examining Table 17–8 in which no test was made for interaction. Obviously, it is important to test for interaction if there is a reasonable possibility it could occur.

TABLE 17–11 ANOVA Output for a Factorial Design

Source of Variation	Degrees of Freedom	Sum of Squares	Mean Square	F	P
Gender	1	6902.04	6902.04	5.47	.021
Brand name	1	900.00	900.00	.71	.401
Name * gender	1	9801.04	9801.04	7.76	.006
Error	96	121,212.92	1262.64		
Total	99	138,816.00			

Name * Gender = interaction of name and gender

ANOVA Assumptions

Using ANOVA properly requires attention to the assumptions underlying the approach. In addition to requiring interval data, all of the versions of ANOVA discussed assume that

1. the sample in each cell is random and independent from samples in the other cells;
2. the dependent variable is normally distributed in each of the populations; and
3. the dependent variable's variance is the same in each population.

In addition to these three general assumptions, the randomized block and Latin square ANOVAs assume that the block and treatment effects are additive. That is, they assume that if a 10 percent price reduction increases sales an average of 10 units a week and a point-of-purchase display increases sales an average of 15 units, using both simultaneously will increase sales by 25 units. The factorial approach allows a test of this assumption. As we saw in the last section, a failure to test for interaction when it exists can result in incorrect decisions.

Summary

Hypothesis tests attempt to ascertain if observed differences between one or more sample values and one or more other values are due to random variations. Two hypotheses are established for each test. The null hypothesis is generally that no real difference exists between the groups the samples represent. The alternate is that there is a difference. The null is tested and either rejected or not rejected. If it is rejected, the alternate can be accepted.

Multivariate hypothesis tests examine the effect of more than one variable at a time. Univariate hypothesis tests focus on only one variable. The appropriate univariate statistic to use depends on (1) the scale level of the data, (2) the number of samples, (3) whether the samples are independent or dependent, and (4) the size of the samples.

Hypotheses are generally tested against a prespecified probability of rejecting the null when it is in fact true (concluding that the groups differ when they do not).

This probability is generally set at .01, .05, or .10. However, there is no logic to support these levels in decisional research. Instead, the exact probability of the null being falsely rejected should always be calculated.

Analysis of variance (ANOVA) is the common approach to test for differences in means caused by more than one variable. It is generally used to analyze experimental results. When no interaction is expected, Latin square or randomized block experimental designs may be used. If interaction is expected, a factorial design is required. Slightly different versions of ANOVA are required for each type of design.

Review Questions

17.1. What are *statistical techniques?*

17.2. What is the purpose of a hypothesis test of differences between groups?

17.3. What is a *univariate hypothesis test?*

17.4. What are the five questions that lead to the selection of an appropriate univariate hypothesis test of differences?

17.5. What characterizes *independent* samples?

17.6. What conditions would lead to the use of _____ ?
   a. Z test of a mean
   b. *t* test of two means
   c. χ^2 two-sample test
   d. Kruskal–Wallis one-way ANOVA
   e. Wilcoxon matched-pairs signed-ranks test
   f. Kolmogorov–Smirnov one-sample test
   g. Mann–Whitney U test
   h. t_r test
   i. one-way ANOVA
   j. Friedman two-way ANOVA
   k. Cochran Q test
   l. McNemar test
   m. χ^2 one-sample test
   n. Z test of two proportions

17.7. What test(s) would be appropriate in the following situations?

Data		Sample Size	Independent Samples?	# Samples
a.	interval	20	Yes	1
b.	nominal	35	Yes	2
c.	interval	100	Yes	2
d.	ordinal	40	No	2
e.	ratio	90	Yes	3
f.	ordinal	100	Yes	4
g.	nominal	36	No	2
h.	interval	120	No	4
i.	interval	80	Yes	1
j.	nominal	45	No	3

Data		Sample Size	Independent Samples?	# Samples
k.	ratio	60	Yes	2
l.	ordinal	50	Yes	2
m.	ordinal	30	No	3
n.	ordinal	21	Yes	1
o.	nominal	100	Yes	1
p.	nominal	80	Yes	6
q.	interval	90	No	2

17.8. What is a *multivariate hypothesis test* of differences between groups?

17.9. What is *interaction?*

17.10. For what kinds of problems is ANOVA used?

17.11. What experimental design is required before ANOVA can be used to detect interaction?

Discussion Questions/Problems

Do you agree that the exact probability should always be reported in decisional research? Why?

Use the data in Table 16–2 to perform the following tests. Use the following definitions: Group 1 = the population represented by males, treatment 1; Group 2 = the population represented by females, treatment 1; Group 3 = the population represented by males, treatment 2; Group 4 = the population represented by females, treatment 2; Group 5 = the population represented by all males; and Group 6 = the population represented by all females. For hypothesis tests use an α of .05 and also report the exact probability.

17.12. Is the mean age of group 1 equal to the mean age of group 2?

17.13. Is the mean age of group 5 equal to the mean age of group 6?

17.14. Are the mean ages of groups 1, 2, 3, and 4 equal?

17.15. Is the mean taste reaction of group 5 greater than 45?

17.16. Is the mean taste reaction of group 4 greater than 55?

17.17. Is the proportion of group 1 having zero consumption equal to the proportion of group 2 having zero consumption?

17.18. Is the proportion of group 6 having a purchase probability of more than .5 greater than a .50?

17.19. Do the ranks assigned *Bravo* by group 1 equal the ranks assigned *Delight* by group 3?

17.20. For groups 5 and 6 combined are there equal numbers of students in the age groups ≤ 19, 20–21, ≥ 22?

17.21. Is there a difference between groups 5 and 6 in the number having a taste reaction ≤ 50, 51–60, or > 60?

17.22. Is there a difference between groups 1, 2, 3, and 4 in the number having a taste reaction ≤ 50, 51–60, > 60?

17.23. Analyze the following data generated by an RBD design.

	Treatment		
Block	A	B	C
1	75	79	99
2	60	73	75
3	77	71	80
4	62	80	75
5	60	57	73
6	47	60	65
7	50	49	50
8	47	53	52
9	45	51	62

17.24. Repeat 17.23 but treat blocks 1–3 as 9 measures within block I, blocks 4–6 as 9 measures within block II, and blocks 7–9 as 9 measures within block III.

17.25. Analyze the following data generated by a Latin square design.

	Design			Results		
	Store Type			Store Type		
Time Period	G	D	S	G	D	S
1	B	A	C	30	53	69
2	A	C	B	51	68	39
3	C	B	A	36	59	51

A, B, C = different P-O-P material
G = Grocery, D = Department, S = Specialty

17.26. Analyze the experimental data in Table 16–2 as though they were obtained from a factorial design with taste reaction as the dependent variable and gender and brand name as treatments.

17.27. Analyze the experimental data in Table 16–2 as though they were obtained from an RBD with gender as the block, brand name as the treatment, and taste reaction as the dependent variable.

17.28. Data from a factorial experiment on the effectiveness of price reductions, P-O-P displays, and newspaper advertising (Ad) are in the following table. The numbers in the table are average weekly units sold under each condition at the 60 stores involved in the study. What impact did each variable have on sales? Were interaction effects present? What would you recommend based on these results?

Regular Price				Price −10%				Price −20%			
P-O-P		No P-O-P		P-O-P		No P-O-P		P-O-P		No P-O-P	
Ad	No Ad	Ad	No Ad	Ad	No Ad	Ad	No Ad	Ad	No Ad	Ad	No Ad
60	45	50	20	75	55	57	22	100	80	77	25
65	40	42	18	68	55	52	20	105	85	82	22
40	50	46	25	65	60	58	23	90	90	91	26
50	35	37	22	70	40	38	26	95	77	70	25
55	40	39	19	80	48	55	21	102	60	62	30

Notes

1. "The Use of Concern Scales as an Alternative to Importance Ratings," *Research on Research* 44 (Chicago: Market Facts, Inc., undated).

2. Additional techniques are described in D. S. Tull, D. I. Hawkins, *Marketing Research* (New York: Macmillan Publishing Company, Inc., 1993). The best source for details on techniques for ordinal and nominal data is S. Siegel, *Nonparametric Statistics* (New York: McGraw-Hill Book Co., Inc., 1956).

3. Details on, and tables for, the small-sample versions are available in Siegel, op. cit., 116–127.

4. Siegel, op. cit., 272–277.

5. When there are a *very* large number of ties, a correction formula should be used. However, even with as many ties as were present in this example, the correction formula only changed Z from 1.05 to 1.09. See ibid., 123–126.

CHAPTER 18

Measures of Association

LEARNING OBJECTIVES

Upon completing this chapter, you should be able to:

1. Describe the nature of association.

2. Explain why one should examine a scatter diagram of the data before conducting a regression analysis.

3. Explain to a manager the meaning of a bivariate regression formula and its coefficient of determination (r^2).

4. Describe the circumstances requiring the use of the Spearman rank correlation coefficient.

5. Explain to a manager the meaning of a multiple regression formula and its coefficient of determination (r^2).

6. Describe the cautions or risks one should be concerned with when using multiple regression analysis.

An Application of Multiple Regression at American Express

American Express, like other credit card firms, earns more from cardholders who use their card extensively than from those who are light users. They also have considerable data on each of their cardholders from their credit application. This information includes such items as age, occupation, area of residence, income, and other financial data. Both mass media such as magazines and mailing lists from direct mail firms have similar data on their subscribers or lists.

One challenge facing American Express is to attract those customers most likely to make extensive use of their card. Target advertising is a means to accomplish this. Thus, American Express needs to be able to understand which demographic data are associated with heavy use of the American Express card. Multiple regression analysis, one of the techniques described in this chapter, can be used for this purpose.

Measuring Association

Association:
two or more
variables
covarying in a
systematic
manner.

Association occurs when two or more variables tend to covary in a systematic manner. Marketing managers are very often interested in the degree of association between variables. That is, they want to know if a high level of one variable tends to be associated with ("go with") a high or low level of another variable. Depending upon the purpose(s) for which the data were obtained, one may be interested in examining the degree of association of such variables as price, amount of advertising, perceived quality, life-cycle stage, social class, income, or education with variables such as purchaser–nonpurchaser of brand, attitudes toward brands, brand preference, sales, or market share.

**Predictor
variables:**
variables whose
levels are used to
predict the level of
other variables.

In analyzing associative relationships, two types of variables are used: **predictor** (independent) **variables** and **criterion** (dependent) **variables.** Predictor variables are used to help predict or "explain" the level of criterion variables. Market share is an example of a criterion variable that such predictor variables as relative price, amount of advertising, and number of outlets are often used to explain.

**Criterion
variables:**
variables whose
level is being
predicted by the
level of other
variables.

Measures of association have two components. First, we want to know the *nature of the association.* That is, we want to be able to predict the level or magnitude of the criterion variable if we know the value of the predictor variable. If our advertising is $1.9 million, what will our sales be?

Second, we want to know the *strength of the association.* That is, we want to know how widely the actual value may vary from the predicted value. This concept is similar to the idea of a confidence interval discussed previously.

Three important considerations in choosing a method of analyzing an associative relationship are (1) *the number of criterion variables,* (2) the number of *predictor variables,* and (3) *the scale(s) used for the measurements.*

Number of Criterion and Predictor Variables.   The minimum number of criterion and predictor variables is one each, because at least two variables are necessary to have an association. The techniques appropriate for analysis of two variable association are known as *bivariate techniques.* When more than two variables are involved in the analysis, the techniques employed are known as *multivariate techniques.* We cover bivariate techniques in the next section of this chapter; multivariate techniques are covered in the final section.

The Scale(s) Used for the Measurement.   As discussed earlier, measurements may be made using a *nominal, ordinal, interval,* or *ratio* scale. Association techniques that are appropriate for analyzing the degree of association between intervally scaled variables may be entirely inappropriate for use with variables measured in other scales. We describe techniques for use with interval and ordinal data.

Misuse of Measures of Association.   Each of the techniques we describe has assumptions that should be met before the technique is used. These are indicated in the appropriate sections. However, a common error in using measures of association is to assume that association represents causation. This is not necessarily the case.

Even if we demonstrate statistically that two (or more) variables vary together in a manner that is unlikely to be due to sampling variation, two problems exist in concluding that changes in variable B cause changes in variable A. The first is *directionality*. Does an increase in overall attitude toward a brand increase brand usage? Or does an increase in brand usage cause an increase in attitude? Or might a third factor be causing both changes?

A second problem often occurs in practice. A number of consumer characteristics, say 20, are measured and one or more measures of purchasing are made. The analyst then runs 20 correlations and finds 2 that are statistically significant at an alpha of .10. However, by chance one would expect to find 2 out of 20 significant results with an alpha of .10. This practice accounts for some of the strange findings of correlations between such things as changes in the daily noon temperatures of some towns and changes in the Dow Jones average. Such findings are termed *spurious correlations*. Thus, one should be very careful in using any measure of association that was not *prespecified* in advance based on theory or practical intuition.

Measures of Association Between Two Variables

Bivariate Measures of Association Using Ratio/Interval Data

Most analyses of association are conducted by computer. However, before the analysis is conducted, the data should be plotted either by hand or by the computer. This plot generally is called a **scatter diagram.** It is important to examine the scatter diagram to determine if the association in the data, if any, is linear or curvilinear. If the data are nonlinear, standard techniques (linear regression analysis) may indicate no relationship when, in fact, there is one. If a nonlinear relationship is indicated, appropriate curve-fitting techniques should be used.

Scatter diagram: a plot of the values of two variables with one variable plotted on one axis and the associated value of the other variable shown on the other axis.

Figure 18–1 contains several scatter diagrams. Diagrams A and F suggest that there is no relationship between X and Y. Diagrams B and C indicate a strong positive and a strong negative relationship, respectively. Diagram D indicates a positive but weaker relationship. A nonlinear relationship between X and Y is indicated in Diagram E.

Let us assume that the taste reaction scores and the purchase probability scores in Table 16–2 are interval data. The first step in analyzing the relationship between the stated purchase probability and the taste reaction for the 20 females who tasted the *Delight* brand is to plot the data, as shown in Figure 18–2.

A visual examination of Figure 18–2 indicates that the purchase probability appears to increase as the taste reaction increases. How can we describe this relationship? The general equation for a straight line fitted to the variables X and Y is

$$Y = a + bX \qquad (18\text{-}1)$$

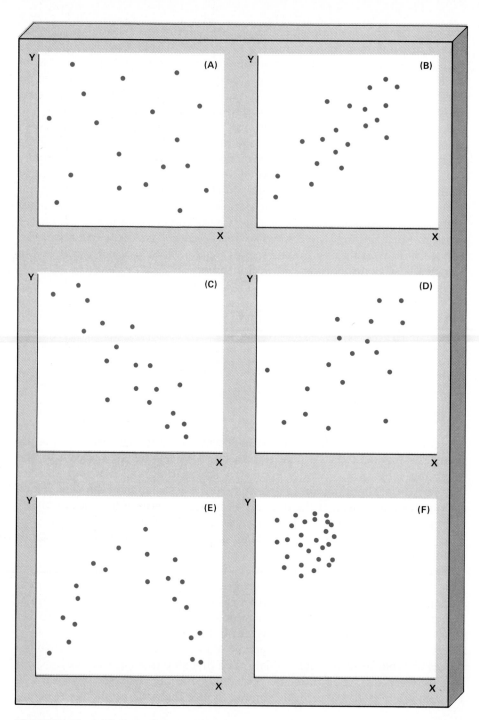

FIGURE 18–1 Various Scatter Diagrams

where Y is the criterion variable, X the predictor variable, a a constant that represents the intercept, and b the amount Y changes for each unit of change in X. Both a and b are unknown and must be calculated.

Approximations to the a and b values may be made by *graphic analysis.* A line can be fitted visually to a plot of the values of the two variables such as shown in Figure 18–2. The line is fitted in such a way as to attempt to make the sum of all the distances of points above the line equal the sum of all those below the line. (The number of points above and below the line need not be equal, however.) The estimate of the a value is the intercept of the Y axis. The estimate of the b value may be determined by solving the equation, $\overline{Y} = a + b\overline{X}$, after substituting in the numerical values of $\overline{Y}$, a, and $\overline{X}$.

Bivariate least-squares regression analysis is the mathematical technique for the fitting of a line to measurements of the two variables such that the algebraic sum of deviations of the measurements from the line are zero and the sum of the squares of the deviations are less than they would be for any other line. Table 18–1 shows the worksheet that is necessary to calculate a

Bivariate least-squares regression analysis: a mathematical technique that measures the relationship between two variables.

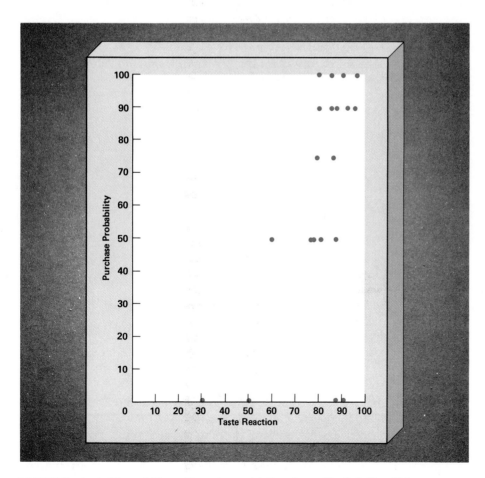

FIGURE 18–2 Plot of Taste Reaction and Purchase Probability Values

TABLE 18–1 Worksheet for Regression Analysis

Respondent No.	Purchase Probability Y	Taste Reaction X	Y^2	X^2	YX
81	100	85	10,000	7,225	8,500
82	90	95	8,100	9,025	8,550
83	0	90	0	8,100	0
.	.	.	.	.	.
.	.	.	.	.	.
.	.	.	.	.	.
100	80	40	6,400	1,600	3,200
Total	1,330	1,548	110,650	126,104	109,335

least-squares regression analysis for our problem. Using the values from this worksheet, we calculate b as follows:

$$b = \frac{\sum_{i=1}^{n} YX - n\overline{Y}\overline{X}}{\sum_{i=1}^{n} X^2 - n(\overline{X})^2} \qquad (18\text{-}2)$$

$$= \frac{109,335 - (20)(66.5)(77.4)}{126,104 - 20(77.4)^2}$$

$$= 1.02$$

The value for a can then be determined as

$$a = \overline{Y} - b\overline{X}$$
$$= 66.5 - 1.02(77.4) \qquad (18\text{-}3)$$
$$= -12.45$$

Thus, our data can be described by the line

$$\hat{Y} = -12.45 + 1.02X$$

This means that for every unit increase in taste reaction (X), the purchase probability tends to increase by about one unit also. Although this is the best mathematical description of our data, nothing in the formula itself indicates how good (accurate) a description it is. Refer again to Figure 18–1. The data in scatter diagrams B and D would be represented by nearly identical lines. However, a visual inspection suggests that the line will describe the data in diagram B more accurately than it will the data in D. Stated another way, the observations (data points) in B will fall much closer to the line than will those in D.

The **coefficient of determination,** generally referred to as r^2, is the measure of the strength of association in a bivariate regression analysis. It can vary from 0 to 1, and represents the proportion of total variation in Y (criterion variable) that is accounted for, or explained, by variation in X (the predictor variable). Thus, an r^2 of 0 indicates that none of the variation in Y is explained by the variation in X whereas one of 1.0 indicates that it all is.

Scatter diagrams A and F in Figure 18–1 would have near 0 r^2 values. Diagram E would also have a near 0 r^2 if a linear rather than a curvilinear trend line were fitted. Diagram D would have an r^2 near .5, indicating that about half the variation in Y is accounted for by variation in X. Finally, diagrams B and C would have r^2 values near .9, indicating that most of the variation in Y is explained by variation in X.

What is the coefficient of determination for our example? Mathematically,

Coefficient of determination (r^2): a measure of the strength of association indicated in a regression formula.

$$r^2 = 1 - \frac{\text{unexplained variance}}{\text{total variance}} = \frac{\text{explained variance}}{\text{total variance}}$$

$$r^2 = 1 - \frac{\displaystyle\sum_{i=1}^{n} (Y_i - \hat{Y}_i)^2}{\displaystyle\sum_{i=1}^{n} (Y_i - \overline{Y})^2} \tag{18-4}$$

where $\hat{Y}_i$ = *the predicted value of Y for the ith data point using the regression formula.*
Thus,

$$r^2 = 1 - \frac{15{,}706}{22{,}205} = .29$$

About 30 percent of the variation in stated purchase probability is accounted for or explained by changes in taste reactions.

Some degree of association often occur between two variables because of random sampling variation. Therefore, it is generally desirable to test the null hypothesis that $r^2 = 0$. This can be tested as

$$t = \frac{r\sqrt{n-2}}{\sqrt{1-r^2}} \quad \text{with } n - 2 \text{ degrees of freedom.} \tag{18-5}$$

For our example,

$$t = \frac{.54\sqrt{20-2}}{\sqrt{1-.29}} = 2.72$$

Examination of Appendix B reveals that an r^2 value this large would occur by chance less than 2 percent of the time. A null hypothesis of no association between taste reaction and purchase probability would therefore have to be rejected if $\alpha \geq .02$.

Bivariate Measures of Association Using Ordinal Data

Spearman rank correlation coefficient (r_s): a common technique for measuring the degree of association between two ordinally scaled variables.

We often want to examine the degree of association between two ordinally scaled variables such as two attitudes or two rank orderings. Suppose we believe that our taste reaction and purchase probability scales produced only ordinal data. How should we analyze them? The **Spearman rank correlation coefficient,** r_s, is the most common approach for measuring the degree of association between two ordinally scaled variables. The steps involved in its calculation are as follows:

1. Establish the null hypothesis that there is no association between taste reaction and purchase probability.
2. Rank order all the observations of Y from 1 to N. Do the same for the sample observations of X.
3. Assign each subject two scores: the rank of his or her value on Y and the rank of his or her value on X.
4. Determine a value, d_i, for each individual by subtracting each person's Y score (rank) from his or her X score (rank). Square this result for each individual and sum for the entire group. Table 18–2 illustrates these steps based on the raw scores from Table 18–1 (assuming that these are ordinal rather than interval).
5. Calculate r_s using the following formula:

$$r_s = 1 - \frac{6\sum_{i=1}^{n} d_i^2}{n^3 - n} \tag{18-6}$$

$$= 1 - \frac{6(638)}{(20)^3 - 20} = .52$$

6. The probability associated with this value (the probability of obtaining a measure of association this strong or stronger given a true null

TABLE 18–2 Worksheet for Spearman Rank Correlation Coefficient

Respondent #	Y	X	di	di²
81	18.5	11.5	−7.0	49.00
82	14.0	19.0	5.0	25.00
83	2.0	16.5	14.5	210.25
.	.	.	.	.
.	.	.	.	.
.	.	.	.	.
99	18.5	20.0	1.5	2.25
100	11.0	2.0	−9.0	81.00

$$\sum_{i=1}^{N} d_i^2 = 638$$

hypothesis of no association) can be determined using a t value calculated as follows:

$$t = r_s \sqrt{\frac{n - 2}{1 - r_s}} \qquad (18\text{-}7)$$

For our example

$$t = .52 \sqrt{\frac{20 - 2}{1 - .52}}$$

$$= 3.18$$

with $n - 2$ degrees of freedom. As Appendix B indicates, an association this strong is very unlikely to occur because of sampling error if the null of no difference were indeed true. We may therefore reject the null and conclude that there is in fact an association between taste reaction and purchase probability.

Multivariate Measures of Association

In this section of this chapter, we cover multivariate measures of association. Like bivariate measures, the appropriate multivariate measure depends on the scale of measurement used (ratio/interval, ordinal, or nominal). In addition, the number of predictor and the number of criterion variables influence the choice of a statistical measure of association. A number of analytical situations require unique statistical measures. In the following section, we describe the most commonly used multivariate measure of association—multiple regression analysis.

Multiple Regression Analysis

Multiple regression analysis is used to examine the relationship between two or more intervally scaled predictor variables and one intervally scaled criterion variable. Ordinal data that are "near interval," such as semantic differential scale data, can generally be used also. In addition, we describe special techniques that allow some nominal predictor variables to be used.

Multiple regression is simply a logical and mathematical extension of bivariate regression, as described in the previous section. However, instead of fitting a straight line through a two-dimensional space, multiple regression fits a plane through a multidimensional space. The output and interpretation are exactly the same as for a bivariate analysis:

$$\hat{Y} = a + b_1 X_1 + b_2 X_2 + b_3 X_3 + \cdots + b_i X_i$$

where $\hat{Y}$ = estimated value of the criterion variable

a = constant derived from the analysis

b_i = coefficients associated with the predictor variables such that a change of one unit in X_i will cause a change of b_i units in $\hat{Y}$. The values for the coefficients are derived from the regression analysis.

X_i = predictor variables that influence the criterion variable

Multiple regression analysis: a mathematical technique to measure the relationship between two or more intervally scaled predictor variables and one intervally scaled criterion variable.

For example,

$$\hat{Y} = 117 + .3X_1 + 6.8X_2$$

where $\hat{Y}$ = sales

X_1 = advertising expenditures

X_2 = number of outlets

would be interpreted as: "Sales tend to increase by .3 units for every unit increase in advertising and 6.8 units for every unit increase in the number of outlets."

An examination of two formulas derived by the General Electric Company will indicate the usefulness of multiple regression. The goal of the GE research project was to isolate the factors associated with a high price for a product relative to one's immediate competitors. A number of industries were examined, and the following partial results were obtained for the consumer durables and capital equipment industries:

$$\text{Consumer Durables: RP} = 60.75 + 0.07\text{RQ} + 0.34\text{RDC} + 0.06\text{ME} + 1.15\text{RS}$$

$$\text{Capital Equipment: RP} = 71.88 + 0.09\text{RQ} + 0.27\text{RDC} + 0.02\text{ME} + 0.43\text{RS}$$

where

RP = firm's price as a percentage of the average price of its leading competitors

RQ = relative product quality

RDC = relative direct cost

ME = marketing effort

RS = relative service

Relative price is influenced by the same variables in both industries (different variables were found for other industries). However, marketing effort (a measure of advertising, sales promotion, and salesforce expenses) is more important (larger *b*) in the consumer durables industry, whereas product quality is more important in the capital equipment industry. Relative direct cost is important in both industries. Such analyses can provide significant marketing strategy implications.

Other marketing applications of multiple regression analysis include

1. *Forecasting* where either company variables such as relative price, relative advertising, and so forth; or external variables such as population growth, disposable income, and so forth; or both are used to forecast sales, demand, or market share.
2. *Outlet location decisions* where traffic counts, location of competitors, square footage available, and so on, are used to analyze the attractiveness of outlet locations for chain stores.
3. *Quota determination* involves using territory size, last period sales, competitor strength, and related variables to determine sales quotas or objectives.
4. *Marketing mix analysis* by analyzing the relationship between elements in the marketing mix and market share or sales.

5. *Determining the relationship between the criterion variable and one predictor variable while the effects of other predictor variables are held constant:* An example is the estimate of the reliance on price as an indicator of quality of furniture while other factors, such as brand of product and stores in which it is available, are held constant.

6. *Estimating values for missing data (item nonresponse) in surveys.* For example, one can estimate income from occupation, age, and education data.

As these examples indicate, multiple regression can serve two primary purposes: (1) to *predict* the level of the criterion variable given certain levels of the predictor variables, or (2) to *gain insights* into the relationships between the predictor variables and the criterion variable.

The Strength of Multiple Regression Measures of Association

Recall from our discussion of bivariate regression that a coefficient of determination, generally called r square (r^2), can be calculated. This statistic can range from 0 to 1 in value and, in multiple regression, indicates the percentage of the variation in the criterion variable that is explained by the entire set of predictor variables. The r^2 for the capital equipment formula shown earlier is .32, which means that 32 percent of the variation in relative price in this industry can be explained by the four variables in the equation.

In addition to measuring the strength of association reflected by the overall regression formula, it is necessary to assess the likelihood that each individual predictor variable's association with the criterion variable is the result of chance. The calculation is routinely performed by all packaged computer programs. The standard output is the probability of error if the null hypothesis of $b_i = 0$ is rejected. Each of the variables in the two GE equations had a probability of error of less than .10.

Multiple regression analysis is invariably conducted through the use of a computer. The computer program places all the predictor variables into the formula unless it is instructed to do otherwise. Therefore, it is customary to specify a cutoff point for inclusion into the final model. The cutoff point in the GE model was specified as .10. Thus, only those predictor variables with a probability of falsely rejecting the null hypothesis, $b_i = 0$, of less than .10 are included in the final model.

No single alpha level is appropriate for all such tests. As discussed in the section on hypothesis tests, it is generally worthwhile to examine the probability level associated with each variable that logically or theoretically "should" influence the criterion variable. The final regression formula should contain predictor variables that (1) are logically related to the criterion variable, and (2) have a probability level that is appropriate for the problem at hand.

Nominal Variables in Regression Analysis

Frequently it is desirable to include nominally scaled predictor variables, such as gender, marital status, or occupational category, in a multiple regression analysis. *Dummy variables* can be used for this purpose as long as there are relatively few such variables. For natural dichotomies, such as gender, one response is coded 0 and the other is coded 1. For polytomous data (multiple categories), such as occupation, each category serves as a variable. Thus, a three-category occupation scale could be coded as three variables:

$X_5 = 1$ (professional/managerial) or 0 (not professional/managerial)
$X_6 = 1$ (white collar) or 0 (not white collar)
$X_7 = 1$ (blue collar) or 0 (not blue collar)

The occupational scale just described could also be coded by using only X_5 and X_6. When these are both coded 0, the respondent must be blue collar. However, interpretation of the equation is easier if all categories are included.

The two GE regression formulas described earlier tested for the effect of patents, a dichotomous (yes/no) variable. For these two industries, patent protection was not associated (with a .10 α level for $b_i = 0$) with relative price. However, for consumer nondurables (whose formula is not shown), it had a b of +2.05. Thus, if a consumer nondurable product had patent protection, its relative price tended to be 2.05 percent higher than competition.

Cautions in Using Multiple Regression

Multiple regression is a very useful technique. However, several cautions need to be observed when using it.

1. Presence of Multicollinearity.   Multiple regression is based on the assumption that the predictor variables are independent (are *not* correlated). If they are, the b values are very unstable. However, the predictive ability of the equation is not affected. Therefore, **multicollinearity** is not a serious problem in forecasting applications but is very serious when the formula is used to gain an understanding of *how* the predictor variables influence the criterion variable.

Multicollinearity: occurs when two or more predictor variables are correlated with each other.

It is always advisable to check for multicollinearity before or during a multiple regression analysis. This is done by requesting the computer to print a *correlation matrix*, which shows the correlation (r) of each variable in the analysis with every other variable in the analysis. The correlation matrix for the variables in the GE capital equipment relative price analysis is shown in Table 18–3.

TABLE 18–3 Correlation Matrix for Relative Price Regression Analysis

	RP	*RQ*	*RDC*	*ME*
RQ	.47			
RDC	.33	.09		
ME	.12	.11	− .03	
RS	.19	− .38	− .12	.19

An examination of the table indicates that relative quality and relative service are modestly correlated. When two predictor variables are correlated above .35, potential distortion of the b_i values should be checked (although serious problems are unlikely unless the r value is well above .50). A simple way to do this is to run the equation with both variables and with each variable separately. The b_i values should be similar in all three cases. If they are not similar, a multicollinearity problem may exist.

Multicollinearity can be dealt with in one of three ways. First, it can be ignored. This is acceptable in forecasting applications but should be avoided in other situations. The second approach is to delete one of the correlated predictors. This is recommended when two variables are clearly measuring the same thing (number of sales personnel and salesforce salary expense) or when one variable has a clearer logical or theoretical link to the criterion variable. Finally, the correlated variables can be combined or otherwise transformed to produce unrelated variables. The marketing effort variable in the GE equation was constructed by combining measures of advertising effort, sales promotion effort, and salesforce effort because the three variables were highly correlated with each other.

2. Interpretation of Coefficients.   Care must be taken in interpreting the coefficients of the predictor variables. Consider the following equation:

$$\hat{Y} = 100 + .01X_1 + .01X_2$$

where

$\hat{Y}$ = sales estimate,

X_1 = advertising in thousands of dollars, and

X_2 = salesforce expenditures in dollars.

At first glance it appears that a dollar spent on advertising and a dollar spent on the salesforce have an equal effect on sales. However, this is not true since different units of measurement (thousands of dollars and dollars) are used for the two variables. Thus, in our example, it would take a $1,000 increase in advertising to equal the effect of a $1 increase in salesforce expenditures.

When it is desirable to compare the relative effects of predictor variables, they should be coded using the same measurement units. If this is not possible, most packaged computer programs will run a regression on standardized scores (each observation is converted to the number of standard deviations it is from its mean). Thus, a standardized predictor coefficient of 1.3 would be interpreted as "a 1 standard deviation change in this predictor will produce a 1.3 standard deviation change in the criterion variable." This allows a direct comparison of the effects of relative changes in variables measured in different units.

3. Causation.   It is very tempting to assume that levels of predictor variables *cause* the level of the criterion variable. However, all they indicate is *association* between the variables. Association is evidence of causation, but it is not proof of it. Assume that a group of firms base their advertising budgets on current

sales. Thus, sales are causing advertising, and changes in sales cause changes in advertising. A regression analysis with sales as the criterion variable and advertising as one of the predictor variables would indicate a strong association. However, to conclude that advertising *causes* sales would not be justified in this case.

This example indicates the critical importance of developing a strong logical or theoretical relationship between the criterion and predictor variables before the analysis is conducted. Even with a strong theoretical base, the results can, at most, be treated only as *evidence* of causation.

Summary

Association occurs when two or more variables tend to covary in a systematic manner. Marketers are interested in using predictor (independent) variables to predict and/or explain criterion (dependent) variables. Managers need to know both the nature of the association between the variables and the strength of the association. The appropriate statistical technique to use to analyze association depends on the number of predictor and criterion variables and the scales used to measure them.

A significant danger in using measures of association is to naively assume that an associative relationship is a causative one. The fact that two variables consistently covary does not necessarily mean that one causes the other.

Bivariate least-squares regression analysis is the most common technique for analyzing the association between two intervally scaled variables. The Spearman rank correlation coefficient is the most common technique for analyzing the association between two ordinally scaled variables. Multivariate least-squares regression analysis is the most common technique for analyzing the association between one criterion variable and two or more intervally scaled predictor variables.

Both bivariate and multiple regression analyses produce a coefficient of determination (r^2) that is the percentage of variation in the criterion variable accounted for by variation in the predictor variables. Multicollinearity, a high degree of correlation between two or more predictor variables, can make the coefficients in a multiple regression analysis difficult to interpret. Care should also be used in assigning relative importance to predictor variables based on the relative size of their coefficients.

Review Questions

18.1. What is a *criterion variable?*

18.2. What is meant by the *nature* of association?

18.3. What is meant by the *strength* of association?

18.4. What is a *scatter diagram?* Why is it useful?

18.5. What is *regression analysis?*

18.6. What is the *coefficient of determination?*

18.7. What does an r^2 of 1.0 mean? .5? 0?

18.8. What technique is used to measure bivariate association in ordinal data?

18.9. What technique is used to measure bivariate association in interval data?

18.10. What purposes does *multiple regression* serve? How is it used in marketing research?

18.11. How is the strength of multiple regression measures of association determined?

18.12. What is a *dummy variable*?

18.13. What is meant by *multicollinearity*? When is it a problem?

18.14. What problems can arise in interpreting the coefficients in a multiple regression equation?

18.15. Discuss the relationship of causation to multiple regression analysis.

Discussion Questions/Problems

18.16. Provide a verbal description of the meaning of each of the following regression analysis outputs.
   a. $\hat{Y} = 34,000 - 1,900X_1$
   b. $\hat{Y} = 700,000 + 1,043X_2$
   c. $\hat{Y} = 432,000 + .129X_3$
   d. $\hat{Y} = 650,000 - .08X_4$

   where
   $$\hat{Y} = \text{predicted annual sales}$$
   $$X_1 = \text{number of competitors within one mile}$$
   $$X_2 = \text{number of outlets}$$
   $$X_3 = \text{annual advertising expenditure}$$
   $$X_4 = \text{average per capita income in the region}$$

18.17. For each of the formulas in 18.16 prepare an explanation to management for the following r^2 values:
   a. $r^2 = .08$
   b. $r^2 = .85$
   c. $r^2 = .58$
   d. $r^2 = .92$

18.18. What is the association between taste reaction and purchase probability for _____ . (Assume interval data using the same group definitions given on page 459.)
   a. Group 2
   b. Group 3
   c. Group 4
   d. Group 5
   e. Group 6

18.19. Repeat 18.18 but assume ordinal data.

18.20. Describe the managerial implications of the following multiple regression formula when $r^2 =$ _____ .
   a. .92
   b. .82
   c. .16
   d. .45

$$Y = 9{,}080 + 780X_1 + 206X_2 - 1{,}880X_3$$

where

Y = annual sales in thousands

X_1 = hourly auto traffic during working hours

X_2 = average household income in thousands within a 2.5-mile radius

X_3 = number of competitors within a 15-minute drive

18.21. Given the following data, what would you estimate the annual sales to be for an outlet of 2,000 square feet, with a traffic flow of 4,000 people per hour, in a shopping center with 300,000 square feet, in a trade area with an average income of $20,000, with customers with an average income of $22,000, and with a competitor in the center? How much confidence would you have in your prediction?

Outlet	Annual Sales (000)	Foot Traffic Per Hour (00)	Center Square Footage	Average Income Shoppers (000)	Outlet Square Footage	Income Trade Area (000)	Competitor in Center
1	$1,300	42	300,000	$10.0	900	$ 8.2	No
2	1,750	20	275,000	17.1	1,500	15.2	Yes
3	950	32	250,000	10.5	1,000	8.4	Yes
4	2,000	48	290,000	20.8	1,800	18.9	No
5	1,350	15	260,000	12.4	1,200	10.2	No
6	1,600	26	280,000	15.7	900	13.6	Yes
7	2,150	31	350,000	23.2	2,000	21.5	Yes
8	1,100	37	200,000	12.1	1,000	10.8	No
9	3,250	22	440,000	26.3	2,200	23.9	Yes
10	2,600	27	360,000	24.8	1,800	22.7	No
11	1,900	29	310,000	20.5	1,600	18.8	No
12	1,500	35	360,000	13.8	1,450	11.2	Yes
13	1,800	31	320,000	16.2	1,700	14.1	No
14	1,650	43	220,000	15.4	1,500	13.8	Yes
15	1,200	36	210,000	13.1	1,200	10.0	No
16	1,760	21	420,000	14.6	1,400	12.5	Yes
17	1,880	18	310,000	15.9	1,200	12.5	No
18	1,950	27	260,000	20.5	1,900	18.9	No
19	2,050	33	290,000	21.3	1,900	19.1	Yes
20	1,720	45	230,000	14.3	1,700	12.8	Yes
21	1,340	19	220,000	12.6	1,300	11.1	Yes
22	1,460	23	290,000	14.2	1,400	13.0	No
23	1,820	28	310,000	17.4	1,700	15.3	No
24	1,990	26	300,000	21.1	1,900	19.2	Yes
25	2,060	30	360,000	22.1	1,800	20.3	No

SECTION IV CASES

CASE IV–1

Weyerhaeuser: Sample Design, Size, and Selection

Weyerhaeuser was very interested in its image compared to that of Georgia-Pacific (review Case II–6). The company's aim was to learn how sponsoring "This Old House" would influence its image over time. Therefore, Weyerhaeuser decided to conduct a benchmark study of DIYers' images of the two firms before the company's sponsorship of the program began. Repeated annually, the study would track changes in consumers' perceptions of the firms.

Initially a national sample was considered, perhaps using an interval panel such as NFO's for a sample frame. The primary reason this option was not chosen was that most lumber companies are not well-known outside their areas of major operations but are very well-known within those areas. A national probability sample would generate respondents from throughout the United States. Determining which respondents were located in areas where a given lumber producer was particularly well-known would be difficult. Furthermore, subsequent surveys would have to match the geographic distribution of the initial survey, or another source of variance would be introduced.

A second reason for not using a national sample is the uneven availability of "This Old House." Since not all towns receive the series, calling into areas where it is not available would add to the cost of the survey.

Based on this logic, Boston, Chicago, Miami, and Phoenix were selected. All four are above-average DIY areas that also have above-average viewing patterns for "This Old House." Thus, they represent important markets and areas where contacting sufficient numbers of viewers would be practical. However, consultations with the interviewing firm resulted in the dropping of Miami as a site, because of the high cost of having to provide bilingual interviewers.

A sample size of 600 completed interviews, 200 per city, was chosen. Available funding was considered but was not a significant constraining factor. The basic logic was that within-city comparisons between viewers and nonviewers, broken down by at least one additional variable, would be desirable. Thus, cell sizes would quickly become too small unless the obtained sample per city were at least 200. The following table indicates how this logic works, given a 60/40 viewer/nonviewer split.

	Phoenix (200)	
	(Viewer = 120)	(Nonviewer = 80)
Heavy DIYer (top 1/3 in expenditures)	40	27
Moderate DIYer (middle 1/3 in expenditures)	40	26
Light DIYer (bottom 1/3 in expenditures)	40	27

Since the primary emphasis was on the effect of sponsorship, a quota sample was used. Viewership of at least once a month was the quota variable, and it was set at 60 percent. All respondents were screened for DIY activity over the past 10 months. Those who spent less than $200 on materials for home improvement were excluded from the survey. The screening questions and quota procedure are shown below.

Gilmore Research Group   RESP.#:_____ 1–3 _____
1100 Olive Way, Suite 250
Seattle, WA 98101-1840

<u>"This Old House" Survey</u>

Tel.#: (___) ___-____ Date:_____
      AC
Interviewer: _____ ID#:_4–6_____
      Stop Time: _____   Total Time: _____   7–8
      Start Time: _____   Male   1
                              Female 9   2

Other Quota Information		
	Area:	
	Viewer	*Non-Viewer*
Boston	1	4
Chicago	2	5
Phoenix	3	6

                                                                  10

Hello, I'm _____ of Gilmore Research Group, a national marketing research firm. We're conducting a brief survey of do-it-yourselfers who have recently completed a home improvement project.

1a. Have you personally done a do-it-yourself home improvement project in 1987?

        Skip To Q.2 ◄———— Yes   1
                       ⌈ No   2
        Ask Q.1b ◄——⌊ Don't know/Refused 3   11

1b. Has anyone else in your household been involved in such a project this year?
Ask to Speak with That Person,
Arrange a Call-back If   ◄———— Yes   1
Required

                          ⌈ No   2
    Thank & Terminate ◄————⌊ Don't know/Refused 3

(2nd Person Introduction:) I'm _____ from Gilmore Research Group. We're conducting a brief survey of do-it-yourselfers. I understand that you have personally done a do-it-yourself home improvement project this year.

2. Approximately how much would you estimate you spent on materials for do-it-yourself home improvement projects in 1987?
(Probe:) We're not interested in an <u>exact</u> amount, just your best estimate.

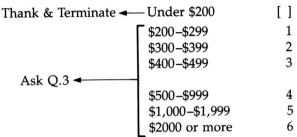

Thank & Terminate ◄— Under $200	[ ]	
$200–$299	1	
$300–$399	2	
$400–$499	3	
Ask Q.3 ◄—		
$500–$999	4	
$1,000–$1,999	5	
$2000 or more	6	

(Probe:)
We're not interested in an <u>exact</u> ◄———[Don't know/Refused   7   12
amount, just your best estimate.
(If Still Unable, Thank & Terminate)

3a. Are you aware of any <u>television programs</u> designed to provide assistance and information on home improvement projects for do-it-yourselfers?
Probe for Names. Do Not Read.

Skip To Q.4 ◄———"This Old House"	1	
Other (Specify):		
Ask Q.3b ◄— _____	2	
_____	2	
Don't know/Aware of none/Refused	3	13

3b. Are you aware of a program on PBS called "This Old House"?

Ask Q.4 ◄—Yes	1	
Check Nonviewer Quota. ◄— No	2	
If Quota Unfilled, Ask Q.4; Don't know/Refused	3	14
If Quota Filled, Thank & Terminate.		

4. How often, if at all, would you say you watch "This Old House" during a typical winter or spring month? Do Not Read.

Nonviewer: Terminate If ◄—Less than once/Never	1	
Quota Full Once	2	
1–2 times	3	
Twice	4	
Ask Q.5 ◄— 2–3 times	5	
3 times	6	
3–4 times	7	
4 or more times	8	

(Probe:) What is your best guess? ◄—Don't know/Refused   9   15
(If Still Don't Know, Count as
Nonviewer & Terminate If Quota Full.)

Discussion Questions

1. Evaluate the sampling procedure used and suggest improvements as appropriate.
2. Develop an alternative sampling plan.

CASE IV–2

Cola Taste Test

Can people really distinguish between New Coke and Classic Coke? Is there a clear preference in taste between New Coke and Pepsi-Cola? Is it mostly younger people who prefer the sweeter colas? Given a choice of a free can of cola, will people tend to take the brand that they have just chosen in a taste test?

To get at the answer to these and other questions, a taste test of Classic Coke, New Coke, and Pepsi-Cola was carried out. It was conducted at two of the entrances to a shopping mall using a sample of 78 persons. The samples of the three colas to be tasted were labeled, "K," "L," and "M." The test was "double blind" in nature, that is, neither the persons administering it nor the persons taking it knew which cola was labeled with which letter.

Each subject was asked to make paired taste comparisons of the cola combinations K/L, K/M, and L/M. The combinations were administered in random order, as were the individual colas in each combination. The subject was asked to rinse out his or her mouth with water after each sample was tasted. After completing the third taste comparison, the subject was interviewed using the following questionnaire.

Cola Questionnaire   Resp. No. ____

Please respond to the following questions as accurately as possible. Thank you for your cooperation and willingness to assist in our research project.

1. For each combination of soft drinks listed below, please indicate which one you prefer.

    a. Brand K or Brand L? _____

    b. Brand L or Brand M? _____

    c. Brand K or Brand M? _____

2. If a free can of cola were offered to you, which would you select?

    a. New Coke _____   d. Other   _____

    b. Classic Coke _____   e. None   _____

    c. Pepsi   _____

3. Gender

    a. female _____

    b. male   _____

4. What is the occupation of the head of your household? _____

5. What is the latest grade of school you have completed?

    a. grade school _____

    b. high school, no diploma _____

    c. graduated high school _____

    d. some college, no degree _____

    e. junior college certificate _____

    f. 4-year college degree _____

    g. some graduate school _____

    h. masters/doctoral degree _____

6. What is your best estimate of the amount of cola you personally drink in one week?

    a. none _____   e. 13–18 cans _____

    b. 1–3 cans _____   f. 19–24 cans _____

    c. 4–6 cans _____   g. 25–36 cans _____

    d. 7–12 cans _____   h. more than 36 cans _____

7. What is your household's yearly family income?

    a. under $10,000 _____

    b. $10,000–$14,999 _____

    c. $15,000–$24,999 _____

    d. $25,000–$34,999 _____

    e. $35,000–$49,999 _____

    f. $50,000 and above _____

8. Age

    a. 14–19 _____   e. 45–54 _____

    b. 20–24 _____   f. 55–64 _____

    c. 25–34 _____   g. 65 and over _____

    d. 35–44 _____

9. Race

    a. white/Caucasian _____   d. Hispanic _____

    b. black _____   e. Oriental _____

    c. Indian _____   f. Other, please specify _____

Cola Taste Test Data

Subject	Pepsi-Cola or Classic Coke	Classic Coke or New Coke	New Coke or Pepsi-Cola	Choice of Free Can	Gender	Head's Occupation	Education Level	Amount Cola/wk.	Income	Age	Race	Best Liked Cola	Least Liked Cola
1	1	3	1	1	1	3	5	2	4	3	1	1	2
2	1	3	1	2	1	5	1	1	2	6	1	1	2
3	2	2	3	4	1	2	4	2	3	6	1	2	1
4	2	3	3	2	2	4	4	4	2	3	1	3	1
5	2	2	1	2	1	4	3	2	1	4	2	2	3
6	1	3	3	2	2	2	2	4	3	7	1	3	2
7	1	3	1	3	2	2	1	1	3	6	1	1	2
8	1	3	1	1	2	3	4	2	5	1	1	1	2
9	1	3	1	2	2	2	4	2	4	1	1	3	2
10	1	3	1	2	2	2	6	3	3	3	1	1	2
11	2	2	3	1	1	2	3	1	3	7	1	2	1
12	2	3	3	1	2	4	3	6	2	3	1	3	1
13	1	3	1	1	1	3	4	1	1	3	1	1	2
14	2	3	3	1	2	3	4	4	5	2	1	3	1
15	1	3	1	2	2	3	4	4	9	2	5	1	2
16	2	3	3	4	1	4	6	4	4	5	1	3	1
17	1	3	1	1	1	2	5	4	5	4	1	1	2
18	1	2	1	1	1	2	3	3	1	7	1	1	3
19	1	2	1	1	1	3	4	3	6	4	1	1	3
20	1	3	3	1	1	3	4	3	6	2	1	3	2
21	1	3	1	2	2	3	4	2	3	6	1	1	2
22	2	2	3	2	2	2	3	2	2	2	1	2	1
23	2	2	3	2	1	2	3	2	3	5	1	2	1
24	2	2	1	1	2	3	4	2	3	3	1	2	3
25	1	3	1	1	1	2	4	4	3	2	1	1	2
26	2	2	3	2	2	1	4	3	2	2	1	2	1
27	2	2	3	4	1	2	5	2	4	4	1	2	1
28	1	3	1	1	1	2	4	3	4	2	1	1	2
29	1	3	1	3	2	3	5	2	5	3	1	1	2
30	2	2	1	2	2	3	5	3	5	3	1	2	3
31	1	3	3	1	2	1	3	6	1	1	1	3	2
32	1	3	1	1	1	3	1	2	9	1	6	1	2
33	1	3	1	1	2	2	2	1	3	7	1	1	2
34	2	2	3	1	1	5	1	1	1	7	1	2	1
35	1	3	1	1	2	2	3	3	6	2	1	1	2
36	1	3	1	1	2	2	3	1	6	2	1	1	2
37	1	3	1	2	1	4	4	1	2	7	1	1	2
38	2	2	1	1	2	1	4	3	1	2	1	2	3
39	1	3	1	2	2	2	2	2	4	1	1	1	2
40	1	3	3	1	1	6	3	2	2	1	1	3	2
41	1	3	3	1	2	2	6	3	5	4	1	3	2

Subject	Pepsi-Cola or Classic Coke	Classic Coke or New Coke	New Coke or Pepsi-Cola	Choice of Free Can	Gender	Head's Occupation	Education Level	Amount Cola/wk.	Income	Age	Race	Best Liked Cola	Least Liked Cola
42	1	3	1	1	2	1	4	1	1	2	5	1	2
43	1	2	1	2	2	4	5	3	6	4	1	1	3
44	1	3	1	1	2	3	6	2	6	5	1	1	2
45	1	3	1	2	1	3	4	2	3	5	1	1	2
46	1	3	1	2	2	3	6	2	4	6	1	1	2
47	1	2	1	2	1	3	4	1	3	7	1	1	3
48	2	2	3	4	2	3	8	2	5	4	1	2	1
49	1	3	3	2	1	2	4	2	2	6	1	3	2
50	2	2	3	1	1	2	3	2	2	6	1	2	1
51	1	3	1	1	1	3	8	6	5	5	1	1	2
52	2	3	3	1	2	2	2	3	2	4	1	3	1
53	1	3	1	1	1	2	3	3	3	5	1	1	2
54	1	3	3	3	2	2	4	2	3	3	1	3	2
55	1	2	1	2	1	2	5	1	3	7	1	1	3
56	2	3	3	2	1	3	2	5	9	1	1	3	1
57	1	2	1	1	1	3	4	8	6	2	1	1	3
58	1	3	3	2	1	3	4	2	5	1	1	3	2
59	1	3	3	2	1	3	4	2	4	1	1	3	2
60	1	3	1	1	1	1	4	1	1	2	1	1	2
61	1	3	1	4	1	1	7	3	2	2	1	1	2
62	1	3	3	2	2	3	4	2	5	2	1	3	2
63	1	3	3	2	2	1	4	2	4	2	1	3	2
64	1	3	1	1	2	1	4	3	1	2	1	1	2
65	1	2	1	2	2	1	7	1	1	2	1	1	3
66	2	3	3	2	1	1	5	2	1	2	1	3	1
67	1	3	1	4	1	2	4	2	3	1	1	1	2
68	1	2	1	2	1	3	4	2	6	2	2	1	3
69	2	2	3	2	2	3	4	4	6	1	1	2	1
70	2	3	3	1	1	3	4	4	6	1	5	3	1
71	1	3	3	1	1	2	4	2	2	1	1	3	2
72	2	3	3	1	2	3	4	2	3	1	1	3	1
73	2	3	3	3	2	3	4	3	6	2	1	3	1
74	1	3	1	1	1	3	4	4	6	1	1	1	2
75	2	2	1	1	2	6	4	2	5	2	1	2	3
76	2	2	3	2	2	3	4	5	6	1	1	2	1
77	1	3	3	2	2	3	4	3	6	1	1	3	2
78	1	3	3	4	2	2	4	2	2	2	1	3	2

Value Labels:

Cola Brands	1 Pepsi-Cola, 2 Classic Coke, 3 New Coke, 4 Other
Gender	1 Female, 2 Male
Occupation	1 Student, 2 Blue Color, 3 White Collar, 4 Service Worker, 5 Housewife, 6 Farmworker
Education	1 Grade School, 2 High School—No Diploma, 3 High School Diploma, 4 Some College, 5 Junior College Graduate, 6 4-Year College Graduate, 7 Some Graduate School, 8 Masters or Doctoral Degree
Amount of Cola (Cans or Equiv) per Week	1, None; 2, 1–3; 3, 4–6; 4, 7–12; 5, 13–18; 6, 19–24; 7, 25–36; 8, More Than 36
Income	1, Under $10,000; 2, $10,000–14,999; 3, $15,000–24,999; 4, $25,000–34,999; 5, $35,000–49,999; 6, $50,000 and Over; 9, Refused
Age	1, 14–19; 2, 20–24; 3, 25–34; 4, 35–44; 5, 45–54; 6, 55–64; 7, 65 and Older
Race	1 White, 2 Black, 3 Indian, 4 Hispanic, 5 Oriental, 6 Other
Best Liked Cola/Least Like Cola	Derived from paired comparisons

Discussion Questions

1. Compare the design of this taste test with that used by Coca-Cola USA (described on page 46). Which design do you think was better? Why?
2. Analyze the results of the test. What do you consider to be the findings that would be relevant to Coca-Cola USA management? To Pepsi-Cola management? Give the supporting analysis for each of these findings.
3. If Coca-Cola and/or Pepsi-Cola management were to take actions based solely on these findings, what should they do? Why?

CASE IV–3

The Toni Company

Toni Company is a manufacturer and marketer of women's home permanents. As women's hair care practices began to change, Toni's management felt a need for detailed information on women's attitudes and behaviors in this area. They planned to use this information to guide product development, advertising, and other marketing activities. To collect the data, a large-scale national at-home personal interview survey was planned. Details of the sampling plan are below.

Definition of population	The population was defined as white females; 15 years and older (element) in households (unit), in the continental U.S. (extent) during the month the sample was taken (time).

Sampling frame used	Three frames were used: (1) a list of the counties and (2) the Standard Metropolitan Statistical Areas (SMSA) in the continental U.S. with (3) maps of the counties/metropolitan areas selected.
Sampling unit used	Households
Sampling method used	*Probability*

A sampling of 228 counties was taken. When a sample county was part of an SMSA, it was used in lieu of the county.

Individual blocks and country segments were then selected by probability sampling methods.

Single unit selection was used. A systematic sample of households was taken from each block. A systematic procedure for selecting households from road intersection starting points was devised for the country open segments.

The population was *unstratified*. However, age group and geographic area comparisons were made with census data to determine the representatives of the sample.

Unequal probability of element selection was used. For example, in the metropolitan areas of the Northeast, where the company had high per capita sales, one woman was interviewed for (approximately) every 15,600 women. In the metropolitan areas of the South Atlantic states, where per capita sales were lower, one woman was interviewed for each 3,900 women.

The sample was a *multistage* design: County/ SMSA to block or open country segment and then systematic selection of households.

Desired sample size	A sample of 6,000 women was specified.
Sampling plan	An entire notebook of materials was prepared and used for training interviewers and field supervisors.
Selection of the sample	Only 5,493 of the interviews were actually completed. A quota sample of 500 cases was added to make up the deficit. The quotas stipulated were such as to compensate in age groups that were underrepresented and to provide added cases in subgroups in which special analyses were desired.

Discussion Questions

1. What other research designs could have provided management the information they needed? Are any of these other approaches superior to the one selected? Why?
2. Why was such a large sample desired?

3. Evaluate the sampling plan. Suggest specific improvements where appropriate.
4. Evaluate the decision to supplement the obtained sample with a quota sample of 500.

CASE IV–4

Carnation's Taste Test Comparison of Coffee-mate and Cream

Carnation ran a series of commercials in which the claim was made that "almost half the coffee drinkers we test think coffee with Coffee-mate is coffee with cream." The basis for this claim is three studies conducted in Pittsburgh, Chicago, and Los Angeles. The methodology, sample size, and results were similar in each study. The methodology used and results obtained in Los Angeles are presented here.

Specifications

A sample of 100 women was specified to participate in a paired comparison taste test of coffee containing Coffee-mate and coffee containing cream. To qualify, each woman had to (1) do most of the grocery shopping, (2) drink a minimum of two cups of coffee a day in her own home, on the average, (3) drink her coffee all or most of the time with a lightener—i.e., not black— and (4) not live in a household where any member was employed in market research, advertising, or any part of the food manufacturing or sales industry.

Recruitment

Interviewers did both phone and street recruiting, screening and scheduling participants who qualified. Phone calls were made to organizations as well as to individuals to recruit respondents.

Testing

An average of 10 women were tested at one time, all well separated in seating arrangements. They were blindfolded, after which the interviewers brought two cups of coffee to each participant. The pair of cups were labeled with different numbers and each cup was placed by its corresponding number on a placemat. Numbers were prerotated for left–right positions. The moderator then gave directions first to taste from the cup on the right and then from the one on the left; then the respondent was to indicate which she thought contained the cream by raising her left or right hand or by keeping both hands down if she could not tell the difference. While all remained blindfolded, interviewers marked each woman's placemat with her choice and turned cards up in front of the cups identifying the Coffee-mate cup and the cream cup. Blindfolds were then removed and respondents were directed to turn the placemats over and write their reactions to the relationship between their guesses (or nonguesses) and the facts.

Results

A total of 105 qualified women were tested. Hand tabulation of their forms showed that a majority of 56 respondents (53 percent) identified the cup with Coffee-mate as containing cream; 8 respondents (9 percent) could not make a choice between the two; and 41 respondents (39 percent) correctly identified the one with cream.

These were the results from the Los Angeles test only. The results from the three test cities combined were that 132 respondents (42 percent) incorrectly identified the cup with Coffee-mate as containing cream, 28 respondents (9 percent) could not tell which cup contained cream, and 153 respondents (49 percent) correctly identified the cup with cream.

Discussion Questions

1. What is the probability that the results of this study are due to sampling error?
2. Evaluate the taste test procedure used and suggest improvements, if appropriate.
3. Is the advertising claim justified by the research design and results?

CASE IV–5

Kermit Steel Supply

Kermit Steel Supply sells iron and steel reinforcing rods. These products are used to provide structural strength to concrete. Thus, they are used almost any time large quantities of concrete are used.

Management has been concerned with the firm's ability to forecast demand. Forecast errors had averaged almost 10 percent during 1991 and 1992 and the error in the first quarter of 1993 had been almost 13 percent.

Sales forecasts were made for two quarters ahead, with a new forecast made each quarter. The forecasting was done by the president and the marketing manager, using what they referred to as their "wet finger in the wind" method. Once each quarter, they met in the president's office with data on orders, construction contract awards for the market area, salesforce call reports, and other information. After reviewing these data, they each wrote their forecasts for the next two quarters on a piece of paper. Differences were discussed and a final sales forecast (usually a compromise that was close to the average of their individual forecasts) was made for each quarter.

As a result of its inability to forecast accurately, the company had been forced to keep large inventories on hand to avoid losing sales when demand was unexpectedly high. The president decided that some means had to be found to make better forecasts so the company could reduce inventories and operating costs.

A consultant was called in to work on the problem. She found that a trade association provided data on reinforcing rod sales each month in each of the counties of Kermit's market area. She ran an analysis of past sales data for the industry and for Kermit and found that Kermit's market share had remained close to 9.2 percent for some time. In discussions with the president and marketing manager, they stated that it was reasonable to expect that the company's share would continue to be at about this same level unless some major change took place in the industry.

The consultant planned to run a simple linear regression analysis with construction contract awards lagged by four through eight months to see which gave the best "fit." She then planned to use the regression equation for the lag period with the best fit to forecast industry reinforcing rod sales for each month for the number of months the equation permitted.

Monthly Construction Activity (X) and Rod Consumption (Y)

Year	Month	X 1992 Dollars (000)	Y Rod Consumption in Meters (000)	Year	Month	X 1992 Dollars (000)	Y Rod Consumption in Meters (000)
				1991	Jan.	97,500	66.9
					Feb.	99,700	71.3
					Mar.	97,500	74.1
					Apr.	100,300	74.9
					May	98,200	82.1
1989	Jan.	84,000	61.0		June	95,700	85.1
	Feb.	84,300	64.6		July	96,300	89.5
	Mar.	82,900	70.6		Aug.	94,900	89.7
	Apr.	85,600	68.3		Sept.	95,600	85.1
	May	82,700	71.6		Oct.	93,200	76.9
	June	78,400	75.5		Nov.	96,300	72.7
	July	76,200	75.6		Dec.	96,000	65.9
	Aug.	76,000	73.9	1992	Jan.	95,300	65.8
	Sept.	80,300	70.8		Feb.	92,000	69.2
	Oct.	82,800	64.2		Mar.	92,500	73.4
	Nov.	80,600	58.1		Apr.	88,500	77.8
	Dec.	81,100	52.6		May	90,100	77.5
1990	Jan.	79,600	53.2		June	90,300	84.2
	Feb.	84,700	60.5		July	91,400	80.5
	Mar.	82,700	65.6		Aug.	95,600	88.1
	Apr.	79,900	65.8		Sept.	95,700	71.2
	May	84,600	66.8		Oct.	97,300	67.1
	June	93,300	71.3		Nov.	99,500	70.2
	July	98,300	77.3		Dec.	102,000	62.0
	Aug.	97,900	76.6	1993	Jan.	103,500	66.4
	Sept.	93,900	67.1		Feb.	95,200	72.8
	Oct.	94,500	65.6		Mar.	92,300	75.0
	Nov.	93,600	73.0				
	Dec.	97,300	66.2				

Discussion Questions

1. What logic supports "lagging" the construction awards?
2. Prepare monthly sales forecasts as far into the future as possible using the optimal lag period.

CASE IV–6

Labaume's Restaurant

Frans Labaume, owner and manager of Labaume's Restaurant, became intrigued by an article indicating that music could influence restaurant patrons' spending levels. He decided to test this by playing light classical music two nights a week, light jazz two nights a week, and no music for two nights a week for 18 weeks. The music was rotated such that each type and the absence of music occurred the same number of times on each day of the week. He used each night's total receipts as his dependent variable (though he did not think of it in those terms). The results of his experiment are shown in the table.

	Jazz		Classical		None	
Mon.	$1,960	$1,690	$1,280	$1,350	$1,520	$1,260
	2,320	1,780	1,860	1,720	1,310	1,150
	1,570	1,430	1,590	1,670	1,630	1,470
Tues.	2,160	2,070	1,890	1,640	1,430	1,790
	1,950	2,000	1,780	1,980	1,820	1,880
	2,030	1,740	2,120	1,760	2,200	1,750
Wed.	1,790	1,680	2,070	2,230	1,890	1,920
	1,980	2,400	1,940	1,710	1,780	1,840
	2,060	1,780	1,750	1,850	1,750	2,030
Thurs.	2,380	2,100	2,170	1,990	1,990	2,060
	2,160	1,860	2,080	1,840	1,840	1,970
	1,970	2,250	1,910	2,170	2,110	1,790
Fri.	2,730	2,630	2,690	2,540	2,180	2,410
	2,410	2,280	2,490	2,360	2,390	2,130
	2,560	2,770	2,310	2,580	2,060	2,190
Sat.	3,060	3,460	3,110	2,920	3,020	2,740
	2,890	2,970	2,910	2,840	2,940	2,800
	3,380	2,890	2,860	3,230	2,910	3,140

Discussion Questions

1. Evaluate the experiment. What potential errors concern you?
2. What do you conclude?

Marketing Research Reports and Ethical Issues

The results of the marketing research project have to be reported effectively if they are to receive the proper attention from management. Marketing research reports are the subject of Chapter 19.

Ethical concerns exist in all activities, and research is no exception. The ethical issues that arise in marketing research, and the practice of corporate espionage, are the topics of Chapter 20.

19

Preparing and Reading Research Reports

LEARNING OBJECTIVES

Upon completing this chapter, you should be able to:

1. Explain the critical importance of focusing on the audience's needs when preparing written and oral research reports.

2. Describe the characteristics of an effective research report.

3. Select and use appropriate visual aids in written and oral research reports.

4. Describe the contents and organization of a research report.

5. Read a research report critically.

A Research Report Disaster
at Coca-Cola

"One of the most popular studies of the past at Coca-Cola nearly went astray. Two days after a three-hour presentation by the researchers who supervised and conducted the study, I was told by a senior top manager, 'We have scheduled a meeting in three weeks for you to tell us what they said. The only thing we're sure of is that there's some important findings in that study.'

"I basically reduced the presentation by leaving out technical details and using the same key charts with minor brands eliminated, and after a four-hour presentation and discussion, everyone was happy with the study."[1]

The results of a research project may be reported in written or oral format, or both. The importance of *effective* reporting cannot be overemphasized. Regardless of the quality of the research process and the accuracy and usefulness of the resulting data, the findings will not be utilized if they are not communicated effectively to the appropriate decision makers.

Furthermore, many executives cannot easily ascertain the quality of a research design, questionnaire, or experiment. They can, however, easily recognize the quality level of a report. Therefore, *the quality of the report is often used as a major indicator of the quality of the research itself.*

Preparing the Written Research Report

Good research reports begin with *clear* thinking on the part of a researcher.[2] The researcher should *analyze the reader's needs* carefully and prepare a detailed outline *prior* to writing the first draft. The first draft should be considered just that—a *first* draft. Few of us write well enough to produce a polished draft the first time. The writer should plan on at least one major rewrite.

Several facts must be kept in mind. First, managers are extremely busy. Second, they are much less interested in the technical and logical aspects of a research problem than the researcher is. Third, they are seldom well versed in research techniques and terminology. Fourth, if there is more than one reader, and there usually is, they are likely to differ in levels of interest, training, and their reasons for reading the report. Finally, managers, like everyone else, prefer interesting reports over dull ones. With these facts in mind, we offer a number of general guides.

Focus on the Audience

The only reason for writing a research report is to communicate something to someone. The *someone* is the most important aspect of the communications process. The entire research project is performed to generate information that will aid one or more decision makers. The research report must convey that information to those decision makers.

Focus on the Objective of the Study

The research was initiated to help make a decision. The report should be built around the decision and how the resultant information is relevant to the decision. This is what the manager is interested in.

Minimize the Reporting of the Technical Aspects of the Project

Researchers have an unfortunate, if natural, tendency to attempt to convince management of their expertise and thoroughness in the research report. This leads to detailed discussions of the sampling plan, explorations of why it is superior to alternative sampling plans, and so on. Yet few executives are interested in this level of detail. However, the research department should keep such a detailed report *internally* to serve as a guide for future studies, and to answer any question that might arise concerning the methodology of the study. Technical details that might be of use to some, but not all readers, should be placed in an appendix.

Use Terminology That Matches the Vocabulary of the Readers

"Few managers can balance a research report, a cup of coffee, and a dictionary at the same time."[3] Terms such as *skewed distribution, correlation coefficient,* or even *significance level* are not necessarily familiar to all marketing managers. In many research reports, it is often necessary to use the concepts that underlie these terms. Three strategies are available for dealing with this problem. The term can be used, followed by a brief description or explanation; the explanation can be provided first followed by the term; or the technical terms can be omitted altogether. Which approach, or combination of approaches, is best depends on the nature of the audience and the message.

Avoid Errors in Grammar and Spelling

One incorrect sentence or misspelled word can undermine the credibility of the entire research project, and it can seriously harm your career. Use a dictionary and grammar guide any time that you are in doubt.

Which of the following words are spelled correctly?

acknowledgement	benificial	correspondant	maintenence
accross	commitee	descrepency	neccessary
astericks	congradulate	inclose	ocurrence

Which of the following sentences are incorrect?

- The firm applied for it's license after the deadline.
- The reports laid there unused for a week.
- I lead a fund drive last year.
- Your prospective on the matter differs from mine.
- I like writing, to read, and cross-country ski trips.

All of the words and sentences listed are incorrect. Since mistakes are hard to detect, two proofreaders should be used for any important document. Word processors with spelling and grammar checks can also be used to minimize such errors.

Develop an Interesting Writing Style

Research reports should be interesting to read. There is no inherent reason for a research report to be dull, tedious, or boring. Consider the following statement written by a well-known research executive:

> The use of analytical techniques of the behavioral sciences will gradually revolutionize the communication arts by predicating their practice upon a body of demonstrably general principles which will be readily available to

creative people for increasing their knowledge of consumer response to advertising communications.[4]

Can you imagine reading a report composed of such statements?

We should strive for simplicity and conciseness. Simplicity does not mean that the audience is talked down to, nor does conciseness mean that the report necessarily be short. However, unnecessary complexity in sentence structure and long-windedness in reporting should be avoided. Consider the following two sentences:

> As Table 6 indicates, our survey found that 86.3 percent of those surveyed said that they would be extremely likely or very likely to purchase Whifle if it were available at their supermarket.

> (versus)

> As Table 6 indicates, consumers are enthusiastic about Whifle.

It is important to "break up" the text of the report. Page after page of type looks dull, and probably is dull. Headings and subheadings with distinct type sizes and styles as well as ample white space are essential. Fortunately, word processors make proper layout easy to achieve. Use bullets (the round or square, black symbols shown in the following) and indentation to highlight key points:

· Key points must stand out
· Break up the text of the report
· Focus on the audience

Use Visual Aids Whenever Practical

Pie chart:
a circle divided into sections such that each section contains the percentage of the total area of the circle associated with one variable.

Bar chart:
has rectangles (bars) placed on the vertical or horizontal axis such that the height or length of the rectangle represents the level of the variable or category associated with it.

Line chart:
has the joint occurrence of two variables, one represented by the horizontal axis and the other by the vertical axis, indicated by a line.

Figure 19–1 illustrates three different ways of presenting numerical data. As a general rule, a sentence in the text of a report should contain no more than two or three numerical values. Sentences containing more numbers than this are difficult to read and understand. The table in the exhibit is much easier to read than the sentence. However, the pie chart contains the same information and provides a quick, strong impression of the relative sales by each department.

A **pie chart** is a circle divided into sections, such that each section represents the percentage of the total area of the circle associated with one variable. Another useful visual aid is the *bar chart*, which may be either vertical or horizontal. A **bar chart** is constructed by placing rectangles or bars over each value or interval of the variable of interest such that the height or length of the bar represents the level of the variable associated with it. Figure 19–2 illustrates two bar charts.

The data shown in the bar chart in Figure 19–2B could also be shown in the form of a **line chart,** such as Figure 19–3. The bar chart is somewhat less complex in appearance and may be more suited to those unaccustomed to dealing with figures. Line charts are generally superior under the following conditions: (1) *when the data involve a long time period*, (2) *when several series are compared on the same chart*, (3) *when the emphasis is on the movement rather than the actual amount*, (4) *when trends rather than a frequency distribution are presented*, (5) *when a multiple-amount scale is used*, and (6) *when estimates, forecasts, interpolations, or extrapolations are to be shown.*

Sentence

Sales by department were appliances, $453,268 (35.1%); hardware, $362,197 (28.0%); drugs and cosmetics, $198,415 (15.4%); household supplies, $169,327 (13.1%); sporting goods, $69,462 (5.4%); and toys, $38,917 (3.0%). Total sales were $1,291,586.

Table   Sales by Department

Department	Sales	Total (%)
Appliances	$ 453,268	35.1
Hardware	362,197	28.0
Drugs and cosmetics	198,415	15.4
Household supplies	169,327	13.1
Sporting goods	69,462	5.4
Toys	38,917	3.0
Total	$1,291,586	100.0

Pie Chart   Sales by Department

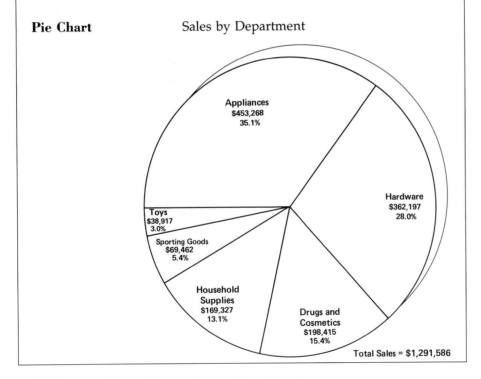

FIGURE 19–1 Three Ways of Presenting Sales Data

A **histogram** is a bar chart in which the height of the bars represents the relative or cumulative frequency of occurrence of the variable of interest. For example, assume that 730 respondents rate the service provided by a restaurant on a six-point semantic differential scale bounded by *poor* on the left and *excellent* on the right. The number of respondents marking each response

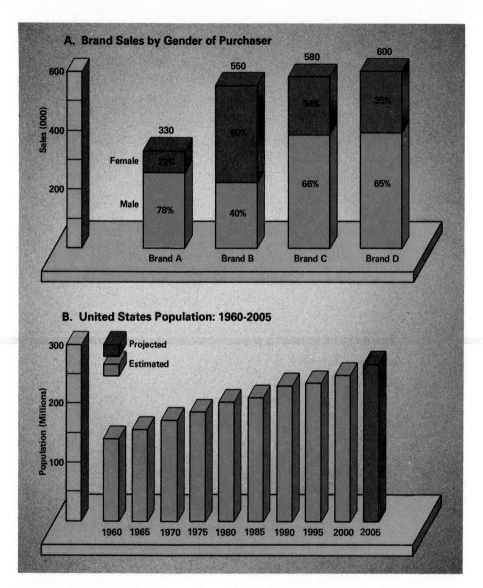

FIGURE 19-2 Bar Charts

Histogram:
a bar chart in which the height of the bars represents the relative or cumulative frequency of occurrence of the variable of interest.

from left to right is 154, 79, 50, 112, 198, and 146. Stated in percentages, the responses from left to right would be 21.2, 10.8, 6.8, 15.3, 25.9, and 20.0. Figure 19–4 demonstrates the advantages of presenting this type of data in the form of a histogram.

The histogram makes clear at a glance the bimodal nature of the response (that is, the fact that responses are clustered in two groups). A textual presentation of the raw data and/or a comment on the fact that the responses were bimodal does not have the same impact on many readers as the histogram.

It is often necessary to present numerical data that cannot be converted to graphic format. When this is the case or when the data underlying the graph

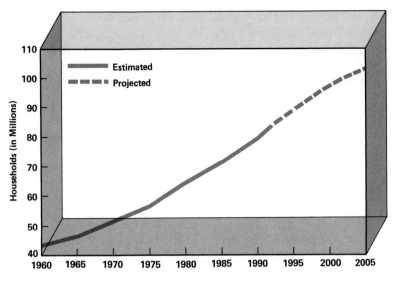

FIGURE 19–3 Line Chart Showing Household Growth, 1960–2005

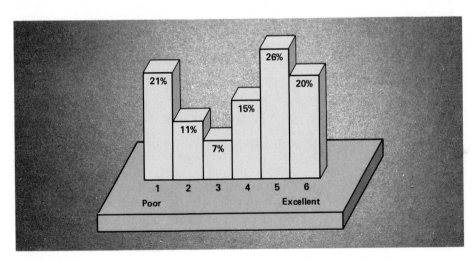

FIGURE 19–4 Relative Frequency Histogram of the Poor Service—
Excellent Service Semantic Differential Item

need to be presented in numerical form as a supplement to the graph, tables
should be used. Figure 19–5 shows both an effective and an ineffective presentation of the same data.

Flow diagrams are a visual presentation of a sequential process or logic.
They are very effective for introducing topics and summarizing results. Figure
19–6 was used to introduce the key areas covered in a study to determine
which individuals in various industries are involved in the purchase and use
of microcomputers.

Most data analysis software programs will prepare standard graphic displays. Likewise, most word processing and spreadsheet software can pro-

Flow diagrams:
a visual
presentation of a
sequential process
or logic.

duce pie charts, bar charts, and so forth. Specialized graphics software can develop elaborate, multicolor charts, graphs, headings, and diagrams. Coupled with high-quality printers, such software has made effective visuals a standard part of research reports. Failure to include such visual aids seriously detracts from the quality of a report.

TABLE 1 United Auto Rental Inc. Performance 1990–1992

Performance Indicator	1990	1991	1992
Days Rental			
All vehicles	3,692	5,402	5,802
Compact	312	1,248	2,621
Standard	2,891	3,469	2,359
Luxury	489	685	822
Mileage			
All vehicles	155,066	246,347	293,981
Compact	20,592	82,368	172,973
Standard	121,422	145,706	99,080
Luxury	13,052	18,273	21,928
Revenue			
All vehicles	$151,963	$223,040	$241,222
Compact	$ 12,973	$ 51,892	$108,973
Standard	$117,193	$140,632	$ 95,630
Luxury	$ 21,797	$ 30,516	$ 36,619

TABLE 2 United Auto Rental Inc. Performance 1990–1992

Performance Indicator	1990	1991	1992
DAYS RENTAL			
Compact	300	1,200	2,600
Standard	2,900	3,500	2,400
Luxury	500	700	800
All Vehicles	3,700	5,400	5,800
MILEAGE			
Compact	21,000	82,000	173,000
Standard	121,000	146,000	99,000
Luxury	13,000	18,000	22,000
All Vehicles	155,000	246,000	294,000
REVENUE			
Compact	$ 13,000	$ 52,000	$109,000
Standard	117,000	141,000	96,000
Luxury	22,000	31,000	37,000
All Vehicles	$152,000	$224,000	$242,000

FIGURE 19–5 Effective and Ineffective Tables

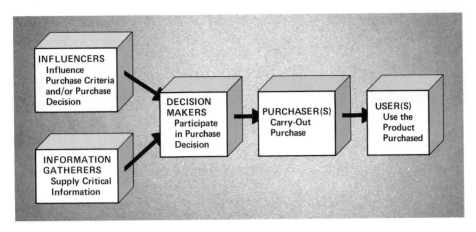

FIGURE 19–6 Use of a Flow Diagram to Introduce a Set of Topics

Rounding of Numbers

All too often one reads statements in research reports such as "the average age of the buyer of standard sized Chevrolets has climbed from 38.72 years in 1985 to 51.65 years in 1992." Such statements are usually the product of a computer analysis having been made in which all calculated numbers are routinely rounded to two places following the decimal point. The analyst then simply copies the data as they are given on the printout, and that is the way they appear in the report.

The reporting of data to a number of decimal places that is either unwarranted or unnecessary is a practice to be avoided. A spurious accuracy is implied by the last two digits for the ages given in the preceding example. There almost certainly were errors in the reporting of ages by buyers when the data were collected that would have made the calculated mean age questionable to an accuracy of more than one year. To imply that the data are accurate to one-hundredth of a year is thus both inaccurate and misleading.

Reporting data to several significant digits is often unnecessary, even when accurate. It is important for Chevrolet officials to know that the average age of the buyers of their standard-sized cars is increasing. It is probably sufficient, however, for this information to be reported as "the average age of the buyers of standard-sized Chevrolets has climbed from just under 40 to just over 50 in the last 8 years."

Writing an interesting research report is not easy. Research Application 19–1 provides several "hints" from an experienced marketing researcher.[5]

The Organization of the Report

No one format is best for all occasions. The nature of the audience and the topic of the report combine to determine the most desirable format. However, a general format is suggested in Table 19–1 that can be altered to meet the requirements of most situations.

RESEARCH APPLICATION 19–1

Hints for Constructing an Interesting Research Report

- Use present tense and active voice. Results and observations expressed in *now* terms sound better. Don't say: *"The respondents liked the taste of Whiffey."* Say, *People like the taste of Whiffey."* Managers use research to make decisions now. If the research results are not valid in the present tense, there is no use presenting them to management.

   The active voice should be used when possible. Why say, *"It is believed that . . ."* when you mean, *"We believe that . . ."?*

- Use information headlines. A headline that says "Convenience is the product's major advantage" is more meaningful and interesting to a manager than a heading such as "Results of Product Benefit Analysis."

- Let tables and charts do the work. The purpose of a table or a chart is to simplify. Use your words to point out significant items

in the table—something that is not readily clear. Or use your words to offer interpretive comments. Use verbatims from sample respondents to support a point. Don't repeat in words what the chart or table already communicates.

- Use the double-sided presentation whenever possible. This format will reduce the verbiage in your report. It simply presents the table on the left side of the open report. Your informative headline and interpretive comments are on the right-hand page.

- Make liberal use of verbatims. Great nuggets of marketing wisdom have come from people's comments. Use verbatims if you have them. They make tables, charts, and text much more interesting. Remember, marketing managers are ultimately interested in the customer's thoughts, not yours.

Title Page.   The title page should identify the topic, for whom the report is prepared, the date of the report, and the researcher(s). If the report is for limited distribution, this fact should also be noted on the title page. The title of the report should indicate the nature of the research project as precisely and as succinctly as possible.

Executive Summary.   The executive summary is the most important part of the research report. It must clearly and concisely present the heart of the report. The objectives, findings, conclusions, and recommendations must be presented forcefully and briefly.

   Many executives will read only this part of the report. In fact, the executive summary may be all that is provided to some managers. Others will use the executive summary to determine if, and what, they should read in the main report.

Table of Contents.   Unless the report is exceptionally brief, it should contain a table of contents, including the page numbers of major sections and sub-

TABLE 19–1 Generalized Format for a Research
Report

I.	Title page
II.	Executive summary
III.	Table of contents
IV.	Introduction
V.	Methodology and limitations
VI.	Findings
VII.	Recommendations
VIII.	Appendixes

divisions within the sections, and a list of all appendixes. If numerous tables or charts are used, they should also be listed on a separate page immediately following the table of contents.

Introduction.   The introduction should provide (1) *background material*, (2) *a clear statement of the research objectives*, and (3) an *overview of the organization of the report*. The first section of the introduction should contain a description of the management problem and the factors that influence it. The researcher cannot assume that everyone who reads the report is familiar with the underlying problem.

The next section of the introduction should be a concise statement of the objectives, which will involve the management problem and its translation into a research problem. The objectives arise out of the background data, but are so critical that they should be stated explicitly. The introduction should conclude with a brief overview of the organization of the report.

Methodology and Limitations.   This section *summarizes* the methodology used to meet the objectives of the research project. Technical details should be minimized. Where necessary, such details should be placed in appendixes. The researcher must remember that, although he or she is deeply interested in research design, managers are not. This should *not* be the major section of the report.

The researcher should not overlook or hide any problems in the research. Furthermore, care should be taken to point out limitations that are apparent to skilled researchers but that a manager might overlook. For example, the danger in generalizing to the national market from local studies or the potential problems of nonresponse error are often overlooked by executives. This section should, without unduly degrading the overall quality of the work, indicate the nature of any potential limitations.

Findings.   The major portion of the report should be devoted to the findings, which should be organized around the objectives of the study. The findings should not consist of an endless series of statistical tables. Instead they should describe, in meaningful terms, what the research found. Summary tables and visual aids (charts, graphs, and the like) should be used to clarify the discussion. Detailed findings are presented in appendixes.

RESEARCH APPLICATION 19–2

Table of Contents from a Research Report

Table of Contents

	Page No.
Major Findings and Recommendations	1
Why This Study Was Done	5
How the Study Was Done	8
Qualitative Phase	
I. What Do Women Say About Margarine?	11
II. What Do They Use It For?	14
III. How Do They Feel About Different Brands?	16
IV. Hypotheses Generated	20
Quantitative Phase	
I. What Does the Market Look Like?	22
II. How Do Premier and Delight Fit into the Margarine Market?	32
III. A Closer Look at Premier	36
IV. A Closer Look at Delight	48
V. What About Butter?	62
VI. Some Special Issues	70
Marketing Implications	76
Detailed Tables	82
Questionnaire Material	104

Recommendations.   This section often has a title like "Marketing Implications" or "Action Recommendations." It should make one or more specific recommendations on each aspect of the management problem the research was designed to assist in solving. These recommendations *must* be explicitly related to the research findings:

> *Since over 80 percent of the respondents preferred the enhanced package design, we do not need to introduce both the standard and the enhanced version.*

Appendixes.   Items that will appeal to only a few readers or that may be needed only for occasional references should be confined to an appendix. Details of the sampling plan, detailed statistical tables, interview verification procedures, copies of questionnaires and interview instructions, and similar items generally belong in an appendix.

An Example.   Many of the points we have been discussing are illustrated in Research Application 19–2. This table of contents was taken from a report conducted for a margarine producer. The purpose of the study was to "gain an understanding of consumer behavior within the margarine market" in order to "create more effective marketing strategies" for the firm's two margarine brands. The impetus for the study was a decline in brand share for both brands. The study involved a series of focus groups followed by a major survey.

Notice that the headings are *action-oriented*—"How the Study Was Done" not "Methodology." This is much more likely to attract the manager's interest. Although the titles are different, the table of contents parallels the one we have recommended. This table of contents serves as an effective invitation to read the report as well as a guide to its contents. The report itself encouraged readership through its quality typing, ample white space, effective graphics, and limited verbiage.

Transmittal Letter.   A research report is not simply dropped on a manager's desk. Instead, it is delivered with a transmittal letter (or memo if it is an internal research department). The transmittal letter (1) identifies the research report, (2) restates the authorization for the study, and (3) indicates who is receiving copies of the report. It may also focus the manager's attention on key aspects of the report. Finally, it is the appropriate place to initiate follow-up research—"I'll call you after you've had a chance to read this to discuss some follow-up suggestions."

Preparing Oral Presentations

Most research proposals and projects involve one or more oral reports. Major projects frequently require a series of interim reports that are generally oral. Oral reports are also commonly made at the proposal and the conclusion of projects. These oral reports may follow or precede the preparation and distribution of a written report. Upper-level managers often base decisions on the oral report. Therefore, we cannot overemphasize how critical this task is. As one successful researcher states: "After working 6 months or more on a project, the researcher may get 30 to 60 minutes of top management's time. The oral report had better be effective!"

The first step in ensuring that the oral report is effective is the same as for a written report—an analysis of the audience. The next step is the development of a detailed report outline or, preferably, a written *script* for the report. Once the oral presentation is prepared, it should be rehearsed. Even highly trained actors and speakers typically rehearse material before they make a formal presentation. Researchers, generally with limited training in oral presentations, should plan on several "dry runs" before making a presentation to management. If practical, these dry runs should be recorded on VCR equipment and carefully analyzed.

The use of visual aids is essential for oral presentations. The oral presentation of a list of several numbers or percentages simply will not register on many listeners. Even the visual presentation of the numbers in a table often does not have the necessary impact. Most people have to "study" a table to understand it. Therefore, oral presentations should make extensive use of the

RESEARCH APPLICATION 19–3

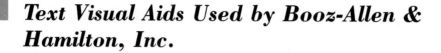

Text Visual Aids Used by Booz-Allen & Hamilton, Inc.

Project Overview . . .
Study results suggest . . .

* Managers have set higher new product targets for the next five years
* A complex external environment will challenge new product managers during the 1990s
* From an internal perspective, a short-term orientation by management is the major obstacle to successful new product development today

* Over the last decade, several refinements have been made to the new product process
  —New products frequently fulfill defined strategic roles
  —Many companies establish formal criteria to measure new product performance
  —Greater prescreening and planning have improved the effectiveness of new product expenditures
  —New product requirements drive the choice of new product organization

various charting techniques referred to earlier as well as any other appropriate visual aids. In fact, most research presentations are built around a complete set of visual aids.

Research Applications 19–3 and 19–4 show two visual aids used in a presentation by Booz-Allen & Hamilton, Inc. Application 19–3 is a chart used to structure and highlight the overview, whereas Application 19–4 presents numerical data.

A *flip chart* is a large pad of blank paper mounted on an easel. Visual aids are drawn on the pages in advance, and the speaker flips to the appropriate chart while progressing through the talk. The use of colored felt-tip pens can increase the impact of the flip chart. Blank pages and/or extra flip charts should be available so that new exhibits can be created as the need arises.

Overhead projectors are widely used to show previously prepared images against a screen or wall. The materials presented in this manner can range from simple charts to complex overlays. An overlay is produced by the successive additions of new images to the screen without removing the previous images. In addition, the speaker can write on the transparency and the writing will appear on the screen.

The potential impact of overhead projectors was reflected in a study involving 36 group meetings in which two speakers presented pro and con positions concerning the introduction of a new product. The use of overhead projectors was systematically varied between the speakers. The results shown in Table 19–2 indicate the positive effect of this visual aid.

Slides of anything that can be photographed can be projected onto a screen. Although these slides are not as flexible as those used on overhead projectors

RESEARCH APPLICATION 19–4

Graphic Visual Aid Used by Booz-Allen & Hamilton, Inc.

CURRENT PRACTICES AND TRENDS . . .

TODAY, ONE THIRD OF THE COMPANIES SURVEYED DO NOT FORMALLY MEASURE NEW PRODUCT PERFORMANCE

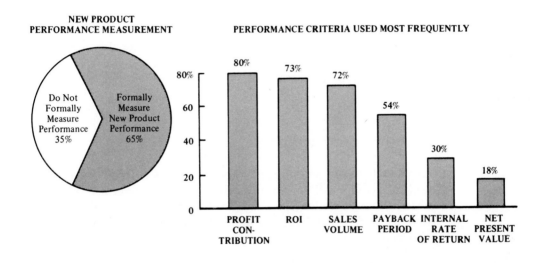

TABLE 19–2 Influence of Overhead Projectors (OHP) on Group Decisions

OHP used to promote "Go" position	Go	67%
	No Go	33%
OHP used to promote "No Go" position	Go	33%
	No Go	67%
No projector used to promote either position	Go	50%
	No Go	50%

SOURCE: The Wharton Applied Research Center, the Wharton School, The University of Pennsylvania (1981).

(that is, they cannot be written on while in use), remote-control, magazine-loaded projectors allow a smooth, evenly paced presentation using this technique. The ability to make color slides directly from computer monitors is a significant advantage of this approach.

Videotape equipment (VCR) coupled with large-screen projectors is gaining use in research presentations. It is particularly useful for presenting parts of focus group interviews, showing how product tests were conducted, and presenting other material that does not lend itself to a static presentation.

Finally, *projectors* similar to VCR projectors can be attached to personal computers to project the monitor image onto a screen. This is particularly useful when mathematical or accounting models or formulas have been developed. Executives can then ask "what if" questions that can be answered immediately.

For example, a research project might forecast a market share of 40 percent for a new product. Part of the report might contain a five-year cash flow and income statement projection. If this is contained in a personal computer, an executive can ask: "What if our market share is actually 35 percent (or 45 percent)?", and the researcher merely needs to enter this one number. The computer will quickly produce new five-year cash flow and income statements that can be projected onto the screen.

Reading Research Reports

Substantially more people read research reports than write them. Managers need to develop skill in reading research reports (and listening to research presentations) in order to evaluate the usefulness of the research results. The Advertising Research Foundation has developed a set of guidelines that managers can follow to evaluate research reports.[6] A brief summary follows.

Origin—What Is Behind the Research. The report should contain a clear statement of why the research was conducted, who sponsored it, and who conducted it. Key questions:

- Does the report identify the organizations (divisions, departments) that requested the research?
- Does it contain a statement of purpose that clearly states what the research was to accomplish?
- Are the organizations that defined and conducted the research identified?

Design—The Concept and the Plan. The research approach, the sample, and the analysis should be described clearly, and they should be appropriate for the purpose of the study. Key questions:

- Is there a complete, nontechnical description of the research design?
- Is the design consistent with the purpose for which the research was conducted?
- Does any aspect of the design, including the measuring instrument(s), induce any bias (particularly bias in favor of the sponsor)?

- Does the design control for patterns of sequence or timing or other external factors that might prejudice the results?
- Are the respondents capable of answering the questions raised?
- Is there a precise statement of the populations the research is to represent?
- Does the sampling frame fairly represent the population?
- Does the report specify the type of sample used and describe the method of sample selection?
- Does the report describe how the data are analyzed?
- Are copies of the questionnaire, field and sampling instructions, and other materials available in the appendix or on file?

Execution—Collecting and Handling the Information.   Data should be carefully collected by competent people using forms and methods appropriate for the task. Key questions:

- Does the report describe the data collection procedures including "quality control" procedures?
- Does the report specify the proportion of the selected sample from which information was collected?
- Were those who collected the data treated in a manner that would minimize any bias they might introduce?

Stability—Sample Size and Reliability.   The sample size should be reported and it should be large enough to yield stable results. Key questions:

- Is the sample large enough to provide stable findings?
- Are sampling error limits shown (if applicable)?
- Is the calculation of sampling error, or the lack of such a calculation, explained?
- Does the treatment of sampling error make clear that it does not include nonsampling error?
- For the major findings, are the reported error tolerances based on direct analysis of the variability of the collected data?

Applicability—Generalizing the Findings.   The research report should clearly indicate the boundaries which limit the findings. Key questions:

- Does the report specify when the data were collected?
- Does the report state clearly whether its results apply beyond the direct source of the data?
- Is it clear which groups, if any, are underrepresented in the data?
- If the research has limited applications, is there a statement describing who or what it represents and the times and conditions under which it applied?

Meaning—Interpretations and Conclusions.   All assumptions and judgments involved in reaching any findings, conclusions, or recommendations should be clearly specified. Key questions:

- Are the measurements described in simple and direct language?
- Does the use of the measurements make sense?

• Are the actual findings clearly differentiated from any interpretation of the findings?
• Has rigorous objectivity and candid reporting been used in interpreting research findings as evidence of causation or as predictive of future behavior?

Candor—Open Reporting and Disclosure.   The research should be an honest, complete description of the research process and outcome. Key questions:

• Is there a full and forthright disclosure of how the research was done?
• Have all the potentially relevant findings been presented?

As a user of a research project, you need to know what the results of the study are and how accurate they are likely to be. The Advertising Research Foundation guidelines can assist you in this evaluation.

Summary

Marketing research is conducted to help management make a decision. A marketing research report should be prepared with this in mind. The objective of a research report is to communicate the results and implications of a research study to management in a concise and interesting manner.

A written research report should follow these guidelines: (1) focus on the objectives of the study, (2) minimize technical details, (3) use an appropriate vocabulary, (4) avoid errors in grammar and spelling, (5) be as interesting as possible, and (6) use visual aids whenever possible. Most research reports are organized as follows: (1) title page, (2) executive summary, (3) table of contents, (4) introduction, (5) methodology and limitations, (6) findings, (7) recommendations, and (8) appendixes.

Oral presentations are based on the same general guidelines as written presentations. Effective visual aids are even more critical in oral presentations.

Managers need to be skilled at reading and listening to research reports critically. This involves questioning seven aspects of the research: (1) its origin, (2) its design, (3) its execution, (4) its stability, (5) its applicability, (6) its meaning, and (6) the candor of the report.

Review Questions

19.1. What is meant by "focus on the audience" when writing a research report?

19.2. How do the objectives of the study relate to the writing of the research report?

19.3. What is a *bar chart?*

19.4. What is a *line chart?*

19.5. When is a *line chart* preferred over a *bar chart?*

19.6. What is a *pie chart?*

19.7. What is a *histogram?*

19.8. What is a *flow diagram?*

19.9. How should numbers be rounded for use in research reports?

19.10. How should a report be organized?

19.11. What should go on the title page?

19.12. What should go in the introduction section?

19.13. What should go in the methodology section?

19.14. What should go in the limitations section?

19.15. What should go in the conclusions section?

19.16. What should go in the transmittal letter?

19.17. How should one prepare for an oral presentation?

19.18. What visual aids are available for oral presentations?

19.19. How does one read or evaluate a research report?

19.20. Why is it critical to avoid spelling and grammar errors in research reports?

Discussion Questions/Problems

19.21. Develop one or more visual aids to present the following data, showing the relationship between store sales and profits and the computer software department's sales and profits. Do you prefer a graphic presentation or the table? Which do you think the typical executive prefers? Why?

	Sales		Profits	
Year	Store	Software	Store	Software
1984	$ 7,500,000	$ 785,000	$ 695,000	$ 98,900
1985	8,700,000	863,000	760,000	108,700
1986	10,056,000	927,000	846,000	117,400
1987	11,624,000	908,000	996,000	121,200
1988	13,681,000	1,101,000	1,052,000	127,600
1989	14,022,000	1,197,000	1,092,000	130,500
1990	15,383,000	2,305,000	1,333,000	148,600
1991	17,766,000	3,536,000	1,567,000	172,200
1992	19,913,000	4,756,000	1,723,000	183,300
1993	21,991,000	5,987,000	1,896,000	200,100

19.22. Using the data in problem 19.22, develop a visual aid to emphasize:
   a. the growth of store sales
   b. the growth of software sales
   c. the growth of store profits
   d. the growth of software profits
   e. the impact of software profits on store profits for 1993
   f. the impact of software sales on store sales for 1993
   g. the change in profits as a percentage of sales over time

19.23. As a new marketing researcher for a medium-sized department store, you have been asked to prepare a report showing what happens to sales revenue after it is received. The report will be presented at the annual stockholders meeting. Investigation reveals the following figures. Prepare a visual aid for use in the report.

Net sales (revenue)	$7,000,000
Cost of goods sold	4,500,000
Salesforce compensation	600,000
Administrative salaries	250,000
Overhead (rent, insurance, etc.)	400,000
Inventory shrinkage (spoilage, theft, etc.)	150,000
Advertising	125,000
Taxes (local, state, and federal)	375,000
Aftertax profit	600,000

19.24. Average daily sales for a grocery store were found to be Monday, $220,000; Tuesday, $100,000; Wednesday, $145,000; Thursday, $100,000; Friday, $140,000; Saturday, $225,000. Prepare a visual aid to show this information.

19.25. A survey produced the following data on television viewing during weekday evenings. Prepare one or more visual aids for presentation of these data.

	Absolute Frequency	Relative Frequency	Cumulative Frequency
Less than 0.1 hrs	12	06.8	06.8
0.1–1.0 hrs	33	18.8	25.6
1.1–2.0 hrs	26	14.8	40.4
2.1–3.0 hrs	50	28.4	68.8
3.1–4.0 hrs	55	31.2	100.0
	176	100.0	

19.26. Prepare a visual aid for presentation of the following annual sales data (in thousands).

1970	$2,220	1976	$2,515	1982	$2,600	1988	$3,400
1971	2,460	1977	3,270	1983	2,510	1989	3,800
1972	2,800	1978	3,770	1984	2,580	1990	4,200
1973	2,815	1979	4,250	1985	2,700	1991	4,375
1974	2,920	1980	4,925	1986	2,880	1992	4,850
1975	2,850	1981	5,030	1987	2,975	1993	5,100

19.27. Using the following data, develop a visual aid to emphasize the growth of sales and profits and a second visual aid to emphasize the change in profits as a percentage of sales.

Year	Sales (000)	Profits (000)	Year	Sales (000)	Profits (000)
1988	$16,200	$2,000	1991	$37,000	$3,900
1989	22,400	2,800	1992	54,100	4,800
1990	29,200	3,200	1993	64,000	6,300

19.28. The following paragraph was part of a research report presented to a group of small retailers. The preceding paragraphs had described a constant-sum scale as "a means of developing interval level quantitative expressions representing individual's internal psychological states."

"Each respondent was required to allocate a number of points to each retail outlet such that the total allocation of points was proportionate to their relative shopping preferences across all the outlets. From their individual allocations across the entire set of stimulus stores, we compiled an overall mean score with a standard deviation for the relative preference of each outlet. These mean scores and their standard deviations were then used to predict respondents' actual allocation of their shopping trips over the study interval. The resulting correlation coefficient between the constant sum allocation and the shopping trip allocation was .92."

Rewrite the paragraph so that it is stated in the way you think is appropriate for the readers (small retailers).

19.29. Two samples of consumers were asked to evaluate two versions of a new product. Attitude measurements were made for one sample for version A and for the other sample for version B.

Write a paragraph describing the fact that the mean attitude score for version A of the new product was 83 compared to a mean score of 74 for version B of the product. Assume that a Z test indicates that the probability of a Type I error is .42. Also assume that the audience for the report does not have a background in statistics.

19.30. Develop a visual aid to introduce and summarize the following discussion:

"We will conduct a series of focus group interviews with retailers and with wholesalers to obtain their attitudes on the issue. At the same time we will conduct an extensive analysis of secondary data. Based on these findings, we will design several alternative packages. These will then be evaluated by separate samples of retailers and wholesalers. The package will be redesigned in light of these evaluations and one or more revised versions will be subjected to a controlled store test to obtain consumer reactions."

19.31. Prepare a visual aid to summarize the following conclusions from a series of focus group interviewers:

"The decision to install a solar hot water heater is determined primarily by the household's overall attitude toward the environment and their perception of the economic savings generated by the solar system. Secondary influencing factors are the length of time the family expects to live in the home and their financial liquidity."

19.32. Convert the following sentence to a table and an appropriate chart:
Between 1980 and 1990, the population of the various age groups in the United States changed as follows: (1) under 5, +3.2 million; (2) 5–13, +0.6 million; (3) 14–17, −3.4 million; (4) 18–24, −5.0 million; (5) 24–34, +4.3 million; (6) 35–44, +10.2 million; (7) 45–54, +2.2 million; (8) 55–64, −0.8 million; and (9) 65 and over, +4.3 million.

Projects/Activities

19.33. Examine the latest two issues of the *Journal of Marketing Research* and the *Harvard Business Review*. Evaluate the differences in reporting style and speculate on the reasons for the differences.

19.34. Examine several issues of the *Journal of Marketing Research* or the *Journal of Marketing*. Find two cases in which data could have been presented more effectively. Prepare a more effective presentation and show both versions to the class.

19.35. Using the data in Table 16–2, write a research report.

19.36. Repeat 19.35, but instead of a report prepare and give an oral presentation.

19.37. Examine the annual reports from several companies. Identify exceptionally good and exceptionally weak presentations of data.

19.38. Read several articles in the *Journal of Marketing Research*. Find five sentences that are unnecessarily complex or are otherwise unclear. Prepare more effective sentences and show both versions to the class.

Notes

1. R. G. Stout, "Intangibles Add to Results," *Advertising Age* (October 20, 1980), S-39.
2. This section is based on A. S. C. Ehrenberg, "Rudiments of Numeracy," in J. Sheth, *Research in Marketing* 2 (New York: JAI Press Inc., 1979), 191–216; and B. D. Sorrels, *Business Communication Fundamentals* (New York: Merrill Publishing, 1984).
3. S. H. Britt, "The Writing of Readable Research Reports," *Journal of Marketing Research* (May 1971), 265.
4. Britt, op. cit.
5. H. L. Gordon, "Eight Ways to Dress a Research Report," *Advertising Age* (October 20, 1980), S-37.
6. Public Affairs Council, *Guidelines for the Public Use of Market and Opinion Research* (New York: Advertising Research Foundation, 1981).

20

Ethical Issues in Marketing Research

LEARNING OBJECTIVES

Upon completion of this chapter, you should be able to:

1. Explain the critical importance of an ethical approach to marketing research.

2. Describe the ethical issues involved in protecting the public.

3. Describe the ethical issues involved in protecting the respondents.

4. Describe the ethical issues involved in protecting the client.

5. Describe the ethical issues involved in protecting the research firm.

6. Describe the ethical issues involved in protecting the research profession.

7. Critically evaluate the ethics of a research proposal or practice.

Ethical Issues in Bristol-Myers' Use of Marketing Research to Support an Advertising Claim

The commercial featured a well-known fashion model saying: "In shampoo tests with over 900 women like me, *Body on Tap* got higher ratings than *Prell* for body. Higher than *Flex* for conditioning. Higher than *Sassoon* for strong, healthy-looking hair."

The supporting research had several groups of approximately 200 women each test just one shampoo. They rated it on a six-step scale, from "outstanding" to "poor," for 27 separate attributes, such as body and conditioning. Nine hundred women did not make product-to-product comparisons between *Body on Tap* and *Sassoon*, or between *Body on Tap* and any of the other brands mentioned. In fact, no woman in the tests tried more than one shampoo.

The basis for the claim that the women preferred *Body on Tap* to *Sassoon* for "strong, healthy looking hair" was to combine the data for the "outstanding" and "excellent" ratings and discard the lower four ratings on the scale. The figures then were 36 percent for *Body on Tap* and 24 percent (of a separate group of women) for *Sassoon*. When the "very good" and "good" ratings were combined with the "outstanding" and "excellent" ratings, however, there was no difference between the two products in the category of "strong, healthy looking hair."

The research was conducted for Bristol-Myers by Marketing Information Systems, Inc. (MISI), using a technique known as blind monadic testing. The president of MISI testified that this method typically is employed when what is wanted is an absolute response to a product "without reference to another specific product." Although he testified that blind monadic testing was used in connection with comparative advertising, that was not the purpose for which Bristol-Myers retained MISI. Rather, they wished to determine consumer reaction to the introduction of *Body on Tap*.

Sassoon also found some other things wrong with the tests and the way they were represented in the Bristol-Myers advertisements. The fashion model said 900 women "like me" tried the shampoos. Actually, one-third of the women were aged 13–18. This was significant because *Body on Tap* appealed disproportionately to teenagers, and the advertising executive

519

who created the campaign for Bristol-Myers testified that its purpose was to attract a large portion of the *adult* women's shampoo market.

Sassoon commissioned its own research to support its legal position. ASI Market Research, Inc. showed the *Body on Tap* commercial, along with other material, to a group of 635 women and then asked them several questions individually.

Some 95 percent of those who responded said each of the 900 women referred to in the commercial had tried two or more brands. And 62 percent said that the tests showed [that] *Body on Tap* was competitively superior.[1]

The Nature of Ethical Issues in Marketing Research

Is it ethical to use research data as Bristol-Myers did in this example? Earlier, both observational and projective techniques were described as means of gathering data that respondents are unable or *unwilling* to provide in response to direct questioning. Should opinions be elicited that the respondent does not want to give? In Chapter 8, we described how many advertising testing firms deceive respondents by indicating that the purpose of the test is to evaluate the program or magazine that contains the ad. Is such deception acceptable?

Many questions such as these—*ethical questions*—are involved in the marketing research process.[2] Research Application 20–1 presents several specific research practices that some individuals might view as being less than completely ethical.

It is essential that we, as marketing research students, practitioners, and professors, develop an awareness of and concern for the ethical issues of our profession. The process of studying and practicing a profession can apparently alter an individual's perceptions of the rights and prerogatives of that profession.[3] Thus, a person engaging in marketing research may unknowingly use techniques and practices that the general public considers unethical. Therefore, we should examine our field for activities that may be questionable in the view of the general public. Such an examination should lead to research practices in line with the general ethical expectations of society.

This approach is not only "good" in some absolute sense, but it is also self-serving. Most of us would prefer to maintain high standards of conduct voluntarily rather than have standards set and enforced by governmental action.[4] However, every year numerous state legislatures consider bills regulating various aspects of the research process. For example, California, Florida, Michigan, New Jersey, Ohio, and Wyoming recently considered laws that would permit persons to have an asterisk beside their names in phone books indicating they do not want unsolicited calls. Survey researchers could be bound by this as would the various telemarketing organizations. If passed,

RESEARCH APPLICATION 20–1

Specific Research Practices with Ethical Implications

1. Research has consistently found that including a small amount of money in a mail survey greatly increases the response rate. Promises of money for returning the questionnaire are much less effective. One explanation is that respondents experience guilt if they do not complete a questionnaire for which they have already been "paid," but find it not worth their while to complete a questionnaire for the amount of money usually promised. Based on this, a research firm puts 25¢ in all its mail surveys.

2. A research firm specializes in telephone surveys. It recently began using voice pitch analysis in an attempt to determine if respondents were distorting their answers to sensitive questions.

3. A mall intercept facility recently installed hidden eye-tracking equipment. Now, when respondents are asked to view advertisements or packages, they are not told that their eye movements are being recorded.

4. The research director of a large corporation is convinced that using the company's name in surveys with consumers produces (1) lowered response rates and (2) distorted answers. Therefore, the firm routinely conducts surveys using the title Public Opinion Institute.

5. A company dramatically cuts the price of its products in a city where a competitor is test marketing a new product.

6. An insurance company uses a variety of projective techniques to assist in preparing advertisements for life insurance. Potential respondents are told that the purpose of the tests is to isolate factors that influence creativity.

7. A survey finds that 80 percent of the doctors responding do not recommend any particular brand of margarine to their patients who are concerned about cholesterol. Five percent recommend Brand A, 4 percent recommend Brand B, and no other brand is recommended by over 2 percent of the doctors. The company runs an advertisement that states: "More doctors recommend Brand A margarine for cholesterol control than any other brand."

such laws could make random digit dialing impossible. Equally restrictive rules are currently under consideration in the EC.[5]

A final benefit from a highly ethical approach to the marketing research process is improved public acceptance. Public acceptance is absolutely essential for the survival of marketing research. This is true for the general public, which provides most of the data, and for managers who base decisions on the data.

Survey research is the type of research most likely to involve the general public directly. Table 20–1 indicates that it enjoys a reasonable degree of acceptance among the general population. However, it should be noted that

TABLE 20–1 Public Perceptions of Survey Research

	1978	1982	1986	1990
Positive Image Attributes	%	%	%	%
The research industry serves a useful purpose	85	84	85	86
Polls and research surveys are used to help manufacturers produce better products	81	80	83	85
Answering questions in polls or surveys is an interesting experience	70	66	67	61
Answering questions in polls or research surveys is in my own best interest	72	68	70	67
Survey research firms maintain the confidentiality of answers	—	61	62	53
Negative Image Attributes				
Some questions asked in polls or research surveys are too personal	42	49	45	47
The term "poll" or "research survey" is used to disguise a sales pitch	43	38	40	40
Polls or research surveys are an invasion of privacy	31	26	24	25
Answering questions in polls or research surveys is a waste of time	17	21	19	18
Last Interview Evaluation				
Pleasant experience	84	83	78	74
Unpleasant experience	6	6	9	10

SOURCE: B. J. Kyzr-Sheeley, "Results of Walker's 1986 Industry Image Study," *The Marketing Researcher*, Vol. 16, No. 3; and *Walker: Industry Image Study* (Indianapolis, Walker Research Inc., 1990). Used with permission from Walker Research Inc.

almost half the households contacted for this "survey on surveys" refused to participate. It is very likely that those who refuse to participate in a survey have substantially more negative attitudes toward research than those who participate.[6]

Unfortunately, we do not have a list of ethical and unethical marketing practices that covers all the situations the marketing researcher may face. Several issues are controversial within the profession. Some widely accepted social values, such as the individual's right to privacy, support one position; whereas equally accepted values, such as the individual's right to seek knowledge, may support an opposing position. Where does one turn for guidance in ethical conduct when engaged in marketing research? Models for ethics in the general field of marketing have been proposed by a number of authors.[7] Each of those models provides useful insights and a general guide for action. However, none is specific enough to provide an unambiguous guide to behavior in specific marketing research situations.

CASRO (Council of American Survey Research Organizations) provides several guidelines for the ethical conduct of survey research. The American Marketing Association provides a Marketing Research Code of Ethics. The International Chamber of Commerce and the European Society for Opinion and Marketing Research have developed the ICC/ESOMAR International

Code of Marketing and Social Research Practice, which is much more detailed and situation specific.[8]

Recent research indicates that the presence of an explicit, *enforced*, company-specific code of ethics has a substantial impact on the behavior of those engaged in the research process.[9] Therefore, organizations should formulate, communicate, and enforce explicit statements of ethical expectations in marketing research. One survey found that 60 percent of research suppliers, 43 percent of field agencies, and 19 percent of corporate clients had written research codes of ethics.[10]

Five distinct entities are affected by the research process: (1) the general public, (2) the respondents in the specific study, (3) the client, (4) the researcher, and (5) the research profession. Specific ethical issues relating to each of these groups are discussed next.

Ethical Issues Involving Protection of the Public

A true profession focuses first on the needs of the public or innocent third parties. A falsified research report used to justify funding for the client by a bank would be unethical (and illegal), despite the fact that it might be economically advantageous to *both* the researcher and the client. Three major areas of concern arise in this context: *incomplete reporting, misleading reporting,* and *nonobjective research.*

Almost a third of the marketing executives and research practitioners responding to a recent survey felt that these three practices are common. (About 40 percent felt they were uncommon.)[11] The Advertising Research Foundation's *Guidelines for the Public Use of Market Research* described in Chapter 19 focuses on these issues. Additional discussion is provided here.

Incomplete Reporting

A client or researcher withholding information that could be useful to the public is analogous to a seller of a product not disclosing potentially damaging information about a product in a sales presentation to the buyer. Both attempt to mislead potential buyers by leaving them uninformed about undesirable features or characteristics of the product.

More common than the temptation to omit negative information is the temptation to avoid reporting situational details that are necessary to interpret the obtained results properly. For example, a common use of test market data is to persuade the trade (wholesalers and retailers) to stock and promote the new item. Therefore, some firms choose to conduct test markets in areas where their distribution or reputation is particularly strong.[12] Failure to report this fact could cause the trade to misinterpret the market response to the item.

Misleading Reporting

Misleading reporting involves presenting the research results in such a manner that the intended audience will draw a conclusion that is not justified by the results. This sometimes occurs when research results are used in advertising campaigns.

For example, an ad claimed that following comparison tests, "an amazing 60 percent" of a sample of consumers said that Triumph cigarettes tasted as good as or better than Merit. This was indeed indicated by the results. However, since many respondents said the brands tasted the same (as good as), the results also indicated that *64 percent said that Merit tasted as good as or better than Triumph!*[13] The public presentation of the results as done for Merit cigarettes would most likely mislead a substantial portion of the general public. The *Body on Tap* story at the beginning of this chapter provides a more detailed example of misleading reporting of research results.

Figure 20–1 illustrates two technically correct ways of presenting the same information. The top version would lead many to conclude that a very significant decrease in unit sales cost had occurred. The bottom chart leaves a different impression.[14]

Nonobjective Research

The researcher, the client, or both would often benefit if certain research findings were obtained. There is no doubt that the "intentional or deliberate misrepresentation of research methods or results," specified in the American Marketing Association code, is unethical. However, research techniques can be selected that will maximize the likelihood of obtaining a given finding.

Conducting test markets in areas where the firm has an unusually strong distribution system or reputation is one example of nonobjective research. The question phrasing used by Burger King to support a comparative advertisement (see page 251) is another example. Calculating and reporting means rather than medians when a few extreme values distort the mean is a third form of nonobjective research.

Ethical Issues Involving Protection of Respondents

Three ethical issues confront researchers in their relationships with respondents; namely, the use of the guise of conducting a survey to sell products, the invasion of the privacy of the respondent, and abuse of the respondents.

Use of "Marketing Research" Guise to Sell Products

The use of the statement, "I am conducting a survey," as a guise for sales presentations or to obtain information for sales leads is a major concern of legitimate researchers. Both telephone and personal "interviews" have been used as an opportunity for sales solicitation. Some mail "surveys" have served to generate sales leads or mailing lists. These practices are termed *sugging* (selling under the guise of research) in the industry and are opposed by all legitimate researchers.

Forty-eight percent of those interviewed in a recent national survey reported exposure to a sales pitch disguised as a survey (21 percent within the past year).[15] Table 20–1 indicates widespread belief that this is a common practice.

A related ploy is to use a "survey" as a guise to solicit funds. This is commonly called *frugging* (fund-raising under the guise of research). Unfortunately, this technique appears to have been used by such respectable orga-

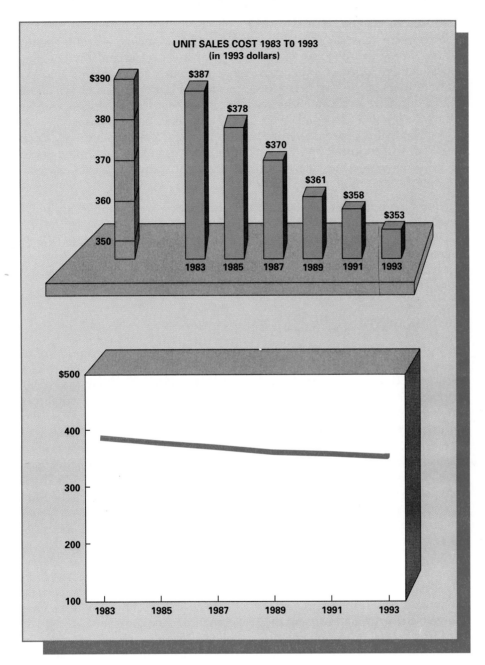

FIGURE 20–1 A Potentially Misleading Data Presentation

nizations as the Democratic Congressional Campaign Committee (DCCC) and the League of Women Voters.

For example, the DCCC sent a mailing with PRESIDENTIAL SURVEY EN-CLOSED, 1984 DEMOCRATIC PRESIDENTIAL SURVEY, in large dark type on the envelope. The heading on the cover letter, OFFICIAL 1984 DEMO-CRATIC PRESIDENTIAL SURVEY, was printed in large, bright blue letters.

The same heading appeared on the "questionnaire" in bright red letters. However, the "questionnaire" contained only two questions and a "contribution" form. The majority of the four-page cover letter and the one-page "questionnaire" focused on encouraging a monetary contribution.

The authors of this text believe that this use of "survey research" is unethical. In our view, any communication described to a respondent as a survey or interview should have the collection of data as its *sole* purpose.

This position is consistent with that taken by the Research Industry Coalition (RIC) and endorsed by all the major research groups in the United States. ESOMAR in Europe has taken a strong stand against these practices as well.[16] RIC specifically prohibits the following:

- Requiring a monetary payment or soliciting monetary contributions as part of a research process
- Offering products or services for sale or using participant contacts to generate sales leads
- Revealing the identity of respondents to a survey or of participants in a research process without their permission.[17]

Invasion of Privacy Respondents

The *right to privacy* refers to the public's general feeling or perception of its ability to restrict the amount of personal data it will make available to outsiders. The three important elements involved in this "right" are the *concept of privacy* itself, the concept of *informed consent* by which an individual can waive the right to privacy, and the concept that *anonymity and confidentiality* can help protect those whose privacy has, to some extent, been invaded.

The *right to privacy is the right of individuals to decide for themselves how much they will share with others* their thoughts, feelings, and the facts of their personal lives. What is private varies between individuals and within individuals from day to day and setting to setting. The essence of the concept is the right of *each individual to decide in each particular setting or compartment of his or her life how much to reveal.* As Table 20–1 shows, the public is concerned about the intrusion of marketing research into their privacy.

Informed consent: respondents agreeing to participate in a research study after having been provided complete information about the study.

Informed Consent.   Because the essence of the right of privacy is the individual's ability to *choose* what will be revealed, the marketing researcher must not abrogate the respondent's ability to choose. This requires the researcher to obtain the **informed consent** of the potential respondents.

Informed means providing potential respondents with sufficient information for them to determine whether participation is worthwhile and desirable, *from their point of view.* In general, this involves a description of the types of questions to be asked or the task required, the subject areas covered, the time and physical effort involved, and the ultimate use to which the resultant data will be put.

Few requests for cooperation for marketing research studies convey all of this information. It is common to withhold both the identity of the sponsor and the true purpose of the research from respondents. While the reason for doing so is to obtain more accurate information, it does make completely informed consent impossible. Research Application 20–2 provides an illus-

RESEARCH APPLICATION 20-2

Deception in Advertising Testing

ASI is a major research firm that conducts tests of advertising copy. ASI (and many other firms involved in advertising tests) recruits respondents to "evaluate" a potential television series or the editorial content of an existing or potential magazine. (See Research Application 8–4.) The actual purpose is to evaluate one or more ads contained in the program or magazine.

Is this ethical?

A Researcher's Perspective: We know from experience that we cannot get as accurate an assessment of the effectiveness of the ads if we inform people in advance that we are evaluating the ads. People will react differently to the ads when they know that the ads are the focal point of the study. No one is pressured to answer the questions about the ads. No one is harmed by this and the development of more effective ads benefits everyone.

A Respondent's View: I agreed to give my time to help develop a television program (magazine). I would not have given my time to develop an ad. I felt pressure to cooperate and answer all the questions in the interview after watching the program. I thought the questions about the ads were to help evaluate the program. I've been lied to. (There is no empirical evidence that respondents actually feel this way.)

---

tration and discussion of this practice. While evidence indicates that respondents expect and understand mild deception in marketing research studies,[18] researchers should engage in such practices only when no other options are available and the respondents are not harmed by the deception.

Observational studies are often conducted in a manner that precludes informed consent. Observing customers as they shop for automobiles or other items or as they consume a meal at a restaurant could lose much of its validity if they were informed that they were being observed. The Code of Conduct of the Market Research Society (United Kingdom) states ". . . *the subject must either give his consent or be in a situation where he could reasonably expect to be seen or heard.*" However, they take a stronger position about filming or recording these same behaviors: ". . . *he must again either give his consent or be in a situation where he could reasonably expect such recording to occur.*"[19]

While there is very little empirical evidence, it appears that most of the general public does not object to being observed while in public. However, a sizable minority does object.[20]

Anonymity and Confidentiality.   To the extent that full informed consent cannot be obtained, *anonymity* and *confidentiality* are important. **Anonymity** means that the identity of the subject is never known to anyone. **Confidentiality** means that the respondent's identity is known to only a limited number of investigators but is otherwise protected from dissemination.

Unfortunately, there is increasing concern about the ability or willingness of research firms to maintain the confidentiality of their data. This increased

Anonymity:
the identity of a subject in a study is never known to anyone.

Confidentiality:
the identity of a subject in a research study is made known only to a limited number of researchers.

concern probably arises from a combination of publicity about (1) the use of research to generate sales leads, (2) the theft and/or transferral of computerized data, and (3) the practice of magazines and other organizations selling their mailing lists.

Abuse of Respondents

Respondents can be abused in a variety of ways. Frequent interviewing of the same respondents is a form of abuse. For example, middle-class, younger (under 35) females are particularly likely to be interviewed frequently.

Overly long interviews are an abuse of the respondents. Table 20–1 indicates that many respondents view their last interview as lasting too long. This is particularly serious when respondents are uninformed or are misled concerning the length of the interview.

Confusing questions, poorly trained interviewers, hard-to-read questionnaires, and other factors that place an unnecessary burden on respondents should be avoided.[21] When respondents agree to give the researcher their time and energy, it is the researcher's responsibility to minimize the effort required of them.

Ethical Issues Involving the Protection of the Client

Every professional is obligated to protect the client in matters relating to their professional relationship. The marketing researcher is no exception. The matters in which the client may expect protection when authorizing a marketing research project include protection against (1) *abuse of position arising from specialized knowledge,* (2) *unnecessary research,* (3) *an unqualified researcher,* (4) *disclosure of identity,* (5) *treating data as nonconfidential and/or nonpropriety,* and (6) *misleading presentation of data.*

Protection Against Abuse of Position

The marketing manager is generally at a substantial disadvantage in discussing a research project. Most researchers have specialized knowledge and experience that the marketing manager cannot match. Therefore, the manager is frequently forced to accept the researcher's suggestions at face value, just as we often accept the advice of medical doctors or lawyers. Like other professionals, the marketing researcher often has the opportunity to take advantage of specialized knowledge to the detriment of the client. Recommending expensive primary data collection when less expensive secondary data would provide adequate information is an example of abuse of position.

Protection Against Unnecessary Research

Researchers are sometimes requested to engage in a specific research project that is unrelated to the underlying problem, has been done before, or is economically unjustified. A marketing researcher has a professional obligation to indicate to the client that, in his or her judgment, the research expenditure is not warranted. If, after this judgment has been *clearly* stated, the client still desires the research, the researcher should feel free to conduct the study. The reason for this is that the researcher can never know for certain the risk preferences and strategies that are guiding the client's behavior.

Protection Against Unqualified Researchers

Another area of concern involves the request for research that is beyond the capabilities or technical expertise of the individual researcher or research organization. The cost, both psychological and economic, of saying, "I cannot do this as well as some other individual" can be quite high. However, accepting a project beyond the researcher's capacities typically results in time delays, higher costs, and decreased accuracy.

Protection of Anonymity of Client

The client will have authorized a marketing research project either to help identify or to help solve marketing problems. In either case, it may well be to the advantage of competitors to know that the study is being done. The researcher is therefore obligated ethically to preserve the anonymity of the client. The fact that a particular firm is sponsoring a study should not be revealed to *any* outside party unless the client so agrees. This includes respondents and other existing and potential clients.

Protection of Confidential and Proprietary Information

The data generated for a particular client and the conclusions and interpretations from those data are the exclusive property of the client. It is obvious that a researcher should not turn over a client's study to one of the client's competitors. However, what if the researcher gathers basic demographic material on a geographic area for one client and the same information is required for a study by a noncompeting client? The American Marketing Association code is not clear on this point, but it seems to suggest that such data cannot be used twice without the explicit consent of the original client. Reuse of the data, assuming that permission is granted, should result in the two clients sharing the cost of this aspect of the research rather than the research organization charging twice.

One researcher clearly expresses the pressures and problems generated by this issue:

> I get involved in a number of proprietary studies. The problem that often arises is that some studies end up covering similar subject matter as previous studies. Our code of ethics states that you cannot use data from one project in a related project for a competitor. However, since I often know some information about an area, I end up compromising my original client. Even though upper management formally states that it should not be done, they also expect it to be done to cut down on expenses. This conflict of interest situation is difficult to deal with. At least in my firm, I don't see a resolution to the issue. It is not a one time situation, but rather a process that perpetuates itself. To make individuals redo portions of studies which have recently been done is ludicrous, and to forgo potential new business is almost impossible from a financial perspective.[22]

Protection Against Misleading Presentations of Data

Reports that are represented orally or are written in such a way as to deliberately give the impression of greater accuracy than the data warrant are obviously not in the best interest of the client. Reports can leave such an impression by a number of means. These include the use of *overly technical jargon, failure to round numbers properly, unnecessary use of complex analytic procedures,* and *incomplete reporting.*

Overly Technical Jargon.   All specialties tend to develop a unique terminology. By and large, this is useful as it allows those familiar with the field to communicate in a more concise and precise way. However, technical jargon and extensive mathematical notation can also convey a false aura of complexity and precision. The research report's primary function is to convey *to the client* the results of the research. It is not the proper place to demonstrate the complexity of sampling formulas or the range of terms that are unique to the research process.

Failure to Round Numbers Properly.   An impression of greater precision than the data warrant can also be created through the failure to round numbers properly. For example, a statement that the average annual expenditure by some group for furniture is $261.17 implies more precision than is generally warranted. If the researcher believes that the data are accurate to the nearest $10, the average should be rounded to $260. If the data were developed from a sample, the use of a confidence interval might be appropriate, as well.

Incomplete Reporting.   Incomplete reporting renders an objective appraisal of the research report impossible. An example should make this point clear. Assume that a sample is drawn from a population of 10,000 firms and the final report shows an obtained sample size of 750. On the surface, this may appear to be a reasonable sample size. However, unless other descriptive data are given, there is no way to estimate the potential impact of nonresponse error. An evaluation of the probable effects of this source of error requires a knowledge of the response rate. The 750 respondents could represent a response rate as low as 10 or 20 percent or as high as 100 percent. One's confidence in the resulting data would vary considerably between these two extremes.

Ethical Issues Involving Protection of the Research Firm

Several issues can arise in the research firm–client relationship in which the research organization needs protection. These include protection against *improper solicitation of proposals, disclosure of proprietary information* or *techniques,* and *misrepresentation of findings.*

Protection Against Improper Solicitation of Proposals

Research proposals should be requested *only* as an aid in deciding whether to conduct the research and/or which research firm to use. Similarly, proposals should be evaluated solely on their merit unless the other criteria (size and/or special capabilities of the research firm) are made known in advance. Proposals from one research firm should not be given to a second firm or an in-house research department for implementation.

Protection Against Disclosure of Proprietary Information or Techniques

Research firms often develop special techniques or information for dealing with certain types of problems. Examples are models predicting the success of new products, models for allocation of advertising expenditures among media, and simulation techniques for predicting effects of changes in the marketing mix variables. Research firms properly regard these techniques as being proprietary. The client should not make these techniques known to other research firms or appropriate them for its own use without the explicit consent of the developer.

Protection Against Misrepresentation of Findings

Suppose the *Honest and Ethical Research Firm* is commissioned to do a study of analgesics by the manufacturer of *Brand A* aspirin. In its report of the findings the statement is made that "Brand A aspirin was reported to be the aspirin most preferred by two of three respondents using only aspirin as an analgesic for headaches." In its advertising on television to consumers, however, the firm makes the statement, "According to a study conducted by the *Honest and Ethical Research Firm*, two of three consumers preferred *Brand A* aspirin to all other products for treatment of headaches."

This is a clear distortion of the findings. It not only misleads the viewer, but is potentially damaging to the research firm as well. Other manufacturers of analgesics will recognize that this is not a true statement and may conclude that the research firm is guilty either of a careless piece of research or of dishonesty in reporting the results.

Ethical Issues Involving Protection of the Research Profession

There is debate as to whether or not marketing research is a profession. It is the belief of your authors that the long-run viability of marketing research hinges on its being recognized as a profession. All of the issues we have described thus far affect the professional status of marketing research. In addition, three other concerns emerge.

Use of Accepted Research Procedures

While there are multiple ways to generate data relevant to most marketing problems, marketing researchers should follow sound research procedures or *clearly* indicate any departures. A profession attempts to "do it right" and treats "doing it right" as an end in itself.

RESEARCH APPLICATION 20–3

The Ethics of Using Marketing Research Technology to Select Juries and Develop Appeals to Juries

• A teenage girl is left a quadriplegic after an automobile accident. The defendant in a lawsuit for damages was the teenage driver of the car in which the girl was riding. The fact that the driver was heavily insured could not be admitted into evidence. The girl's lawyer was afraid the jury would be reluctant to impose a large judgment against the teenager.

The girl's lawyer hired a marketing research firm to conduct a community survey to determine the demographic characteristics of people most likely to hold a teenager liable for large damages. This information was used by the attorney to guide his jury selection.

• A simulated jury is a group of individuals with similar characteristics—such as age, gender, and political affiliation—as the members of the actual jury. The simulated jury either sits in the audience of the courtroom and reports its reactions to the actual proceedings or listens to lawyers present arguments that they plan to use in the trial and responds to both the content and the style of the presentation.

A simulated jury was used by IBM in a $300 million antitrust suit. Six individuals with backgrounds similar to the actual jury were paid to attend the trial each day (they did not know which side employed them). They weighed the evidence and reported their impressions each evening. IBM developed much of its strategy around this information. It won the case.

MCI Communications used simulated juries in an antitrust suit against AT&T. It used several mock juries that allowed its attorneys to try out various arguments *before* presenting them in front of the real jury. It won the largest award in history.

Marketing research professionals recognize that research that produces wrong managerial decisions harms the entire practice of marketing research. If marketing research is to become a true profession, quotations such as the one that follows must become nonexistent:

> The most difficult moral problem is how to handle a situation in which our company has made a mistake in study design (or in study execution) which results in obtaining results that are unreliable or invalid. We try to bury the mistake and concentrate on the valid parts of the study in those cases.[23]

Would you like your doctor to have this attitude?

Certification

In the U.S. as well as Europe and Japan, anyone can simply declare themselves to be marketing researchers. They can claim any specialization within the field of marketing research. There are no rules or regulations whatsoever concerning qualifications required for marketing researchers. Furthermore, there are no rules concerning membership in most professional marketing research societies or organizations. Thus, anyone can declare themselves marketing researchers and, if they have paid their dues, also indicate that they are members in good standing of the American Marketing Association.

Given the wide array of skills and specialties in marketing research, any type of certification will require substantial flexibility as well as creativity.[24] However, other complex disciplines such as law and accounting have benefited greatly from certification programs, as have their clients. For marketing research to become a true, respected profession, some form of certification is probably necessary.

Inappropriate Use of Marketing Research Techniques

Marketing research firms and others often use marketing research techniques in areas that at least some of the public feel should not be studied in this manner.

Most major political campaigns make extensive use of marketing research. There is concern about our national leaders using marketing research to develop positions that reflect what the public wants rather than trying to persuade the public to support what it needs. In addition, the early and frequent release of opinion poll results influences the ability of candidates to raise funds and otherwise gain support.

Research Application 20–3 describes another controversial use of marketing research technology.[25] Although there are no easy answers to the ethical questions raised by applying marketing research methodologies in courtroom situations, these questions have serious implications for both legal practice and marketing research.[26]

Summary

Marketing research should be conducted at the highest ethical level because (1) this is the right way to conduct any business activity, (2) such conduct reduces the likelihood of overly restrictive legislation, and (3) such conduct helps preserve the public acceptance that is essential for the continued existence of marketing research.

Five distinct entities can be adversely affected by unethical marketing research. The general public or other third parties can be harmed by incomplete reporting, misleading reporting, and nonobjective research. Respondents are harmed when research invades their privacy, is used as a guise to sell products or raise funds, or is abusive of their cooperation. Clients require protection from abuse of position, unnecessary research, unqualified researchers, disclosure of their identity, release of confidential data, and misleading presentations of data.

The research firm requires protection from improper solicitation of proposals, disclosure of proprietary techniques or information, and misrepresentation of findings. Any abuse of clients, respondents, the general public, or research firms also hurts the research profession. In addition, the profession is concerned with the use of nonstandard or inadequate research designs, the use of research techniques in inappropriate situations, and the lack of certification procedures for marketing researchers.

Review Questions

20.1. Why is an ethical approach to marketing important?

20.2. Describe the ethical issues involving the *protection of the public.*

20.3. Describe the ethical issues involving the *protection of the client.*

20.4. Describe the ethical issues involving the *protection of the research firm.*

20.5. Describe the ethical issues involving the *protection of the respondents.*

20.6. What is *informed consent?*

20.7. What is the difference between *anonymity* and *confidentiality?*

20.8. Describe the ethical issues involving the *protection of the marketing research profession.*

Discussion Questions/Problems

20.9. Discuss the ethical issues involved in the situations described in Research Application 20–1.

20.10. Discuss the ethical implications involved in Research Application 20–2.

20.11. Evaluate the code of ethics presented in Research Application 20–2.

20.12. Discuss the ethical implications of the practices described in Research Application 20–3.

20.13. Discuss the ethical implications of the following situations:[27]

   a. A project director recently came in to request permission to use ultraviolet ink in precoding questionnaires on a mail survey. He pointed out that the cover letter referred to an anonymous survey, but he said he needed respondent identification to permit adequate cross tabulations of the data. The M. R. director gave his approval.

   b. One product of the X company is brassieres, and the firm has recently been having difficulty making some decisions on a new line. Information was critically needed concerning the manner in which women put on their brassieres. So the M. R. director designed a study in which two local stores cooperated in putting one-way mirrors in their foundations dressing rooms. Observers behind these mirrors successfully gathered the necessary information.

   c. In a study intended to probe rather deeply into the buying motivations of a group of wholesale customers by use of a semistructured personal interview form, the M. R. director authorized the use of the department's special attaché case equipped with hidden tape recorders.

   d. Some of X company's customers are busy executives, hard to reach by normal interviewing methods. Accordingly, the market research department recently conducted a study in which interviewers called "long distance" from nearby cities. They were successful in getting through to busy executives in almost every instance.

e. In another study, this one concerning magazine reading habits, the M. R. director decided to contact a sample of consumers under the name of Media Research Institute. This fictitious company name successfully camouflaged the identity of the sponsor of the study.

f. In the trial run of a major presentation to the board of directors, the marketing vice-president deliberately distorted some recent research findings. After some thought, the M. R. director decided to ignore the matter since the marketing head obviously knew what he was doing.

20.14. Is it ethical to utilize projective techniques to determine an individual's attitudes about a product without disclosing the reason? Justify your answer.

20.15. A manufacturer of small appliances issues a guarantee with each appliance that covers more variables and a longer time period than any of its competitors. This guarantee is featured in the firm's advertising and on the product packages. However, for the guarantee to be effective, the consumer must first complete a questionnaire designed by the marketing research department. Is this an ethical approach to data collection?

20.16. "Individuals acquire telephones so that they can talk with whomever they wish and so that those wishing to talk with them can do so easily. If they do not wish to be called by people other than those they select, they can obtain an unlisted phone number. Therefore, marketing research techniques such as random digit dialing, which results in contacts with persons with unlisted numbers, are a direct invasion of a person's privacy. These techniques should be illegal. They are clearly unethical." Comment.

20.17. "Observational studies in which the subjects are not first informed that their behavior is being observed are unethical." Comment.

20.18. Would your answer to 20.17 change if the behavior were being videotaped? Why?

20.19. Clients sometimes request and even insist that a specific question be included in a questionnaire. How should the researcher react to this if it is felt that the question will produce biased data?

20.20. Develop a marketing research code of ethics. How, if at all, would this code be enforced?

20.21. Discuss the ethical implications of the following situations:[28]
a. Researcher poses as graduate student working on a thesis in order to gain information that competitors might not otherwise give.
b. Researcher calls the vice-president while he is at lunch, hoping to find the secretary who may have some information but is less likely to be suspicious about researcher's motives.
c. Researcher calls competitor's suppliers and distributors, pretending to do a study of the entire industry. Researcher poses as a representative of a private research firm and works at home during the project so that the company's identity is protected.

d. The competitor's representative is coming to a local college to recruit employees. Researcher poses as a student job-seeker to learn recruiting practices and other general information about competitor.

e. Researcher is asked to verify rumors that the competitor is planning to open a new plant in a small southern town. Researcher poses as an agent from a manufacturer looking for a site similar to the one that the competitor supposedly would need. Researcher uses this cover to become friendly with local representatives of the Chamber of Commerce, newspapers, realtors, etc.

f. Researcher corners a competitor's employee at a national conference and offers to buy drinks at the hotel bar. Several drinks later, the researcher asks the hard questions.

g. Researcher hires an individual who works for the competitor to serve as an informant to researcher's company.

20.22. Discuss the ethics of the following situations:

Pretests show that the average time to complete a particular telephone interview is 20 minutes. They also show a sharp drop in the response rate if respondents are told in advance that the interview will last 20 minutes. Telling them it will take 15 minutes does *not* reduce the response rate. The researcher

a. does not provide any information in advance on the length of the interview.

b. tells the respondent it "will take only a few minutes."

c. tells the respondent it "will take about 15 minutes."

20.23. How can a researcher honor a client's request for anonymity and a respondent's need for informed consent?

Projects/Activities

20.24. Develop a 10-point "ethical–unethical" and a 10-point "common–uncommon" scale for each of the situations in problem 20–13. Have 25 marketing majors and 25 nonbusiness majors evaluate each situation. Analyze the results and prepare a report.

20.25. Repeat 20.24 using the situations in problem 20.21.

20.26. Repeat 20.24 using the situations in Research Application 20–1.

20.27. Repeat 20.24 using a nonstudent group for the 25 nonbusiness majors.

20.28. Repeat 20.25 using a nonstudent group for the 25 nonbusiness majors.

20.29. Repeat 20.26 using a nonstudent group for the 25 nonbusiness majors.

20.30. Interview a marketing researcher. Report on his or her perceptions of the major ethical problems in the field.

20.31. Read (a) "Mind Control in the Courtroom," *Psychology Today* (March 1982), 66–73; and (b) "Marketing Research and Corporate Ligation," *Journal of Business Ethics* 3 (1984), 185–194. Prepare a report presenting your evaluation of the ethics of this use of marketing research.

20.32. Conduct two focus groups, one with business majors and one with liberal arts majors. Discuss the deception in Research Application 20–3 and report your results.

Notes

1. S. A. Diamond, "Market Research Latest Target in Ad Claims," *Advertising Age* (January 25, 1982), 52. Used with permission.
2. S. D. Hunt, L. B. Chonko, J. B. Wilcox, "Ethical Problems of Marketing Researchers," *Journal of Marketing Research* (August 1984), 309–324; and I. P. Akaah, E. A. Riordan, "Judgments of Marketing Professionals About Ethical Issues in Marketing Research," *Journal of Marketing Research* (February 1989), 112–120.
3. See W. French, M. Ebner, "A Practical Look at Research Ethics," *Journal of Data Collection* (Fall 1986), 49–53; and O. C. Ferrell, S. J. Skinner, "Ethical Behavior and Bureaucratic Structure in Marketing Research Organizations," *Journal of Marketing Research* (February 1988), 103–109.
4. C. J. Frey, T. C. Kinnear, "Legal Constraints and Marketing Research," *Journal of Marketing Research* (August 1979), 295–302; and R. Schweizer, "Present and Future Data Flow Legislation," *European Research* (January 1986), 29–34.
5. "Self-Regulated Research," *Marketing News* (January 2, 1987), 1; and J. Honomichl, "Legislation Threatens Research by Phone," *Marketing News* (June 24, 1991), 4.
6. See also S. W. McDaniel, P. Verille, C. S. Madden, "The Threats to Marketing Research," *Journal of Marketing Research* (February 1985), 74–80; and J. Goyder, "Surveys on Surveys," *Public Opinion Quarterly* (Spring 1986), 27–41.
7. See G. R. Laczniak, P. E. Murphy, *Marketing Ethics* (Lexington, MA: Lexington Books, 1985); O. C. Ferrell, L. G. Gresham, "A Contingency Framework for Understanding Ethical Decision Making in Marketing," *Journal of Marketing Research* (Summer 1985), 87–96; S. D. Hunt, S. Vitell, "A General Theory of Marketing Ethics," *Journal of Macromarketing* (Spring 1986), 5–16; A. J. Dubinsky, B. Loken, "Analyzing Ethical Decision Making in Marketing," *Journal of Business Research* (September 1989), 83–107; and M. A. Mayo, L. J. Marks, "An Empirical Investigation of a General Theory of Marketing Ethics," and S. Hunt, "Commentary" both in *Journal of the Academy of Marketing Science* (Spring 1990), 163–172, 173–178.
8. C. H. Winquist, C. C. J. de Koning, "ICC/ESOMAR International Code of Marketing and Social Research Practice," in R. Worcester, J. Downham, *Consumer Market Research Handbook* (New York: North-Holland, 1986), 813–826.
9. Ferrell, Skinner, op. cit. However, the presence of a written code without executive support has little impact (Mayo, Marks, op. cit.).
10. "Important Issues for the '90s," *Industry Image Study* (Indianapolis: Walker Research, Inc., 1990), 7.
11. I. P. Akaah, E. A. Riordan, "The Incidence of Unethical Practices in Marketing Research," *Journal of the Academy of Marketing Science* (Spring 1990), 143–152.
12. C. L. Hodock, "Intellectual Dishonesty," *Marketing News* (January 20, 1984), 1.
13. S. A. Diamond, "Market Research Latest Target in Ad Claims," *Advertising Age* (January 25, 1982), 52.
14. See S. J. Tordella, "How to Create Good Graphs," *American Demographics* (October 1988), 40–41.
15. "About the Interview Experience," *Industry Image Study* (Indianapolis: Walker Research, Inc., 1990), 5.
16. M. Bartram, P. Bartram, "Ethical Dilemmas of the Market Researcher," *European Research* (November 1988), 208–214.
17. "Research Group to Warn Violators," *Marketing News* (November 12, 1990), 5.
18. D. Toy, J. Olsen, L. Wright, "Effects of Debriefing in Marketing Research Involving 'Mild' Deceptions," *Psychology and Marketing* (Spring 1989), 69–85.
19. For an excellent discussion of informed consent, see S. Robson "Ethics," *Journal of the Market Research Society* (January 1991), 19–29.
20. A. Finn, "Consumer Observation in a Shopping Center" in P. Bloom, et al., eds. *Enhancing Knowledge Development in Marketing* (Chicago: American Marketing Association, 1989), 176–181.
21. See L. M. Sharp, J. Frankel, "Respondent Burden," *Public Opinion Quarterly* (Spring 1983), 36–53.
22. Hunt, Chonko, Wilcox, op. cit., 314.
23. Ibid.
24. See H. Schlossberg, "Consensus Eludes Certification Issue," *Marketing News* (September 11, 1989), 1.
25. L. B. Andrews, "Mind Control in the Courtroom," *Psychology Today* (March 1982), 66–73.
26. S. M. Smith, "Marketing Research and Corporate Litigation," *Journal of Business Ethics* 3 (1984), 185–194; and C. Schleier, "Lawyers, Court Help in Jury Selection," *Advertising Age* (November 14, 1985), 30–32.
27. C. M. Crawford, "Attitudes of Marketing Executives Toward Ethics in Marketing Research," *Journal of Marketing* (April 1970), 46–52. Used with permission of the American Marketing Association. See also I. P. Akaah, E. A. Riordan, "Judgments of Marketing Professionals About Ethical Issues in Marketing Research" *Journal of Marketing Research* (February 1989), 112–120.
28. Adopted from B. Whalen, "Business Ethics Are Taking a Beating," *Marketing News* (May 25, 1984), 1+.

CASE V–1

Greenpeace Questionnaire

The following questionnaire (page 539) was recently sent out by the environmental group Greenpeace. The original questionnaire was on one side of an 8.5 × 14 inch piece of paper.

Discussion Questions

1. Evaluate the questionnaire, suggesting improvements where appropriate.
2. Are any ethical issues raised by this questionnaire? If so, what are they and what is the appropriate course of action?

CASE V–2

Methodology Section of a Telephone Provider Awareness Survey

The methodology section of a survey conducted for US WEST is reproduced here. The purpose of the survey was to measure the awareness and knowledge of household and business consumers about telephone service providers after the breakup of AT&T.

Methodology

Sample Recruitment

Telephone interviews were conducted among cells of business and household local phone users in three distinct geographic regions, each in the territory of a different Regional Holding Company (RHC). Within US WEST's region, telephone interviews were conducted among cells of business and household

GREENPEACE

Community Toxic Report

Greenpeace
P.O. Box 3720
Washington, D.C. 20007

COMMUNITY TOXIC REPORT

NUMBER 052561

Your participation in this community survey on hazardous
wastes is urgently requested. The questions are easy to
answer. Estimated time of response is 2-3 minutes. Please
complete and return to GREENPEACE within ten days.

1. Each year, more than 300 million tons of hazardous waste are produced in the U.S. alone. Do you believe your state, local, and federal authorities are doing all they can to protect you and your community from these wastes?

☐ Yes   ☐ No   ☐ No opinion

2. Rather than reducing production of toxic wastes, chemical and industrial giants propose "new" and "better" ways of disposing of them. What would be your response to locating the following waste disposal facilities in or near your community:

A. Toxic waste
incinerator   ☐ Opposed   ☐ Unopposed

B. Toxic storage
facility   ☐ Opposed   ☐ Unopposed

C. Toxic
landfill   ☐ Opposed   ☐ Unopposed

D. Injection
well   ☐ Opposed   ☐ Unopposed

3. Do you feel safe with the quality of drinking water in your community?

☐ Yes   ☐ No   ☐ No opinion

4. The use of pesticides, herbicides and other chemicals by U.S. agribusiness is a major source of toxic pollution in our water, soil, and food supplies. Would you favor more vigorous regulation of agricultural chemicals?

☐ Yes   ☐ No   ☐ No opinion

5. Toxic chemicals are suspected to be causing the deaths of dolphins, beluga whales and other animals. Do you think Greenpeace should invest its resources in investigating the impact of toxic pollution on wildlife habitats?

☐ Yes   ☐ No   ☐ No opinion

6. Rather than waste disposal or toxic waste management, Greenpeace believes that the best solution to the problem of hazardous wastes is to stop it before it starts, to reduce the quantity and toxicity of these wastes by improving industrial processes—*source reduction*. Do you agree that source reduction would be an effective way of reducing pollution?

☐ Agree   ☐ Disagree   ☐ No opinion

7. Recent surveys show that many Americans consider toxic wastes to be a serious threat to their health, but feel incapable of doing anything about it. How would you characterize your attitude toward toxic wastes?

☐ Serious problem, and
   want to do something about it

☐ Serious problem, but
   feel I can't do anything about it

☐ Not a serious problem

8. Would you be willing to spend just a few cents a day to help Greenpeace expose and confront the major toxic polluters—and to establish source reduction as a policy of major industrial nations as soon as possible?

☐ Yes   ☐ No

If your answer is "yes," Greenpeace invites you to join our historic effort to reduce and eventually eliminate toxic wastes from our communities. Simply check the appropriate box below, and return this form with your contribution today.

☐ Yes, I want to help Greenpeace's efforts to eliminate toxic wastes around the world by becoming a supporter of Greenpeace. Enclosed is my contribution in the amount of:

☐ $15   ☐ $25   ☐ $35

☐ $50   ☐ $100   ☐ Other_____

For your contribution of $15 or more, you will receive our lively, informative magazine, *Greenpeace*, to keep you up to date on our campaign to eliminate toxic pollution, and on all of Greenpeace's other work to preserve life and the environment around the world.

Thanks, from
GREENPEACE
P.O. Box 3720
Washington, D.C. 20007

SOURCE: Used with permission.

users in regions serviced by each of US WEST's Bell Operating Companies (BOCs). The following diagram summarizes the study's sample:

Cell One:	Business Users (384 Total Respondents)
	76 persons drawn from the Ameritech region
	75 persons drawn from the Pacific Telesis region
	233 persons drawn from the US WEST region, *including:*
	80 respondents from the Pacific Northwest Bell region
	77 respondents from the Northwestern Bell region
	76 respondents from the Mountain Bell region
Cell Two:	Household Users (376 Total Respondents)
	75 persons drawn from the Ameritech region
	75 persons drawn from the Pacific Telesis region
	226 persons drawn from the US WEST region, *including:*
	75 respondents from the Pacific Northwest Bell region
	75 respondents from the Northwestern Bell region
	76 respondents from the Mountain Bell region

Specific geographic areas covered by each of these RHCs and BOCs is appended.

It is important to note that respondents were drawn from geographic areas served by each of the three RHCs. However, respondents' local phone service was *not necessarily* provided by a subsidiary of that RHC. Indeed, in each of these geographic regions, local phone service may have been supplied by GTE or another non-BOC provider. Thus, *some* of the awareness/image scores detailed in this report may have been skewed by the fact that *some* respondents (we do not know how many) were, in fact, *noncustomers* of the BOCs. As *noncustomers*, they could not be expected to know much about the BOC or the parent company of that BOC.

Once interviewing was completed, weights were separately applied to the business and consumer samples in each of US WEST's BOC regions in order to bring the number of interviews in each region into their proper proportion to the population. The bases for all tables in this report reflect the sample as it was weighted.

Definition of Cells

The executives interviewed were limited only to those individuals responsible for planning and selecting the telecommunications services used by the company. The businesses selected for inclusion in the sample were further defined as follows:

- Those with SIC codes of 20–70 (including financial institutions and manufacturing concerns)—500 or more employees;
- Those with SIC codes of 71–89 (including service—i.e., telephone intensive—industries)—100 or more employees.

Descriptions of each of these SIC codes are appended.

Respondents selected for consumer interviews were male/female heads of households. An equal number of interviews was conducted with males and females.

Administration of Study

Fieldwork was conducted by the Opinion Research Corporation of Princeton, NJ, during late July. Analysis of the data was performed by the Research Department of FMR.

Definition of Terms

It is important to note that respondents were *not* exposed to the technical telecommunications terminology; questions were phrased in consumer lexicon. For example, respondents were asked for the name of their "local service provider"; they were not asked the name of their "Bell Operating Company." Obviously, the numbers in this report would be significantly lower had the questions not been "translated" into a consumer vocabulary.

Discussion Question

Evaluate the adequacy of this methodology section. (No other methodological information was provided in the report. However, a copy of the questionnaire was contained in an appendix.)

CASE V–3

Weyerhaeuser Report Format

The table of contents and several pages of an advertising effectiveness study conducted for Weyerhaeuser are reproduced here. The Executive Summary was one page with 12 bullets each with a one- or two-sentence summary of a key finding. The Introduction was one page of text. It described the authorization and purpose of the study and its relationship to a previous study on the same general topic. It also gave an overview of the methodology.

Sections II, III, and IV consisted of facing pages such that the top (left-hand) page contained a graph and the bottom (right-hand) page contained one to six "bullets" which provided the key points or insights provided by the graph. Four of these graphs are included in this case. In the actual report, the bulleted key points were on a separate page facing the graph.

Discussion Question

Evaluate the table of contents and the format used for this report.

Table of Contents

Executive Summary i
Introduction 1
Section I—General Reactions To The Weyerhaeuser and Georgia-Pacific Ads 3
    Ad Awareness 4
    Reasons for Noticing the Ad 6
    Description of the Ad Content 8
    Is Believable 10
    Is Informative 12
    Projects A Quality Image 14
    Is Eye Catching 16
    Positively Impacts Attitudes 18
    Captures Attention 20
    Is Similar to Other Ads 22
    Offers Important Products/Services 24
    Inspires Me to Call for More Information 26
Section II—Specific Reactions to the Weyerhaeuser Ad 29
    Meaning of the Ad 30
    Reactions to George Weyerhaeuser as a Spokesman 32
    Recall of Prior George Weyerhaeuser Ads 34
    Perceived Effectiveness of George Weyerhaeuser Ads 36
    Desirability of Continuing George Weyerhaeuser Ads 38
    Reasons for Continuing/Discontinuing George Weyerhaeuser Ads 40
    Meaning of "100% Satisfaction on Quality" 42
    Weyerhaeuser Action If Not Satisfied with Quality 44
    Meaning of "100% Satisfaction on Service" 46
    Reasons for Using the Customer Satisfaction Line 48
    Expectations from Using the Customer Satisfaction Line 50
Section III—Specific Reactions to the Georgia-Pacific Ad 53
    Meaning of "It's Simple. Georgia-Pacific" 54
    Importance of Designer Based Paneling 56
    Importance of a Single Source of Supply 58
    Believability of Georgia-Pacific as a Single Source 60
Section IV—Sample Characteristics 63
    Job Titles 64
    Lumber/Plywood Purchases 66
    Nonwood Building Material Purchases 68
    Retail Sales 70
    Number of Stores in the Company 72
Section V—Questionnaire 75

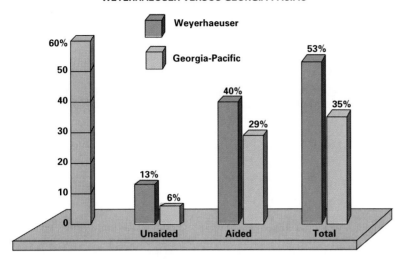

**AD AWARENESS:
WEYERHAEUSER VERSUS GEORGIA-PACIFIC**

- Reported awareness of ads for Weyerhaeuser was substantially higher than reported awareness of ads for Georgia-Pacific.

- Weyerhaeuser's advantage exists in both unaided and aided recall.

- This is an improvement over the 1988 figures when the total recall figures for Weyerhaeuser and Georgia-Pacific were 43 and 41 percent, respectively.

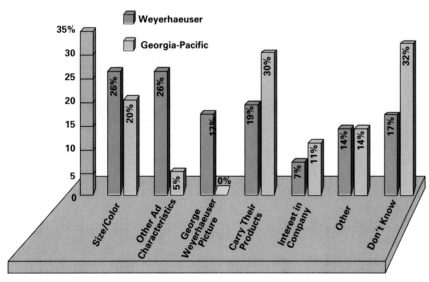

**REASONS FOR NOTICING AD:
WEYERHAEUSER VERSUS GEORGIA-PACIFIC***

- Respondents are better able to state why they noticed the Weyerhaeuser ad.

- George Weyerhaeuser's picture is memorable.

- Interest in the company and/or its products and physical charcateristics of the ad are primary reasons for noticing an ad.

- The Weyerhaeuser ad produces more ad specific reasons for recall.

*Weyerhaeuser = 133; Georgia-Pacific = 87.

543

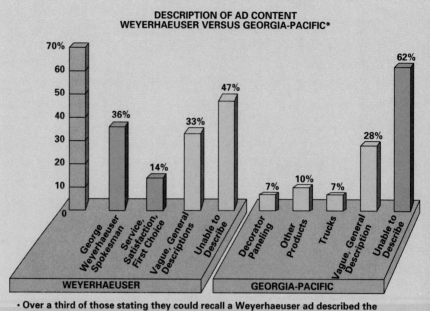

- Over a third of those stating they could recall a Weyerhaeuser ad described the content in terms of George Weyerhaeuser and an additional 14 percent described service satisfaction.

- Those claiming to recall seeing a Georgia-Pacific ad were generally unable to recall its content.

- The Weyerhaeuser scores are improved from the 1988 study while the Georgia-Pacific scores have declined.

* Weyerhaeuser = 133; Georgia-Pacific = 87.

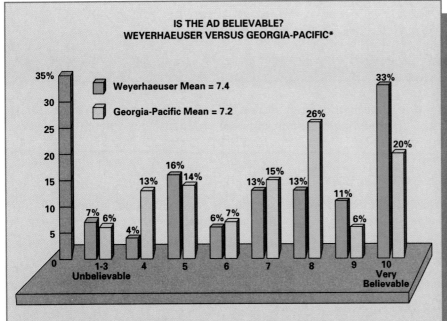

IS THE AD BELIEVABLE?
WEYERHAEUSER VERSUS GEORGIA-PACIFIC*

Weyerhaeuser Mean = 7.4

Georgia-Pacific Mean = 7.2

- Both ads are viewed as believable by respondents looking at the ads.

- Believability ratings are approximately the same as in the 1988 study.

- One-third of the respondents give the Weyerhauser ad the highest possible rating compared to the one-fifth for the Georgia-Pacific ad.

- Based on the 121 respondents actually looking at the ad. Ten respondents answered "Don't Know."

CASE V-4

Methodology Report for a Home Improvement Study

Following is the methodology section of a report describing a conjoint analysis study. The study involved four different products (four different evaluations per respondent).

Discussion Question

Evaluate the adequacy of this section (no other methodological details were provided except for a copy of the questionnaire).

Methodology

The study was conducted by means of personal interviews with consumers at stores selling home improvement materials in three markets during the last week of October through the third week in November. A total of 592 interviews were conducted, 201 in Chicago and Boston and 190 in Los Angeles.

Store customers were screened to ensure that they had done a home improvement project in the past 10 months. They were also screened regarding the amount spent on home improvement projects during this time period. A maximum of 20 per market who had spent between $100 and $200 were allowed to be included, while the remainder were required to have spent more than $200. A $5 gift certificate redeemable in the store in which the interview was conducted was used as an incentive to encourage participation.

The questionnaire required about 15 minutes to complete. Consumers were asked to perform two card-sorting tasks in which they ranked various combinations of product attributes and levels for two products, as well as respond to a series of open-ended "first-thought" type of items. Interviews were conducted at various times of day on weekends and weekdays.

CASE V-5

Hydra Products

Hydra Products manufactures and markets a number of products, including a low-cholesterol cooking oil. The firm's brand, H-P Oil, is the leading selling oil. As part of a major evaluation of the marketing mix used for H-P Oil, the firm hired a nationally known marketing research firm to assess physicians' knowledge, attitudes, and behavior with respect to this product category.

The researchers interviewed 2,000 physicians in a nationwide survey. One of their most significant conclusions was that "Most physicians lack sufficient knowledge of the relationship between heart disease and diet to provide meaningful recommendations on diet to their patients." In addition, the following specific findings were of particular interest to Hydra Products' management.

1. Of the 2,000 doctors surveyed, 1,400 recommended the use of a low-cholesterol cooking oil to patients who need to lower their cholesterol levels. Of those 1,400, 600 doctors recommended a specific brand. However, a doctor's recommendation often appeared to be based on factors other than a depth of knowledge of the health-related attributes of the various brands. The distribution of those doctors recommending a specific brand was as follows:

Brand	%
H-P Oil	34
A	15
B	14
C	12
D	8
All others	17

2. Of the 2,000 doctors surveyed, 1,200 were unaware of the brand of oil used in their own homes. The distribution of brands among those who were aware of the brand used was as follows:

Brand	%
H-P Oil	14
A	12
B	10
C	6
D	6
All others	52

Based on these findings, Hydra Products developed a new advertising campaign that featured the following claims:

- Of those doctors interviewed in a national survey, more than twice as many recommend H-P Oil than any other brand to their patients.
- Of those doctors interviewed in a national survey, more reported using H-P Oil in their own home than any other brand.

Discussion Questions

1. Was Hydra Products' use of the research data ethical? Why?
2. Assume that the Federal Trade Commission believed that the advertisements were misleading. Devise a research project that would provide information on whether the advertisements were, in fact, misleading.

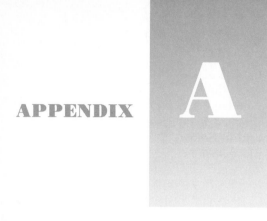

Area Under the Normal Curve

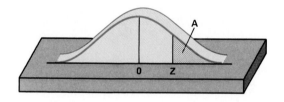

Z	A	Z	A	Z	A	Z	A
0.00	.5000	0.36	.3594	0.72	.2358	1.06	.1446
0.02	.4920	0.38	.3520	0.74	.2296	1.08	.1401
0.04	.4840	0.40	.3446	0.76	.2236	1.10	.1357
0.06	.4761	0.42	.3372	0.78	.2177	1.12	.1314
0.08	.4681	0.44	.3300	0.80	.2119	1.14	.1271
0.10	.4602	0.46	.3228			1.16	.1230
0.12	.4522	0.48	.3156	0.82	.2061	1.18	.1190
0.14	.4443	0.50	.3085	0.84	.2005	1.20	.1151
0.16	.4364	0.52	.3015	0.86	.1949	1.22	.1112
0.18	.4286	0.54	.2946	0.88	.1894	1.24	.1075
0.20	.4207	0.56	.2877	0.90	.1841	1.26	.1038
0.22	.4129	0.58	.2810	0.92	.1788	1.28	.1003
0.24	.4052	0.60	.2743	0.94	.1736	1.30	.0968
0.26	.3974	0.62	.2676	0.96	.1685	1.32	.0934
0.28	.3897	0.64	.2611	0.98	.1635	1.34	.0901
0.30	.3821	0.66	.2546	1.00	.1587	1.36	.0885
0.32	.3745	0.68	.2483	1.02	.1539	1.38	.0838
0.34	.3669	0.70	.2420	1.04	.1492	1.40	.0808

Z	A	Z	A	Z	A	Z	A
1.42	.0778	1.86	.0314	2.34	.0096	2.80	.0026
1.44	.0749	1.88	.0301	2.36	.0091	2.82	.0024
1.46	.0721	1.90	.0287	2.38	.0087	2.84	.0023
1.48	.0694	1.92	.0274	2.40	.0082	2.86	.0021
1.50	.0668	1.94	.0262	2.42	.0078	2.88	.0020
1.52	.0643	1.96	.0250			2.90	.0019
1.54	.0618	1.98	.0239	2.44	.0073	2.92	.0018
1.56	.0594	2.00	.0228	2.46	.0070	2.94	.0016
1.58	.0571	2.02	.0217	2.48	.0066	2.96	.0015
		2.04	.0207	2.50	.0062	2.98	.0014
1.60	.0548	2.06	.0197	2.52	.0059	3.00	.0014
		2.08	.0188	2.54	.0055	3.05	.0011
1.62	.0526	2.10	.0179	2.56	.0052	3.10	.0010
1.64	.0505	2.12	.0170	2.58	.0049	3.15	.0008
1.66	.0485	2.14	.0162	2.60	.0047	3.20	.0007
1.68	.0465	2.16	.0154	2.62	.0044	3.25	.0006
1.70	.0446	2.18	.0146	2.64	.0042	3.30	.0005
1.72	.0427	2.20	.0139	2.66	.0039	3.35	.0004
1.74	.0409	2.22	.0132	2.68	.0037	3.40	.0003
1.76	.0392	2.24	.0125	2.70	.0035	3.45	.0003
1.78	.0375	2.26	.0119	2.72	.0033	3.50	.0002
1.80	.0359	2.28	.0113	2.74	.0031		
1.82	.0344	2.30	.0107	2.76	.0029	3.55	.0002
1.84	.0329	2.32	.0102	2.78	.0027	3.60	.0002

Percentiles of the t Distribution (One- and Two-Tailed Tests)*

df	.30 (.15)	.20 (.10)	.10 (.05)	.050 (.025)	.02 (.01)	.01 (.005)
1	1.963	3.078	6.314	12.706	31.821	63.657
2	1.386	1.886	2.920	4.303	6.965	9.925
3	1.250	1.638	2.353	3.182	4.541	5.841
4	1.190	1.533	2.132	2.776	3.747	4.604
5	1.156	1.476	2.015	2.571	3.365	4.032
6	1.134	1.440	1.943	2.447	3.143	3.707
7	1.119	1.415	1.895	2.365	2.998	3.499
8	1.108	1.397	1.860	2.306	2.896	3.355
9	1.100	1.383	1.833	2.262	2.821	3.250
10	1.093	1.372	1.812	2.228	2.764	3.169
11	1.088	1.363	1.796	2.201	2.718	3.106
12	1.083	1.356	1.782	2.179	2.681	3.055
13	1.079	1.350	1.771	2.160	2.650	3.012
14	1.076	1.345	1.761	2.145	2.624	2.977
15	1.074	1.341	1.753	2.131	2.602	2.947
16	1.071	1.337	1.746	2.120	2.583	2.921
17	1.069	1.333	1.740	2.110	2.567	2.898
18	1.067	1.330	1.734	2.101	2.552	2.878
19	1.066	1.328	1.729	2.093	2.539	2.861
20	1.064	1.325	1.725	2.086	2.528	2.845
21	1.063	1.323	1.721	2.080	2.518	2.831
22	1.061	1.321	1.717	2.074	2.508	2.819

df	.30 (.15)	.20 (.10)	.10 (.05)	.050 (.025)	.02 (.01)	.01 (.005)
23	1.060	1.319	1.714	2.069	2.500	2.807
24	1.059	1.318	1.711	2.064	2.492	2.797
25	1.058	1.316	1.708	2.060	2.485	2.787
26	1.058	1.315	1.706	2.056	2.479	2.779
27	1.057	1.314	1.703	2.052	2.473	2.771
28	1.056	1.313	1.701	2.048	2.467	2.763
29	1.055	1.311	1.699	2.045	2.462	2.756
30	1.055	1.310	1.697	2.042	2.457	2.750

*The probability in parenthesis is for a one-tailed test.

SOURCE: R. A. Fisher, *Statistical Methods for Research Workers*, 14th ed. (Copyright © 1972 by Hafner Press, a division of Macmillan Publishing Company, Inc.).

Percentiles of the F-Distribution for α Values of .01, .05, and .10

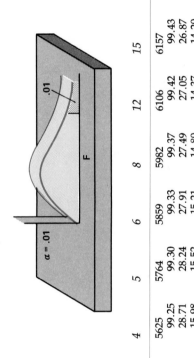

$\alpha = .01$

v_2/v_1^*	1	2	3	4	5	6	8	12	15	20	30	60	∞
1	4052	4999.5	5403	5625	5764	5859	5982	6106	6157	6209	6261	6313	6366
2	98.50	99.00	99.17	99.25	99.30	99.33	99.37	99.42	99.43	99.45	99.47	99.48	99.50
3	34.12	30.82	29.46	28.71	28.24	27.91	27.49	27.05	26.87	26.69	26.50	26.32	26.13
4	21.20	18.00	16.69	15.98	15.52	15.21	14.80	14.37	14.20	14.02	13.84	13.65	13.46
5	16.27	13.26	12.06	11.39	10.97	10.67	10.29	9.89	9.72	9.55	9.38	9.20	9.02
6	13.75	10.92	9.78	9.15	8.75	8.47	8.10	7.72	7.56	7.40	7.23	7.06	6.88
7	12.25	9.55	8.45	7.85	7.46	7.19	6.84	6.47	6.31	6.16	5.99	5.82	5.65
8	11.26	8.65	7.59	7.01	6.63	6.37	6.03	5.67	5.52	5.36	5.20	5.03	4.86
9	10.56	8.02	6.99	6.42	6.06	5.80	5.47	5.11	4.96	4.81	4.65	4.48	4.31
10	10.04	7.56	6.55	5.99	5.64	5.39	5.06	4.71	4.56	4.41	4.25	4.08	3.91
11	9.65	7.21	6.22	5.67	5.32	5.07	4.74	4.40	4.25	4.10	3.94	3.78	3.60
12	9.33	6.93	5.95	5.41	5.06	4.82	4.50	4.16	4.01	3.86	3.70	3.54	3.36
13	9.07	6.70	5.74	5.21	4.86	4.62	4.30	3.96	3.82	3.66	3.51	3.34	3.17
14	8.86	6.51	5.56	5.04	4.69	4.46	4.14	3.80	3.66	3.51	3.35	3.18	3.00
15	8.68	6.36	5.42	4.89	4.56	4.32	4.00	3.67	3.52	3.37	3.21	3.05	2.87
16	8.53	6.23	5.29	4.77	4.44	4.20	3.89	3.55	3.41	3.26	3.10	2.93	2.75
17	8.40	6.11	5.18	4.67	4.34	4.10	3.79	3.46	3.31	3.16	3.00	2.83	2.65
18	8.29	6.01	5.09	4.58	4.25	4.01	3.71	3.37	3.23	3.08	2.92	2.75	2.57
19	8.18	5.93	5.01	4.50	4.17	3.94	3.63	3.30	3.15	3.00	2.84	2.67	2.49
20	8.10	5.85	4.94	4.43	4.10	3.87	3.56	3.23	3.09	2.94	2.78	2.61	2.42
21	8.02	5.78	4.87	4.37	4.04	3.81	3.51	3.17	3.03	2.88	2.72	2.55	2.36
22	7.95	5.72	4.82	4.31	3.99	3.76	3.45	3.12	2.98	2.83	2.67	2.50	2.31
23	7.88	5.66	4.76	4.26	3.94	3.71	3.41	3.07	2.93	2.78	2.62	2.45	2.26
24	7.82	5.61	4.72	4.22	3.90	3.67	3.36	3.03	2.89	2.74	2.58	2.40	2.21
25	7.77	5.57	4.68	4.18	3.85	3.63	3.32	2.99	2.85	2.70	2.54	2.36	2.17
26	7.72	5.53	4.64	4.14	3.82	3.59	3.29	2.96	2.81	2.66	2.50	2.33	2.13
27	7.68	5.49	4.60	4.11	3.78	3.56	3.26	2.93	2.78	2.63	2.47	2.29	2.10
28	7.64	5.45	4.57	4.07	3.75	3.53	3.23	2.90	2.75	2.60	2.44	2.26	2.06
29	7.60	5.42	4.54	4.04	3.73	3.50	3.20	2.87	2.73	2.57	2.41	2.23	2.03
30	7.56	5.39	4.51	4.02	3.70	3.47	3.17	2.84	2.70	2.55	2.39	2.21	2.01
40	7.31	5.18	4.31	3.83	3.51	3.29	2.99	2.66	2.52	2.37	2.20	2.02	1.80
60	7.08	4.98	4.13	3.65	3.34	3.12	2.82	2.50	2.35	2.20	2.03	1.84	1.60
120	6.85	4.79	3.95	3.48	3.17	2.96	2.66	2.34	2.19	2.03	1.86	1.66	1.38
∞	6.63	4.61	3.78	3.32	3.02	2.80	2.51	2.18	2.04	1.88	1.70	1.47	1.00

*v_1 = degrees of freedom in numerator; v_2 = degrees of freedom for denominator.

553

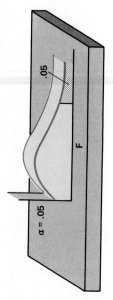

$\alpha = .05$

v_2/v_1^*	1	2	3	4	5	6	8	12	15	20	30	60	∞
1	161.4	199.5	215.7	224.6	230.2	234.0	238.9	243.9	245.9	248.0	250.1	252.2	254.3
2	18.51	19.00	19.16	19.25	19.30	19.33	19.37	19.41	19.43	19.45	19.46	19.48	19.50
3	10.13	9.55	9.28	9.12	9.01	8.94	8.85	8.74	8.70	8.66	8.62	8.57	8.53
4	7.71	6.94	6.59	6.39	6.26	6.16	6.04	5.91	5.86	5.80	5.75	5.69	5.63
5	6.61	5.79	5.41	5.19	5.05	4.95	4.82	4.68	4.62	4.56	4.50	4.43	4.36
6	5.99	5.14	4.76	4.53	4.39	4.28	4.15	4.00	3.94	3.87	3.81	3.74	3.67
7	5.59	4.74	4.35	4.12	3.97	3.87	3.73	3.57	3.51	3.44	3.38	3.30	3.23
8	5.32	4.46	4.07	3.84	3.69	3.58	3.44	3.28	3.22	3.15	3.08	3.01	2.93
9	5.12	4.26	3.86	3.63	3.48	3.37	3.23	3.07	3.01	2.94	2.86	2.79	2.71
10	4.96	4.10	3.71	3.48	3.33	3.22	3.07	2.91	2.85	2.77	2.70	2.62	2.54
11	4.84	3.98	3.59	3.36	3.20	3.09	2.95	2.79	2.72	2.65	2.57	2.49	2.40
12	4.75	3.89	3.49	3.26	3.11	3.00	2.85	2.69	2.62	2.54	2.47	2.38	2.30
13	4.67	3.81	3.41	3.18	3.03	2.92	2.77	2.60	2.53	2.46	2.38	2.30	2.21
14	4.60	3.74	3.34	3.11	2.96	2.85	2.70	2.53	2.46	2.39	2.31	2.22	2.13
15	4.54	3.68	3.29	3.06	2.90	2.79	2.64	2.48	2.40	2.33	2.25	2.16	2.07
16	4.49	3.63	3.24	3.01	2.85	2.74	2.59	2.42	2.35	2.28	2.19	2.11	2.01
17	4.45	3.59	3.20	2.96	2.81	2.70	2.55	2.38	2.31	2.23	2.15	2.06	1.96
18	4.41	3.55	3.16	2.93	2.77	2.66	2.51	2.34	2.27	2.19	2.11	2.02	1.92
19	4.38	3.52	3.13	2.90	2.74	2.63	2.48	2.31	2.23	2.16	2.07	1.98	1.88
20	4.35	3.49	3.10	2.87	2.71	2.60	2.45	2.28	2.20	2.12	2.04	1.95	1.84
21	4.32	3.47	3.07	2.84	2.68	2.57	2.42	2.25	2.18	2.10	2.01	1.92	1.81
22	4.30	3.44	3.05	2.82	2.66	2.55	2.40	2.23	2.15	2.07	1.98	1.89	1.78
23	4.28	3.42	3.03	2.80	2.64	2.53	2.37	2.20	2.13	2.05	1.96	1.86	1.76
24	4.26	3.40	3.01	2.78	2.62	2.51	2.36	2.18	2.11	2.03	1.94	1.84	1.73
25	4.24	3.39	2.99	2.76	2.60	2.49	2.34	2.16	2.09	2.01	1.92	1.82	1.71
26	4.23	3.37	2.98	2.74	2.59	2.47	2.32	2.15	2.07	1.99	1.90	1.80	1.69
27	4.21	3.35	2.96	2.73	2.57	2.46	2.31	2.13	2.06	1.97	1.88	1.79	1.67
28	4.20	3.34	2.95	2.71	2.56	2.45	2.29	2.12	2.04	1.96	1.87	1.77	1.65
29	4.18	3.33	2.93	2.70	2.55	2.43	2.28	2.10	2.03	1.94	1.85	1.75	1.64
30	4.17	3.32	2.92	2.69	2.53	2.42	2.27	2.09	2.01	1.93	1.84	1.74	1.62
40	4.08	3.23	2.84	2.61	2.45	2.34	2.18	2.00	1.92	1.84	1.74	1.64	1.51
60	4.00	3.15	2.76	2.53	2.37	2.25	2.10	1.92	1.84	1.75	1.65	1.53	1.39
120	3.92	3.07	2.68	2.45	2.29	2.17	2.02	1.83	1.75	1.66	1.55	1.43	1.25
∞	3.84	3.00	2.60	2.37	2.21	2.10	1.94	1.75	1.67	1.57	1.46	1.32	1.00

*v_1 = degrees of freedom in numerator; v_2 = degrees of freedom for denominator.

$\alpha = .10$

.10

v_2/v_1*	1	2	3	4	5	6	8	12	15	20	30	60	∞
1	39.86	49.50	53.59	55.83	57.24	58.20	59.44	60.71	61.22	61.74	62.26	62.79	63.33
2	8.53	9.00	9.16	9.24	9.29	9.33	9.37	9.41	9.42	9.44	9.46	9.47	9.49
3	5.54	5.46	5.39	5.34	5.31	5.28	5.25	5.22	5.20	5.18	5.17	5.15	5.13
4	4.54	4.32	4.19	4.11	4.05	4.01	3.95	3.90	3.87	3.84	3.82	3.79	3.76
5	4.06	3.78	3.62	3.52	3.45	3.40	3.34	3.27	3.24	3.21	3.17	3.14	3.10
6	3.78	3.46	3.29	3.18	3.11	3.05	2.98	2.90	2.87	2.84	2.80	2.76	2.72
7	3.59	3.26	3.07	2.96	2.88	2.83	2.75	2.67	2.63	2.59	2.56	2.51	2.47
8	3.46	3.11	2.92	2.81	2.73	2.67	2.59	2.50	2.46	2.42	2.38	2.34	2.29
9	3.36	3.01	2.81	2.69	2.61	2.55	2.47	2.38	2.34	2.30	2.25	2.21	2.16
10	3.29	2.92	2.73	2.61	2.52	2.46	2.38	2.28	2.24	2.20	2.16	2.11	2.06
11	3.23	2.86	2.66	2.54	2.45	2.39	2.30	2.21	2.17	2.12	2.08	2.03	1.97
12	3.18	2.81	2.61	2.48	2.39	2.33	2.24	2.15	2.10	2.06	2.01	1.96	1.90
13	3.14	2.76	2.56	2.43	2.35	2.28	2.20	2.10	2.05	2.01	1.96	1.90	1.85
14	3.10	2.73	2.52	2.39	2.31	2.24	2.15	2.05	2.01	1.96	1.91	1.86	1.80
15	3.07	2.70	2.49	2.36	2.27	2.21	2.12	2.02	1.97	1.92	1.87	1.82	1.76
16	3.05	2.67	2.46	2.33	2.24	2.18	2.09	1.99	1.94	1.89	1.84	1.78	1.72
17	3.03	2.64	2.44	2.31	2.22	2.15	2.06	1.96	1.91	1.86	1.81	1.75	1.69
18	3.01	2.62	2.42	2.29	2.20	2.13	2.04	1.93	1.89	1.84	1.78	1.72	1.66
19	2.99	2.61	2.40	2.27	2.18	2.11	2.02	1.91	1.86	1.81	1.76	1.70	1.63
20	2.97	2.59	2.38	2.25	2.16	2.09	2.00	1.89	1.84	1.79	1.74	1.68	1.61
21	2.96	2.57	2.36	2.23	2.14	2.08	1.98	1.87	1.83	1.78	1.72	1.66	1.59
22	2.95	2.56	2.35	2.22	2.13	2.06	1.97	1.86	1.81	1.76	1.70	1.64	1.57
23	2.94	2.55	2.34	2.21	2.11	2.05	1.95	1.84	1.80	1.74	1.69	1.62	1.55
24	2.93	2.54	2.33	2.19	2.10	2.04	1.94	1.83	1.78	1.73	1.67	1.61	1.53
25	2.92	2.53	2.32	2.18	2.09	2.02	1.93	1.82	1.77	1.72	1.66	1.59	1.52
26	2.91	2.52	2.31	2.17	2.08	2.01	1.92	1.81	1.76	1.71	1.65	1.58	1.50
27	2.90	2.51	2.30	2.17	2.07	2.00	1.91	1.80	1.75	1.70	1.64	1.57	1.49
28	2.89	2.50	2.29	2.16	2.06	2.00	1.90	1.79	1.74	1.69	1.63	1.56	1.48
29	2.89	2.50	2.28	2.15	2.06	1.99	1.89	1.78	1.73	1.68	1.62	1.55	1.47
30	2.88	2.49	2.28	2.14	2.05	1.98	1.88	1.77	1.72	1.67	1.61	1.54	1.46
40	2.84	2.44	2.23	2.09	2.00	1.93	1.83	1.71	1.66	1.61	1.54	1.47	1.38
60	2.79	2.39	2.18	2.04	1.95	1.87	1.77	1.66	1.60	1.54	1.48	1.40	1.29
120	2.75	2.35	2.13	1.99	1.90	1.82	1.72	1.60	1.55	1.48	1.41	1.32	1.19
∞	2.71	2.30	2.08	1.94	1.85	1.77	1.67	1.55	1.49	1.42	1.34	1.24	1.00

*v_1 = degrees of freedom in numerator; v_2 = degrees of freedom for denominator.

SOURCE: M. Abramewitz, I. A. Stegan, *Handbook of Mathematical Functions—AMS 55*, National Bureau of Standards and Applied Mathematics, Series (Washington, D.C.: U.S. Government Printing Office, 1964).

D

Table of Values of Chi Square

How to use the table and interpret the probability found:

1. Find the *degrees of freedom (df)* of the contingency table for the problem by multiplying the number of rows minus one $(r - 1)$ times the number of columns minus one $(k - 1)$:

$$df = (r - 1)(k - 1)$$

2. Look up the probability for the number of degrees of freedom and the calculated value of χ^2, approximating if necessary. This will be the *probability that the differences between the observed and the expected values occurred because of sampling variation.*

Probability of χ² Occurring Because of Sampling Variation

df	.99	.98	.95	.90	.80	.70	.50	.30	.20	.10	.05	.02	.01	.001
1	.00016	.00063	.0039	.016	.064	.15	.46	1.07	1.64	2.71	3.84	5.41	6.64	10.83
2	.02	.04	.10	.21	.45	.71	1.39	2.41	3.22	4.60	5.99	7.82	9.21	13.82
3	.12	.18	.35	.58	1.00	1.42	2.37	3.66	4.64	6.25	7.82	9.84	11.34	16.27
4	.30	.43	.71	1.06	1.65	2.20	3.36	4.88	5.99	7.78	9.49	11.67	13.28	18.46
5	.55	.75	1.14	1.61	2.34	3.00	4.35	6.06	7.29	9.24	11.07	13.39	15.09	20.52
6	.87	1.13	1.64	2.20	3.07	3.83	5.35	7.23	8.56	10.64	12.59	15.03	16.81	22.46
7	1.24	1.56	2.17	2.83	3.82	4.67	6.35	8.38	9.80	12.02	14.07	16.62	18.48	24.32
8	1.65	2.03	2.73	3.49	4.59	5.53	7.34	9.52	11.03	13.36	15.51	18.17	20.09	26.12
9	2.09	2.53	3.32	4.17	5.38	6.39	8.34	10.66	12.24	14.68	16.92	19.68	21.67	27.88
10	2.56	3.06	3.94	4.86	6.18	7.27	9.34	11.78	13.44	15.99	18.31	21.16	23.21	29.59
11	3.05	3.61	4.58	5.53	6.99	8.15	10.34	12.90	14.63	17.28	19.68	22.62	24.72	31.26
12	3.57	4.18	5.23	6.30	7.81	9.03	11.34	14.01	15.81	18.55	21.03	24.05	26.22	32.91
13	4.11	4.76	5.89	7.04	8.63	9.93	12.34	15.12	16.98	19.81	22.36	25.47	27.69	34.53
14	4.66	5.37	6.57	7.79	9.47	10.82	13.34	16.22	18.15	21.06	23.68	26.87	29.14	36.12
15	5.23	5.98	7.26	8.55	10.31	11.72	14.34	17.32	19.31	22.31	25.00	28.26	30.58	37.70
16	5.81	6.61	7.96	9.31	11.15	12.62	15.34	18.42	20.46	23.54	26.30	29.63	32.00	39.29
17	6.41	7.26	8.67	10.08	12.00	13.53	16.34	19.51	21.62	24.77	27.59	31.00	33.41	40.75
18	7.02	7.91	9.39	10.86	12.86	14.44	17.34	20.60	22.76	25.99	28.87	32.35	34.80	42.31
19	7.63	8.57	10.12	11.65	13.72	15.35	18.34	21.69	23.90	27.20	30.14	33.69	36.19	43.82
20	8.26	9.24	10.85	12.44	14.58	16.27	19.34	22.78	25.04	28.41	31.41	35.02	37.57	45.32
21	8.90	9.92	11.59	13.24	15.44	17.18	20.34	23.86	26.17	29.62	32.67	36.34	38.93	46.80
22	9.54	10.60	12.34	14.04	16.31	18.10	21.34	24.94	27.30	30.81	33.92	37.66	40.29	48.27
23	10.20	11.29	13.09	14.85	17.19	19.02	22.34	26.02	28.43	32.01	35.17	38.97	41.64	49.73
24	10.86	11.99	13.85	15.66	18.06	19.94	23.34	27.10	29.55	33.20	36.42	40.27	42.98	51.18
25	11.52	12.70	14.61	16.47	18.94	20.87	24.34	28.17	30.68	34.38	37.65	41.57	44.31	52.62
26	12.20	13.41	15.38	17.29	19.82	21.79	25.34	29.25	31.80	35.56	38.88	42.86	45.64	54.05
27	12.88	14.12	16.15	18.11	20.70	22.72	26.34	30.32	32.91	36.74	40.11	44.14	46.96	55.48
28	13.56	14.85	16.93	18.94	21.59	23.65	27.34	31.39	34.03	37.92	41.34	45.42	48.28	56.89
29	14.26	15.57	17.71	19.77	22.48	24.48	28.34	32.46	35.14	39.09	42.56	46.69	49.59	58.30
30	14.95	16.31	18.49	20.00	23.36	25.51	29.34	33.53	36.25	40.26	43.77	47.96	50.89	59.70

SOURCE: R. A. Fisher, *Statistical Methods for Research Workers*, 14th ed. (Copyright © 1972 by Hafner Press, a Division of Macmillan Publishing Company, Inc.)

Table of Random Numbers

69	47	26	60	28	33	65	51	63	91	41	07	85	54	48	47	89	89	28	16	53	63	25	95	88
36	14	60	08	90	71	30	34	43	18	96	70	86	34	51	06	51	11	14	03	33	67	85	71	90
62	16	07	76	94	09	32	30	74	76	86	78	75	52	70	37	57	13	08	29	32	23	91	70	56
75	46	96	99	49	03	54	14	38	20	58	77	01	14	85	16	66	99	28	95	46	57	76	48	08
32	53	72	54	45	60	27	95	50	61	94	74	24	19	78	12	00	75	85	97	32	75	62	45	62
66	09	42	47	16	57	33	42	44	67	41	75	32	43	09	79	78	39	01	27	21	30	48	49	20
12	56	30	19	62	47	50	43	45	05	13	13	79	58	36	73	10	71	17	77	56	92	66	44	72
93	63	44	66	76	44	76	82	75	38	09	46	79	96	66	80	57	46	23	99	32	05	27	34	43
99	96	86	08	57	19	62	73	25	37	61	76	95	17	07	61	40	57	34	44	54	85	84	40	08
92	95	55	56	71	43	44	26	00	73	43	15	01	66	82	74	35	10	28	92	17	90	92	95	63
88	77	70	08	13	16	60	87	60	67	80	97	39	58	27	90	59	22	75	49	43	63	83	03	90
71	43	59	44	65	08	48	18	95	88	73	16	98	95	53	70	49	86	71	25	87	37	88	73	79
81	71	50	68	32	00	95	95	39	17	83	77	07	95	65	90	61	10	52	48	74	48	32	49	54
85	35	17	54	65	57	99	07	07	65	21	93	79	91	42	77	75	10	96	19	13	78	19	34	56
97	98	88	17	00	58	81	12	61	35	25	42	21	18	68	84	37	73	30	88	85	19	59	16	47
40	50	04	89	66	51	21	91	82	71	15	80	17	88	38	27	49	65	30	34	49	28	22	14	67
22	73	51	48	82	14	87	85	46	89	19	46	67	54	20	61	33	11	68	14	55	25	25	25	92
21	29	99	31	69	64	45	42	00	84	18	46	43	44	30	16	40	07	95	26	63	24	69	37	48
18	09	90	67	79	82	33	35	05	92	31	34	64	39	62	35	51	99	31	87	41	61	85	97	94
26	72	96	60	46	44	75	28	54	62	38	92	97	05	53	34	53	64	56	43	93	64	05	68	42
66	28	80	86	71	43	11	46	59	63	17	27	36	56	92	37	11	11	86	57	44	98	34	87	82
62	99	58	99	85	78	25	10	31	75	63	00	87	08	78	22	12	12	52	85	49	86	18	07	70
55	60	57	69	48	19	41	83	50	67	59	12	99	19	02	00	28	19	08	11	96	28	36	61	43
76	62	89	95	48	58	09	12	03	61	59	06	54	85	46	84	63	96	51	96	65	12	98	54	11
94	66	26	20	23	40	59	39	40	32	15	16	54	81	79	63	12	78	47	16	58	70	58	97	02
50	73	51	48	98	54	66	93	14	37	81	30	87	07	65	99	95	12	72	94	81	51	49	09	37
94	11	04	04	22	92	49	83	08	57	01	85	53	53	23	75	41	14	29	11	66	15	93	94	90
97	87	81	59	36	66	29	96	73	78	67	53	01	98	78	74	15	70	42	62	68	10	52	98	34
46	50	73	23	03	04	37	49	13	66	97	24	11	63	83	18	23	87	99	66	21	91	79	12	63
43	85	00	91	54	39	67	34	53	17	21	10	43	16	80	81	09	79	08	82	51	07	40	95	83
18	20	00	87	87	11	61	72	26	45	62	83	74	27	48	29	35	71	96	66	24	78	91	94	06
68	94	94	68	84	27	04	78	14	17	14	84	79	82	01	96	90	62	31	73	19	12	96	97	05
04	19	46	04	41	94	03	09	64	84	26	45	84	77	37	82	23	36	75	78	06	25	19	44	15
18	58	79	01	03	59	56	25	50	68	29	21	93	72	00	20	31	12	49	91	03	44	85	01	90

Name Index

Aaker, D. A., 303
Abernethy, A. M., 129
Abramewitz, M., 555
Abrams, B., 248
Achabal, D. D., 186
Adams, A., 248
Adams, A. J., 400
Adler, L., 213
Akaah, I. P., 537
Albaum, G., 62, 159, 278, 303
Alpert, M. I., 323
Alsop, R., 323, 342
Alwin, D. F., 279
Anderson, C., 323
Anderson, J. C., 248
Andreason, A. R., 62
Andrews, L. B., 537
Angelus, T., 213
Aquilino, W. S., 158
Arroyo, R. D., 21
Assael, H., 129, 158
Atkins, C. K., 342
Ayidia, S. A., 279
Azhari, A. G., 3, 20

Bagozzi, R. P., 249
Bailey, L., 62
Baim, J., 152, 153, 159
Banks, M. J., 158
Banks, S., 186
Barnard, N. R., 303
Barnes, J. H., Jr., 279
Bartos, R., 103
Bartram, M., 537
Bartram, P., 21, 537
Bass, F. M., 303
Batra, R., 303
Batsell, R. R., 278
Bayer, J., 39
Bender, S. D. F. G., 135
Berbie, D. R., 159
Best, R. J., 129, 248, 278, 303

Betak, J. F., 323
Billington, M., 158
Bishop, W. R., Jr., 122
Blair, J., 158
Blankenship, A. B., 279
Blattberg, R. L., 122
Bloom, P., 158, 342
Blyth, J. S., 21
Bogart, L., 186
Bolstein, R., 159
Bolton, R. M., 323
Bond, J. R., 39
Booth, L., 174
Borg, M. J., 158
Bradburn, N., 279
Brandt, R., 21
Brasive, H. B., 159
Bratzman, J., 86
Brennan, J. M., 158
Brinkhoff, H. G. M., 39
Britt, S. H., 516
Brokhoff, K., 39
Bronkhorst, T. M., 323
Brown, C. E., 213
Brown, S. W., 39
Brunn, B. J., 159
Buchanan, B., 303
Buckley, M. R., 248
Burroughs, W. J., 303
Burton, J. P., 278
Bush, C. M., 39

Cacioppo, J. T., 342
Cagley, J. W., 278
Calantone, R. J., 180, 186
Caller, L., 21
Camacho, F. E., 20
Carsen, T., 21
Carter, J., 5, 173
Casley, D. J., 380
Chapin, F. S., 187
Chapman, R. G., 62

Chatterjee, R., 213
Checkman, D., 323
Chonko, L. B., 537
Churchill, G. A., Jr., 213, 248
Coleman, L. G., 21, 129
Collins, L. F., 323
Collins, M., 380
Colwell, J., 323
Conant, J. S., 159
Coney, K. A., 129, 248, 278, 303
Cook, W. A., 278
Cooper, H., 159
Cooper, P., 323
Cornish, P., 380
Cote, J. A., 248
Cox, A. D., 278
Cox, S., 158
Craig, C. S., 279
Crask, M. R., 159, 248, 303
Crawford, C. M., 537
Czepiel, J., 303
Czinkota, M., 21

Dalvi, N., 129
Davis, J. E., 21
Day, D., 303
Day, E., 323
Day, R. L., 249
deAlmeida, P. M., 103
de Koning, C. C. J., 537
Delphos, W. A., 103
Diamond, S. A., 537
Dillman, D. A., 278
Dommeyer, C. J., 159
Donsbach, W., 159
Dotson, M. J., 279
Douglas, S. P., 279
Dowling, G. R., 248
Downham, J., 323, 537
Downs, P. E., 278
Draper, P., 129, 159
Dubinsky, A. J., 537
Duffy, J. E., 21
Duncan, O. D., 303
Dupont, T. D., 381
Durant, R. F., 158
Durgee, J. T., 323
Durvasula, S., 248

Ebner, M., 537
Edel, R., 21
Edwards, L., 213
Ehrenberg, A. S. C., 129, 303, 516
Esslemont, D., 303
Etmekjian, C., 26, 39

Fahey, A., 248
Fairley, D., 159

Fedder, C. J., 323
Feinberg, B. M., 159
Feinberg, R. A., 303
Ferber, R., 323
Ferrell, O. C., 537
Finkel, S. E., 158
Finn, A., 342, 537
Fischer, P. M., 347
Fisher, R. A., 557
Foltz, K., 342
Ford, J. B., 278
Foreman, J., 380
Fountain, E., 21
Fox, J. A., 278
Fox, R. J., 159, 248, 303
Frankel, J., 537
Frankel, M. R., 380
Freeman, L., 213
Freeman, P., 129
French, W., 537
Frey, C. J., 537
Frey, J. H., 278
Friedman, H. H., 303
Friedman, L. W., 303
Fujitake, K., 129
Fuld, L., 39, 87

Gabriel, C., 323
Geer, J. G., 279
Gendall, P., 303
Gerbing, D. W., 248
Giges, N., 186, 323, 342
Gillett, R., 303, 400
Givon, M., 303
Glassman, M., 278
Gluck, B., 303
Goerne, C., 248
Goldberg, M. E., 187
Golden, L. L., 303, 323
Goldman, A., 303
Goldsmith, R. E., 278
Gomes, R., 39
Goodyear, M., 323
Gordon, H. L., 516
Goslar, M. D., 39
Goyder, J., 537
Goydon, R., 278
Greco, A. J., 35, 39
Grede, J., 26, 39
Green, P. E., 278
Gregg, J. P.
Gresham, L. G., 537
Griggs, S., 323
Groves, R. M., 158
Gupta, S., 186
Guterbock, T. M., 158

Haire, M., 323
Hansen, J., 129

Hapoienu, S. L., 213
Harter, R., 39
Havice, M. J., 158
Hawkins, D. I., 62, 129, 159, 248, 278, 303, 461
Hekmat, F., 158
Hernandez, S. A., 158
Herring, J. P., 38
Higgins, K. T., 21
Higgins, L. F., 38
Hinds, E. E., 21
Hink, D. R. W., 39
Hippler, H. J., 279
Hodock, C. L., 21, 365, 537
Hogue, J. T., 35, 39
Holbrook, M. B., 303
Holman, R. H., 333
Homma, N., 21
Honomichl, J., 21, 62, 537
Horton, C., 103
Howard, N., 213
Howe, G. R., 183
Howell, R., 248
Hume, S., 158, 279, 400
Hunt, S. D., 279, 537
Hyatt, C., 333
Hyatt, E. M., 186

Ingoassia, L., 213

Jackson, D. W., Jr., 278
James, J. M., 159
Jamieson, L. F., 303
Jaroslovsky, R., 278
Jobber, D., 158, 159
Johansson, J. K., 21
Johnson, J. C., 278
Johnson, R. L., 278
Johnson, R. M., 303
Jones, S., 62
Juárez, N. F., 158
Jussaume, R. A., Jr., 159

Kamen, J. M., 20
Karimahahy, H., 159
Kassarjian, H. H., 323
Katori, K., 334
Kaufman, C. J., 158
Kedia, P. K., 278
Kelly, J. P., 186
Keon, Jr., 158
Kerin, R. A., 145, 158, 159
Kerlinger, F. N., 213, 248
Kernan, J. B., 303
Kerr, J. R., 278
Kiecker, P. L., 158
Kilburn, D., 205
Kim, J., 159
Kinnear, T. C., 537

Klein, F. C., 342
Klose, A., 159
Knain, D. M., 20
Kobayashi, K., 129, 159
Kolbert, E., 400
Kosbab, W. H., 86
Kotabe, M., 21
Kreisman, R., 213
Krosnick, J. A., 279
Kruzas, A. T., 87
Kuga, M., 50
Kulka, R. A., 159
Kyzr-Sheeley, B. J., 159, 522

LaBarbera, P., 303
Laczniak, G. R., 537
Lambert, D. M., 103
Langer, J., 323
Lansing, J. B., 413
Laric, M. L., 39
Larkin, J., 129
Lehman, C., 186
Leigh, L. E., 248
Levin, G., 303
Lichtenstein, D. R., 248
Lieb, M. E., 213
Liefeld, J. P., 158
Liesse, J., 21, 248
Lifton, D., 159
Lilien, G. L., 39
Linda, G., 213
Lituack, D. S., 180, 186
Locander, W. B., 378
Loken, B., 303, 537
LoSciuto, L. A., 158
Lury, D. A., 380
Lusch, R. F., 303
Lyons, W., 158
Lysaker, R. L., 342

MacFarlane, I., 103
MacLachlan, J., 291
Madden, C. S., 159, 537
Madigan, K., 230
Magiera, M., 279
Magilavy, L. J., 158
Maguire, R., 428
Malhotra, N. K., 159
Malnight, T. W., 21
Marbeau, Y., 98, 103
Marks, L. J., 537
Marmorstein, H., 103
Marsh, C., 380
Martin, C. R., Jr., 187
Mason, J. B., 186
Mayo, M. A., 537
McClendon, M. J., 279
McDaniel, S. W., 159, 537

McDonald, W. J., 323
McIntyre, S. C., 38
McIntyre, S. H., 135
McKinnon, G. T., 186
Mehrotra, S., 248
Meier, E., 159
Mentzer, J. T., 39
Meredith, L., 38, 39
Metzger, G. D., 129
Meyers, G., 135
Middleton, L., 137
Midgley, D. F., 248
Miller, A., 323, 342
Miller, P. V., 158
Mitchell, A. A., 39
Mitchell, D., 380
Mohn, N. C., 303
Morgan, J. N., 413
Morgan, R. P., 39
Morita, A., 11
Morrison, D. G., 303
Mueller, C., 202
Mulcahy, P., 11
Mulholland, H., 323
Murphy, P. E., 537
Myers, J. G., 291
Myers-Levy, J., 342

Neelankavil, J. P., 286
Nelson, J. E., 158
Nelson, P. H., 103
Nelson, T. A., 87
Netemeyer, R. G., 248
Nikhil, R. S., 278
Noazin, S., 303
Nonaka, I., 21
Nowell, C., 381
Noyes, H. C., 319

O'Brien, J. V., 286
Ohlon, J. E., 39
Olsen, J., 537
Oostreen, J., 21
Opatow, L., 158
O'Rourke, D., 158
Overholser, C. E., 21

Paksog, C., 186
Parker, I., 21
Parket, I. R., 21
Parlin, C. C., 11
Payne, J. L., 20
Payne, M. S., 323
Pearl, D. K., 159
Perreault, W. D., Jr., 248
Peter, J. P., 248
Peterson, R. A., 145, 158, 159
Petty, R. E., 342

Piekarski, L., 158, 159
Pierson, S. A., 159
PiHenger, D. B., 103
Plath, D. A., 39
Plummer, J. T., 323
Pol, L. G., 158, 159
Poltrack, D. F., 129
Ponzurick, T. G., 158, 159
Presser, S., 278, 279
Prince, M., 129
Pyle, D. L., 158

Raine, C. G., 38
Rangaswamy, A., 39
Raphael, J., 21
Rasinski, K. A., 279
Reilly, M. D., 323
Revett, J., 213
Richer, J., 342
Riordan, E. A., 537
Robinson, E. D., 186
Robinson, L., 159
Robson, S., 323, 537
Rothman, J., 380
Rothschild, M. L., 342
Roy, P. L., 159
Rudelius, W., 144
Russick, B., 144
Russo, J. E., 39
Rust, L., 333
Ryan, P., 21

Sampson, P., 323
Samuels, J., 21
Scarbrough, E., 380
Schaeffer, N. C., 278
Schauer, J. A., 21
Schertzer, C. B., 303
Schiavone, N., 21
Schiller, Z., 21
Schitler, L., 260
Schleier, C., 537
Schlinger, M. J. R., 248
Schlossberg, H., 537
Schmalenese, D. H., 129
Schneider, K. C., 278
Schröder, S., 279
Schuman, H., 278, 279
Schwartz, N., 278, 279
Schweizer, R., 537
Scott, D. N., 213
Segal, M. N., 158
Serafin, R., 21, 103
Seymour, D. T., 323
Sharma, A., 103
Sharot, T., 159
Sharp, L. M., 537
Sheth, J., 516
Shiffler, R. E., 400

Shimp, T. A., 186, 278
Siegel, S., 461
Singh, S. N., 213
Sinkula, J. M., 21, 129
Sisodia, R. S., 39
Skinner, S. J., 537
Smart, D. T., 159
Smead, R. J., 159
Smith, D., 62
Smith, J. W., 62
Smith, L., 380
Smith, S. M., 537
Smithies, R. H., 303
Snyder, D. J., 186
Solomon, M. R., 333
Soong, P., 129
Sopariwala, D. R., 159
Sorrels, B. D., 516
Spagna, G. J., 269
Sparkman, R. D., Jr., 279
Stamen, J. P., 35, 39
Stanley, L. R., 381
Steele, H. C., 159, 380
Stegan, I. A., 555
Steinhorst, R. K., 278
Stem, D. E., Jr., 278, 303
Stenbeck, M., 303
Stevens, S. S., 237
Stevenson, T. H., 39
Stiff, R., 21, 39
Stoddard, L. R., Jr., 129
Stout, R. G., 129, 516
Strandskov, J., 159
Strauss, A., 5, 173
Strnad, P., 103
Sudman, S., 399
Sykes, W., 323
Synodinos, N. E., 158

Tashjian, R., 286
Tordella, S. J., 537
Tourangeau, R., 279
Toy, D., 537
Tracy, P. E., 278
Treasure, J., 103
Tsiantar, D., 323
Tuckel, P. S., 159
Tull, D. S., 62, 159, 461
Tyebjee, T. T., 303

Van Auken, S., 248
van Hammersveld, M., 21
Varekamp, Sullivan, L., 87
Veltzhöffer, J., 21
Venkatesh, B., 233
Verille, P., 159, 537
Vigderhous, G., 248
Vitell, S., 537
von Arx, D. W., 20
von Keitz, B., 342

Wakshlag, J., 129
Walker, B. J., 159
Walker, D., 213
Wallis, L. A., 35
Walstra, B., 278
Walters, H., 278
Ward, J. C., 144
Wardle, J., 323
Warren, M., 323
Warshaw, P. R., 180, 186
Wasserman, P., et.al., 86, 87
Weeks, M. F., 159
Weinstein, S., 336
Wells, S., 323
Westbrook, R. A., 285
Whalen, B., 537
White, J. D., 278
Wickerhauser, H., 103
Wicks, A., 129
Wilcox, J., 159
Wilcox, J. B., 279, 537
Wilkinson, J. B., 186
Wilkinson, W., 21
Williams, J., 279
Wilson, T. C., 428
Wind, Y., 278
Winquist, C. H., 537
Wiseman, F., 158, 159
Wood, V. R., 248
Worcester, R. M., 323, 537
Wouters, J., 21
Wright, L., 537

Yamada, Y., 159
Yorovich, B. G., 213
Young, E., 339
Yu, J., 159

Zimmer, M., 303

Subject Index

ABI/Inform, 88, 99
Abuse of respondents, 528
Accounting records, as data source,
  82–83
Accuracy
  census versus sample, 362
  of measurements, 240–244
  of secondary data, 81
Add-a-digit dialing, 141–142
ADI, 119–120
Advertisements, testing of, 193–197,
  198
Advertising, and media usage data,
  119–120, 124
Affective value distance (AVD) scale,
  290–291
After-only design, 169–170
After-only with control design, 172–174
Aggregate analysis, 296–297
Aided recall, 258–259
Alpha error, 432–433
Alternate hypothesis, 432–433
Alternative-form reliability, 241–242
Ambiguous answers on questionnaires,
  410–411
Analysis, data reduction in, 403–423
Analysis of variance (ANOVA),
  442–446, 451–457
  assumptions in, 457
  factorial designs, 456–457
  with interaction, 456–457
  for Latin square designs, 453–455
  for randomized block designs,
    451–453
  univariate or one-way, 442–446
  without interaction, 451–455
Anonymity
  of clients, 529
  of respondents, 527–528
Area of dominant influence (ADI),
  119–120
Area under normal curve, 548–549
Artifacts, demand, 167

Association measures, 462–476
  bivariate, 465–471
    ordinal data in, 470–471
    ratio/interval data in, 465–469
  criterion and predictor variables in, 464
  directionality in, 465
  misuse of, 464–465
  multiple regression analysis in,
    471–476
  multivariate, 471–476
Association projective techniques, 314
Associations as data sources, 91
Attitude scales, 294–298
  Likert, 297–298
  ratings in, 283–294. See also Rating
    scales
  semantic differential, 294–297
Attitude surveys, 124–125
Audits, 113–115
  applications, 122
  pantry, 332
  product, 115
  retail distribution, 115
  store, 113–114
Availability of secondary data, 80

Balanced rating scale, 286
Banners, to display cross tabulations,
  417
Bar charts, 498
Base value, 235
BASES system, 15
Basic data array, 409
  development of, 409–417
Basic experimental designs, 169–175
Bayesian statistical model, 385–386
Before-after design, 170–171
Before-after with control design,
  171–172
BehaviorScan, 385–386
Benefit chain, in word association, 314
Beta error, 433
Bias, 240

Biased words, 263–264
Bibliographic databases, 88–89
Bivariate measures of association, 465–471
Blind tests, 197, 283
  monadic, 283
Blocking groups, randomized, 176
Bogus recall, 256–257
Brain-wave analysis, 335
Branching instructions in questionnaire, 270
Branded research products, 15
Buying Power Index (BPI), 96

Campbell-Fiske procedure, 244
Cartoon techniques, 315–316
Case analyses, 48
Categories of research, 42–43
CATI, 134–136
Causal research, 43
Census, compared to sampling, 362
Central tendency, measures of, 418
Certification of marketing researchers, 532–533
Charts, use of, 498–502, 507–510
Chi square X^2 test, 448–451
  table of values for, 556–557
Children
  observation of, 326, 327
  rating scales for, 285–286
Chip testing, 293–294
Client protection, ethical issues in, 528–530
Cluster sampling, 369–370
CMP interval panel, 110
Code of ethics, in marketing research, 522–523
Coding of data, 411–412
  by interviewers, 266–267
  postcoding in, 412
  precoding in, 412
Coefficient
  alpha, 242
  of determination, 469, 473
Commercial surveys, 108–113
Comparative rating scales, 287–294
Competitor intelligence, 29–30
Completion projective techniques, 314–315
Computer assisted telephone interviews, 134–136
Computer interviews, 136–137
Computer use
  in decision support systems, 34
  in editing of data, 411
  in interviews, 61, 134–137, 153
    multinational, 153
    strengths, 143
    in telephone interviews, 134–136

Computerized databases, 87–91
  bibliographic, 88–89
  numeric, 89–90
  systems, 90–91
Concept tests, 6
Conceptual definitions, 231
Concern scale, 431
Concomitant variation, 43
Concurrent validity, 243
Confidence coefficient of estimates, 390
Confidence interval, 390
Confidentiality of data
  for clients, 529
  for respondents, 527–528
Consent, informed, 526–527
Consistent preference discrimination test, 289–290
Constant sum scale, 292–293
Construct validity, 244
Construction projective techniques, 315–318
Consumer panels, 117–121
Consumer price index (CPI), 230
Content validity, 242–243
Continuous panels, 108, 115–121
Contrived observations, 328
Control groups, 162
Controlled-store tests, 206–207
Convenience samples, 367
Convergent validity, 244
Correlation matrix, 474
Cost
  census versus sample, 362
  of interviews, 142
  survey, 142
Counterbiasing statements, 261
Creation, and recall, 257
Criterion-related validity, 243–244
Criterion variables, 464
Critical path method (CPM), 53, 54
Critical value, in null hypothesis, 435
Cross tabulations, 416–417
Cumulative frequency distribution, 414–415
Custom research, 14–15

Data analysis, 403–423, 431–457
  estimation techniques in, 386–391, 420–423
  reduction of data in, 403–423. *See also* Reduction of data
Data array, basic, development of, 409–414
Data collection, 49–51
Databases, computerized, 87–91. *See also* Computerized databases
Day-after recall (DAR), 198, 365
Debriefing, 272
Deception, in advertising testing, 527

Decision-making process, 7–13
Decision support systems, 30–35
    applications of, 35
    computers in, 34
    data in, 34
    interface, 34–35
    managers in, 35
    models in, 31–34
Demand artifacts, 167
Demand characteristics, 167
Dependent variable, 162
Depth interviews, 306–313
    focus group, 309–313
    individual, 306–309
    mini-group, 313
Descriptive research, 43
Design, experimental, 169–181
    basic, 169–175
        after-only, 169–170
        after-only with control, 172–174
        before-after, 170–172
        before-after with control, 171–172
        completely randomized designs
            (CRD), 173–174
        potential errors in, 163–168
        simulated before-after, 172
        Solomon four-group, 174
    ex post facto, 181–183
    guide for selection of, 182
    statistical, 175–181
        factorial, 179–181
        Latin square, 177–179
        randomized block, 175–177
Deviation. See Standard deviation
DIALOG, 91
Diary panels, 117–119
Dichotomous questions, 269
Direct observation, 330–332
Directionality, in measures of
    association, 465
Directories, 95
    international, 105
Discriminant validity, 244
Disguised observations, 329
Distortions by respondents, 261–262
Distribution, sampling, 386–391
Double-paired comparisons, 289
Double triangle discrimination test,
    290
Double triangle preference test, 290
Dummy data, 52
Dummy variables in regression analysis,
    473–474

Editing of data, 409–411
    accuracy and quality of responses in,
        411
    ambiguous answers in, 410–411
    computer use in, 411

missing data in, 410
    plug values for, 410
Electronic panels, 119–120
Electronic Point-of-Sale systems (EPOS),
    115–116
Electronic test markets (ETMs), 207
Embarrassing information requests,
    responses to, 261–262
Emotional Measurement System, 299
Emotions, measurement of, 298–299
Employment data, 94
Encyclopedia of Associations, 91
Encyclopedia of Business Information
    Sources, 85
Equal unit probability sampling, 371
Errors
    affecting experimental results,
        56, 163–168
    frame, 57, 364
    measurement, 56, 236–239
    in projective techniques, 318–320
    of recall, 256–259
    in research design, 55–59
    standard, 387–391
        of the mean, 387–391
        of the proportion, 391
    strategies for dealing with, 58–59
    systematic, 240
    variable, 240
Estimates, 390–395
    confidence coefficient of, 390
    confidence interval, 390
    interval, 390–391
    of most representative amount, 419
    point, 390, 421
    of population mean, 390–391,
        421–423
    of population proportion, 391, 421, 423
    of population total, 419
    of standard deviation of population,
        391
    of variances for rating scales, 393
Estimation techniques, 390–395,
    420–423
Ethical issues, 52–53, 519–533
    client protection in, 528–530
    code of ethics in, 522–523
    nature of, 520–523
    in observational approach, 328, 527
    public protection in, 523–524
    research firm protection in, 530–531
    research profession protection in,
        531–533
    respondent protection in, 524–528
Ethnography, marketing, 334
Experimental error, 56, 163–168
Experimentation, 162–183
    control groups, 162
    defined, 162

Experimentation, (*Continued*)
  design of. *See* Design, experimental,
    169–181
  environments in, 191–210
    field, 198–210
    laboratory, 191–197
  errors affecting results, 56, 163–168
    history, 165
    instrumentation, 165–166
    interaction, 164–165
    maturation, 165
    measurement timing, 167–168
    mortality, 166–167
    premeasurement, 164
    reactive, 167
    selection, 166
    surrogate situation, 168
  treatment groups, 162
Experimenter effects, 167, 193
Expert systems, 36
Experts
  external, 95, 96
    international data from, 105
  internal, 84
Exploratory research, 43
Ex post facto studies, 181–183
Expressive projective techniques, 318
Extended use tests, 197
External experts, 95, 97
  international data from, 105
External sources of secondary data,
    85–97, 98–100, 104–105
  international, 98–100, 104–105
External validity, 192
Eye tracking, 335–339

F distribution table, 552–555
Face validity, 242–243
Factorial designs, 179–181
  ANOVA for, 456–457
Fantasy scenarios, 317
Field controls, 409
Field experiments, 198–210
  advertising copy tests, 198
  test marketing, 198–211
Field organizations, 15
Financial requirements, estimates of, 53
FIND/SVP, 87, 99
Flip charts, 508
Flow diagrams, 501
Focus group interviews, 309–313
Forced rating scale, 287
Forgetful respondents, 257–259
Frame error, 57, 364
Frame of reference, 264–265
Frames for sampling, 364
  errors in, 57, 364
Frequency distributions, tabulation of,
    414–417
Frugging, 525

Garbage analysis, 327, 332
Government data sources, 91–94, 99, 104
  on foreign markets, 99, 104
Graphic analysis, 467
Graphic displays in research reports,
    498–503, 507–510
Graphic positioning scale, 295

Hemispheral lateralization, 335
Hidden-issue questioning, 307
Histogram, 499–500
History, as source of experimental error,
    165
Home interviews, 132–133
Household purchase data, 123
Housing data, 92
Hypothesis tests, 432–457
  multivariate, 451–457. *See also*
    Analysis of variance (ANOVA)
  nature of, 432–433
  univariate, 433–451. *See also*
    Univariate hypothesis tests
    interval data in, 433–446
    nominal data in, 448–451
    ordinal data in, 446–448

Implied alternatives, 264
Implied assumptions, 264
Inarticulate respondents, 259
Incidence, and sample size
    determination, 395–396
Income data, 92
Incomplete reporting, 523, 530
Independent variable, 162
Index numbers, 235
Indirect observation, 330–332
Individual depth interviews, 306–309
Information
  and decision making, 7–13
  embarrassing, 261
  personal, 259–260
  prestige-oriented, 262
  surrogate, errors in, 55–56
  types in marketing information
    system, 25–27
  value of, 12–13
    estimation of, 48
Information brokers, 85, 87
Informed consent, 526–527
InfoScan, 116–117
INRABUS, 125
In-store intercept interviews, 134, 135
Instrumentation experimental error,
    165–166
Interaction
  defined, 179
  errors from, 164–165
  measurement of, 456–457
  test for, 456–457
Intercept interviews, 132–134

Interface, decision support system, 34
Internal-comparison reliability, 242
Internal experts, 84
Internal sources of secondary data,
    82–85, 97–98
  international, 97–98
Internal validity, 191
International commercial surveys,
    audits, and panels, 125–126
International Research, 13 See
    Multinational Research
International research industry, 16
International secondary data, 97–100,
    104–105
International Trade Administration
    (ITA), 99, 104
Interval data, 235–236
Interval estimates
  of the mean, 390–391, 421–423
  of proportions, 391, 423
Interval measurements, 235–236
Interval panels, 108–110
Interviewer code, 409
Interviewer effects, 140
Interviews
  cheating in, 140
  computer, 136–137, 153
    multinational, 153
    strengths, 143
  cost of, 142
  depth, 306–313
    individual, 306–309
  focus group, 309–313
  intercept, 132–134, 153
  interviewer effects in, 140
  mail, 136
    multinational, 152–153
    nonresponses, 148–150
    strengths, 143
  mall intercept, 132–134
  minigroup, 313
  nonresponse errors, 143–151
  personal, 132–134
    multinational, 153
    nonresponses, 145–148
    strengths, 143
  respondent numbers for, 409
  sensitive questions in, 139
  telephone, 134–136
    computer-assisted, 134–136
    multinational, 152
    nonresponses, 145–148
    random digit dial, 141–142
    strengths, 143
  validation or verification of, 140
Invariant association, 43
Item nonresponse, 410
Itemized rating scales, 284–289
  comparative, 287–289
  noncomparative, 284–287

Jamming tactics, 204
Judgment samples, 368
Jury selection, marketing research
    techniques in, 532–533
Juster Scale, 284

Laboratory experiments, 191–198
  advertising tests, 193–197
  applications of, 193–197
  package tests, 193
  product tests, 197
  reactive errors in, 192–193
  simulated test markets, 207–211
Laddering, 306–307
Language in phrasing of questions,
    262–265
  in multinational questionnaire, 273
Latin square designs, 177–179
  ANOVA for, 453–455
Layout of questionnaires, 270
Leading questions, 263–264
Leasing squares regression analysis,
    465–469, 470–476
Likert scale, 297–298
Line charts, 498–499
Loaded questions, 263

Mail interviews, 136, 148–150
Mall intercept interviews, 132–134, 153
Management problem, 42
Mann-Whitney U test, 446–448
Marketing decisions, 7–13
  support systems in. See Decision
    support systems
Marketing ethnography, 334
Marketing information systems, 24–30
  compared to decision support
    systems, 30
  for competitor intelligence, 29–30
  defined, 24
  nature of, 24
  specialized, 27–28
  types of information in, 24–27
Marketing research
  careers, 16–18
  definition of, 4
  design. See Research design
  departments, 13–14
  ethical issues in, 519–533
  function of, 4–7
  industry, 14–16
  international, 13
  limitations, 12–13
  measurements in. See Measurements
  mission statements, 4–5
  process, 42
  reports, 495–512
    oral, 507–510
    reading of, 510–512
    written, 496–507

Matching of treatment and control
    groups, 163
Maturation error experiments, 165
Mean
    arithmetic, 418
    interval estimate of, 390–391, 421–423
    in multivariate hypothesis tests,
        451–457
    point estimates of, 390, 421
    sampling distribution of, 386–391
    in univariate hypothesis tests,
        434–437, 438–440, 442–446
Measurements, 228–244
    accuracy of, 240–244
    assignment of numbers in, 228–229
    components of, 236–239
    conceptual definitions, 231
    defined, 228–229
    of emotions, 298–299
    errors in, 56, 236–239
        timing, 167–168
    evaluation of, 229–230
    interval, 235–236
    nominal, 232–234
    operational definitions, 231–232
    ordinal, 234–235
    physiological, 334–339
    ratio, 236
    reality and, 229–230
    scales of, 232–236
Media usage data, 124
Median, 418
Minigroup interviews, 313
Minimarket tests, 206–207
Misleading reporting, 523–524, 530
Misrepresentation of findings, 531
Missing data on questionnaires, 410
    plug values for, 410
Mission statements, 4–5
Mode, 418
Models
    in decision support systems, 31–34
    situation, 47–48
Modular research, 309–310
Monadic scales, 283
Monitoring
    in field controls, 409
    of information, 26
Mortality errors in experiments, 166–167
Multicollinearity, in multiple regression
    analysis, 474–475
Multinational research, 13
    commercial surveys and panels in,
        125–126
    design of, 59
    focus groups in Europe, 309
    industry, 16
    questionnaire design in, 272–274
    sampling in, 374–375

secondary data for, 97–100, 104–105
surveys in, 151–154
test marketing in, 202–203
Multiple-choice questions, 267–269
Multiple regression analysis, 471–476
    causation in, 475–476
    cautions in, 474–476
    dummy variables in, 473–474
    interpretation of coefficients in, 475
    multicollinearity in, 474–475
    nominal variables in, 473–474
    strength of, 473
Multistage sampling, 371
Multitrait-multimethod matrix, 244
Multivariate measures of association,
    471–476
Mystery-shopper programs, 328

n-way frequency distribution, 416–417
National Restaurant Market Index, 109
National Technical Information Service
    (NTIS), 94
NEXIS, 91
NFO interval panel, 110
Nielsen Retail Index, 113–115
Nominal data, 232–234
    in measures of association, 473–474
    in univariate hypothesis tests,
        448–451
Nominal measurements, 232–234
Nominal variables in multiple regression
    analysis, 473–474
Nomological validity, 244
Noncomparative rating scales, 283–287
Nonobjective research, 524
Nonprobability samples, 367–369
Nonresponse, 143–151
    error, 143–151
    item, 410
    missing questionnaire data, 410
    and sample size determination,
        395–396
Nonresponse error, 143–151
    imputation estimates of, 151
    mail, 148–150
    personal, 145–148
    reduction of, 145–150
    strategies for dealing with, 150–151
    subjective estimates of, 150–151
    subsample measures of, 151
    telephone, 145–148
    trend analysis of, 151
Normal curve, 387–390
    area under, 548–549
Normative answers, 262
Null hypothesis, 432–433
Numbers
    index, 235
    random, table of, 558

rounding of, in reports, 503, 530
rules for assignment of, 228–232
Numeric databases, 89–90
Numerical comparative scale, 295

Observational approach, 326–334
conditions for use, 326
direct versus indirect, 330–332
ethical issues, 328, 527
human versus mechanical, 332
natural versus contrived situation, 328
open versus disguised, 329
preference for, 326–328
structured versus unstructured, 330
Observer effects, 329
Omission by respondents, 257–259
Omnibus surveys, 110–113
One-on-one interviews, 306–309
One-tailed tests, 432
One-way ANOVA, 442–446
One-way frequency distributions, 414–415
Open-ended questions, 266–267
Operational definitions, 231–232
Opportunity
identification of, 7–9
resolution of, 10–12
selection of, 9–10
Oral presentations, 507–510
Ordinal data, 234–235
in measures of association, 470–471
in univariate hypothesis tests, 446–448
Ordinal measurements, 234–235
Organization of Economic Cooperation and Development (OECD), 100, 105

Package tests, 193
Paired comparisons, 289
Panel surveys, 108–110
Panels, 108–110, 115–125
applications, 122–125
consumer, 117–121
diary, 117–119
electronic, 119–120
international, 125–126
single-source data, 120–121
UPC scanners, 120
continuous, 108, 115–121
interval, 108–110
retail, 115–117
Pantry audits, 332
People meters, 119
Percentages, sampling distribution of, 391
Periodic surveys, 108, 109
Personal information requests, responses to, 259–260

Personal interviews, 132–134, 153
Personification techniques, 317
PERT, 53, 54
Physical traces, observation of, 332
Physiological measures, 334–339
brain-wave analysis, 335
eye tracking, 335–339
psychogalvanometer, 339
Picture response, 317
Pie charts, 498
Plug values, for missing data, 410
Plus-one dialing, 141–142
Point estimates
of population means, 390–391, 421
of population proportions, 391, 421
Political organizations, international, 99–100
Population data, 92
Population for sampling
definition of, 363–364
specification error, 56–57
Position bias, 268–269
Postmeasurements, 167–168
Power of a test, 433
Precoding, 267
Predicasts, 88–89, 99
Predictive validity, 192, 243–244
Predictor variables, 464
Preference ranking, 289–294
Premeasurements, 167–168
effects of, 164
Prestige-oriented questions, 262
Pretesting, 270–272
Primary data, 80
PRISM, 15
Privacy of respondents, 526–528
Probability samples, 367
Problem definition, 45–48
Problem/opportunity
identification of, 7–9
resolution of, 10–12
selection of, 9–10
Product audits, 115
Product tests, 197
Profile analysis, 297
Program evaluation review technique (PERT), 53, 54
Projective techniques, 313–321
association, 314
benefits of, 318–321
completion, 314–315
construction, 315–318
expressive, 318
problems with, 318–321
PromotionScan, 122
PROMPT, 88, 99
Proportions
interval estimate of, 394–395, 423
point estimates of, 421

Proportions, (*Continued*)
    sampling distribution of, 391
    in univariate hypothesis tests, 437,
        440–441
Proprietary information, protection of,
    531
Protocol analysis, 272
Psychogalvanometer, 339
Purchase intercept technique (PIT), 135
Purposive samples, 369

Quadric comparisons, 292
Qualitative research, 304–321
    depth interviews, 306–313
        focus group, 309–313
        individual, 306–309
        minigroup, 313
    projective techniques, 313–321
        association, 314
        benefits of, 318–321
        completion, 314–315
        construction, 315–318
        expressive, 318
        problems with, 318–321
Questionnaires, 252–274
    ambiguous answers in, 410–411
    complexity of, 138–139
    decision areas in, 253–272
    information required, 253
    interview technique. *See* Interviews
    measurement error in, 56, 236–239
    missing data in, 410
    multinational, 272–274
    physical characteristics, 270
    pretesting, 270–272
    question content, 255–262
        ability to produce data, 255–256
        ability of respondent to answer
            accurately, 256–259
        external events affecting, 262
        need for data, 255
        willingness of respondent to answer
            accurately, 259–262
    question phrasing, 262–265
        biased words and leading
            questions, 263–264
        frame of reference, 264
        implied alternatives, 264
        implied assumptions, 264
        meaning of words, 263
    question sequence, 270
    response format, 266–269
        dichotomous questions, 269
        multiple-choice questions, 267–269
        open-ended questions, 266–267
Quota samples, 368–369

R-square measure of fit, 469
Random digit dialed surveys, 141–142

Random numbers, table of, 558
Random samples, 367
Randomization, 162–163
Randomized blocks design, 175–177
    ANOVA for, 451–453
Randomized response techniques,
    261–262
Range, in dispersion of data, 420
Rank order rating scale, 292
Rating scales, 283–294
    attitude, 294–298
    comparative, 287–294
        consistent preference discrimination
            test, 289–290
        constant sum measures, 292–293
        double-paired comparisons, 289
        double triangle discrimination test,
            290
        double triangle preference test, 290
        Juster Scale, 284
        paired comparisons, 289
        rank order method, 292
        response latency, 290–291
        simulated-purchase chip testing,
            293–294
        triangle discrimination test, 290
        triangle preference test, 290
    noncomparative, 283–287
        balanced versus unbalanced, 286
        category descriptions, 284–285
        forced versus unforced, 287
        itemized, 284–287
        number of categories, 285
        odd or even number of categories,
            286
    variances in, estimates of, 393
Ratio measurements, 236
Reactive errors in experiments, 167,
    192–193
Reading test markets, 204–205
Recall, 257–259
    aided, 258–259
    bogus, 256–257
    day-after, 198, 365
    in tests of advertisements, 198, 365
    unaided, 257–258
Recurrent information, 25
Reduction of data, 409–420
    coding in, 411–412
    editing in, 409–410
    field controls in, 409
    generating new variables in, 414
    summarizing statistics in, 417–420
    tabulation of frequency distributions
        in, 414–417
    transcribing in, 412
Refusal to answer questions, 259–262
Regression analysis, 465–469, 470–476
    bivariate, 465–469

dummy-variable, 473–474
multiple, 470–476
Relevance of secondary data, 80–81
Reliability, 240–242
alternative-form, 241–242
coefficient alpha, 242
internal-comparison, 242
scorer, 242
split-half, 242
test-retest, 241
Replicability of laboratory experiments,
191
Reports, 495–512
ethical issues, 523–524
oral, 507–510
reading of, 510–512
written, 496–507
Requested information, 27
Research design, 42–59
causal, 43
defined, 42, 43
descriptive, 43
errors, 55–59
experimental, 56
frame, 57
handling strategies, 58–59
measurement, 56
nonresponse, 57–58
population specification, 56–57
sampling, 57
selection, 57
surrogate information, 55–56
exploratory, 43
goals, 42
multinational, 59
steps, 43–55
analysis method selection, 52
case analyses, 48
data collection approach, 49–50
ethical guidelines, 52–53
financial requirement estimation, 53
information requirements, 48
information value estimation, 48
management problem/opportunity
clarification, 45
measurement technique selection,
51
model development, 47–48
research problem definition, 45–48
research proposal preparation,
53–55
sample selection, 51–52
situation analysis, 45–47
time estimation, 53
types of, 42–43
Research problem, 42
Research proposal, 53, 55
Research reports, 495–512
Respondent numbers for interviews, 409

Respondents
forgetful, 257–259
inarticulate, 259
protection of, 524–528
refusal to answer questions, 259–262
situational characteristics of, 239
stable characteristics of, 238
temporary characteristics of, 238–239
uninformed, 256–257
Response error, 239
Response latency measures, 290–291
Retail distribution audits, 115
Retail panels, 115–117
Retail sales measures, 122
Retail scanner data, 115–117, 122
Role playing, projective technique, 318
Rounding of numbers in reports,
503, 530

Sales data for product categories, 92
Sales force reports, as data source, 83
Sample size determination, 371, 383–396
all-you-can-afford method, 384
Bayesian statistical model, 385–386
incidence and nonresponse in,
395–396
largest size required in, 396
in multinational sampling, 395
required size per cell, 385
and sampling distribution, 386–391
traditional statistical methods in, 386,
392–395
typical sizes in, 385
unaided judgment in, 384
Sampling, 361–377, 383–396
applications, 375–377
compared to census, 362
control, 140–141
convenience samples, 367
data analysis in. See Data analysis
distribution, 386–391
of the mean, 386–391
of the proportion, 391
errors in, 57
and estimation techniques, 390–391
frame error in, 57, 364
frame specification, 364
in multinational sampling, 374
judgment samples, 368
method selection, 367–371
equal unit probability versus
unequal unit probability, 371
in multinational sampling, 375
probability versus nonprobability,
367–369
single stage versus multistage, 371
single-unit versus cluster, 369–370
unstratified versus stratified,
370–371

Sampling, (*Continued*)
  multinational, 374–375
  plan specification, 372
    in multinational sampling, 375
  population definition, 363–364
    in multinational sampling, 374
  purposive samples, 369
  quota samples, 368–369
  selection error in, 57
  simple random sample, 367
  size determination, 371, 383–396
  subsampling of nonrespondents, 151
  unit specification, 364–366
    in multinational sampling, 374
Sampling distribution, 386–391
  of the mean, 386–391
  of the proportion, 391
Satisfaction measures, 285
Scales of measurement, 232–236
Scanner data, 115–117, 120–121
  retail sales, 115–117
  in UPC consumer panels, 120–121
SCANTRACK, 116–117, 120
Scatter diagram, 465–467
Scorer reliability, 242
SDC/Orbit, 91
Secondary data, 80–100, 104–105
  accuracy, 81
  advantages, 80
  availability, 80
  external sources, 85–97
    associations, 91
    bibliographic databases, 88–89
    computerized databases, 87–91
    database systems, 90–91
    directories, 95
    external experts, 95, 96
    government agencies, 91–94
    international, 98–100, 104–105
    numeric databases, 89–90
    Predicasts PTS, 88–89
    syndicated services, 94
  guides to, 85–87
  internal sources, 82–85, 97–98
    accounting records, 82–83
    internal experts, 84
    international, 97–98
    miscellaneous reports, 83–84
    sales force reports, 83
  international, 97–100, 104–105
    external sources, 98–100, 104–105
    internal sources, 97–98
  problems, 80–82
  relevance, 80–81
  sufficiency, 81
Securities and Exchange Commission
  (SEC), 94
Selection errors in experiments, 166

Selective Dissemination of Information
  (SDI), 91
Semantic differential scale, 294–297
Sensitive questions, 139
Sensitivity analysis, 32
Sentence completion technique, 314–315
Sequence of occurrence, 43
Service shopping, 328
Shared surveys, 110–113
SIC, 92–93
Simple random sample (srs), 367
Simulated before-after design, 172
Simulated-purchase chip testing,
  293–294
Simulated test markets (STMs), 207–210
Single-source data, 120–121
  in electronic test markets, 207
Single-stage sampling, 371
Single-unit sampling, 369–370
Size determination in sampling, 383–396
Skip instructions in questionnaires, 138
Smiling face scale, 286
Solomon four-group design, 174
Spearman rank correlation coefficient,
  470–471
Split-ballot technique, 269
Split-half reliability, 242
Spurious awareness, 256–257
Spurious correlations, 465
Standard deviation, 419
  calculation from frequency table, 428
  estimate of, 391
  formula for, 419
  and standard error of the mean, 387
Standard error, 387–391
  of the mean, 387–391
  of the proportion, 391
Standard Industrial Classification (SIC),
  92–93
Standard market tests, 201–206
Statistical estimation techniques,
  390–391, 420–423
Statistical experimental designs, 169,
  175–181
Statistical models
  Bayesian, 385–386
  traditional, 386–395
Statistics, 417–420
Store audits, 113–115
Story completion technique, 315
Stratified sampling, 370–371
Structured observation, 330
Sufficiency of secondary data, 82
Sugging, 524
Summarizing statistics, 417–420
  measures of central tendency in,
    418–419
  measures of dispersion in, 419–420

Surrogate data, 55–56
Surrogate information error, 55–56
Surrogate situation error, 168
Survey research, 108–113, 132–154
  computer, 136–137
  international, 151–154
  interviews in. *See* Interviews
  mall intercept, 132
  method selection criteria, 138–143
    accuracy of data, 139–140
    amount of data, 139
    computer strengths, 143
    cost, 142
    mail strengths, 143
    personal strengths, 143
    questionnaire complexity, 138–139
    response rate, 142–151
    sample control, 140–142
    telephone strengths, 143
    time requirements, 142
  multinational, 151–154
  nonresponse errors, 143–151
    imputation estimates of, 151
    mail, 148–150
    personal, 145–148
    reduction of, 145–150
    strategies for dealing with, 150–151
    subjective estimates of, 150–151
    subsample measurements of, 151
    telephone, 145–148
    trend analysis of, 151
  panel, 108–110
    continuous, 108–109
    interval, 108–110
  periodic, 108
  personal, 132–134
  random digit dialing, 141–142
  shared, 110–113
  single-source data, 120–121
  telephone, 134–136
  types of, 132–137
Symbolic questioning, 307
Syndicated services, 15, 107–126
Systematic errors, 240

t distribution table, 550–551
t test, 438–439, 440
Tab houses, 15
Tabulation of frequency distributions, 414–417
  banners in, 417
  cross tabulations in, 416–417
  one-way distributions in, 414–415
Tachistoscopic tests, 193, 196
Telephone interviews, 134–136, 152
Telescoping, 257
  10-K report, 94
  10-Q report, 94

Test markets, 198–210
  controlled-store, 206–207
  electronic, 207
  international, 202–203
  jamming of, 204
  minimarket, 206–207
  read by competitors, 204–205
  simulated, 207–210
  standard, 201–206
    advantages of, 205–206
    analysis of, 203
    disadvantages of, 203–205
    site selection in, 201–203
Test-retest reliability, 241
Theater tests, 197
Third-person techniques, 316–317
Tiger system, 92
Time-lapse photography, 332
Timing of measurements, errors in, 167–168
Top box score, 284
Trade associations, 91
Traditional statistical model, 392–395
Traffic counts, 328, 332
Transcription of data, 412
Translations, 273
  back, 273
  parallel, 273
Treatment groups, 162
Trend analysis, 151
Triangle discrimination test, 290
  double, 290
Triangle preference test, 290
  double, 290
Two-tailed tests, 432–433
Two-way frequency distribution, 415–417
Type I error, 432–433
Type II error, 432–433

Unaided recall, 257–258
Unbalanced rating scale, 286
Unequal unit probability sampling, 371
Uninformed respondents, 256–257
United Nations (UN), 99–100, 105
Univariate ANOVA, 442–446
Univariate hypothesis tests, 433–451
  interval data in, 433–446
    mean, one sample, 434–437, 438–439
    proportion, one sample, 437–438
    two means, independent samples, 439–440
    two or more means, independent samples, 446
    two proportions, independent samples, 440–441

Univariate hypothesis tests, (*Continued*)
  nominal data in, 448–451
    single sample, 448–449
    two independent samples, 449–450
    two or more independent samples,
      450–451
  ordinal data in, 446–448
    rank order, two independent
      samples, 446–448
Universal product code (UPC), 115–116
  consumer scanner panels, 120
Unnecessary research, 528–529
Unqualified researchers, 529
Unstratified sampling, 370–371
Unstructured observation, 330
Upgraded semantic differential scale, 295

Validation
  in field controls, 409
  of quota samples, 368
Validity, 240, 242–244
  concurrent, 243
  construct, 244
  content, 242–243
  convergent, 244
  criterion-related, 243–244
  discriminant, 244
  external, 192
  face, 242–243

  internal, 191
  nomological, 244
  predictive, 192, 243–244
Variable errors, 240
Variables
  dependent, 162
  independent, 162
Variance
  analysis of. *See* Analysis of variance
    (ANOVA)
  in dispersion of data, 420
  estimates for rating scales, 393
Video cameras, use of, 332, 527
Visual aids in reports, 498–503, 507–510

What-if analysis, 31–33
Word association, 314
  free, 314
  successive, 314
World Bank, 100, 105

X^2 test, 448–451
  k-sample, 450–451
  one-sample, 448–449
  table of values for, 556–557
  two-sample, 449–450

Z test, 434–438, 439–441
Z value, 388